Theology and Sociology

Theology and Sociology:

A Reader

edited and introduced by
Robin Gill

New and Enlarged Edition

CASSELL

Cassell

Wellington House, 125 Strand, London WC2R 0BB
127 West 24th Street, New York, NY 10011

First published 1996

British Library Cataloguing-in-Publication Data
A catalogue record for this book is available from the British Library.

ISBN 0 304 33839 7

Typeset by York House Typographic Ltd, London
Printed and bound in Great Britain by Biddles, Guildford and King's Lynn

Contents

SECTION THREE   Implications for Biblical Studies

SECTION FOUR   Implications for Applied Theology

SECTION FIVE   Implications for Postmodern Culture

Introduction

The first edition of this book tried to reflect a remarkable change that took place within academic theology in the 1970s and early 1980s. After years of neglect, theologians and biblical scholars started to take sociology seriously, to read the classical studies of Weber, Durkheim and Troeltsch, and to lose some of their old fears about 'sociological reductionism'. Many New Testament scholars, in particular, went through a major transformation. Brought up in a world of exegesis, they now faced a very different environment of interpretation. After years of struggling with such issues as the original meaning of a particular text, its date, authorship and sources, they now became more interested in the different communities that have variously interpreted texts. Questions about social context and social shaping came to the fore.

It became fashionable for theologians to read sociology. But herein lay a major problem. How could theologians become sufficiently expert in handling sociological tools and in learning to differentiate between more and less sophisticated uses of sociology? Many theologians had been trained professionally as philosophers, but as yet only a few of us as sociologists. There seemed to be an increasing awareness that theology makes frequent assumptions about the nature of society, that it is itself shaped by differing societies, and that it may at times be a factor in shaping those societies. Yet there was also a fear that many theologians were relatively unskilled in the critical discipline that is concerned with analysing these social interactions — namely sociology.

It was for this very reason that I produced the first edition of *Theology and Sociology* (1987). It reflected my own involvement with the Blackfriars Symposia on Theology and Sociology. These Symposia started in 1978 as a result of a dispute between two sociologists/theologians about my first book, *The Social Context of Theology* (1975).[1] These disputes were reflected, albeit gently, in our only joint book, edited by David Martin, John Orme Mills and W. S. F. Pickering, *Sociology and Theology: Alliance and Conflict*

1

(1980).[2] After meeting for a decade, the Symposia ceased, significantly, with a paper from John Milbank, as yet to produce his intensely provocative and challenging book *Theology and Social Theory: Beyond Secular Reason* (1990).[3] The Catholic sociologist Kieran Flanagan quipped later that, after the publication of the Symposia collection, 'the battlefield separating the two disciplines has been a bit too quiet. Milbank's new book disrupts that peace.'[4]

The radical challenge of postmodernism — represented here by Milbank — does need to be taken seriously in any up-to-date account of theology and sociology. This new and enlarged edition seeks to do just that. I have retained the original structure and conventions (such as paragraph numbering for teaching purposes), but have added an entirely new section at the end on 'Implications for Postmodern Culture'. The predominant style of sociology in the early sections is still 'interactionist' — an approach to sociology typified by the work of Max Weber, which is concerned with the *mutual* interaction between ideas and behaviour (ideas-shaping-behaviour and behaviour-shaping-ideas). However, a few extracts reflect a style of sociology which is more concerned with social function — following in the important tradition of Durkheim. Sociology — like theology itself — is not a unified discipline. It offers a variety of perspectives — interactionist, functionalist and even Marxist — so theologians should be clearly warned that they must make choices between these perspectives if they are to find them intelligible. Postmodernism merely adds yet another perspective, or set of perspectives, to an already confusing array. If my book can help theologians to map a path through this array, then it will have fulfilled its purpose.

Section One: Classical Sociological Studies

Interactionist Sociology

By focusing on Weberian/interactionist sociology, the emphasis is placed on theology seen as both a dependent and an independent social variable. I set out this understanding in *Extract 11*, but for the moment this approach to theology as a cognitive discipline pays attention both to the ways it is shaped by differing societies and, in turn, to the ways it may actually shape these societies. Weber gave classic expression to this social understanding of theology in his *The Protestant Ethic and the Spirit of Capitalism*. In this he sought to trace the extent to which the theological changes that occured with the Reformation were connected with the new 'spirit' that made possible the rise of Western rational capitalism. The validity of the so-called Protestant Ethic Thesis has been much discussed by sociologists (it is outlined in Roderick Martin's **Extract 8**). Its importance here, however, lies in the way Weber approached theology. **Extract 1** shows him discussing the social significance of Luther's notion of the calling. It well demonstrates both the careful and sophisticated nature of his argument and the distinctively sociological way in which he approached theology. He was fully aware that his approach to the subject of theology differed significantly from that of theologians. In a telling footnote in the work, he wrote:

> From theologians I have received numerous valuable suggestions in connection with this study. Its reception on their part has been in general friendly and impersonal, in spite of wide differences of opinion on particular points. This is the more welcome to me since I should not have wondered at a certain antipathy to the manner in which these matters must necessarily be treated here. What to a theologian is valuable in his religion cannot play a very large part in this study. We are concerned with what, from a religious point of view, are often quite superficial and unrefined aspects of religious life, but which, and precisely because they were superficial and unrefined, have often influenced outward behaviour most profoundly (p. 187, n.1).

The same interactionist approach to sociology is apparent in **Extract 2**. Here Weber considers the role of the religious prophet, and particularly the charismatic prophet. For Weber, the latter is a figure who can effect radical social change (he clearly regarded both Jesus and Muhammad as such figures) but is also subject to social constraints. In this extract he also outlines the influential theory of the routinisation of charisma which sets out the dilemma every religious movement which is dependent on a charismatic prophet faces when that prophet dies or ceases to be effective. The theory has numerous implications for those studying earliest Christianity.

Functionalist Theory

Extract 3, from Emile Durkheim's classic study of suicide, provides a contrast with Weber. Like Weber in *The Protestant Ethic and the Spirit of Capitalism*, Durkheim notes differences between Catholic and Protestant behaviour. But unlike Weber, he does not allow that it is theological differences between Catholics and Protestants (and Jews) which shape this behaviour. His treatment of theological factors is characteristically brief and dismissive. As a functionalist, he tends to interpret beliefs in terms of patterns of belonging and seldom entertains the notion that beliefs may effect social changes. So he concludes this extract with the celebrated claim that it is not the beliefs of religion that reduce suicide rates, but rather the degree to which religion 'is a society'. This eminently social and functional (but also deeply conservative) understanding of religion was to receive full expression in Durkheim's monumental *The Elementary Forms of the Religious Life,* which was first published in 1915.

Although the predominant style among the extracts is Weberian (including Troeltsch and Niebuhr), the influence of Durkheim can be seen at several points. It is particularly evident in Robert Bocock's *Extract 26.* His discussion of ritual and liturgy is predominantly functionalist and 'external' (as is Turner's anthropological account of pilgrimage in *Extract 27*). In contrast, David Martin's discussion of theological and liturgical symbols in *Extract 13* is clearly more Weberian and 'internal'. Together they demonstrate that both approaches yield interesting results when analysing liturgy and ritual, although the Weberian approach may in the end prove to be the more theologically interesting. If our concern were the sociology of religion, the choice between these two approaches would be far more arbitrary. But since the focus here is on the needs of the theologian and on theology as a cognitive discipline, rather than on religion in general, the choice becomes clearer.

On 'sect' and 'church'

Ernst Troeltsch's *The Social Teaching of the Christian Churches* has continued to be of interest both to sociologists and to theologians. In some respects this is rather surprising, since the work contains a number of explicit theological criteria and objectives. The central distinction between a 'church' and a 'sect', which is outlined in *Extract 4,* involves the use of Christian doctrinal distinctions and is ultimately framed in terms of an understanding of the gospel. It may seem curious, then, that it has played so seminal a role in typologies within the sociology of religion. Certainly recent sociologists of religion have frequently bemoaned the fact that the distinction as presented by Troeltsch is too tied to the Christian religion. However, for those interested in the relation between sociology and Christian theology this is hardly a problem. Whatever stratagems must be adopted to make the typology fit other religious situations (and these proliferate further every year), their relevance here is apparent. Once it is realised that the relationship a religious institution has to society at large shapes the boundaries of its theological and ethical positions, this relevance can be appreciated by the theologian. The broad distinction between a church and a sect is especially relevant to the extracts concerned with New Testament sociology and to those in Section Four on applied theology.

H. Richard Niebuhr's *The Social Sources of Denominationalism,* in contrast, has suffered periods of comparative neglect both by theologians and by sociologists. The latter have shown periodic interest in Niebuhr's central thesis that sects tend either to die out or to denominationalise in the second generation. But it was often argued that the thesis was over-drawn and too culturally specific to American religious history. Now, with the major use of the thesis by Rodney Stark and William Sims Bainbridge in their *The Future of Religion*,[5] this situation is surely going to change. **Extract 5** shows that the work is also of central interest to those concerned with the relation between theology and sociology. Niebuhr demonstrates how socio-economic factors can be taken seriously by those interested in Christian history, without any necessary commitment to a thoroughgoing Marxist analysis. This is particularly relevant to Gerd Theissen's **Extract 20**.

Relationism

Karl Mannheim's **Extract 6** sets a rather different tone. His *Ideology and Utopia* describes itself as an 'Introduction to the Sociology of Knowledge'. Although Mannheim does not make extensive use of theology in this work, his comments are always pertinent and fruitful. Indeed, Gregory Baum's **Extract 10** shows that Mannheim has been a central influence on his thought in this area (earlier in the article Baum describes him as 'one of my favourite sociologists'). In contrast to Marx and Engels' *The German Ideology*, Mannheim does not use 'ideology' as a reductionist term. Indeed, his point about not using the sociology of knowledge as a 'weapon', since the 'laying bare of the unconscious sources of intellectual existence' applies as much to one's own ideas as those of others, is foundational for an interactionist understanding of theology and sociology. It provides the agenda for, and removes some of the reductionist threat to, the discipline. As I argue in **Extract 11**, there is nothing new about theologians claiming that their *opponents'* views are socially conditioned. In the light of Mannheim, such polemical uses of sociology may seem misdirected: if ideas are to be discredited simply because they are shown to be socially conditioned, then one's own ideas appear equally vulnerable: a thoroughly sociological understanding of knowledge would soon be driven into the absurd position of discrediting *all* knowledge, including its own. Edward Schillebeeckx is sometimes vulnerable to this charge in the way he maps out (to discredit) the social roots of sacerdotal understandings of priesthood — although in **Extract 28** he shows that he is aware of a more interactionist understanding of the role of sociology *vis-à-vis* theology. It is this last understanding which Mannheim chooses to call relationism rather than relativism: a frank admission of the social rootedness of all ideas, without a relativistic attempt to discredit them.

Should a Reader dedicated to 'theology and sociology' not offer a full range of Marxist analyses of theology, as well as recent theological analyses of Marxism, in addition to the literature which looks back to Weber and (somewhat differently) to Durkheim? The popularity of liberation theology has meant that there are already quite a number of sophisticated Marxist sociological/theological analyses, and indeed several useful Readers in this area. Important as these are, they are distinct from types of sociology which attempt to be less value-laden (few sociologists today would claim that their discipline is ever entirely value-free) and which are not at the outset prescriptive. The shadow of Marx is behind many of the extracts, but it is a shadow and not a credal frame.

It was for this reason that it was decided not to include extracts from Marx. It was very tempting to include a passage from Marx and Engels' *The German Ideology*. In the sociology of knowledge this has proved a seminal work, and it does have some (mainly abusive) comments on contemporary theology and on Feuerbach's anthropocentric account of theology. In that work, theology is seen as a form of 'ideology', and ideology, in turn, is seen as a mere expression of the privileged ruling classes and as a product of a spurious division between mental and material behaviour. And against Feuerbach they argue that 'the "liberation" of "man" is not advanced a single step by reducing philosophy, theology, substance and all that trash to "self-consciousness" and by liberating man from the domination of these phrases, which have never held him in thrall': rather, 'liberation is an historical and not a mental act, and it is brought about by historical conditions, the development of industry, commerce, agriculture' (p. 61).[6] These propositions have proved particularly formative in Liberation theology, providing it with both a critique of much Western theology and a *modus operandi* for future theology. This overtly evaluative function of Marxist sociology is important, and has strong implications for theology which are noted particularly by Gregory Baum in *Extract 10*. None the less, it is not the central focus of this Reader, and the inclusion of adequate Marx extracts would have radically altered this focus. In contrast, Mannheim's more restrained, interactionist approach offers the theologian many largely unexplored insights.

Section Two: Implications for Theological Studies

The extracts in the second section have been chosen to illustrate some of the ways that theologians and interested sociologists in the 1970s and 1980s related the two disciplines. A version of my own *Extract 11* and Timothy Radcliffe's *Extract 12* were first published in the Blackfriars Symposia collection (Radcliffe was later to become Master of the Dominicans). An earlier collection of an Oxford conference of theologians and sociologists, *Sociology, Theology and Conflict* (ed. D. E. H. Whiteley and R. Martin),[7] was more disappointing, with the exception of Roderick Martin's very stimulating *Extract 8*. It is interesting that Martin's article was written so soon after Peter Berger's *Extract 7* and yet displays the sort of openness and sophistication in both disciplines that Berger thought was absent. Both Gregory Baum and David Martin have been contributing members of the Blackfriars Symposium, and wrote articles for its publication. Parts of David Martin's *The Breaking of the Image*[8] were first delivered to this Symposium. Further, its influence can even be seen in the work of another of its members, Stephen Sykes, in his *The Identity of Christianity*,[9] to which I shall return presently.

Methodological Groundwork

Extract 7 represents a transition in Berger's theological orientation. In it he rejects his previous sympathies with neo-orthodoxy and, in particular, with the differentiation between 'religion' and 'Christian faith' which he had once thought empirically tenable. As a result, theology, viewed as a social reality, becomes much more vulnerable to sociological analysis. A purely ancillary role for sociology *vis-à-vis* theology is no longer acceptable (see further my *Extract 22*). In his more theological books, *A Rumour of Angels* (1967),[10] *The Heretical Imperative* (1979)[11] and *A Far Glory: The Quest for Faith in an Age of Credulity* (1992),[12] he explores more fully the theological implications of this sociological understanding. The first of these books develops a very successful critique of sociological imperialism (a critique he depicts as a process of 'relativising the relativisers'). It also introduces the idea of 'signals of transcendence', upon which he believes that theological vision can be built. He expands this idea further in *A Far Glory*:

> I have long thought that the signals we can find in ordinary, everyday life are of decisive importance: The recurring urge of human beings to find meaningful order in the world, from the overarching edifices constructed by great minds to the assurance that a mother gives to her frightened child; the redemptive experiences of play and humor; the ineradicable capacity to hope; the overwhelming conviction that certain deeds of inhumanity merit absolute condemnation, and the contrary conviction as to the absolute goodness of certain actions of humanity; the sometimes searing experience of beauty, be it in nature or the works of man ... Each of these ... points toward a reality that lies beyond the ordinary (p. 139).

In *The Heretical Imperative*, the outside links that he seeks to make are with differing religious faith traditions. In a situation of modern fluidity, he looks to a new 'open-minded encounter with other religious possibilities on the level of their truth claims' (p. 167). He believes that this will inevitably lead theologians to question the 'status of particular historical revelations' (p. 169). What he offers in these books is a fascinating mixture of socially structured realities and moments of individual awareness of 'truth' beyond them.

The links with the sort of 'openness' sought in *Extract 7* are clear. Once particular theological traditions are recognised as socially conditioned, claims to a sole possession of religious truth appear distinctly less plausible. It is no longer considered legitimate to 'discredit' other traditions as social products while exempting one's own. Further, it is a fact (at an intellectual level at least) that modern theological faculties are today better and more sympathetically informed about non-Christian religious traditions than once they were. Despite his tendency to distinguish too sharply between 'modernism' and 'pre-modernism', some of the changes Berger outlines are already apparent within the theological world. He sets an important theological agenda, even though remaining vague about its actual contents.

Roderick Martin's *Extract 8* is a useful addition to the Reader for a number of reasons. For those less familiar with the writings of Weber and Durkheim, it provides a convenient and accurate outline. But for those who are already familiar with them, it provides an unusual attempt to uncover the theological roots of these classic works. A number of liberation theologians — most obviously José Porfirio Miranda in *Marx Against the Marxists* (1980)[13] — have sought to show the degree to which Marx's writings presuppose values which he had inherited from the Judaeo-Christian tradition. It is less common to find theologians noting the similar indebtedness of Durkheim and Weber. Yet it should not prove too surprising that Durkheim, whose father and grandfather were both rabbis, and Weber, who spent an active Christian youth, should, despite their subsequent religious agnosticism, have such debts. Martin is commendably restrained in the use to which he puts these observations, but a theologian might wish to take them further. Indeed, it is possible that theologians should be concerned about the extent to which Judaeo-Christian values that have become transposed into a predominantly secular society still require their theological roots for their adequate elaboration and even legitimation. John Habgood has used this point to good effect in his *Church and Nation in a Secular Age*.[14] From a more evangelical perspective, David Lyon's *Sociology and the Human Image*[15] and *The Steeple's Shadow*[16] make sharp and interesting points about values in sociology as a whole.

Roderick Martin's restraint compares interestingly with the ambitious claims of Robert Bellah in **Extract 9**. Bellah, like Peter Berger, has been a major influence on the sociology of religion, particularly in the United States. His pioneering work on American 'civil religion' — which he published in *The Broken Covenant: American Civil Religion in Time of Trial*[17] — has been widely accepted and used by other sociologists. Like Berger, too, Bellah has also written explicitly about his religious beliefs and feelings, although, in contrast to Berger, he has been less concerned to differentiate between his work as a sociologist of religion and his personal commitment as a religious person. Part of the fascination of **Extract 9** is that in it he is happy to see sociology and theology conflated in an approach based upon 'symbolic realism'. In his book *Beyond Belief*,[18] in which the article that formed this extract was reprinted, Bellah outlined his own religious history, linking it at every stage with his work as a sociologist. His early Marxism was tempered both by Stalinism and by Paul Tillich's *The Courage to Be*, and he became convinced of the need, both sociologically and theologically, for a new religious consciousness. He now argued that the fact that Durkheim, Weber and Freud, 'these three great nonbelievers, the most seminal minds in modern social science, each in his own way ran up against nonrational, noncognitive factors of central importance to the understanding of human action, but which did not yield readily to any available conceptual resources, is in itself a fact of great significance for religion in the twentieth century' (p. 240). This approach can be compared interestingly with David Martin's **Extract 13**. It does, however, tend to remove the sociology of religion from the main stream of sociology as a whole. His two more recent collaborative works, *Habits of the Heart: Middle America Observed* (1985)[19] and *The Good Society* (1992),[20] have gone some way to meet this criticism. Both are written from an empirical perspective, albeit with an underlying regret about the plurality of values apparent in America today.

Sociology of Knowledge and Theology

The theologian Gregory Baum has played a very significant role in exploring the relationship between theology and sociology. He first produced *Religion and Alienation: A Theological Reading of Sociology*[21] after a two-year leave of absence from teaching theology in the University of Toronto to study sociology at the New School for Social Research in New York. His reasons for doing this are instructive:

> I was interested in sociology largely because I could not understand why the Catholic Church, despite the good will of clergy and laity and the extraordinary institutional event of Vatican II, had been unable to move

and adopt the new style of Catholicism outlined in the conciliar documents. I thought that sociology, as the systematic enquiry into society,
should be able to answer this question. But what I did not expect was the
profound influence that the study of sociology would have on my entire
theological thinking. I became convinced that the great sociological literature of the 19th and early 20th centuries records human insight and
human wisdom as much as philosophical writings, and that it ought to have
a special place in the education of philosophers and theologians (p. 1).

Focusing as it does on alienation, the book provides a very useful
introduction for theologians to the classic sociologists including
Marx. **Extract 10** was written just after this book was completed
and was later reprinted in Baum's collection *The Social Imperative:
Essays on the Critical Issues that Confront the Christian Churches.*[22] It
summarises particularly effectively the theological implications of a
sociology of knowledge approach to theology. In his work with the
review *Concilium*, and in his *Essays in Critical Theology* (1994),[23]
Baum has continued to explore this particular interaction between
theology and sociology.

Social Role of Theology

My own path as a theologian to studying sociology at university was
rather different. It was while completing my PhD in modern
Christology, at the time of *Honest to God* and secular theology, that
I began to notice both that theologians on either side of the debate
tended to make uncritical assumptions about the nature of society,
and especially about secularisation, and that the theology of the
debate itself exercised a social role. Indeed, my theological super-
visor E. L. Mascall, in his *The Secularisation of Christianity*,[24]
specifically argued that secular theologians were themselves contributing to the very process of secularisation to which they were
ostensibly responding. By extending this argument to all those
engaged in the debate, it became increasingly clear that sociology
did have a role to play in critical theology. The three distinct
sociological approaches that emerged from this observation in my
first two books, *The Social Context of Theology*[25] and *Theology and
Social Structure*,[26] are summarised at the beginning of **Extract 11**.
However, as a result of reading Baum and then Alfredo Fierro's *The
Militant Gospel*,[27] I also became convinced that sociology could at
times play a more critical role in assessing the validity of particular
theological understandings. The work of Baum and others on the
theological roots of anti-Semitism provided the initial evidence for
this. Without adopting the fully Marxist position of Fierro, I realised
that it was possible to use Weberian interactionism as the middle
point of what I term in the extract 'praxis theology'. The first point

would be the theological task of seeking to unpack the social implications of the gospel, albeit using the critical tools of the biblical exegete and systematic theologian. The middle point would be the sociological task of analysing the actual, possible and potential social effects of the theological notions emerging from the first. And the third point would be theological again, attempting to assess the validity of these notions in the light of their likely social effects and the congruence of the latter with the gospel as a whole.

What is 'theology'?

Timothy Radcliffe's **Extract 12** provides a contrast with my own. It is clear that we have rather different understandings of what theology is. In **Extract 22** my definition of theology as 'the written and critical explication of the *sequelae* of individual religious beliefs and of the correlations and interactions between religious beliefs in general' is intentionally academic, cognitive and descriptive/critical. In seeing theology as 'the attempt to make sense of the gospel and the world in the mutually illuminating moment of their encounter', Radcliffe is opting for a more experiential and less academic approach which would not distinguish between spirituality, mysticism, religious poetry and art, and the more academic works which might appear on the shelves of a university library under 'theology'. In the subsequent debate between us at the Blackfriars Symposium, it was suggested that the issue should be decided empirically. But the trouble is that the term 'theology' is used empirically in a variety of ways in Western society. For some it denotes an academic enterprise, but for others not. For some (even within the churches) it is a term of abuse, whereas for others it is evidence of critical faith. For some it is to be used across religious traditions, whereas for others it is a specifically Christian undertaking (as Radcliffe's definition appears to be). Once again, choices cannot be avoided.

David Martin's understanding of theology seems to contain features of both of the previous understandings. In his own contribution to the Blackfriars collection he identifies theology as an intellectual discipline and sees sociology in Weberian terms as concerned with social bonds and boundaries. But then he argues, in terms that would seem to allow for the broader understanding of Radcliffe, that theology 'articulates a "set" or frame which gathers together into one an approach to our personal and social being, a relation of temporal and eternal, a location or image or focus for harmony and perfection, a meaning which lies beyond our immediate apprehensions and which informs the world of natural and historic process' (*Sociology and Theology: Alliance and Conflict*, p. 46). At the same time this understanding is not so explicitly limited to Christianity. In *The Breaking of the Image* this understanding of theology becomes clearer. Most of his books, including his pioneering *A Sociology of English Religion*[28] and his *magnum opus, A General Theory of Secularization,*[29] abide by the conventions of Weberian sociology. But **Extract 13** appears to go beyond this and teases the reader with its final claim that 'in all this nothing has been said about God since reflection on social processes can know nothing whatever about God'. It is evident that his understanding of theological symbolism has been influenced by the studies of signs and symbols in semiotics. The rich potential of such study is only now beginning to be realised, and it is possible that *The Breaking of the Image* may come to be judged to be Martin's most innovative and creative work. However, in discussing the roots, bonds, boundaries and possibilities of religious signs, David Martin, as a sociologist of religion, begins, like Bellah, to sound little different from a descriptive/critical theologian.

Niklas Luhmann is quite clearly a sociologist, albeit one with an unusually central conception of the social function of theology. Garrett Green's **Extract 14** offers both an overview and a critique of this social interpretation of theology. For Luhmann, it is through religion that people can give shape to a highly complex and relative world, and it is through the reflective (and changing) discipline of theology that the identity of religion itself can be shaped and maintained. Few sociologists have given attention to the social role of theologians. In this respect Luhmann is unusual. Green, however, warns fellow theologians not to embrace his analysis of this role too enthusiastically, since he believes that it would 'fundamentally alter' the nature of theology and 'betray its basic commitments'.

Section Three: Implications for Biblical Studies

The extracts in the third section represent one of the fastest-growing areas of biblical scholarship. Old Testament scholars, especially, have a long tradition of drawing upon the social sciences, going back at least to W. Robertson Smith and Julius Wellhausen. Indeed, Weber himself made use of this research, as can be seen in **Extract 2** and **Extract 16**. New Testament scholars have in the past appeared more wary of using, for example, the insights of Troeltsch's **Extract 4**. This has been the case despite the fact that Bultmann gave a strong stress to social context (*Sitz im Leben*) in his historical writings. Perhaps the fear of reductionism was greater among New Testament than among Old Testament scholars, since it was felt that sociology would almost inevitably represent Jesus as a 'mere' charismatic prophet and the early church as a 'mere' conversionist/

millenarian sect. (This fear is somewhat curious among a group of scholars so rigorously critical in other respects.) However, it is only in the last two decades that the social sciences have been used by biblical scholars so systematically. The extracts here have been chosen to represent some of the more sophisticated explorations in this field, and to raise some of the problems they face.

Interpreting Socio-economic Factors

Norman Gottwald's *The Tribes of Israel: A Sociology of the Religion of Liberated Israel*[30] established him as one of the leading Old Testament scholars making active use of sociological methods. *Extract 15* was specifically written to explain the methodological framework of this book and was subsequently reprinted in his influential collection *The Bible and Liberation: Political and Social Hermeneutics*.[31] Gottwald's *The Hebrew Bible: A Socio-Literary Introduction*[32] compares this with more traditional critical methods. His work tends to mix Marxist and Weberian approaches (and sometimes also functionalism). However, the methodological issues raised in this extract also apply to a specifically Weberian approach to sociology. Gottwald faces squarely the objections that are often made by biblical scholars — and that are made very expertly in *Extract 16* by Cyril Rodd — to the use of sociology in their study. Two objections are found more commonly than most. First, it is frequently argued that the socio-economic evidence about Old or even New Testament communities is far too thin to form the basis for any sustainable sociological analysis. And second, it is argued that it is faulty methodology to apply theories developed through studying late nineteenth- and twentieth-century industrial societies to communities that existed two to three thousand years ago. As Rodd correctly points out, Gerd Theissen's work is vulnerable at times to these objections. In response, Gottwald maintains that scholars should be careful in the assumptions they make about socio-economic evidence (Wayne Meeks' *The First Urban Christians*[33] is a striking example of such a careful approach) and should be equally careful about making cross-cultural comparisons (Robert Carroll's *Extract 17* and John Gager's *Extract 19* supply good examples of how this can be done). And finally he sets out an agenda for the sort of historico-territorial and topological studies that could assist theoretical development in this area. If it is still objected that the socio-economic evidence is never going to be complete and that, as a result, the scholar will never be sure that modern sociological theories are entirely appropriate, it can be responded that certainty is not a feature of any other area of biblical research. The scholar will have to make some imaginative assumptions. Gottwald does just that in interpreting earliest Israel as a social revolutionary peasant movement. The point is not: can he substantiate this model beyond reasonable doubt? (of course he cannot), but rather: is it at all credible, and does it generate new and fruitful insights? But that is surely all that can be expected from any biblical analysis. Biblical sociology is in this respect little different from other more traditional methods. Where it is different is in the new insights and connections it can suggest in a scholarly area which has sometimes become repetitive and constrained. It is surely for this reason that biblical sociology is now receiving so much attention.

Cognitive Dissonance

It is possible that a more rather than less theoretical approach will best meet these methodological objections. Both Carroll and Gager are clearly convinced that this is the case. They make an interesting comparison in that they both use the theory of cognitive dissonance to interpret biblical material. Carroll uses it to interpret the prophetic traditions of Isaiah and Haggai-Zechariah. *Extract 17* summarises the approach that he sets out in full in his pioneering study *When Prophecy Failed: Reactions and Responses to Failure in the Old Testament Prophetic Traditions.*[34] Gager uses it to interpret earliest Christianity in his seminal *Kingdom and Community,*[35] from which *Extract 19* is taken. They both start from the premise that Festinger's *When Prophecy Fails*[36] sets out the framework for understanding how religious communities cope with the failure of their predictions to materialise. The theory is not intended to be specific to a particular culture or time, and therefore in principle ought to be applicable even to ancient communities. It intends to set out the options and constraints that *any* community faces in the event of such failure. If this characteristic of the theory is accepted, then the question for the biblical scholar using it becomes: is there evidence to suggest that biblical communities ever faced such failure? The failure of the *parousia* to materialise within the time-span of the New Testament is then an obvious candidate for the theory. Unfortunately for both Carroll and Gager, there must now be considerable doubt about Festinger's study and about the specific conclusions that he drew from it. In *Competing Convictions* (1989)[37] I argue that the key feature in the theory — namely, that increased proselytism results from cognitive dissonance — has proved difficult to substantiate in subsequent case studies. It is even difficult to assess the veracity of Festinger's original case study. Instead, all that can be safely rescued from the theory is that groups at odds with the rest of society tend to resolve cognitive dissonance in a number of different ways — such as denial, blaming others or even each other, and/or a search for new explanations or techniques. The behaviour of Jehovah's Witnesses in the twentieth century, after their various predictions of the *parousia* have appeared unreliable, provides clear evidence of this. Gager himself, while not doubting the original theory, does add interestingly to it.

Routinisation of Charisma

Another example of such a theoretical approach might be provided if the New Testament scholar used the theory of the routinisation of charisma set out in Weber's **Extract 2** (and used by Bocock in **Extract 26**). This theory has received considerable attention among sociologists. Roy Wallis, for example, in his *The Elementary Forms of the New Religious Life*[38] set out a number of ways contemporary sects/cults cope with the problem of routinisation. Together they provide the New Testament scholar with a rich series of possibilities through which to interpret the diachronics of the earliest church. Again the assumption is made that any movement so dependent on a single prophetic figure faces problems when that figure dies or ceases to be effective. Contemporary movements such as Scientology or The Children of God have shown the patterns of social behaviour necessary to cope with this problem. Without intending to 'reduce' the early church to 'nothing but' a Scientology-like sect, the New Testament scholar can still learn from the comparison. This is a methodological, not an ontological approach: it is an attempt to learn through a comparative method; it is not an ontological claim that the early church is 'nothing but' a deviant millenarian sect.

Critical Analysis

Robin Scroggs' **Extract 18** provides a very useful overview and introduction to the three extracts that follow: Gager (**Extract 19**); Theissen (**Extract 20**); and Meeks (**Extract 21**). Gager has already been discussed and a weakness of Theissen has already been noted. Theissen's significance in this area however should not be underrated. His two studies, *The First Followers of Jesus,*[39] from which **Extract 20** is taken, and *The Social Setting of Pauline Christianity*[40] together prompted much of the recent research in this area. He is a stimulating, if eclectic, scholar. This eclecticism stems from a central concern to express faith in terms that take full account of current intellectual forms of criticism. This emerges most clearly in his earlier work *On Having a Critical Faith.*[41] He describes the motivation behind this work in the opening chapter:

If we take seriously the problem of historical relativity, the concern for empirical verification, and present-day ideological scepticism, how much of Christianity can really stand up to criticism? In other words, once we stop assuming that Christianity is a privileged tradition, and give up the claim that the truth is contained, once and for all, in one particular tradition, what is left? What is left if we question whether we are competent to say anything at all about areas beyond the realm of potential experience? What is left once we stop playing the defensive trick of declaring our own particular sanctuaries out of bounds to psychological and sociological criticisms, as though these criticisms were concerned only with marginal phenomena and other religions . . . For all its obscenities, illusions and daydreams, I believe that Christianity has an authenticity which can make it supremely significant for human life. Most Christians are not so confident. As a result, they are allergic to historical, empiricist and ideological criticism. They mistrust arguments. They prefer to say that faith is a miracle which defies all argument (p. 1).

This quotation describes very well both the sort of critical theological attitude to faith which can accept the challenge of biblical sociology, and the reason why some theologians still remain suspicious of it. Theissen's own form of theological tough-mindedness has led him into a rich variety of areas. For example, in *Biblical Faith: An Evolutionary Approach* (1984)[42] he examines the implications of evolutionary theory for theology and, more recently, in *The Sign Language of Faith* (1995)[43] he looks at preaching and symbolic language. At a more popular level, many have found his little book *The Shadow of the Galilean* (1987)[44] to be highly evocative.

Wayne Meeks' work is less overtly apologetic. His *The First Urban Christians: The Social World of the Apostle Paul*[45] quickly established itself as one of the most comprehensive in current New Testament sociology. It successfully demonstrates that the misgivings expressed in Rodd's **Extract 16** need not deter further research in this area. Indeed, such research is only just beginning. The article from which **Extract 21** is taken acted as a forerunner to this research. It is admittedly speculative, but it does show how a sociological perspective can bring new light to well-known textual problems. Instead of treating the paradoxical language of the Fourth Gospel as a literary problem, Meeks suggests that it is also a social problem. More specifically, he attempts to produce an outline of the community from which it emerged. An interest in the particular communities implicit in the New Testament, and in the (often very similar) communities in the pagan world surrounding the early Christians, has been crucial to his most recent research. The fruits of this interest are brilliantly set out in his *The Origins of Christian Morality: The First Two Centuries* (1993).[46]

Section Four: Implications for Applied Theology

This section of the Reader could easily have dominated it. There is
after all a history of some decades of churches using some sociological techniques to further their work. Most churches are aware
now of the importance of keeping accurate statistics of their affili-
ation and membership patterns. In France, since soon after the last
war, the Roman Catholic 'religious sociology' movement under le
Bras and Boulard (summarised in Fernand Boulard's *An Introduction to Religious Sociology*[47]) used a variety of sociological techniques
to further the mission of the rural church. In the United States, the
Roman Catholic sociologist J. H. Fichter paid particular attention
to churches in urban areas (e.g. in his *Social Relations in the Urban
Parish*[48]). And in Britain, evangelicals have been most active in
measuring churchgoing patterns (e.g. in the MARC surveys). Further, many church bodies have used professional sociologists in
compiling reports on moral/social issues. However, important
though this work is for other purposes, it has not been noticeably
theoretical in orientation and, as a result, has seldom contributed
significantly to academic theology. Since that is the focus of this
Reader, such work has therefore been excluded. The mere use of
some sociological techniques has not been considered sufficient for
inclusion. Instead, all of the contributions that appear have been
selected for their theoretical and professional contribution to the
discipline. In addition, they have been selected to demonstrate
some of the range of areas within applied theology that can benefit
from sociological theory.

Social Consequences and Theological Validity

In *Extract 22* I review some of the ancillary uses that have been
made of sociology within practical/pastoral theology and Christian
ethics, before suggesting more integral relations between the two
disciplines. In some respects it is somewhat artificial to distinguish
between, say, 'systematic theology' and 'applied theology'. My own
definition of theology (which includes both the *sequelae* of and the
correlations and interactions between religious beliefs) rather precludes this. Liberation theology also precludes this distinction,
since it insists that praxis and belief are mutually related and should
not be treated separately. In contrast, the conventional distinction
presupposes that systematic theology can be studied apart from its
application, and vice versa. It is also clear that the final point in this
extract relates to the central point of *Extract 11* — i.e. that the
social consequences of theological notions are relevant to a theological assessment of their validity. In a theologian like Edward

Schillebeeckx this point becomes increasingly clear. The implication of all of this is that the very term 'applied theology' is at most only a convenient way of ordering material and not a separate branch of theology.

Sociology and Christian Ethics

David Martin's **Extract 23** provides a very clear account of the ways sociology can be used integrally in ethics/Christian ethics. It is commonplace to find social data being used in ethical discussions of socio-political issues, but Martin's suggestions go considerably beyond this. By tracing the social antecedents of, constraints upon, and possibilities for, particular issues, the sociologist enters into a serious role in ethics and can help to clarify the 'quagmire of compromises' that comprise political decision-making. In *A Textbook of Christian Ethics*[49] I attempt to show at length how such sociological analysis can form an integral part of doing Christian ethics. For me, an adequate understanding of Christian ethics involves moral, philosophical, theological *and* social forms of analysis. There can be little doubt that this places heavy demands upon those doing Christian ethics, but a work like Thomas Ogletree's *The Use of the Bible in Christian Ethics*[50] shows that this is both possible and necessary. Once it is observed that Christian ethics is itself pluralistic (not least in its varying uses of the Bible), sociological understanding can be seen to be an important means of self-understanding within the discipline.

Sociology and Church Organisation

There have been a number of attempts to apply the sociology of organisations to the churches. These tend to be based upon Weber's theories about differing types of organisation, and the variants that have been suggested since Weber. Peter F. Rudge's *Ministry and Management: The Study of Ecclesiastical Administration*[51] provides a clear example of how these can be applied to theological concepts of the church. Stewart Ranson, Alan Bryman and Bob Hinings' *Clergy, Ministers and Priests*[52] shows how they can also be applied to an analysis of religious professionals. Neither study, however, has the range or verve of Mady A. Thung's *The Precarious Organisation: Sociological Explorations of the Church's Mission and Structure.*[53] This work is well informed in three areas: the sociology of religion, the sociology of organisations, and theology. **Extract 24** provides a convenient summary of this long and detailed study. Thung takes seriously the degree to which churches as churches are socially constrained, and then attempts to construct a model which could act as a blueprint for a church which was able to be genuinely prophetic in society. She offers, in effect, a structural pattern which could allow churches to exercise the kind of ethical role suggested in Martin's *Extract 23*. Whether such a blueprint could ever be put into practice, or even whether it is desirable that it ever should be put into practice (for some it may in the end appear too sectarian), it *is* theologically interesting. What it demonstrates is that utopian models (in Mannheim's sense) can be constructed by combining theological and sociological skills, and that they may, once constructed, help the theologian to understand better the function of the churches. This theoretical model-building role for sociology contrasts sharply with the mundane role it occupied in the French religious sociology movement. Clare Watkins in *Extract 29* places both Rudge and Thung into a wider critical context of theologians who have used insights from the sociology of organisations.

Sociology and Pastoral Care

Mady Thung is aware of the need for pastoral care in her church model, although she gives few details. The dominant models within the field of pastoral care and counselling have been individualistic and psycho-therapeutic. Nevertheless, there has been a small but persistent voice even within such approaches calling for a more social model of pastoral care. This has stemmed from the recognition that an adequate system of pastoral care for individuals must also pay attention to their social context. E. Mansell Pattison's *Extract 25* was a rather isolated call when it first appeared. It was strongly reinforced by his subsequent book, *Pastor and Parish — A Systems Approach*.[54] However, it has now received far greater support from those writing from the perspective of liberation theology. For example, the seminal work, Gustavo Gutiérrez's *A Theology of Liberation*,[55] saw pastoral activity as essentially belonging to the Christian community and as giving rise to a theology which has 'a clear and critical attitude regarding economic and socio-cultural issues in the life and reflection of the Christian community' (p. 11). However, Pattison demonstrates that it is not essential to adopt a Marxist approach to appreciate the relevance of social factors in pastoral care. The discipline remains individualistic, but there are important signs of change, and once again sociological models could assist and clarify this change.

Sociology and Liturgy

Liturgists have as yet given surprisingly little theoretical attention to sociology, despite being in the vanguard of religious change, and despite having at times used social data and techniques. It may be more important than they realise that they examine their own social role if they are to understand contemporary Christianity. Certainly if Stephen Sykes' position is adopted (or that of Luhmann in *Extract 14*), that the identity of Christianity is strongly related to Christian worship, liturgy and ritual, then his questions about the power of theologians become relevant. Following an analysis using insights from the sociology of power, he argues, in *The Identity of Christianity*,[56] as follows:

> In a situation of internal conflict about the identity of Christianity . . . the necessary decisions are taken in the light of the clarification of the issues provided by theologians. Theologians are active across the entire range of dimensions of Christianity, from doctrines and ethics to ritual and social embodiment, because in each case a theological, or interpretative discipline has grown up in order to make meanings as precise as possible. Theologians are, therefore, necessarily involved in the internal power struggles which conflicts provoke (p. 76).

Kieran Flanagan's *Sociology and Liturgy* (1991)[57] provides one of the fullest sociological accounts of liturgy. For Flanagan, liturgies attempt 'to deal in hidden meanings produced through ambiguous and indeterminate social means'. If these meanings are finally for philosophers and theologians to discuss, he argues that the means (functional as well as dysfunctional) are appropriate objects of sociological curiosity. Since Section Five has an extract from Flanagan, *Extract 26* is taken instead from Robert Bocock's pioneering study *Ritual in Industrial Society* (1974).[58] Bocock's functionalism makes a sharp contrast with David Martin's interactionism and subtle nuances in *Extract 13*. However, what it does demonstrate is that Durkheim's social understanding of ritual (albeit with slight modifications) can successfully be applied to ritual in an industrial society. The work also shows numerous ways ritual persists even within 'secular' society. Another very imaginative attempt to show this persistence (in communist Russian society) is in Christel Lane's *The Rites of Rulers*.[59] A rather different use of the social sciences in liturgy would involve the sort of use of semiotics evident in *Extract 13*. It is here perhaps that the most far-reaching results might be achieved. Social anthropologists, sociologists and socio-linguists might all be able to make substantial contributions to liturgical studies in ways that are still emerging.

Sociology, not social anthropology, forms the main focus of this Reader. However, liturgists have been particularly influenced by the work of the late Victor Turner. His *The Ritual Process*[60] (1969) convinced many that social anthropology can make an important contribution to this area of applied theology. *Extract 27* comes from his *Image and Pilgrimage in Christian Culture*,[61] which appeared nine years later (written with his wife Edith). It offers a startling example of ritual, that of pilgrimage, which contrasts strongly with the cognitive discipline of theology, and exposes central differences between Roman Catholic and Protestant perspectives. For the theologian, the concept of 'liminality' that he outlines has especial relevance.

Sociology, Ministry and Ecclesiology

Extract 28 is a short piece from Edward Schillebeeckx's *Ministry: A Case for Change* (revised as *The Church with a Human Face* — a revision which does not change the substantive thesis represented here).[62] There has been a considerable amount of attention given to ordained ministry by sociologists of religion. Much of this has been concerned with the roles of ministers in a predominantly secular society, and with the question of whether or not ministry is still to be considered a 'profession'. In this context Anthony Russell's *The Clerical Profession*[63] provides a useful socio-historical analysis and Robert Towler and A. P. M. Coxon's *The Fate of the Anglican Clergy*[64] provides a polemical, but sociologically informed, analysis of ministry within the Church of England. These studies, however, have seldom contributed substantially to theological discussions of ministry. In this respect Schillebeeckx's study is quite different. Less diffuse than Bernard Cooke in *Ministry to Word and Sacraments*,[65] Schillebeeckx writes as a theologian, albeit as a theologian using socio-historical methods to uncover particular patterns and understandings of ministry as they relate to changing social contexts. Despite his occasional polemical use of this method, he successfully shows that a theological analysis of Christian ministry throughout the ages should not ignore its social determinants. Once it is observed that Christian history (let alone the contemporary churches) does not offer a single understanding or pattern of ordained ministry, the role of the sociologist again becomes evident. For some, this observation will undoubtedly lead to a relativisation of all understandings of ordained ministry (or an attempt to bypass the analysis altogether by insisting that one form is exempt and sacrosanct). Schillebeeckx, however, seems to adopt a position closer to Mannheim's relationism. In this understanding, all forms of ministry are recognised as socially rooted, so it becomes incumbent on the theologian (albeit using sociological analysis) to ask which forms are most appropriate for present-day society. Sociology is thus afforded an integral role in a theological enterprise.

Clare Watkins' *Extract 29* brings this section to a useful conclusion. She clearly sees the importance of using the social sciences judiciously in ecclesial areas. However, she is also well aware of some of the dangers. In the longer article from which this extract is taken, she argues that 'the use of social-science perspectives in ecclesiology is rooted in a traditional tension of church life — the tension between the Church which is the object of our faith and the erring community in which we live and worship — and represents a serious attempt to understand this tension more fully and fruitfully' (p. 692). This is indeed a tension which drives many of us who work in this area of theological–sociological research.

Section Five: Implications for Postmodern Culture

This final section of the Reader seeks to reflect the challenge of postmodernism that has increasingly been discussed in recent theology. Sometimes this takes the form of theologians attempting to understand the changing nature of societies and cultures today. Richard Roberts' *Extract 35* provides a good example of this — examining as it does the possible religious implications of globalisation. However, more radically, it takes the Milbank form — theology challenging 'secular' disciplines such as sociology itself. Most of the other contributors to this Reader regard sociology as a critical perspective which can, if used judiciously, sharpen and deepen theology. Milbank, in contrast, uses theology as a means to vanquish sociology.

John Milbank sets out his polemic against the sociology of religion in chapter 5 of his *Theology and Social Theory*.[66] In this chapter he attempts 'to show how all twentieth-century sociology of religion can be exposed as a secular policing of the sublime. Deconsructed in this fashion, the entire project evaporates into the pure ether of the secular will-to-power' (p. 106). There are several extremely ambitious claims here.

Milbank's first claim is that apparently he does mean *all* twentieth-century sociology of religion. To emphasise this point, he ends the chapter by claiming that 'if the analysis given in this chapter is correct, the sociology of religion ought to come to an end' (p. 139). Kieran Flanagan's *Extract 33* points out the obvious difficulty facing such an all-encompassing claim. To be properly substantiated, it would need to include a critique of theologically nuanced sociologists of religion such as David Martin, Richard Fenn or Flanagan himself. Yet it is significant that their work is nowhere mentioned in *Theology and Social Theory*.

A second claim is that the sociology of religion can be seen as 'a *secular* policing of the sublime'. For Milbank sociology of religion is secular in the sense of being positively secularist. He seeks to show that a secularism which presumes the dominance of the social over the religious is implicit (and sometimes explicit) throughout the discipline. Again, Flanagan has little difficulty pointing out that, while positivism may indeed have been presumed by some of the early sociologists of religion, it is scarcely a position held by all present-day exponents of the discipline or even by Weber himself. Flanagan's own writings — and especially his recent book *The Enchantment of Sociology* (1996)[67] — demonstrate this clearly. What Flanagan seeks to do in this book is to offer a route through sociology which makes contact with a specifically Catholic theology. He examines at length some of the dilemmas facing modern sociology — such as the problems of detachment, relativism, and disenchantment — and seeks to show that such features as reflexivity, habitus and re-enchantment offer positive points of sociological contact which are indeed relevant to theology. In the process he offers an account of Weber's own sociology of religion which is considerably removed from positivism/secularism.

Milbank's third and most original claim is that the sociology of religion represents an attempt at 'policing of the sublime'. Once this is recognised, the discipline can then be 'deconstructed' and unmasked as a 'secular will-to-power'. It is precisely this element in his polemic that has been so attractive to a number of theologians. It neatly reverses Nietzsche, and offers theologians a way of showing that 'every secular positivism is revealed to be also a positivist theology'. With more than a hint of irony, Milbank concludes that 'sociology could still continue, but it would have to define itself as a "faith" ' (p. 139). Thus, after years of being patronised by philosophers and social scientists, theologians can now turn the tables and unmask these secular understandings of religion as being themselves forms of secular theology. In effect, theologians can call the ideological bluff of sociologists of religion. As Fergus Kerr's *Extract 30* argues: 'Milbank's thesis is simplicity itself. There is no need to bring theology and social theory together, theology is *already* social theory, and social theory is *already* theology.' Theology is able to unmask the theological pretensions of the social sciences and to offer instead an alternative, and indeed better, means of understanding social reality. Christian theology, and the church which carries and sustains this theology, alone overcomes the ills of Western ideology.

This high and exclusive claim for Christian theology, and in turn for 'the Church', has attracted fierce critics as well as strong supporters. It is certainly very different from Peter Berger's 'step-by-step correlation' and from the sort of cautious use of sociology envisaged by earlier extracts in this Reader. The Anglican theologian Rowan Williams in *Extract 31* and the Catholic theologian Aidan Nichols in *Extract 32* both offer thoughtful criticisms of this understanding of theology and the weight it places upon particular churches.

Gregory Baum, while sympathetic to the idea of theology offering a social critique, is also uncomfortable with the exclusivism of Milbank's claims. Baum believes 'against Milbank that the Church must be open to its critics, whether they be the victims of society or the modern masters of suspicion'. He argues:

> Basing himself on postmodern theory and his exclusivist christology, Milbank rejects all dialogue across the boundaries of the Church. He regards dialogue across cultural boundaries as a modern illusion ... Milbank argues that the Church's stance toward world religions should not be dialogue but suspicion. In my opinion, to defend such a position in contemporary England troubled by racial, cultural and religious diversity creates a discourse that encourages violence. This takes us to Milbank's fateful decision to shield the Church from the critiques of modernity issued by Marx, Freud, Nietzsche and many others. The critiques derived from secular reason, Milbank has argued, perpetuate the violence implicit in the Enlightenment project. What this committed pacifist fails to acknowledge is that Christian practice itself, almost from the beginning, contained dimensions of violence ... Symbolic of the dark side of Christian practice was the negation of Jewish existence (in action and theory) associated from the beginning with the proclamation of Jesus as Lord (*Essays in Critical Theology*, p. 70).

In *Extract 34* Milbank responds to some of his critics. He remains convinced that it is possible to articulate a (postmodern) understanding of the church and Christian theology which offers a radical alternative to 'secular reason'.

Richard Roberts' *Extract 35* and Stephen Pattison's *Extract 36* offer a sharp contrast to Milbank. Whereas Milbank sees radical discontinuities between theological and sociological perspectives, Roberts and Pattison tend instead to see continuities. So Roberts maintains that the social process of globalisation has important implications for present-day theology. And Pattison argues that theology can both challenge and be challenged by management studies. But for Milbank it is Christianity alone which can unmask the ills of Western ideology.

Roberts believes that it is religion within and beyond the boundaries of Christianity which can become a socially significant global resource. The world's religions have the potential to become 'an effective cultural capital, a dynamic resource for a modern/postmodern world system'. Of course he is well aware of the fragile optimism that lies behind this claim. Pattison is somewhat more modest. He argues that the theologian can unmask some of the implicit faith and theology of management theory and practice and, in the process, teach managers to be more nuanced and critically aware. In effect, managers should become critical theologians!

The postmodern debate has generated a good deal of energy recently among theologians. It suggests that the interaction between theology and sociology is not yet over. Nothing is (or perhaps ever could be) finally settled. There is much fruitful work to be done.

Notes

1. Mowbrays, Oxford, 1975.
2. Harvester, Sussex, 1980.
3. Blackwell, Oxford, 1990.
4. Kieran Flanagan, 'Preface', *New Blackfriars*, Vol. 73 No. 861, June 1992, p. 302.
5. University of California Press, Berkeley, 1985.
6. Karl Marx and Frederick Engels, *The German Ideology*, ed. C. J. Arthur; Lawrence and Wishart, London and New York, 1970.
7. Blackwell, Oxford, 1969.
8. Blackwell, Oxford, 1980.
9. SPCK, London, 1984.
10. Doubleday, New York, 1967; Pelican, Harmondsworth, Middlesex, 1969.
11. Anchor/Doubleday, New York, 1979; Collins, London, 1980.
12. Free Press, New York, 1992.
13. SCM Press, London, 1980.
14. Darton, Longman and Todd, 1983.
15. Inter-Varsity Press, Leicester, 1983.
16. SPCK, London, 1985.
17. Seabury Press, New York, 1975.
18. Harper and Row, New York and London, 1970.
19. Robert Bellah, Richard Madsen, William M. Sullivan, Ann Swidler, Steven M. Tipton, *Habits of the Heart*, University of California Press, 1985; Hutchinson, London, 1988.
20. Robert Bellah, Richard Madsen, William M. Sullivan, Ann Swidler, Steven M. Tipton, *The Good Society*, Vintage, New York, 1992.
21. Paulist Press, New York, 1975.
22. Paulist Press, New York, 1979.
23. Sheed and Ward, Kansas City, 1994.
24. Darton, Longman and Todd, 1965.
25. Mowbrays, Oxford, 1975.
26. Mowbrays, Oxford, 1977.
27. SCM Press, London, 1977.
28. Heinemann, London, 1968.
29. Blackwell, Oxford, 1978.
30. Orbis Books, Maryknoll, New York, 1979.
31. Orbis Books, Maryknoll, New York, 1983.

32. Fortress, Philadelphia, 1987.
33. Yale University Press, New Haven and London, 1983.
34. SCM Press, London, 1979.
35. Prentice-Hall, Englewood Cliffs, New Jersey, 1975.
36. Minneapolis, 1956.
37. SCM Press, London, 1989.
38. Routledge and Kegan Paul, London, 1984.
39. Christian Kaiser Verlag, Munich, 1977; ET, SCM Press, London, 1978.
40. Fortress Press, Philadelphia; T. and T. Clark, Edinburgh, 1982.
41. Christian Kaiser Verlag, Munich, 1978; ET, SCM Press, London, 1979.
42. Christian Kaiser Verlag, Munich, 1984; ET, SCM Press, London, 1984.
43. SCM Press, London, 1995.
44. SCM Press, London, 1987.
45. Yale University Press, New Haven and London, 1983.
46. Yale University Press, New Haven and London, 1993.
47. Darton, Longman and Todd, London, 1960.
48. University of Chicago Press, 1954.
49. T. and T. Clark, Edinburgh, 1985 (revised edition, 1995).
50. Blackwell, Oxford, 1985.
51. Tavistock, London, 1969.
52. Routledge and Kegan Paul, London, 1977.
53. Mouton, Gravenhage, 1976.
54. Fortress Press, Philadelphia, 1977.
55. Orbis Books, Maryknoll, New York, 1973; SCM Press, London, 1974; see also Stephen Pattison, *Pastoral Care and Liberation Theology*, Cambridge University Press, 1994.
56. SPCK, London, 1984.
57. Macmillan, London, 1991.
58. Peters, London, 1974.
59. Cambridge University Press, 1981.
60. Aldine, Chicago; Routledge and Kegan Paul, London, 1969.
61. Columbia University Press, New York; Blackwell, Oxford, 1978.
62. New York, Crossroad; SCM Press, London, 1981.
63. SPCK, London, 1980.
64. Macmillan, London, 1979.
65. Fortress Press, Philadelphia, 1976.
66. Blackwell, Oxford, 1990.
67. Macmillan, London, 1996.

SECTION ONE

Classical
Sociological Studies

1

Max Weber
Luther's Conception of the Calling

This Extract constitutes the third chapter of *The Protestant Ethic and the Spirit of Capitalism* (first published 1904–05). In the first chapter Weber (1864–1920) observed that 'business leaders and owners of capital, as well as the higher grades of skilled labour, and even more the technically and commercially trained personnel of modern enterprises, are overwhelmingly Protestant' (p. 35). Other differences between Roman Catholics and Protestants were noted by Durkheim in *Extract 3* and Turner in *Extract 27*. Before trying to identify the way these differences are related to the rise of Western capitalism, Weber outlined, in the second chapter, what he termed the 'spirit' of capitalism. He found the writings of Benjamin Franklin in the eighteenth century particularly instructive: 'all Franklin's moral attitudes are coloured with utilitarianism. Honesty is useful, because it assures; so are punctuality, industry, frugality, and that is the reason they are virtues' (p. 52). Weber thought this odd in two ways. Firstly, such a utilitarian approach makes social appearance more important than actuality: it is more important that someone in business *appears* to be honest (because this generates business confidence) than that this person is actually honest. And secondly, the combination of Franklin's virtues is odd: the spirit of capitalism demands both industry (particularly in the making of money) and frugality (this money is to be spent not on personal enjoyment but on building up the business). It is to account for these oddities that Weber turned back to the Reformation to see whether it (incidentally) effected such moral changes in society. As this Extract indicates (*1.9f.*), he was to find in popular Calvinism the fullest expression of the Protestant ethic (with its very strong stress on election and predestination). But chapter 3 marks the crucial transition in the book and, in the context of attempts to understand theology sociologically, sets out the ground-rules of what is to follow. Of particular importance here is the stress upon the social effects of theology (not always congenial to the theologian), the distinction between popular Lutheranism and Luther's own attitudes towards economic realities, and the modest role (*1.15*) that Weber afforded his theory (many critics of the theory have ignored Weber's own careful qualifications). Whatever the merits of the theory as a whole, Weber's method in examining the social role of theology remains a model for present-day research in this area.

Further Reading

Michael Hill, *A Sociology of Religion* (Heinemann, 1973) provides a useful account of Weber's theory and sets it into the larger context of the sociology of religion (see also *Extract 8*). Gordon Marshall, *In Search of the Spirit of Capitalism: an Essay on Max Weber's Protestant Ethic Thesis* (Hutchinson, 1982) and Gianfranco Poggi, *Calvinism and the Capitalist Spirit* (Macmillan, 1983) provide a full account in the light of recent research.

Task of the Investigation

1.1 Now it is unmistakable that even in the German word *Beruf*, and perhaps still more clearly in the English *calling*, a religious conception, that of a task set by God, is at least suggested. The more emphasis is put upon the word in a concrete case, the more evident is the connotation. And if we trace the history of the word through the civilized languages, it appears that neither the predominantly Catholic peoples nor those of classical antiquity have possessed any expression of similar connotation for what we know as a calling (in the sense of a life-task, a definite field in which to work), while one has existed for all predominantly Protestant peoples. It may be further shown that this is not due to any ethnical peculiarity of the languages concerned. It is not, for instance, the product of a Germanic spirit, but in its modern meaning the word comes from the Bible translations, through the spirit of the translator, not that of the original. In Luther's translation of the Bible it appears to have first been used at a point in Jesus Sirach (xi, 20 and 21) precisely in our modern sense. After that it speedily took on its present meaning in the everyday speech of all Protestant peoples, while earlier not even a suggestion of such a meaning could be found in the secular literature of any of them, and even, in religious writings, so far as I can ascertain, it is only found in one of the German mystics whose influence on Luther is well known.

1.2 Like the meaning of the word, the idea is new, a product of the Reformation. This may be assumed as generally known.

It is true that certain suggestions of the positive valuation of routine activity in the world, which is contained in this conception of the calling, had already existed in the Middle Ages, and even in late Hellenistic antiquity. We shall speak of that later. But at least one thing was unquestionably new: the valuation of the fulfilment of duty in worldly affairs as the highest form which the moral activity of the individual could assume. This it was which inevitably gave every-day worldly activity a religious significance, and which first created the conception of the calling in this sense. The conception of the calling thus brings out that central dogma of all Protestant denominations which the Catholic division of ethical precepts into *præcepta* and *consilia* discards. The only way of living acceptably to God was not to surpass worldly morality in monastic asceticism, but solely through the fulfilment of the obligations imposed upon the individual by his position in the world. That was his calling.

1.3 Luther developed the conception in the course of the first decade of his activity as a reformer. At first, quite in harmony with the prevailing tradition of the Middle Ages, as represented, for example, by Thomas Aquinas, he thought of activity in the world as a thing of the flesh, even though willed by God. It is the indispensable natural condition of a life of faith, but in itself, like eating and drinking, morally neutral. But with the development of the conception of *sola fide* in all its consequences, and its logical result, the increasingly sharp emphasis against the Catholic *consilia evangelica* of the monks as dictates of the devil, the calling grew in importance. The monastic life is not only quite devoid of value as a means of justification before God, but he also looks upon its renunciation of the duties of this world as the product of selfishness, withdrawing from temporal obligations. In contrast, labour in a calling appears to him as the outward expression of brotherly love. This he proves by the observation that the division of labour forces every individual to work for others, but his view-point is highly naïve, forming an almost grotesque contrast to Adam Smith's well-known statements on the same subject. However, this justification, which is evidently essentially scholastic, soon disappears again, and there remains, more and more strongly emphasized, the statement that the fulfilment of worldly duties is under all circumstances the only way to live acceptably to God. It and it alone is the will of God, and hence every legitimate calling has exactly the same worth in the sight of God.

1.4 That this moral justification of worldly activity was one of the most important results of the Reformation, especially of Luther's part in it, is beyond doubt, and may even be considered a platitude. This attitude is worlds removed from the deep hatred of Pascal, in his contemplative moods, for all worldly activity, which he was deeply convinced could only be understood in terms of vanity or low cunning. And it differs even more from the liberal utilitarian compromise with the world at which the Jesuits arrived. But just what the practical significance of this achievement of Protestantism was in detail is dimly felt rather than clearly perceived.

1.5 In the first place it is hardly necessary to point out that Luther cannot be claimed for the spirit of capitalism in the sense in which we have used that term above, or for that matter in any sense whatever. The religious circles which to-day most enthusiastically celebrate that great achievement of the Reformation are by no means friendly to capitalism in any sense. And Luther himself would, without doubt, have sharply repudiated any connection with a point of view like that of Franklin. Of course, one cannot consider his complaints against the great merchants of his time, such as the Fuggers, as evidence in this case. For the struggle against the privileged position, legal or actual, of single great trading companies in the sixteenth and seventeenth centuries may best be compared with the modern campaign against the trusts, and can no more justly be considered in itself an expression of a traditionalistic point of view. Against these people, against the Lombards, the monopolists, speculators, and bankers patronized by the Anglican Church and the kings and parliaments of England and France, both the Puritans and the Huguenots carried on a bitter struggle. Cromwell, after the battle of Dunbar (September 1650), wrote to the Long Parliament: 'Be pleased to reform the abuses of all professions: and if there be any one that makes many poor to make a few rich, that suits not a Commonwealth'. But, nevertheless, we will find Cromwell following a quite specifically capitalistic line of thought. On the other hand, Luther's numerous statements against usury or interest in any form reveal a conception of the nature of capitalistic acquisition which, compared with that of late Scholasticism, is, from a capitalistic view-point, definitely backward. Especially, of course, the doctrine of the sterility of money which Anthony of Florence had already refuted.

1.6 But it is unnecessary to go into detail. For, above all, the consequences of the conception of the calling in the religious sense for worldly conduct were susceptible to quite different interpretations. The effect of the Reformation as such was only that, as compared with the Catholic attitude, the moral emphasis on and the religious sanction of, organized worldly labour in a calling was mightily increased. The way in which the concept of the calling, which expressed this change, should develop further depended upon the religious evolution which now took place in the different Protestant Churches. The authority of the Bible, from which Luther thought he had derived his idea of the calling, on the whole favoured a traditionalistic interpretation. The old Testament, in particular, though in the genuine prophets it showed no sign of a tendency to excel worldly morality, and elsewhere only in quite isolated rudiments and suggestions, contained a similar religious idea entirely in this traditionalistic sense. Everyone should abide by his living and let the godless run after gain. That is the sense of all the statements which bear directly on worldly activities. Not until the Talmud is a partially, but not even then fundamentally, different attitude to be found. The personal attitude of Jesus is characterized in classical purity by the typical antique-Oriental plea: 'Give us this day our daily bread'. The element of radical repudiation of the world, as expressed in the *mamōnas tēs adikias*, excluded the possibility that the modern idea of a calling should be based on his personal authority. In the apostolic era as expressed in the New Testament, especially in St Paul, the Christian looked upon worldly activity either with indifference, or at least essentially traditionalistically; for those first generations were filled with eschatological hopes. Since everyone was simply waiting for the coming of the Lord, there was nothing to do but remain in the station and in the worldly occupation in which the call of the Lord had found him, and labour as before. Thus he would not burden his brothers as an object of charity, and it would only be for a little while. Luther read the Bible through the spectacles of his whole attitude; at the time and in the course of his development from about 1518 to 1530 this not only remained traditionalistic but became ever more so.

1.7 In the first years of his activity as a reformer he was, since he thought of the calling as primarily of the flesh, dominated by an attitude closely related, in so far as the form of worldly activity was concerned, to the Pauline eschatological indifference as expressed in 1 Cor. vii. One may attain salvation in any walk of life; on the short pilgrimage of life there is no use in laying weight on the form of occupation. The pursuit of material gain beyond personal needs must thus appear as a symptom of lack of grace, and since it can apparently only be attained at the expense of others, directly reprehensible. As he became increasingly involved in the affairs of the world, he came to value work in the world more highly. But in the concrete calling an individual pursued he saw more and more a special command of God to fulfil these particular duties which the Divine Will had imposed upon him. And after the conflict with the Fanatics and the peasant disturbances, the objective historical order of things in which the individual has been placed by God becomes for Luther more and more a direct manifestation of divine will. The stronger and stronger emphasis on the providential element, even in particular events of life, led more and more to a traditionalistic interpretation based on the idea of Providence. The individual should remain once and for all in the station and calling in which God had placed him, and should restrain his worldly activity within the limits imposed by his established station in life. While his economic traditionalism was originally the result of Pauline indifference, it later became that of a more and more intense belief in divine providence, which identified absolute obedience to God's will, with absolute acceptance of things as they were. Starting from this background, it was impossible for Luther to establish a new or in any way fundamental connection between worldly activity and religious principles. His acceptance of purity of doctrine as the one infallible criterion of the Church, which became more and more irrevocable after the struggles of the 'twenties, was in itself sufficient to check the development of new points of view in ethical matters.

1.8 Thus for Luther the concept of the calling remained traditionalistic. His calling is something which man has to accept as a divine ordinance, to which he must adapt himself. This aspect outweighed the other idea which was also present, that work in the calling was a, or rather *the*, task set by God. And in its further development, orthodox Lutheranism emphasized this aspect still more. Thus, for the time being, the only ethical result was negative; worldly duties were no longer subordinated to ascetic ones; obedience to authority and the acceptance of things as they were, were preached. In this Lutheran form the idea of a calling had, as will be shown in our discussion of mediæval religious ethics, to a considerable extent been anticipated by the German mystics. Especially in Tauler's equalization of the values of religious and worldly occupations, and the decline in valuation of the traditional forms of ascetic practices on account of the decisive significance of the ecstatic-contemplative absorption of the divine spirit by the soul. To a certain extent Lutheranism means a step backward from the mystics, in so far as Luther, and still more his Church, had, as compared with the mystics, partly undermined the psychological foundations for a rational ethics. (The mystic attitude on this point is reminiscent partly of the Pietist and partly of the Quaker psychology of faith.) That was precisely because he could not but suspect the tendency to ascetic self-discipline of leading to salvation by works, and hence he and his Church were forced to keep it more and more in the background.

1.9 Thus the mere idea of the calling in the Lutheran sense is at best of questionable importance for the problems in which we are interested. This was all that was meant to be determined here. But this is not in the least to say that even the Lutheran form of the renewal of the religious life may not have had some practical significance for the objects of our investigation; quite the contrary. Only that significance evidently cannot be derived directly from the attitude of Luther and his Church to worldly activity, and is perhaps not altogether so easily grasped as the connection with other branches of Protestantism. It is thus well for us next to look into those forms in which a relation between practical life and a religious motivation can be more easily perceived than in Lutheranism. We have already called attention to the conspicuous part played by Calvinism and the Protestant sects in the history of capitalistic development. As Luther found a different spirit at work in Zwingli than in himself, so did his spiritual successors in Calvinism. And Catholicism has to the present day looked upon Calvinism as its real opponent.

1.10 Now that may be partly explained on purely political grounds. Although the Reformation is unthinkable without Luther's own personal religious development, and was spiritually long influenced by his personality, without Calvinism his work could not have had permanent concrete success. Nevertheless, the reason for this common repugnance of Catholics and Lutherans lies, at least partly, in the ethical peculiarities of Calvinism. A purely superficial glance shows that there is here quite a different relationship between the religious life and earthly activity than in either Catholicism or Lutheranism. Even in literature motivated purely by religious factors that is evident. Take for instance the end of the *Divine Comedy*, where the poet in Paradise stands speechless in his passive contemplation of the secrets of God, and compare it with the poem which has come to be called the *Divine Comedy of Puritanism*. Milton closes the last song of *Paradise Lost* after describing the *expulsion* from paradise as follows:

> They, looking back, all the eastern side beheld
> Of paradise, so late their happy seat,
> Waved over by that flaming brand; the gate
> With dreadful faces thronged and fiery arms.
> Some natural tears they dropped, but wiped them soon:
> The world was all before them, there to choose
> Their place of rest, and Providence their guide.

And only a little before Michael had said to Adam:

> '. . . Only add
> Deeds to thy knowledge answerable; add faith;
> Add virtue, patience, temperance; add love,
> By name to come called Charity, the soul
> Of all the rest: then wilt thou not be loth
> To leave this Paradise, but shall possess
> A Paradise within thee, happier far.'

1.11 One feels at once that this powerful expression of the Puritan's serious attention to this world, his acceptance of his life in the world as a task, could not possibly have come from the pen of a mediæval writer. But it is just as uncongenial to Lutheranism, as expressed for instance in Luther's and Paul Gerhard's chorales. It is now our task to replace this vague feeling by a somewhat more precise logical formulation, and to investigate the fundamental basis of these differences. The appeal to national character is generally a mere confession of ignorance, and in this case it is entirely untenable. To ascribe a unified national character to the Englishmen of the seventeenth century would be simply to falsify history. Cavaliers and Roundheads did not appeal to each other simply as two parties, but as radically distinct species of men, and whoever looks into the matter carefully must agree with them. On the other hand, a difference of character between the English merchant adventurers and the old Hanseatic merchants is not to be found; nor can any other fundamental difference between the English and German characters at the end of the Middle Ages, which cannot easily be explained by the differences of their political history. It was the power of religious influence, not alone, but more than anything else, which created the differences of which we are conscious to-day.

1.12 We thus take as our starting-point in the investigation of the relationship between the old Protestant ethic and the spirit of capitalism the works of Calvin, of Calvinism, and the other Puritan sects. But it is not to be understood that we expect to find any of the founders or representatives of these religious movements considering the promotion of what we have called the spirit of capitalism as in any sense the end of his life-work. We cannot well maintain that the pursuit of worldly goods, conceived as an end in itself, was to any of them of positive ethical value. Once and for all it must be remembered that programmes of ethical reform never were at the centre of interest for any of the religious reformers (among whom, for our purposes, we must include men like Menno, George Fox, and Wesley). They were not the founders of societies for ethical culture nor the proponents of humanitarian projects for social reform or cultural ideals. The salvation of the soul and that alone was the centre of their life and work. Their ethical ideals and the practical results of their doctrines were all based on that alone, and were the consequences of purely religious motives. We shall thus have to admit that the cultural consequences of the Reformation were to a great extent, perhaps in the particular aspects with which we are dealing predominantly, unforeseen and even unwished-for results of the labours of the reformers. They were often far removed from or even in contradiction to all that they themselves thought to attain.

1.13 The following study may thus perhaps in a modest way form a contribution to the understanding of the manner in which ideas become effective forces in history. In order, however, to

avoid any misunderstanding of the sense in which any such effectiveness of purely ideal motives is claimed at all, I may perhaps be
permitted a few remarks in conclusion to this introductory discussion.

1.14 In such a study, it may at once be definitely stated, no
attempt is made to evaluate the ideas of the Reformation
in any sense, whether it concern their social or their religious worth.
We have continually to deal with aspects of the Reformation which
must appear to the truly religious consciousness as incidental and even
superficial. For we are merely attempting to clarify the part which
religious forces have played in forming the developing web of our
specifically worldly modern culture, in the complex interaction of
innumerable different historical factors. We are thus inquiring only to
what extent certain characteristic features of this culture can be
imputed to the influence of the Reformation. At the same time we
must free ourselves from the idea that it is possible to deduce the
Reformation, as a historically necessary result, from certain economic
changes. Countless historical circumstances, which cannot be reduced to any economic law, and are not susceptible to economic
explanation of any sort, especially purely political processes, had to
concur in order that the newly created Churches should survive at all.

1.15 On the other hand, however, we have no intention whatever of maintaining such a foolish and doctrinaire thesis is
that the spirit of capitalism (in the provisional sense of the term
explained above) could only have arisen as the result of certain effects
of the Reformation, or even that capitalism as an economic system is a
creation of the Reformation. In itself, the fact that certain important
forms of capitalistic business organization are known to be considerably older than the Reformation is a sufficient refutation of such a
claim. On the contrary, we only wish to ascertain whether and to what
extent religious forces have taken part in the qualitative formation and
the quantitative expansion of that spirit over the world. Furthermore,
what concrete aspects of our capitalistic culture can be traced to them.
In view of the tremendous confusion of interdependent influences
between the material basis, the forms of social and political organization, and the ideas current in the time of the Reformation, we can only
proceed by investigating whether and at what points certain correlations between forms of religious belief and practical ethics can be
worked out. At the same time we shall as far as possible clarify the
manner and the general *direction* in which, by virtue of those relationships, the religious movements have influenced the development
of material culture. Only when this has been determined with reasonable accuracy can the attempt be made to estimate to what extent the
historical development of modern culture can be attributed to those
religious forces and to what extent to others.

2

Max Weber
Prophets and the Routinisation of Charisma

This Extract is taken from the first part of chapter 5 of *The Sociology of Religion*, entitled 'The Religious Congregation, Preaching, and Pastoral Care'. The work as a whole was first published posthumously in 1922 under the title *Religionssoziologie*. As a result it contains more mature thoughts of Weber than *The Protestant Ethic and the Spirit of Capitalism* did, but at the same time, because it was never completed, it lacks the overall coherence of the latter. In earlier chapters Weber considered questions surrounding the rise of religions and functionaries such as magicians, priests and then prophets. In later chapters he examined such issues as religion and class relationships, theodicy as a social phenomenon, and those raised in his earlier work. This Extract has been chosen because it raises a number of issues surrounding prophecy, religious communities, and especially the key concept of the routinisation of charisma, which have played so central a role in social analyses of earliest Christianity (see the Extracts in **Section Three**). In the previous chapter Weber defined a 'prophet' as 'a purely individual bearer of charisma, who by virtue of his mission proclaims a religious doctrine or divine commandment' (p. 46). So the prophet is distinguished by a personal (and often idiosyncratic) call — unlike the priest who claims authority by virtue of service in a sacred tradition (prophets usually being lay figures for Weber). He also distinguished between 'exemplary' prophets, like the Buddha, 'who, by his personal example, demonstrates to others the way to religious salvation' (p. 55), and 'ethical' prophets, like Muhammad, who appear as 'an instrument for the proclamation of a god and his will . . . he demands obedience as an ethical duty' (p. 55). It is to the latter that the Old Testament prophets belong (for a critique of Weber at this point see **Extract 16**). The present Extract sets out the transition that can take place from the sect gathered around the prophet (especially the ethical prophet) to the churchly congregation within which the priest operates. The prophet, in this sense, and the priest represent very different social communities and serve very different social functions. The priest is essentially a conservative figure, whereas the ethical prophet can be a figure of radical social change. So tension between the two can frequently be expected (*2.15*). If the latter tends to challenge existing authority, the priest is concerned with conserving authority, with maintaining tradition and with propagating canons of sacred scripture. The distinction between 'church' and 'sect' is fundamental to *Extract 4* and *Extract 5*. For Weber the distinction rested on the criterion that the 'church' is an inclusive social body whereas the 'sect' is exclusive (both in its doctrine and, as a result, in its membership).

2.1 If his prophecy is successful, the prophet succeeds in winning permanent helpers. These may be apostles (as Bartholomaeus translates the term of the Gathas), disciples (Old Testament and Hindu), comrades (Hindu and Islamic), or followers (Isaiah and the New Testament). In all cases they are personal devotees of the prophet, in contrast to priests and soothsayers who are organized into guilds or official hierarchies. We shall devote additional consideration to this relationship in our analysis of the forms of domination. Moreover, in addition to these permanent helpers, who are active co-workers with the prophet in his mission and who generally also possess some special charismatic qualifications, there is a circle of followers comprising those who support him with lodging, money, and services and who expect to obtain their salvation through his mission. These may, on occasion, group themselves into a congregation for a particular temporary activity or on a continuous basis.

2.2 A 'community' or 'congregation' in the specifically religious sense (for this term is also employed to denote an association of neighboring groups which may have originated for economic or for fiscal or other political purposes) does not arise solely in connection with prophecy in the particular sense used here. Nor does it arise in connection with every type of prophecy. Primarily, a religious community arises in connection with a prophetic movement as a result of routinization (*Veralltäglichung*), i.e., as a result of the process whereby either the prophet himself or his disciples secure the permanence of his preaching and the congregation's distribution of grace, hence insuring the economic existence of the enterprise and those who man it, and thereby monopolizing as well the privileges reserved for those charged with religious functions.

2.3 It follows from this primacy of routinization in the formation of religious congregations that congregations may also be formed around mystagogues and priests of nonprophetic religions. For the mystagogue, indeed, the presence of a congregation is a normal phenomenon. The magician, in contrast, exercises his craft independently or, if a member of a guild, serves a particular neighborhood or political group, not a specific religious congregation. The congregation of the mystagogues, like those of the Eleusinian practitioners of mysteries, generally remained associations that were open to the outer world and fluid in form. Whoever was desirous of salvation would enter into a relationship, generally temporary, with the mystagogue and his assistants. The Eleusinian mysteries, for example, always remained a regional community, independent of particular localities.

2.4 The situation was quite different in the case of exemplary prophets who unconditionally demonstrated the way of salvation by their personal example, as did, for example, the mendicant monks of Mahavira and the Buddha, who belonged to a narrower exemplary community. Within this narrower community the disciples, who might still have been personally associated with the prophet, would exert particular authority. Outside of the exemplary community, however, there were pious devotees (e.g., the *Upasakas* of India) who did not go the whole way of salvation for themselves, but sought to achieve a relative optimum of salvation by demonstrating their devotion to the exemplary saint. These devotees tended to lack altogether any fixed status in the religious community, as was originally the case with the Buddhist *Upasakas*. Or even might they be organized into some special group with fixed rules and obligations. This regularly happened when priests, priest-like counselors, or mystagogues like the Buddhist *bonzes*, who were entrusted with particular responsibilities, were separated out from the exemplary community. This had not been the case in the earliest stages of Buddhism, but the prevailing Buddhist practice was the free organization of devotees into occasional religious communities, which the majority of mystagogues and exemplary prophets shared with the temple priesthoods of particular deities from the organized pantheon. The economic existence of these congregations was secured by endowments and maintained by sacrificial offerings and other gifts provided by persons with religious needs.

2.5 At this stage there was still no trace of a permanent congregation of laymen. Our present conceptions of membership in a religious denomination are not applicable to the situation of that period. As yet the individual was a devotee of a god, approximately in the sense that an Italian is a devotee of a particular saint. There is an almost ineradicable vulgar error that the majority or even all of the Chinese are to be regarded as Buddhists in religion. The source of this misconception is the fact that many Chinese have been brought up in the Confucian ethic (which alone enjoys official approbation) yet still consult Taoist divining priests before building a house, and that Chinese will mourn deceased relatives according to the Confucian rule while also arranging for Buddhist masses to be performed in their memory. Apart from those who participate in the cult of a god on a continuous basis and ultimately form a narrow circle having a permanent interest in it, all that we have at this stage are occasional laymen or, if one is permitted to use metaphorically a modern political designation, 'independent voters'.

2.6 Naturally, this condition does not satisfy the interests of those who man the cult, if only because of purely economic considerations. Consequently, in this kind of situation they endeavor to create a congregation whereby the personal following of the cult will assume the form of a permanent organization and become a community with fixed rights and duties. Such a transformation of a personal following into a permanent congregation is the normal process by which the doctrine of the prophets enters into everyday life, as the function of a permanent institution. The disciples or apostles of the prophets thereupon become mystagogues, teachers, priests or pastors (or a combination of them all), serving an organization dedicated to exclusively religious purposes, namely a congregation of laymen.

2.7 But the same result can be reached from other starting points. We have seen that the priests, whose function evolved from that of magicians to that of generic priesthood, were either scions of landed priestly families, domestic court priests of landed magnates or noblemen, or trained priests of a sacrificial cult who had become organized into a separate class. Individuals or groups applied to these priests for assistance as the need arose, but normally they were engaged in any occupation not deemed dishonorable to their status group. One other possibility is that priests might become attached to particular organizations, vocational or otherwise, and especially those in the service of a political association. But in all these cases there is no actual congregation which is separate from all other associations.

2.8 Such a congregation may arise when a clan of sacrificing priest succeeds in organizing the particular followers of their god into an exclusive association. Another and more usual way for a religious community to arise is as a consequence of the destruction of a political association, wherever the religious adherents of the tribal god and his priests continue as a religious congregation. The first of these types is to be found in India and the Near East, in numerous intermediate gradations associated with the transition of mystagogic and exemplary prophecy or of religious reform movements into a permanent organization of congregations. Many small Hindu denominations developed as a result of such processes.

2.9 By contrast, the transition from a priesthood serving a political association into a religious congregation was associated primarily with the rise of the great world empires of the Near East, especially Persia. Political associations were annihilated and the population disarmed; their priesthoods, however, were assigned certain political powers and were rendered secure in their positions. This was done because the religious congregation was regarded as a valuable instrument for pacifying the conquered, just as the coercive community resulting from the neighborhood association was found to be useful for the protection of financial interests. Thus, by virtue of decrees promulgated by the Persian kings from Cyrus to Artaxerxes, Judaism evolved into a religious community under royal protection, with a theocratic center in Jerusalem. It was probably the Persian victory that brought similar chances and opportunities to the Delphic Apollo and to the priestly class servicing other gods, and possibly also to the Orphic prophets. In Egypt, after the decline of political independence, the national priesthood built a sort of 'church' organization, apparently the first of its kind, with synods. On the other hand, religious congregations in India arose in the more limited sense as exemplary congregations. There, the integral status of the Brahmin estate, as well as the regulations of asceticism, survived the multiplicity of ephemeral political structures, and as a consequence, the various systems of ethical salvation transcended all political boundaries. In Iran, the Zoroastrian priests succeeded during the course of the centuries in propagandizing a closed religious organization which under the Sassanides became a political 'denomination'. (The Achaemenides, as their documents demonstrate, were not Zoroastrians, but rather, followers of Mazda.)

2.10 The relationships between political authority and religious community, from which the concept of religious denomination (*Konfession*) derived, belong in the analysis of domination (*Herrschaft*). At this point it suffices to note that congregational religion is a phenomenon of diverse manifestations and great fluidity. Here we desire to consider its status only where the laity has been organized into a continuous pattern of communal behavior, in which it actively participates in some manner. Where one finds a tiny island of administrative concern which delimits the prerogatives of priests, this is a parish, but not yet a congregational community. But even the concept of a parish, as a grouping different from the secular, political, or economic community, is missing in the religions of China and ancient India. Again, the Greek and other ancient phratries and similar cultic communities were not parishes, but political or other types of associations whose collective actions stood under the guardianship of some god. As for the parish of ancient Buddhism, moreover, this was only a district in which temporarily resident mendicant monks were required to participate in the semi-monthly convocations.

2.11 In medieval Christianity in the Occident, in post-Reformation Lutheranism and Anglicanism, and in both Christianity and Islam in the Near East, the parish was essentially a passive ecclesiastical association and the jurisdictional district of a priest. In these religions the laymen generally lacked completely the character of a congregation. To be sure, small vestiges of community rights have been retained in certain oriental churches and have also been found in Occidental Catholicism and Lutheranism. On the other hand, ancient Buddhist monasticism, like the warrior class of ancient Islam, Judaism, and ancient Christianity, had religious communities with an entirely different principle of social organization. Without going into any details, it will suffice to say that it was far more rigid. Furthermore, a certain actual influence of the laity may be combined with the absence of a rigidly regulated local congregational organization. An example of this would be Islam, where the laity wields considerable power, particularly in the Shiite sect, even though this is not legally secure; the Shah never appointed priests without being certain of the consent of the local laity.

2.12 On the other hand, it is the distinctive characteristic of every sect, in the technical sense of the term (a subject we shall consider later), that it is based on a restricted association of individual local congregations. From this principle, which is represented in Protestantism by the Baptists and Independents, and later by the Congregationalists, a gradual transition leads to the typical organization of the Reformed Church. Even when the latter has actually become a universal organization, it nevertheless makes membership conditional upon a quasi-contractual entry into some particular congregation. We shall return later to some of the problems which arise from these diversities. At the moment, we are particularly interested in just one consequence of the development of genuine congregational religion, which has very important results.

2.13 With the development of a congregation, the relationship between priesthood and laity within the community is of crucial significance for the practical effect of the religion. As the organization assumes the specific character of a congregation, the very powerful position of the priest is increasingly confronted with the necessity of keeping in mind the needs of the laity, in the interest of maintaining and enlarging the membership of the community. Actually, every type of priesthood is to some extent in a similar position. In order to maintain its own status, the priesthood must frequently meet the needs of the laity in a very considerable measure.

The three forces operative within the laity with which the priesthood must come to grips are: (a) prophecy, (b) the traditionalism of the laity, and (c) lay intellectualism. In contrast to these forces, another decisive factor at work here derives from the necessities and tendencies of the priestly enterprise as such. A few words need to be said about this last factor in its relation to those mentioned earlier.

2.14 As a rule, the ethical and exemplary prophet is himself a layman, and his power position depends on his lay followers. Every prophecy by its very nature devalues the magical elements of the priestly enterprise, but in very different degrees. The Buddha and others like him, as well as the prophets of Israel, rejected and denounced adherence to knowledgeable magicians and soothsayers, and indeed they scorned all magic as inherently useless. Salvation could be achieved only by a distinctively religious and meaningful relationship to the eternal. Among the Buddhists it was regarded as a mortal sin to boast vainly of magical capacities; yet the existence of the latter among the unfaithful was never denied by the prophets of either India or Israel, nor denied by the Christian apostles or the ancient Christian tradition as such. All ethical prophets, by virtue of their rejection of magic, were necessarily skeptical of the priestly enterprise, though in varying degrees and fashions. The god of the Israelite prophets desired not burnt offerings, but obedience to his commandments. The Buddhist would have nothing to do with Vedic knowledge and ritual in his quest for salvation; and the sacrifice of soma so esteemed by priests was represented in the oldest *Gathas* as an abomination to *Ahura-mazda*.

2.15 Thus, tensions between the prophets and their lay followers on the one hand, and between the prophets and the representatives of the priestly tradition on the other existed everywhere. To what degree the prophet would succeed in fulfilling his mission, or would become a martyr, depended on the outcome of the struggle for power, which in some instances, e.g., in Israel, was determined by the international situation. Apart from his own family, Zoroaster depended on the clans of the nobles and princes for support in his struggle against the nameless counter-prophets; this was also the case in India and with Muhammad. On the other hand, the Israelite prophets depended on the support of the urban and rural middle class. All of them, however, made use of the prestige which their prophetic charisma, as opposed to the charisma held by technicians of the routine cults, had gained for them among the laity. The sacredness of a new revelation opposed that of tradition; and depending on the success of the propaganda by each side, the priesthood might compromise with the new policy, surpass its doctrine, or conquer it, unless it were subjugated itself.

2.16 In every case, however, the priesthood had to assume the obligation of codifying either the victorious new doctrine or the old doctrine which had maintained itself despite an attack by the prophets. The priesthood had to delimit what must and must not be regarded as sacred and had to infuse its views into the religion of the laity, if it was to secure its own position. Such a development might have causes other than an effort by hostile prophets to imperil the position of the priesthood, as for example in India, where this took place very early. The simple interest of the priesthood in securing its own position against possible attack, and the necessity of insuring the traditional practice against the scepticism of the laity might produce similar results. Wherever this development took place it produced two phenomena, viz., canonical writings and dogmas, both of which might be of very different scope, particularly the latter. Canonical scriptures contain the revelations and traditions themselves, whereas dogmas are priestly interpretations of their meaning.

2.17 The collection of the prophetic religious revelations or, in the other case, of the traditionally transmitted sacred lore, may take place in the form of oral tradition. Throughout many centuries the sacred knowledge of the Brahmins was transmitted orally, and setting it down in writing was actually prohibited. This of course left a permanent mark on the literary form of this knowledge and also accounts for the not inconsiderable discrepancies in the texts of individual schools (*Shakhas*), the reason being that this knowledge was meant to be possessed only by qualified persons, namely the twice-born. To transmit such knowledge to anyone who had not experienced the second birth or who was excluded by virtue of his caste position (*Shudra*) was a heinous sin. Understandably, all magical lore originally has this character of secret knowledge, to protect the professional interest of the guild. But there are also aspects of this magical knowledge which everywhere become the material for the systematic instruction of other members of the group. At the root of the oldest and most universally diffused magical system of education is the animistic assumption that just as the magician himself requires rebirth and the possession of a new soul for his art, so heroism rests on a charisma which must be aroused, tested, and controlled in the hero by magical manipulations. In this way, therefore, the warrior is reborn into heroism. Charismatic education in this sense, with its novitiates, trials of strength, tortures, gradations of holiness and honor, initiation of youths, and preparation for battle is an almost universal institution of all societies which have experienced warfare.

2.18 When the guild of magicians finally develops into the priesthood, this extremely important function of educating the laity does not cease, and the priesthood always concerns itself with maintaining this function. More and more, secret lore recedes and the priestly doctrine becomes a scripturally established tradition which the priesthood interprets by means of dogmas. Such a scriptural tradition subsequently becomes the basis of every system of religion, not only for the professional members of the priestly class, but also for the laity, indeed especially for the laity.

2.19 Most, though not all, canonical sacred collections became officially closed against secular or religiously undesirable additions as a consequence of a struggle between various competing groups and prophecies for the control of the community. Wherever such a struggle failed to occur or wherever it did not threaten the content of the tradition, the formal canonization of the scriptures took place very slowly. The canon of the Jewish scriptures was not fixed until the year 90 A.D., shortly after the destruction of the theocratic state, when it was fixed by the synod of Jamnia as a dam against apostolic prophecies, and even then the canon was closed only in principle. In the case of the Vedas the scriptural canon was established in opposition to intellectual heterodoxy. The Christian canon was formalized because of the threat to the piety of the lower middle classes from the intellectual salvation doctrine of the Gnostics. On the other hand, the soteriology of the intellectual classes of ancient Buddhism was crystallized in the Pali canon as a result of the danger posed by the missionizing popular salvation religion of the *Mahayana*. The classical writings of Confucianism, like the priestly code of Ezra, were imposed by political force. But they did not on that account take on the quality of authentic sacredness, which is always the result of priestly activity. Indeed, the aforementioned legislation of Ezra received this accolade only later. Only the Quran underwent immediate editing, by command of the Caliph, and became sacred at once, because the semi-literate Muhammad held that the existence of a holy book automatically carries with it the mark of prestige for a religion. This view of prestige was related to widely diffused notions concerning the taboo quality and the magical significance of scriptural documents. Long before the establishment of the biblical canon, it was held that to touch the Pentateuch and the authentic prophetic writings 'rendered the hands unclean'.

2.20 The details of this process and the scope of the writings that were taken into the canonical sacred scriptures do not concern us here and can only be touched upon. It was due to the magical status of sacred bards that there were admitted into the Vedas not only the heroic epics but also sarcastic poems about the intoxicated Indra, as well as other poetry of every conceivable content. Similarly, a love poem and various personal details involved with the prophetic utterances were received into the Old Testament canon.

Finally, the New Testament included a purely personal letter of Paul, and the Quran found room in a number of *suras* for records of the most personal kind of family vexations in the life of its prophet.

2.21 The closing of the canon was generally accounted for by the theory that only a certain epoch in the past history of the religion had been blessed with prophetic charisma. According to the theory of the rabbis, this was the period from Moses to Alexander, while from the Roman Catholic point of view the period was the Apostolic Age. On the whole, these theories correctly express recognition of the contrast between prophetic and priestly systematization. Prophets systematized religion with a view to simplifying the relationship of man to the world, by reference to an ultimate and integrated value position. On the other hand, priests systematized the content of prophecy or of the sacred traditions by supplying them with a casuistical, rationalistic framework of analysis, and by adapting them to the customs of life and thought of their own class and of the laity whom they controlled.

3

Emile Durkheim
Theology and Egoistic Suicide

When Durkheim's *Suicide: A Study in Sociology* first appeared in 1897
it represented a very remarkable attempt to analyse and explain that
seemingly most individual of acts, suicide, in specifically *social* terms.
Although its particular statistics relating to suicide have long since
been questioned (including those assumed in this Extract) it remains a
model of sociological enquiry. It is also vital for understanding
Durkheim's developing theory about the social function of religion
(and the comparative lack of function of theology), which was to find
full expression in *The Elementary Forms of the Religious Life* in 1915. In
Suicide Durkheim (1858–1917) distinguished between three different
theoretical or 'ideal' types of suicide — altruistic, anomic and egoistic.
Altruistic suicide is characterised by a strong sense of duty to commit
suicide in certain situations (e.g. widows in some societies on the
death of their husbands). Anomic suicide often takes the form of
suicide in the face of some social or even economic crisis (e.g. the
collapse of the stock market). However Durkheim gave the greatest
attention to egoistic suicide: suicide which is individualistically motivated and which might be thought to be the least susceptible type of
suicide to sociological explanation. It is under this heading that he
noted major difference of suicide rates between Protestants on the one
hand and Roman Catholics and Jews on the other. Having set out the
statistical evidence from Europe as a whole, suggesting that Protestants were twice as likely to commit suicide as Catholics or Jews, he
then attempted to account for this phenomenon. It is at this point that
this Extract begins. It was clear to Durkheim that (given the statistical
evidence) straightforward theological explanations would not be
adequate, since Jews and Catholics shared a joint pattern of suicide
but not the same theology (*3.4* and *3.16*). Durkheim also considered
educational differences between the three groups (*3.11f.*). Right up to
the final paragraph Durkheim was attempting to exclude variables —
i.e. to eliminate non-causal differences between Catholics, Protestants and Jews in relation to suicide. He finally concluded that it was

the strong nature of Catholicism and Judaism as *societies* or moral communities (and the relative weakness of individualistic Protestantism) which was the causal factor (*3.16*). Thus for him it was less the actual beliefs or theological differences between the three forms of religion which accounted for this situation than the different abilities of the three to act as religious communities effecting social 'integration'.

Further Reading

W. S. F. Pickering, *Durkheim's Sociology of Religion: Themes and Theories* (Routledge and Kegan Paul, 1984) provides the fullest recent account of Durkheim's understanding of religion and society. Readings, with background information, from this and Durkheim's other works can be found in W. S. F. Pickering (ed.), *Durkheim on Religion* (Routledge and Kegan Paul, 1975).

3.1 If we consider that the Jews are everywhere in a very small minority and that in most societies where the foregoing observations were made, Catholics are in the minority, we are tempted to find in these facts the cause explaining the relative rarity of voluntary deaths in these two confessions. Obviously, the less numerous confessions, facing the hostility of the surrounding populations, in order to maintain themselves are obliged to exercise severe control over themselves and subject themselves to an especially rigorous discipline. To justify the always precarious tolerance granted them, they have to practice greater morality. Besides these considerations, certain facts seem really to imply that this special factor has some influence. In Prussia, the minority status of Catholics is very pronounced, since they are only a third of the whole population. They kill themselves only one third as often as the Protestants. The difference decreases in Bavaria where two thirds of the inhabitants are Catholics; the voluntary deaths of the latter are here only in the proportion of 100 to 275 of those of Protestants or else of 100 to 238, according to the period. Finally, in the almost entirely Catholic Empire of Austria, only 155 Protestants to 100 Catholic suicides are found. It would seem then that where Protestantism becomes a minority its tendency to suicide decreases.

3.2 But first, suicide is too little an object of public condemnation for the slight measure of blame attaching to it to have such influence, even on minorities obliged by their situation to pay special heed to public opinion. As it is an act without offense to others, it involves no great reproach to the groups more inclined to it than others, and is not apt to increase greatly their relative ostracism as would certainly be the case with a greater frequency of crime and misdemeanor. Besides, when religious intolerance is very pronounced, it often produces an opposite effect. Instead of exciting the dissenters to respect opinion more, it accustoms them to disregard it. When one feels himself an object of inescapable hostility, one abandons the idea of conciliating it and is the more resolute in his most unpopular observances. This has frequently happened to the Jews and thus their exceptional immunity probably has another cause.

3.3 Anyway, this explanation would not account for the respective situation of Protestants and Catholics. For though the protective influence of Catholicism is less in Austria and Bavaria, where it is in the majority, it is still considerable. Catholicism does not therefore owe this solely to its minority status. More generally, whatever the proportional share of these two confessions in the total population, wherever their comparison has been possible from the point of view of suicide, Protestants are found to kill themselves much more often than Catholics. There are even countries like the Upper Palatinate and Upper Bavaria, where the population is almost wholly Catholic (92 and 96 per cent) and where there are nevertheless 300 and 423 Protestant suicides to 100 Catholic suicides. The proportion even rises to 528 per cent in Lower Bavaria where the reformed religion has not quite one follower to 100 inhabitants. Therefore, even if the prudence incumbent on minorities were a partial cause of the great difference between the two religions, the greatest share is certainly due to other causes.

3.4 We shall find these other causes in the nature of these two religious systems. Yet they both prohibit suicide with equal emphasis; not only do they penalize it morally with great severity, but both teach that a new life begins beyond the tomb where men are punished for their evil actions, and Protestantism just as well as Catholicism numbers suicide among them. Finally, in both cults these prohibitions are of divine origin; they are represented not as the logical conclusion of correct reason, but God Himself is their authority. Therefore, if Protestantism is less unfavorable to the development of suicide, it is not because of a different attitude from that of Catholicism. Thus, if both religions have the same precepts with respect to this particular matter, their dissimilar influence on suicide must proceed from one of the more general characteristics differentiating them.

3.5 The only essential difference between Catholicism and Protestantism is that the second permits free inquiry to a far greater degree than the first. Of course, Catholicism by the very fact that it is an idealistic religion concedes a far greater place to thought and reflection than Greco-Latin polytheism or Hebrew monotheism.

It is not restricted to mechanical ceremonies but seeks the control of the conscience. So it appeals to conscience, and even when demanding blind submission of reason, does so by employing the language of reason. None the less, the Catholic accepts his faith ready made, without scrutiny. He may not even submit it to historical examination since the original texts that serve as its basis are proscribed. A whole hierarchical system of authority is devised, with marvelous ingenuity, to render tradition invariable. All *variation* is abhorrent to Catholic thought. The Protestant is far more the author of his faith. The Bible is put in his hands and no interpretation is imposed upon him. The very structure of the reformed cult stresses this state of religious individualism. Nowhere but in England is the Protestant clergy a hierarchy; like the worshippers, the priest has no other source but himself and his conscience. He is a more instructed guide than the run of worshippers but with no special authority for fixing dogma. But what best proves that this freedom of inquiry proclaimed by the founders of the Reformation has not remained a Platonic affirmation is the increasing multiplicity of all sorts of sects so strikingly in contrast with the indivisible unity of the Catholic Church.

3.6 We thus reach our first conclusion, that the proclivity of Protestantism for suicide must relate to the spirit of free inquiry that animates this religion. Let us understand this relationship correctly. Free inquiry itself is only the effect of another cause. When it appears, when men, after having long received their ready made faith from tradition, claim the right to shape it for themselves, this is not because of the intrinsic desirability of free inquiry, for the latter involves as much sorrow as happiness. But it is because men henceforth need this liberty. This very need can have only one cause: the overthrow of traditional beliefs. If they still asserted themselves with equal energy, it would never occur to men to criticize them. If they still had the same authority, men would not demand the right to verify the source of this authority. Reflection develops only if its development becomes imperative, that is, if certain ideas and instinctive sentiments which have hitherto adequately guided conduct are found to have lost their efficacy. Then reflection intervenes to fill the gap that has appeared, but which it has not created. Just as reflection disappears to the extent that thought and action take the form of automatic habits, it awakes only when accepted habits become disorganized. It asserts its rights against public opinion only when the latter loses strength, that is, when it is no longer prevalent to the same extent. If these assertions occur not merely occasionally and as passing crises, but become chronic; if individual consciences keep reaffirming their autonomy, it is because they are constantly subject to conflicting impulses, because a new opinion has not been formed to replace the one no longer existing. If a new system of beliefs were constituted which seemed as indisputable to everyone as the old, no one would think of discussing it any longer. Its discussion would no longer even be permitted; for ideas shared by an entire society draw from this consensus an authority that makes them sacrosanct and raises them above dispute. For them to have become more tolerant, they must first already have become the object of less general and complete assent and been weakened by preliminary controversy.

3.7 Thus, if it is correct to say that free inquiry once proclaimed, multiplies schisms, it must be added that it presupposes them and derives from them, for it is claimed and instituted as a principle only in order to permit latent or half-declared schisms to develop more freely. So if Protestantism concedes a greater freedom to individual thought than Catholicism, it is because it has fewer common beliefs and practices. Now, a religious society cannot exist without a collective *credo* and the more extensive the *credo* the more unified and strong is the society. For it does not unite men by an exchange and reciprocity of services, a temporal bond of union which permits and even presupposes differences, but which a religious society cannot form. It socializes men only by attaching them completely to an identical body of doctrine and socializes them in proportion as this body of doctrine is extensive and firm. The more numerous the manners of action and thought of a religious character are, which are accordingly removed from free inquiry, the more the idea of God presents itself in all details of existence, and makes individual wills converge to one identical goal. Inversely, the greater concessions a confessional group makes to individual judgment, the less it dominates lives, the less its cohesion and vitality. We thus reach the conclusion that the superiority of Protestantism with respect to suicide results from its being a less strongly integrated church than the Catholic church.

3.8 This also explains the situation of Judaism. Indeed, the reproach to which the Jews have for so long been exposed by Christianity has created feelings of unusual solidarity among them. Their need of resisting a general hostility, the very impossibility of free communication with the rest of the population, has forced them to strict union among themselves. Consequently, each community became a small, compact and coherent society with a strong feeling of self-consciousness and unity. Everyone thought and lived alike; individual divergences were made almost impossible by the community of existence and the close and constant surveillance of all over each. The Jewish church has thus been more strongly united than any other, from its dependence on itself because of being the object of intolerance. By analogy with what has just been observed apropos of Protestantism, the same cause must therefore be assumed for the slight tendency of the Jews to suicide in spite of all sorts of circumstances which might on the contrary incline them to it. Doubtless they owe this immunity in a sense to the hostility surrounding them. But if this is its influence, it is not because it imposes a higher morality but because it obliges them to live in greater union. They are immune to this degree because their religious society is of such solidarity. Besides, the ostracism to which they are subject is only one of the causes producing this result; the very nature of Jewish beliefs must contribute largely to it. Judaism, in fact, like all early religions, consists basically of a body of practices minutely governing all the details of life and leaving little free room to individual judgment.

2

Several facts confirm this explanation.

3.9 First, of all great Protestant countries, England is the one where suicide is least developed. In fact, only about 80 suicides per million inhabitants are found there, whereas the reformed societies of Germany have from 140 to 400; and yet the general activity of ideas and business seems no less great than elsewhere. Now, it happens at the same time that the Anglican church is far more powerfully integrated than other Protestant churches. To be sure, England has been customarily regarded as the classic land of individual freedom; but actually many facts indicate that the number of common, obligatory beliefs and practices, which are thus withdrawn from free inquiry by individuals, is greater than in Germany. First, the law still sanctions many religious requirements: such as the law of the observance of Sunday, that forbidding stage representations of any character from Holy Scripture; the one until recently requiring some profession of faith from every member of political representative bodies, etc. Next, respect for tradition is known to be general and powerful in England: it must extend to matters of religion as well as others. But a highly developed traditionalism always more or less restricts activity of the individual. Finally, the Anglican clergy is the only Protestant clergy organized in a hierarchy. This external organization clearly shows an inner unity incompatible with a pronounced religious individualism.

3.10 Besides, England has the largest number of clergymen of any Protestant country. In 1876 there averaged 908 church-goers for every minister, compared with 932 in Hungary, 1,100 in Holland, 1,300 in Denmark, 1,440 in Switzerland and 1,600 in Germany. The number of priests is not an insignificant detail nor a superficial characteristic but one related to the intrinsic nature of religion. The proof of this is that the Catholic clergy is everywhere much more numerous than the Protestant. In Italy there is a priest for every 267 Catholics, in Spain for 419, in Portugal for 536, in Switzerland for 540, in France for 823, in Belgium for 1,050. This is because the priest is the natural organ of faith and tradition and because here as elsewhere the organ inevitably develops in exact proportion to its function. The more intense religious life, the more men are needed to direct it. The greater the number of dogmas and precepts the interpretation of which is not left to individual consciences, the more authorities are required to tell their meaning; moreover, the more numerous these authorities, the more closely they surround and the better they restrain the individual. Thus, far from weakening our theory, the case of England verifies it. If Protestantism there does not produce the same results as on the continent, it is because religious society there is much more strongly constituted and to this extent resembles the Catholic church.

Here, however, is a more general proof in confirmation of our thesis.

3.11 The taste for free inquiry can be aroused only if accompanied by that for learning. Knowledge is free thought's only means of achieving its purposes. When irrational beliefs or practices have lost their hold, appeal must be made, in the search for others, to the enlightened consciousness of which knowledge is only the highest form. Fundamentally, these two tendencies are one and spring from the same source. Men generally have the desire for self-instruction only in so far as they are freed from the yoke of tradition; for as long as the latter governs intelligence it is all-sufficient and jealous of any rival. On the other hand, light is sought as soon as customs whose origins are lost in obscurity no longer correspond to new necessities. This is why philosophy, the first, synthetic form of knowledge, appears as soon as religion has lost its sway, and only then; and is then followed progressively by the many single sciences with the further development of the very need which produced philosophy. Unless we are mistaken, if the progressive weakening of collective and customary prejudices produces a trend to suicide and if Protestantism derives thence its special pre-disposition to it, the two following facts should be noted: 1, the desire for learning must be stronger among Protestants than among Catholics; 2, in so far as this denotes a weakening of common beliefs it should vary with suicide, fairly generally. Do facts confirm this twofold hypothesis?

3.12 If Catholic France is compared with Protestant Germany merely at their highest levels, that is, if only the upper classes of both are compared, it seems that France may bear the comparison. In the great centers of our country, knowledge is no less honored or widespread than among our neighbors; we even decidedly outdistance several Protestant countries in this respect. But if the desire for learning is equally felt in the upper reaches of the two societies, it is not so on their lower levels; and whereas the maximal intensity is approximately the same in both, the average intensity is less among us. The same is true of the aggregate of Catholic nations compared with Protestant nations. Even assuming that the highest culture of the former is about the same as the latter's, the situation is quite otherwise as regards popular education. Whereas among the Protestant peoples of Saxony, Norway, Sweden, Baden, Denmark and Prussia, from 1877–1878 among 1,000 children of school age, that is, from 6 to 12 years, an average of 957 attended school, the Catholic peoples, France, Austria-Hungary, Spain and Italy, had only 667, or 31 per cent less. Proportions are the same for the periods of 1874–75 and 1860–61. Prussia, the Protestant country having the lowest figure here, is yet far above France at the head of the Catholic countries; the former has 897 pupils per 1,000 children, the latter only 766. In all of Germany, Bavaria has most Catholics and also most illiterates. Of all Bavarian provinces, the Upper Palatinate is one of the most profoundly Catholic and has also the most conscripted men who do not know how to read or write (15 per cent in 1871). In Prussia the same is true for the duchy of Posen and the province of Prussia. Finally, in the whole kingdom there numbered in 1871, 66 illiterates to every 1,000 Protestants and 152 to 1,000 Catholics. The relation is the same for the women of both faiths.

3.13 Perhaps it will be objected that primary instruction can be no measure of general education. The degree of a people's education, it is often said, does not depend on the greater or smaller number of illiterates. Let us agree to this qualification, though the various degrees of education are perhaps more closely interrelated than seems to be the case and the development of one is difficult without the simultaneous growth of the others. In any case, although the level of primary instruction may only imperfectly reflect that of scientific culture, it has a certain reference to the extent of the desire for knowledge of a people as a whole. A people must feel this need very keenly to try to spread its elements even among the lowest classes. Thus to place the means of learning within everyone's reach, and even legally to forbid ignorance, shows a national awareness of the indispensability of broadened and enlightened intelligence of the individual for the nation's own existence. Actually, Protestant nations have so stressed primary instruction because they held that each individual must be able to understand the Bible. Our present search is for the average intensity of this need, the value attached by each people to knowledge, not the standing of its scholars and their discoveries. From this special point of view, the state of advanced learning and truly scientific production would be a poor criterion; for it would show only what goes on in a limited sector of society. Popular and general education is a more accurate index. . . .

3

Two important conclusions derive from this chapter.

3.14 First, we see why as a rule suicide increases with knowledge. Knowledge does not determine this progress. It is innocent; nothing is more unjust than to accuse it, and the example of the Jews proves this conclusively. But these two facts result simultaneously from a single general state which they translate into different forms. Man seeks to learn and man kills himself because of the loss of cohesion in his religious society; he does not kill himself because of his learning. It is certainly not the learning he acquires that disorganizes religion; but the desire for knowledge wakens because religion becomes disorganized. Knowledge is not sought as a means to destroy accepted opinions but because their destruction has commenced. To be sure, once knowledge exists, it may battle in its own name and in its own cause, and set up as an antagonist to traditional sentiments. But its attacks would be ineffective if these sentiments still possessed vitality; or rather, would not even take place. Faith is not uprooted by dialectic proof; it must already be deeply shaken by other causes to be unable to withstand the shock of argument.

3.15 Far from knowledge being the source of the evil, it is its remedy, the only remedy we have. Once established beliefs have been carried away by the current of affairs, they cannot be artificially reestablished; only reflection can guide us in life, after this. Once the social instinct is blunted, intelligence is the only guide left us and we have to reconstruct a conscience by its means. Dangerous as is the undertaking there can be no hesitation, for we have no choice. Let those who view anxiously and sadly the ruins of ancient beliefs, who feel all the difficulties of these critical times, not ascribe to science an evil it has not caused but rather which it tries to cure! Beware of treating it as an enemy! It has not the dissolvent effect ascribed to it, but is the only weapon for our battle against the dissolution which gives birth to science itself. It is no answer to denounce it. The authority of vanished traditions will never be restored by silencing it; we shall be only more powerless to replace them. We must, to be sure, be equally careful to avoid seeing a self-sufficient end in education, whereas it is only a means. If minds cannot be made to lose the desire for freedom by artificially enslaving them, neither can they recover their equilibrium by mere freedom. They must use this freedom fittingly.

3.16 Secondly, we see why, generally speaking, religion has a prophylactic effect upon suicide. It is not, as has sometimes been said, because it condemns it more unhesitatingly than secular morality, nor because the idea of God gives its precepts exceptional authority which subdues the will, nor because the prospect of a future life and the terrible punishments there awaiting the guilty give its proscriptions a greater sanction than that of human laws. The Protestant believes in God and the immortality of the soul no less than the Catholic. More than this, the religion with least inclination to suicide, Judaism, is the very one not formally proscribing it and also the one in which the idea of immortality plays the least role. Indeed, the Bible contains no law forbidding man to kill himself and, on the other hand, its beliefs in a future life are most vague. Doubtless, in both matters, rabbinical teaching has gradually supplied the omissions of the sacred book; but they have not its authority. The beneficent influence of religion is therefore not due to the special nature of religious conceptions. If religion protects man against the desire for self-destruction, it is not that it preaches the respect for his own person to him with arguments *sui generis*; but because it is a society. What constitutes this society is the existence of a certain number of beliefs and practices common to all the faithful, traditional and thus obligatory. The more numerous and strong these collective states of mind are, the stronger the integration of the religious community, and also the greater its preservative value. The details of dogmas and rites are secondary. The essential thing is that they be capable of supporting a sufficiently intense collective life. And because the Protestant church has less consistency than the others it has less moderating effect upon suicide.

4

Ernst Troeltsch
Churches and Sects

Troeltsch (1866–1923) was a friend of Weber and was much influenced by some of his central understandings of religion and theology as social phenomena. However, Troeltsch was also a theologian and it is clear from this Extract that he believed that there were theological implications that could be drawn from a social analysis of religious institutions. The Extract is taken from the summary that he made at the end of the first volume of *The Social Teaching of the Christian Churches* (first published as *Die Soziallehren der christlichen Kirchen und Gruppen* in 1911). This volume sought to trace the social development of Christianity from New Testament times to mediaeval Catholicism. From these studies Troeltsch believed that it was possible to differentiate three distinct 'types' of religious institution: churches, sects, and mysticism. The third of these types, a purely individualistic and inward religious orientation, plays no part here (although in recent sociology of religion it has sometimes been used to denote some modern, individualistic cults). This Extract begins with an outline of 'churches' and 'sects' as distinct social types: differentiated by their relations to the secular order, by size, by social status, by ethical orientations, as well as by their specifically supernatural or doctrinal commitments. From this sociological/historical perspective Troeltsch then moved to a discussion of their relative theological merits and weaknesses. He was fully aware (*4.7*) that the term 'sect' tends to be used pejoratively by churches (a clear instance of a power relationship). But in this remarkable passage he insisted that *both* churches and sects are a 'logical result of the Gospel' (*4.15*) and that they separately bring essential theological emphases. If the church can 'represent the objective treasury of grace' (*4.13*), the sect can represent moral demands 'founded only upon the Law and the Example of Christ' (*4.10*). The implications of this analysis for theology and Christian ethics are only slowly being realised in the theological world today. Troeltsch's typology is not without difficulties — there have long been doubts, given its explicitly Christian depiction, about its applicability to other religions (although see *4.15*) — yet its general framework still offers powerful insights which are evident in *Extract 5*, *Section Three*, and *Extract 24*.

Further Reading

Betty Scharf, *The Sociological Study of Religion* (Hutchinson, 1970), provides a clear introduction to Troeltsch's typology. I make considerable use of it in relation to theology and Christian ethics in *Theology and Social Structure* (Mowbrays, 1977) and in *Prophecy and Praxis* (Marshall, Morgan and Scott, 1981). Criticisms of the typology from the perspective of the sociology of religion can be found in Bryan Wilson, *Religion in Sociological Perspective* (OUP, 1982).

4.1 The Church is that type of organization which is overwhelmingly conservative, which to a certain extent accepts the secular order, and dominates the masses; in principle, therefore, it is universal, i.e. it desires to cover the whole life of humanity. The sects, on the other hand, are comparatively small groups; they aspire after personal inward perfection, and they aim at a direct personal fellowship between the members of each group. From the very beginning, therefore, they are forced to organize themselves in small groups, and to renounce the idea of dominating the world. Their attitude towards the world, the State, and Society may be indifferent, tolerant, or hostile, since they have no desire to control and incorporate these forms of social life; on the contrary, they tend to avoid them; their aim is usually either to tolerate their presence alongside of their own body, or even to replace those social institutions by their own society.

4.2 Further, both types are in close connection with the actual situation and with the development of Society. The fully developed Church, however, utilizes the State and the ruling classes, and weaves these elements into her own life; she then becomes an integral part of the existing social order; from this standpoint, then, the Church both stabilizes and determines the social order; in so doing, however, she becomes dependent upon the upper classes, and upon their development. The sects, on the other hand, are connected with the lower classes, or at least with those elements in Society which are opposed to the State and to Society; they work upwards from below, and not downwards from above.

4.3 Finally, too, both types vary a good deal in their attitude towards the supernatural and transcendent element in Christianity, and also in their view of its system of asceticism. The

Church relates the whole of the secular order as a means and a preparation to the supernatural aim of life, and it incorporates genuine asceticism into its structure as one element in this preparation, all under the very definite direction of the Church. The sects refer their members directly to the supernatural aim of life, and in them the individualistic, directly religious character of asceticism, as a means of union with God, is developed more strongly and fully; the attitude of opposition to the world and its powers, to which the secularized Church now also belongs, tends to develop a theoretical and general asceticism. It must, however, be admitted that asceticism in the Church, and in ecclesiastical monasticism, has a different meaning from that of the renunciation of or hostility to the world which characterises the asceticism of the sects.

4.4 The asceticism of the Church is a method of acquiring virtue, and a special high watermark of religious achievement, connected chiefly with the repression of the senses, or expressing itself in special achievements of a peculiar character; otherwise, however, it presupposes the life of the world as the general background, and the contrast of an average morality which is on relatively good terms with the world. Along these lines, therefore, ecclesiastical asceticism is connected with the asceticism of the redemption cults of late antiquity, and with the detachment required for the contemplative life; in any case, it is connected with a moral dualism.

4.5 The asceticism of the sects, on the other hand, is merely the simple principle of detachment from the world, and is expressed in the refusal to use the law, to swear in a court of justice, to own property, to exercise dominion over others, or to take part in war. The sects take the Sermon on the Mount as their ideal; they lay stress on the simple but radical opposition of the Kingdom of God to all secular interests and institutions. They practise renunciation only as a means of charity, as the basis of a thorough-going communism of love, and, since their rules are equally binding upon all, they do not encourage extravagant and heroic deeds, nor the vicarious heroism of some to make up for the worldliness and average morality of others. The ascetic ideal of the sects consists simply in opposition to the world and to its social institutions, but it is not opposition to the sense-life, nor to the average life of humanity. It is therefore only related with the asceticism of monasticism in so far as the latter also creates special conditions, within which it is possible to lead a life according to the Sermon on the Mount, and in harmony with the ideal of the communism of love. In the main, however, the ascetic ideal of the sects is fundamentally different from that of monasticism, in so far as the latter implies emphasis upon the mortification of the senses, and upon works of supererogation in poverty and obedience for their own sake.

In all things the ideal of the sects is essentially not one which aims at the destruction of the sense life and of natural self-feeling, but a union in love which is not affected by the social inequalities and struggles of the world.

4.6 All these differences which actually existed between the late Mediaeval Church and the sects, must have had their foundation in some way or another within the interior structure of the twofold sociological edifice. If, then, in reality both types claim, and rightly claim, a relationship with the Primitive Church, it is clear that the final cause for this dualistic development must lie within primitive Christianity itself. Once this point becomes clear, therefore, it will also shed light upon the whole problem of the sociological understanding of Christianity in general. Since it is only at this point that the difference between the two elements emerges very clearly as a permanent difference, only now have we reached the stage at which it can be discussed. It is also very important to understand this question thoroughly at this stage, since it explains the later developments of Church History, in which the sect stands out ever more clearly alongside of the Church. In the whole previous development of the Church this question was less vital, for during the early centuries the Church itself fluctuated a great deal between the sect and the Church-type; indeed, it only achieved the development of the Church-type with the development of sacerdotal and sacramental doctrine; precisely for that reason, in its process of development up to this time, the Church had only witnessed a sect development alongside of itself to a small extent, and the differences between them and the Church were still not clear. The problem first appears clearly in the opposition between the sacramental-hierarchical Church conception of Augustine and the Donatists. But with the disappearance of African Christianity this opposition also disappeared, and it only reappeared in a decisive form after the completion of the idea of the Church in the Gregorian church reform.

4.7 The word 'sect', however, gives an erroneous impression. Originally the word was used in a polemical and apologetic sense, and it was used to describe groups which separated themselves from the official Church, while they retained certain fundamental elements of Christian thought; by the very fact, however, that they were outside the corporate life of the ecclesiastical tradition — a position, moreover, which was usually forced upon them — they were regarded as inferior side-issues, one-sided phenomena, exaggerations or abbreviations of ecclesiastical Christianity. That is, naturally, solely the viewpoint of the dominant churches, based on the belief that the ecclesiastical type alone has any right to exist. Ecclesiastical law within the modern State definitely denotes as 'sects' those religious groups which exist alongside of the official privileged State Churches, by law established, groups which the State either does not recognize at all, or, if it does recognize them, grants them fewer rights and privileges than the official State Churches. Such a conception, however, confuses the actual issue. Very often in the so-called 'sects' it is precisely the essential elements of the Gospel which are fully expressed; they themselves always appeal to the Gospel and to Primitive Christianity, and accuse the Church of having fallen away from its ideal; these impulses are always those which have been either suppressed or undeveloped in the official churches, of course for good and characteristic reasons, which again are not taken into account by the passionate party polemics of the sects. There can, however, be no doubt about the actual fact: the sects, with their greater independence of the world, and their continual emphasis upon the original ideals of Christianity, often represent in a very direct and characteristic way the essential fundamental ideas of Christianity; to a very great extent they are a most important factor in the study of the development of the sociological consequences of Christian thought. This statement is proved conclusively by all those who make a close study of the sect movements, which were especially numerous in the latter mediaeval period — movements which played their part in the general disintegration of the mediaeval social order. This comes out very clearly in the great works of Sebastian Franck, and especially of Gottfried Arnold, which were written later in defence of the sects.

4.8 The main stream of Christian development, however, flows along the channel prepared by the Church-type. The reason for this is clear: the Church-type represents the longing for a universal all-embracing ideal, the desire to control great masses of men, and therefore the urge to dominate the world and civilization in general. Paulinism, in spite of its strongly individualistic and 'enthusiastic' features, had already led the way along this line: it desired to conquer the world for Christ; it came to terms with the order of the State by interpreting it as an institution ordained and permitted by God; it accepted the existing order with its professions and its habits and customs. The only union it desired was that which arose out of a common share in the energy of grace which the Body of Christ contained; out of this union the new life ought to spring up naturally from within through the power of the Holy Spirit, thus preparing the way for the speedy coming of the Kingdom of God, as the real universal end of all things. The more that Christendom renounced the life of this supernatural and eschatological fulfilment of its universal ideal, and tried to achieve this end by missionary effort and organization, the more was it forced to make its Divine and Christian character independent of the subjective character and service of believers;

henceforth it sought to concentrate all its emphasis upon the objective possession of religious truth and religious power, which were contained in the tradition of Christ, and in the Divine guidance of the Church which fills and penetrates the whole Body. From this objective basis subjective energies could ever flow forth afresh, exerting a renewing influence, but the objective basis did not coincide with these results. Only thus was it possible to have a popular Church at all, and it was only thus that the relative acceptance of the world, the State, of Society, and of the existing culture, which this required, did no harm to the objective foundation. The Divine nature of the Church was retained in its objective basis, and from this centre there welled up continually fresh streams of vital spiritual force. It was the aim of the leaders of the Church to render this basis as objective as possible, by means of tradition, priesthood, and sacrament; to secure in it, objectively, the sociological point of contact; if that were once firmly established the subjective influence of the Church was considered secure; it was only in detail that it could not be controlled. In this way the fundamental religious sense of possessing something Divinely 'given' and 'redeeming' was ensured, while the universalizing tendency was also made effective, since it established the Church, the organ of Divine grace, in the supreme position of power. When to that was added the Sacrament of Penance, the power of spiritual direction, the law against heretics, and the general supervision of the faith, the Church was then able to gain an inward dominion over the hearts of men.

4.9 Under these circumstances, however, the Church found it impossible to avoid making a compromise with the State, with the social order, and with economic conditions, and the Thomist doctrine worked this out in a very able, comprehensive theory, which vigorously maintained the ultimate supernatural orientation of life. In all this it is claimed that the whole is derived, quite logically, from the Gospel; it is clear that this point of view became possible as soon as the Gospel was conceived as a universal way of life, offering redemption to all, whose influence radiates from the knowledge given by the Gospel, coupled with the assurance of salvation given by the Church. It was precisely the development of an objective sociological point of reference, its establishment on a stable basis, and its endeavour to go forward from that point to organize the conquest of the world, which led to this development. It is, however, equally obvious that in so doing the radical individualism of the Gospel, with its urge towards the utmost personal achievement, its radical fellowship of love, uniting all in the most personal centre of life, with its heroic indifference towards the world, the State and civilization, with its mistrust of the spiritual danger of distraction and error inherent in the possession of or the desire for great possessions, has been given a secondary place, or even given up altogether; these features now appear as mere factors within the system; they are no longer ruling principles.

4.10 It was precisely this aspect of the Gospel, however, which the sects developed still farther, or, rather, it was this aspect which they were continually re-emphasizing and bringing into fresh prominence. In general, the following are their characteristic features: lay Christianity, personal achievement in ethics and in religion, the radical fellowship of love, religious equality and brotherly love, indifference towards the authority of the State and the ruling classes, dislike of technical law and of the oath, the separation of the religious life from the economic struggle by means of the ideal of poverty and frugality, or occasionally in a charity which becomes communism, the directness of the personal religious relationship, criticism of official spiritual guides and theologians, the appeal to the New Testament and to the Primitive Church. The sociological point of contact, which here forms the starting-point for the growth of the religious community, differs clearly from that upon which the Church has been formed. Whereas the Church assumes the objective concrete holiness of the sacerdotal office, of Apostolic Succession, of the *Depositum fidei* and of the sacraments, and appeals to the extension of the Incarnation which takes place permanently through the priesthood, the sect, on the other hand, appeals to the ever new common performance of the moral demands, which, at bottom, are founded only upon the Law and the Example of Christ. In this, it must be admitted that they are in direct contact with the Teaching of Jesus. Consciously or unconsciously, therefore, this implies a different attitude to the early history of Christianity, and a different conception of Christian doctrine. Scripture history and the history of the Primitive Church are permanent ideals, to be accepted in their literal sense, not the starting-point, historically limited and defined, for the development of the Church. Christ is not the God-Man, eternally at work within the Church, leading it into all Truth, but He is the direct Head of the Church, binding the Church to Himself through His Law in the Scriptures. On the one hand, there is development and compromise, on the other literal obedience and radicalism.

4.11 It is this point of view, however, which makes the sects incapable of forming large mass organizations, and limits their development to small groups, united on a basis of personal intimacy; it is also responsible for the necessity for a constant renewal of the ideal, their lack of continuity, their pronounced individualism, and their affinity with all the oppressed and idealistic groups within the lower classes. These also are the groups in which an ardent desire for the improvement of their lot goes hand in hand with a complete ignorance of the complicated conditions of life, in which therefore an idealistic orthodoxy finds no difficulty in expecting to see the world transformed by the purely moral principles of love. In this way the sects gained on the side of intensity in Christian life, but they lost in the spirit of universalism, since they felt obliged to consider the Church as degenerate, and they did not believe that the world could be conquered by human power and effort; that is why they were always forced to adopt eschatological views. On the side of personal Christian piety they score, and they are in closer touch with the radical individualism of the Gospel, but they lose spontaneity and the spirit of grateful surrender to the Divine revelation of grace; they look upon the New Testament as the Law of God, and, in their active realization of personal fellowship in love, they tend towards legalism and an emphasis upon 'good works'. They gain in specific Christian piety, but they lose spiritual breadth and the power to be receptive, and they thus revise the whole vast process of assimilation which the Church had completed, and which she was able to complete because she had placed personal Christian piety upon an objective basis. The Church emphasizes the idea of Grace and makes it objective; the sect emphasizes and realizes the idea of subjective holiness. In the Scriptures the Church adheres to the source of redemption, whereas the sect adheres to the Law of God and of Christ.

4.12 Although this description of the sect-type represents in the main its prevailing sociological characteristics, the distinctive significance of the sect-type contrasted with the Church-type still has a good concrete basis. (There is no need to consider here the particular groups which were founded purely upon dogma; they were indeed rare, and the pantheistic philosophical sects of the Middle Ages merge almost imperceptibly into sects of the practical religious kind.) In reality, the sects are essentially different from the Church and the churches. The word 'sect', however, does not mean that these movements are undeveloped expressions of the Church-type; it stands for an independent sociological type of Christian thought.

4.13 The essence of the Church is its objective institutional character. The individual is born into it, and through infant baptism he comes under its miraculous influence. The priesthood and the hierarchy, which hold the keys to the tradition of the Church, to sacramental grace and ecclesiastical jurisdiction, represent the objective treasury of grace, even when the individual priest may happen to be unworthy; this Divine treasure only needs to be set always upon the lampstand and made effective through the sacraments, and it will inevitably do its work by virtue of the miraculous power which the Church contains. The Church means the eternal existence of the God-Man; it is the extension of the Incarnation, the objective organization of miraculous power, from which, by means of the Divine Providential government of the world, subjective results will appear quite naturally. From this point of view compromise with the world, and the connection with the preparatory stages and dispositions which it contained, was possible; for in spite of all individual inadequacy the institution remains holy and Divine, and it contains the promise of its capacity to overcome the world by means of the miraculous power which dwells within it. Universalism, however, also only becomes possible on the basis of this compromise; it means an actual domination of the institution as such, and a believing confidence in its invincible power of inward influence. Personal effort and service, however fully they may be emphasized, even when they go to the limits of extreme legalism, are still only secondary; the main thing is the objective possession of grace and its universally recognized dominion; to everything else these words apply: *et cetera adjicientur vobis.* The one vitally important thing is that every individual should come within the range of the influence of these saving energies of grace; hence the Church is forced to dominate Society, compelling all the members of Society to come under its sphere and influence; but, on the other hand, her stability is entirely unaffected by the fact of the extent to which her influence over all individuals is actually attained. The Church is the great educator of the nations, and like all educators she knows how to allow for various degrees of capacity and maturity, and how to attain her end only by a process of adaptation and compromise.

4.14 Compared with this institutional principle of an objective organism, however, the sect is a voluntary community whose members join it of their own free will. The very life of the sect, therefore, depends on actual personal service and co-operation; as an independent member each individual has his part within the fellowship; the bond of union has not been indirectly imparted through the common possession of Divine grace, but it is directly realized in the personal relationships of life. An individual is not born into a sect; he enters it on the basis of conscious conversion; infant baptism, which, indeed, was only introduced at a later date, is almost always a stumbling-block. In the sect spiritual progress does not depend upon the objective impartation of Grace through the Sacrament, but upon individual personal effort; sooner or later, therefore, the sect always criticizes the sacramental idea. This does not mean that the spirit of fellowship is weakened by individualism; indeed, it is strengthened, since each individual proves that he is entitled to membership by the very fact of his services to the fellowship. It is, however, naturally a somewhat limited form of fellowship, and the expenditure of so much effort in the maintenance and exercise of this particular kind of fellowship produces a certain indifference towards other forms of fellowship which are based upon secular interests; on the other hand, all secular interests are drawn into the narrow framework of the sect and tested by its standards, in so far as the sect is able to assimilate these interests at all. Whatever cannot be related to the group of interests controlled by the sect, and by the Scriptural ideal, is rejected and avoided. The sect, therefore, does not educate nations in the mass, but it gathers a select group of the elect, and places it in sharp opposition to the world. In so far as the sect-type maintains Christian universalism at all, like the Gospel, the only form it knows is that of eschatology; this is the reason why it always finally revives the eschatology of the Bible. That also naturally explains the greater tendency of the sect towards 'ascetic' life and thought, even though the original ideal of the New Testament had not pointed in that direction. The final activity of the group and of the individual consists precisely in the practical austerity of a purely religious attitude towards life which is not affected by cultural influences. That is, however, a different kind of asceticism, and this is the reason for that difference between it and the asceticism of the Church-type which has already been stated. It is not the heroic special achievement of a special class, restricted by its very nature to particular instances, nor the mortification of the senses in order to further the higher religious life; it is simply detachment from the world, the reduction of worldly pleasure to a minimum, and the highest possible development of fellowship in love; all this is interpreted in the old Scriptural sense. Since the sect-type is rooted in the teaching of Jesus, its asceticism also is that of primitive Christianity and of the Sermon on the Mount, not that of the Church and of the contemplative life; it is narrower and more scrupulous than that of Jesus, but, literally understood, it is still the continuation of the attitude of Jesus towards the world. The concentration on personal effort, and the sociological connection with a practical ideal, makes an extremely exacting claim on individual effort, and avoidance of all other forms of human association. The asceticism of the sect is not an attempt to popularize and universalize an ideal which the Church had prescribed only for special classes and in special circumstances. The Church ideal of asceticism can never be conceived as a universal ethic; it is essentially unique and heroic. The ascetic ideal of the sect, on the contrary, is, as a matter of course, an ideal which is possible to all, and appointed for all, which, according to its conception, united the fellowship instead of dividing it, and according to its content is also capable of a general realization in so far as the circle of the elect is concerned.

4.15 Thus, in reality we are faced with two different sociological types. This is true in spite of the fact (which is quite immaterial) that incidentally in actual practice they may often impinge upon one another. If objections are raised to the terms 'Church' and 'Sect', and if all sociological groups which are based on and inspired by monotheistic, universalized, religious motives are described (in a terminology which is in itself quite appropriate) as 'Churches', we would then have to make the distinction between institutional churches and voluntary churches. It does not really matter which expression is used. The all-important point is this: that both types are a logical result of the Gospel, and only conjointly do they exhaust the whole range of its sociological influence, and thus also indirectly of its social results, which are always connected with the religious organization.

4.16 In reality, the Church does not represent a mere deterioration of the Gospel, however much that may appear to be the case when we contrast its hierarchical organization and its sacramental system with the teaching of Jesus. For wherever the Gospel is conceived as primarily a free gift, as pure grace, and wherever it is offered to us in the picture which faith creates of Christ as a Divine institution, wherever the inner freedom of the Spirit, contrasted with all human effort and organization, is felt to be the spirit of Jesus, and wherever His splendid indifference towards secular matters is felt, in the sense of a spiritual and inner independence, while these secular things are used outwardly, there the institution of the Church may be regarded as a natural continuation and transformation of the Gospel. At the same time, with its unlimited universalism, it still contains the fundamental impulse of the evangelic message; the only difference is that whereas the Gospel had left all questions of possible realization to the miraculous coming of the Kingdom of God, a Church which had to work in a world which was not going to pass away had to organize and arrange matters for itself, and in so doing it was forced into a position of compromise.

4.17 On the other hand, the essence of the sect does not consist merely in a one-sided emphasis upon certain vital elements of the Church-type, but it is itself a direct continuation of the idea of the Gospel. Only within it is there a full recognition of the value of radical individualism and of the idea of love; it is the sect alone which instinctively builds up its ideal of fellowship from this point of view, and this is the very reason why it attains such a strong subjective and inward unity, instead of merely external membership in an institution. For the same reason the sect also maintains the original radicalism of the Christian ideal and its hostility towards the world, and it retains the fundamental demand for personal service, which indeed it is also able to regard as a work of grace: in the idea of grace, however, the sect emphasizes the subjective realization and the effects of grace, and not the objective assurance of its presence. The sect does not live on the miracles of the past, nor on the miraculous nature of the institution, but on the constantly renewed miracle of the Presence of Christ, and on the subjective reality of the individual mastery of life.

4.18 The starting-point of the Church is the Apostolic Message of the Exalted Christ, and faith in Christ the Redeemer, into which the Gospel has developed; this constitutes its objective treasure, which it makes still more objective in its sacramental-sacerdotal institution. To this extent the Church can trace its descent from Paulinism, which contained the germ of the sacramental idea, which, however, also contained some very unecclesiastical elements in its pneumatic enthusiasm, and in its urgent demand for the personal holiness of the 'new creature'.

4.19 The sect, on the contrary, starts from the teaching and the example of Jesus, from the subjective work of the apostles and the pattern of their life of poverty, and unites the religious individualism preached by the Gospel with the religious fellowship, in which the office of the ministry is not based upon ecclesiastical ordination and tradition, but upon religious service and power, and which therefore can also devolve entirely upon laymen.

4.20 The Church administers the sacraments without reference to the personal worthiness of the priests; the sect distrusts the ecclesiastical sacraments, and either permits them to be administered by laymen, or makes them dependent upon the personal character of the celebrant, or even discards them altogether. The individualism of the sect urges it towards the direct intercourse of the individual with God; frequently, therefore, it replaces the ecclesiastical doctrine of the sacraments by the Primitive Christian doctrine of the Spirit and by 'enthusiasm'. The Church has its priests and its sacraments; it dominates the world and is therefore also dominated by the world. The sect is lay Christianity, independent of the world, and is therefore inclined towards asceticism and mysticism. Both these tendencies are based upon fundamental impulses of the Gospel. The Gospel contains the idea of an objective possession of salvation in the knowledge and revelation of God, and in developing this idea it becomes the Church. It contains, however, also the idea of an absolute personal religion and of an absolute personal fellowship, and in following out this idea it becomes a sect. The teaching of Jesus, which cherishes the expectation of the End of the Age and the Coming of the Kingdom of God, which gathers into one body all who are resolute in their determination to confess Christ before men and to leave the world to its fate, tends to develop the sect-type. The apostolic faith which looks back to a miracle of redemption and to the Person of Jesus, and which lives in the powers of its heavenly Lord: this faith which leans upon something achieved and objective, in which it unites the faithful and allows them to rest, tends to develop the Church-type. Thus the New Testament helps to develop both the Church and the sect; it has done so from the beginning, but the Church had the start, and its great world mission. Only when the objectification of the Church had been developed to its fullest extent did the sectarian tendency assert itself and react against this excessive objectification. Further, just as the objectification of the Church was achieved in connection with the feudal society of the Early Middle Ages, the reappearance of the tendency to form sects was connected with the social transformation, and the developments of city-civilization in the central period of the Middle Ages and in its period of decline — with the growth of individualism and the gathering of masses of people in the towns themselves — and with the reflex effect of this city formation upon the rural population and the aristocracy.

5

H. Richard Niebuhr
The Churches of the Disinherited

Niebuhr (1894–1962), unlike many other theologians, was directly influenced by the writings of Weber and Troeltsch, even before their translation into English. *The Social Sources of Denominationalism* was first published in 1929 and established his reputation as a major thinker in social ethics and theology. More sociological in orientation than his older brother Reinhold Niebuhr, he sought to show how the churches could learn to identify, and then transcend, their social roots. To this end, he set out in the first chapter the ethical dilemma facing a socially determined church: 'Christendom has often achieved apparent success by ignoring the precepts of its founder. The church, as an organization interested in self-preservation and in the gain of power, has sometimes found the counsel of the Cross quite as inexpedient as have national and economic groups' (p. 3). Faced with such issues as war, slavery, and social inequality, the church has allied itself to 'power and prestige' rather than the demands of the Gospel. Niebuhr adopted Troeltsch's church–sect typology (as in *5.5*) and added to it the observation that, although the sect represents 'the child of an outcast minority', yet by 'its very nature the sectarian type of organization is valid only for one generation' (p. 19). After the first generation sects, too, learn to compromise with the world and become interested in self-preservation and the gain of power. A cycle of sects-turning-into-denominations-followed-by-new-sects becomes apparent (*5.3* and *5.14*). Following this Extract Niebuhr analysed the churches as expressions of the middle classes, and then as expressions of (and reinforcers of) sectional, racial, and political differences. He concluded that, viewed from a denominational perspective, (American) Christianity 'has become part and parcel of the world, one social institution alongside of many others, a phase of the total civilization more frequently conditioned by other cultural tendencies than conditioning them. The old vision of the time when the kingdom of this world should be transformed into a kingdom of our Lord and of his Christ has faded into the light of a common day in which the brute

facts of an unchanging human nature, of the invincible fortifications
of economic and political society, of racial pride, economic self-
interest and *Realpolitik* appear in their grim reality' (pp. 264–265).
The only way to overcome this is for the churches to find a fresh vision
of the Kingdom of God which transcends these socio-economic
boundaries. The present Extract clearly forms an important part of
this overall socio-theological analysis. It is also important in the
present context for the way it views doctrine as socially related but not
thereby solely reduced to social terms (*5.2*); for its insistence that
ethical positions within Christianity are related to social factors (*5.7*);
and for its extended treatment of Luther (*5.11*). Indeed, in Luther
Niebuhr saw the two poles of his analysis: 'The Luther who began the
Reformation belonged to mankind . . . But the Luther who founded
the Lutheran church as a separate, nationalist denomination was a
Germanized Luther, who needed to attenuate his heroic conceptions
in order that German nationalism might save Christianity from its
Latinic degeneracy' (p. 133). Niebuhr always remained hopeful that
the first Luther, and the vision of Christianity represented by him,
was a possibility for the present-day churches despite their social
conditioning.

Further Reading

Bryan Wilson, *Sects and Society* (Heinemann, 1955) provides an
important empirical critique of Niebuhr's sect–denomination cycle,
but Rodney Stark and William Sims Bainbridge, *The Future of
Religion* (University of California Press, 1985) provide an extended
and spirited reinstatement of the theory at a purely sociological level. I
discuss the issues facing a socially conditioned church further in
Prophecy and Praxis (Marshall, Morgan and Scott, 1981), and in
Beyond Decline (SCM Press, 1988).

5.1 One phase of denominationalism is largely explicable by
means of a modified economic interpretation of religious
history; for the divisions of the church have been occasioned more
frequently by the direct and indirect operation of economic factors
than by the influence of any other major interest of man. Furthermore, it is evident that economic stratification is often responsible for
maintaining divisions which were originally due to differences of
another sort. Social history demonstrates how a racial class may retain
its solidarity and distinction by becoming an economic class, and
religious history offers examples of churches which were originally

racial in character but maintained their separateness under new conditions because the racial group developed into an economic entity. It is true, of course, in this case as in that of others, that no one element, the religious or the economic or the racial, operates alone. Economic classes tend to take on a cultural character and economic differences between groups result in educational and psychological distinctions between them. The interaction of the various factors is well exemplified in the history of immigrant groups in the United States. These are distinguished at first by racial or national character, but they are usually also the lowest groups in the economic and cultural scale during the first generation and, therefore, their distinction from other groups is triply fortified. Their churches, as a result, are distinguished economically and culturally as well as racially from the denominations of previous immigrants who have risen in the economic scale while losing their specifically national or racial character.

5.2 An exclusively economic interpretation of denominationalism would, because of this interaction, be as erroneous as the exclusively economic interpretation of political history is bound to be. It is quite unjustifiable, above all, to leave the religious factor itself out of account in dealing with religious movements. Only because the inspiration of such movements is religious do they develop the tremendous energy they display in history. Yet an exclusively religious interpretation, especially a doctrinal one, is likely to miss the point of the whole development even more completely than does an exclusively economic explanation. For if religion supplies the energy, the goal, and the motive of sectarian movements, social factors no less decidedly supply the occasion, and determine the form the religious dynamic will take. Were spiritual energies to develop unchecked they would scarcely issue in the formation of such denominations as now compose Christianity. Religious energies are dammed up, confined to narrow channels, split into parallel streams, by the non-religious distinctions and classifications of Christians. The source of a religious movement, therefore, need not be economic for its results to take on a definitely economic character. On the other hand, economic conditions may supply the occasion for the rise of a new religious movement without determining its religious value. In any case, however, the character of the denomination issuing from the movement is explicable only if the influence of economic factors be taken into consideration.

5.3 So regarded, one phase of the history of denominationalism reveals itself as the story of the religiously neglected poor, who fashion a new type of Christianity which corresponds to their distinctive needs, who rise in the economic scale under the influence of religious discipline, and who, in the midst of a freshly acquired cultural respectability, neglect the new poor succeeding them on the lower plane. This pattern recurs with remarkable regularity in the history of Christianity. Anabaptists, Quakers, Methodists, Salvation Army, and more recent sects of like type illustrate this rise and progress of the churches of the disinherited.

5.4 Not only the religious revolutions of the poor, however, have left their impress on the denominational history of Christendom. One may also speak with G. K. Chesterton of the revolt of the rich against the poor. Some of the earlier churches of the Reformation received much of their specific character from their alliance with rising commercialism and set forth an interpretation of Christianity conformable with their major economic interests. To this group belong especially the Calvinistic churches, as has been shown by Weber, Cunningham, and Tawney. Other sects, whose origins are not so readily identifiable with economic movements, have preserved their separate character because of the economic status of their members and are distinguished from their sister denominations less by doctrine than by their wealth and the consequent conservatism of ethics and thought.

1

5.5 That astute historian of the social ethics of the churches, Ernst Troeltsch, once wrote: 'The really creative, church-forming, religious movements are the work of the lower strata. Here only can one find that union of unimpaired imagination, simplicity in emotional life, unreflective character of thought, spontaneity of energy and vehement force of need, out of which an unconditioned faith in a divine revelation, the naïveté of complete surrender and the intransigence of certitude can rise. Need upon the one hand and the absence of an all-relativizing culture of reflection on the other hand are at home only in these strata. All great community-building revelations have come forth again and again out of such circles and the significance and power for further development in such religious movements have always been dependent upon the force of the original impetus given in such naïve revelations as well as on the energy of the conviction which made this impetus absolute and divine.' This passage not only describes the character of the religious movements which originate in the culturally lower strata of society but also indicates wherein the religious expatriation of these classes consists and shows the dialectic of the process which gives rise to ever new movements.

5.6 The religion of the untutored and economically disfranchised classes has distinct ethical and psychological characteristics, corresponding to the needs of these groups. Emotional fervor is one common mark. Where the power of abstract thought has not been highly developed and where inhibitions on emotional expression have not been set up by a system of polite conventions, religion must and will express itself in emotional terms. Under these circumstances spontaneity and energy of religious feeling rather than conformity to an abstract creed are regarded as the tests of religious genuineness. Hence also the formality of ritual is displaced in such groups by an informality which gives opportunity for the expression of emotional faith and for a simple, often crude, symbolism. An intellectually trained and liturgically minded clergy is rejected in favor of lay leaders who serve the emotional needs of this religion more adequately and who, on the other hand, are not allied by culture and interest with those ruling classes whose superior manner of life is too obviously purchased at the expense of the poor.

5.7 Ethically, as well as psychologically, such religion bears a distinct character. The salvation which it seeks and sets forth is the salvation of the socially disinherited. Intellectual naïveté and practical need combine to create a marked propensity toward millenarianism, with its promise of tangible goods and of the reversal of all present social systems of rank. From the first century onward, apocalypticism has always been most at home among the disinherited. The same combination of need and social experience brings forth in these classes a deeper appreciation of the radical character of the ethics of the gospel and greater resistance to the tendency to compromise with the morality of power than is found among their more fortunate brethren. Again, the religion of the poor is characterized by the exaltation of the typical virtues of the class and by the apprehension under the influence of the gospel of the moral values resident in its necessities. Hence one finds here, more than elsewhere, appreciation of the religious worth of solidarity and equality, of sympathy and mutual aid, of rigorous honesty in matters of debt, and the religious evaluation of simplicity in dress and manner, of the wisdom hidden to the wise and prudent but revealed to babes, of poverty of spirit, of humility and meekness. Simple and direct in its apprehension of the faith, the religion of the poor shuns the relativizations of ethical and intellectual sophistication and by its fruits in conduct often demonstrates its moral and religious superiority.

5.8 Whenever Christianity has become the religion of the fortunate and cultured and has grown philosophical, abstract, formal, and ethically harmless in the process, the lower strata of society find themselves religiously expatriated by a faith which neither meets their psychological needs nor sets forth an appealing ethical ideal. In such a situation the right leader finds little difficulty in launching a new movement which will, as a rule, give rise to a new denomination. When, however, the religious leader does not appear and religion remains bound in the forms of middle-class culture, the secularization of the masses and the transfer of their religious fervor to secular movements, which hold some promise of salvation from the evils that afflict them, is the probable result.

5.9 The development of the religion of the disinherited is illustrated not only by the history of various sects in Christianity but by the rise of that faith itself. It began as a religion of the poor, of those who had been denied a stake in contemporary civilization. It was not a socialist movement, as some have sought to show, but a religious revolution, centering in no mundane Paradise but in the cult of Christ. Yet it was addressed to the poor in the land, to fishermen and peasants, to publicans and outcasts. In Corinth as in Galilee, in Rome as in Antioch, not many 'wise after the flesh, not many mighty, not many noble were called'; and this condition continued far down into the third century. Origen and Tertullian as well as the opponents of Christianity, notably Celsus, bear ample testimony to the fact that 'the uneducated are always in a majority with us'. But the new faith became the religion of the cultured, of the rulers, of the sophisticated; it lost its spontaneous energy amid the quibblings of abstract theologies; it sacrificed its ethical rigorousness in compromise with the policies of governments and nobilities; it abandoned its apocalyptic hopes as irrelevant to the well-being of a successful church. Now began the successive waves of religious revolution, the constant recrudescences of religions of the poor who sought an emotionally and ethically more satisfying faith than was the metaphysical and formal cult Christianity had come to be. Montanism, the Franciscan movement, Lollardy, Waldensianism, and many similar tendencies are intelligible only as the efforts of the religiously disinherited to discover again the sources of effective faith. Yet on the whole it is true that the Roman Church, with its ritual, its pageantry, and its authoritative doctrine, supplied to the unsophisticated groups a type of religion which largely satisfied their longings; for under the necessity of adapting itself to the inundation of the northern tribes it had evolved a system of leadership and worship congenial to the naïve mind and had learned to set forth salvation in terms not abstract but tangible and real though remote. The Roman Church, despite the evident failings of scholasticism and papal policy and sacerdotal luxury, was unable to maintain its integrity not so much because it did not meet the needs of the lower strata as because it did not sufficiently accommodate itself to the new middle classes represented by humanism, the new capitalism and nationalism, as well as for reasons not primarily connected with the economic and cultural stratification of society.

2

5.10 The failure of the Reformation to meet the religious needs of peasants and other disfranchised groups is a chapter writ large in history. With all of its native religious fervor it remained the religion of the middle classes and the nobility. The Peasants' War and the Anabaptist movement were the result; for distinct as these two movements were, their close relationships are evident in history. Thomas Muenzer, the arch-enemy of Luther, was Anabaptist as well as revolutionary leader. The Zwickau prophets and Melchior Hoffmann represented the political and economic as well as the religious interests of the poor in proclaiming a faith which promised not only the salvation of emotional experience wherein the believer transcended the problems of a toilsome, humdrum life, but also gave assurance of deliverance from political and social oppressions through the establishment of Christ's perfect brotherhood.

5.11 Honestly and naïvely the peasants of Germany had believed that Luther's appeal to the New Testament was an appeal not to Pauline theology alone but to the ethics of the Sermon on the Mount as well. All too soon they discovered that the new Protestantism they had espoused so heartily protested less against their masters than against their masters' enemies and that the new faith dealt with their extreme necessities even less effectively than did the old. The priesthood of all believers, they found, meant deliverance neither from the abstruseness of dogma and the formality of sacramentalism nor from the inequalities of political and economic ethics. From Luther they learned that they could not look to Protestantism for salvation from the dual standard which bade rulers rule in accordance with the code of Old Testament precepts of strict reward and punishment while it required subjects to obey their political and economic masters in the spirit of a Christian and self-sacrificing meekness. Had not Luther said to them, 'Listen, dear Christians, to your Christian right. Thus speaks your supreme Lord Christ, whose name you bear: Ye shall not resist evil, but whosoever shall compel thee to go one mile, go with him two, and if any would take away thy coat, let him have thy cloak also, and whosoever smiteth thee on thy right cheek, turn to him the other also. Do you hear, you Christian congregation? How does your project agree with this right? You will not bear that anyone inflict evil or injustice upon you, but want to be free and suffer only complete goodness and justice. . . . If you do not want to bear such a right, then you had better put away the Christian name and boast of another name in accordance with your deeds, or Christ himself will snatch his name away from you, so that it will be too hard for you to bear.' But not long thereafter this same Luther had addressed their masters in other terms in his pamphlet 'Against the Thieving and Murderous Hordes of Peasants' — a production which has well been called a 'disgrace to literature, to say nothing of religion'. 'Dear masters', he wrote in this pamphlet, 'deliver here, save here, help here, have mercy upon the poor people. Stab, hit, kill here, whoever can; and though you die in this, happy are you, for a more blessed death you can never find; for you die in obedience to the divine word and command (Romans 13) and in the service of love, to save your neighbor from the bonds of hell and devil.' 'Here let whoever can give blows, strangle, stab — secretly or openly — and remember that nothing can be more poisonous, harmful, and devilish than a revolutionary; just as one must kill a mad dog, for if you do not slay him he will slay you and a whole land with you.' All of this, it is true, Luther justified by ample appeal not to the Old Testament but to the New. 'It does not help the peasants', he wrote, 'that they claim that in Genesis I and II all things were created free and common and that we have all been equally baptized. For in the New Testament Moses counts for nothing, but there stands our Master Christ and casts us with body and possessions under the Kaiser's and worldly law when he says, "Give to Cæsar the things that are Cæsar's".' So the disinherited were ruled out of Protestantism and discovered their last estate to be worse than the former, for the dualism of Catholic social ethics had been in favor of a spiritual, not primarily of a political and economic, aristocracy, while the new faith proclaimed that 'the ass will have blows and the people will be ruled by force'. Thus, in the very first years of the new movement the tendency towards cleavage along economic lines, so baneful for all later Protestantism, came to expression. 'As the poor found their spiritual needs best supplied in the conventicle of dissent, official Lutheranism became an established church, predominantly an aristocratic and middle-class party of vested interest and privilege.'

5.12 The Swiss Reformation resulted in the same division between the Christianity of the bourgeoisie and that of the poor. In fact it was in Zurich that the representatives of the new emotional and social religion had first appeared. There they had met, after an early friendship with Zwingli, that reformer's rebuff, for 'the humanist could have little sympathy with an uncultured and ignorant group — such they were, in spite of the fact that a few leaders were university graduates — and the statesman could not admit in his categories a purpose that was sectarian as against the state church and democratic as against the existing aristocracy'. Accused of communism, which Zwingli considered a sin in the light of a divine sanction of private property implied in the sixth commandment, the leaders of the Protestantism of the poor were fined, banished, and, in some instances, executed.

5.13 In the Netherlands, in Poland, in England, at last in America also, the Anabaptists met a similar fate and the expatriation of the poor and uneducated from the new church went on with violence and much shedding of blood. Neither Lutheranism nor Calvinism had a message for them and both resented, with the vehemence of those whose economic rather than religious interests are threatened, the attempt to found a religion which met the need for a Christianity of emotional fervor and for a social reconstruction.

5.14 Under such circumstances the rise of the first Protestant sect, as distinct from the churches of the Reformation, took place. 'It was a movement', as Bax points out, 'constituted in the main of the disinherited classes of the time, the peasants, the poorer handicraftsmen, and the journeymen of the towns, to whose oppressed position, economically and politically, it powerfully appealed.' Its ethical interests came into appearance not only in the early revolutionary movements but even more in the later practice of pacific and non-resistant morality, in the rejection of the oath, in the refusal to participate in warfare and in government, in the practice of equality and mutual aid as well as in the frequent communism of individual groups. Its religious character was made evident in the insistence on voluntary membership, on adult baptism of the converted, in the democratic election and ordination of pastors by local churches, in lay preaching and congregational organization, and especially in the phenomena of revivalism. Persecuted vindictively on the continent and lacking adequate leadership, Anabaptism all but disappeared there leaving the peoples who had been disappointed by the failure readier for the message of the old Catholicism than for that of the new Protestanism. A remnant was gathered by Menno Simons, founder of the now much divided Mennonites. But with Simons began also the inevitable tendency accompanying the rise of a religious group in fortune and culture — the tendency toward a relaxation of the ethical demand and toward formalization of the cult. From violent revolution the path of development led through stubborn non-resistance and unyielding assertion by non-assertion of the principles of equality and love to an accommodating quietism. The Anabaptists, however, were too broken by the Protestant Inquisition to become a strong church, affiliated with wealth and prestige. Isolated by persecution, as the Jews had been isolated, they formed a narrow sect, cut off from other churches not only by the caste-consciousness of early Lutherans and

Calvinists but by their own social loyalties to their outcast group. A splendid devotion to principles remains among many of the heirs of the sixteenth-century prophets to the disinherited, but even more effective is the consciousness of kind. And that is another phase of the tragedy of caste in the church of Christ, for castes make outcasts and outcasts form castes.

6

Karl Mannheim
Theology and the Sociology of Knowledge

Karl Mannheim's *Ideology and Utopia* marks a crucial transition both for Mannheim himself and for the sociology of knowledge. For Mannheim it bridged his move, in the troubled 1930s, from a chair in sociology in the University of Frankfurt to one at the London School of Economics and Political Science. The work first appeared in English in 1936 and the introduction, from which the first part of this Extract is taken, was especially written for this edition. The second part of the Extract was originally a part of *Ideologie und Utopie*, first published in Bonn in 1929. Mannheim's struggle with the concepts of 'ideology' and 'utopia' clearly reflect the ideological struggles of that time. But they also represent a decisive intellectual break with Marxist, polemical uses of the concept of 'ideology' (*6.3*). This placed him in an ideal position to examine the cognitive implications of pluralism (*6.8*) and what appeared to be sociological relativism (*6.19*). He was not particularly interested in theology, as such, but when he did use theological illustrations his remarks were always pertinent. The example here (*6.13*) is clearly relevant to *Extract 5* and acts as an important reminder in this context (and especially to the Extracts in *Section Three*) that the researcher should not be tempted to treat such sociological propositions in too mechanistic a manner: he or she always participates 'evaluationally' in such enterprises. The effect of this observation is to force a recognition that social conditioning can be traced in all but the most formal thought: it is relational (*6.19*). Mannheim was also aware that such an understanding of the sociology of knowledge militates against thoroughgoing positivism (*6.22*). Once applied to theological ideas, a relational understanding no longer presents the threats of relativism and reductionism that are often feared most by the theologian — see further *Extract 10*.

Further Reading

Gregory Baum is the theologian who has done most to work out the theological implications of Mannheim, particularly in his *Religion and*

Alienation: a Theological Reading of Sociology (Paulist, 1975) and *The Social Imperative* (Paulist, 1979); J. E. Curtis and J. W. Petras (eds), *The Sociology of Knowledge: a Reader* (Duckworth, 1970) and Peter Hamilton, *Knowledge and Social Structure* (Routledge and Kegan Paul, 1974) set Mannheim into the context of the sociology of knowledge as a discipline.

6.1 In political discussion in modern democracies where ideas were more clearly representative of certain groups, the social and existential determination of thought became more easily visible. In principle it was politics which first discovered the sociological method in the study of intellectual phenomena. Basically it was in political struggles that for the first time men became aware of the unconscious collective motivations which had always guided the direction of thought. Political discussion is, from the very first, more than theoretical argumentation; it is the tearing off of disguises — the unmasking of those unconscious motives which bind the group existence to its cultural aspirations and its theoretical arguments. To the extent, however, that modern politics fought its battles with theoretical weapons, the process of unmasking penetrated to the social roots of theory.

6.2 The discovery of the social-situational roots of thought at first, therefore, took the form of unmasking. In addition to the gradual dissolution of the unitary objective world-view, which to the simple man in the street took the form of a plurality of divergent conceptions of the world, and to the intellectuals presented itself as the irreconcilable plurality of thought-styles, there entered into the public mind the tendency to unmask the unconscious situational motivations in group thinking. This final intensification of the intellectual crisis can be characterized by two slogan-like concepts 'ideology and utopia' which because of their symbolic significance have been chosen as the title for this book.

6.3 The concept 'ideology' reflects the one discovery which emerged from political conflict, namely, that ruling groups can in their thinking become so intensively interest-bound to a situation that they are simply no longer able to see certain facts which would undermine their sense of domination. There is implicit in the word 'ideology' the insight that in certain situations the collective unconscious of certain groups obscures the real condition of society both to itself and to others and thereby stabilizes it.

6.4 The concept of *utopian* thinking reflects the opposite discovery of the political struggle, namely that certain oppressed groups are intellectually so strongly interested in the destruction and transformation of a given condition of society that they unwittingly see only those elements in the situation which tend to negate it. Their thinking is incapable of correctly diagnosing an existing condition of society. They are not at all concerned with what really exists; rather in their thinking they already seek to change the situation that exists. Their thought is never a diagnosis of the situation; it can be used only as a direction for action. In the utopian mentality, the collective unconscious, guided by wishful representation and the will to action, hides certain aspects of reality. It turns its back on everything which would shake its belief or paralyse its desire to change things.

6.5 The collective unconscious and the activity impelled by it serve to disguise certain aspects of social reality from two directions. It is possible, furthermore, as we have seen above, to designate specifically the source and direction of the distortion. It is the task of this volume to trace out, in the two directions indicated, the most significant phases in the emergence of this discovery of the role of the unconscious as it appears in the history of ideology and utopia. At this point we are concerned only with delineating that state of mind which followed upon these insights since it is characteristic of the situation from which this book came forth.

6.6 At first those parties which possessed the new 'intellectual weapons', the unmasking of the unconscious, had a terrific advantage over their adversaries. It was stupefying for the latter when it was demonstrated that their ideas were merely distorted reflections of their situation in life, anticipations of their unconscious interests. The mere fact that it could be convincingly demonstrated to the adversary that motives which had hitherto been hidden from him were at work must have filled him with terror and awakened in the person using the weapon a feeling of marvellous superiority. It was at the same time the dawning of a level of consciousness which mankind had hitherto always hidden from itself with the greatest tenacity. Nor was it by chance that this invasion of the unconscious was dared only by the attacker while the attacked was doubly overwhelmed — first, through the laying bare of the unconscious itself and then, in addition to this, through the fact that the unconscious was laid bare and pushed into prominence in a spirit of enmity. For it is clear that it makes a considerable difference whether the unconscious is dealt with for purposes of aiding and curing or for the purpose of unmasking.

6.7 To-day, however, we have reached a stage in which this weapon of the reciprocal unmasking and laying bare of the unconscious sources of intellectual existence has become the property not of one group among many but of all of them. But in the measure that the various groups sought to destroy their adversaries' confidence in their thinking by this most modern intellectual weapon of radical unmasking, they also destroyed, as all positions gradually came to be subjected to analysis, man's confidence in human thought in general. The process of exposing the problematic elements in thought which had been latent since the collapse of the Middle Ages culminated at last in the collapse of confidence in thought in general. There is nothing accidental but rather more of the inevitable in the fact that more and more people took flight into scepticism or irrationalism.

6.8 Two powerful currents flow together here and reinforce one another with an overwhelming pressure: one, the disappearance of a unitary intellectual world with fixed values and norms; and, two, the sudden surge of the hitherto hidden unconscious into the bright daylight of consciousness. Man's thought had from time immemorial appeared to him as a segment of his spiritual existence and not simply as a discrete objective fact. Reorientation had in the past frequently meant a change in man himself. In these earlier periods it was mostly a case of slow shifts in values and norms, of a gradual transformation of the frame of reference from which men's actions derived their ultimate orientation. But in modern times it is a much more profoundly disorganizing affair. The resort to the unconscious tended to dig up the soil out of which the varying points of views emerged. The roots from which human thought had hitherto derived its nourishment were exposed. Gradually it becomes clear to all of us that we cannot go on living in the same way once we know about our unconscious motives as we did when we were ignorant of them. What we now experience is more than a new idea, and the questions we raise constitute more than a new problem. What we are concerned with here is the elemental perplexity of our time, which can be epitomized in the symptomatic question 'How is it possible for man to continue to think and live in a time when the problems of ideology and utopia are being radically raised and thought through in all their implications?'

6.9 It is possible, of course, to escape from this situation in which the plurality of thought-styles has become visible and the existence of collective-unconscious motivations recognized simply by hiding these processes from ourselves. One can take flight into a supra-temporal logic and assert that truth as such is unsullied and has neither a plurality of forms nor any connection with unconscious motivations. But in a world in which the problem is not just an interesting subject for discussion but rather an inner perplexity, someone will soon come forth who will insist against these views that 'our problem is not truth as such; it is our thinking as we find it in its rootedness in action in the social situation, in unconscious motivations. Show us how we can advance from our concrete perceptions to your absolute definitions. Do not speak of truth as such but show us the way in which our statements, stemming from our social existence, can be translated into a sphere in which the partisanship, the fragmentariness of human vision, can be transcended, in which the social origin and the dominance of the unconscious in thinking will lead to controlled observations rather than to chaos'. The absoluteness of thought is not attained by warranting, through a general principle, that one has it or by proceeding to label some particular limited viewpoint (usually one's own) as supra-partisan and authoritative.

6.10 Nor are we aided when we are directed to a few propositions in which the content is so formal and abstract (e.g. in mathematics, geometry, and pure economics) that in fact they seem to be completely detached from the thinking social individual. The battle is not about these propositions but about that greater wealth of factual determinations in which man concretely diagnoses his individual and social situation, in which concrete interdependences in life are perceived and in which happenings external to us are first correctly understood. The battle rages concerning those propositions in which every concept is meaningfully oriented from the first, in which we use words like conflict, breakdown, alienation, insurrection, resentment — words which do not reduce complex situations for the sake of an externalizing, formal description without ever being able to build them up again and which would lose their content if their orientation, their evaluative elements, were dropped out.

6.11 We have already shown elsewhere that the development of modern science led to the growth of a technique of thought by means of which all that was only meaningfully intelligible was excluded. Behaviourism has pushed to the foreground this tendency towards concentration on entirely externally perceivable reactions, and has sought to construct a world of facts in which there will exist only measurable data, only correlations between series of factors in which the degree of probability of modes of behaviour in certain situations will be predictable. It is possible, and even probable, that sociology must pass through this stage in which its contents will undergo a mechanistic dehumanization and formalization, just as psychology did, so that out of devotion to an ideal of narrow exactitude nothing will remain except statistical data, tests, surveys, etc., and in the end every significant formulation of a problem will be excluded. All that can be said here is that this reduction of everything to a measurable or inventory-like describability is significant as a serious attempt to determine what is unambiguously ascertainable and, further, to think through what becomes of our psychic and social world when it is restricted to purely externally measurable relationships. There can no longer be any doubt that no real penetration into social reality is possible through this approach. Let us take for example the relatively simple phenomenon denoted by the term 'situation'. What is left of it, or is it even at all intelligible when it is reduced to an external constellation of various reciprocally related but only externally visible patterns of behaviour? It is clear, on the other hand, that a human situation is characterizable only when one has also taken into account those conceptions which the participants have of it, how they experience their tensions in this situation and how they react to the tensions so conceived. Or, let us take some milieu; for instance, the milieu in which a certain family exists. Are not the norms which prevail in this family, and which are intelligible only through meaningful interpretation, at least as much a part of the milieu as the landscape or the furniture of the household? Still further, must not this same family, other things being equal, be considered as a completely different milieu (e.g. from the point of the training of the children) if its norms have changed? If we wish to comprehend such a concrete phenomenon as a situation or the normative content of a milieu, the purely mechanistic scheme of approach will never suffice and there must be introduced in addition concepts adequate for the understanding of meaningful and non-mensurative elements.

6.12 But it would be false to assume that the relations between these elements are less clear and less precisely perceivable than those that obtain between purely measurable phenomena. Quite on the contrary, the reciprocal interdependence of the elements making up an event is much more intimately comprehensible than that of strictly external formalized elements. Here that approach which, following Dilthey, I should like to designate as the understanding of the primary interdependence of experience (*das verstehende Erfassen des 'ursprünglichen Lebenszusammenhanges'*) comes into its own. In this approach, by use of the technique of understanding, the reciprocal functional interpenetration of psychic experiences and social situations becomes immediately intelligible. We are confronted here with a realm of existence in which the emergence of psychic reactions from within becomes evident of necessity and is not comprehensible merely as is an external causality, according to the degree of probability of its frequency.

6.13 Let us take certain of the observations which sociology has worked up by the use of the method of understanding and consider the nature of its scientific evidence. When one has stated concerning the ethics of the earliest Christian communities, that it was primarily intelligible in terms of the resentment of oppressed strata, and when others have added that this ethical outlook was entirely unpolitical because it corresponded to the mentality of that stratum which had as yet no real aspirations to rule ('Render unto Caesar the things that are Caesar's'), and when it has been said further that this ethic is not a tribal ethic but a world ethic, since it arose from the soil of the already disintegrated tribal structure of the Roman Empire, it is clear that these interconnections between social situations on the one hand and psychic-ethical modes of behaviour on the other are not, it is true, measurable but can none the less be much more intensively penetrated in their essential character than if coefficients of correlation were established between the various factors. The interconnections are evident because we have used an understanding approach to those primary interdependences of experience from which these norms arose.

6.14 It has become clear that the principal propositions of the social sciences are neither mechanistically external nor formal, nor do they represent purely quantitative correlations but rather situational diagnoses in which we use, by and large, the same concrete concepts and thought-models which were created for activistic purposes in real life. It is clear, furthermore, that every social science diagnosis is closely connected with the evaluations and unconscious orientations of the observer and that the critical self-clarification of the social sciences is intimately bound up with the critical self-clarification of our orientation in the everyday world. An observer who is not fundamentally interested in the social roots of the changing ethics of the period in which he himself lives, who does not think through the problems of social life in terms of the tensions between social strata, and who has not also discovered the fruitful aspect of resentment in his own experience, will never be in a position to see that phase of Christian ethics described above, to say nothing of being able to understand it. It is precisely in the degree in which he participates evaluationally (sympathetically or antagonistically) in the struggle for ascendancy of the lower strata, in the degree that he evaluates resentment positively or negatively, that he becomes aware of the dynamic significance of social tension and resentment. 'Lower class', 'social ascendancy', 'resentment' instead of being formal concepts are meaningfully oriented concepts. If they were to be formalized, and the evaluations they contain distilled out of them, the thought-model characteristic of the situation, in which it is precisely resentment which produced the good and novel fruitful norm, would be totally inconceivable. The more closely one examines the word 'resentment' the more clear it becomes that this apparently non-evaluative descriptive term for an attitude is replete with evaluations. If these evaluations are left out, the idea loses its concreteness. Furthermore, if the thinker had no interest in reconstructing the feeling of resentment, the tension which permeated the above-described situation of early Christianity would be entirely inaccessible to him. Thus here, too, the purposefully oriented will is the source of the understanding of the situation. . . .

2

The non-evaluative conception of ideology

6.15 The investigator who undertakes the historical studies suggested above need not be concerned with the problem of what is ultimate truth. Interrelationships have now become evident, both in the present and in history, which formerly could never have been analysed so thoroughly. The recognition of this fact in all its ramifications gives to the modern investigator a tremendous advantage. He will no longer be inclined to raise the question as to which of the contending parties has the truth on its side, but rather he will direct his attention to discovering the approximate truth as it emerges in the course of historical development out of the complex social process. The modern investigator can answer, if he is accused of evading the problem of what is truth, that the indirect approach to truth through social history will in the end be more fruitful than a direct logical attack. Even though he does not discover 'truth itself', he will discover the cultural setting and many hitherto unknown 'circumstances' which are relevant to the discovery of truth. As a matter of fact, if we believe that we already have the truth, we will lose interest in obtaining those very insights which might lead us to an approximate understanding of the situation. It is precisely our uncertainty which brings us a good deal closer to reality than was possible in former periods which had faith in the absolute.

6.16 It is now quite clear that only in a rapidly and profoundly changing intellectual world could ideas and values, formerly regarded as fixed, have been subjected to a thoroughgoing criticism. In no other situation could men have been alert enough to discover the ideological element in all thinking. It is true, of course, that men have fought the ideas of their adversaries, but in the past, for the most part, they have done so only in order to cling to their own absolutes the more stubbornly. To-day, there are too many points of view of equal value and prestige, each showing the relativity of the other, to permit us to take any one position and to regard it as impregnable and absolute. Only this socially disorganized intellectual situation makes possible the insight, hidden until now by a generally stable social structure and the practicability of certain traditional norms, that every point of view is particular to a social situation.[1] It may indeed be true that in order to act we need a certain amount of self-confidence and intellectual self-assurance. It may also be true that the very form of expression, in which we clothe our thoughts, tends to impose upon them an absolute tone. In our epoch, however, it is precisely the function of historical investigation (and, as we shall see, of those social groups from which the scholars are to be recruited), to analyse the elements that make up our self-assurance, so indispensable for action in immediate, concrete situations, and to counteract the bias which might arise from what we, as individuals, take for granted. This is possible only through incessant care and the determination to reduce to a minimum the tendency to self-apotheosis. Through this effort the one-sidedness of our own point of view is counteracted, and conflicting intellectual positions may actually come to supplement one another.

6.17 It is imperative in the present transitional period to make use of the intellectual twilight which dominates our epoch and in which all values and points of view appear in their genuine relativity. We must realize once and for all that the meanings which make up our world are simply an historically determined and continuously developing structure in which man develops, and are in no sense absolute.

6.18 At this point in history when all things which concern man and the structure and elements of history itself are suddenly revealed to us in a new light, it behooves us in our scientific thinking to become masters of the situation, for it is not inconceivable that sooner than we suspect, as has often been the case before in history, this vision may disappear, the opportunity may be lost, and the world will once again present a static, uniform, and inflexible countenance.

6.19 This first non-evaluative insight into history does not inevitably lead to relativism, but rather to relationism. Knowledge, as seen in the light of the total conception of ideology, is by no means an illusory experience, for ideology in its relational concept is not at all identical with illusion. Knowledge arising out of our experience in actual life situations, though not absolute, is knowledge none the less. The norms arising out of such actual life situations do not exist in a social vacuum, but are effective as real sanctions for conduct. Relationism signifies merely that all of the elements of meaning in a given situation have reference to one another and derive their significance from this reciprocal interrelationship in a given frame of thought. Such a system of meanings is possible and valid only in a given type of historical existence, to which, for a time, it furnishes appropriate expression. When the social situation changes, the system of norms to which it had previously given birth ceases to be in harmony with it. The same estrangement goes on with reference to knowledge and to the historical perspective. All knowledge is oriented toward some object and is influenced in its approach by the nature of the object with which it is preoccupied. But the mode of approach to the object to be known is dependent upon the nature of the knower. This is true, first of all, with regard to the qualitative depth of our knowledge (particularly when we are attempting to arrive at an 'understanding' of something where the degree of insight to be obtained presupposes the mental or intellectual kinship of the understander and of the understood). It is true, in the second place, with regard to the possibility of intellectually formulating our knowledge, especially since in order to be transmuted into knowledge, every perception is and must be ordered and organized into categories. The extent, however, to which we can organize and express our experience in such conceptual forms is, in turn, dependent upon the frames of reference which happen to be available at a given historical moment. The concepts which we have and the universe of discourse in which we move, together with the directions in which they tend to elaborate themselves, are dependent largely upon the historical-social situation of the intellectually active and responsible members of the group. We have, then, as the theme of this non-evaluative study of ideology, the relationship of all partial knowledge and its component elements to the larger body of meaning, and ultimately to the structure of historical reality. If, instead of fully reckoning with this insight and its implications, we were to disregard it, we would be surrendering an advanced position of intellectual achievement which has been painfully won.

6.20 Hence it has become extremely questionable whether, in the flux of life, it is a genuinely worthwhile intellectual problem to seek to discover fixed and immutable ideas or absolutes. It is a more worthy intellectual task perhaps to learn to think dynamically and relationally rather than statically. In our contemporary social and intellectual plight, it is nothing less than shocking to discover that those persons who claim to have discovered an absolute are usually the same people who also pretend to be superior to the rest. To find people in our day attempting to pass off to the world and recommending to others some nostrum of the absolute which they claim to have discovered is merely a sign of the loss of and the need for intellectual and moral certainty, felt by broad sections of the population who are unable to look life in the face. It may possibly be true that, to continue to live on and to act in a world like ours, it is vitally necessary to seek a way out of this uncertainty of multiple alternatives; and accordingly people may be led to embrace some immediate goal as if it were absolute, by which they hope to make their problems appear concrete and real. But it is not primarily the man of action who seeks the absolute and immutable, but rather it is he who wishes to induce others to hold on to the *status quo* because he feels comfortable and smug under conditions as they are. Those who are satisfied with the existing order of things are only too likely to set up the chance situation of the moment as absolute and eternal in order to have something stable to hold on to and to minimize the hazardousness of life. This cannot be done, however, without resorting to all sorts of romantic notions and myths. Thus we are faced with the curiously appalling trend of modern thought, in which the absolute which was once a means of entering into communion with the divine, has now become an instrument used by those who profit from it, to distort, pervert, and conceal the meaning of the present.

The Transition from the Non-Evaluative to the Evaluative Conception of Ideology

6.21 Thus it appears that beginning with the non-evaluative conception of ideology, which we used primarily to grasp the flux of continuously changing realities, we have been unwittingly led to an evaluative-epistemological, and finally an ontological-metaphysical approach. In our argument thus far the non-evaluative, dynamic point of view inadvertently became a weapon against a certain intellectual position. What was originally simply a methodological technique disclosed itself ultimately as a *Weltanschauung* and an instrument from the use of which the non-evaluative view of the world emerged. Here, as in so many other cases, only at the end of our activity do we at last become aware of those motives which at the beginning drove us to set every established value in motion, considering it as a part of a general historical movement.

6.22 We see then that we have employed metaphysical-ontological value-judgements of which we have not been aware. But only those will be alarmed by this recognition who are prey to the positivistic prejudices of past generation, and who still believe in the possibility of being completely emancipated in their thinking from ontological, metaphysical, and ethical presuppositions. In fact, the more aware one becomes of the presuppositions underlying his thinking, in the interest of truly empirical research, the more it is apparent that this empirical procedure (in the social sciences, at least) can be carried on only on the basis of certain meta-empirical, ontological, and metaphysical judgments and the expectations and hypotheses that follow from them. He who makes no decisions has no questions to raise and is not even able to formulate a tentative hypothesis which enables him to set a problem and to search history for its answer. Fortunately positivism did commit itself to certain metaphysical and ontological judgments, despite its anti-metaphysical prejudices and its pretensions to the contrary. Its faith in progress and its naïve realism in specific cases are examples of such ontological judgments. It was precisely those presuppositions which enabled positivism to make so many significant contributions, some of which will have to be reckoned with for some time to come. The danger in presuppositions does not lie merely in the fact that they exist or that they are prior to empirical knowledge. It lies rather in the fact that an ontology handed down through tradition obstructs new developments, especially in the basic modes of thinking, and as long as the particularity of the conventional theoretical framework remains unquestioned we will remain in the toils of a static mode of thought which is inadequate to our present stage of historical and intellectual development. What is needed, therefore, is a continual readiness to recognize that every point of view is particular to a certain definite situation, and to find out through analysis of what this particularity consists. A clear and explicit avowal of the implicit metaphysical presuppositions which underlie and make possible empirical know-ledge will do more for the clarification and advancement of research than a verbal denial of the existence of these presuppositions accompanied by their surreptitious admission through the back door.

Note

1. By social stability we do not mean uneventfulness or the personal security of individuals, but rather the relative fixity of the existing total social structure, which guarantees the stability of the dominant values and ideas.

SECTION TWO

Implications for Theological Studies

7

Peter L. Berger
Sociological and Theological Perspectives

This Extract formed an appendix to Berger's major sociological interpretation of religion, *The Sacred Canopy*, which was published in the USA in 1967 (and published in Britain in 1969 as *The Social Reality of Religion*). The fact that he was attempting to write a sociological book explains the first paragraph (*7.1*). However, as a sociologist who has also public theological sympathies (*7.2*), he is particularly concerned to distinguish the sociological approach to religion which he has earlier termed 'methodological atheism' from an ontological approach treating atheism as a matter of faith (*7.3f.*). He insists that the sociological interpretation of religion *purely* as a social phenomenon is a methodological position and not an attempt to exclude the possibility that, viewed from a different perspective, it will appear as more than a human projection. At the same time he insists that sociology does raise crucial questions which relate directly to theology, particularly since the latter involves some socio-historical presuppositions (*7.7*). It also, and most radically, raises the problem of relativity (*7.9*). This final problem has occupied Berger in much of his subsequent socio-theological writings: Christianity apparently makes certain exclusive truth claims which under the pressure of modern pluralism (or 'modernity' as he terms it later) seem increasingly implausible. He is well aware that 'implausibility' is not the same as falsifiability: ideas may be implausible but still true. But it does naturally undermine contemporary confidence. Once he resolved this dilemma by distinguishing between 'religion' and 'Christianity' (excluding the latter from some of the analysis present in the sociology of religion), in the manner of some neo-orthodox theologians (though see *14.24*). But now he rejects this approach (*7.12f.*). He looks instead to a liberal theology which is able 'to take with utmost seriousness the historicity of religion' (*7.15*). Whether or not this is identified as 'liberal' theology, some such approach seems a prerequisite of using sociology seriously as a means of understanding theology. Berger is professor of sociology at Boston University, Massachusetts.

7.1 The argument in this book has moved strictly within the frame of reference of sociological theory. No theological or, for that matter, anti-theological implications are to be sought anywhere in the argument — if anyone should believe such implications to be present *sub rosa*, I can only assure him that he is mistaken. Nor is there an intrinsic necessity for sociological theory, as here understood, to engage in a 'dialogue' with theology. The notion, still prevalent among some theologians, that the sociologist simply raises certain questions, which must then be answered by the theological partner in the 'dialogue', must be rejected on very simple methodological grounds. Questions raised within the frame of reference of an empirical discipline (and I would emphatically consider sociological theory to be within such a frame of reference) are not susceptible to answers coming out of the frame of reference of a non-empirical and normative discipline, just as the reverse procedure is inadmissible. Questions raised by sociological theory must be answered in terms falling within the latter's universe of discourse. This methodological platitude, however, does not preclude the fact that certain sociological perspectives may be *relevant* for the theologian, though in that case he will be well advised to keep the afore-mentioned discrepancy in mind when he tries to articulate that relevance within *his* universe of discourse. In sum, the argument of this book stands or falls as an enterprise of sociological theorizing and, as such, is not amenable to either theological support or theological critique.

7.2 But having said this I want, after all, to make some comments here about the relevance of this perspective to theological thinking. I have two reasons for this. First, there is the simple desire not to be misunderstood, especially not by the theologically concerned reader (for whom, let it be admitted, I have specially warm feelings). Second, I have in previous writings made statements about the relationship between sociological and theological perspectives that I no longer regard as tenable (particularly in my book *The Precarious Vision*, 1961), and I have the perhaps slightly old-fashioned notion that one ought to correct in print what one has previously said in print and no longer holds to.

7.3 Within the argument of this book itself I have felt it necessary in a few places to state that any statements made there strictly bracket the ultimate status of religious definitions of reality. I have done this particularly where I sensed the danger that the 'methodological atheism' of this type of theorizing could be misinterpreted as atheism *tout court*. I would like to stress this point again here, as strongly as I can. The essential perspective of the sociological theory here proposed is that religion is to be understood as a human projection, grounded in specific infrastructures of human history. It can be seen without much difficulty that, from the viewpoint of certain religious or ethical values, there can be both 'good' and 'bad' implications to this perspective. Thus one might feel that it is 'good' that religion protects men against anomy, but that it is 'bad' that it alienates them from the world produced by their own activity. Such valuations must be kept strictly apart from the theoretical analysis of religion as nomos and of religion as false consciousness, an analysis that, within this frame of reference, remains value-free with regard to both these aspects.

7.4 Put differently, sociological theory (and, indeed, any other theory moving within the framework of empirical disciplines) will always view religion *sub specie temporis*, thus of necessity leaving open the question whether and how it might *also* be viewed *sub specie aeternitatis*. Thus sociological theory must, by its own logic, view religion as a human projection, and by the same logic can have nothing to say about the possibility that this projection may refer to something other than the being of its projector. In other words, to say that religion is a human projection does not logically preclude the possibility that the projected meanings may have an ultimate status independent of man. Indeed, if a religious view of the world is posited, the anthropological ground of these projections may itself be the reflection of a reality that *includes* both world and man, so that man's ejaculations of meaning into the universe ultimately point to an all-embracing meaning in which he himself is grounded. It is not without interest to observe in this connection that it was just such a conception that underlay Hegel's early development of the idea of the dialectic. To be grateful, *qua* sociologist, to Marx for his inversion of the Hegelian dialectic in the interest of an empirical understanding of human affairs does not preclude the possibility that, *qua* theologian, one might once more stand Marx on *his* head — just as long as one is very clear that the two dialectical constructions take place in strictly discrepant frames of reference. Put simply, this would imply that man projects ultimate meanings into reality because that reality is, indeed, ultimately meaningful, and because his own being (the empirical ground of these projections) contains and intends these same ultimate meanings. Such a theological procedure, if feasible, would be an interesting ploy on Feuerbach — the reduction of theology to anthropology would end in the reconstruction of anthropology in a theological mode. Regretfully, I am not in a position to offer such an intellectual man-bites-dog feat here, but I want at least to suggest the possibility to the theologian.

7.5 The case of mathematics is rather instructive in this connection. Without any doubt mathematics is a projection on to reality of certain structures of human consciousness. Yet the most amazing fact about modern science is that these structures have turned out to correspond to something 'out there' (to quote the good Bishop Robinson). Mathematicians, physical scientists, and philosophers of science are still trying hard to understand just how this is possible. What is more, it is possible to show sociologically that the development of these projections in the history of modern thought has its origins in very specific infrastructures without which this development is most unlikely ever to have taken place. So far nobody has suggested that *therefore* modern science is to be regarded as a great illusion. The parallel with the case of religion, of course, is not perfect, but it is worth reflecting on.

7.6 All this leads to the commonplace observation, frequently found in the opening pages of works in the sociology of religion, that the theologian *qua* theologian should not worry unduly over anything the sociologist may have to say about religion. At the same time, it would be foolish to maintain that *all* theological positions are equally immune to injury from the side of sociology. Logically, the theologian *will* have to worry whenever his position includes propositions that are subject to empirical disconfirmation. For example, a proposition that religion in itself is a constitutive factor of psychological well-being has a lot to worry about if subjected to sociological and social-psychological scrutiny. The logic here is similar to that of the historian's study of religion. To be sure, it can be maintained that historical and theological assertions take place in discrepant, mutually immune frames of reference. But if the theologian asserts something that can be shown to have never taken place historically or to have taken place in quite a different way from what he asserts, and if this assertion is essential to his position, then he can no longer be reassured that he has nothing to fear from the historian's work. The historical study of the Bible offers plentiful examples of this.

7.7 Sociology thus raises questions for the theologian to the extent that the latter's positions hinge on certain socio-historical presuppositions. For better or for worse, such presuppositions are particularly characteristic of theological thought in the Judaeo-Christian orbit, for reasons that are well known and have to do with the radically historical orientation of the Biblical tradition. The Christian theologian is, therefore, ill-advised if he simply views sociology as an ancillary discipline that will help him (or, more likely, help the practical churchman) to understand certain 'external' problems of the social environment in which his Church is located. To be sure, there are types of sociology (such as the quasi-sociological research approach that has become so popular in recent years in Church organizations) that are quite 'harmless' in this sense and can readily be appropriated for pragmatic ecclesiastical purposes. The worst that the churchman may expect from the sociologist doing religious market research for him is the unwelcome news that fewer people go to church than he thinks should go. But he will still be wise if he is careful about letting sociological analysis go too far. He may be getting more than he bargained for. Specifically, he may be getting a wider sociological perspective that may lead him on to see his over-all activity in a different light.

7.8 To repeat: on strictly methodological grounds it will be possible for the theologian to dismiss this new perspective as irrelevant to his *opus proprium*. This will become much more difficult, however, as soon as he reflects that, after all, he was not born as a theologian, that he existed as a person in a particular socio-historical situation before he ever began to do theology — in sum, that he himself, if not his theology, is illuminated by the lighting apparatus of the sociologist. At this point he may suddenly find himself ejected from the methodological sanctuary of his theologizing and find himself repeating, albeit in a very different sense, Augustine's complaint that '*Factum eram ipse mihi magna quaestio*'. He is likely to find further that, unless he can somehow neutralize this disturbing perspective in his own mind, it will be relevant to his theologizing as well. Put simply, *methodologically*, in terms of theology as a disembodied universe of discourse, sociology may be looked on as quite 'harmless' — *existentially*, in terms of the theologian as a living person with a social location and a social biography, sociology can be a very dangerous business indeed.

7.9 The *magna quaestio* of sociology is formally very similar to that of history: How, in a world of socio-historical relativity, can one arrive at an 'Archimedean point' from which to make cognitively valid statements about religious matters? In terms of sociological theory there are certain variants to this question: If all religious propositions are, at least, *also* projections grounded in specific infrastructures, how is one to distinguish between those infrastructures that give birth to truth from those that give birth to error? And if all religious plausibility is susceptible to 'social engineering', how can one be sure that those religious propositions (or, for that matter, 'religious experiences') that are plausible to oneself are not just that — products of 'social engineering' — and nothing else? It may readily be admitted that there were analogues to these questions long before sociology appeared on the scene. These may be found in the problem of Jeremiah of how to distinguish genuine and false prophecy, in the terrible doubt that apparently plagued Thomas Aquinas as to whether his own belief in the arguments for the existence of God may not after all be a matter of 'habit', in the tormenting question of numberless Christians (particularly since the Protestant schisms) of how to find the true Church. In the sociological perspective, however, such questions attain a new virulence, precisely because sociology, on its own level of analysis, gives a kind of answer to them. The vertigo of relativity that historical scholarship has brought over theological thought may thus be said to deepen in the perspective of sociology. At this point one is not much helped by the methodological assurance that theology, after all, takes place in a different frame of reference. That assurance comforts only if one is safely established in that frame of reference, if, so to speak, one already has a theology going. The existential question, however, is how one may begin to theologize in the first place.

7.10 Orthodox theological positions typically ignore this question — 'innocently' or in *mauvaise foi*, as the case may be. And indeed, for anyone who can today hold such a position 'innocently' (that is, one who has, for whatever reasons, not been touched by the vertigo of relativity) the question does not exist. Extreme theological liberalism of the variety that now calls itself 'radical theology' may be said to have despaired of finding an answer to the question and to have abandoned the attempt. Between these two extremes there is the very interesting attempt, typical of neo-orthodoxy, to have one's cake and eat it too — that is, to absorb the full impact of the relativizing perspective, but nevertheless to posit an 'Archimedean point' in a sphere immune to relativization. This is the sphere of 'the Word', as proclaimed in the *kerygma* of the Church and as grasped by faith. A particularly interesting point in this attempt is the differentiation between 'religion' and 'Christianity', or between 'religion' and 'faith'. 'Christianity' and 'Christian faith' are interpreted as being something quite different from 'religion'. The latter can then be cheerfully thrown to the Cerberus of relativizing analysis (historical, sociological, psychological, or what have you), while the theologian, whose concern, of course, is with 'Christianity'-which-is-not-'religion', can proceed with his work in splendid 'objectivity'. Karl Barth performed this exercise with brilliant consequence (most importantly in volume I/2 of the *Kirchliche Dogmatik* — and with highly instructive results in his essay on Feuerbach's *Essence of Christianity*). The same procedure allowed a good many neo-orthodox theologians to come to terms with Rudolf Bultmann's 'demythologization' programme. Dietrich Bonhoeffer's fragmentary ideas on a 'religionless Christianity' were probably tending in the same direction.

7.11 It is interesting, incidentally, that a very similar possibility exists where Christianity is understood in fundamentally mystical terms. Already Meister Eckhart could distinguish be- tween 'God' and the 'Godhead', and then go on to envisage the becoming and disbecoming of 'God'. Wherever one can maintain that, in the words of Eckhart, 'All that one can think of God, that God is not', an immune sphere is posited *ipso facto*. Relativity then touches only that which 'one can think of God' — a sphere already defined as ultimately irrelevant to the mystical truth. Simone Weil represents this possibility in recent Christian thought with great clarity.

7.12 The differentiation between 'religion' and 'Christian faith' was an important ingredient in the argument of *The Precarious Vision*, which took a neo-orthodox approach at least at that point (something, incidentally, that was perceived more clearly by some critics than by myself at the time). This differentiation, and the consequences drawn from it, now seem quite inadmissible to me. The *same* analytical tools (of historical scholarship, of sociology, and so on) can be applied to 'religion' and to 'faith'. Indeed, in any empirical discipline the 'Christian faith' is simply another case of the phenomenon 'religion'. Empirically, the differentiation makes no sense. It can only be postulated as a theological *a priori*. If one can manage this, the problem disappears. One can then deal with Feuerbach in the manner of Barth (a procedure, incidentally, that is very handy in any Christian 'dialogue' with Marxism — as long as the Marxists are agreeable to this theoretical legerdemain). But I, for one, cannot get myself into a position from which I can launch theological *a prioris*. I am forced, therefore, to abandon a differentiation that is senseless from any *a posteriori* vantage point.

7.13 If one shares this inability to hoist oneself on to an epistemologically safe platform, then no privileged status with regard to relativizing analyses can be accorded to Christianity or to any other historical manifestation of religion. The contents of Christianity, like those of any other religious tradition, will have to be analysed as human projections, and the Christian theologian will have to come to terms with the obvious discomforts caused thereby. Christianity and its various historical forms will be understood as projections similar in kind to other religious projections, grounded in specific infrastructures and maintained as subjectively real by specific procession of plausibility-generation. It seems to me that, once this is really accepted by a theologian, both the neo-orthodox and the 'radical' or neo-liberal short cut, in answer to the question as to what *else* these projections may be, are precluded. The theologian is consequently deprived of the psychologically liberating possibility of either radical commitment or radical negation. What he is left with, I think, is the necessity for a step-by-step re-evaluation of the traditional affirmations in terms of his own cognitive criteria (which need *not* necessarily be those of a putative 'modern consciousness'). Is this or that in the tradition true? Or is it false? I don't think that there are short-cut answers to such questions, neither by means of 'leaps of faith' nor by the methods of any secular discipline.

7.14 It further seems to me that such a definition of the theological situation takes one back, if not to the details, to the spirit of classical Protestant liberalism. To be sure, very few of the answers proffered by that liberalism can be replicated today in good conscience. The liberal notions of religious evolution, of the relationship between Christianity and the other world religions, of the moral dimensions of religion, and particularly of the 'ethic of Jesus' — all these can be shown to rest on untenable empirical presuppositions that very few people today would be tempted to salvage. Nor is the liberal mood of cultural optimism likely of resurrection in our own situation. The spirit of this theology, however, is more than the sum of its particular misconstructions. It is, above all, a spirit of intellectual courage that is equally removed from the cognitive retrenchment of orthodoxy and the cognitive timidity of what passes for neo-liberalism today. And it should be, one may add, a spirit that also has the courage to find itself in a cognitive minority — not only within the Church (which is hardly very painful today), but in the circles of secular intellectuals that today form the principal reference group for most theologians.

7.15 Specifically, liberal theology means to take with utmost seriousness the historicity of religion, without such theoretical subterfuges as differentiating between *Historie* and *Geschichte*, and thereby to take seriously the character of religion as a human product. This, it seems to me, must be the starting point. Only after the theologian has confronted the historical relativity of religion can he genuinely ask where in this history it may, perhaps, be possible to speak of *discoveries* — discoveries, that is, that transcend the relative character of their infrastructures. And only after he has really grasped what it means to say that religion is a human product or projection can he begin to search, *within* this array of projections, for what may turn out to be signals of transcendence. I strongly suspect that such an inquiry will turn increasingly from the projections to the projector, that is, will become an enterprise in anthropology. An 'empirical theology' is, of course, methodologicaly impossible. But a theology that proceeds in a step-by-step correlation with what can be said about man empirically is well worth a serious try.

7.16 It is in such an enterprise that a conversation between sociology and theology is most likely to bear intellectual fruits. It will be clear from the above that this will require partners, on both sides, with a high degree of openness. In the absence of such partners, silence is by far the better course.

8

Roderick Martin
Sociology and Theology: Alienation and Original
Sin

Roderick Martin contributed this Extract to the symposium edited by
himself, as a sociologist and fellow of Jesus College, Oxford, and
D. E. H. Whiteley, as the chaplain there, *Sociology, Theology and
Conflict* (Blackwell, 1969). The initial section, not included here, sets
out the way sociology can make a contribution 'to understanding
problems theologians attempt to resolve in their own terms' (p. 14), as
distinct from ecclesiastical or purely sociological uses of the discipline. He proposes to do this by examining the concept of 'alienation'
from the perspectives offered by Durkheim, Weber and Marx, before
turning to a specifically theological interpretation (a fuller analysis of
the same issue is offered by Gregory Baum's *Religion and Alienation*).
He argues that sociology is both an empirical and also a value-laden
discipline: 'For the "founding fathers" of sociology — Marx, Weber,
Durkheim, Toennies and others — were inspired by essentially moral
considerations: the need to comprehend, and often prevent, the
corrosive effects of industrial development upon society and the
individual . . . the early sociologists were both social scientists and
social critics' (pp. 18-19). By focusing his discussion in this way
Martin is able in this Extract to give a lucid account of some of the
central features of Durkheim's (*8.1–7*), Weber's (*8.8–13*) and Marx's
(*8.14–20*) social perspectives as they relate to theology. Particularly
important in the present context is Martin's contention that, in
relation to the concept of 'alienation', there 'is a clear path from the
Old Testament to Marx, through St Paul, Augustine, Luther and
Hegel' (*8.21*). Unfortunately, despite the challenge of the concluding
paragraphs of this Extract, subsequent contributors to the symposium did not trace this path further.

8.1 According to one recent sociological theorist, the central
question sociological theory attempts to answer is: 'What is
the basis of social order?'[10] How do societies cohere despite the
multitude of conflicting individual and group interests they contain?
Nowhere is this central focus clearer than in Durkheim's work: his

central theoretical concern was with the problem of social cohesion, his central moral concern the threat rapid industrial development, individualism — 'the disease of the western world' — and 'vaunted ambition' pose for individual and social integration. Industrialism, mass democracy, and secularism were destroying 'that sense of society which alone can maintain individuality'. At a group level this involved the collapse of social solidarity, at an individual level anomie or normlessness.[11]

8.2 By social solidarity Durkheim meant the institutions — family, community and occupational group — and their concomitant we-feelings which held society together. History is seen as the development from mechanical solidarity, the solidarity of similarity, of moral and social homogeneity re-inforced by the discipline of the small community, to organic solidarity, the solidarity of inter-dependent difference. Modern industrial society is based upon organic solidarity, the division of labour (although he later came to see that this pre-supposed at least a degree of homogeneity). Institutional coherence and integration is given strength and supplemented, both for the individual and for the group, by 'collective representations', especially those expressed through religious ritual. Religion, as a belief system and a behavioural pattern, is a 'collective representation' of group life. The internalisation of this collective representation and the code of behaviour it enjoins provides the basis for the specifically human elements in homo sapiens. Man is a human being in so far as he is a social being. The collapse of social solidarity, the weakening of social bonds and the emergence of discord between the individual and the group which Durkheim saw industrialisation producing caused a state of anomie or normlessness, shared by society and the individual alike.

8.3 The related concepts of social solidarity and anomie have provided the theoretical basis for much later empirical work in fields as diverse as the sociology of religion and criminology. The role of religious institutions in strengthening social solidarity and maintaining social coherence by providing symbolic representation of the group is a commonplace in social anthropology, and in diluted form informs the sociological study of religion in complex industrial societies.[12] For example, in Will Herberg, *Protestant, Catholic, Jew*, the high level of religious activity in the United States at the present time is related to the problem of integrating immigrant populations into a new nation.[13] Religious institutions help society to absorb and mould into a common framework a heterogeneous immigrant population: the Protestant, Catholic, and Jewish churches provide for individual and collective integration, for underlying the surface differences between the churches is a fundamental agreement upon acceptance of the American way of life. Solidarity, and marginal differences, are reinforced simultaneously. For the individual, the high rate of geographical and social mobility which characterises the United States has created rootlessness, a loss of community, which only some form of communal identification wider than the nuclear family, yet smaller than society as a whole, can provide.

8.4 The concept of anomie has proved even more fruitful, especially in criminological research. 'The degree of anomie in a social system is indicated by the extent to which there is a lack of consensus on norms judged to be legitimate, with its attendant uncertainty and insecurity in social relations.'[14] This lack of consensus leads to 'avoidance behaviour', and often to criminal activity. The sources of this lack of consensus lie either in society at large (normlessness understood in a strict sense, produced by society's inability to modify norms to keep pace with rapid social change), or in the conflict between different social groups, often finding expression in role conflicts within the individual (norm conflict), or in the individual himself (norm ignorance). Normlessness has been related specifically to the position of underprivileged youth in the United States and in Britain.[15] Deprived adolescents are seen as facing an inherently contradictory and consequently conflictful situation: a contradiction between the goals prescribed by society as a whole for its members, and the accessibility of legitimate means for achieving these goals. Juvenile delinquency is caused by this contradiction between the universal acceptance of the goal of material success and the lack of any legitimate means for achieving it. Inevitably, the dispossessed either repudiate the goal, as, for example, the hippies, or seek illegitimate means for achieving the goal, as in robbery with violence. Norm conflict, the second category of anomie, arises most acutely from the multiplicity of the individual's group affiliations. Individuals are members of more than one social group — or, to use slightly different language, perform more than one role — and are likely to suffer from any conflict which may emerge from these different roles. In normal circumstances church membership and political party membership may not be incompatible: but they may be, as they were in Nazi Germany. Similarly, behaviour appropriate to the role of uncle may be in conflict with behaviour appropriate to the role of business men, for example, in the selection of applicants for a particular job. The number of examples of conflict between group memberships, and between different roles, is infinite. The result, for the individual, is internal conflict leading to 'avoidance behaviour', a stressful adjustment, or inaction. As voting studies have shown, cross pressurisation stemming from multiple group membership often results in political apathy.[16] Norm conflict may produce apathy, norm ignorance may result in simple disregard for socially prescribed behaviour. The degree to which ignorance is culpable no doubt varies but there are sections of the population ignorant of the norms governing behaviour. This is most obviously the case for example, with recent immigrants, whose knowledge of the prevailing norms is limited, and whose transgressions are accordingly frequent. Indeed, one school of thought attributes a large degree of British colour prejudice to precisely this immigrant ignorance of the unspoken norms of British life.[17] It may similarly be the case with adolescents unaware of the responsibilities of the adult role, for example over credit obligations.

8.5 The moral thread which holds Durkheim's thought together is his concern, muted but nonetheless real, with the problem of social order. Although his work has a sophisticated intellectual theoretical coherence of its own, at the risk of considerable over-simplification social solidarity and anomie can be seen within a moral and political framework. He was concerned, as is clearly revealed in his work *The Division of Labour*, with the effect of industrialism upon community, and the danger of social disintegration. With Durkheim's main English-speaking heirs, the functionalists, this concern with the problem of order is overt. Functionalists are primarily concerned to analyse social structures in terms of their function or role in sustaining the total social system: 'Society is usefully conceived as a dynamic equilibrium of various functional parts, each with its own independent function to perform for society as a whole, but each limited by, because it is inter-dependent with, the other parts'.[18] The analogy is, of course, with the human body; social institutions are, like members of the body, parts of an integrated, normally healthy whole. This very general formulation has been refined and elaborated, most notably in the work of Talcott Parsons. Parsons has attempted to specify the conditions which need to be fulfilled if society is to survive. According to Parsons all societies face the same problems, and must develop mechanisms for solving these problems if they are to survive.[19] The main problems societies must solve are: goal attainment, or agreement on 'the purpose or aim of any cycle of social action, involving decisions about the allocation of resources to particular ends'; adaptation, the acquisition of sufficient resources from the physical environment to achieve these ends; integration, the maintenance of relations between the units of the system in achieving these ends; and finally tension management, 'the problem of maintaining adequate motivations among the elements in the system and resolving tensions generated by internal interaction'. Although all social institutions help to resolve more than one of these problems, the political system is primarily concerned with goal attainment, the economy with adaptation, religious institutions with integration, and the family with tension management.

8.6 The specification of these common problems, or 'functional pre-requisites', which face society is the first step towards constructing a model of the social system. The second step involves closer discussion of relations between specific institutions and specific problems. This is, of course, an enormous task, and it has attracted the particular concern of developmental sociologists. According to the predominant view, that advanced by Clark Kerr and his colleagues, the achievement of industrial society involves solving specific problems in particular ways. Industrialisation requires the acceptance of rational, scientific technology; individual achievement; geographical and social mobility; a loose-knit network; an educational system 'functionally related to the skills and professions imperative to technology . . . and not primarily concerned with conserving traditional values or perpetuating the classics'; and finally a pluralist democratic political system. Whether this model of industrial society and the prescriptions for action derived from it is confirmed, or at least proven to be effective, remains to be seen. It is too early to say yet — but the American government recognised the utility of this systems approach to the extent of granting fifty million dollars to examine it more closely (only withdrawing the grant after protests by developing countries against academic imperialism).[10]

8.7 Although the fully fledged Parsonian approach has not yet been tested, attempts have already been made to apply his approach to specific institutions. The most controversial is the attempt to explain social stratification, the nature and basis of social inequality, in functionalist terms.[21] According to this functional analysis, the system of social stratification helps to solve two problems, those of adaptation and of integration. Inequality, whether material or symbolic, performs an adaptive function by providing incentives, stimulating the more able members of society to sustain the deprivations of extended training and the responsibility of performing socially important tasks. Moreover, 'to the extent that the stratification system is an expression or result of differential ranking judgements in terms of some common set of values, it serves to integrate the society. Men have a sense of justice fulfilled and of virtue rewarded when they feel that they are fairly ranked as superior and inferior by the moral standards of their own community'.

8.8 If Durkheim's major fear was that industrialisation and the limitless ambition which economic life encouraged would destroy social and individual integration, Weber's main preoccupation was with the threat rationalisation posed to individual autonomy. As he declared in a moving speech to the University of Munich eighteen months before his death in 1919: 'the fate of our times is characterized by rationalization and intellectualization and, above all, by the "disenchantment of the world". Precisely the ultimate and most sublime values have retreated from public life, either into the transcendental realm of mystic life or into the brotherliness of direct and personal human relations. It is not accidental that our greatest art is intimate and not monumental, nor is it accidental that today only within the smallest intimate circles, in personal human situations, in *pianissimo*, that something is pulsating that corresponds to the prophetic pneuma, which in former times swept through the great communities like a firebrand, welding them together. Rationality, the removal of the magical elements in human thought, was the distinctive characteristic of European development' — and the peculiar tragedy, which took almost personal form in Weber's own case.[22] It was most clearly seen in his fear that the organisational expression of rationality, bureaucracy, would destroy individual autonomy.

8.9 Bureaucracy, rationally the most efficient administrative system, is based upon two fundamental principles; predictability and impersonality. Predictability is ensured by strict adherence to the rules, impersonality by a rigid separation between official and personal life. Organisationally, bureaucracy is characterised by a functional rather than a personal relation between office-holders, a clearly defined hierarchy with a graded career structure, appointment rather than election, preferably on the basis of competitive examination, payment by fixed salaries rather than fees, and strict discipline.

8.10 In Weber's terms this is an 'ideal-type' construction. Although few bureaucracies have achieved this rational perfection, all will possess some elements and as history progresses will possess more. As a concept it has serious difficulties, including a fundamentally ambiguous status. 'Ideal' and 'typical' are very different categories: in the present world what is ideal cannot, by definition, be typical, and what is typical cannot be ideal. Moreover, the relation between the different items in his specification is unclear.[23] Authority based upon expertise and authority based upon discipline are not necessarily the same, and may not even work in the same direction. Even more fundamentally, later empirical work suggests that predictability and efficiency, the basic criteria for bureaucracy, are not necessarily correlated. In a changing environment impersonal adherence to the rules is inefficient; in a much quoted phrase, the bureaucrat is sometimes 'fit with an unfit fitness'.

8.11 Despite these logical difficulties Weber's discussion of legal rational authority and bureaucracy has provided the starting point for much later work, especially on organisations. Organisational theory begins with Weber, and an account of Weber's influence on the subject would be an account of the subject's history.

But amongst a multitude of theoretical and empirical studies following his work A. W. Gouldner's *Patterns of Industrial Bureaucracy* remains one of the best.[24] In a case study of a gypsum mining and manufacturing plant Gouldner discovered that different environments produced different types of bureaucracy: in one situation a 'representative' bureaucracy, based upon consensus and expertise, emerged, in another a 'punishment centred' bureaucracy (resembling Weber's type), based upon authority and discipline, emerged. Moreover, he discovered that the degree of bureaucratisation did not depend upon the need for efficiency, but upon political considerations, particularly the need for the new plant manager to assert his position over his predecessor's lieutenants. Rule enforcement was a result of personal uncertainty and inadequate information, not the need for efficiency. The success of rule enforcement depended upon the degree of resistance to it, which in turn was most successful in technological conditions fostering informal solidarity.

8.12 Although later research following Weber's directives has been predominantly concerned with the microscopic examination of contemporary society, he himself was primarily concerned with a broad historical sweep, attempting to discover the distinctive characteristics of Western European civilisation. The *differentia specifica* of European civilisation was the distinctive role of rationality in West European culture. Its roots lay partly in specific economic conditions, the money economy and its specific European form, capitalism, and partly in a continously evolving value system; economics and ideals worked together to enthrone rationality. Although Weber never stated his position in general terms, 'believing that historical truth would be best served by leaving general conclusions until the end of the exhaustive empirical investigation', his position was well stated in the work of one of his pupils, Otto Hinze. 'Everywhere the first impulse to social action is given as a rule by real interests, i.e., by political and economic interests. But ideal interests lend wings to these real interests, give them a spiritual meaning, and serve to justify them . . . in pursuing [his interest] he develops his capacities to the highest extent only if he believes that in so doing he serves a higher rather than a purely egoistic purpose. . . . Wherever interests are vigorously pursued, an ideology tends to be developed also to give meaning, reinforcement, and justification to these interests. And this ideology is as "real" as the real interests themselves, for ideology is an indispensable part of the life process which is expressed in action. And conversely: whenever ideas are to conquer the world, they require the leverage of real interests, although frequently ideas will more or less distract these interests from their original aim. . . .'[25] That this relation between economic interest and ideal interests and their mutual inter-action is producing the distinctive tone of West European civilisation, was clearly revealed in Weber's classic account of *The Protestant Ethic and the Spirit of Capitalism*. Weber defined the spirit of capitalism in terms of individual acceptance of the obligation to work regardless of extrinsic reward, which is 'calling'.[26] He was concerned to show how this secular ethic emerged from sixteenth century protestantism by relating moral attitudes to capital accumulation with theological doctrine. The religious foundations of 'worldly asceticism' and their relation to capitalist accumulation were exemplified for Weber in Richard Baxter's *Christian Dictionary*: 'If God show you a way in which you may lawfully get more than in another way, if you refuse this, and use the less gainful way, you cross one of the ends of your calling, and you refuse to be God's steward, and to accept his gifts and use them for him when he requireth; you may labour to be rich for God, but not for the flesh and sin'. Methodologically and substantively Weber's analysis is open to criticism. Methodologically, his reliance upon seventeenth and eighteenth century writers to assess the influence of sixteenth century doctrines ignores the importance of intervening developments: seventeenth century Calvinism was perverted Calvinism, not Genevan Calvinism, and reflected the adaptation of the economic ethics of the original doctrines to new circumstances. Substantively, his analysis ignores the Calvinist aspiration to form a 'Godly commonwealth', characterised by a stern collective discipline. In fact, Puritans tended to be 'narrow and conservative in their economic views, urging men to seek no more wealth than they needed for a modest life, or alternatively, to use up their surplus in charitable givings'. The Puritan judgement on the pursuit of money was better expressed by John Bunyan than by the (Unitarian) Benjamin Franklin; Mr Moneylove and Mr Sureall were thoroughly despised.[27]

8.13 Although Weber was primarily concerned with the general question of the distinctive characteristics of western civilisation, his corpus includes a number of fruitful fragments. Amongst the most important is his short but perceptive analysis of the relation between class, status and power. Like Marx he defined class in economic terms: 'We may speak of a class when (1) a number of people have in common a specific causal component of their chances, in so far as (2) this component is represented exclusively by economic interests in the possession of goods and opportunities for income, and (3) is represented under the conditions of the commodity or labour markets'.[28] Unlike Marx, however, he did not regard class as the basic determinant of status, i.e. prestige, or as the basic determinant of power, i.e. the ability to obtain the compliance of others to one's own wishes independently of their own. For Weber, understanding the social structure involved understanding these three separate, but related dimensions. In many societies, for example modern capitalism, class may be the major determinant of status; but in others, for example feudalism, legal status is the determinant of class; in yet others, e.g. in contemporary Eastern Europe, political power may determine both class and status. Although this analysis of class, status and power is only a small part of Weber's work it has proved a major source of insight into the nature of modern society. According to the Marxist tradition, social class divisions retain their fundamental importance in modern capitalism, muted but not obliterated by the increase in wealth for the proletariat. The working classes remain powerless and deprived. However, society can no longer be analysed in these simple dichotomous economic terms. For class conflict has been replaced by individual status seeking, status being indicated by a particular way of life and its evaluation by others. This view is evident most clearly in the United States, where more attention has been paid both by sociologists and the population at large to status strata than to economic classes. In W. L. Warner's study of *Yankee City* the community was divided into six social strata, each consisting of individuals symbolically placed by the majority of the population. Social position depended upon the group which admitted you, and the evaluation of your position by the community; the criteria for evaluation were multiple, including length of residence in the community, type of house, and general way of life. Income was not a direct determinant of status.

8.14 If the fear of social disintegration preoccupied Durkheim and the aweful clarity of the disenchanted world Weber, the moral thread running through Marx's work is the dehumanisation and alienation of the worker under capitalism. Marx's rejection of Hegel, his critique of capitalism, and his vision of a Communist Utopia is informed by the sight of alienated man and the vision of unalienated man. For Marx, alienation involved man's experience of himself as the passive object of external forces, not as a self-activating agent. 'Man does not experience himself as the acting agent in his grasp of the world, but that the world (nature, others and himself) remain alien to him.'[29] Although alienation was to be found in all areas of social life, including politics and religion, it was to be found most acutely in the world of work. Man is alienated from himself as a 'species being', from the act of production, and from the product of his labour. As Marx movingly wrote in the *Economic and Philosophical Manuscripts in 1844*, 'in what does this alienation of labour consist? First, that the work is *external* to the worker, that it is not a part of his nature, that consequently he does not fulfil himself in his work but denies himself, has a feeling of misery, not of well-being, does not develop freely a physical and mental energy, but is physically exhausted and mentally debased. The worker, therefore, feels himself at home only during his leisure, whereas at work he feels homeless. His work is not voluntary but imposed, *forced labour*. It is not the satisfaction of a need, but only a means for satisfying other needs. Its alien character is clearly shown by the fact that as soon as there is no physical or other compulsion it is avoided like the plague. Finally, the alienated character of work for the worker appears in the fact that it is not his work but work for someone else, that in work he does not belong to himself but to another person'.

8.15 Alienated labour derives ultimately from commodity fetishism, the money economy, and private property. Labour becomes externalised as a commodity: 'The product of labour is labour which has been embodied in an object, and turned into a physical thing; this product is an *objectification* of labour. The performance of work is at the same time its objectification. This performance of work appears, in the sphere of political economy, as a vitiation of the worker, objectification as a loss. . . '. 'The worker puts his life into the object, and his life then belongs no longer to him but to the object . . . what is embodied in the product of his labour is no longer his . . . the alienation of the worker in his product means not only that his labour becomes an object, takes on its own existence, but that it exists outside him, independently . . . and that it stands opposed to him as an autonomous power.' Money, as the medium of exchange, 'the reflection in a single commodity of the value relations between all commodities', symbolises this subordination to external objects. As Marx declared, 'money is the jealous One God of Israel, beside which no other God may stand. Money dethrones all the gods of man and turns them into a commodity. Money is the universal, independently constituted value of all things. It has, therefore, deprived the whole world, both the world of man and nature, of its value. Money is the alienated essence of man's work and his being. This alien being rules over him and he worships it'.[30] It is the expropriation of this externalised object by the bourgeoisie which constitutes the peculiar exploitation of capitalism; it was this expropriation, and thus exploitation, which would cease with the socialist revolution, and the emancipation of society from private property.

8.16 In recent years alienation has become a popular catchword, a portmanteau concept covering everything from individual Angst to general social disintegration. As one sociologist commented, 'it has become a popular vehicle of virtually every kind of analysis, from the prediction of voting behaviour to the search for *The Sane Society*'. It has been used to refer to an objective social condition, one in which the system of social relations is characterised by money fetishism, to an individual's experience of his relations with the external world, and to an individual state of mind.[31] At a social psychological level it refers to the 'sense of the splitting asunder what was once together, the breaking of the seamless mould in which values, behaviour, and expectations were once cast into interlocking forms', and at a psychological level to the neurotic disintegration of the personality. Indeed one writer has gone so far as to argue, 'Alienation is used to convey the emotional tone which accompanies any behaviour in which the person is compelled to act self-destructively'.[32] Despite the difficulties which this widespread use of the concept creates, it still remains possible to use the term in a strictly sociological context, and to relate it to empirical research. By ignoring the ontological antecedents of the concept, by discarding Marx's programmatic prescriptions but retaining his socio-historical emphasis, by replacing property relations with the division of labour, and by breaking the concept down into its constituent elements and elaborating them, it is possible to use the concept of alienation as a sociological tool, as sociologists like Melvin Seeman and especially Robert Blauner, have done.

8.17 Alienation refers to a syndrome of 'objective conditions and subjective feeling states'.[33] It comprises a state of mind associated with a given external social situation, and that social situation itself. The state of mind comprises four distinct categories of fragmentation: powerlessness, meaninglessness, isolation, and self-estrangement. A person experiences powerlessness when he is an object controlled and manipulated by other persons or by an impersonal system such as technology, and when he cannot assert himself as a subject to change or modify this domination. A person experiences meaninglessness when his actions seem to have no relation to a broader life programme, or when his activities do not seem to have any organic connection with the whole of which they are a part. Isolation comprises 'the feeling of being in, but not of, society, a sense of remoteness from the larger social order, an absence of loyalties to intermediate collectivities'. Finally, self-estrangement refers to the experience of work as being a means to an end rather than an end in itself, and a heightened awareness of time resulting from a split between present engagements and future considerations. All these four items are to be discovered in the modern industrial work situation. In modern industry the worker experiences powerlessness, for his speed of work is dictated by the machine he is operating, and the individual expertise of the craftsman has been built into the machine. Meaninglessness stems from the individual's fragmented relation to his work; the subdivision of tasks has diminished the area of understanding as well as responsibility. The worker is isolated both from the product of his labour by the non-ownership of the product produced, and often from his fellow workers by the layout of the factory. Finally, the worker is self-estranged; work has become an instrumental activity subordinated to the most animal needs for food and shelter, rather than an end in itself. Alienation, in these terms, can be viewed as the result of employment in large-scale enterprises, and the division of labour, rather than as a result of capitalist exploitation. It is the task of the industrial sociologists to relate these feelings and experiences to specific industrial situations.

8.18 The objective conditions which cause alienation are basically determined by industrial technology and market forces. Different types of industrial technology allow industrial workers varying degrees of power, meaning, and integration within the work place. In a craft technology, like the printing industry and parts of the building industry, alienating conditions are at a minimum: the lack of standardisation of the product prevents the rationalisation of the work process, preserving the individual worker's discretion. The printer largely sets his own pace of work, can readily see the meaning of his own activity in relation to the whole process, and is integrated into a meaningful occupational community. The standardisation of the product in mass consumption industries like the textile and car industries produces a very different situation. Expertise is built into the machine, limiting the discretion of the individual worker, individual tasks are minutely sub-divided parts of a whole, and the worker is isolated from his fellow workers. In both 'machine minding' technologies like the textile industry and assembly line technologies like the car industry the worker's experience of powerlessness, meaninglessness, and isolation is most acute. The worker's powerlessness 'is expressed in a constant work pressure and inability to control movement, meaninglessness in a fragmented production process, and isolation in lack of contact with others and lack of commitment to institutional goals'. However, this experience is not universal in modern industry. In contrast to the textile and motor car industries the chemical and petroleum industries, characterised by a continuous process technology, offer their work force considerable freedom from pressure, control over their pace of work, responsibility for maintaining a high quality product, choice of how to do the job, and the freedom of physical movement. Although the individual worker no longer uses his individual skill to manufacture a product, he retains discretion over the allocation of his own time and effort. In continuous process technology the worker's main task is to ensure that the process is operating smoothly by watching instruments, and where breakdowns occur seeing that maintenance staff are called. Responsibility replaces skill as a source of the worker's human dignity, and of his self-realisation.

8.19 Blauner's approach to the study of alienation and its roots in modern industrial technology is derived directly from Marx. Like Marx, he holds up an image of what the work role might be, and sees that in many situations reality falls short of his image. The industrial worker should be an autonomous, integrated individual, discovering meaning and self-realisation in the work place. Instead, he is often the passive object of industrial technology, a mutilated fragment in a domineering process he does not understand. In approaching the subject in this way Blauner raises a crucial question for social scientists, the role of values in social science. For some critics, the important question is not the actual as compared with the ideal, but the actual as compared with the participant's expectations. Whether a given technology is alienating or not depends upon the actor, as well as upon the actual situation. Alienation occurs when work expectations are not fulfilled, not when the situation fails to measure up to some ideal. Where workers have adjusted their expectations to the reality of the work situation, expecting little, it is a waste of time to discuss alienation in Marxist terms. As a recent investigation into a British car plant revealed, many car workers have a purely 'instrumental orientation' to their work, regarding it as a means towards an end not as an end in itself.[34] They expect work to be financially rewarding, not to be interesting, and will be more disappointed by inadequate financial rewards than with dreary work — they expect work to be dreary.

8.20 Yet this 'accepting' attitude towards the social structure is a sharp departure from the 'classical' attitude towards social research. As we have seen, the works of Durkheim, Weber, and Marx reveal clearly the inseparability of social diagnosis and social research. The concepts which have provided the basis for the most fruitful modern research, including the most self-consciously objective empirical research, were initially presented as part of a critique of contemporary society that was often moral and ideological in origin. The continued importance in the sociological perspective of concepts like social solidarity, anomie, rationality, legal rational authority, bureaucracy and alienation illustrates one simple truth: above the most elementary level it is only possible to understand what is by envisaging what might be — and to understand what might be by discovering what is. Nowhere is this clearer than with the concept of alienation.

2

8.21 On its first emergence in the early nineteenth century sociology 'inherited the unresolved dilemmas of traditional metaphysics'.[35] It has attempted, in its own way, to solve them ever since. Nowhere is this doubt and this struggle clearer than in the discussion of the industrial work role and the analysis of alienation. A direct line can be drawn from Christian theology via Hegel and Marx to modern sociology. As Philip Rieff has remarked, 'alienation was originally neither a Marxist nor a psychiatric tool of understanding the human condition, but theological and specifically Christian'.[36] The concept of alienation has its origin in the parable of the Fall of Man. 'In the act of cognition — of desiring to become something more or other than what one might merely continue to be — the old Adam disobeyed God and thereby became estranged from the Divine in himself.' In the original Christian doctrine this alienation of man from God, and from himself ('self-estrangement'), can only be overcome by accepting divine forgiveness through Christ, and obedience to the divine commandment 'love thy neighbour as thyself'. There is a clear path from the Old Testament to Marx, through St Paul, Augustine, Luther and Hegel.

8.22 The pre-Marxist history of the concept of alienation is more interesting to historians of philosophy than to sociologists, but a short discussion of the relation between Hegel and Marx will be enough to reveal the metaphysical and philosophical roots of the sociological concept. For Hegel alienation was 'an ontological fact, in the structure of grammar as well as of life, for the self, the individual, was not just an "I" seeking to shape the world according to its intentions, but also a "me", an object whose identity is built up by the picture that *others* have of "me" '.[37] Man is both subject, striving to control his own fate, and object, manipulated by others. Human consciousness had externalised itself in spirit; it was man's task to repossess the externalised object and to be born again, reintegrated. For Marx, Hegel's concern only with the spirit, and explanation of alienation in human nature, was inadequate. Marx explicitly translated alienation from the realm of Hegelian philosophy to that of socio-economic development, and sociology.

8.23 In Marx's hands the concept of alienation became a tool of social analysis and social criticism. Under capitalism man's condition was one of alienation, and exploitation, of submission to the tyranny of external objects, appropriated by others. Man's future condition could be one of self-realisation, of freedom and spontaneity. Proletarian revolution, which would bring the machinery of bourgeois exploitation crashing down, would usher in a new social order and a new man. Subsequent writers have discarded the political programmes which would bring this ideal state nearer, but have retained the vision, and the contrast between the vision and reality. Without it sociology and social criticism would be considerably poorer.

8.24 It was a common concern with the apparent alienation of men in the contemporary world which united the very diverse participants in the conference. Although we did not spend our time bewailing the wickedness of the world, we shared a common interest in analysing the causes of our present discontents and looking for a way forward. To some social scientists this may seem a betrayal of scientific objectivity, a retreat from scientific sociology into the old-fashioned humanist tradition. But in fact it is simply a restatement of the 'classical' view, a view which has proved more fruitful than more modern, and more anaemic, attitudes. There is no contradiction between the social science method and traditional philosophical and humanitarian concerns: the criteria of falsifiability are as applicable to hypotheses concerning the industrial worker's alienation as they are to less value-laden problems. And criticism based upon objective facts is obviously preferable to criticism based upon random anecdotes.

8.25 As we have seen, sociology has developed historically from the philosophical, moral, and political concerns of the early nineteenth century, of the years following the French and industrial revolutions. It drew its theoretical concepts from sources as diverse as Christian theology, enlightenment rationalism, German idealism, the conservative reaction to the French and industrial revolutions, and many others. In recent years there has been a tendency to deny this past condition, to maintain a self-consciously value-free stance, asserting sociology's scientific status, disciplinary autonomy, and distinctiveness from political ideologies like socialism with which it had been wrongly associated. This period of insecure aggressiveness is, hopefully, now over. Substantial scientific achievements, and substantial institutional safeguards, fortify its present status. Perhaps sociology, social diagnosis, social, political and moral philosophy, and moral theology can once more come together, as they did in the writings of the classic nineteenth century theorists.

8.26 In the guise of an introductory essay to a volume of essays intended for the general, socially concerned, predominantly religious public, I have attempted to show how far sociology has been concerned with important social issues. By illustrating the fusion between social research and social criticism in the classic nineteenth century writers and their more empirical descendants, rather than by an empirical account of current social problems, I have attempted to show how 'relevant' sociology is for the socially conscious Christian. By illustrating the metaphysical roots of the sociological concept of alienation — the concept which serves to unite the different contributions to this conference — I have suggested that sociologists have, whether they recognise it or not, a common heritage with theology, and that they might profitably look to their past, present and future in company with theologians. Sociology and theology both share a common concern in understanding and explaining human behaviour, and especially contemporary social problems. They both provide 'models' for the explanation of such behaviour (although I do not claim to understand the status of theological models). As became clear in the discussion of alienation and original sin during the conference proceedings, the human experience which sociologists explain in terms of social forces the theologian explains in terms of parable. Both modes of explanation are valid in their own terms, and in terms of a common usefulness in providing guide-lines for the future.

Notes

10. P. S. Cohen, *Modern Social Theory* (Heinemann, 1968), cap. 2.
11. R. A. Nisbet, *The Sociological Tradition* (Heinemann, 1967), pp. 300–4. The relevant parts of Durkheim's work for the present purposes are: *The Division of Labour in Society* (Trans. by G. Simpson, The Free Press, 1933); *Suicide: A Study in Sociology* (Trans. by J. A. Spaulding and G. Simpson, Routledge and Kegan Paul, 1952) [see *Extract 3* above]; *The Elementary Forms of Religious Life* (Trans. by J. W. Swain, Routledge and Kegan Paul, 1915).
12. J. Beattie, *Other Cultures* (Routledge and Kegan Paul, 1966).
13. W. Herberg, *Protestant, Catholic, Jew* (Doubleday, 1955); G. Lenski, *The Religious Factor* (Doubleday, 1963); a useful illustration of the role of the church in providing a social home for migrant Americans is H. J. Gans, *The Levittowners* (Allen Lane: The Penguin Press, 1967), cap. iv.
14. G. Rose, 'Anomie and Deviation — A Conceptual Framework for Empirical Studies' (*British Journal of Sociology*, 1964), pp. 29 seq.
15. R. K. Merton, *Social Theory and Social Structure* (The Free Press, 1957), caps. 4 and 5; a number of empirical studies of deviant behaviour have discussed this approach (A. B. Clinard, *Anomie and Deviant Behaviour*, The Free Press, 1964).
16. A. Campbell et al., *The American Voter* (John Wiley, 1960), p. 85.
17. M. Banton, *Race Relations* (Tavistock Publications, 1967), cap. 15.
18. A. R. Radcliffe-Brown, 'The Concept of Function', reprinted in E. F. Borgatta and H. J. Meyer, *Sociological Theory* (Knopf, 1956), pp. 263–9.
19. T. Parsons, *The Social System* (Routledge and Kegan Paul, 1951); a useful summary of his work is R. Devereux, Jnr, 'Parsons' Sociological Theory' in ed. M. Black, *The Social Theories of Talcott Parsons* (Prentice Hall, 1964), pp. 1–63.
20. C. Kerr et al., *Industrialism and Industrial Man* (Heinemann, 1962), esp. p. 36; I. L. Horowitz, *The Rise and Fall of Project Camelot* (MIT, 1967).
21. The major articles in the controversy are reprinted in R. Bendix and S. M. Lipset, *Class Status and Power* (Routledge and Kegan Paul, 1967), pp. 47–69; B. Barber, *Social Stratification* (Harcourt, Brace and World, 1957), pp. 7–8.

22. Ed. H. H. Gerth and C. Wright Mills, *From Max Weber* (Routledge and Kegan Paul, 1948), p. 155.

23. *Ibid.*, cap.8; R.K. Merton et al., *Reader in Bureaucracy* (The Free Press, 1952), esp. pp. 18–33.

24. A. W. Gouldner, *Patterns of Industrial Bureaucracy* (The Free Press, 1954); a useful historical survey of recent work on bureaucracy is N. P. Mouzelis, *Organization and Bureaucracy: An Analysis of Modern Theories* (Routledge and Kegan Paul, 1967).

25. Quoted in R. Bendix, *Max Weber: An Intellectual Portrait* (Heinemann, 1960), p. 69.

26. M. Weber, *The Protestant Ethic and the Spirit of Capitalism* (Trans. by T. Parsons, Allen and Unwin, 1930) [see *Extract 1* above].

27. M. Waltzer, *The Revolution of the Saints* (Weidenfeld and Nicolson, 1966), pp. 304–5.

28. Gerth and Mills, *op. cit.*, p. 181; W. L. Warner and P. S. Lunt, *The Social Life of a Modern Community* (Yale U.P., 1941); W. L. Warner, *Structure of American Life* (Edinburgh U.P., 1952), caps. 1 and 2.

29. T. Bottomore and M. Rubel, *Karl Marx: Selected Writings in Sociology and Social Philosophy* (Penguin Books, 1963), pp. 175–86; R. Nisbet, *op. cit.*, pp. 284–92.

30. Quoted in R. Tucker, *Philosophy and Myth in Karl Marx* (Cambridge U.P., 1965), p. 111.

31. M. Seeman, 'On the Meaning of Alienation', reprinted in L. Coser and B. Rosenberg, *Sociological Theory: A Book of Readings* (Macmillan (N.Y.), 1957), p. 526; S. M. Lukes, 'Alienation and Anomie' in W. G. Runciman and P. Laslett, *Politics, Philosophy and Society*, 3rd series (Basil Blackwell, 1967), p. 136.

32. L. Feuer, 'What is Alienation? The Career of a Concept', reprinted in M. Stein and M. Vidich, *Sociology on Trial* (Prentice-Hall, 1963), p. 143.

33. R. Blauner, *Alienation and Freedom* (Chicago U.P., 1964), passim.

34. J. H. Goldthorpe et al., *The Affluent Worker: Industrial Attitudes and Behaviour* (Cambridge U.P., 1968).

35. G. Lichtheim, 'Alienation' in *International Encyclopaedia of the Social Sciences* (Collier-Macmillan, 1967), vol. 1, p. 268.

36. P. Rieff, *The Triumph of the Therapeutic* (Chatto and Windus, 1966), pp. 206–7.

37. D. Bell, *The End of Ideology* (Collier Books, 1961), p. 358.

9

Robert N. Bellah
Theology and Symbolic Realism

When it was first given as a lecture to the Society for the Scientific Study of Religion, this Extract caused very considerable interest amongst both sociologists of religion and theologians. Bellah delivered it as professor of sociology and comparative studies and chairman of the Center for Japanese and Korean Studies at the University of California. This environment proved particularly receptive to suggestions about a new religious consciousness and indeed for the next few years Bellah was engaged in a major interdisciplinary research project on the phenomenon in California — published as ed. Charles Y. Glock and Robert N. Bellah, *The New Religious Consciousness* (University of California Press, Berkeley, 1976). Nonetheless, few sociologists of religion have fully accepted the symbolic realist approach that he advocates here: within the American and British traditions, at least, most remain committed to a more empirical approach to religion, such as is evident in Berger's specifically sociological writings. In this Extract Bellah seeks to differentiate his own approach from that of 'historical realist' theologians (*9.2*) and 'reductionist' critics of theology (*9.3f.*). Bellah is particularly critical of those pioneer social scientists who 'convey the feeling that the scientific observer cannot finally take seriously the beliefs he is studying' (*9.9*). In contrast, he is impressed with the way noncognitive and nonscientific symbols are crucial to the work of both Durkheim and Freud and also to modern scientists. He argues that 'religious symbolization and religious experience are inherent in the structure of human existence' (*9.17*). It is at this point that he believes that the work of the theologian and the sociologist come together. Indeed, it is clear that Bellah sees the new consciousness that might emerge from this fusion as important to the very survival of mankind. His later writings show him to be deeply critical of 'the exclusive dominance of technical reason'; 'Priorities would shift away from endless accumulation of wealth and power to a greater concern for harmony with nature and between human beings. . . . Science, which would ultimately have to be shackled in a traditional authoritarian regime, would continue to be pursued in the revolutionary culture, but it would not be idolized as in the liberal model. In all these respects the values, attitudes, and beliefs of the oriental religious groups, the human-potential movement, and even a group like the Christian World Liberation Front, as well as the more flexible of the radical political groups, would be consonant with the new regime and its needs . . . the new groups would be, under such an option, the vanguard of a new age' (*The New Religious Consciousness*, pp. 351–352).

9.1 There is probably nothing more important than intellectual history to help us understand how our culture has become so fragmented and dissociated that we find it almost impossible to communicate the integrated meaning our young people so passionately require of us. Aware of my lack of competence in intellectual history, I must nonetheless venture into it in order to deal with one central aspect of this fragmentation, namely, the split between theological and scientific (and here I mean mainly social scientific) language about Christianity or, more generally, the split between religious man and scientific man in the West.

9.2 Without going back before the seventeenth century, one can perhaps say that from that time almost to the present the dominant theological defense of Christianity has been what may be called 'historical realism'. The roots of this historical realism can be traced back to biblical historicism, Greek rationalism, and the new awareness of scientific method emerging in the seventeenth century. The figural and symbolic interpretation of Scripture that was characteristic of medieval thought was almost eliminated by Reformation and counter-Reformation theology. Modern consciousness required clear and distinct ideas, definite unambiguous relationships, and a conception of the past 'as it actually was'. The proponents of 'reasonable Christianity' worked out a theology that seemed to fit these requirements. It is true that some of the most significant theological minds — such as Blaise Pascal, Jonathan Edwards, Friedrich Schleiermacher, and Kierkegaard — don't quite fit this formulation. Nevertheless for broad strata of educated laymen, and above all for the secular intellectuals, it was this understanding of Christianity that was decisive. Lest anyone think this kind of Christian thought is dead let him pause for a moment to consider the recent popularity of apologists who have argued that 'Christ must have been who he said he was or he was the greatest fraud in history'.

9.3 There have always been those willing to pick up the gauntlet with that kind of argument. Particularly in the eighteenth century many secular intellectuals argued that Christ, or if not Christ certainly the priests, were indeed frauds. Meeting Christianity on the ground of historical realism they rejected it. When faced with the inevitable question of how something clearly fraudulent and indeed absurd could have been so powerful in human history, they answered that religion was propagated for the sake of political despotism, maintained by an unholy alliance of priestcraft and political despotism. This argument was a species of 'consequential reductionism', the explanation of religion in terms of its functional consequences, which in cruder or subtler form has been a standard piece of intellectual equipment in the modern secular intellectuals' understanding of religion ever since.

9.4 The nineteenth century began with a partial reaction against the abstract rationalism of the Enlightenment and saw a growing awareness of the complex role of religion in the development of human consciousness. Yet at the same time the certainty grew among the secular intellectuals that Christianity, still defended largely by the old arguments and the old formulas, and with it religion generally, could not be taken seriously in its own terms. There grew up alongside of the continuing use of consequential reductionism several varieties of what I would call 'symbolic reductionism'. From this point of view religion is not entirely fraudulent. It contains a certain truth. But it is necessary for the modern intellectual to discover what that truth is that is hidden in the fantastic myths and rituals of religion. Much of nineteenth-century social science developed out of the search for the kernel of truth hidden in the falsity of religion.

9.5 One of the great intellectual strategies of the symbolic reductionists was to treat religion as a phase in the history of science. Primitive man, unable to understand the great natural phenomena of night and day, summer and winter, storm and drought, developed the fantastic hypotheses of religion to account or them. This kind of evolutionary rationalism has been enormously pervasive and has influenced religious thought as well as secular. How convenient for the Sunday school teacher to be able to explain the strange dietary rules of the ancient Hebrews in terms of hygiene — an intuitive awareness that shellfish and pork easily spoil under the warm climatic conditions of the Middle East! Another version of evolutionary rationalism that the nineteenth century developed with vast persuasiveness was the conception of religion as a stage in the development of human morality. The hidden truth of religion was the gradually growing perception of man's ethical responsibilities. The monotheistic God of the Bible could then be considered as the expression of a high ideal of man's ethical action.

9.6 For those perplexed that religion should continue to survive even in scientifically and ethically enlightened times, more immediate, more existential forms of symbolic reductionism were developed. Following Ludwig Feuerbach's treatment of religion as the projection of human nature, Marx developed his famous conception of religion as the opium of the people. This is usually treated as a form of consequential reductionism, which it perhaps is, but if we look at the *locus classicus* we can see that it is even more an existential version of symbolic reductionism. In his introduction to the 'Critique of Hegel's Philosophy of Right', Marx wrote: '*Religious* suffering is at the same time an *expression* of real suffering and a *protest* against real suffering. Religion is the sigh of the oppressed creature, the heart of a heartless world, and the soul of soulless conditions. It is the *opium* of the people'.[9]

9.7 From the early decades of the twentieth century symbolic reductionist theories of religion gained new subtlety and new complexity. Freud and Durkheim developed comprehensive formulas for the translation of religious symbols into their real meanings. Freud, first in *Totem and Taboo*, and then more starkly in *The Future of an Illusion*, disclosed that the real meaning of religion is to be found in the Oedipus complex that it symbolically expresses. The biblical God stands for the primordial father toward whom the sons feel both rebellious and guilty. Christ sums up a whole set of conflicting Oedipal wishes: the wish to kill the father, the wish to be killed for one's guilty wishes, and the wish to be raised to the right hand of the father. Finally, for Freud, the psychologically courageous man will discard the religious symbols that cloak his neurosis and face his inner problems directly.

9.8 For Durkheim the reality behind the symbol was not the Oedipus complex but society, and the morality that expresses it. In one of his most important essays 'Individualism and the Intellectuals',[10] he attempts to describe the religion and morality appropriate to his own society. He finds this in a religion of humanity and a morality of ethical individualism. How does he treat Christianity? 'It is a singular error', he says, 'to present individualist morality as the antagonist of Christian morality; on the contrary it is derived from it.' In contrast to the religion of the ancient city-state, he says, Christianity moved the center of the moral life from outside to within the individual, who becomes the sovereign judge of his conduct without having to render account to anyone but himself and God. But, he says, today this morality does not need to be disguised under symbols or dissimulated with the aid of metaphors. A developed individualism, the appropriate morality of modern society, does not need the symbolic clothing of Christianity.[11]

9.9 Unlike Marx, Freud, and Durkheim, Max Weber made no claim to have the key to the reality that lies behind the façade of religious symbolization. He treated religions as systems of meaning to be understood in their own terms from the point of view of those who believe in them, even though in the observer they strike no personal response. In this attitude he was at one with a whole tradition of German cultural historians and phenomenologists. For all the sensitivity with which he treats Calvinism, for example, it is the consequences for the actions of the believers that interest him, not the beliefs themselves. Without ever quite taking the position of consequential reductionism, Weber still manages to convey the feeling that the scientific observer cannot finally take seriously the beliefs he is studying even though he must take seriously the fact that beliefs have profound social consequences.

9.10 For the moment I am not trying to refute any of these theories of religion. They all have a great deal of truth in them as far as they go. But it is notable that the best minds in social science by the third decade of the twentieth century were deeply alienated from the Western religious tradition. None of them were believers in the ordinary sense of that word. All of them believed themselves to be in possession of a truth superior to that of religion. But since none of them except very hesitantly and partially wanted to fill the role that religion had previously played, they contributed to the deep split in our culture between religion and science, a break just at that highest level of meaning where integration is of the greatest importance.

9.11 Meanwhile, back at the seminary, things went on much as usual. The same old books were picked up, thumbed through, and put down again. The contemporary proponents of the historical realist position cut and trimmed what no longer seemed tenable and hoped for the best. A Karl Barth had the courage to give vivid expression to the grand themes of biblical and Reformation theology as though nothing had happened intellectually in the nineteenth and twentieth centuries, at least nothing that could not be refuted with the magnificent rhetoric of divine initiative and revelation. A few — one thinks of Martin Buber and Paul Tillich — saw the problem and tried to heal the split. In their more ecstatic moments it is even possible to say that they did heal the split. But neither was quite able to come up with a theoretical formulation that would spell out their ecstatic insights.

9.12 It is my contention that implicit in the work of the great symbolic reductionists was another possible position with entirely different implications for the place of religion in our culture, a position I will call 'symbolic realism' and will spend the rest of this essay trying to describe. Not only the great social scientists but many philosophical, literary, linguistic, and religious thinkers have contributed to this position, which has been gestating for a long time and has become increasingly explicit in the last twenty years.

9.13 Both consequential reductionism and symbolic reductionism are expressions of an objective cognitive bias that has dominated Western thought ever since the discovery of scientific method in the seventeenth century. This position has held that the only valid knowledge is in the form of falsifiable scientific hypotheses. The task then with respect to religion has been to discover the falsifiable propositions hidden within it, to discard the unverifiable assertions and those clearly false, and, even with respect to the ones that seem valid, to abandon the symbolic and metaphorical disguise in which they are cloaked. Both Durkheim and Freud, who are worth considering for a moment in this connection, ardently held to this conception of knowledge. Yet the work of both contains deep inner contradictions precisely with respect to this point.

9.14 Durkheim came to see that the most fundamental cultural forms, the collective representations, are not the product of the isolated reflective intelligence but are born out of the intense atmosphere of collective effervescence. Collective representations are based first of all on the sentiment of respect that they exact from individuals, and it is only through their discipline that rational thought becomes possible. Rational inquiry, then, rests on a necessary substratum of sentiments and representations that have neither the form nor the function of scientific hypotheses. Nor did Durkheim believe that the element of the sacred, which is what he called the symbolic expression of the collective vitality at the basis of society and culture, could ever be outgrown. It would always be an essential feature of social life, and the great terms which moved him and which he felt were so essential to modern society — individuality, reason, truth, morality, and society itself — were, as he knew, symbols, collective representations. In fact, he came to see that society itself is a symbolic reality. In his own terms, finally, symbolic reductionism comes to be self-contradictory and self-destructive. It is the reality of symbols that his life work goes to prove.

9.15 Freud's greatest discovery was the existence and nature of the unconscious. In his first and in many ways most fundamental major work, *The Interpretation of Dreams*, he showed that dreams are the royal road to the unconscious. Only through dreamlike symbolism can the primary process of the unconscious express itself. Although the rational understanding that he called secondary process can gradually increase its effective control, Freud never thought it could replace the unconscious. Indeed, he emphasized the relative weakness and fragility of rational processes. And in his own work he again and again abandoned the form of scientific hypothesis for the language of myth, image, and symbol, much to the dismay of subsequent academic psychologists. He named his most important psychological complex after a Greek myth. In his late years he constructed his own myth, the myth of the struggle of Eros and the death-instinct, in order to express his deepest intuitions. The unmasker of all symbols finally if implicitly admitted the necessity and reality of symbols themselves.

9.16 In recent years the knowledge that noncognitive and nonscientific symbols are constitutive of human personality and society, are real in the fullest sense of the word, has deepened and consolidated. Rather than the norm of scientific objectivity invading all spheres of human experience, the role of noncognitive factors in science itself have become increasingly recognized. As the philosopher of science Michael Polanyi says, ' . . . into every act of knowing there enters a passionate contribution of the person knowing. . . . This coefficient is no mere imperfection but a vital component of his knowledge'.[12] What this signals is a shift away from the mechanical model of early natural science, in which reality was seen as residing in the object, the function of the observer was simply to find out the laws in accordance with which the object behaves, and 'subjective' was synonymous with 'unreal', 'untrue', and 'fallacious'. For this mechanical model there has increasingly been substituted the interactionist model of social science, or what Talcott Parsons calls 'action theory'. Here reality is seen to reside not just in the object but in the subject, and particularly in the relation between subject and object. The canons of empirical science apply primarily to symbols that attempt to express the nature of objects, but there are nonobjective symbols that express the feelings, values, and hopes of subjects, or that organize and regulate the flow of interaction between subjects and objects, or that attempt to sum up the whole subject-object complex or even point to the context or ground of that whole. These symbols, too, express reality and are not reducible to empirical propositions. This is the position of symbolic realism.

9.17 If we define religion as that symbol system that serves to evoke what Herbert Richardson calls the 'felt-whole',[13] that is, the totality that includes subject and object and provides the context in which life and action finally have meaning, then I am prepared to claim that as Durkheim said of society, religion is a reality *sui generis*. To put it bluntly, religion is true. This is not to say that every religious symbol is equally valid any more than every scientific theory is equally valid. But it does mean that since religious symbolization and religious experience are inherent in the structure of human existence, all reductionism must be abandoned. Symbolic realism is the only adequate basis for the social scientific study of religion. When I say religion is a reality *sui generis* I am certainly not supporting the claims of the historical realist theologians, who are still working with a cognitive conception of religious belief that makes it paralled to objectivist scientific description. But if the theologian comes to his subject with the assumptions of symbolic realism, as many seem to be doing, then we are in a situation where for the first time in centuries theologian and secular intellectual can speak the same language. What this can mean for the reintegration of our fragmented culture is almost beyond calculation.

9.18 But if a new integration is incipient, fragmentation still describes the present reality. Concentrating so heavily on the mastery of objects, we have too long neglected what Anais Nin calls the 'Cities of the Interior',[14] and everywhere these neglected cities are in revolt. We have concentrated too much on what Polanyi calls explicit knowledge and too little on what he calls implicit knowing, and we have forgotten that the implicit knowing is the more fundamental, for all explicit knowledge depends on its unconscious assumptions.[15] As Yeats says,

Whatever flames upon the night
Man's own resinous heart has fed.[16]

We see the flames but we have forgotten the heart and its reasons that reason knows not of. The price of this neglect of the interior life (and I use interior not only to refer to the individual; there is a collective interior that contains vast forces) is the reification of the superficial, an entrapment in the world of existing objects and structures.

9.19 But the life of the interior, though blocked, is never destroyed. When thwarted and repressed the interior life takes its revenge in the form of demonic possession. Just those who feel they are most completely rational and pragmatic, and most fully objective in their assessment of reality, are most in the power of deep unconscious fantasies. Whole nations in this century have blindly acted out dark myths of destruction all the while imagining their actions dictated by external necessity. In our own country both the National Security Council and the Students for a Democratic Society (SDS) claim to be acting in accordance with the iron laws of politics at the same time that they seem trapped dreamlike in their own unconscious scenarios. All of this is the price we have paid for relegating art to the periphery of life, denying the central integrating role of myth and ritual, and letting our morality be dictated by our politics. For these reasons the issues of concern here are not academic, are not, to use a word that I have come to loathe in recent months, irrelevant. The future of our society, perhaps of life on this planet, depends on how we face them.

9.20 Perhaps the first fruit of symbolic realism, of taking seriously noncognitive symbols and the realms of experience they express, is to introduce a note of skepticism about all talk of reality. 'Reality is never as real as we think.'[17] Since for human beings reality is never simply 'out there', but always also involves an 'in here' and some way in which the two are related, it is almost certain that anything 'out there' will have many meanings. Even a natural scientist selects those aspects of the external world for study that have an inner meaning to him, that reflect some often hidden inner conflict. But this is true of all of us. We must develop multiple schemas of interpretation with respect not only to others but ourselves. We must learn to keep the channels of communication open between the various levels of consciousness. We must realize with Alfred Schutz that there are multiple realities[18] and that human growth requires the ability to move easily between them and will be blocked by setting up one as a despot to tyrannize over the others. Perhaps this is partly what is meant by what today is called 'multimedia communication', but it is even more important to remember that any one medium or any one symbol has many meanings and many contexts of interpretation.

9.21 Let me conclude by applying these general remarks to the field of religion and to the problems that face those of us who think about religion today. If art and literature primarily express the realm of inner meaning and are free to explore even the most aberrant and idiosyncratic wishes, hopes, and anxieties, religion is always concerned with the link between subject and object, with the whole that contains them and forms their ground. Though religion is not primarily subjective it is not objective either. It symbolizes unities in which we participate, which we know, in Polanyi's words, not by observing but by dwelling in them.[19] While neither the churches nor our secular culture seem to be doing a terribly good job of providing the symbols that evoke the wholeness of life and give meaning to our participation in it, we must nonetheless look to whatever in our own culture or in any culture has played this role.

9.22 If we think especially of contemporary Christianity there are a number of theologians whose work seems relevant; such names as Wilfred Smith, Richard Niebuhr, Gordon Kaufmann, and Herbert Richardson come to mind. But for me Paul Tillich is still the great theologian of the century, perhaps because it was through his work that Christian symbols first began to live again for me after my adolescent loss of faith. Certainly no one had a clearer sense of the fatal consequences of objectivism in religion. When Tillich objected to such phrases as 'God exists' or 'God is a Being' or 'the Supreme Being', it was because he felt they made God into an object, something finite, a being alongside other beings. His own conception of God was far more transcendent than the neofundamentalists ever realized. And yet even Tillich succumbed perhaps too much to the mania for interpretation, for discovering the rational core beneath the symbol, and the metaphysical structure in which he restated the fundamental Christian truths is after all not very persuasive. As one more schema of interpretation alongside others it certainly has its uses, but when he says that the statement 'God is being-itself' is not symbolic he seems to be engaging in a kind of metaphysical reductionism.[20] Perhaps his greatest contribution and the line of work that is still worth pursuing today was his restless quest for the 'dimension of depth' in all human social and cultural forms. This was his great contribution to breaking out of the institutional ghetto and seeing once more, as Augustine did, the figure of Christ in the whole world.

9.23 Two secular intellectuals have made major contributions in recent years to the position I am trying to set forth: Herbert Fingarette in *The Self in Transformation*[21] and Norman O. Brown in *Love's Body*.[22] Both of them oppose any kind of symbolic reductionism; both of them know that reality is inner as well as outer and that the symbol is not decoration but our only way of apprehending the real. They both have much to teach us about the multiplicity of vision — poetic, Buddhist, primitive, as well as Christian — which has become a possibility and, indeed, a necessity in the modern world. The work of these men is the most vivid illustration I know of the rapprochement between the language of religion and the language of the scientific analysis of religion.

9.24 As a sociologist I am by no means prepared to abandon the work of the great consequential and symbolic reductionists. They have pointed out valid implications of religious life that were not previously understood. But I am prepared to reject their assumption that they spoke from a higher level of truth than the religious systems they studied. I would point out instead their own implicit religious positions. Most of all I am not prepared to accept the implication that the religious issue is dead and that religious symbols have nothing directly to say to us.

9.25 Superficially the phenomenological school seems preferable on this score since it insists on describing religious symbols as closely as possible in the terms of those who hold them. But here there is the temptation to treat religious systems as embalmed specimens that could not possibly speak directly to those outside the charmed circle of believers.

9.26 I believe that those of us who study religion must have a kind of double vision; at the same time that we try to study religious systems as objects we need also to apprehend them as ourselves religious subjects. Neither evolutionist nor historical relativist nor theological triumphalist positions should allow us to deny that religion is one. I don't mean to say that all religions are saying the same thing in doctrinal or ethical terms; obviously they are not. But religion is one for the same reason that science is one — though in different ways — because man is one. No expression of man's attempt to grasp the meaning and unity of his existence, not even a myth of a primitive Australian, is without meaning and value to me. Perhaps this assertion will seem less radical to many young people today, for example to the young anthropologist Carlos Castaneda who apprenticed himself to a Yaqui shaman, than it does to those trained in my generation. I am not advocating the abandonment of the canons of scientific objectivity or value neutrality, those austere disciplines that will always have their place in scientific work. But those canons were never meant to be ends in themselves, certainly not by Weber, who was passionately committed to ethical and political concerns. They are methodological strictures. They neither relieve us of the obligation to study our subject as whole persons, which means in part as religious persons, nor do they relieve us of the burden of communicating to our students the meaning and value of religion along with its analysis. If this seems to confuse the role of theologian and scientist, of teaching religion and teaching about religion, then so be it.[23] The radical split between knowledge and commitment that exists in our culture and in our universities is not ultimately tenable. Differentiation has gone about as far as it can go. It is time for a new integration.

Notes

9. Karl Marx, *Early Writings* (New York: McGraw-Hill, 1964), pp. 43–44.
10. Emile Durkheim, 'L'Individualisme et les intellectuels', *Revue Bleue*, 4e ser. 10 (1898): 7–13.
11. *Ibid.*, p. 11.
12. Michael Polanyi, *Personal Knowledge* (New York: Harper & Row, Harper Torchbooks, 1964), p. xiv.
13. Herbert W. Richardson, *Toward an American Theology* (New York: Harper & Row, 1967), chap. 3, esp. p. 64.
14. The title of her multivolume 'continuous novel'.
15. Polanyi, *op. cit.*, p. x.
16. William Butler Yeats, *The Variorum Edition of the Poems* (New York: Macmillan Co., 1968), p. 438.
17. Daniel Stern, in Anais Nin, *The Novel of the Future* (New York: Macmillan Co., 1968), p. 200.
18. Alfred Schutz, *Collected Papers*, vol. 1 (The Hague: Nijhoff, 1962), pp. 209–59.

19. Polanyi, *op. cit.*
20. Paul Tillich, *Systematic Theology*, vol. 1 (Chicago: Univ. of Chicago Press, 1951), p. 238.
21. Herbert Fingarette, *The Self in Transformation* (New York: Harper & Row, Harper Torchbooks, 1965).
22. Norman O. Brown, *Love's Body* (New York: Random House, Vintage Books, 1968).
23. Randall Huntsberry, of the Department of Religion, Wesleyan University, has recently discussed the untenability of the distinction between teaching religion and teaching about religion in an unpublished paper, 'Secular Education and Its Religion'.

10

Gregory Baum
The Impact of Sociology on Catholic Theology

This Extract, like *Extract 8*, offers a useful overview of relationships between sociology and theology, this time from a Roman Catholic perspective. Gregory Baum is professor of theology and religious studies at St Michael's College, University of Toronto, and also has had sociological training. The Extract is a part of a paper which first appeared in the proceedings of the Catholic Theological Society of America in 1975. Baum is particularly concerned here to examine the implications for theology of the sociology of knowledge. In the first part, not included here, Baum sets out the cognitive changes in the Catholic world, most evident in Vatican II, which he believes should encourage theologians to take the sociology of knowledge seriously. He faces the issue of social determinism and relativism and sets out Mannheim's distinction between this and 'relationism' (see *6.19*). Indeed, he insists that 'we have never paid sufficient attention to the plural character of religion within the Catholic Church': pluralism is a fact within Christianity and sociology offers an obvious means of seeking to understand it (p. 106). For Baum this demands that the theologian take social context more seriously. Thus 'the social foundation of ideas or the historicity of truth is implicitly recognized in ecumenical dialogue' (p. 110). It is at this point in Baum's discussion that this Extract begins. Such a social perspective raises serious questions about the 'truth' of the Gospel (*10.1*). Like Roderick Martin, Baum is not convinced that sociology can be 'value-neutral' and argues against a static, atemporal understanding of 'truth' in theology. As a result, he argues that both sociology and theology can contribute to a 'symbolic realist' approach to the Gospel (*10.7–13*). He then turns from a discussion of the historicity of truth in theology, represented in Mannheim, to Marxist interpretations of theology which view the latter in terms of 'error' (*10.14f.*). It is here that Baum believes that sociologists can make their most critical contribution to theology in identifying ideological distortions in theology. This powerful section represents a very different tradition within sociology to the Weberian interactionism which forms the central focus of this Reader. But it is included here for completeness and also to show how it differs from a less explicitly ideological approach. In *Extract 11* I set out a critical use for sociology in theology which is dependent on a more distinctly Weberian approach.

10.1 How can we defend the truth of the Gospel and still hold to the authenticity of its various historical formulations? This is the problem of 'historicism', in which sociologists have been as interested as historians and philosophers. Since sociologists insist that all truth is historical, are they still able, we ask, to acknowledge that some truth transcends the culture in which and by which it was formulated? If the answer to this question were no, sociologists would have to abandon their science. Usually sociologists assume that if the truth is abstract enough, if it deals not with reality but with an ideal order, then such transcendence is possible. Such cultural transcendence is found in mathematics and it may also be found in the natural sciences. Yet even here some sociologists go on questioning under what social conditions science was first developed and what social conditions must obtain so that science achieves cultural power and generates an ever wider application to human life. Who knows? Perhaps modern science is so closely linked to the technological, bureaucratic society that what appears to us as its universality is rather the sign of the cultural victory of the West and hence represents a universality of power and aggression. But is there a truth transcending culture apart from mathematics and the natural sciences?

10.2 Sociology, as I mentioned above, presupposes the possibility of universal human communication and hence inevitably edges toward metaphysics. Karl Mannheim was very much aware of this.[11] In his sociology of knowledge he insisted that all truth was historical. But if we look at the critical edge of this truth and the orientation it induces in human life, then one might imagine a truth that is universal — even if it could never be possessed except perspectively. Mannheim thought that in every society people wrestle with the problems of their lives and learn to distinguish between truth and error, right and wrong. In this social quest truth appears as a critique of the current notions and the orientation of social and personal life. If we compare the various systems of values and ideas, we may find that they are quite different, but if we set them into their socio-political context, we see that they perform a similar function: they criticize oppressive trends and practices, they promote human life, they reach out for wider communication. It is not unreasonable to suppose that from a vantage point not yet available to us (and possibly never to be available to us) these various systems of truth and values are perspectives of a single truth. Mannheim held that unless sociologists acknowledged such a drift toward humanization and the presence of a universal dynamics in man, they would either undermine the entire work of sociology by a total relativism or else reify one historical system as the final and total truth. While the sociology of knowledge convinced Mannheim that all truth is historical, it also made him affirm the unity of truth in a common, relational orientation. Mannheim realized, of course, that this brought him to the edge of metaphysics, but he preferred not to develop this line of thought.

10.3 Truth as critique and orientation appeals to theologians who seek an understanding of religious truth that allows them to affirm the self-identity of the Gospel and its manifold historical formulations. As long as the notion of religious truth was drawn from neo-Scholasticism it was impossible to account for the passage from the old to the new and to reconcile the historicity of Christian doctrine with its transcendent unity. But if religious truth is critique of an existing culture and orientation toward renewed life, then it is possible that one and the same message acquires different meanings in various historical circumstances. Theologians have turned to hermeneutics, the theory of interpretation to be able to read and reread the biblical message out of different sets of presuppositions and hence reconcile the unity with the plural form of the Christian Gospel.

10.4 This is not the place to discuss theological hermeneutics. Since I am interested in the impact of sociology on theology I wish to make two remarks in this connection. First, the hermeneutical circle is also of interest to the sociologists. In the important controversies between sociologists who try to assimilate sociology as much as possible to the natural sciences and sociologists who insist that the human sciences (*Geisteswissenschaften*), including sociology, have a specific methodology, the latter have attempted to clarify the hermeneutics involved in the exercise of sociological research.[12] While natural sciences take for granted the separation of subject (the observer) and the object (the observed), except in some limiting cases, the human sciences — including sociology — acknowledge an interrelation of subject and object. Both the social scientist and the social action studied by them have been produced by the same history. The social scientists do not stand on neutral ground; they find themselves in a position that has been affected by the object they intend to study. In other words, they find themselves within the hermeneutical circle and before they can read correctly the empirical data they have collected, they must determine the precise place which they occupy in this circle. They must discover how the social action they study has affected their own self-understanding, and, conversely, if they study events more or less contemporary to them how the world with which they are identified has affected the object of their research. From Wilhelm Dilthey and Ernst Troeltsch to the contemporary critical sociologists of North America (C. Wright Mills, Robert W. Friedrichs, Alvin Gouldner, John O'Neil to mention a few), the struggle of sociology against the illusory ideal of value-neutrality and the quest of sociology for a new kind of objectivity are expressed in a body of literature that deals basically with hermeneutics, even if this particular term is not used.[13]

10.5 My second remark has to do with a principle of interpretation used in sociological research that would be helpful in theological studies. Since sociologists hold that consciousness and its cultural expressions are created by the social reality (in the sense explained above), it is possible to understand a particular social event in two ways: first, there is the meaning which the social event has to the actors involved in it, and, secondly, there is the meaning the event has, possibly unknown to the actors, as an expression of the wider social reality with which the actors are identified. Karl Mannheim calls this second 'documentary meaning'.[14] It is possible to study football in terms of the meaning which the players assign to the game, but it is also possible to study football as an expression of the socio-economic reality to which the players and the spectators belong, an approach that might account for the extraordinary power football holds over the imagination of contemporary society. Since the social institutions in which we live create a certain mind-set or consciousness, more is expressed in people's self-expression than their personal intention: the society expresses something about itself in the words and gestures of its members, even if this remains unknown to them. When idealists talk of the *Geist* of a community that expresses itself in works of art and literature, we may object to the metaphysical implications of their language, but we have to admit that it accurately records the sociological reality.

10.6 If we apply this principle to the reading of biblical literature, then we must take into account two distinct meanings of a text, one the literal meaning which is intended by the author and the other the documentary meaning which expresses something of the sociologically defined community to which the author belongs. In other words, there is a hidden meaning in a biblical passage that transcends the literal sense. The same principle can be applied in ecclesiology to give more precise meaning to the reliance of Catholics, including the Catholic theologian, on the wisdom produced in and by the community. Catholics have stressed more than Protestants that in the search for the understanding of the Gospel the theologians are not alone and that they should not surrender themselves fully to their own insights unless they are supported in this by a significant section of the believing community. In other words, the believing community itself is involved in the discernment of Christian truth. This position makes good sociological sense. For if consciousness is created by society, then the ideas people have reflect the common institutions and the socio-political conditions in which they live. A reading of the Gospel can be authentic only if it is shared by many. This explains, moreover, why the same religious development takes place in a good number of people dispersed in the same society, even though there is no direct communication between them. Only if theologians are confirmed by a significant movement in the Church do they know that more expresses itself in their interpretation of the Gospel than their own conscious insights: what they think also expresses something of the community's wrestling with its own conditions of life.

10.7 Theologians, I have said, try to solve the problems raised by the passage from the old to the new, and by the one and the many, through the application of hermeneutics to normative texts. There is, however, another way of dealing with these problems — a way, derived from the sociology of religion, that does not contradict the preceding way but parallels and supplements it. Beginning with Emile Durkheim, many sociologists have come to understand religion as a set of symbols that offers people an interpretation of the whole of reality, dominates their imagination and their hearts and orients their action in a certain way. Durkheim and some of his followers did not believe in God, and hence there was a reductionist tendency in their brilliant analyses. They presented religion as the sacred canopy protecting society and hinted that its creation was due to nothing but society's quest for stability. Other sociologists used the same symbolic understanding of religion non-reductively. Robert Bellah distinguishes two trends in the sociological approach to the study of religion as symbol system — 'symbolic reductionism' and 'symbolic realism'.[15] By symbolic realism he means the view that does not simply regard religious symbols as a reflection of society and its aspirations but acknowledges them as possessing a creativity of their own (and hence as remaining open to a metaphysical interpretation).

10.8 Christian theology is able to make use of the approach to religion derived from symbolic realism. For it is possible to regard divine revelation in Israel and Jesus Christ as the manifestation of God's hidden gracious presence to human history (this is shared by much of modern theology) and look upon this revelation not primarily as truth addressed to the mind but as stories and symbols through which the believing community interprets reality, understands itself and its mission, and opens itself to the divine self-communication. It is possible, in other words, to regard divine revelation as symbolic.

10.9 The so-called Modernists, we recall, tried to look upon divine revelation as symbolic. They did this to overcome the rationalistic understanding of religious truth operative in the theology of their day. However, the Modernists did not derive their understanding of symbols from the incipient social sciences contemporary to them. For them symbols were signs addressed to the memory, recalling significant events of the past and hence exercising power on people's emotions. Symbols communicated religious sentiment. We note that the notion of symbols, derived from the sociology of religion, is quite different. Here religious symbols are the form of the imagination, through which people lay hold of reality, understand themselves, their origin and their destiny, and move forward in creating their history.

10.10 Does this symbolic understanding derived from sociology neglect the noetic component of divine revelation? This is usually the first question that theologians ask. It seems to me that this approach does relegate this noetic component to a subordinate position. What divine revelation communicates directly is new consciousness. Through the story of Israel and the life and personality of Jesus the believing community comes to see reality in a certain way and by remaining faithful to this it eventually recreates its history in keeping with the divine promises. God acts in the community's history through the revealed symbols. In order to protect these divinely revealed symbols and repudiate false interpretations, the Christian community tried to lay hold of these symbols in a conceptual way and thus produced a set of doctrines. But these doctrines by themselves do not mediate the divine revelation. They initiate people into divine salvation only if they are grasped in their connection with, and dependence on, the revealed symbols. By putting primary stress on the noetic component of the Gospel, we have obscured the power of divine revelation; we have separated doctrines from the symbols they were meant to affirm and transformed them into conceptual information (usually quite unbelievable) about the divinity. By making use of the sociology of religion, the theologian is able to recover a broader, more action-oriented understanding of divine revelation and discover meaning and power in the Christian religion that has often been overlooked.

10.11 This is the approach we find in the writings of the sociologist Andrew Greeley.[16] While his writings are occasionally marred by outrageous generalizations and angry polemics against somebody else's position, his constructive effort to join theology and the sociology of religion in the interpretation of the Christian Gospel for modern society has been original and successful — and deserves the serious attention of theologians. As I have written elsewhere, I regard this application of symbol analysis to the understanding of the Gospel as the most fruitful trend in American theology.[17] Greeley has worked out his concept of symbol in line with the sociological studies of Talcott Parsons, Robert Bellah and Clifford Geertz, and after he applied this concept in a theological way to the interpretation of the Christian religion, he found himself, possibly to his surprise, very close to Paul Tillich's theological use of the symbolic. Greeley often adopts the Tillichian formulation that the Christian symbols shed light on human life and history, that they disclose the basic ambiguity of existence and reveal the divine graciousness operative at the heart of it. Christian symbols make known the hidden structure of reality; they reveal the divine judgment on the world and the hidden divine life present to the world, grounding and orienting the forward movement of life and history. (This recalls my earlier remarks on truth as critique and orientation.)

10.12 The constructive theological work of Rosemary Ruether, the most important section of which exists so far only in manuscript form, also uses symbols as the central instrument for interpreting the meaning and power of religion. Her understanding of symbol, however, is derived not from the sociology of religion, even if it is not in contradiction with it, but from her original training in classics and the study of ancient religions.

10.13 How does the symbolic understanding of divine revelation help theologians to solve the problems raised by the one and the many and the passage from the old to the new? Symbols have many meanings. In different cultural and sociopolitical situations the Christian symbols speak different languages. Since these symbols reveal the ambiguity of life and since the face of evil changes in various societies, the symbols will produce new meaning as the societies undergo significant changes. We touch here upon the extraordinary creativity of religion. Andrew Greeley, following his sociological method, trusts that symbols are resourceful; they give rise to many meanings. When the Christian community finds itself in a new social and cultural situation, the inherited symbols associated with the inherited meaning may at first fail to make sense or fail to illumine the life in which people actually find themselves, but as Christians wrestle with their religious inheritance in the new situation, the identical symbols will produce new meaning. They will eventually shed critical light on the concrete form of life and bring people in touch with the divine mystery present of them and carrying them forward. In his *The New Agenda*, Greeley uses this approach to explain the shift from the old to the new in the recent American Catholic experience. In other writings of his he has applied this method to interpret the covenant story and the Jesus story to our times. What remains constant and unchanging in the Christian religion are the symbols revealed in Israel and in Jesus Christ; what changes is their meaning. The formal function of these symbols remains the same in all ages and societies, yet their actual meaning undergoes significant transformations. While Andrew Greeley does not treat this approach in a speculative manner, his method offers a new and original way of reconciling the unity of the Gospel with its changing manifestations.

2

10.14 We now turn to another line, along which sociology has had an impact on Catholic theology. The first line had to do with the historicity of truth. The second one, which I wish to discuss in the remaining pages, has to do with the historicity of error.

10.15 Every age and every group of people produce their own form of blindness. This is an insight that is shared by those sociologists who have been willing to enter into dialogue with Karl Marx. Each group of people, through a largely unconscious process, creates an understanding of reality that legitimates its power and privileges. This, in Marxian language, is ideology. Ideology is the distortion of truth for the sake of social interest. We are all subject to some false consciousness. The sinfulness of the world, to use theological language, affects the very structure of human reason. This basic Marxian insight, which is so appealing to Augustinian theologians with their stress on the universality of sin, has been lifted from its original Marxian context and applied in a variety of ways in sociological approaches that have nothing to do with Marxism. Max Weber, who followed Marx neither in the view that economics is the primary social variable nor in his political eschatology, was quite willing to admit that the ideas of people and their religion always tend to fulfill a particular legitimating function in regard to their power and privileges. Max Weber did not reduce the meaning of ideas, culture and religion to this legitimating function, but he was willing to detect in them the ideological moment.

10.16 Let me add that a similar unconscious trend to produce false consciousness is also described in Freudian psychoanalysis, for there we are told that operative in our lives is the trend to build 'defenses'. To the extent that we are afraid and unwilling to deal with our instinctual conflicts and the unintegrated aspects of our personality, we build defenses — by a process of which we are unaware — that prevent us from seeing ourselves and the world as they really are. None of us is ever completely free of false consciousness even from this point of view. Even here we remain in need of on-going *metanoia*.

10.17 In sociology and psychology, then, we find a significant intellectual movement that looks upon error in human life not as accidental; error is just as profoundly rooted in our history as truth — and often just as revealing.

10.18 What is the relationship of ideology and religion? For Marx, religion was purely and simply false consciousness, even though he also wrote that 'religious distress is at the same time the expression of real distress'. 'Religion', he continued, 'is the sigh of the oppressed creature, the heart of a heartless world, the soul of soulless conditions.'[18] Sociologists of religion did not follow Marx in seeing religion almost exclusively as ideological defense of the existing power relations. In three famous chapters of his *The Sociology of Religion*, Max Weber examined the relation of religion and class and showed that religion always had different layers and trends, some of which were conservative and some critical.[19] Weber readily admitted that there are situations where one and the same religion serves as the legitimation of the ruling class and the consolation of the lower classes. Since Weber's time a good deal of sociological research has been done on the social function of religion. While some sociologists put more emphasis on those aspects or trends of religion that legitimate the social and political status quo — religion as sacred canopy — others have focused more on prophetic and innovative religion, following Max Weber, and brought out the radical potential in the religious traditions.

10.19 Theologians can no longer stand back from the ideological critique of the Christian religion, to which the sociologists have led them. The time has come that we too must acknowledge the historicity of error. In the past we tended to attribute to human weakness the failings of the Church and the failure of the Christian religion in some situations to ally itself with the historical movements for truth and justice. We were of course ready to admit that we and our ancestors were fools and sinners. But today we can no longer regard these failings and failures as unfortunate and regrettable accidents. We must ask whether they were produced by the discrepancies built into our institutions and the identification of religion with the interests of the dominant classes. The worst we have done is closely linked to the best we have inherited. This is, alas, the human condition.

10.20 The power of ideological distortion of the truth impressed itself on me many years ago when I studied the anti-Jewish trends present in the Christian religion and their link to the formation of Western culture. Christians became contemptuous of the Jewish people not because they, the Christians, were sinners and failed to live up to the Christian call to love; they learned to despise the Jews and denigrate their religion because of the ideological framework in which the Gospel was proclaimed. Woven into the most precious things we have are the distortions, produced by social interest, that eventually translate themselves into institutional forces of destruction. The defense of the Christian claims against the synagogal reading of the Scriptures produced a Christian language that made the Jews appear as an inferior people and, as Rosemary Ruether has recently shown in her *Faith and Fratricide*,[20] eventually led to the negation of their social existence altogether. Contemporary theologians, I repeat, find it impossible to stand back from submitting their religion to an ideological critique. This is what I mean by the historicity of error. Theologians believe, moreover, that it is ultimately the Spirit of God who leads them to engage in this critique.

10.21 How can ideological distortion or false consciousness be overcome? From a sociological point of view, false consciousness cannot be overcome by science or philosophy. New thinking alone will not do. Since the particular forms of blindness are rooted in the societal reality of the people struck by it, what is necessary is that they resituate themselves in regard to this society. What is needed is commitment and action. Ideas change when their 'bearers' undergo significant societal changes.

10.22 From the theological point of view, we have to say that the process of conversion, commitment and action by which people are delivered from ideological distortion is summoned forth by God's Word and moved by God's Spirit. Hence theologians are quite willing to examine critically their own tradition, even if they find discrepancies built into its language and its institutions that seem to threaten the integrity of the whole. We have to be willing to feel the ground shake under us. Marx believed that by identification with the most oppressed class, true conciousness becomes available to people. This is not enough, for wherever people are situated, they are in need of an on-going critique. Christians want to add to the Marxian formula that it is through identification in faith with the oppressed and crucified man Jesus that they began to detect the structures of domination in the several institutions to which they belong and thus move toward overcoming the layers of false consciousness.

10.23 Let me add that this view of the historicity of error has introduced vehement controversies in the social sciences. The sociologists who defend the value-free nature of social science suppose that the error in sociological research is due to mistakes in measurement and failures in the use of logic. To gain more reliable results the social scientist must refine his measuring instruments and perfect his conceptual tools, sociologists who repudiate the value-neutrality of social science add that error in sociological research may also be due to an ideological distortion of the researcher's consciousness. What may be required, as we suggested above, is that scientists discover their actual place in the hermeneutical circle, and this may demand a raising of consciousness. Today sociology departments are divided on this methodological issue.

10.24 Contemporary Catholic theology has opened itself to the historicity of error. Theologians on the whole have been willing to submit their religion and even their theology to an ideological critique. I already mentioned the scholarly effort to discern and come to grips with the anti-Jewish ideology operative in the Christian tradition. Much work has also been done on the anti-feminist ideology of biblical religion, Judaism and Christianity. An outstanding example of this research is *Religion and Sexism*, a collection of several articles on the image of women during various periods of Western religion, edited by Rosemary Ruether.[21] These studies show that the images of women, drawn from several distinct traditions, were various forms legitimating the existing structures that subjugated women and excluded them from public life.

10.25 We can think of many other examples of ideological deformations affecting the Christian religion. The question has been raised whether the tradition of monocratic power in the Catholic Church, according to which all ecclesiastical institutions are hierarchically ordered and government is exercised on every level, including the highest, by a single man, is grounded in a divinely revealed disposition or whether it is an ideological trend through which the monocratic episcopate that evolved more or less accidentally in the early Church was able to legitimate its claims and powers. This is an important question, for the experience of authority mediated to people through their religion has a profound effect on their social and political ideals. Sociologists have often pointed out the interaction between democratic structures of the Protestant churches and the democratic ideals of the political order. The question has been asked in Catholic theology whether the centralizing power of the papacy is a historical development guided by the Spirit, as it is usually supposed, or whether it is an ideological development that should be overcome. A growing number of Catholic theologians have adopted the latter view.[22]

10.26 In this context one should mention the issue raised by Max Weber and Ernst Troeltsch according to whom the so-called Protestant ethic has contributed to the creation of capitalism and remains its legitimation.[23] The Protestant religion is here seen as creating hard-working, individualist, self-reliant men who appreciate free enterprise and honest competition as the basis of economic life. According to Weber and Troeltsch these ideals were at odds with the older Christian tradition which placed the community at the center of people's awareness and presented individual life as a participation, albeit at a rather fixed place, in the life of the community. Weber's and Troeltsch's thesis has been confirmed by sociologists working in North America — for instance by Richard Niebuhr in the United States[24] and S. D. Clark in Canada.[25] According to Bryan Wilson, the British sociologist, it has been the genius of Protestantism to supply every rising class with the religious motivation and inward power to climb on the social and economic scale.[26] According to Will Herberg and Andrew Greeley this ethos is not confined to Protestantism in America; it is equally shared by Catholics and Jews.[27] It would appear, then, that the religion we have inherited is the inward spirit of what is excellent in capitalism, summoning people to the virtues necessary to make the system work and proscribing as sin the outlook and attitudes that undermine it. We note that this theory was by no means first proposed by Marxist sociologists. On the contrary, it represents a central theme in the sociology of religion. Ernst Troeltsch believed that the churches that have become successful, in whatever age, have allied themselves with the dominant classes and created a fusion between cultural ideals and religious aspirations.[28] At the same time, Troeltsch held that Christianity would again and again produce critical religious movements that tend to undermine the dominant values and provide people with a new vision of social life. In our days Christian theologians have taken these studies seriously and try to examine to what extent our inherited Church life is the legitimation of the prevalent economic system and its political consequences.

10.27 The 'political theology' of Germany and 'liberation theology' of Latin America are particularly sensitive to the historicity of error. According to these theological trends, in order to proclaim the Gospel it is necessary to make a sociological analysis of evil and injustice in society, then criticize the inherited religion to the extent that it legitimates these ills, and finally, relying on new commitment and religious experience, formulate the Christian message as God's promise to deliver the people from the sinful and demonic forces that distort their humanity. I mentioned above that American Catholics are sometimes overenthusiastic in regard to theologies produced in other parts of the world and try to incorporate these into their own thinking without first examining how they can be applied in North America. If theologians want to develop a critical

theology for North America they will have to turn to social studies to
clarify the structure of evil on this continent. Under the impact of
sociology, Catholic theology is turning more consistently to the
discernment of ideology in religion and culture. It has been suggested
that consciousness-raising is the blameworthy invention of Paolo
Freire; as a matter of fact the raising of consciousness is deeply rooted
in the sociological tradition. Thanks to the influence of this sociological trend, there are a growing number of theologians who hold, with
Edward Schillebeeckx, that unless we are committed to the emancipation or liberation of mankind, we are unable to free ourselves from
ideology and formulate in a credible way the Christian message.[29]

10.28 The saving message of Jesus Christ intends to deliver
people from false consciousness and appoints them to
transform the world. This is not sociologically demonstrable, but this
is what Christians believe. Jesus has come to deliver people from all of
the enemies of life. This is the prophetic text with which Jesus
introduced himself: 'The Spirit of the Lord is upon me, because he
has appointed me to preach good news to the poor; he has sent me to
proclaim release to the captives and recovering of sight to the blind,
to set at liberty those who are oppressed, to proclaim the acceptable
year of the Lord' (cf. Lk. 4:18–19). While this perception of divine
redemption has not been formulated with its political implications
prior to the impact of sociology on theology, the foundations of this
wide view are amply present in Scripture and the Catholic tradition.
In Jesus Christ God has acted on behalf of all of humankind; in Jesus
Christ God has united himself not only with one man but through him
with the entire human family; in Jesus Christ God has revealed that
there is a single destiny for all men and women, Christian and
non-Christian alike. Jesus came to usher in a new age. Jesus is the
instrument of God's kingdom which is promised to us at the end of
time but which is anticipated by us in special moments of our history
when we pass from sin to grace, from oppression to freedom, from
blindness to sight. In the past, under the influence of individualistic
cultural trends, we have often privatized the Gospel, i.e., we have
often understood the Christian message as if it were addressed only to
individuals. Today, largely under the impact of sociological thinking,
theologians are recovering their Christian foundation: they recognize
that the Gospel has meaning for persons as well as societies. One of the
tasks of contemporary religious thought is the deprivatization of the
Christian message.

10.29 The impact of sociology on Catholic theology that I
have examined in these pages lies in the application of
two principles — the historicity of truth and the historicity of error.
These two principles must be jointly applied in theological research

and reflection — and this is not always easy. It is very difficult to decide whether a certain aspect of the religious tradition should be interpreted as an authentic expression of the Gospel in a given situation or as an ideological deformation of the truth. In his book *Infallible?* Hans Küng presents two interpretations of the teaching of Vatican I on infallibility.[30] This teaching may either have been the only way in which the Church could affirm its reliance on divine guidance in a culture in which truth was regarded in highly rationalistic terms (historicity of truth), or it may have been an ideological distortion of the Christian message on divine guidance, prompted by the quest for more papal power and ecclesiastical security (historicity of error). Küng does not decide between these two theories of interpretation. A one-sided emphasis on the historicity of error would eventually undermine all sources of wisdom inherited from the past, and a one-sided stress on the historicity of truth would lead to a theological method that could reconcile with the Gospel any and every development, however strange, in the life of the Church. Here again theologians are confronted by problems that also preoccupy sociologists. Shall they study societies mainly in terms of what they contribute to human well-being or rather in terms of the damage they do to people? Is there a set of criteria that enable sociologists to make such a decision in each concrete case? Or do they depend in this decision on a choice that is not derived from their science at all?

10.30 It is my view that sociologists (and the theologian) should approach the object of their study from a perspective that promises to make their work a contribution to the humanization of life. This raises many important issues which contemporary sociologists are no longer able to avoid. Social science, too, must serve the emancipation of the human race.

Notes

11. K. Mannheim, *Ideology and Utopia* (New York: Harcourt, Brace & World, 1936), pp. 88–94.
12. Cf. G. Baum, 'Science and Commitment: Historical Truth According to Ernst Troeltsch', *Journal of Philosophy of the Social Sciences* 1 (1971), 259–77.
13. The search for a new 'objectivity' is found especially in the Frankfurt School of social thought and its followers in North America. Cf. Martin Jay, *The Dialectical Imagination* (Boston: Little, Brown and Company, 1973).
14. K. Mannheim, 'On the Interpretation of "Weltanschauung" ', *Essays on the Sociology of Knowledge* (London: Routledge & Kegan Paul, 1952), p. 44.

15. R. Bellah, *Beyond Belief* (New York: Harper & Row, 1970), pp. 246–57 [see above, *Extract 9*].
16. A. Greeley, *What a Modern Catholic Believes About God* (Chicago: Thomas More Press, 1971): *The Jesus Myth* (New York: Doubleday, 1971); *The Sinai Myth* (New York: Doubleday, 1972).
17. A. Greeley, *The New Agenda* (New York: Doubleday, 1973), Foreword, pp. 11–34.
18. *Marx and Engels on Religion*, intr. by Reinhold Niebuhr (Schocken Books, 1964), p. 42.
19. M. Weber, *The Sociology of Religion* (Boston: Beacon Press, 1968), pp. 80–137.
20. R. Ruether, *Faith and Fratricide* (New York: Seabury Press, 1974).
21. R. Ruether, ed., *Religion and Sexism* (New York: Simon and Schuster, 1974).
22. Cf. P. Misner, 'Papal Primacy in a Pluriform Polity', *Journal of Ecumenical Studies* 11 (1974), pp. 239–62.
23. M. Weber, *The Protestant Ethic and the Spirit of Capitalism* [see above, *Extract 1*]. For a collection of articles discussing the Weber thesis, see S. N. Eisenstadt, ed., *Protestant Ethic and Modernization* (New York: Basic Books, 1968).
24. H. Richard Niebuhr, *The Social Sources of Denominationalism* (New York: Meridian Books, 1957) [see above, *Extract 5*].
25. S. D. Clark, *Church and Sect in Canada* (University of Toronto Press, 1948).
26. Bryan Wilson, *Religion in Secular Society* (London: Penguin Books, 1969), p. 42.
27. W. Herberg, *Protestant, Catholic, Jew* (New York: Doubleday, 1955); A. Greeley, 'The Protestant Ethic: Time for a Moratorium', *Sociological Analysis* 25 (1964), pp. 20–33.
28. E. Troeltsch, *The Social Teaching of the Christian Churches* (New York: Harper & Row, 1960), p. 331 [see above, *Extract 4*].
29. 'In contemporary society, it is impossible to believe in a Christianity that is not at one with the movement to emancipate mankind': Edward Schillebeeckx, 'Critical Theories and Christian Political Commitment', *Concilium* 84 (New York: Herder & Herder, 1974), p. 55.
30. H. Küng, *Infallible? An Inquiry* (New York: Doubleday, 1971), pp. 151–6.

11

Robin Gill
Sociology Assessing Theology

This Extract is taken from the sixth chapter of my *Prophecy and Praxis* which appeared in 1981. In the first part of the chapter, not included here, I argued for a greater use by theologians of the social sciences if they are to understand better relationships between faith and practice. In particular, I argued that the social sciences could form an important part of critical self-understanding within theology. The Extract itself attempts to set out how this is possible. The chapter, originally entitled 'Prophecy as Praxis', finished with a discussion of the relevance of the argument contained in the Extract for Christian prophecy. The book as a whole was an attempt to work out how genuine prophecy is still possible in churches that are at the same time socially determined. If churches as churches (in the sense of *Extract 4* and *Extract 5*) have a strong tendency to adjust to the world and to be shaped by the societies in which they are located, in what sense can they be prophetic to those societies? Christian ethicists and theologians have usually been rather reluctant to face this question. Yet, as soon as a sociological approach is used by the theologian, it becomes a very pressing question indeed. I have tried to find an answer to it at length in my *A Textbook of Christian Ethics*. In this Extract, however, I set out the three sociological approaches to theology which have formed the basis of my work (*11.7–9*). The second approach, a study of the social determinants of theology, seems initially to pose the greatest challenge to theology. Most obviously it raises the problem of reductionism, or, at the very least, that of relativism (*11.14–22*). But it is the third approach, a study of the social significance of theology, which I believe really raises the most serious critical challenge for the theologian. Unlike those adopting a more explicitly Marxist position (cf. *10.14f.*), I maintain on specifically theological, rather than sociological, grounds that an adequate assessment of the validity of particular theological notions must take into account their potential or actual social effects (*11.23f.*). I set out the theological basis of this claim (*11.41–42*) only after noting parallels with Marxist and Liberationist perspectives (*11.26–39*). It is clear that I do not wholly subscribe to

145

the latter, despite the parallels, which is why I believe that it is important to identify this as a theological rather than sociological commitment (*11.44–50*). It is, though, a commitment which makes a critical use of sociology as the means to identify the various social effects of differing theological stances.

11.1 As a theologian, I believe that it is essential for theology to continue rigorous self-criticism: theology is essentially a dynamic discipline in which concepts are tested and re-tested afresh in each age and culture. In our own age and culture the social sciences should be playing a more important role, alongside philosophical and historical methods, in this dynamic process of discovery and re-discovery.

11.2 Once this point is conceded, there arise fresh possibilities for theology. Instead of concentrating upon the purely cognitive aspects of theology, as the philosopher is inclined to do, the theologian may be encouraged to explore the dynamic between faith and practice. This point will be made in more detail later, but for the moment, the suggestion is that, if the theologian resorts to the social sciences, in his task of rigorous self-criticism, s/he may eventually be encouraged to undertake a theology of practice, as well as the current more formally cognitive type of theology. For convenience, this possibility is referred to as 'praxis theology'.

11.3 There are two basic features of praxis theology. Most contentiously, I will maintain that sociological (and perhaps psychological, though this must be left to other specialists) techniques and theories can be used actually to arbitrate on the validity of differing theological notions — or, at the very least, on the validity of particular interpretations of theological notions. Clearly, this notion of arbitration goes considerably beyond the three socio-logical approaches to theology that I have previously studied and which will be outlined shortly. It will need careful qualification later, but obviously it belongs specifically to theology rather than to sociology.

11.4 The other major aspect of a praxis theology would be this: — such a theology would attempt systematically to un-pack the social implications of particular theological positions and notions. It will become apparent soon that this, too, raises numerous problems for theologians. Nonetheless, on this aspect of praxis theology, there is much wider agreement amongst them. Thus, although individual theologians might differ with each other on the exact social implications of their views, most might agree broadly that (with one or two important exceptions) their views do indeed have social implications. Certainly most contemporary theologians are not 'Political theologians'. However, most would still agree that their theological views are relevant to such social issues as abortion and euthanasia. On the other hand few might concede that the social effects of their theological positions are actually relevant to the validity of these positions.

11.5 Already a distinction has been introduced, between the social effects and the social implications, of theological positions. For the sake of clarity, one may confine the first to largely unconscious consequences of theological positions and the second to deliberate, intended, or conscious consequences of such positions. Specifically sociological techniques and theories are more relevant to a study of the first, than to the second. It *is* appropriate for the interested sociologist to investigate the way in which particular theological positions have, or even could have, particular effects upon society. The theologian can then use such investigations to become more self-critical. However, the intended social implications of a particular theologian's positions are not so subject to sociological investigation. They belong more fully to the specific task of the theologian himself. Here there are better established areas of conflict and methods of procedure actually within theology itself.

11.6 Before seeking to justify the claim that a praxis theology would in part be concerned with assessing the validity of theological notions in the light of their social effects, I must indicate how such a study differs from my more specifically sociological attempt to analyse theology. I have suggested three distinct sociological approaches to theology[1]: —

11.7 A. **A Study of the Social Context of Theology**: this approach depends upon the assumption that theology does not work in a vacuum, but that theologians tend to make claims about the society or culture within which they operate and then incorporate these claims into their theology. Precisely because the theologian is concerned to communicate with his contemporaries, he is obliged to respond (sometimes critically) to contemporary plausibility structures. This was most evident in the Secular theology movement, in which theologians deliberately wrote in response to a supposed process of secularisation within society at large. However, it is also apparent in contemporary Liberation theology, particularly in its conscious espousal of social and political models from the Third World. Bonino, for example, insists that it is necessary to devote the first half of a *theological* book to 'a discussion of sociological analysis and political trends and options'.[2] Sociological analysis could provide incisive and rigorous tools for the theologian to understand better the social context within which he operates.

11.8 B. **A Study of the Social Determinants of Theology**: the focus here is less upon the task of the theologian than upon theology itself. This approach assumes that, as a human enterprise, theology is socially determined. It suggests a correlation between social structures and theology, regarding the latter as a product of the former. Theology (like all other ideologies and explications of beliefs) is viewed as a human product or as a social construction — whatever else it might be. On the basis of this approach, it becomes possible to use techniques, developed in the sociology of knowledge, in order to study the ways in which differing theological positions are correlated with differing social structures.

11.9 C. **A Study of the Social Significance of Theology**: here the possibility is explored that theology, even as a product of society, may in turn have an influence upon that society. If the previous approach regards theology as a dependent variable within society, this one allows for the possibility that theology may also act as an independent variable. Overall, theology is seen as a socially constructed reality — that is, as something that is both socially constructed *and* a social reality. To give a single example, certain forms of Marxist theory would suggest that theology is the product and expression of certain socio-economic divisions within society and, in particular, the expression of the rulers over-and-against the ruled. In these terms theology is seen as a social construction. But there is also a possibility that Marx and Engels were themselves unwittingly influenced by the prevailing Hegelian theologies[3] of their day and an even stronger possibility that certain versions of Liberation theology, having incorporated a Marxist critique actually into their discipline, are proving influential within parts of the Third World. An extraordinarily complex web of interactions between theology and society emerges; Hegelian theological ideas may have influenced Marx and Engels' critique of theology, which, in turn, has been adopted by certain influential versions of Liberation theology. A combination of approaches B and C, then, presents a view of the role of theology within society which the sociology of knowledge can do much to clarify.

11.10 All this has already been covered and argued at length elsewhere.[1] Taken together, these three sociological approaches to theology seek to offer the theologian a relatively unexplored, but, nonetheless, incisive and rigorously academic, means of examining his discipline.

11.11 It is important not to over-state the 'newness' of these three approaches to theology. Implicitly and, sometimes, even explicitly, critical theologians have often alluded to their particular social context and shown an awareness of the social determinants and significance of their discipline. It is a common-place of theological polemic to demonstrate how opponents' views are inadequate responses to their social context, products of certain social factors, or lead to undesirable social consequences. Further, various forms of Existentialist theology have made systematic use of the concept of *Sitz im Leben* or social context — arguing that contemporary theology must respond directly to contemporary thought-forms and not to those of First Century Christians. In addition, both biblical and doctrinal criticism have shown a considerable awareness of the relation between ideas and beliefs, on the one hand, and social or cultural factors, on the other. Finally, church historians have frequently emphasised the role of specifically theological elements in the shaping of religious and political events. A combination of hermeneutics, historical research, apologetics and even theological polemics, has already made considerable use of these three sociological approaches to theology. But, what theologians have seldom done, is to use these approaches systematically or with any reference to the obvious fund of scholarship provided by the discipline of sociology itself. Too much has been just too amateur.

11.12 Once these three approaches are studied systematically and rigorously, each raises rather different problems for the theologian. Whilst he has come to accept a variety of philosophical and historical means of assessing the validity of theological notions, he has yet to adopt more specifically sociological ones. Thus he has faced the criticisms of the Logical Positivists, the Functional Analysts, those requiring evidence of meaningfulness and clarity, those checking christological claims against the shadows of the 'historical Jesus' or the beliefs of the Early Church, and so forth. What he has yet to realise, is that these three sociological approaches themselves raise crucial problems for Christian theology.

11.13 The first approach, based on a study of the social context of theology, raises problems more of communication and plausibility than of validity as such. 'True' theology may indeed be able to ignore its social context, either by expressing 'timeless' truths or by using terms designed for other social contexts. Whilst it may not thereby be rendered invalid, it might be regarded by many as largely irrelevant. The consequence of ignoring contemporary plausibility structures, is for theologians to produce work which may appear increasingly anachronistic.[4] Clearly this was a matter which concerned Bultmann deeply, even if one might dissent from the analysis of actual plausibility structures that he provided.[5] This is also a matter which currently concerns those attempting to develop 'indigenous' theologies in non-Western contexts. In fact, while it is perfectly possible for theologians to ignore totally the social context in which they operate, few have actually done so in the past, or do so in the present.

11.14 The second approach, based on a study of the social determinants of theology, does, at first, appear to raise the problem of validity in a critical way. The systematic attempt to explain theological ideas as products of particular social structures, does seem to be an attempt, by the sociologist, to falsify them, or, at least, to support a relativist position. Even when a distinction is made, between 'explaining' something and 'explaining it away' and a further distinction is made between the 'origins' and 'validity' of ideas, a problem of validation remains — if not for the sociologist, at least for the theologian. As Mannheim argued, the social source of ideas *is* usually construed to be relevant to their truth or falsity, whether or not a formal logical relationship exists.[6] Thus, as maintained, at length, in *The Social Context of Theology*, if we successfully demonstrate a disreputable source for something, we usually distrust it thereafter — genetic fallacy or no genetic fallacy.

11.15 On the other hand, there is a somewhat disconcerting element within Christian theology which almost glories in disreputable origins. For Paul the *skandalon* created, for Jews and Gentiles, by the origins of Christianity, was almost something to boast about. And for theologians like Kierkegaard, Christianity was considered to be both outrageous and nevertheless true. Further, various types of Mystical theology have delighted in paradoxes verging on outright inconsistencies.

11.16 Yet, there is still an aspect of this sociological approach to theology which does concern its validity. If, for example, a Marxist critique of the discipline is adopted, whereby it is seen as an expression of the ruling-class, and contemporary confirmation for this is gathered from the middle-class bias of most Western churches, then it might become more difficult to trust its 'universality'. Or again, if, as argued in the first chapter, it is evident that the churches' pronouncements on ethical issues, such as abortion, tend to follow, rather than to lead, public opinion, it might become more difficult wholly to trust them in the future.

11.17 In this last situation, the theologian is faced with a number of options. He may question, either the particular findings, or the methodological bias, of the sociologist. Alternatively, he may return to a complete separation between origins and validity, claiming that, whatever the social source of his theological notions, they are still valid. However, if he resorts to none of these options he may have to revise his claims or his ideas. In the process, he would be affording sociological analysis a more central role than hitherto in the validation of theological notions, since it is such analysis which provides him with the initial suspicion of the invalidity of the notions. This is certainly not to claim that sociological analysis can directly discredit particular theological positions. Such a claim would result in the sort of confusion of sociological and theological concepts that has unfortunately characterised several previous attempts to correlate the two disciplines. Rather, it is to claim, more modestly, that sociological analysis may, at times, raise theological suspicions — suspicions which must then be investigated, not in the light of further sociological analysis, but in the light of the claims of the Gospel as a whole. It is just such suspicions that I am attempting to raise in this book's analysis of prophecy in the contemporary churches.

11.18 It is interesting to note, in passing, that this whole approach could form an important plank in Christian-Marxist dialogue. Certainly, Alfredo Fierro takes it as the initial starting-point for his political theology. He is deeply critical of Miranda's[7] approach to this dialogue, arguing that, in the end, he 'engages in an apologetics of coincidence and convergence . . . the result — or rather, the aim which governs his work from the very start — is to make Marx nothing less than a prophet beholden to biblical tradition'.[8] For Fierro, it is simply not sufficient to demonstrate a convergence between biblical and Marxist concepts; 'it is hardly surprising that one might find ideas from the Bible in Marx or any other Western thinker. It only confirms what we have known for a long time: that biblical thought has penetrated deeply into Western civilization and left a real mark on it'.[9] Rather, the question he seeks to face is, 'assuming the Marxist theory as correct, is any faith or theology possible at all?'.[10] This is an explicitly methodological position. He is not seeking to sanctify Marxist theory as such: instead, he believes that it is the job of the theologian, in any age, to explore contemporary theories (whether Marxist, Freudian, Existentialist, or whatever) to see whether or not faith or theology is possible on their basis. In his attempt to answer this specific question, he suggests a starting-point for Christians and Marxists alike, founded on the Marxist principle of analysing 'social relationships as being conditioned or determined by the economic base'.[11]

11.19 Fierro's work is rich with insights and has many resonances with the theoretical position here, but only a few of these can be isolated now. Some of the most important are contained in the following quotation:

The first and primary thesis of a historical-materialist theology entails the adoption of Marxist theory and maintains that ideas and beliefs are determined or conditioned by the economic base, by the production relationships in a given society. This applies to religious ideas and beliefs as well. Even in this initial thesis, however, one may see an irreducible opposition arising between believers and Marxists. Are they strictly determined by the economic base, or only conditioned by it? Orthodox Marxists ought to maintain that ideas and beliefs are rigorously determined by the economic structure whereas orthodox Christians could not maintain that; Christians could only say that religious ideas and beliefs are at most conditioned by socioeconomic factors.[12]

11.20 He argues, however, that this apparent opposition is based on an out-dated understanding of the relationship between cause and effect. In fact, 'modern thought is abandoning the etiological approach that looks for cause and effect relationships; it is now more interested in investigating relationships and correspondences between different phenomena'.[13] Certainly a number of contemporary sociologists[14] are critical of what they consider to be a pre-Humean understanding of causality and, as I argued in the first chapter, an exact specification is unnecessary. The theologian is asked only to concede that there *is* a relationship between 'purely' theological ideas and social structures and that the latter constrain the former.

11.21 Once this point is conceded, then Fierro's analysis follows. Given that he is concerned with the social determinants of theological ideas from an explicitly Marxist perspective, he maintains that the theologian can never avoid social determination, he can only choose by what kind of social determinants his ideas are to be fashioned. Like many others influenced by South American Liberation theology, he concludes that genuine theology must always side with the oppressed and with the working-classes. Thus, he admits that *all* ideas (one's own, as well as those of one's opponents) are socially determined or constrained: no one can escape this. He avoids the mistake of some exponents of Liberation theology in imagining that it is simply 'bourgeois' Western theology which is socially structured. The individual can only opt for one kind of social determination rather than another.

11.22 This specific solution is obviously directly related to his adoption of a Marxist perspective and, as such, is highly relevant to the contemporary Marxist-Christian dialogue. A more general point, though, also emerges from his analysis. He maintains that an understanding of the socially structured nature of theology should lead to less absolutist theological claims in the future: 'if we accept the hypothesis of historical materialism, we can only have a theology that is not all transcendent vis-à-vis the realm of other human ideas'.[15] At the very least, a sociology of knowledge (whether Marxist or not) might help, on this basis, to generate a degree of theological humility.

11.23 However, it is the third approach, based on a study of the social significance of theology, which offers the theologian the most serious problems of validation. What appears to the sociologist as the social significance of theology, appears to the theologian as its social importance. There is an inescapable evaluative element in the latter's response to this phenomenon which the former usually attempts to avoid. The claim that will be developed now, from the theological (emphatically not the sociological) perspective, is that an adequate assessment of the validity of particular theological notions must take into account their potential or actual social effects. Further, if these effects appear to be at variance with the Gospel as a whole, the theologian is given *a priori* grounds for distrusting their validity. If accepted, this peculiarly social criterion for assessing the validity of theological notions has radical implications for theology at large. It could serve to break the current virtual monopoly within the discipline of philosophical and historical criteria.

11.24 Before attempting to substantiate these claims, two initial points must be made to avoid confusion. Firstly, it is important to recognise that there has always been some concern about the social effects of theology. It has been a common-place of theological polemic to maintain that 'heretical' beliefs tend to lead to wrong and often 'immoral' actions. 'Orthodoxy' and 'orthopraxis' have frequently been seen as inseparably correlated. Nevertheless, outside these one-sided and, often, un-self-critical, accounts, attention to the social effects of differing theological positions is rare and rigorous study of them still rarer. In short, this is largely unexplored territory. And secondly, I do not believe that it is a part of the task of theology to call into question the validity of the Gospel as a whole. Certainly it belongs to the task of the philosophy of religion. But theology, as theology, assumes the overall validity of Christianity: it operates 'as if' the Christian Gospel is fundamentally valid and seeks a critical explication of it, not a critique of its foundations. This position accords with my definition of theology as 'written and critical explication of the "sequelae" of individual religious beliefs and of the correlations and interactions between religious beliefs in general'.[16] Accordingly the problems of validation of concern here are always partial. It is the validity of particular theological notions and positions which are under inspection, not the overall claims of the Gospel. This point is crucial, if confusion with the philosophy of religion is to be avoided. The concern is primarily with the 'inner coherence' of the social effects of particular theological positions with the Gospel as a whole.

11.25 The following section will focus upon these social effects, whilst the section beyond it will return to the problems raised by claims about the social implications of theology.

Faith Tested By Practice

11.26 The claim that the potential or actual social effects of particular theological notions are relevant to their validity, points to a deep rift within much Western, intellectual thought. Despite the fact that philosophy and the emerging social sciences were scarcely differentiated until the late 19th Century, the prevailing wisdom within the West today suggests that, the study of 'ideas', as 'ideas', belongs largely to the discipline of philosophy and that, the study of human behaviour belongs to the social sciences. In general, social scientists have tended to avoid epistemological questions, whereas philosophers have tended to overlook the socially structured nature of ideas. Given this sharp division between the study of 'ideas' and the study of 'behaviour', immediate hostility must be expected for any attempt to suggest a relationship between the social effects and validity of theological notions.

11.27 There is, however, a radical alternative to this prevailing wisdom, suggested by Marxist thinkers. In various ways they have tended to reject the study of 'ideas', simply as 'ideas', and unrelated to empirical 'behaviour' and have attempted to offer, instead, a synthesis of the two. Amongst Marxist writers, the division between philosophers and social scientists is not nearly so apparent as it is amongst non-Marxist intellectuals. Further, although there are very sharp divisions amongst Marxists themselves, there might be widespread agreement that 'ideas' can be fully understood only in relation to 'behaviour' and *vice versa*. For the Marxist, the problem with Western philosophy is, that it is overly cognitive and, all too often, chooses to ignore empirical factors and determinants, such as class, power-structures and economic-structures. The problem with the Western social scientist, on the other hand, is that, from the perspective of the Marxist, he tries (and fails) to be 'value free' and ignores the moral and political context within which he operates and devises his research. So, a Marxist philosopher will tend to carry a concern for socio-political structures actually into his philosophy and the Marxist social scientist will filter his empirical research through a self-conscious philosophical/ideological commitment.

11.28 The germ of this radically different orientation can be traced back at least to Karl Marx and Frederick Engels' *The German Ideology* of 1844. In this extended polemic against the prevailing Hegelian and Young-Hegelian forms of theology and philosophy, the two authors sought to show the basis of 'ideas' and consciousness in class structures and material behaviour. They contended that, despite its stress on the social significance of ideas, Hegelianism was 'ideology', itself reflecting a spurious division between mental and material behaviour and, in turn, an equally spurious division between the privileged rulers and the disprivileged ruled. There is much debate, of course, about the exact import of their term 'ideology' and whether, or not, they explained its origins solely in terms of economic sub-structures. What *is* interesting here is that they contended that 'ideas' which are left unrelated to 'actions' are vacuous and that even the socially concerned Feuerbach ignored the social basis of ideas.

11.29 The following quotation from *The German Ideology* well illustrates the opposing perspectives of the Hegelians and Marx and Engels:

> In direct contrast to German philosophy which descends from heaven to earth, here we ascend from earth to heaven. That is to say, we do not set out from what men say, imagine, conceive, nor from men as narrated, thought of, imagined, conceived, in order to arrive at men in the flesh. We set out from real, active men, and on the basis of their real life-process we demonstrate the development of the ideological reflexes and echoes of this life-process. The phantoms formed in the human brain are also, necessarily, sublimates of their material life-process, which is empirically verifiable and bound to material premises.[17]

The blend of empirical and philosophical elements and the correlation between 'actions' and the validity of 'ideas', evident in this passage, are quite alien to much contemporary Western thought.

11.30 Not surprisingly, they are also alien to much contemporary theology. The cognitive orientation of contemporary philosophy has proved too attractive for most recent systematic theologians.[18] Doubtless through a desire to produce theological/philosophical correlations which appear plausible to twentieth-century man, the theologian has often been happy to consider 'faith' in isolation from 'practice'. Encouraged by the apparent relevance to theology of Continental philosophy, he has concentrated upon 'faith' and upon the grounds for faith and not upon 'faith', as it relates to and is tested and made intelligible, by 'practice'.

11.31 Of course there have been a few theologians who have been concerned to relate 'faith' and 'practice'. Since the rise of Liberation theology they have become more plentiful. Some have adopted the Marxist critique of knowledge and society *in toto* into their theologies: some have even used this critique to assess the validity of particular theological positions. Nevertheless, for most Western theologians (as distinct from Third World theologians) this critique is no longer thought to supply a relevant analysis of the societies within which they operate. Although a correlation between Marxist and Christian thought would have undoubted usefulness in certain contexts — indeed it has been attempted on several occasions over the last thirty years — it is doubtful if it would receive widespread support in the present Western context.

11.32 Whatever the merits or demerits of the Marxist perspective within philosophy or the social sciences, it is arguable that its insistence upon the inseparability of 'ideas' and 'actions' is peculiarly pertinent to Christianity. Without any overall commitment to the Marxist critique of society, it is possible to maintain that 'faith' and 'practice' will be badly misunderstood within Christian theology if they are treated separately. For Christians, 'beliefs' are not usually statements merely about 'the way things are', that is, they are not simply cognitive. Credal statements, for example, are not just recitations of religious knowledge or opinion: when used within the liturgical context they are expressions of religious commitment. As Talcott Parsons observes, 'acceptance of a religious belief is . . . a commitment to its implementation in action in a sense in which acceptance of a philosophical belief is not . . . religious ideas may be speculative in the philosophical sense, but the attitude towards them is not speculative in the sense that "well, I wonder if it would make sense to look at it this way?" '.[19] At the very least, some degree of correlation between 'faith' and 'practice' would appear essential within Christian theology, in a way that it might not be elsewhere. Indeed, I prefer to use the term 'faith', in this context, to 'belief', precisely because an element of commitment is implicit within it. In addition, it avoids some of the philosophical and sociological difficulties attached to the concept of 'belief'. The term 'practice', on the other hand, is intentionally wide — covering both intended and unintended modes of behaviour. Prophecy belongs more to the former than the latter.

11.33 Once the possibility is allowed, that the social effects of theological notions might be relevant to their validity, then the reason for much of the polemic within the history of Christian theology becomes evident. The christological and trinitarian controversies that took place within the Early Church, were not fired by a desire for correct 'religious knowledge'. In part, the struggles before Chalcedon were politically and culturally based, reflecting the balance of power and difference of milieu between East and West. But, in part, they were also fired by the fear that distorted Christian faith would lead to distorted practice. If this were not the case, then the extraordinary degree of bitterness caused over a single Greek letter in the *homoousios/homoiousios* debate would be without adequate explanation. At the heart of this debate and many another between Docetists, Arians, Apollinarians and so forth, lay the fear that if Christ was only 'like' God or only 'like' men, then he could not have effected man's redemption and, in turn, man's sinful nature could not have been changed. A christology that expressed anything less than the incarnation of God in the world was thought, at Chalcedon, to be socially ineffective. A docetic christology denied that Christ ever became man, whereas an adoptionist christology denied that he was ever fully God. The result of either was thought to be the same; the incarnation would have been ineffective and mankind would have been left unredeemed.

11.34 A double link, then, can be seen in the Early Church's correlation of faith and practice. Wrong faith was to be feared, both because it had the immediate social effect of 'anarchy' and 'immorality', and because it had the eschatological effect of eternal damnation. Just as orthodoxy and orthopraxis were deemed to go hand-in-hand, so conversely did 'heresy', 'anarchy', 'immorality' and 'damnation'. In the Medieval Church, too, and in the bitter controversies engendered by the Reformation, the same correlations are to be found. Religious tolerance, regarded as a desirable virtue, is a comparatively modern phenomenon and is possible only when 'heresy' is no longer widely feared. In ages of religious intolerance much depended upon accurate theology!

11.35 Even within some of the more radical contemporary sects, 'heresy' is still perceived, in part, as a challenge to their authority. Movements, like those of the Jehovah's Witnesses and the Scientologists, go to great lengths in devising social mechanisms for controlling 'heretical' views. In the case of the Scientologists this meant changing from a somewhat diffuse counselling movement or 'cult'[20] to a strictly controlled, bureaucratic sect. In the instance of the Jehovah's Witnesses, 'orthodoxy' is only maintained at the expense of a high loss of members.[21] Yet in either movement 'heresy', if allowed, would entail, not merely a change of faith, but also a change of practice. Once dissuaded from his ardent millenarianism, the Jehovah's Witness might lose much of his enthusiasm for proselytism and, once allowed to experiment with differing counselling techniques, the Scientologist might lose much of his commitment to the techniques and metaphysical beliefs of the movement as a whole. In both sects, the social effects of 'heresy' are to be feared: a rigid orthodoxy is offered as a means to control these effects.

11.36 A stress upon the social effects of faith is also to be found in certain types of contemporary Existentialist theology. Here, the emphasis is less on the evil effects of 'heresy', than upon the beneficial effects of the Gospel. The Gospel is to be trusted, not because the events it describes are historically accurate, even less because the Church claims that they are to be trusted, but rather because it still has the power to change people. It is the Gospel itself, regarded as proclamation, which is seen as salvific, not the events portrayed in the Gospel. Various theologians have held this position in the last one hundred years — ranging from the proponents of 'symbolic christology', through followers of Bultmann, to some present-day exponents of the Gospel as 'story'. They have in common, a disinterest in the 'historical Jesus' as seriously affecting the Gospel today, a distrust of metaphysics and an emphasis upon the social effects of the Gospel.

11.37 A rather different stress upon the social effects of faith is to be found in some current versions of Liberation theology. Closer to the traditional understanding of 'heresy' than the emphasis of Existentialist theology, exponents tend to point to the harmful social effects of opposing view-points. Thus, they have suggested a close correlation between Western theology and Western imperialism and colonialism (or sometimes just between Western theology and Western male chauvinism). This is usually linked to a positive stress on the 'liberating' social effects of Liberation theology itself, but, until recently, a negative emphasis frequently predominated. Whilst a Marxist critique of society is by no means essential to this approach to theology, it is in fact often adopted within it.

11.38 A firm stress on the vital connection between faith and practice, is certainly one of the chief characteristics of the whole Political theology movement in recent theology. As Moltmann has emphasised, 'the new criterion of theology and faith resides in praxis'.[22] For Gutiérrez, this emphasis is captured in the phrase 'theology as critical reflection on praxis'.[23] A study of praxis for him, is relevant to the actual verification of theology.

'To do the truth', as the Gospel says . . . acquires a precise and concrete meaning in terms of the importance of action in Christian life. Faith in a God who loves us and calls us to the gift of full communion with him and brotherhood among men not only is not foreign to the transformation of the world; it leads necessarily to the building up of that brotherhood and communion in history. Moreover, only by doing this truth will our faith be 'veri-fied', in the etymological sense of the word. From this notion has recently been derived the term *orthopraxis*, which still disturbs the sensitivities of some. The intention, however, is not to deny the meaning of *orthodoxy*, understood as a proclamation of and reflection on statements considered to be true. Rather, the goal is to balance and even to reject the primacy and almost exclusiveness which doctrine has enjoyed in Christian life and above all to modify the emphasis, often obsessive, upon the attainment of an orthodoxy which is often nothing more than fidelity to an obsolete tradition or a debatable interpretation. In a more positive vein, the intention is to recognize the work and importance of concrete behaviour, of deeds, of action, of praxis in the Christian life.[24]

11.39 This passage demonstrates well the new stress upon practice in Liberation and Political theology. Of course, there is a growing amount of internal criticism within the movement and real methodological differences are now emerging.[25] But all might agree on the centrality of practice vis-à-vis faith. As Segundo argues, for Liberation theologians, 'faith . . . is not a universal, atemporal, pithy body of content summing up divine revelation', but rather 'the possibility of fully and conscientiously carrying out the ideological task on which the real-life liberation of human beings depends'.[26]

11.40 Of course, the fact that a correlation between faith and practice has often been made within Christian theology (even if it is largely absent from recent systematic theology), does not of itself demonstrate that it ought to be made. Still less does it demonstrate that the social effects of theological notions are relevant to their validity. This is especially the case when it is admitted that, so much of this correlation has been made on a now thoroughly un-fashionable understanding of 'heresy' (even if it is still evident in some versions of Liberation theology).[27] Few may wish to return to the attacks against 'heresy' and the fiery theological polemics that have bedevilled so much Christian history. Most might now regard as distortions of the Gospel past correlations of opposing theological convictions with 'anarchy', 'immorality' and 'eternal damnation'. It is, nonetheless, still possible that previous attempts to link faith and practice (however distorted) were pointing to a correlation wrongly ignored by contemporary systematic theology.

11.41 This possibility is further strengthened by a study of the New Testament. The mysterious, eschatological parable of the sheep and the goats lays stress upon both the positive and the negative social effects of faith: 'anything you did for one of my brothers here, however humble, you did for me' and 'anything you did not do for one of these, you did not do for me' (Matt. 25.40 & 45). The parable denies, neither the importance of faith nor its eschatological consequences, yet it makes a clear connection between faith and practice. Again, there is the frequent mention by Paul of the 'fruit of the Spirit' and of the changes effected by our life 'in Christ' — all of which are discernible *ante mortem*. And the Johannine Epistles constantly connect faith with its social effects: 'love must not be a matter of words or talk; it must be genuine, and show itself in action' and 'if a man says, "I love God", while hating his brother, he is a liar' (1 John 3.18 & 4.19). James 2 is clearly not alone in connecting faith with practice.

11.42 This connection is again supported by those interpretations of the Synoptic Gospels which hold together the parables and miracles of Jesus. Just as the Synoptic parables are not generally advanced as moral tales, so the miracles are not pre-sented as *ad hoc* acts of human kindness. Instead, both find a common purpose as proclamations and even demonstrations of the Kingdom of God: 'if it is by the finger of God that I drive out the devils, then be sure the Kingdom of God has already come upon you' (Luke 11.20). Further, the whole Passion story in these Gospels becomes, not just an expression of Jesus' faith, but a demonstration of this faith. For Matthew, in particular, as his constant use of Old Testament 'proof texts' indicates, the Passion events served to verify the faith that lay behind them. Here faith was tested, and indeed vindicated, by practice.

11.43 The specific connection here, between the social effects and the validity of particular theological notions must be qualified in a number of ways:

11.44 First, it should be stressed, again, that this is a specifi-cally theological, and not a sociological, claim. From the perspective of the sociologist of religion, there can be no legitimate jump from the social effects of faith to the validity of that faith. In the framework of the type of sociology of religion I proposed in *The Social Context of Theology*, there can be no concern for theological validity. Durkheim's celebrated claim that 'there are no religions which are false . . . all are true in their own fashion',[28] was, it is important to note, a specifically sociological claim. He expressed the conviction that 'it is inadmissible that systems of ideas like religions, which have so considerable a place in history, and to which, in all times, men have come to receive the energy which they must have to live, should be made up of a tissue of illusions'.[29] For Durkheim, religious belief and ritual were 'true', not because he himself was a religious believer (he was not), but because, as a sociologist, he observed that it was a social reality exercising a crucial social function. Similarly, the sociological identification of theology with theodicy[30] affords theology a crucial social function: since theodicy is an omni-present cultural phe-nomenon, theology is, by definition, an omni-present social reality. Nevertheless, in neither instance does the sociologist, as a sociologist, wish to claim that religion or theology really reflect 'the way things are', or that particular expressions of faith 'do justice to God'. The claim is only that religion is a genuine human response to genuine human problems. The theological claim, in contrast, obviously does wish to go further: the Christian theologian *is* concerned to assess how far particular theological notions adequately reflect the object of Christian worship and the claims of the Gospel.

11.45 Secondly, this proposal does not replace the traditional methods of assessing the validity of theological no-tions. One of the criticisms frequently made of Bultmann's theology is that, despite his prodigious biblical scholarship, his whole emphasis is upon the contemporary effects of the Gospel. He shows no interest in historical 'checks' for those effects and leaves us little reason to believe that they are the same today as they always have been.[31] In contrast, my own position does not question the admissibility of historical and philosophical means of assessing particular theological positions. It claims only that social means have been wrongly neglected.

11.46   Thirdly, only provisional validation or falsification can be gleaned from a study of the social effects of theological positions. There are two sides to this crucial claim, one positive and the other negative.

11.47   Negatively, if it can be shown that certain theological notions, as perceived by others, lead to social effects that appear inconsistent with the claims of the Gospel as a whole, then the theologian is given provisional warning that, either they, or the way they are understood, may be false. Naturally, particular theological notions may have different social effects in different social contexts. For example Matt. 27.26 (the so-called Christ-Killer text) has quite different connotations — and possibly effects — today, after the Nazi holocaust, to those intended by the Gospel writer. Theological notions may, indeed, have several effects upon societies. Again, it may not always be easy to be sure of the 'claims of the Gospel' in any particular situation. Modern understandings of the pluriformity of the Gospel makes this particularly difficult.[32] Nonetheless, without having to resort to even more arbitrary external criteria or values, a concern for inner coherence is usually thought to be a proper part of the theologian's task.

11.48   Positively, it is tempting to verify theological notions by the simple pragmatic principle of whether or not they 'work'.[33] Indeed, most people may validate their particular expressions of faith by some such principle, not by their supposed 'empirical fit',[34] or by the additional belief that they will be 'eschatologically verified'.[35] Such a straightforward theological (as distinct from general philosophical) pragmatism has obvious attractions: the social effects of theological notions which accord with the Gospel and with general Christian practice (and in this sense 'work'), would act as 'proof' of the validity of these notions. Unfortunately, expressions of faith that 'work' may still be false. So, the faith of the Jehovah's Witness, that God is to bring the world to an end in the next few years, has undoubted benefits. The individual, thus persuaded, is given a clear incentive to strive hard for the Gospel, to concentrate exclusively upon the Kingdom of God and to live a devoted and faithful life. All of these effects seem to accord thoroughly with the claims of the Gospel and with general Christian practice. An exclusive use of social effects to assess the validity of theological notions — without a parallel philosophical analysis of the grounds on which they are held and an historical analysis of the way God is thought to act by past Christian thinkers — may lead to some curious results.[36] Social means of assessing theological notions can offer only provisional validation or falsification.

11.49 Fourthly, an obvious objection to this proposal is that theologians cannot be held responsible for the social effects of their notions. Thus, if Weber is correct and there really was a connection between the theological notions of Calvin, as popularly perceived, and the moral ideas necessary for the spirit of Capitalism at its inception in the West,[37] Calvin cannot himself be held accountable. According to this view, a theologian should be held accountable only for the ideas he in fact proposes and not for the ideas others perceive him to propose. Thus, the fact that, in the United States, some particularistic expressions of christology and soteriology appear to be strongly correlated with anti-semitism,[38] would not, of itself, necessarily worry their exponents.

11.50 Naturally it may be difficult, at times, actually to demonstrate a link between certain types of practice and particular expressions of faith. From a sociological perspective, measuring the social significance of particular theological positions is undoubtedly difficult — though, as I have tried to demonstrate elsewhere,[39] by no means impossible. However, from a theological perspective, the concept of 'accountability' in this objection involves ethical, rather than theological, considerations. Nevertheless, if sustained, it might place the theologian in an even more isolated role than at present. It has already been argued that he is concerned with communication and that, on this account, he must take seriously the social context within which he operates. What is now claimed is that, in future, his concern for this context should also lead him to study the ways in which his notions are perceived by others and with the potential and actual effects these notions might then have upon them. It is precisely this element of responsibility which many churchmen may feel is lacking amongst a number of critical theologians today and which may lead them to complain so often about the gap between pew and theological faculty. An essential part of the theological task might involve a systematic attempt to assess the possible social effects of *all* theological ideas and positions.

Notes

1. See further, Robin Gill, *The Social Context of Theology* (Mowbrays, 1975) and *Theology and Social Structure* (Mowbrays, 1977).

2. José Míguez Bonino, *Revolutionary Theology Comes of Age* (SPCK, 1975), p. 61.

3. See Roderick Martin, 'Sociology and Theology' in ed. D. E. H. Whiteley and R. Martin, *Sociology, Theology and Conflict* (Blackwell, 1969) [above, *8.21–22*].

4. See further, Gill, *op. cit.* (1975). The concept of 'plausibility structures' is derived from Berger — see especially Peter L. Berger and Thomas Luckmann, *The Social Construction of Reality* (Penguin, 1971) and Berger, *A Rumour of Angels* (Pelican, 1969).

5. One of the main problems in interpreting Bultmann's position lies in his celebrated claim that 'myth should be interpreted not cosmologically, but anthropologically, or better still, existentially' when he has already defined 'mythology' as 'the use of imagery to express the other worldly in terms of this world and the divine in terms of human life' (Rudolf Bultmann, 'New Testament and Mythology' in ed. H. W. Bartsch, *Kerygma and Myth* (SPCK, 1953), p. 10). He makes the claim, precisely because he believes it to be demanded by the scientific view-point of 20th Century man. A number of the contributors to *Kerygma and Myth*, including Thielicke and Schumann, criticise this claim. G. Vaughan Jones, *Christology and Myth in the New Testament* (London, 1965), H. P. Owen in *Kerygma and Myth* and *Revelation and Existence* (Cardiff, 1957), and John Macquarrie, *The Scope of Demythologizing* (SCM, 1960), all raise important difficulties about Bultmann's position.

6. See Karl Mannheim, *Ideology and Utopia* (Routledge and Kegan Paul, 1936) [above, *Extract 6*]; see also D. W. D. Shaw, *The Dissuaders* (SCM, 1978) on reductionist arguments.

7. José Porfirio Miranda, *Marx and the Bible* (Maryknoll, Orbis, 1974): see further, Robin Gill, *A Textbook of Christian Ethics* (T. & T. Clark, 1985).

8. Alfredo Fierro, *The Militant Gospel* (SCM, 1977), p. 373.

9. *Ibid.*

10. *Ibid.* p. 375.

11. *Ibid.* p. 377.

12. *Ibid.* pp. 378–9.

13. *Ibid.* p. 379.

14. Cf. John Rex, *Key Problems of Sociological Theory* (Routledge & Kegan Paul, 1961), and Bernard Barber, 'Toward a New View of the Sociology of Knowledge' in ed. Lewis A. Coser, *The Idea of Social Structure* (Harcourt Brace Jovanovich, 1975).

15. Fierro, *op. cit.*, p. 382.
Cf. Werner Stark, *The Sociology of Knowledge* (Routledge & Kegan Paul, 1956), pp. 26f: though, see Gill, *op. cit.* (1977), pp. 16f.

16. Gill, *op. cit.* (1977), pp. 2–5.

17. Karl Marx and Frederick Engels, *The German Ideology*, ed. C. J. Arthur (Lawrence & Wishart, 1970), p. 47.

18. A very important recent exception is Geoffrey Wainwright's *Doxology* (Epworth, 1980).

19. Talcott Parsons, *The Social System* (Routledge & Kegan Paul, 1951), p. 367.

20. See Roy Wallis, *The Road to Total Freedom: A Sociological Analysis of Scientology* (Heinemann, 1976).

21. See James A. Beckford, *The Trumpet Call of Prophecy* (Blackwell, 1975).
22. Jürgen Moltmann, 'Gott in der Revolution', quoted by Fierro, p. 396.
23. Gustavo Gutiérrez, *A Theology of Liberation* (SCM, 1974), pp. 6f.
24. *Ibid.* p. 10.
25. See especially Bonino, *op. cit.*, and Fierro, *op. cit.*
26. Juan Luis Segundo, *The Liberation of Theology* (Gill and Macmillan, 1977), p. 122.
27. Bonino, *op. cit.*, makes important criticisms of this feature of some Liberation theology.
28. Emile Durkheim, *The Elementary Forms of the Religious Life* (George Allen & Unwin, 1976), p. 3.
29. *Ibid.* p. 69.
30. E.g. by Peter L. Berger in *The Social Reality of Religion* (Faber & Faber, 1969) [see above, **Extract 7**].
31. See further the critics in *Kerygma and Myth* and elsewhere, cited in n. 5 above.
32. Cf. James D. G. Dunn, *Unity and Diversity in the New Testament* (SCM, 1977).
33. Cf. Gutiérrez, *op. cit.*, pp. 10f.
34. See I. T. Ramsey, *Religious Language* (SCM, 1957).
35. See John Hick, 'Theology and Verification' in ed. Hick, *The Existence of God* (Macmillan, 1964).
36. Cf. Fierro, *op. cit.*, pp. 392f.
37. See Max Weber, *The Protestant Ethic and the 'Spirit' of Capitalism* (Scribner, 1958) [above, **Extract 1**].
38. See Charles Y. Glock and Rodney Stark, *Christian Beliefs and Anti-Semitism* (Harper, 1966), and Richard L. Gorsuch and Daniel Aleshire, 'Christian Faith and Prejudice: Review of Research', *Journal for the Scientific Study of Religion*, Vol. 13, No. 3 (1974).
39. See Gill, *op. cit.* (1977).

12

Timothy Radcliffe
A Theological Assessment of Sociological Explanation

This Extract formed chapter 9 of the collection from the Blackfriars Symposium, ed. David Martin, John Orme Mills and W. S. F. Pickering, *Sociology and Theology: Alliance and Conflict* (Harvester, 1980). It originally had the lengthy title, 'Relativizing the Relativizers: a theologian's assessment of the role of sociological explanation of religious phenomena and theology today'. Radcliffe wrote this as a Dominican himself and as Vice-Regent of Studies for the Dominicans in England. It is clear that he writes as a theologian, albeit as one who has an active interest in the sociology of religion and particularly in the work of Peter Berger. Throughout the Extract Radcliffe rejects any form of sociological reductionism (e.g. *12.2* and *12.21*) and insists that 'creative' elements in human thought cannot be 'explained' (or, as I would prefer to say, 'explained away') sociologically. He concludes that sociology does have a positive role in liberating theology from the 'tyranny of the past' (*12.23*) by showing that particular theological controversies are rooted in past social contexts. However, the major part of the Extract is concerned to show that theology and sociology are not complementary disciplines. Theology is rather a 'creative praxis' which can transform our understanding of the world, and even of sociology itself (*12.25*). Indeed, for Radcliffe theology 'explains' nothing: it is an attempt to 'articulate meaning' (*12.4*). Nonetheless, it can be contradicted by various types of explanation (*12.5*): there is a real possibility that sociology and theology may at times conflict with each other. He believes that the genuinely creative aspect of theology is simply inexplicable in sociological terms (*12.14*) and argues at length that Peter Berger's *The Sacred Canopy* (or *The Social Reality of Religion*, its British title, from which **Extract 7** is taken) misunderstands this point (*12.16f.*).

12.1 This book opened with sociologists writing, from different angles, about the ways in which sociology might be a challenge to theology. It is not my intention here to go back over their ground. Mills, in Chapter 8, has tried to illustrate how confused one can sometimes be nowadays about what is 'sociological' and what is 'theological' thinking. It is my aim here to review from a specifically theological standpoint the major issues which have been the concern of this book. First of all we shall look again briefly at the relationship between the sociological explanation of religious phenomena and theological statements about them. Then I shall suggest the limitations of the sociological explanation of *theology itself*. I shall attempt to show why the sociologist is, in reality, neither the theologian's rival nor his executioner, and why, on the contrary, sociological explanation may have an immensely important function within the practice of theology itself.

12.2 It is commonly assumed that sociology and theology provide alternative explanations of religious phenomena. Sociology explains what happens by reference to patterns of social interaction; theology by reference to God's intervention. It would follow, of course, that if the sociological explanation was accepted then the theological explanation would be redundant; there would be no need to bring in God at all. But if one conceives of the relationship between sociological and theological statements in this way, then one is being deceived by the superficial resemblance of their language. Theological references to divine intervention are not, or should not be, understood as explanatory at all. Rather, they are claiming that the events in question are, in some sense, revelatory.

12.3 Let us take the example of the Exodus. The sociologist could attempt to produce a coherent explanation of the event of the Exodus in terms of the social conditions of Egypt in the thirteenth century B.C. He could examine the conflicts between Haipiru and other classes of that society and seek to establish whether they could be identified with the Hebrews of the Bible or not. In principle it might be shown that the Exodus is perfectly comprehensible as one of a number of attempts by oppressed groups within that society to slip across the border and take refuge in the desert. What room would there be left for the theological claim that it was God who led the Israelites out of Egypt? It looks as if the theologian is presenting an alternative explanation of the event, which he would have to justify by demonstrating that there were certain aspects of the Exodus that the sociologist had failed to explain. But this is not the case. The theological claim that it was God who caused the Exodus does not explain how the event happened; it is the recognition of the event as revelatory of God and his purposes. The theological statement is made within the context of a belief in the ultimate destiny of mankind, a destiny that is revealed and achieved in a history. It is claimed that this event is, in some sense, constitutive of this history and revelatory of that destiny. This is not to say that if you were to observe the Exodus you would see the hand of God at work in it, or that the event would have some numinous quality about it that would puzzle the sociologist. The theologian would see just what the sociologist saw, but he would claim to have discerned its significance and its meaning. The point that I am making is not too dissimilar to Evans-Pritchard's insistence that when the Azande explain events in terms of witchcraft they are not rejecting perfectly natural explanations. 'Witchcraft explains *why* events are harmful to man and *how* they happen. A Zande perceives how they happen just as we do. He does not see a witch charge a man but an elephant. He does not see a witch push over the granary, but termites gnawing away its supports. He does not see psychical flame igniting the thatch, but an ordinary lighted bundle of straw. His perception of how events occur is as clear as our own.'[1]

12.4 This distinction between understanding an event, declaring its significance and explaining it, does not mean that the theologian will be utterly indifferent to all possible explanations of religious phenomena, that they are none of his business. Some 'understandings' will clearly exclude some 'explanations'. For example, if I say that God raised Jesus from the dead I am not explaining the emptiness of the tomb but rather articulating the meaning of its emptiness. But my interpretation of the meaning of its emptiness will clearly exclude certain, possibly all, explanations. If someone were to explain that the tomb was empty because the disciples stole the body then this would contradict my understanding of the meaning of the empty tomb.

12.5 Let us take a more trivial example in which the relationship between understanding and explanation is more complex. After the first papal election of 1978, while Cardinal Hume was declaring that Pope John Paul I was 'God's candidate', Vatican watchers were carefully analyzing possible voting combinations and producing a fairly coherent explanation of his election. Of course, Hume would not maintain that he was making a serious theological claim, but it is worth asking whether all possible explanations of the event would be compatible with his interpretation. If it emerged, for example, that Luciani had bribed most of the electorate, then Hume might well wonder whether his interpretation was justified, not because he had been confronted with an alternative and more convincing explanation of the event but because the election would have been shown to be an event of a different sort. He had understood the election to be pregnant with meaning, a revelation of God's purpose for the Church, because he believed it to be the election of a good man. If Luciani turned out to be a wicked briber then his election would have been a different event, the election of a bad man. So if there are conflicts between sociological and theological statements about religious phenomena, then this will not be because they are competing as forms of explanation, but because it might so happen that the sociological explanation implied such a radical redescription of the event that the theologian would have to conclude that it was not in fact open to the sort of significance that he had attributed to it. If a sociologist, for example, explained the career of Jesus in terms of the popular Galilean revolutionary movements of his time, if he saw him as just another Zealot, then he would find himself in conflict with the theologians because the life of such a Jesus could not have been open to the sort of significance that the theologian was claiming to find there. The theologian, therefore, would not be ruling out *all* sociological explanations of the career of Jesus, but merely those implying such a radical redescription of who Jesus was that he could not have been revelatory of God in the way that the theologians claim that he was.

12.6 It is worth remembering that even sociological theories are not value-free. The explanations proposed always derive from and express some prior implicit or explicit interpretation of the meaning of man's existence and destiny. If this interpretation is in profound contradiction with the professed beliefs of the theologian, then it is likely that the theologian will find that the sociological explanations of the events offered will be in contradiction with his interpretation of their meaning and significance. A Marxist sociological explanation of Christianity will be threatening or useful to the theologian to the extent that the ideology that it expresses and of which it is symptomatic is held to be compatible or incompatible with Christian belief. A radically incompatible interpretation of man's destiny and meaning is likely to beget explanations of religious phenomena with which the theologian is unhappy. Of course, the theologian cannot simply dismiss these explanations by showing that they derive from an unacceptable interpretation of the world. If he accepts the validity of sociology as a discipline he will have to maintain that these explanations can be refuted sociologically.

12.7 So far I have been performing a merely negative task by suggesting how sociology and theology do not relate, that is, as alternative forms of explanation. Many sociologists of religion believe that one could describe the relationship between the disciplines more positively as one of complementarity. For example, Robin Gill, in his book *The Social Context of Theology*, maintains that they offer alternative perspectives on the world, that they work in terms of alternative 'as if' methodologies which do not compete but which complement each other. Unfortunately Gill never spells out at length what constitutes the theological perspective and therefore what sort of complementarity it might have with the sociological perspective; but he does give an example which is illuminating. He refers to Maurice Wiles' suggestion that when the theologian considers the doctrine of creation he is obliged to employ two 'stories', the one scientific-historical and the other mythological. He quotes Wiles:

> On the one hand we tell the scientific story of evolution; it is the real world as it has developed with which the doctrine of creation is concerned, not with some ideal world of the theological imagination. But in addition we tell a frankly mythological story about the spirit of God moving on the face of the chaotic waters, about God taking the dust of the earth, making man in his own image, and breathing upon him so that he becomes a living soul. If we know what we are doing we can weave the two stories together in poetically creative ways — as indeed the poet combines logically disparate images into new and illuminating wholes.[2]

12.8 Like Gill, I accept this description of the task of the theologian, but we interpret Wiles' position quite differently. Gill sees here an example of the complementarity of two 'as if' methodologies, that of the theologian and that of the scientist, and in this a model for the relationship between sociology and theology. He says, 'Wiles' depiction of the theologian's task in terms of "mythology" may or may not be satisfactory. Yet his main point remains. It is important to maintain that the theologian's methodology is complementary, not in opposition, to scientific methodology'.[3] But I understand Wiles to be suggesting that the theologian's task is to weave together the mythological and scientific 'stories' in a creative and illuminating way. The mythological story is not for us a transparent theological statement, and it is certainly not the task of the theologian to repeat it. He has to make sense of it by establishing a relationship between it and contemporary understandings of creation. So what we have here is not an example of the complementarity of the scientific and theological methodologies, but a description of the theologian's task as the establishment of an illuminating relationship between two disparate accounts of the origins of our world. The theologian is only able to perform this task in so far as he can transcend the mythological perspective himself and so bring it into an illuminating relationship with a quite different perspective. The theological 'perspective' is the product of the encounter of these two 'stories'.

12.9 The time has come to propose a definition of theology that will enable us to specify its relationship with sociology. Cornelius Ernst defined theology thus: 'Theology is an encounter of Church and world in which the meaning of the gospel becomes articulate as an illumination of the world'.[4] The theologian has the essentially creative task of making sense of the gospel in the light of contemporary experience, and of making sense of contemporary experience in the light of the gospel. His role is not simply to repeat religious formulae, whether they come from the gospels or from his own tradition, but to illuminate them by bringing them into relationship with the contemporary experience of meaning. The New Testament is a theological work precisely because it represents the initial encounter of Church and world, in which the gospel became articulate as an illumination of that world. It expresses that first encounter of the gospel with Judaism and Hellenism. It remains the permanently normative instance of creative transformation. We will all recognize in our respective traditions other, though less normative, theological 'monuments'. For a Roman Catholic one might be that encounter of the gospel and Aristotelianism in the thirteenth century that culminated in the theology of Thomas Aquinas, the disclosure of a new, deep understanding of the gospel and a transformation of Aristotelianism. It should be clear now why I do not think that it is legitimate to talk of a 'theological perspective'. If the task of the theologian is to provoke and enable a mutually illuminating encounter between the gospel and contemporary understandings of man and his destiny, then he cannot bring to that task a ready-made perspective. Whatever perspective may arise must be engendered by the encounter and not brought to it. One might, for example, wish to talk of a Thomist perspective, a Thomist 'way of looking at things', but would it make more sense to say that Thomas shared this perspective with non-Christian Aristotelians or with non-Aristotelian Christians? The question is obviously inappropriate. One might even wish to say that theology does not have a permanent and coherent language of its own. Of course, there is a whole vocabulary of theological words such as 'grace', 'justification', 'salvation', etc., but they only remain properly 'theological' for us as long as they remain capable of making possible that creative encounter.

12.10 So theology is not a 'discipline' in any ordinary sense of the word, and its relationship to sociology cannot, therefore, be that of one discipline to another. They are not complementary perspectives or methodologies, for theology, in itself, has neither a particular perspective or methodology. It is rather that praxis or activity by which the meaning of the gospel becomes articulate as the illumination of the world, and by which the meaning that men succeed in making of themselves and their experience is transformed to become a disclosure of that meaning of meaning that we call God.

12.11 One might object at this point that it is nonsense to deny that theology is an academic discipline, given that there are, whether one likes it or not, 'professional' theologians, degrees in theology, theological journals and so on. I would reply that these 'theological disciplines' which we find practised in the universities are properly theological not because they employ rational, coherent and critical modes of discourse, but because such forms of discourse, especially philosophy and history, have been important ways in which man has attempted to interpret his experience, and therefore are potentially theological. It follows that the relationship between theology and sociology within our universities will often be that between a philosophical or historical perspective that has been transformed in the light of the gospel and a sociology which has not been so transformed. But there is no reason why sociology itself should not provide an alternative locus for the encounter of gospel and world. One must remember, however, that there are all sorts of other less academic ways in which men seek to make sense of their experience, through poetry, drama, painting, music, etc., and any of these activities are potentially theological in that the meaning they make is capable of disclosing that most ultimate depth of meaning which we believe was revealed in the life, death and resurrection of Jesus Christ. I would not be happy with any definition of theology that excluded, for example, the poems of St John of the Cross, which are the secular love songs he heard outside his prison walls transformed in the light of the gospel.

12.12 One might also protest that if one identifies theology as an essentially creative praxis, then one is excluding from the fold all those theologians who write the boring humdrum books that fill the shelves of our theological libraries. I would reply that they can be accepted as genuine theologians only in the sense that they perpetuate or extend some original and creative theological insight. Thus the theological perspectives of Thomas, Luther, Barth, etc., will continue to be explored by their disciples, but many of these disciples will only be creative by virtue of some sort of participation in the original, founding, creative praxis of their masters.

12.13 Having made those provisos, I would still wish to assert that theology is, in itself, neither an explanation of the world, nor a perspective, nor a methodology. But the fact still remains that theologians make theological statements. In what sense may sociology be said to explain these statements? Theological statements are, after all, examples of language, and one of the functions of sociology is to explain the relationship between social structures and language. Could sociology therefore demonstrate that theological statements are merely epiphenomenal, the products of patterns of social interaction? Theology may not fear sociology as a rival, but might not sociology relativize theology out of existence?

12.14 If theology is the attempt to make sense of the gospel and the world in the mutually illuminating moment of their encounter, then the limitations of sociological explanation will be determined by the extent to which sociology can be held to explain man's attempts to make sense creatively of himself and the world. Theology is as inexplicable in sociological terms as those other activities that man practises when he attempts to explore and establish the meaning of his existence, whether through philosophy, poetry, drama or even sociology! A sociologist who explores the relationship between social structures and language will misunderstand the limitations of the explanations that he proposes if he misconceives the relationship between language and meaning.

12.15 A poem or a piece of theology or a play is meaningful not merely in virtue of being an example of a particular language but because of what it *does* with that language. *Hamlet*, for instance, is certainly significant and meaningful as an example of Elizabethan English. If there had not been such a thing as Elizabethan English then there could never have been that play which we call *Hamlet*. A sociologist could establish a relationship between that language and the structures of Elizabethan society, and in that sense he could be said to 'explain' *Hamlet*. But of course this play is not merely an instance of Elizabethan English but a creative use of it. It stretches the language in all sorts of unaccustomed ways, uses metaphors and analogies and poetically engenders new meaning in a way that a knowledge of Elizabethan English would not enable one to anticipate. Therein lies the limitations of sociological explanation confronted with any creative praxis, including theology.

12.16 I shall illustrate my thesis by looking at the work of one social theorist, Peter Berger, who does misconceive the relationship between language and meaning and who therefore, I believe, misrepresents the relationship between sociological explanation and theology. It is true that he is primarily concerned not with theology but with religion, but it is clear that he believes that his sort of explanation would apply to theology itself, particularly when he is considering the question of theodicy.

12.17 Throughout his book *The Sacred Canopy* Berger makes an explicit identification between meaning and order or *nomos*. The meaning that man projects upon the universe, the order that he establishes, is always threatened by collapse and potential chaos because of the inability of any order to organize the whole of human experience. Man therefore requires religion to legitimize this projected order, this *nomos*, by claiming that it is inevitable and sacred.

> Religion legitimates so effectively because it relates the precarious reality constructions of empirical societies with ultimate reality. The tenuous realities of the social world are grounded in the sacred *realissimum*, which by

definition is beyond the contingencies of human meanings and human activity.[5]

Berger therefore maintains that religion is inherently a conservative force, since its function is to consecrate the *status quo*. If the task of religion, and so of theology, is to bestow or reveal some ultimate meaning, and if meaning is the order that society projects upon the universe, then religion cannot but be seen as the consecration of the structures of society.

12.18 Can we really be satisfied with such a definition of meaning? Is meaning simply equatable with order? Berger tells us that animals live in perfectly ordered worlds determined by their instinctual structures. Does this mean that the mouse rejoices in a plenitude of meaning that man can never hope to enjoy? On the contrary, I believe that man is only driven to question the meaning of anything and everything because he finds himself at the intersection of many orders, employing many languages, playing many roles. It is the plurality of *nomoi* that provokes the question of meaning. The mouse could never ask about the meaning of being a mouse because he could never be anything else. Because the structures and order of its life are unalterably given, the question of meaning could not arise. Now sociology can demonstrate the relationship between social structures and the various languages that are employed within a society, but it cannot explain the creative interpretations that man makes of his experience when he finds himself at the point of intersection of different roles and discourses. It is precisely at these moments that men find themselves driven to articulate their self-understanding, whether in terms of philosophy, theology or poetry, not through the affirmation of the given orders of meaning but rather through the evocation of an order that cannot be fully stated. If theology, or indeed any other creative praxis, simply legitimized society with all its contradictions and conflicts then it would not give meaning to man's experience. It would simply rule out the question of meaning and make man's experience of meaninglessness appear to be inevitable.

12.19 When Berger is considering the role of theology as theodicy, he appeals to the book of Job. But in Job the sufferings of the innocent man are never legitimized by the articulation of an explicit overarching *nomos* in which they are given meaning. These sufferings only make sense in terms of an order, 'the wisdom of God', which can never be made explicit, merely glimpsed. In the final moment of vision, Job confesses: 'I have heard of thee by the hearing of the ear, but now my eye sees thee: therefore I despise myself and repent in dust and ashes'.[6] Berger cites only the second half of Job's confession and claims it as evidence that Job's sufferings are justified by his sinfulness. This is a misinterpretation of the whole book. Job suffers because he and his companions have absolutized a *nomos*, the wisdom tradition, which is unable to interpret his experience and which therefore drives him to accuse God. He only comes to understanding in that vision of God, which explains nothing. The book of Job is not an example of the legitimization of suffering by the affirmation of a *nomos* which confirms the structures of society. It demonstrates the way in which our *nomoi* break down in their attempts to explain. Job passes from explanation to understanding in a moment of vision — from theory to *theoria*.

12.20 Berger himself is unable to sustain this oversimple identification of meaning and order. In the second half of the book he operates with an alternative and implicit definition of meaning which might be described as 'self-awareness'. All true knowledge is knowledge of oneself. The ultimate truth is the truth of man himself. This becomes particularly evident in Berger's interpretation of the relationship between religion and alienation. He defines alienation as 'the process whereby the dialectical relationship between the individual and his world is lost to consciousness. The individual "forgets" that this world was and continues to be co-produced by him'.[7] Religion is an alienating force because, by consecrating the meaningful order that man projects upon the universe, it conceals from man the fact that order derives from himself. Thus it induces a 'false consciousness'. The implication is that true salvation, the return to 'true consciousness', is achieved in that moment in which man becomes aware of himself as the origin of the meaningful order that he has projected. The same *nomos* which in the first part of the book was identified with meaning is here claimed to be 'the alien', that which stands between man and true self-awareness. I believe that the plot or play of Berger's book hinges upon the uneasy and shifting relationship between these two definitions of meaning as order and as self-awareness. Meaning as order must always seek to establish itself as total and all-embracing; meaning as self-awareness must always attempt to undermine the facticity and givenness of the projected order. Of course religion and theology have to be identified with meaning as order, since the alternative definition excludes the knowledge of anything other than man himself.

12.21 I have attempted this analysis of Berger's text in order to illustrate my thesis that man's attempts to make sense of his experience always involve a creative praxis, in this case involving the play between two definitions of meaning. Sociology can demonstrate the relationship between social structures and forms of language, but man's search for meaning involves an irreducible creativity which it cannot explain. Berger invites us to relativize the relativizers. It would be amusing to do just that and attempt a sociological analysis of *The Sacred Canopy*. Berger was born in Vienna in 1929 and came to America when he was seventeen. His formative years were spent in a highly structured society threatened by *anomie*. He then experienced the transition to a far more fluid, mobile and individualistic society with a different value system and a different conception of meaning. It would be tempting to explain this text as a product of the experience of these two societies, a conversation between a Viennese past and an American present. My thesis is that even if we did produce a convincing sociological analysis of the text we would still have failed to explain what he had done with these experiences. We could analyze what he said in terms of the different social structures in which he had been formed, but we could not explain his creative attempt to make sense of this complex experience. One may either participate in it as an event of meaning or not. Even one's relativizing of the relativizers is limited.

12.22 On 30 June 1860, when Wilberforce, the Bishop of Oxford, attempted to refute Darwinism during his confrontation with Huxley in the University Museum, he defined man as *homo poeticus*. Even though I do not agree with Wilberforce's conclusions, I believe that one should justify theology, and indeed any other creative praxis, in the face of any attempt at sociological reductionism, by an appeal to man as 'poetic' or creative. Man is the one who is capable of new meaning. This novelty is achieved through what Eliot called 'the intolerable wrestle with words', through metaphor and analogy, through the creative interplay of different modes of discourse. Any such discourse can be said to be 'theological' when the meaning that it generates is claimed to be revelatory of the meaning of meaning that we call God, when this new meaning is accepted as a disclosure of 'the transcendent novelty of the God who creates, liberates and renews'.[8]

12.23 Having suggested what are, I believe, the limitations of the sociological explanation of religious phenomena and of theology, I shall now attempt to say why, nevertheless, I believe sociology to be potentially a very useful and liberating discipline for the theologian. In *A Rumour of Angels*, Berger tells us that 'while other analytical disciplines free us from the dead weight of the past, sociology frees us from the tyranny of the present'.[9] I think that sociology can free the theologian from the tyranny of the past as well. By showing how the theological statements of his tradition are in fact formulated in languages that reflect the social structures of quite different societies, the sociologist can free the theological from the temptation merely to repeat what has been said before. Once the theologian has been brought to see how the language that is used is a

human product, the function of particular patterns of social interaction, then he is liberated from naive biblical or dogmatic literalism.
Of course, one hopes that this initial distancing of the text is just the
first step towards a more profound re-appropriation. But once he has
come to discern the strangeness of the language, as the product of an
alien way of life, then he might be able to see how it is more than that:
that it is a creative and revelatory use of that language. He must let the
text be drawn far from him if he is to come close to it again and
participate in it as an event of meaning, just as in one's ordinary
experience of human relationships one must sometimes discover how
different someone is from oneself before one can rediscover a unity at
a more profound depth of one's humanity.

12.24 Let us take the example of the Chalcedonian Definition. All too often Roman Catholic theologians have
given up biblical fundamentalism, only to cling all the more firmly to
dogmatic literalism. But one can only discover a proper loyalty to the
Chalcedonian Definition if one has come to understand it not as an
eternal solution to the 'problem' of the person of Christ but as an
attempt to evoke the mystery of his person through the creative
interplay of two quite different theological languages, Alexandrian
and Antiochean. These two theological languages, in turn, must be
understood as reflecting the two quite different societies that produced them; Alexandria with its philosophical tradition and history of
autocratic government, and Antioch with its tradition of rhetoric and
democracy. It is only when one has distanced oneself from the text
through some such sociological analysis that one can re-appropriate the
Definition as a subtle and profound attempt to lead one into the
mystery of Christ's person through the mutual qualification of these
different discourses. One has to lose the text in order to rediscover it as
poetic, creative and deeply theological, and thus come to see what
loyalty to its insights might demand. The sociologist can liberate the
theologian by helping him to let go.

12.25 These appear, then, to be two ways in which theology
and sociology might relate. First of all, the sociological
exploration of the relationship between language and social structures
can liberate the theologian from a false understanding of his own
tradition. Second, the theologian should recognize that sociology is
not merely explanatory. It is one valid way in which man attempts to
make sense of himself and his experience. And so sociology can itself
provide a locus for the encounter of gospel and world. This encounter
would take place not through the theologian importing a particular
'theological perspective', but rather by the internal transformation of
sociology itself.

Notes

1. Evans-Pritchard, E. E. *Witchcraft, Oracles and Magic among the Azande* (Oxford, 1937) p. 72.
2. Wiles, M. F. 'Does Christianity Rest on a Mistake?' in S. W. Sykes and J. P. Clayton (eds) *Christ, Faith and History* (London, 1972) p. 8.
3. Gill, R. *The Social Context of Theology* (London & Oxford, 1975) p. 134.
4. Ernst, G. 'Theological Methodology' in Karl Rahner *et al.* (ed.) *Sacramentum Mundi*, English translation Vol. 6 (London & New York) p. 218.
5. Berger, P. L. *The Sacred Canopy* (New York, 1967); Eng. edn *The Social Reality of Religion* (Harmondsworth) p. 41.
6. Job 42: 5f. (RSV tr.)
7. Berger, *op. cit.* p. 92.
8. Ernst, C. *The Theology of Grace* (Cork, 1974) p. 80.
9. Berger, P. L. *A Rumour of Angels* (New York, 1968); Eng. edn (Harmondsworth) p. 62.

13

David Martin
Transcendence and Unity

This Extract is the first chapter of David Martin's *The Breaking of the Image* (Blackwell, 1980) originally delivered by Martin, professor of sociology at the London School of Economics and subsequently also a non-stipendiary Anglican priest, as the Gore Lectures at Westminster Abbey in 1977. Characteristically the book reflects both Martin's interests as a sociologist and also his theological, and especially liturgical, interests. The central concern of the book is with religious signs and symbols. Martin maintains that they are crucial means of religious socialisation, that they both constrain religious communities and thereby give them an identity, and that they also provide the means for religions to shape society and to be socially significant. Because these signs and symbols are of interest to him as both sociologist and theologian it is sometimes difficult to be certain which mode of understanding is uppermost. In this Extract he focuses upon the key symbols/signs of 'transcendence' (*13.3f.*) and 'unity' (*13.16f.*). He is aware that viewing symbols/signs as social phenomena produces a confusing picture. In the next chapter he describes the paradox that becomes evident as follows: 'the aspiration to unity and the abolition of partitions has to be protected by the distinction between church and world and between church and state. This runs parallel to the paradox that the hope of equality is kept in being by the discipline of hierarchy among the brothers. And the possibility of revolutionary change has to be conserved in the cycle of liturgy . . . revolutions are so intensely conservative' (p. 26). Martin is fully aware that churches as churches tend to adjust to the world in a manner less typical of sects (*13.33* — cf. *Extract 4* and *Extract 5*), but towards the end of the book he maintains that liturgy, and especially the eucharist, is sometimes able to go beyond this: here there is an impulse 'towards a unification: the breaking down of the middle wall of partition, the abolition of the rail between sacred and secular or between church and world, the creation of a new, unified space where "they may all be one". But the recalcitrance of "the world" means that we must still distinguish between church and world, and the limits of our situation means that we must re-build partitions' (pp. 126–127). From this, and from the Extract itself, it is evident that Martin treats religious signs and symbols both as dependent social variables (entities that are shaped by society) and as independent social variables (entities that may in turn shape society). The subtlety of his analysis is that he moves so often between these two possibilities. However, it is this subtlety, combined with his combination of sociological and theological perspectives, which makes this Extract surprisingly difficult to assimilate. Martin's own summary at the start of the next chapter is helpful: 'The sign of transcendence concerns the beyond and therefore implies that men must go into that beyond. What is still to come has an open texture, it may be named, and yet may not be named. Men seek after it and are impelled to choose it. The sign of transcendence creates movement and *the* movement: it is a sign for coming and going. The sign of unity is cognate with the sign of transcendence. It contains the most powerful and wide-ranging resonance: the unity of God's people, the solidarity of man, the idea of solidarity against evil, the aspiration for the one true primal speech, the unity of knowledge and science and of the world itself. The potent idea of the one and the true, the truth of unity and the unity of truth, is a two-edged sword. Those who unite in truth and solidarity are divided from those who do not. Unity is a social wedge, cutting into the diversity of cultures and gods, creating division' (p. 17).

13.1 A sociologist has no remit to talk about God. If he were to talk directly about God he would immediately convert himself into a theologian or a philosopher of history or a prophet. To speak of God in the world is an act of unveiling. A prophet looks at the seeming flux of events and discerns the finger of God. He brings out the invisible writing and identifies it as *the* true Word. It is no business of the sociologist to distinguish the true and lively word from any other statement.

13.2 Sociologists are scientific scribes concerned with verifiable and falsifiable statements and with more or less correct propositions about social processes. They try to transcribe what happens as accurately as they can and give a reasoned account of the rules that undergird what happens. They make connected sense out of the patterns that are thrown onto their field of social vision and hope that this connected sense is more controlled, more rich and rigorous than everyday observation. Most everyday observation is *ad hoc* wisdom, or proverbial *nous*, broad expectations built out of the stuff of experience, without much attempt at refinement or interconnection. Sociologists are specialists in social connections and in making that web of connection tighter and more comprehensive. But that has nothing to do with finding the finger of God, unless of course his finger is in the making of every social pie. If that is so they may safely ignore him. If God is up to everything then his activity may be elided. A God who contributes nothing distinctive does not matter, so far as social science is concerned.

13.3 So sociologists cannot point out 'God' because that is a normative activity outside the remit of science; and they cannot take account of what is merely coextensive with the whole. It is impossible to pick out a particular word and say *this* is *the* Word or to identify the Word of God with the sum total of everything that is said. So what is there to say?

13.4 Suppose we ask how men transcend their situations. Perhaps the proper adjunct to thinking normatively about God's activity is thinking positively about man's activity. I do not mean that one can make a transition from describing the activity of man to discerning the activity of God. But it could be that the act of describing, interpreting and ordering man's activity, that is sociology, can be used to circumscribe how we talk about God.

13.5 So when we describe man's activity as a social being we cannot insert a separate mysterious X as a God variable. God is not part of the ensemble of variables. Nor is he a residual factor left over when the rest of the variance has been satisfactorily accounted for. Of course, sociology is constantly confronted by left-overs. That doesn't mean we can identify God as the murky residuum of multi-variate analysis. So I have already excluded two notions. God is not the Ensemble of all that is, that is the Totality, the All. Nor is He an Unexplained Remainder. There is not much interest in a God who is nothing in particular because everything in general, nor in a God who has been remaindered.[1] To put the matter epigrammatically: God is not *the* whole, nor is he *a* hole. A hole-in-the-multi-factor-analysis God will not *do* and cannot *be*.

13.6 The point can be extended a little before passing on. Social activity comprises rule-governed processes which are in principle understandable and explicable. We may find them surprising from time to time, but they do not come as bolts from the blue. Social activity is no more visited from the blue than meteorology is disturbed by bolts from heaven. It follows that there is no room for a trickster-God or a being who suddenly suspends the rules for a brief period of pure inexplicable activity. A social mutation may occur but it does so within the ambit of understandable processes in which we discern no intruding arbitrary element. Social mutations are on all fours with natural mutations insofar as our webs of explanation do not require a randy spontaneous Divine Pusher. Indeed, there is another similarity. Most natural mutations are regressive, and only a few are eventually selected out of the range of mutations. Likewise most social mutations are defective and only a few survive the complex challenges of changing social environments.

13.7 However, at this point we have to pause and distinguish rather carefully. Social mutations are not discrete entities, confronting an environment. Societies are organic and continuous, and involve constant shifts, adaptations, adjustments. They absorb shock and incorporate experience. This does not mean that they are entirely shaped by the learning process, because they already possess a semi-determinate character. They have acquired profiles and their mode of adaptation is consistent with those profiles. A social group is of a particular sort and it will breed characteristic kinds of action and response. Yet the human beings who comprise a social group are not determined. They learn over time and envisage alternatives or variations. Men cognize their situation and recognize certain potentialities in those situations. Thus once cultural evolution takes off it is relatively swift in its operations.

13.8 This cultural evolution is one aspect of consciousness. We do not know how the germ of consciousness grew but it is abundantly clear that awareness of self and others and the world enormously accelerates the processes of change. It is equally clear that there is a further acceleration once men grasp the fact that they can play a part in their own development and can re-act back on the slower processes of biological change. Consciousness is one great shift; consciousness of what consciousness can achieve is another great shift.

13.9 These standard observations are a necessary prolegomenon to the main issue, which is man's ability to transcend and transform his situation. However, this potential is rooted in limitation and constriction. An enormous amount has to be 'given' before men can even begin to envisage that which is not 'given'. The open-ended possibility cannot occur without an antecedent programme which is both genetic and social. Unless the biological base is automatic and the social base carefully programmed in terms of rote, role and rite the take-off cannot occur. Of course there is much dispute at the moment between sociobiologists, biologists and sociologists as to the precise point where the programmes initiated by socialization take over from the basic biological programmes. For this present discussion the line of demarcation hardly matters. The enormous variability of man's social arrangements and his cultural worlds at least suggests that a substantial sector of biological openness has been preempted by socialization. And since the patterns of socialization once set up remain fairly stable it seems that socialization involves a substantial degree of closure. So the human being is doubly stabilized by biological inheritance and by the patterning of culture as imprinted by socialization.

13.10 The central point is that man cannot envisage what transcends his situation unless he is built up and stabilized by heavy programming. What is not set cannot see. A man cannot speak a new word unless the basic grammar has been already imprinted in his system. He cannot initiate a new practice unless socialization has cut down the enormous range of social options to a limited more or less coherent sector. Socialization selects a limited group out of the overall range of social options and gives them a minimal coherence. Without the bio-grammar and the pre-selection of a particular limited language of social intercourse the human being would be destabilized.

13.11 Without stability and without fixed points in the social universe it is impossible to generate new combinations and initiate alternatives. Without the given there can be no alternatives: no Alter, no Other. This is not to say that every set of givens contains equal potential for alternatives. Some of the options selected by socialization contain more potential for alternatives than others. Some societies, perhaps most, succeed too well in the primary task of stabilization. They over-conform to the pattern, and the imprint of the sacred template bites too deep to move beyond stability. Conquest or cultural contact may distrupt the stability but without such intrusions and disruptions the pattern tends to reproduction rather than development. Since the necessary condition of any creativity is a given and accepted pattern the majority of societies become over-adjusted and stabilized.

13.12 So we have an array of social patterns each of which has cut a limited sector out of the full arc of social possibilities. All of them embody closure in order to survive but some embody more closure than others. It is, for example, perfectly possible for the bio-grammar to be supplemented by a completely formulaic version of socialization. The little sect of John the Baptist Christians is organized almost entirely in terms of verbal and ritual formulae. Or again, upper-class Tibetans employ forms of speech bound in by proverbs and formulae. The formulae ensure stability but inhibit creativity. No contrary vision can disturb the repetitions. Culture becomes almost entirely cyclic. It turns for ever round and round. The cycle is necessary to existence, but once it becomes all-pervasive transformation is inhibited.

13.13 The cycles of repetition and stabilization are not inevitable. Some societies will explore those sectors of social option which allow a historical trajectory: the idea of moving through time to a new era. They will achieve a creative balance between necessary stability and destructive openness. Their view of the world will have an open texture which can be exploited. How does that open texture work?

13.14 In such societies the basic images, words and acts go beyond reflection of what already exists. These societies contain possibilities and potentialities as well as reflections of the *status quo*. The Word and the Image transcend the ensemble of what is, and are able to suggest what might be. In the vast majority of societies of course the images and words will project what is, providing a screen on which the social order is writ large. That screen will contain the credits of the society, its company charter, its foundation stories, its sense of distinctive identity, its sanctions and prescriptions, the categories in which it organizes the social and natural worlds. Indeed, every society will project its identity onto a screen and individual members will then absorb and introject that projection, making the social image their own. A society *is* a shared image; and it is also an idea as to which groups are brought together by that image. Not even those societies where the images encapsulate other possibilities can escape the compulsory screening of the *status quo* and the limiting definitions of social self and social identity.

13.15 What are the alternative possibilities I have mentioned above? How do they work? Here I must restrict myself to some of the possibilities and potentialities best known to ourselves in our own society and derived from the Jewish tradition. The Confucian tradition, for example, lies closer to the extant reality of societies. In India some traditions reject the social image wholesale in order to protect the comprehensive withdrawal from the given found in classical Buddhism. One thing only needs to be said at this juncture about the major religions which stem from roots other than that of Judaism. Taken together with religions based on Judaism, they comprise a basic limited set of perspectives on the world. Out of the immense variety of projections and possible social perspectives, there seems to emerge a limited number of basic generators, each of which contains a more or less coherent splay of potentialities and correlative limitations. In the world religions the chaos of options is dramatically reduced to half a dozen or so fundamental visions, each of which allows a particular range of developments, a set of possibilities. The sets overlap; they may meet, mingle and combine. But the distinctive, logically separate roots remain. There are various criteria by which these roots may be categorized and distinguished, such as, for example, Weber's 'Religious Rejections of the World and their direction'. Perhaps the fundamental criterion turns on the vision of 'the world'. Is God (or Truth) to be discovered in the world as it is, or in the world as it may be, or in a harmonized version of the present world, or away from the world in the recesses of self and not-self? There is, in other words, a continuum of degrees and kinds of transcendence.

13.16 As I have suggested, each root contains a specific range of potentialities and constraints. In the case of those religions deriving from the Judaic stem, the potentiality centres on positive transcendence and the idea of unity. The transcendent God is one. This is the word and the image. Men grasp at what goes beyond them and at the concept of the One. Because the one God transcends the world as it is and as we know it, His name and His image are both known and unknown. He is revealed and hidden; his name can be spoken and must not be spoken; He is like unto this and like unto that but He has no graven image. To whom then will ye liken God?

13.17 To what does the unity of God refer? To transcend is to go beyond. So we must name it and refuse to name it. Men point towards something and declare that it resists definition and nomenclature. Out of this positive and this negative various possibilities may emerge. One is to bow before the decree of the unknown. The Almighty One has spoken: we obey. Another is to embody that decree in human exploits, more especially conquests, crusades, and holy wars. God's people enforce God's will. Yet another is to refuse to identify any human concept or notion or institution with the transcendent, and therefore to leave an open space in which man may share an undisclosed future with God. This is the way of negative theology: God is not a body, He is without passions or parts. So the idea of transcendence allows various combinations of obedience and co-operative sharing, of certainty and uncertainty. Men are not entirely disobedient to the heavenly vision and are ready to place their will in the hand of God, going out not knowing whither they go. Clearly this vision is open-ended, demanding and requiring move-ment and obedience, but not specifying the end or filling in the objective. It is a mighty Rorschach blot from which men draw ends and conclusions. They may pursue a holy war in the name of the supreme decree, or go on a pilgrimage to the holy land, or journey to some undiscovered country or celestial city. But whether it is holy war, pilgrimage or journey, there is certainly movement. The very ideas of movement and of *the* movement lie embedded in the apprehension of transcendence. To go beyond is to go *into* the beyond.

13.18 It follows that the idea of transcendence must include the possibility of alienation. The alien looks forward, upward and away. Of course, if a man bows before the supreme decree and sees God's rule in all that is, he may consent to the world as presently constituted and be at home in it. Islam is just such a way of being at home in the world, and there is much in Judaism that rejoices in the constitution of things as they are. This acceptance of the world is only a limited good. When men are too much at home in things as they are, and suppose that 'whatever is, is right' then they are aliens to the possibility of a new heaven and new earth. Yet those who already claim their citizenship is in heaven can be alien to the normal joys of creation, procreation and recreation. There is a very nice point between the pleasures of earth and the hope of heaven which is impossible to reach and sustain. Moreover, although it is true that transcendence allows the emergence of open alternatives, yet the inevitable association between the transcendent cosmic powers and human political powers means that the forces of change may need to attack even the idea of transcendence from time to time. In so doing they are undermining their own long-term foundations.

13.19 Yet the radical strain remains active, capable of taking men away from home, or turning them into aliens who seek after another home. The beyond intrudes on the given, revealing its limits and inciting men to uncover new potentialities. The transcendent makes limitation visible. It works in the imperative mood and employs the verbs of coming and going:

'Arise, go down to meet Ahab King of Israel.'
'Arise, go to Nineveh, that great city.'
'Let us now go even unto Bethlehem . . . '
'Go ye into all the world . . . '
'Surely I come quickly . . . '
'The Spirit and the bride say, Come . . . '

Coming and going are the verbs of movement. Command is the characteristic mood of the Word.

13.20 Coming and going, alienation and movement are associated with roads and highways, and also with the imagery of marching and battle. These comings and goings can be cast in the mould of actual warfare, crusades and holy wars. Or else they can be cast in the mould of spiritual warfare. There is on the one hand the marchings of Joshua, Mahomet, Cromwell, or Charlemagne; and on the other hand there are the journeys of Paul, or Francis, or Columba, or George Fox. The military comings and goings demand discipline; the spiritual warfare demands discipleship. This brings us back to the idea of obedience and of subjection. The freedom to move and to create movements depends on discipline and obedience. Every army, and every peaceful brotherhood for that matter, obeys a rule. Freedom is linked to authority. The transcendent impels. When men envisage their freedom to move they are moved by an impulsion. This is the source of very paradoxical language and of considerable philosophical perplexity. When a man is confronted by the transcendent claim there is no choice but to obey. He makes God's will his own and is thereby free. He finds that service is perfect freedom.[2]

13.21 So the idea of the transcendent includes in it a wide-ranging vocabulary: a fundamental grammar of motives. This comprises coming and going, pursuit and alienation, pilgrimage and arrival, the free acceptance of service, the compelling nature of choice. The characteristic images are the highway and the city, the exodus and the promised land. One says that the idea of the transcendent *includes* this vocabulary because there seems to be a dialectic of quiescence and movement. Transcendence can also be deployed as the legitimation of whatever is established. Things are established by God so that they *cannot* be moved. A commandment descends from God to man and man must obey the rules. Man bows before the weight of the given and cannot imagine how anything might be otherwise. How should he question what 'Th' unsearchable dispose of highest wisdom brings about'?

13.22 So much for part of the vocabulary of motives pendant on the idea of transcendence. It is not that there is a unique association between transcendence and movement or that movement is impossible without the idea of transcendence. There is no need to assert unique correlations. It is simply that movement is one important potentiality lying within transcendence. It is at least notable that the three movements deriving from this idea — Christianity, Islam and Marxism — comprise cultural areas which now contain the majority of the human race.

13.23 What then of unity? God goes beyond the given; He is also *one*.

13.24 Speaking of the oneness of God I am largely setting on one side generalized ideas of a high god, or a president of the immortals, or intimations of One who lies beyond the apparent diversity of phenomena and above the godlings which represent those phenomena. I am thinking rather of the divine unity as a fiercely apprehended principle which disdains the idols of the heathen and rejects henotheistic compromise. 'The Lord our God is one Lord, beside Him is none else.' The faith in the divine unity *also* generates a vocabulary of motives. These are centred first of all around the invocation of unity in general: the unity of a People and then the unity of mankind. But those who resist unity constitute the 'other', the contrary. There is no invocation of the one which does not engender the contrary; and no unification which does not encounter diversity. Unity must engender duality: us, them, those who inherit the promises and those who do not.

13.25 If God is one, then His people must be one, and the rest are those who lie outside the house and covenant of Israel. A passionate belief in unity unifies the community and expels all those who do not share the faith or honour the covenant between God and His people. The unity of God means that men may fall away from Him and from His people. The ordinary distinctions between in-group and out-group acquire a new edge. Indeed, the seductions of the diverse world outside reinforce that edge. The divine unity is encased in the corporate consciousness of Israel. The normal tendency to remove intrusive elements and maintain minimal group homogeneity is reinforced by the belief in the homogeneity of the divine. The demarcations which mark off a people are reinforced by the boundaries between truth and falsity, true God and idols. Taboos which mark off a People become rules defining the Ark of Salvation. Oneness creates a sharp line of demarcation: 'Little children, keep yourselves from idols'. Oneness is easily associated with the idea of a peculiar people, a covenant, the elect.

13.26 From the unity of God springs the unity of the people of God, the unity of the human race, the unity of belief, the unity of human speech. Implicit in unity is the concept of something absolutely inclusive, and that in turn implies exclusion. Unity creates duality and encounters diversity. In the Jewish case, of course, the impulse to unity is held in check by the fact that the truth is located on a biological basis, the peoplehood of Israel. This lowers the tension with diversity, and all but destroys any impulse to bring everybody into the one fold. The capsule of the peculiar people does not expand or take off: it stays as an irreducible peculiarity, co-existing with other peoples.

13.27 Indeed, the pressure against Israel from the universal impulse of Christianity or Islam or Marxism makes the Jewish people into an instance of unreduced *diversity*. For that matter the Peoplehood of the Hebrews is a problem for all three universal faiths. Each faith has to 'place' the others. Every universal religion has to see the other as lacking something which could be realized by submission to the one true faith. Insofar as the rival versions of unity do *not* submit they have to be accepted as redoubts of diversity.

13.28 Unification is dialectically related to duality and to diversity. This is dramatically illustrated in the aspiration to one, true speech. The tongues of Pentecost united all men in a single speech. Even a sacred language is an archaic expression of an eschatological idea: the united speech of humankind. (Perhaps I may add in parenthesis that the passionate desire for the unity of science, including even the reductionist impulse, may also derive from the overall notion of the divine unity.) The notion of the divine unity is related to the perception of a world which is a universe not a multiverse.

13.29 This vocabulary of unification and opposition, the people of God and the heathen, the people and the class enemy, the social boundaries of truth and unreclaimed soil or unreclaimed souls is part of the fundamental structure of all those movements springing from the Judaic root. It envisages unity as solidarity in faith or in the covenant relationship. Like the vocabulary of coming and going, pilgrimage and alienation, it has a tendency to militant imagery. The warrior, either the soldier of Christ or the class struggler, is the natural symbol of solidarity.

13.30 However, I suggested earlier that transcendence and unity include the possibility of passivity as well as of militancy, of stasis as well as ecstasis. This is partly because there is a steady social pressure to maintain continuity. Societies cannot exist without continuity, so elements of quiescence and passivity are necessary to social existence. There is however another reason: the reservoir of potentiality has to be built up over time. Before a great movement emerges there seems to be a gestation in which there is a gathering together of resources. The Church is a dam and builds up enormous potentiality inside it. Unless the divine is held back in sacred space, inside churches, or behind altar rails under priestly control, there will be no build-up. Without quiescence, latency and passivity there is no power, only wastage. So the institutional church is a channel of power and also a temporary but necessary barrier against the premature realization of power. In any case, as Marx pointed out, mankind only takes up those problems for which it is nearly ready.

13.31 So far I have suggested that transcendence and unity together breed a powerful vocabulary: a Word comes with power. I have also suggested that it takes the active form of 'the movement' and a passive, quiescent form. However, that is not the same thing as a pacifist form and I want to underline the pacifist tradition in the splay of possibilities deriving from the Jewish root. It is a possibility much more associated with Christianity than Islam and it is positively repudiated by Marxism. This is not pacifism simply in the restricted sense of the refusal to bear arms, but realized more profoundly in the acceptance of redemptive suffering. The acceptance of redemptive suffering is central to Christianity and generates some of the social forms more characteristic of that religion: the peaceable but revolutionary sect, the radical but loving fraternity.

13.32 Christianity stands accused of masochistic quiescence before human pain and social injustice. The vocabulary of peaceable love and redemptive suffering is charged with being just another form of religious quiescence. It is true that peaceable love recognizes the resistance of structures and is reluctant to engage in the violent overthrow of those structures. Love creates, instead, in-numerable social experiments, each encountering different con-straints and exploiting different possibilities. They all have to find some partial solution to the problems of ownership and sexuality and they have to inaugurate equality by some form of discipline. The first experiments are the monastic orders, trying to operate outside the frame of necessary social violence and attempting to realize the kingdom in the enclave or in the isolated spot. The later experiments include the radical sectarians of the Reformation and the utopian Christian communities of the eighteenth and nineteenth centuries.

13.33 Each of these experiments repeated in little certain aspects of the more central assault on society by the institutional Church. One such aspect is the sharp social edge of the community: the unity of the brethren demands demarcation. Another aspect is the period of imprinting or latency in which the reservoir of potency is built up. The constant repetition is the means whereby the ink of the word bites deep into the substance of the collective Soul. However, the sect or the radical brotherhood can be exemplary in a way the Church cannot because it has siphoned off a spiritual elect. The elect are a tight capsule of possibilities maintained in being by strict limitations. When those possibilities have cut deep enough they may slip gradually through the protective covering. Again, this differs somewhat from the Church at large. The Church has to link itself with things as they are and can only manage to infiltrate the realm of images rather than of structural realities. Nevertheless these images lie poised in the realm of symbols awaiting the moment of release. And when they are released they fragment and disperse in the collective psyche, achieving their end by another route and under another name. The images poised by the Church in the ideal realm often enter and subvert reality in disguise, as well as under their native name.

13.34 What are these images, realized in the communal experiments of sects and monasteries and infiltrating the symbolic canopy of society at large through the agency of the Church? They include the image of inversion: he who is lord of all must be servant of all. They also include the underlying oxymoron of Christianity: when I am weak I am strong, when I fall I rise, in my end is my beginning.[3] They utilize the points of ignominy, ugliness and vulnerability in the human situation as the redoubts of redemption. The process of imprinting the signs of inversion and paradox takes centuries: it was a thousand years and more before the suffering God and vulnerable child replaced the signs of simple, triumphant potency. Nevertheless these signs eventually reach the deepest level of the imagination, so that men can envisage the peaceable kingdom where the child plays on the hole of the asp and there is no violence in all the holy mountain. Men understand what it would be for a valley to be exalted and a mountain and a hill to be brought low. The interior of faith is appropriated.

13.35 In all this nothing has been said about God since reflection on social processes can know nothing whatever about God. Nevertheless God is meaningful to men through word and image and these images are the means of transcendence. Signs are the means of grace: God is known in the making of signs.

Notes

1. I may add that the idea of freedom is often remaindered in the same way. Indeed it is all too easy to phrase the problem so that the autonomy of God and the autonomy of man are rival claimants for what science leaves over.
2. Or as the Latin of the collect has it: 'whom to serve is to *reign*'.
3. This idea I owe to Donald Davie, *A Gathered Church: the Literature of the English Dissenting Interest 1700–1930*, London: Routledge and Kegan Paul, 1978.

14

Garrett Green
The Sociology of Dogmatics: Niklas Luhmann's
Challenge to Theology

Garrett Green's article on Luhmann was published in 1982, when
Green was associate professor of religious studies at Connecticut
College. For two years he was an Alexander von Humboldt Research
Fellow at the University of Tübingen, where he did his research on
Luhmann. The complete article which forms this Extract provides an
important overview of the ambitious sociological understanding of
religion and theology presented by Niklas Luhmann, professor of
sociology at the University of Bielefeld. Because the latter's work is
still relatively little known in the English-speaking world and because
it is written at a level of high-critical theory characteristic of critical
theorists like Habermas, to whom he responds (*14.6*), Green's article
is particularly useful. Luhmann's theory of the social function of
religion goes considerably beyond that of Durkheim (*Extract 3*).
Religion does not simply serve to integrate society, it is actually a
means of giving shape to a highly complex world of relativities
(*14.11–15*). All knowledge is to be seen in relative or relational terms
(cf. *Extract 6* and *Extract 10*): religion, too, is subject to social
change and variety (*14.14*), even whilst still acting as a transformer of
complexity. Theology, as distinct from religion, is the reflective
aspect of religion. As such it has a specific social function in coordinating the whole religious system: it has a particular concern to provide
and maintain the identity of the system (*14.16–20*). Like David
Martin, Luhmann stresses the social significance of theological symbols, signs or ciphers. For both sociologists, a religious community
receives its identity through them and it is this identity which can
shape surrounding society. But unlike Martin, he accords religion
(and thus theology as well) a more privileged role in shaping Western
society. However, in the process Green argues that he presents a
reductionist threat to theology that would, if accepted, fundamentally
alter its central basic aims and commitments (*14.21f.*).

14.1 Demands that theology take seriously its social and cultural context have been voiced repeatedly in recent years,

both by theologians themselves and by their interpreters and critics in other fields. It has long been apparent that insights into the sociology of knowledge have important implications for theology as for all areas of human inquiry. The growth of religious studies as a field — and increasingly as the intellectual and institutional environment for theologians in the English-speaking world — has intensified pressures to take account of the external social world in which theology is done. Though these pressures have led theologians to pay more attention to sociology, social anthropology, and social history, the only concrete result seems to have been a proliferation of methodological proposals and programmatic essays.

14.2 Another demand frequently heard in the midst of the disciplinary identity crisis through which theology has been struggling since the passing of the great systematicians who dominated the 1930s, 40s, and 50s is for an alternative to theologies based on metaphysical presuppositions or ontological principles. This appeal was sounded earlier by Karl Barth, but neither his alternative nor any other has achieved widespread acceptance by contemporary theologians, who continue to insist on the need for a new kind of fundamental or foundational theology.

14.3 For the most part, of course, these theological frustrations have remained an in-house affair, attracting little attention from other disciplines. Recently, however, a notable exception has appeared on the scholarly horizon: a comprehensive theory of religion, by a thoroughly 'secular' sociologist, which assigns a major social function not just to religion generally but to dogmatic theology in particular. From the prolific pen of Niklas Luhmann, sociologist at the University of Bielefeld in West Germany, comes a theory that restores religion to a central position in sociology, ascribes to 're-ligious dogmatics' a crucial role in the guidance of religion, and even enables a detailed sociological analysis and critique of specific Christ-ian doctrines. The dialogue with theologians that Luhmann expressly invites has begun to take shape in Germany,[1] especially since the publication of *Funktion der Religion*, in which his theory of religion — including an attempt to provide a sociological grounding of theology — appears in its most developed formulation. Ecclesiastical interest in Luhmann has also spread beyond the theological faculties to leaders of the West German Protestant churches, who have engaged his services as a consultant.

14.4 The opportunity for intensive dialogue between sociology and theology at a sophisticated theoretical level is to be welcomed, and theologians should be appreciative of a social-scientific theory that takes the theological enterprise seriously enough to enter into its problems and procedures in detail. Luhmann offers a refreshing change from sociological theories that treat theology, if at all, merely as an epiphenomenal superstructure obscuring the underlying economic, political, and cultural realities of religious behavior. But theologians (and church leaders) should also beware of being flattered into accepting too quickly a definition of their own enterprise which offers answers to fundamental questions that they have been unable to answer for themselves. For Luhmann makes the bold claim, in contrast to most of the tradition of sociology, that sociological analysis can explain not only the 'external' actions of religious individuals and institutions but also the 'inner' realm of faith and religious experience that has been so jealously guarded by modern theology as its exclusive preserve. Luhmann himself warns that 'the relations that could be established between sociological theory and religious dogmatics are closer, more abstract, more fruitful, and more dangerous than one commonly assumes' (1977:73).

14.5 Luhmann's thought is of particular relevance to theologians, because it speaks directly to the two issues mentioned at the outset, which continue both to fascinate and to frustrate the work of theology: the social location and significance of the theological enterprise itself, and the need for a new kind of theory independent of metaphysical and ontological presuppositions. In view of the exceptional linguistic and conceptual demands that Luhmann makes on his readers, and the nearly total absence of English translations of his work,[2] the first step must be a brief description of the nature and aim of his theory as a whole (I), followed by an attempt to recount the broad outlines of his theory of religion (II) and the special role of 'religious dogmatics' (III). Then on the basis of this account I want to highlight the challenges posed by the theory for Christian theology and to suggest the direction that an adequate theological response should take (IV).

I

14.6 Luhmann emerged as a social theorist to be reckoned with in a published debate with Jürgen Habermas which attracted the attention of German academics beyond the ranks of professional sociologists. After a late start in academic life — he first studied law and had a career in public administration — Luhmann has been making up for lost time at a breathtaking pace in a series of essays and books covering most of the main areas of modern society. His work is tied together by a general theory of society both comprehensive in scope and grounded in a conceptuality in sharp contrast to other European sociology.

14.7 But to consider Luhmann's theory simply from the point of view of sociology as that field has usually been understood would be to risk seriously misconstruing both its content and its significance for theology. For Luhmann makes some bold — even audacious — claims on behalf of his theory that put him in competition not only with the theories of other sociologists but also with the main traditions of Western philosophy. One critic maintains that the motive underlying all of Luhmann's work, and its chief weakness, is his attempt to solve philosophical problems by sociological means (Hondrich:89ff.). Luhmann, for his part, is quite explicit about his designs on territory traditionally occupied by philosophy, openly announcing his intention to 'resolve epistemology into an instance of the application of systems theory' (1977:17). He sees himself as the proponent of a qualitatively new kind of theory, frankly relativistic, lacking any fixed points of reference, and characterized by the ability to combine high degrees of both choice (*Beliebigkeit*) and specification (1975:200–201). He repeatedly contrasts this type of theory to old-style metaphysical and ontological theories, for which his favorite pejorative is *alteuropäisch* (e.g. 1974:196–97). 'The goal of knowledge', he claims, 'is no longer the establishment of unchangeable, self-identical substance in its essence, but control over alternatives' (1974:36). To achieve this goal, he proposes not simply a particular sociological theory but rather a complex and multifacted '*Supertheorie*' (1978:9–27), a comprehensive framework for all special scientific endeavors.

14.8 Luhmann normally refers to his program as functional systems theory, and he draws many of his key concepts from Talcott Parsons (cf., e.g., 1951, 1968). (In a reversal of the German-laden English prose familiar to theologians, Luhmann's works are sprinkled with anglicized German and sociological English — 'adaptive upgrading', 'loose coupling'.) This Parsonian base has been developed further by the use of concepts derived from Husserlian phenomenology. To make matters even more complex (*not* a drawback according to Luhmann's criteria), he links up systems theory with two other recent theoretical enterprises, evolutionary theory and communications theory (1975:193–203). These various theory elements cannot be reduced to a unified base, yet they 'mutually presuppose one another'. Each of them is a 'self-referential' complex of concepts, which can be combined with elements from the others in a process of 'relationizing' to achieve new and more sophisticated means for analyzing particular social phenomena. Although Luhmann affirms the goal of combining these independent elements into 'a coherent theory', he acknowledges that the results are extremely complicated; he likens them to the patterns created by the intersecting concentric waves produced by three stones thrown simultaneously into the water. He characterizes the resulting mode of argumentation as 'neither linear, nor circular, but labyrinthine' — and few of his readers are likely to disagree.

14.9 One further way in which Luhmann seeks to overcome the limitations of the old European tradition is especially important for his theory of religion. In order to avoid fixed ontological presuppositions, he replaces unitary concepts with relations. In analyzing social experience and behaviour, he thus endeavors to establish not unchanging entities or structures of being but rather abstract reference-points from which apparently diverse social phenomena can be fruitfully compared. Such a theoretical point of reference can be fixed by locating a particular problem for which the social system seeks a solution. When viewed from the perspective of such a 'reference-problem', 'different possibilities of behavior [and] social circumstances that appear externally to be quite diverse can be treated as functionally equivalent' (1974:35). Luhmann calls this kind of theory functional-structural, in contrast to the structural-functional systems theory advocated by Parsons and others. In the latter theory, the structure of the system is presupposed as the basis for investigating the functional achievements required to maintain the system. Luhmann argues that functional-structural systems theory has the major advantage of being able to treat the systematic structure itself as a question and to investigate the meaning and function of system-building in general (1974:113–14).

II

14.10 The point of departure for Luhmann's theory of religion is the problem of *complexity*, 'the ultimate attainable material reference-problem of functional inquiry'. Complexity means that the world 'has no limits'; it always contains more possibilities than can be realized, or even recognized (1973: 3–5). The basic concepts of systems theory, *system* and *environment*, are directed to this problem: systems are structured arrangements for reducing complexity by limiting and controlling contacts with the environment; the environment is defined relatively as everything lying beyond the boundaries of the system. Stated most simply, 'a system *is* its difference from the environment, an order for defining and maintaining a boundary' (1975:211, emphasis added). The function of the system is to maintain a complexity-differential between itself and its environment, which it does by selectivity, by strictly limiting the quantity and nature of contacts with the environment. But all selection entails the risk of omission and error.

14.11 As a result of the process of selection, the environment is necessarily twofold: it consists of what has been selected systematically, or determinate complexity; and also of what has not been selected, indeterminate complexity. The definitive problem for religion — its reference-problem — is the transformation of indeterminate into determinate complexity. Precisely because the problem is insoluble it becomes the 'catalyst' for the development of religion (1977:20). This extremely abstract description can be rendered somewhat more specific by concentrating on those systems of special concern to the sociologist: what Luhmann calls 'meaning-constitutive psychic and social systems' — in other words, human individuals and societies. Here the selection necessary for meaningful experience and action precipitates the following twofold environment: on the one hand, an accessible environment of ordered and familiar things and events subject to normal expectations and probabilities; on the other hand, the inaccessible environment beyond, experienced as the unexpected, the surprising, the disappointing ('intangible like a bang behind one's back' [1977:17]). Luhmann, adapting terms from Husserl's phenomenology, calls the first experience representation and the second appresentation; they correspond to what in traditional terms would be called reality and possibility. Their simultaneous presence in all human life is the fundamental fact to which religion responds. 'In all meaningful experience and action', Luhmann writes, 'more is continually appresented than can be represented' (1977:22). The social system is therefore subjected to a continuous pressure to give shape to the elusive transcendence beyond the accessible environment, to represent and formulate it; but because representation always takes place in a context of further appresentation, the world forever eludes definitive formulation. Religion performs the social function of transforming this indeterminable world into a determinable one, one which can compensate for the inevitable risk of selection and protect against the threat of arbitrary change in the relationship of system and environment. In order to carry out this task, religion must itself venture to give representational form to indetermine appresentation. 'But over the course of a long history', Luhmann explains, 'it specializes its particular efforts on representations that absorb the risk of representation' (1977:27).

14.12 Religion fulfills this function by 'sacralizing' the realm of the indeterminate through a process of 'ciphering'. Ciphers are not simply symbols, since their purpose is not to point to something different; 'they have their meaning not in any relation to something else but are it themselves'. They replace the indeterminate, and also hide it, leaving it a mere 'empty horizon' without reality

(1977:33). Ciphers, unlike signs, are not substitutable, since they disguise and replace their origin, thereby 'generating knowledge by reductive determination' (1977:84–85). For this reason the function of religion in transforming indeterminate into determinate complexity remains 'latent', both for religious experience and for dogmatics. An example of religious ciphering — the most important one in Western culture — is the formula *God*, to which we will return below.

14.13 Indeterminate complexity thus serves as the general reference-problem for which religion assumes special responsibility in the social system. Luhmann analyzes it, using the concepts of modal logic, as the problem of contingency. In simplest terms, he is saying that social choices always take place in a context of further unrealized possibilities. This situation poses the problem of contingency, logically defined as the negation of both necessity and impossibility, and experienced as the sense that anything actual might also be otherwise: why is the world like *this* instead of any number of other possible ways? The function of religion is to deal with this problem, 'to transform indeterminable into determinable contingency' (1977:189).

14.14 But Luhmann's concept of religion is not sufficiently defined by describing the reference-problem. Although the *functional* aspect of religion is thereby given, Luhmann's concept also contains an *evolutionary* dimension. The basic problem posed by the twofold environment and the need to transform complexity or contingency does not simply produce a stable functional structure but rather initiates a developmental process. The continuous pressure of the reference-problem 'catalyzes' the development of a wide range of religious forms, which vary according to cultural and historical conditions. Religious institutions, in a way analogous to biological evolution, are exposed to ceaseless evolutionary influences, producing a long history in which various forms are generated, undergo change, and die out. But even the reference-problem does not remain unchanged but splits apart into relatively more concrete and soluble special problems. Luhmann discusses two examples (1977:114ff.). The first is the so-called rites of passage, which function to determine the indeterminate in the specific case of individual status-transformations, as in the Christian rites of baptism, confirmation, marriage, and burial. A second example is the religious function of explaining and absorbing disappointments, which are experienced either as anxiety in anticipation of future possibilities or as insecurity occasioned by past disappointments.

14.15 Luhmann's theory makes it impossible to define religion either solely by its reference-problem or solely in terms of the functions it develops in response to this problem. He claims that this 'detached conceptuality' is precisely the advantage of functional analysis over 'a definitory-categorizing procedure'. He also finds it superior to monofunctional definitions of religion solely on the basis of its *integrating* function, which is contradicted by the facts, or its *interpretive* function, which 'short-circuits' analysis by simply presupposing the need to interpret as an unexamined given (1977:10–12). His aim is to replace two-term functional relations with three-term relations that can determine the function of religion both positively, in relation to a particular problem, and negatively, in contrast to solutions offered by functionally equivalent forms. His concept of religion thus tries to account for both the unity and variety of religion, to do justice to its diverse forms in such a way that 'one can nevertheless also say that they "always mean the same thing" ' (1977:20).

III

14.16 Luhmann's sociology of theology is a further development of his general theory of religion but one that plays a particularly crucial role and constitutes the most original feature of the theory. Traditionally, sociologists who have produced general theories of religion (Marx and Durkheim, for example) have had little to say about the specific contents of theology; while those who have produced sociological analyses of particular doctrines (such as Max Weber's work on capitalism and Protestantism) have not provided a comprehensive account of the sociological meaning of theology as such. Luhmann lays claim to a theoretical perspective from which he can not only explain religious dogmatics generally but also analyze the social functions of particular doctrines, even to the extent of proposing explicit theological reforms.

14.17 Theology, or 'religious dogmatics' — Luhmann uses the terms almost interchangeably — emerges in the course of the religious evolution of Western Christendom. Two sorts of differentiation that occur in social evolution must be distinguished, both of which play a role in the emergence of theology. First, the social system develops in such a way that the religious function comes to be differentiated as a special subsystem enjoying considerable independence from the total system as well as from other subsystems. Modern global society has largely moved beyond the earlier stages of segmentary stratified organization, becoming highly differentiated into autonomous functional subsystems for politics, economy, science, religion, etc. The religious system retains a connection to the total society but specializes in fulfilling a particular function. A second kind of differentiation is meanwhile occurring within the subsystem in response to its increased autonomy and to obstacles encountered in performing its function. As in all self-referential systems, three types of relations are internally differentiated: (1) the relation of the subsystem to the total social system takes the form of *function*; (2) the relation to other subsystems within society is *performance*; and (3) its relation to itself is differentiated as *reflection*. In the religious system of the modern West (Luhmann apparently has only the Christianity of Europe and North America in view) these three appear, respectively, as church, social service, and theology (1977:54–59).

14.18 Assigning to theology responsibility for the reflection of the religious system means that its primary subject matter is the identity of the system itself. Theology accordingly emerges in social evolution in response to threats to religious identity, which may be occasioned practically by the failure of religious intentions in reality, socially by encounters with other religious systems, and temporally by increasing distance from its historical origin and source of revelation (1977:59–61). But the deepest roots of religious dogmatics are embedded in the original ciphering of the religious function. Luhmann argues both that religion performs the task of transforming indeterminate into determinate complexity and that it remains unconscious of this function. If the function were to become explicitly thematic, religion would be exposed to comparison and possible replacement. Dogmatics therefore grows up as a kind of ersatz for the latent function, a replacement for the missing functional consciousness of religion. As religion becomes increasingly free of specific situations in the course of social evolution, it develops a need for interpretation. Religious dogmatics can be defined as the 'verbal and conceptual equipment for this interpretive function' at any given cultural and historical point in its development. The task performed by ritual at an earlier stage of religious evolution is transformed by 'adaptive upgrading' into dogmatic interpretation. Dogmatics does not treat its social function as an explicit theme but reflects on religious themes and symbols, which in turn are related to experience. In this regard theology can be most fruitfully compared not with science but with jurisprudence (1977:85–88). Particularly significant in contrast to other sociological theories of religion is the central function that Luhmann assigns to theology for the coordination of the whole religious system. Under the impact of the functional differentiation of society, experienced in the religious system as 'secularization', the theological function has become more rather than less important in the modern era, thus increasing the interest and potential fruitfulness of a dialogue between sociologists and theologians.

14.19 The seriousness with which Luhmann takes theology is most evident in the detailed analysis he devotes to a wide range of particular Christian doctrines. These analyses include some of his most interesting and original observations. Undoubtedly the most important of these doctrinal excursuses is Luhmann's interpretation of the concept *God* as the 'contingency formula' of Western religion. Contingency formulas are defined as 'symbols or groups of symbols that serve to translate the indeterminate contingency of a particular functional sphere into determinable contingency' (1977:201). An example from another social sphere is the formula *scarcity* in the economic system, which reduces to calculable proportions the arbitrary possibilities expressed in the wish to have more or to have something else. The religious formula *God* has traditionally reduced the complexity of the world by grounding its contingency in a supreme principle conceived as both perfect and personal. Luhmann believes that theology has encountered difficulty since the eighteenth century because perfection has been replaced by the principle of development as the highest ideal of bourgeois society. A theology that responds to contingency today with a concept of a perfect God thus comes into conflict with an evolution-oriented science, including sociology (1977:133). One wonders whether Luhmann might revise this judgment if he were aware of recent process theology.

14.20 A second doctrinal issue particularly important in Luhmann's theory of religion is his thesis that *faith* functions as the religious 'communications medium', analogous to truth, love, money, art, and power in other functional spheres. 'Communications media', according to his definition, 'are symbolic codes that establish the rules for the possible combination of symbols and are thereby able simultaneously to insure a transfer of selective achievements' (1977:91). In the case of religion, the immediacy of religious experience requires some means of regulation and control as soon as it becomes the content of communication among individuals. The church as the arena of 'spiritual communication' provides the institutional structure. Dogmatics has the task of overseeing the communications medium — for example, it must guard against both 'inflation' and 'deflation' of faith by holding it in balance between the extremes of inflexible fixation and vapid neutralization. Luhmann cites 'civil religion' as an example of religious inflation, fundamentalism as an example of deflation (1977:124).

IV

14.21 Luhmann's theory presents a challenge to theology in the double sense of the word: it contains dangers to which theology must not fall prey, but it also offers constructive possibilities by provoking theologians to rethink their own enterprise, by throwing fresh light on old issues, and by demonstrating new conceptual resources. Even a theory which theology dare not accept uncritically or on its own terms may nevertheless contain useful insights and suggest theoretical models which theologians can put to work for their own purposes and according to their own proper criteria.

14.22 The persistent problem of relating theology to its social environment would seem to be the point at which functional systems theory could make its greatest contribution to the work of theology. Luhmann explicitly offers the aid of his theory in the diagnosis of social structures in their interaction with religion. He invites theology, in its role as the reflective sphere of religion, to employ the analytical tools of systems theory as a basis for its guidance of the religious system (1977:271). In accepting this invitation, however, theology would be acquiescing in a definition of its own work that would fundamentally alter its nature and betray its basic commitments.

14.23 The crucial issue is posed by Luhmann's identification of Christian theology with 'religious dogmatics'. The issue of the theological significance of religion was raised by Karl Barth's theological critique of religion and debated vigorously for a time in response to Dietrich Bonhoeffer's poignant but elliptical rejection of religion in his prison letters. More recently, however, most theologians seem either to have ignored the issue or quietly acquiesced to a consensus that their work serves the enterprise called religion.[3] If Luhmann is right, theology in fact has no other ground, subject matter, or raison d'être than religion, it is by definition the self-reflection of religion, the instrument by which the religious subsystem maintains its identity and regulates its intercourse with the whole social system and with its sister subsystems. It is to be judged by its success in enabling religion to perform its social function smoothly and efficiently, avoiding either a loss of identity or disruptive conflicts with other systems such as politics or the economy. Luhmann wants to assist theologians in carrying out their task by offering them a theoretical instrument designed to lay bare the functional structures underlying their own 'media-code'. They will then be in a position to achieve greater 'structural compatibility' with modern functionally-differentiated society. They might choose, for instance, to exchange their contingency formula *God* for one more in keeping with a development-oriented culture; or they might follow Luhmann's advice to abandon the 'supplementary myth of the resurrection' in favor of a concept of divine self-negation without a 'happy end' as a more promising means for mediating the duality of suffering and salvation (cf. 1977:198–200).

14.24 A half-century ago Barth argued that modern Protestant theology, in a process that began as far back as the orthodox schools of the seventeenth century and reached its zenith in the liberalism of his own theological teachers, had managed 'to exchange its own birthright for the concept of religion' (*KD* I/2:320; cf. *CD* I/2:294). The dependence of theology on a nontheological concept of religion seems hardly to have lessened in the meantime; indeed, if theologians like Rahner, Lonergan, and Tracy are representative, one would now have to include Roman Catholics, too. Contrary to a common assumption, the point of Barth's critique of religion was never to deny that Christianity is a religion[4] or to suggest that theology has nothing to do with religious studies. In fact, Barth argues that to deny that revelation can be understood as religion is to deny revelation itself (*KD* I/2:308; *CD* I/2:283). God's revelation in Christ was, is, and will remain bound to the Christian religion as one religion among others, with which it has significant continuities.

14.25 The crucial point is the error of making religion the *criterion* for theology; and it is just this point that Luhmann's sociology of dogmatics brings clearly into focus. Pannenberg, who dismisses the theological critique of religion at the outset of his reply to Luhmann as 'a self-destructive impulse' in the theology of the recent past, misses this central issue. By misstating the theological alternative as 'the separation of biblical revelation from the religious life of humanity' (1978:99), he forfeits the basis for an effective critique of Luhmann's account of the theological task. The real issue raised by Luhmann for theology is contained in Barth's question whether 'that which we think we know about the essence and phenomenon of religion is to serve as the standard and explanatory principle for God's revelation, or vice versa' (*KD* I/2:309; cf. *CD* I/2:284). Luhmann — who of course makes no pretense to being a theologian — quite obviously chooses the first option. He by no means denies revelation; on the contrary, he treats it as the key concept of dogmatics. But its importance is precisely its role as 'the most functional dogma', able to ground the concept of dogma itself as the self-revelation of revelation. He can then add: '*Theology* formulates this self-reference as God's identity' (1977:173). For Luhmann the criterion of theology is its social function, which can be understood only with the help of functionalistic sociology: left to itself, 'religious dogmatics' is only the fig leaf covering the functional nakedness of religion.

14.26 Once the normative consequences implicit in Luhmann's account of the relationship between theology and society have been uncovered, it becomes clear why theologians must decline his offer of assistance with this problem. The difficulty is inherent in his concept of theory and the claims he advances on behalf of it. A theory, according to Luhmann, is an instrument for dealing with social problems, and it is subject to the criterion not of truth but of success in problem-solving. Such a theory is fixed in none of its terms, any one of which can be modified if the need should arise. The very modesty of this concept of theory becomes the basis for Luhmann's immodest claim to present a super-theory (Messner:1), a sociology conceived as the queen — a more fitting title would be manager — of the sciences, theology included. Here the danger is not reductionism, which has so often been the case with social-scientific theories of religion, but imperialism. And theology, having learned the dangers of disciplinary imperialism the hard way, should be especially wary of becoming anyone else's handmaid. However justified Luhmann may be in seeking to ferret out the social function of dogmatics, he is unable to show why this function ought to be taken as the norm for theology. Indeed, he does not even try but simply assumes that sociological theory is an adequate groundwork for dogmatics. This uncritical assumption is finally self-contradictory, for his claim that dogmatics takes the place of functional consciousness in religion implies that it is incompatible with a sociological analysis of its function. Indeed, seen in this light, Luhmann appears to be proposing that theologians abandon dogmatics in favor of functional systems theory. The implication, though Luhmann never advances the claim, seems to be that his social theory is the functional equivalent of dogmatics.

14.27 The very real danger represented by Luhmann's transformation of social function into dogmatic norm ought not to frighten off theologians too quickly, however. For Luhmann belongs to that select group of thinkers whose failures can be more interesting and instructive than the successes of less gifted and more timid minds. In the first place, even if he cannot tell theologians what they ought to be doing, he can at least do them the service of shedding new light on religion. Even his sociology of dogmatics succeeds at least in showing the intimate and intricate ways in which all religious experience and action, including the 'inner' world of faith and dogma, is implicated in the functioning of society. Luhmann's vision of the social world, and of religion as one of its aspects, is surely one of the most original, sophisticated, and conceptually powerful theories to come along for some time; it has already succeeded in undermining the unquestioned preeminence of the Frankfurt School in German social thought.

14.28 But the main potential of Luhmann's theory for contributing positively to Christian theology lies in that other perennial concern of modern dogmatics, mentioned at the outset: the quest for a qualitatively new kind of foundational theory, one free of any prior commitment to a metaphysics or to ontological first principles. Luhmann contributes to this task more implicitly than explicitly, more by analogy than by design. In brief, he presents in his own social theory an example of a relativistic or relational thinking that aims at illuminating its subject in a manner that is coherent yet never systematically complete. The result is a conceptual arrangement that is flexible and adaptable, admittedly circular, and able to bring otherwise unrelated phenomena into comparative relationships based on *their* relations to a common problem. 'Foundational security', he claims, 'is in fact scientifically dispensable' (1975:201).

14.29 Now such a manner of thinking bears a striking formal resemblance to much of the theological tradition. For example, Luhmann's rejection of 'foundational security' (*Grundlagensicherheit*) sounds very much like Karl Barth's refusal on principle to offer any philosophical or methodological grounding for dogmatics (e.g. *KD* I/2:954ff.; *CD* I/2:853ff.). Barth eschews the notion that theology should be a 'system', understood as a 'closed and complete interconnection of principles and corollaries constructed under the presupposition of a certain *basic intuition* (*Gründanschauung*) by the use of certain sources of knowledge and certain axioms' (*KD* I/2:963; cf. *CD* I/2:861). Rather, theology must always retain an 'open center', resisting every temptation to fill it with some kind of presupposition or first principle (such as 'religion'). Systems theory as defined by Luhmann is quite obviously *not* a 'system' in this sense, on the contrary, it has formal similarities to Barth's own procedure.

14.30 Such parallels between sociological systems theory and a nonsystematic theological method — all the more remarkable in view of their virtually total divergence in content — invite further comparative exploration. Might theologians use Luhmann's thought heuristically to construct a truly *theological* systems theory? Such a program would mean taking Luhmann's description of the ideal modern theory more seriously and consistently than he does himself. He maintains that there are no rules governing the selection of reference-problems to be explored and consequently no absolute basis for determining what is to be taken as a system in the first place; these choices spring from an original theory-commitment (*Theorieentscheidung*; cf. Messner:2). Luhmann himself makes such a commitment on behalf of sociology, whose theme he takes to be human activity. 'My proposal', he says, 'is to choose the problem of complexity itself as the ultimate reference-point of functional analyses, to conceive all systems as the comprehension and reduction of complexity, and to assess them in this extremely abstract perspective as comparable and exchangeable' (1974:260). A theological program is conceivable on the basis of a different, but formally comparable, theory-commitment. Let me conclude with a brief sketch of how such a program might look.

14.31 The theme of theology, God, can be paraphrased (in terms parallel to Luhmann's sociological program) as divine activity. Christian dogmatics has chosen to pursue this theme in relation to the ultimate reference-point of Jesus Christ. This 'theory-commitment' is formally comparable to that of the sociologist, notwithstanding the fact that it is existentially of a different order, since the theological theory-commitment is only one aspect of a Christian faith-commitment. Faith, though it serves as the personal precondition for the theologian, does *not* function as a metaphysical presupposition for theology. Formally, the ultimate source of theology in personal faith is equivalent to the preliminary but 'ungroundable' decisions necessary for any theoretical enterprise.

14.32 Theology, understood as a theoretical undertaking in which the problem of God's activity is explored in relation to Jesus Christ, permits a 'relationizing' (*Relationierung*, Luhmann's cumbersome but important concept) of dogmatic issues. For example, the first great controversy in the history of dogma, which culminated in the Nicene doctrine of the Trinity, involved a relational issue: 'Is the Divine which appeared on the earth and has made its presence actively felt [in Jesus Christ] identical with the supreme Divine that rules heaven and earth?' (Harnack:1). The theological attempt to conceive God in relation to Jesus Christ led to a relational (nonmetaphysical) concept of God as a Trinity, whose individual members are not parts of a whole but are constituted by their interrelations: 'they mutually presuppose one another' (Luhmann, 1975:201; cf. [*14.8*] above). This 'relationizing' of the concept of God was followed by a 'relationizing' of Christology in the formula of Chalcedon, in which the identity of the incarnate Logos is understood to be constituted by the relation of his relations to divinity and humanity. The central doctrines of the Reformation allow a similar analysis. The Protestant doctrine of justification replaces the Roman Catholic metaphysical concept of faith as an infused *habitus* with a relational definition: from the perspective of Jesus Christ as the ultimate point of reference, faith is conceived as the relation between two other relations — that of the believer to Christ, and that of Christ to the Father. From this perspective faith appears as the functional equivalent of works, with which it can then be fruitfully compared. Might not a corresponding method be of help in resolving characteristically modern dogmatic issues, such as the relationship between Christian faith and other religions?

14.33 Such a view of theology employs Luhmann's own theoretical tools on behalf of a dialogue between sociological and theological theory. What emerges is a way of conceiving sociological systems theory as indeed the functional equivalent of Christian dogmatics — but in a radically different sense from Luhmann's own account of theology as 'religious dogmatics'. Luhmann can even be cited in support of such a theological appropriation of his theory, for he claims that functional analysis proceeds 'neither deductively nor inductively, but heuristically' (1973:2). Luhmann deserves the dialogue with theology that he has requested. If theologians are bold enough to accept the challenge, it will not be the first time they have confronted a theory that proposes an *Aufhebung* of their own enterprise. It is a risky business, but one that might offer a worthwhile alternative to sterile in-house discussions of the nature of theology, and to unbecoming chasing after the skirts of cultural fads.

Notes

1. The most notable examples to have appeared so far are Rendtorff and the exchange between Luhmann and Pannenberg. The present article depends, in addition to the items listed explicitly as 'Works Consulted', on various working papers and discussions of the theological study group on Luhmann's theory in Tübingen under the leadership of Dr Michael Welker. I would also like to thank the Alexander von Humboldt Foundation for travel and fellowship support that enabled me to participate in the Tübingen group.
2. The Edwin Mellen Press of Toronto has announced plans to publish the second chapter of Luhmann's book on religion (1977) as a separate volume, to be entitled *Religious Dogmatics and the Evolution of Societies*, translated with an introduction by Peter Beyer.
3. A notable exception to this trend is the work of Jürgen Moltmann (see, e.g. 1974:32ff., 321ff.).
4. This common misinterpretation in the English-speaking world is due in part to one of the most egregious translation errors in modern theology. In the title of §17 of the *Church Dogmatics* ('Gottes Offenbarung als Aufhebung der Religion'), the translator has rendered *Aufhebung* with 'Abolition' (*KD* I/2:304; *CD* I/2:280). To make matters worse, the key occurrences of the same term in the final sentences of both the first and second subsections have been translated differently each time, as 'abolition' and 'abrogation' (*KD* I/2:324, 356; *CD* I/2:297, 325). The context makes unmistakably clear that Barth uses the term in the deliberately ambiguous sense first introduced by Hegel to signify the crucial dialectical transition in his philosophy ('the negation of the negative'): *Aufhebung* in this sense

means *both* 'annulment' *and* 'preservation' or 'elevation'. The title of the third subsection of §17 ('True Religion') should remove any doubts about Barth's intention to use *Aufhebung* in both its senses.

Works Consulted

Barth, Karl (CD I/2) *Church Dogmatics*. Eds G. W. Bromiley and T. F. Torrance. Vol. 1, *The Doctrine of the World of God*, pt. 2. Trans. G. T. Thomson and Harold Knight. Edinburgh: T. & T. Clark, 1956.

———, (*KD* I/2) *Die kirchliche Dogmatik*. Vol. 1, *Die Lehre vom Wort Gottes*, pt. 2. 6th ed. Zurich: Theologischer Verlag Zürich, 1975.

Habermas, Jürgen, and Luhmann, Niklas (1971) *Theorie der Gesellschaft oder Sozialtechnologie — Was leistet die Systemforschung?* Frankfurt am Main: Suhrkamp Verlag.

Harnack, Adolf (1961) *History of Dogma*. Vol. 4. Trans. Neil Buchanan. Reprint ed. New York: Dover.

Hondrich, Karl Otto (1973) 'Systemtheorie als Instrument der Gesellschafts-analyse: Forschungsbezogene Kritik eines Theorieansatzes.' In *Theorie der Gesellschaft oder Sozialtechnologie: Beiträge zur Habermas-Luhmann-Diskussion* (Theorie-Diskussion Supplement 1), edited by Franz Macie-jewski, pp. 88–114. Frankfurt am Main: Suhrkamp Verlag.

Luhmann, Niklas (1973) *Vertrauen: Ein Mechanismus der Reduktion sozialer Komplexität*. 2nd ed. Stuttgart: Ferdinand Enke Verlag.

———, (1974) *Soziologische Aufklärung: Aufsätze zur Theorie sozialer Systeme*. Vol. 1. 4th ed. Opladen: Westdeutscher Verlag.

———, (1975) *Soziologische Aufklärung: Aufsätze zur Theorie der Gesellschaft*. Vol. 2. Opladen: Westdeutscher Verlag.

———, (1977) *Funktion der Religion*. Frankfurt am Main: Suhrkamp Verlag.

———, (1978) 'Soziologie der Moral.' In *Theorietechnik und Moral*, edited by Niklas Luhmann and Stephan H. Pfürtner, pp. 8–116. Frankfurt am Main: Suhrkamp Verlag.

Luhmann, Niklas, and Pannenberg, Wolfhart (1978) 'Die Allgemeingültig-keit der Religion: Diskussion über Luhmanns Religionssoziologie.' *Evangelische Kommentare* 11:350, 355–57.

Messner, Brigitta (1980) 'Der Anspruch der Theorie Niklas Luhmanns.' Unpublished working paper for the theological study group on Luhmann's theory. Tübingen.

Moltmann, Jürgen (1974) *The Crucified God: The Cross of Christ as the Foundation and Criticism of Christian Theology*. Trans. R. A. Wilson and John Bowden. New York: Harper & Row.

Pannenberg, Wolfhart (1978) 'Religion in der säkularen Gesellschaft: Niklas Luhmanns Religionssoziologie.' *Evangelische Kommentare* 11:99–103.

Parsons, Talcott, (1951) *The Social System*. Glencoe, IL: Free Press.

———, (1968) 'Systems Analysis II: Social Systems.' *International Encyclopedia of the Social Sciences* 15:458–73. Ed. David L. Sills. N.p.: Macmillan, and Free Press.

Rendtorff, Trutz (1975) *Gesellschaft ohne Religion? Theologische Aspekte einer sozialtheoretischen Kontroverse (Luhmann/Habermas).* Munich: R. Piper & Co.

SECTION THREE

Implications for Biblical Studies

15

Norman K. Gottwald
Sociological Method in the Study of Ancient Israel

This Extract first appeared in ed. M. J. Buss, *Encounter with the Text: Form and History in the Hebrew Bible* in 1979. The author is professor of biblical studies at New York Theological Seminary. In this Extract Gottwald sets out careful ground-rules for the use of sociology in biblical research. These ground-rules receive added authority from the fact that they have been worked out in his own major study *Tribes of Yahweh: A Sociology of the Religion of Liberated Israel, 1250–1050 B.C.E.* (Orbis, 1979). He claims that sociology can be particularly useful in the examination 'of how biblical texts with similar social data function in relation to texts or traditions of a similar nature among other peoples' (*15.9*). For the biblical scholar sociology is clearly only one tool amongst others (*15.10*). However, he argues that particular sociological models can provide new ways of understanding well-known texts (*15.12f.*). It is this, above all else, which has encouraged most of those scholars working in this area: carefully constructed and deployed sociological models can offer fresh perspectives on over-familiar material. Gottwald distinguishes two levels of social analysis in considering the origins and operations of early Israelite society. The first is concerned with the internal structure of this society (*15.16–17*), whereas the second is concerned with this particular social structure as it compares and contrasts with other social systems (*15.18f.*). If the first involves problems of collecting sufficient data (cf. *Extract 20*), the second involves the problem of knowing whether these data really are comparable to other cross-cultural examples (cf. *Extract 17*). Both of these are persisting problems in this developing discipline, of which Gottwald is fully aware (*15.21f.*). Indeed, he insists that if they are to be met it is vital that a number of socio-economic and cultural tools are developed further by the biblical scholar (*15.30f.*). What emerges is a programme which could serve to initiate a considerable amount of future research.

15.1 Historical method and sociological method are different but compatible methods for reconstructing ancient

Israelite life and thought. Historical study of ancient Israel aims at grasping the sequential articulation of Israel's experience and the rich variety of its cultural products, outstandingly its literature and religion. Sociological study of ancient Israel aims at grasping the typical patterns of human relations in their structure and function, both at a given moment or stage (synchronics) and in their trajectories of change over specified time spans (diachronics). The hypothetically 'typical' in collective human behavior is sought by comparative study of societies and expressed theoretically in 'laws', 'regularities', or 'tendencies' that attempt to abstract translocal and transtemporal structural or processual realities within the great mass of spatiotemporal particularities. In such terms, the tribal phase of Israel's social history is greatly illuminated by a theoretical design of social organization (as developed by Sahlins and Fried, among others).[1]

15.2 Historical method embraces all the methods of inquiry drawn from the humanities (e.g., literary criticism, form criticism, tradition history, rhetorical criticism, redaction criticism, history, history of religion, biblical theology). Sociological method includes all the methods of inquiry proper to the social sciences (e.g. anthropology, sociology, political science, economics). Sociological method in data collection and theory building enables us to analyze, synthesize, abstract, and interpret Israelite life and thought along different axes and with different tools and constructs from those familiar to us from historical method. Sociological inquiry recognizes people as social actors and symbolizers who 'perform' according to interconnecting regularities and within boundaries or limits (social systems).

15.3 If we wish to reconstruct ancient Israel as a lived totality, historical method and sociological method are requisite complementary disciplines. Historical method has long recognized the need for collaboration with archaeology, which as a discipline does not fit immediately or comfortably into the molds of the humanities. It is increasingly clear that the need of historical method for sociological inquiry into ancient Israel is just as urgent as its need for archaeology.

15.4 The social system of ancient Israel signifies the whole complex of communal interactions embracing functions, roles, institutions, customs, norms, symbols, and the processes and networks distinctive to the sub-systems of social organization (economic production, political order, military defense, judicatory procedure, religious organization, etc.). This social system must be grasped in its activity both in the communal production of goods, services, and ideas and in the communal control of their distribution and use.

15.5 We must resist the tendency to objectify Israel's social system into a static and monolithic hypostasis. It developed unevenly, underwent change, and incorporated tension and conflict. It was a framework for human interaction in which stability struggled against change and change eroded away stability. To call this complex of human interaction a social system is meaningful in that it was something more than an aggregation of discrete interhuman relations. There were regularities in the ways that Israelites organized their actions and thoughts, cooperated and contended with one another and with outside groups. These regularities form an analyzable system in the additional sense that they placed Israelite behavior and valuing under impulses and pressures toward normativeness or standardization. The social system tended to validate particular uses and distributions of natural and human resources and to delimit the exercises and distributions of personal and public power. The social system supplied the constraints of physical coercion and symbolic persuasion. By carefully noting the regularities and normative tendencies, it is possible to identify deviations and idiosyncrasies, both those that appear to have been 'social waste' and those that augured 'social innovation'.

15.6 The materials for sociological study of ancient Israel are the biblical text and all available extrabiblical evidence, written and material. In addition, the contents, structures, and developmental trajectories of other social systems — whether in Israel's immediate milieu or far beyond in time and space — are potentially relevant for comparative study. What is vital is that those contents, structures, and trajectories be examined in their total contexts and that they be compared with Israel in its total context. Alleged comparison of isolated social data torn out of systemic context is not comparison at all, but superficial juxtaposition lacking criteria for evaluation.

15.7 Sociological method works as a totality with its own analytic tools and theoretical perspectives quite as much as does historical method. Since historical method has already 'staked out' the field of biblical study, sociological method tends to arrive on the scene as a 'tacked on' adjunct to the customary privileged methods. As long as it performs in the role of supplying addenda or trying to do 'rescue work' on texts and historical problems that are momentarily resistant to historical methods, sociological method in biblical study will appear tangential and quixotic, as a problematic interloper.[2]

15.8 In any given text the sociological data may be no more than traces or shattered torsos. What are we to make, for example, of the kinship and marriage patterns attested in the patriarchal accounts? When sociologial method is called in to assist on this problem, it must try to contextualize the fragments within their larger complexes. So far, what is loosely called 'sociological' inquiry in this instance is a ransacking of ancient Near Eastern societies for parallel social phenomena. As in the appeal to Nuzi parallels to patriarchal kinship and marriage practices, insufficient attention is paid to the nature of the compared texts and to the social systems presupposed by the texts.

15.9 We are becoming freshly aware of the scandalous imprecision of such 'sociological' dabbling in the patriarchal traditions. The historical and social loci of the patriarchal traditions are simply not specifiable with any degree of confidence, and, in fact, there is every reason to believe that the historical and social horizons of the separate units and cycles of tradition are highly diverse.[3] In this stalemated situation, sociological inquiry can be most helpful when it extends the examination of how biblical texts with similar social data function in relation to texts or traditions of a similar nature among other peoples, whether literate or preliterate. Working on its own ground, sociological method will try to build up a body of knowledge about types or families of texts and traditions containing social data of certain kinds. How do these tradition types reflect or refract social reality in various types of social systems? How, for example, do genealogies function in oral and written traditions, as separate pieces and as elements within larger compositions, in tribal and in statist societies, etc.?[4]

15.10 In other words, a sociology of ancient Israel can be a proper complement to literary and historical inquiry only as it pursues its own proper object of reconstructing the Israelite social system as a totality, without prejudging which of its results are likely to be germane to understanding specific texts or historical problems and without diverting too much energy at the start to narrowly or obscurely framed 'social puzzles' in idiosyncratic literary and historical contexts.

15.11 In order to approximate comprehensive reconstruction of the Israelite social system, sociological method depends upon literary and historical criticism to undertake their tasks in a similarly comprehensive and systemic way. It also relies upon archaeology to break loose from the domination of historically framed orientations and to become an instrument for recovering the total material life of ancient Israelites irrespective of immediate applications to texts or to historical and sociological problems.

15.12 We may illustrate the way the integral projects of sociological method intersect with historical methods by noting the impact of the introduction of a new model for understanding the origins of Israel within its Canaanite matrix. The proposal that earliest Israel was not an invading or infiltrating people but a social revolutionary peasant movement within Canaan is at least a quasi-sociological model.[5] This heuristic model gives a new way of looking at all the old texts, biblical and extrabiblical, and the material remains.[6] Its effect has been to shift attention away from the precise historical circumstances of Israel's occupation of Canaan and toward the social processes by which Israel came to dominance. The effort to reconstruct a history of the occupation has long been deadended by the sparse historical data. A sociological model in this case provides a way of re-viewing the fragmentary historical data and in the end may help us to understand why the historical data are as obscure as they are. Finally, the specifically historical project of identifying the agents and spatiotemporal course of the emergent dominion of Israel in Canaan may be freshly facilitated by the working out of a different conception of the process at work in that achievement.

15.13 The effect of the peasant-revolt model of the origins of Israel has been to replace uncritical cultural assumptions about Israel's alleged pastoral nomadism with sharper sociological inquiry into the internal composition of early Israel, demographically and socioeconomically.[7] What exactly was this formation of people called Israel which took control in Canaan and whose social system took form as it gained the upper hand in the land? From what social spaces in Syro-Palestine did these people derive? What brought them together, enabled them to collaborate and to succeed? What were the goals these people shared and what social instrumentalities and material conditions contributed to their accomplishment? How does this social system of earliest Israel relate to those that preceded it and those against which it was counterposed? In other words, a proper model of the Israelite emergence in Canaan is not attainable apart from a proper model of the social system of the people who gained dominion in the land.[8] And of course neither the historical course of Israel's coming to power nor its emergent social system can be grasped without an understanding of the cultic-ideological process of tradition formation.

15.14 Up to the present, biblical studies have grappled with a model of the settlement and with a model of the cultic production of traditions, but there has been no adequate mediation between these two forms of inquiry within a larger analytic model of the social system involved in the twin process of taking power in the land and of building its own traditions. Martin Noth and George Mendenhall have made suggestive, incomplete, and at times mistaken attempts at an encompassing societal model. By drawing together the seminal contributions of Noth and Mendenhall, while weeding out their errors and false starts, we have the beginnings of a comprehensive social model for early Israel — or, more precisely, we have an inventory of the questions to be pursued and a general sense of the appropriate range of model options.[9]

15.15 A theoretical model of the origins and operations of early Israelite society will entail two axes of investigation: (1) the analysis of Israel's internal composition and structure at its several organizational levels and in its sectoral subsystems; (2) the characterization of Israel's social system as an operational and developing totality in comparison and contrast with other social systems. Both types of inquiry have synchronic and diachronic dimensions, and both types of inquiry will proceed dialectically in movement back and forth between concrete data about specific social systems and more abstract heuristic models, such as a theoretical design of 'tribalism'.[10]

15.16 As for the first task, evidence of the internal composition and eclectic structure of early Israel is largely biblical, but there are significant checkpoints in the Ugaritic, Alalakh, and Amarna texts, as well as rich resources concerning the material culture which have yet to be sufficiently mined. These immediate social data must be reflected upon against the backdrop of the large body of information and theory we now possess as a consequence of anthropological field studies, work in pre-history, and theorizing about social organization.

15.17 To what levels, ranges, and functions of social organization do the designations *shēvet̤, mishpaḥāh*, and *beth-'āv* refer? To date it has seemed sufficient to give them the native meanings of 'tribe', 'clan', and 'household' or 'extended family', without further ado. If early Israel is conceivable as a form of 'retribalization', what were the bonding organizational elements for holding together the segmented 'tribes' of diverse origin? Noth provided the summary answer of 'a sacral league', but his analogy between the Greek amphictyony and the intertribal league of Israel holds good at such an abstract level that it is of doubtful value in illuminating the crucial features of Israel's retribalization process. If Israel was a revolutionary movement within Canaanite society, how did matters develop from the uncoordinated restiveness of peasants and *'apiru* in Amarna days into the coalition of Israelite tribes? So far only Alt has offered a bare sketch of diachronic possibilities.[11] Merely appealing to Mosaic traditions and Yahwistic faith as 'explanations' for this coalescing process does not clarify and reconstruct the arduous struggle by which Israel put itself together in Canaan.

15.18 As for the second task, what was the over-all character of Israel's social system in comparison with other preceding and contemporary social systems? Such a comparison depends upon prior analysis of the social systems compared, and this analysis must follow an inventory of social desiderata so that we do not simply accept at face value either the form or the preponderance of specific social data as they happen to appear to us in texts. The comparison of social systems must constantly contextualize social systems and subsystems within the systems as a whole and in terms of the direction of their movement (e.g., expansion, differentiation, decline, transition to new systems, etc.).

15.19 Whether two different social complexes can be meaningfully compared is of course a matter of much discussion.[12] In biblical studies there has been an abundance of hasty and superficial cross-cultural comparisons. With each new discovery in the ancient Near East — such as the Amarna, Mari, Ugaritic, or Ebla texts — there has been a rush of claims for direct correlations between them and the biblical text, or for wholesale borrowing of systems or institutions or offices by Israel. On more careful analysis these 'parallels' either vanish or are greatly scaled down and nuanced. Such defaults establish the urgency of developing more reliable ways of comparing and contrasting social data and systems. If we wish, for example, to compare early Israelite society with its Canaanite counterpart and matrix, we face serious gaps in our knowledge of aspects of both entities, but these difficulties need to be brought out more systematically so that we will be clearer about the explanatory strength or weakness of our theory and thereby more aware of the kinds of research needed to test and improve theory.

15.20 It is evident that comparison of early Israel with other contemporary social systems entails diachronic and synchronic approaches. The social systems under comparison were not static, isolated entities; they developed internally and stood in varying relations to one another over spans of time and in different regions. A great deal of nuancing in treating these societal interfaces is required, often dismally lacking, for example, in the way 'Canaan' and 'Israel' are counterposed by biblical scholars, like characters in a morality play. According to all known analogies of revolutionary movements, we should expect that by no means all of the people of Canaan will have been 'polarized' by the nascent Israelite movement. It should be expected that as the Canaanite and rising Israelite social systems collided and conflicted, there will have been many people — probably a majority at first — who were conflicted in their own feelings and stances toward the two options. We should expect to find those who strove for neutrality, by choice or necessity, some who were half-hearted converts and those who switched sides, others who were secret supporters and yet others who were opportunist in their allegiances.[13] A re-examination of Israel's early traditions in terms of these dynamics of social revolutionary movements will reveal unexpected results toward a clearer conception of how Israel arose. The result is likely to be that the initially simplistic-appearing peasant revolt model will turn out to be even more complex and nuanced than the previous conquest and immigration models of Israel's origins.

15.21 In pursuing the comparative approach to Israelite society a major issue is how we are to decide which social systems should be compared with Israel's. Here we encounter the vexed problem of determining the boundaries of social systems in relation to the boundaries of the various historic state, tribal, and cultural formations which appear under various, vaguely depicted proper names and gentilics in the biblical and extrabiblical texts. No doubt we should identify the Canaanite city-state system as the dominant and definitive social system within earliest Israel's horizon.[14] But do the *'apiru* of the Amarna period form another such system? Here the time trajectory enters into consideration. The *'apiru* appear as a sub-set within Amarna 'feudalism' or 'Asiatic mode of production',[15] but insofar as the *'apiru* are seen as forerunners and one of the contributors to early Israel, they may indeed merit attention as another social system in embryo or as one trajectory along which the Canaanite social system declined and the Israelite social system rose. And it would be a grave methodological error to assume that early Israel arose along only one such trajectory. More often than not, the relation of the *'apiru* to early Israel has been examined as though it was the only or the primary pertinent relationship and that, if the *'apiru* data could not account for all or most of the features of early Israel, then they were irrelevant.

15.22 Pastoral nomadism as the supposed socioeconomic condition of early Israel might be viewed as another social system, but we now see how doubtful it is that we can locate an autonomous pastoral nomadic system in the immediate environment of Canaan contemporary with early Israel. The transhumant, village-based pastoral nomadism of Israel's environment was a minor sub-set of village tribalism subordinated socioeconomically and politically to sedentary Canaan. This pastoral nomadism was at most a minor contributor to early Israel. Nonetheless, it is necessary that this pastoral nomadic sub-specialization of village tribalism be carefully analyzed in order to reassess properly its vastly overstated role in Israelite origins.[16]

15.23 Other possible social systems in Israel's milieu come to mind. Do the Philistines constitute a new social system or are they merely heirs of the Canaanite system with new organizational twists, mostly of a political and military nature?[17] And what are we to make of the Ammonites, Moabites, and Edomites, whose origins were roughly contemporary with Israel and yet who did not become a part of Israel? Did these people feel the tug of Israel's social mutation, did some of them actually engage in social revolution, and if so, why did they accept kingship earlier than did Israel itself?[18]

15.24 Against this methodological sketch, we can see why the patriarchal traditions are particularly resistant to sociological analysis. From all appearances, those traditions belong to any number of peoples moving along various trajectories toward their convergence in early Israel. The patriarchal groups are proto-Israelites. Just as Noth recognized that the patriarchal traditions can only be approached backwards, working out of the congealing traditions of united Israel in Canaan, so the sociological analysis of the patriarchal communities must be approached backwards from the coalescing peoples of the intertribal community in Israelite Canaan. No sociological wonders will be workable on the patriarchal traditions until much more is known of their literary form and function, of their temporal horizons, and of their rootage in one or another of the social trajectories along which sectors of the Syro-Palestinian peoples converged toward their unity in Israel.[19]

15.25 An instance of the great difficulties in precise sociological analysis of the groups represented in the patriarchal traditions of Genesis 25–35 is the practice of using the connubium reported in Genesis 34 between Shechemites and Israelites as evidence for clan exogamy, a habit that goes back at least to the nineteenth-century anthropologist E. B. Tylor.

15.26 Genesis 34 tells us only that the two parties began to reach agreement on an alliance that was to include the exchange of wives. It does *not* tell us that a presupposition for the proposed wife-exchange was that Israelites or Shechemites could not marry among themselves and thus were obliged to get wives from outside. It does *not* tell us that the wives to be exchanged between the group constituted all or most of the marriage arrangements to be made by Israelites and Shechemites, thereby sharply reducing or excluding intragroup marriages or intermarriage with other groups. In other words, since we do not know the actual scope demographically or the internal social structure of the two contracting entities in Genesis 34, we have to try out various hypotheses to see how clan-exogamous they look on close examination. The results are not reassuring.

15.27 If, for example, 'Israel' in Genesis 34 was actually only a relatively small social group (still proto-Israelite), the connubium formulat might be read — especially noting the phrase 'we will become one people' (v.16) — as alluding to an early endeavor to meld together two groups of people into one tribal formation as complementary moieties. We might in that case be witnessing an initial act by which a member of later Israel (Manasseh or a section of Manasseh?) was formed from two originally separate groups that become segments practicing exogamy and thus exchanging wives within the newly shaped tribe. Granted that the formation was not carried through according to Genesis 34, it could at least be construed that connubium covenant was a means by which some peoples did come together as tribal entities within Israel, the tribes being built up by exogamous clans.

15.28 If, on the other hand, we imagine (as the final state of the text certainly does), that many Israelite tribes are present and that this is an 'external' arrangement between autonomous entities, a matter of intertribal 'foreign policy', we could say that Israel developed, or sought to develop, peaceful relations with some surrounding peoples by connubium covenant. But would a tribal organization (Israel) and a city organization (Shechem) be likely to enter into such an exogamous connubium? Would a large assemblage of tribes be able to get enough wives from one city for an exclusive connubium if exogamy forbade marriage of Israelites to fellow Israelites? The anthropological evidence is that whole tribes are not exogamous; it is clans within a tribe that are exogamous and that take wives from and give wives to other exogamous clans, the tribe as a whole remaining endogamous (although marriages may be allowed or prescribed outside the tribe in certain cases). The more large-scale the Israelite partner in the proposed connubium is conceived to have been, the more likely it becomes that the group already would have worked out marriage patterns, exogamous or otherwise (that cannot be known from the text), among its member units, and thus the more peripheral the connubium with Shechem would become as a wife-exchange mechanism and the more it would look like an alliance sealed with limited intermarriage bearing no correlation whatsoever with exogamy rules. Maybe the difficulties can be eased by conceiving the proposed connubium as an arrangement involving only a single clan or group of clans (of Manasseh?) located in the vicinity of Shechem. In that way a possible symmetrical, exogamously-based exchange of wives could be made plausible, but that hypothesis still fails to deal with the issue of whether a city would be interested in, or capable of, wholesale exogamy.

15.29 The farther our analysis and speculation about alternatives runs, the more evident it becomes that even if Genesis 34 goes back to early times, the obstacles to perceiving its exact sociohistoric context, the parties involved, and the mechanisms posited, are insuperably opposed to any reasonable confidence that this tradition shows the existence of exogamous clans in early Israel. A careful examination of other early biblical traditions thought to attest to clan exogamy yields similarly doubtful or flatly negative results.[20]

15.30 A main sociological task in the study of early Israel is the development of an adequate socioeconomic and cultural material inventory. This will require further historico-territorial and topological studies (of the sort begun by Alt and carried on by Rowton). Archaeology will have to attend not only to fortified cities but to the agricultural village/neighborhood complexes that included settlements, roads, fields, springs, irrigation, terrace systems, etc. Renewed attention will have to be given to population size, density, and distribution. The role of technological factors taken in combination will have to be explored more thoroughly: the introduction of iron, waterproof cisterns, improved terracing, and irrigation works. The archaeology of biblical Israel, previously overwhelmingly oriented to direct synchronizations with biblical literature and history (e.g. who were the kings of Genesis 14:1?), will increasingly offer a wider spectrum of data for the social and cultural reconstruction of the early Israelite movement. More and more we can hope for the collaboration of all methodologies in clarifying the material and socioreligious processes by which the Israelites came into dominance in the hill country of Canaan.[21]

15.31 The sociological inquiry which I have here illustrated in the instance of Israel's origins will equally apply to the major social transition to the monarchy and the resulting tensions and conflicts between state, empire, and tribe, as well as to the later period of the disintegration of the Israelite states and the survival and reconstruction of social forms into the postexilic age. It is obvious that in this task it will be necessary to call upon a host of specialists so far only sporadically enlisted in the task of reconstructing ancient Israel, e.g., agronomists, botanists, hydrologists, geologists, demographers, etc. The reconstructed cultural-material complexes will bear important indicators for social, military, and religious organization, especially when contextually compared with agrarian complexes and urban center/rural periphery complexes of similar sorts that can be studied at first hand by contemporary ethnologists.

15.32 In sum, it is essential that we devise a constructive model of the Israelite social system in its own right, firmly rooted in its material conditions, a model which delineates the major subsystems and segmented organization, as well as a model that grasps the integrating mechanisms and the solidifying ideology of the social whole.[22] This model will necessarily be viewed genetically in order to show how Israel arose, achieved its first cohesive form, and then passed over into other forms in the course of time through a combination of internal and external pressures. Synchronics and diachronics, internal dynamics and external interfaces and inter-penetrations will be drawn together under the principle or law of internal relations whereby an alteration in any element of the whole will be seen to bring about alterations in the entire system.

15.33 A model of the Israelite social system will incorporate the highly centralized and richly articulated religion of Yahweh. But it must do so sociologically by understanding the religion as a social phenomenon (institutionally and symbolically) and therefore related to all the other social phenomena within the system by the law of internal relations. This socioreligious inquiry must proceed without simplistic recourse to the tautological, philosophically idealist claim that because religion was central to the social system, it can be posited as the unmoved mover of the Israelite mutation.[23]

15.34 The sociological contribution to biblical hermeneutics is that the Israelite traditions must not only be interpreted within their original matrices, but must be interpreted from out of the social matrix of the interpreter. In the end it will be learned that an adequate biblical hermeneutics will require the investigation of the evolution of social forms and systems from biblical times until the present![24] Any interpreter who claims continuity with the biblical texts must also assume the continuity of the history of social forms as an indispensable precondition of the hermeneutical task.

Notes

1. Marshall Sahlins, *Tribesmen* (Englewood Cliffs, N.J.: Prentice-Hall, 1968); Morton H. Fried, *The Evolution of Political Society: An Evolutionary View* (New York: Random House, 1968).
2. Frank S. Frick and Norman K. Gottwald, 'The Social World of Ancient Israel', *SBL 1975 Seminar Papers* I (1975), pp. 165–78. See also Article 10 in that volume.
3. The precariousness of attaching patriarchal tradition to Bronze Age historical and social settings is independently demonstrated by Thomas L. Thompson, *The Historicity of the Patriarchal Narratives: The Quest for the Historical Abraham* (Berlin: de Gruyter, 1974) and John Van Seters, *Abraham in History and Tradition* (New Haven: Yale University Press, 1975).
4. Renger, working with Amorite texts in which he finds exogamous clan organizations, posits patriarchal exogamy for the biblical patriarchs, but can only succeed by capriciously regarding the biblical genealogies as actual descent lineages and sometimes as fictitious or eponymous constructs (J. Renger, '*mārat ilim*: Exogamie bei den semitischen Nomaden

des 2. Jahrtausends', *Archiv für Orientforschung* 14 [1973]: 103–7). Much more sophisticated in using comparative methods and thus advancing our comprehension of biblical genealogies are Abraham Malamat, 'Tribal Societies: Biblical Genealogies and African Lineage Systems', *Archives Européennes de Sociologie* 14 (1973): 126–36, and Robert R. Wilson, *Genealogy and History in the Biblical World*, Yale Near Eastern Researches, 7 (New Haven: Yale University Press, 1977). See also Norman K. Gottwald, *The Tribes of Yahweh: A Sociology of the Religion of Liberated Israel, 1250–1050 B.C.E.* (Maryknoll, N.Y.: Orbis Books, 1979), pp. 308–10, 334–37.

5. See George E. Mendenhall, 'The Hebrew Conquest of Palestine', *BA* 25 (1962): 66–87, and *The Tenth Generation: The Origins of the Biblical Tradition* (Baltimore: Johns Hopkins University Press, 1973). The same broad conclusion that early Israel was 'the *first* ideologically based socio-political revolution in the history of the world' was reached independently by Jan Dus, 'Moses or Joshua? On the Problem of the Founder of the Israelite Religion', *Radical Religion* 2, nos. 2 and 3 (1975): 26–41. See also the discussions in the May 1978 issue of *JSOT*: by Alan J. Hauser, 'Israel's Conquest of Palestine: A Peasants' Rebellion?', pp. 2–19; Thomas L. Thompson, 'Historical Notes on "Israel's Conquest of Palestine: A Peasants' Rebellion?" ', pp. 20–27; and Norman K. Gottwald, 'The Hypothesis of the Revolutionary Origins of Ancient Israel: A Response to Hauser and Thompson', pp. 37–52.

6. A striking example of heuristic value of a sociological model for textual criticism and historical reconstruction is Marvin L. Chaney, 'ḤDL-II and the "Song of Deborah": Textual, Philological, and Sociological Studies in Judges 5, with Special Reference to the Occurrences of ḤDL in Biblical Hebrew' (Ph.D. diss., Harvard University, 1976).

7. Norman K. Gottwald, 'Were the Early Israelites Pastoral Nomads?' in *Rhetorical Criticism: Essays in Honor of James Muilenburg*, ed. J. J. Jackson and M. Kessler (Pittsburgh: Pickwick, 1974), pp. 223–55; idem, 'Nomadism', *IDBSup* (1976), pp. 629–31; idem, *The Tribes of Yahweh*, pp. 464–92.

8. Gottwald, *Tribes of Yahweh*, pp. 493–587.

9. My critiques of Noth's and Mendenhall's models for early Israel will be found in *Tribes of Yahweh*, pp. 220–33, 345–57, 376–86, 599–602. See Note 5 above for Mendenhall, and Martin Noth, *A History of the Pentateuchal Traditions* (1948) (Englewood Cliffs, N.J.: Prentice-Hall, 1972).

10. For an elaboration of this programmatic statement, see *Tribes of Yahweh*, pp. 228–33, and for provisional conclusions on the content see pp. 237–587.

11. Albrecht Alt, 'The Settlement of the Israelites in Palestine' in *Essays in Old Testament History and Religion* (1925) (Oxford: Blackwell, 1966), pp. 175–204.

12. Walter R. Goldschmidt, *Comparative Functionalism: An Essay in Anthropological Theory* (Berkeley: University of California Press, 1966).

13. For an analysis of Israel's Canaanite converts, allies, and neutrals, see *Tribes of Yahweh*, pp. 555–583.

14. W. Helck, *Die Beziehungen Aegyptens zu Vorderasien im 3. und 2. Jahrtausend v. Chr.* (Wiesbaden: Harrassowitz, 1962); M.A.K. Mohammad, 'The Administration of Syro-Palestine during the New Kingdom', *Annales du Service des Antiquités de l'Egypte* (Cairo) 56 (1959): 105–37; Giorgio Buccellati, *Cities and Nations of Ancient Syria*, Studi Semitici, 26 (Rome: Università di Roma, 1967).

15. Norman K. Gottwald, 'Early Israel and "The Asiatic Mode of Production" in Canaan', *SBL 1976 Seminar Papers* (1976), pp. 145–54.

16. On classificatory typology of pastoral nomadism, see Douglas L. Johnson, *The Nature of Nomadism* (Chicago: University of Chicago Press, 1969), and for ancient Near East pastoral nomadism, see M. B. Rowton, 'Autonomy and Nomadism in Western Asia', *Orientalia* 42 (1973): 247–58, and 'Urban Autonomy in a Nomadic Environment', *JNES* 32 (1973): 201–15.

17. Cf. Albrecht Alt, 'Aegyptische Tempel in Palaestina und die Landnahme der Philister' in *Kleine Schriften*, I (1944) (Munich: Beck, 1953), pp. 216–30; Hanna E. Kassis, 'Gath and the Structure of the "Philistine" Society', *JBL* 84 (1965): 259–71.

18. Cf. S. H. Horn, 'Ammon, Ammonites', *IDBSup* (1976): 20; J. R. Bartlett, 'The Rise and Fall of the Kingdom of Edom', *PEQ* (1972), pp. 26–37, and 'The Moabites and the Edomites' in *Peoples of Old Testament Times*, ed. D. J. Wiseman (Oxford: Clarendon, 1973), pp. 229–58.

19. Gottwald, *Tribes of Yahweh*, pp. 32–44, 105–10.

20. Ibid., pp. 301–15.

21. Ibid., pp. 642–63.

22. Ibid., pp. 191–663.

23. Ibid., pp. 591–691.

24. Ibid., pp. 692–709.

16

Cyril S. Rodd
Max Weber and Ancient Judaism

This Extract first appeared as an article in the *Scottish Journal of Theology* in 1979. Cyril Rodd, editor of the distinguished *Expository Times*, is qualified both as a sociologist and as a biblical specialist. This brings to the Extract an unusual authority, even though it is clear (*pace* his remarks on Theissen in *16.25*) that most of the later Extracts in this Section are fully aware of the methodological difficulties that he raises. Quite apart from Rodd's sociological critique, this Extract is useful because of the continuing influence of Weber on biblical sociologists. In the first part of this Extract Rodd examines Weber's *Ancient Judaism* in the light of subsequent Old Testament research (*16.2–13*). The new archaeological evidence is obviously crucial (cf. *15.30*). However the shifts of interpretation, which produce the ironic situation that 'Weber strikes the modern reader as more up-to-date than many of the older text-books' (*16.11*), might be of more interest to the sociologist than Rodd seems to allow. Luhmann's understanding of the social role of the theologian/biblical scholar (***Extract 14***) might be applied here to good effect: each generation of biblical scholars apparently believes that it has 'established results' and protects these 'results' whilst being aware that they have been held and rejected before. Biblical interpretation is ripe for the attention of the sociologist of knowledge (Dennis Nineham's *The Use and Abuse of the Bible* (SPCK, 1976), starts to do this, but without a solid grounding in the sociology of knowledge). The second part of the article provides a useful critical account of *Ancient Judaism* from a specifically sociological perspective (*16.14–19*) and the third makes overall criticisms of the attempt to use sociology so directly in biblical research (*16.20–25*). Both of the major problems that Rodd sees in such uses of sociology — the adequacy of cross-cultural comparisons through time (i.e. diachronic comparisons) and the unavailability of vital socio-economic evidence of ancient communities – are discussed further in Gottwald's ***Extract 15***.

16.1 Anyone who attempts to assess Max Weber's study of ancient Judaism must adopt two stances, those of the Old

Testament specialist and of the sociologist, and I shall use these two view-points to provide the main structure of this article. I hope, nevertheless, to avoid becoming completely schizophrenic by drawing the two interpretations together in a final section. I should also make it clear that the discussion is based mainly upon those essays which were translated by Gerth and Martindale as *Ancient Judaism*, although these by no means exhaust the studies which Weber made of Hebrew religion.

1. *Ancient Judaism* in the light of Old Testament Studies

16.2 In his introduction to the English edition of Weber's *Sociology of Religion* Talcott Parsons writes, 'A great service could be done by a careful appraisal of what difference it would make in Weber's interpretations and generalizations on the sociology of religion if account were taken of the materials, both specifically factual and interpretive, which have become available since Weber wrote'.[1] While I am not competent to undertake such a 'careful appraisal', this desideratum indicates the main way in which I shall consider Weber's account of ancient Israel.

16.3 The translators have noted the humble caution with which Weber undertook his study.[2] Yet few readers can fail to be impressed by his mastery of the material. That unwillingness to accept secondary evidence which led him to learn Hebrew when he was sent to confirmation classes, so that he could read the Old Testament in the original language, drove him to master the main works in the Old Testament scholarship of his day. Seldom is he inaccurate in matters of fact. His survey of the literature is marked by a breadth of knowledge and critical acumen. Unfortunately, his policy of refraining from providing references except where there was some point of material detail at issue[3] makes it difficult to examine whether he failed to take into account important studies which were available to him, and I do not possess the detailed knowledge of the German literature up to about 1920 needed to do this.

16.4 Apart from specialised work in philology, the debate about hermeneutics and the appearance of several notable Theologies of the Old Testament, there are four major advances in Old Testament research since Max Weber wrote his essays that would affect his conclusions.

16.5 (a) The most important source of new knowledge has been the expansion of archaeological exploration throughout the whole of the Middle East, and this has influenced every aspect of the study of Israel. Weber was well aware of the importance of such discoveries. He refers to the Tell-el-Amarna tablets, the stories of Sinuhe and Wen Amun, the law code of Hammurabi, the Elephantine papyri, the Murashu documents and the discoveries at Boghazköy, while the reconstruction of the history of Israel which underlies his whole work is heavily dependent upon the Egyptology and Assyriology of his day. Four major groups of discoveries made since 1919 would certainly have forced Weber to modify details of his arguments, even if he judged that his general theoretical approach might remain unchanged. When he wrote these essays the only ancient laws from countries near Palestine which could be compared with the Old Testament laws were those of Hammurabi. (Neo-Babylonian laws were available, but there is no evidence that he knew of these.) Since then laws from very early times, Middle Assyrian laws and Hittite laws have been discovered and translated. In addition some scholars have seized upon Hittite treaty forms as shedding light upon the Israelite ideas of covenant. These discoveries are important because they enable us to reconstruct the social conditions of the different areas, and in view of Weber's preoccupation with the comparative method in sociology, he would surely have regarded them as indispensable evidence. In particular, for his purposes, the essential differences between the 'class' societies in these more advanced countries and the equality which is presupposed by Israelite laws would have been significant. Moreover, the form criticism of the laws which has followed the pioneering work of Alt would certainly have appealed to Weber.

16.6 Secondly, there are the discoveries at Ras Shamra, which permit a much greater understanding of Canaanite religion than had been possible when the main evidence was found in the writings of Philo of Byblos (a late source) and the Old Testament (a hostile witness). Here Weber might have found confirmatory evidence for his view of the 'orgiastic' nature of Baal religion. The discoveries also provide evidence for the social life in Ugarit which have been utilised in the study of Israelite society.

16.7 Thirdly, Weber wrote at a time when the historicity of the patriarchs was in doubt. The length of time between the date of Abraham according to the traditions and the time when the stories were written down made most scholars regard the narratives as evidence only for the later period. The debate has not ended, and contrasting attitudes can be seen in the histories of Martin Noth and John Bright and the detailed work of T. L. Thompson, de Vaux, and others. The pendulum has, in fact, swung first towards a greater readiness to accept that the stories fit the second millennium B.C. and therefore to credit the details with substantial accuracy, and more recently has returned to a scepticism similar to that of Weber's time.

16.8 Finally, there have been the dramatic discoveries by the Dead Sea. Weber showed great interest in the Essenes, the information about whom he presumably derived from Josephus, Philo and the elder Pliny.[4] Weber would certainly have used the new material, for it reveals both the separation from others which he stressed and an emphasis on prophecy which he regarded as central to the development of Judaism.

16.9 Besides these written sources, archaeology has unearthed a vast amount of non-epigraphic material which is highly important for the study of the interaction between social organisations and ideas. To give but one example, excavations at Tirzah show the social changes which occurred between the tenth and eighth centuries B.C., changes from a broadly egalitarian society with houses of similar size to a developing class society in which the rich and poor were segregated into different parts of the town.[5]

16.10 The other three developments in Old Testament research to which I wish to draw attention concern interpretation rather than factual knowledge and can be dealt with rather more briefly.

16.11 (b) At the time when Weber was writing, there was a widespread feeling among scholars that the general framework for a reconstruction of the history of Israel was firmly established. Wellhausen, coming at the end of a fruitful period of study, had cogently argued both for a particular documentary hypothesis of the formation of the Pentateuch and for the development of Israelite religion on this basis. Debates were still taking place, and Weber notes some of these, but the first two decades of the twentieth century were the age of 'critical orthodoxy', when there was a broad consensus of opinion that the main outlines of Israelite history and religion had been finally determined. Thus Weber tends to view ancient Israel as more unified than it probably was, although his sociological awareness of different social strata and the links between social structure and thought saved him from accepting this uncritically. He refused to accept a simple evolutionary scheme and was more ready to stress similarities and co-operation between priests (levites) and prophets than some other writers. He also saw the importance of Gunkel's form-critical approach. More recent scholarship has tended to be less sympathetic to the Wellhausen schema, and in some ways Weber strikes the modern reader as more up-to-date than many of the older text-books. His stress on the importance of the amphictyony of Israelite tribes and on the covenant is in line with modern approaches, though, as with the attitude to the patriarchs, most recently these have been under attack.

16.12 (c) Old Testament research has always applied insights derived from other disciplines to the biblical sources. Some of the most fruitful of these have come from social anthropology. Weber was aware of this, but he rightly criticised those who used it indiscriminately and claimed that religion everywhere developed along a single path from animism to monotheism. He was also sharply critical of those who found totemism in Israel, and again modern scholarship has sided with him. In more recent times exciting expositions of Israelite thought have been produced by scholars who carefully examined the Old Testament records in the light of the theories of contemporary anthropologists. Thus Pedersen drew inspiration from Grønbech, and Aubrey Johnson acknowledges the stimulation of the writings of Lévy-Bruhl and van der Leeuw. But again, while there is no wish to deny the value of the insights which social anthropology can provide, there has been considerable criticism of the way it has been applied. The criticisms which J. R. Porter and J. Rogerson have levelled at the concept of 'corporate personality' are an example of this.

16.13 (d) The emphasis upon the supposed conflict between prophet and priest tended to undervalue the place of worship for the religious life of the people. This tendency is found in Weber, who did not escape from an over-intellectualised and ethicised approach to Israelite religion. Not long after his death, however, the whole complexion of Old Testament scholarship was radically transformed with the publication of Mowinckel's *Psalmenstudien*. Some of Mowinckel's suggestions have not survived later criticism, but his emphasis upon the temple worship as a ritual drama and his stress upon the place of feeling in the religious consciousness of the Israelite have been widely accepted, although they have not gone unchallenged. If the worshipper apprehended the divine presence and power through psychological experiences which he obtained during the ritual of the temple worship, Israelite religion was not as sharply differentiated from the 'orgiastic' Canaanite religion as Weber supposed, and the advance towards rationality was less prominent than he asserted.

It is time, however, to consider Weber's essays from the aspect of sociology.

2. The Sociological Theory implicit in *Ancient Judaism*

16.14 It is common-place to point out that Weber's study of Judaism formed part of a much larger intellectual exercise intended to examine the relationship between religion and the development of the industrial capitalism of modern society. Yet while the Protestant Ethic is the key to all his writings in the sociology of religion, it is a key which can lock the door to a true understanding of his thought as well as open it. One thing must be emphasised from the start. Even if Weber viewed Judaism as a precursor to Christianity, and therefore as in a sense a precondition of the development of the Protestant ethic, he is quite certain that Judaism did not develop either an inner-worldly asceticism or economic rationality.[6] Unfortunately Weber makes little of his theory explicit in *Ancient Judaism*, and I cannot attempt to trace out the implications of his essentially descriptive narrative.[7] Five themes, however, appear to be central to his thought: (i) the interaction of society and ideas; (ii) the importance of covenant and prophecy over against the historical circumstances which brought disaster to the nation of Israel — the prophets are central to this as being the great innovators whose activity was chiefly responsible for the creation of Judaism;[8] (iii) the increasingly rationalised religion and ethics of Israel, in contrast to the orgiastic Baal religion of Canaan and magic in Babylon; (iv) the contrast between the world-accepting religion of Judaism and a world-denying religion such as the religion of India, seen especially in the difference between the Old Testament prophet, who was a demagogue with a mission, and the Indian contemplative, whose stance was that of 'exemplary prophecy';[9] (v) the interpretation of Israel as a 'pariah' people, with the consequent emphasis upon the *gēr* (resident alien, metic) in Israel and the marginal status of later Judaism.

16.15 Since we are considering these themes only in relation to the wider significance of Weber's book, we can be content with a very brief comment at this point. As in all his writings, Weber is never content with a one-sided causal analysis of any social phenomenon. He recognises that prophecy developed at a time of economic and social change, when peasants were becoming impoverished landless labourers or tenants of urban landlords, yet he refuses to accept that the prophets were simply champions of the poor. But more than in some other studies, perhaps because the material he was dealing with was almost entirely history-writing in one form or another (for he never wrote an analysis of the psalms or the wisdom writings), he lays considerable stress upon the historical vicissitudes which befell Israel. His interpretation of prophecy hardly makes sense without this emphasis upon the significance of historical disasters. Despite these reservations, the interaction of society and ideas must be regarded as the dominant theme. We shall have to consider later whether Weber's handling of this was satisfactory and whether the evidence permits such a study.

16.16 Weber looked upon rationality with the accompanying 'disenchantment of the world' as the major factor in the evolution of modern society. It is this which provides the link between the studies of ancient Israel and of Puritanism. In his essay on 'The Social Psychology of World Religions'[10] Weber attempts to analyse the different meanings of the term. He limits 'economic rationality' to the type of behaviour found in the West since the sixteenth and seventeenth centuries. Rationality, however, can also mean 'systematising thought' in terms of abstract concepts, and the calculation of means to attain definite ends. 'Rational' can be the opposite of 'religious', and yet as meaning the *systematic* orientation of means to goals and the distinguishing of 'valid' means from what is empirically given, there can be 'rational' methods to achieve religious ends. There are many more occasions when Weber uses 'rational' and 'rationalisation' in *Ancient Judaism* than the thirty or so listed in the index, but within these thirty occurrences 'rational' is contrasted with such things as blind chance, magic, mysticism, unsystematic ethical demands, divination, ecstasy, and religious philosophies which are not readily understandable. Thus the basic sense of rationality is that systematisation which removes inconsistencies of thought or action and produces a self-consistent and purposeful way of life. It is this rationality in religious ideas and ethics which Weber finds developing in Israel. He does not seem to make much of rationality as a motivation.

16.17 Despite this emphasis upon rationality, the essential nature of later Judaism as a 'pariah' people, living on the edge of society and not fully subject to its norms is the central feature of Weber's interpretation of the economic activity of medieval and modern Jews.[11] In Weber's view, although prophecy contributed to this, it was the Exile which finally brought it about, through the ritual separation of the Jews from the surrounding nations in order to preserve their identity as a people.[12] This feature of Judaism's later existence enabled the Jews to engage in the commercial capitalism for which they became famous, without motivating them to the Puritan industrial capitalism.[13]

These have been fragmentary comments, but it is necessary to move on to consider Weber's book more generally.

16.18 The debate about the central thesis of *The Protestant Ethic* continues. On the one hand historians and economists tend to be critical (we may note Samuelsson as an example of one who collects an array of malcontents and adds his own rapier thrusts), while Marxists claim that Weber muddied the argument by introducing non-economic factors and independent variables; on the other hand sociologists of development (chiefly Americans) have claimed that a substitute for the Protestant ethic will have to be found before underdeveloped countries can modernise their economy and social structure, and Bellah finds an equivalent of Calvinistic predestination in the sense of endless obligation taught by some of the Japanese sects. The essential feature of *The Protestant Ethic*, however, was Weber's attempt to offer an explanation which would link religious beliefs with economic motivation, and he found this in unintended psychological consequences of Calvinistic teaching. Put over-simplistically, what he argued was that the removal of priestly mediation placed the individual alone before his God, and when this was coupled with absolute predestination the individual in his isolation sought reassurance that he was among the saved through the success which accompanied his application of hard work and thrift. We may, if we will, criticise his introduction of psychology and demand a sociological explanation, but Weber *did* posit causal links. This is missing in much of *Ancient Judaism*. Even where psychology is discussed (and Weber followed Hölscher in regarding the canonical prophets as ecstatics, though he thought that they were distinct from the earlier *nᵉbîʾîm*) the rationalisation is mainly intellectual and explicit. Both levites and prophets tend to be aware of what they were doing. The chief place where sociological explanation is offered is in the later 'separation' of the pariah people, which aimed at religious purity but led to important economic consequences in medieval times.

16.19 We must ask, therefore, whether Peter Berger is correct when he suggests that by the time he wrote *Ancient Judaism* Weber had moved away from a central concern with economic rationality to a realisation that it is a wider rationality which is the characteristic of modern society, in a word, that he is tracing the development of secularisation.[14] The word itself occurs only once in *Ancient Judaism*, and there in a non-technical sense — the law of Deuteronomy which permitted the eating of flesh without the offering of sacrifice.[15] In some of his other studies in the sociology of religion Weber mentions 'secular', always as the opposite of some aspect of religion such as contemplation.[16] Thus he does not refer explicitly to the process of secularisation, and the word 'disenchantment' does not, I believe, occur in *Ancient Judaism*. Nevertheless, rationalisation of the religious ethic is an important step on the road towards secularisation of the whole of life, and to this extent Weber has pointed to one factor in the growth of secular society.

3. A Synoptic View

16.20 From this point we can proceed no further without linking together our two perspectives. One of the strongest emphases in Old Testament study today, induced perhaps by the large amount of data presented by the archaeology of the ancient Near East, is the need to set Israelite life and religion within the context of the cultures of the surrounding nations. This modern approach is very different from the pan-Babylonianism of Weber's time which he himself criticised.[17] It is true that the attempt to construct a common pattern of myth and ritual throughout the ancient Near East has been generally abandoned, but the rituals of Babylon and the myths of Ugarit have had a considerable influence upon studies of the Israelite cult and the place of the king in the nation. Much more attention is now turned towards differences between these cultures and that of Israel, both in such features as royal ideology and in the use of myth. The important study by Henri Frankfort and others traces the emancipation of thought from the mythological ways of thinking that were prevalent in Egypt and Babylon. The authors argue that the decisive break with myth was made in ancient Israel and that it was this break which led, through Greek philosophy, to the modern Western scientific understanding of the world. Thus they examine the same problem which concerned Max Weber but over a narrower sector of man's culture. The feature of this and other studies to which attention must be drawn is that it is with other *ancient* cultures that comparisons are made.

16.21 Weber makes many references to Egypt and Babylon, and he notes such features as the effect of the Egyptian bureaucracies upon the development of ecstasy and the care of the poor,[18] but his main comparisons are with Indian and, to a lesser extent, Chinese religion. We note particularly the first sentence of the book: 'The problem of ancient Jewry, although unique in the socio-historical study of religion, can best be understood in comparison with the problem of the Indian caste order'. This was partly due to the range of his own knowledge, partly because of the aim of his studies in religion. He was aware of the importance of archaeological discoveries, but he did not examine them systematically. At this point Old Testament scholars become uneasy about his approach. To some extent this is due to the difference between an historical and a sociological approach, but it is more than merely a difference of perspective and it raises important questions as to how far comparisons between societies widely separated in time and by geography are valid. We have noted that Weber uses relatively few theoretical constructs in his interpretation of the development of ancient Israel. The student of the Old Testament, being aware of the complexity of the Israelite society and that of neighbouring countries and stressing the gulf which separates ancient Israel from modern Western society, regards it as inappropriate to apply the broader generalisation of sociological theory to the Old Testament records. Basically what I am suggesting is that Weber tended to work backward from late Judaism, which he interpreted in terms of two key concepts, rationality and the pariah people, and tried to discover how this social group developed out of ancient Israel. Old Testament scholarship would prefer to focus attention upon the world out of which Israel arose and to ask what caused the sharp differences which appear at a very early stage of Israel's history.

16.22 I have noted already that Weber is conscious of historical factors in the development of Judaism, but he is essentially a sociologist who seeks to discover general patterns of social relationships. I suspect that this was an additional reason why he introduced the comparisons with India and China, and also with other societies such as those around the Mediterranean and in medieval towns. It is akin to the comparisons which Edmund Leach, a social anthropologist, likes to make. As a sociologist Weber was right in accepting as a basic presupposition the belief that such comparisons would reveal causal relations, because the comparative method is the only way to isolate variables in societies where laboratory experiment is impossible, but the Old Testament specialist will regard his use of terms like peasants, plebeians and petty bourgeoisie as a misleading terminology which may highlight features about the society that might otherwise be overlooked, but which has the same danger as is contained in describing the racial divisions in the Southern United States as a caste system. Similarly today scholars with an awareness of social anthropology are cautious about the use of the term nomad.

16.23 Finally I must revert to an issue which was glanced at earlier. One of Weber's main aims was to trace the interaction between society and ideas. For this reason his analysis of Israelite society is highly important. Difficulties arise, however, when we ask upon what basis Weber erects his reconstructions and theories. The Old Testament consists solely of religious texts, even though a number of them are also historical narratives and many contain allusions to society. Not merely is it a selection from a much larger literature which once existed, but at no point does it specifically describe the social institutions of Israel. Thus the social life has to be reconstructed from the documents, which include narratives, laws, prophetic oracles and other forms of literature, all coming from a wide range of dates and settings in life. Some scholars have even used metaphors in their descriptions of society.[19] As we have noted, archaeology now has much to offer, although the evidence from Palestine is mainly non-epigraphic and is subject to conflicting interpretations. Unless, therefore, a close control is kept upon the evidence, the arguments will run the risk of being circular. It is by no means clear that what Weber attempted is possible on the basis of the data available. Sometimes he has to argue for probabilities in Israel on the basis of conditions in societies which he regarded as similar. Although scholars such as de Vaux produce convincing accounts of Israelite institutions, the two variables of society and ideas cannot be set out with the independence needed to carry through this part of Weber's proposed analysis. Weber, as I have tried to show, was too great a scholar not to be aware of the great difficulties involved in dealing with the Old Testament literature. Philology, textual criticism, a critical analysis of the documents, the study of the forms of the traditions, the assessment of the historical value of the material and its chronology, and the interpretation of Hebrew concepts are essential preliminaries to the kind of sociological analysis which he attempted. He recognised this, yet he does not seem to be fully aware of the complexities involved.

16.24 What I have been arguing is this. Old Testament research since Weber's time shows that it is impossible to carry out the programme which he attempted because of the state of the evidence available. It is not possible now, and it was not possible in his day. Weber thought that he could carry it through because the leading scholars of the time believed that the history and religious development of Israel had been recovered with substantial accuracy. A work such as *Israelite & Judaean History*, edited by John H. Hayes and J. Maxwell Miller, reveals just how far the present lack of confidence has gone. Moreover, because of the state of biblical scholarship, the gaps between ancient Israel and both other ancient civilisations and more recent societies appeared smaller than we now know them to be.

16.25 This leads me to ask whether the past is ever amenable to sociological analysis, since Weber's attempt to conduct such an analysis of an ancient civilisation set the problem in high relief. The difficulty is not simply a matter of the paucity of data, although for more distant periods this will almost always be a factor. The basic problem lies in the fact that the evidence has 'set' and cannot be forced by the researcher to reveal a choice between two or more options. The sociologist can neither decide what set of empirical facts he will collect nor posit and test hypotheses, both of which operations are central to scientific sociology, if the study of man in society can ever be truly 'scientific'. My own research into the social teaching of the churches underlined the difference between the historical part of the study and the survey of attitudes among church members today. Should we not be well advised, then, to leave the past to the historian, albeit the historian who is aware of sociological factors, and limit the sociologist to explaining the present by means of the ever-advancing future which will support or disprove his hypotheses? At any rate *Ancient Judaism* appears as both a pioneer work and the climax of an intellectual tradition to which we can never return. I find it interesting that the most recent attempt to carry sociology into the biblical area, Gerd Theissen's *The First Followers of Jesus* (London, 1978), contains the same weakness that we have seen in Weber's study of Israel.

Notes

1. Max Weber, *Sociology of Religion* (London, 1965), p. xxvi, n. 8.
2. Cf. *Ancient Judaism* (Glencoe, 1952), pp. ix, 425–9.
3. Ibid., p. 429.
4. Cf. ibid., p. 74. The Damascus Rule or Zadokite Document was published in 1910, but I do not think Weber refers to it.
5. Cf. R. de Vaux, 'Tirzah' (in *Archaeology and Old Testament Study*, ed. D. W. Thomas, Oxford, 1967). De Vaux actually uses the term 'urban proletariat' in his description of Stratum II (p. 378).
6. Cf., e.g., *Sociology of Religion*, pp. 246–54, *Ancient Judaism*, p. 343, 'Rational economic activity on the basis of formal legality never could and never has been religiously valued in the manner characteristic of Puritanism'; also pp. 254, 401, 403.
7. Few detailed studies of *Ancient Judaism* have been made, and on the whole sociologists fight shy of it. One of the most important is Julius Guttmann, 'Max Webers Soziologie des antiken Judentums', *Monatsschrift für Geschichte und Wissenschaft des Judentums*, LXIX (1925), pp. 195–223. See also H. F. Hahn, *The Old Testament in Modern Research* (Philadelphia, 1966), pp. 159ff.; Reinhard Bendix, *Max Weber, an Intellectual Portrait* (London, 1966), chaps. VII and VIII.
8. Bendix (op. cit., pp. 264f., 289) claims that *Ancient Judaism* is a study in the sociology of innovation. Cf. Talcott Parsons' stress on the importance of the 'breakthrough' for Weber (*Sociology of Religion*, pp. xxxiii–xxxiv).
9. *From Max Weber* (ed. H. H. Gerth and C. Wright Mills, London, 1948), p. 285. Cf. Talcott Parsons' analysis of Weber's theory in *Sociology of Religion*, pp. xix–lxvii.
10. *From Max Weber*, p. 293; cf. Bendix, op. cit., pp. 278f.; Talcott Parsons, op. cit., pp. xxxiif.
11. *Ancient Judaism*, pp. 3–5.
12. Ibid., pp. 336ff., 356, 363f., 417.
13. *Sociology of Religion*. pp. 248ff.
14. Peter Berger, *The Social Reality of Religion* (London, 1969), pp. 113ff. Hahn also suggests that Weber's discussion of rationalisation 'has some bearing on the problem of how and when Israel outgrew the "pre-logical" type of thinking characteristic of primitive peoples' (op. cit., p. 165) — an assertion which is questionable in the form in which it is expressed.
15. *Ancient Judaism*, p. 186.
16. *Sociology of Religion*, pp. 171, 175, 204, 213, 257.
17. *Ancient Judaism*, p. 427.

18. Ibid., pp. 96, 256.
19. E.g. R. H. Kennett, *Ancient Hebrew Social Life and Custom as indicated in Law, Narrative and Metaphor* (Schweich Lecture, 1931).

17

Robert P. Carroll
Ancient Israelite Prophecy and Dissonance Theory

Extract 17 first appeared as an article in *Numen* in 1977 and acted as a forerunner to Carroll's *When Prophecy Failed: Reactions and Responses to Failure in the Old Testament Prophetic Traditions* (SCM, 1979). Carroll, now a reader in Old Testament studies at the University of Glasgow, uses the theory of cognitive dissonance from social psychology as a means to understand better elements within Old Testament prophecy. The Extract is useful because it contains a clear account of cognitive dissonance (*17.3–5*), which is also relevant to *Extract 19*, and because it faces the problems of lack of evidence and of diachronic cross-cultural comparisons raised in the preceding Extract by Cyril Rodd. Indeed, the Extract is remarkable in that it makes few positive observations about the use of dissonance theory until it is more than half completed (*17.14f.*). Having set out the theory, Carroll argues that even the material which is most suitable for examination — Isaiah, Jeremiah and the post-exilic prophets — contains many features which do not satisfy the conditions of Festinger's thesis (*17.7f.*). It is difficult to find unequivocal predictions which are clearly disconfirmed, which are known to be disconfirmed by the prophets themselves, and which cannot simply be blamed upon the bad behaviour of the people to whom the predictions were originally made. Fully admitting all this, Carroll sees the relevance of the theory as a general indicator of 'the problems facing any prophet in a given situation in which expectation of a particular nature comes under pressure from events outside the prophet' (*17.14*). This is a modest, but nonetheless highly significant, claim for this social theory as it relates to biblical evidence. Carroll clearly believes that Festinger's, admittedly twentieth-century, study has set out in general terms the problems facing *any* prophet whose predictions have apparently failed. If this is accepted (and that in itself is naturally a matter for debate amongst social scientists), then the problems of diachronic cross-cultural comparison are not insuperable. Evidence may still be hard to establish (*17.23*), but such comparisons cannot be ruled out as illegitimate even before they are attempted. Rather the scholar should ask whether or not Carroll's particular analyses of prophets such as Isaiah (*17.15*) are sustainable.

17.1 Among the dialectical structures of ancient Israelite prophecy the tension between the critique of society (threat oracles) and predictions of future wellbeing (salvation oracles) is the most striking. The trenchant criticism of society's corrupt, oppressive practices has become a hallmark of prophecy as has its equally characteristic prophesying of a golden future when Israel would live securely under a Davidic king and Jerusalem would be the focus of religious attention for the nations. In dialectical terms the elements of judgment and promise represent prophecy's No and Yes to Israelite society. Now it is generally acknowledged that the social criticism of the prophets was a percipient description of Israel's socio-political state and their predictions of doom accurately anticipated the future. But the salvation oracles, their positive hopes for the future, were a complete failure to foresee the longterm propects with any degree of accuracy. The conventional idiom of these oracular hopes (e.g. Am. 9: 11–15; Is. 2: 2–4; 9: 2–7; 11: 1–9; Jer. 31: 31–34) suggests that the prophets had given little thought to the shape of the future other than to believe that there would be a future. By its very nature predicting the future is precarious yet this was considered to be the business of the prophet (cf. Dt. 18: 22). This failure of prophecy raises questions about the nature of prophecy and the prophet's apperception of his own work in relation to the world at large. In particular this paper is devoted to a consideration of the problem of whether the prophet was aware of his failure and endeavoured to bridge the gap between expectation and reality or simply had a different view of reality which permitted him to avoid confrontations with possible failure.

17.2 Before examining the material available for such an approach it is necessary to consider briefly some views of prophecy which would reduce the above problem to a pseudo-problem. Thus any view of the prophetic books which maintained that only oracles of judgment were authentic in the eighth century prophets would dismiss the presence of salvation oracles in Amos, Isaiah of Jerusalem and Micah as secondary interpolations.[1] This would effectively rule out the notion of failure in these prophets and only leave the subsequent prophets open to such a criticism. The cultic approach to prophecy which sees the prophet as a cult functionary proclaiming salvation and judgment as part of his ministry of the covenant cult would make salvation and judgment purely formal elements of a sacred liturgy.[2] The cultic view of reality may be seen in the royal psalms where the often beleaguered Israelite king is regarded as the scourge of the nations (Pss. 2: 7–9; 45: 2–5; cf. 72: 8–11). Problems too difficult to solve elsewhere found resolution in a cultic context (cf. Ps. 73; Hab. 3). This cultic interpretation of prophetic statements can be linked to a formal linguistic approach to their utterances whereby the fulfilment of any prediction is a matter of linguistic usage.[3] Thus a spiritual understanding of what a prophet predicted might constitute its fulfilment. Any of these three approaches would seriously modify the claim that predictions of salvation in the prophets were open to the charge of having failed to be fulfilled. However, apart from the proponents of these views, most scholars tend to reject the cultic interpretation of prophecy and many regard the salvation promises of Is. 9: 2–7; 11 : 1–9 as not improbably from Isaiah himself.[4] There can be little doubt that Second Isaiah was a prophet of salvation who fully expected the return from exile to be a triumphalist affair. As such he is a classical example of a prophet seriously compromised by the event as it later materialised. But this view of the prophet as a foreteller of the future is in keeping with the biblical presentation of the prophet. The deuteronomistic history, Joshua – 2 Kings, presents much of its history as the unfolding of the prophetic word, the deuteronomic legislation for the prophet concerns itself with the fulfilment of predictions (Dt. 18: 20), and the clash between the prophets Jeremiah and Hananiah (Jer. 28) is one of conflicting predictions about the future. Thus it is reasonable to pursue this line of enquiry in terms of predictive prophecy and its failure.

17.3 Where prophecy failed there must have been a gap between expectations encouraged by the prophets and the reality in which they lived without any evidence of fulfilment. This gap between belief and reality may have affected the prophet and his followers in varying ways, ranging from the ability to ignore it altogether to such loss of confidence as to silence the prophet. The real problem in dealing with this issue in Old Testament prophecy is the paucity of data about the prophet's self-awareness of such crises. In order to maximise the exploration of this subject I wish to have recourse to dissonance theory. The theory of cognitive dissonance was put forward by Leon Festinger in 1957.[5] It is essentially a psychological description of how people react to problems arising out of clashes between belief and behaviour. In simple behavioural terms dissonance is said to exist where there is a conflict between an attitude, e.g. the belief that certain indulgences are bad for one's health, and a practice, e.g. the persistent performing of such indulgences. Attempts to modify or resolve the dissonance may include refusing to think about the issue, or a denial of the existence of a conflict, or avoiding the company of people who insist on pointing out the discrepancy between belief and behaviour, or even the maintenance of the view that in spite of the harmful effects of such practices the overall gains outweigh any possible damage done to health. The intensity of dissonance resolution will depend entirely upon the degree of conflict existing in a situation and the pressures put on a person to establish an equilibrium between attitude and behaviour. In this way dissonance reduction can be seen as 'the psychological analogue of the physiological mechanisms which maintain homoeostasis in the body'.[6] Perhaps the most important aspect of eliminating dissonance is the role of social support, i.e. the social group provides the individual with a context of cognitive factors with which he can identify and which can protect him from dissonance producing opinions.[7]

17.4 The theory of cognitive dissonance has had an immense impact in the field of social psychology, particularly in relation to post-decision studies.[8] But it is Festinger's work on groups with specific predictive expectations which is most relevant for biblical studies. In his book *When Prophecy Fails* Festinger and his colleagues studied a group who had received a message from outer space informing them of an imminent flood about to destroy their part of the world.[9] When the flood failed to materialise on the expected date, instead of the group disintegrating as might be expected, the Seekers, as they were called, went public and even began to seek converts for their beliefs.[10] This reaction illustrates one of the conclusions generated by dissonance theory 'when people are committed to a belief and a course of action, clear disconfirming evidence may simply result in deepened conviction and increased proselyting'.[11] However further research has suggested that this principle requires some modification so as to take into account whether the group's environment is hostile or friendly. Thus where there is minimal social support and the group is ridiculed there will be a drive towards proselytising but where there is more social support and the group is not ridiculed by outsiders there may be little need to convert others.[12] As the function of conversion in dissonance theory is to reduce dissonance by persuading more and more people that the system of belief is correct and thus increase the social support within the group so there is less need for such tactics when the public at large is not overtly hostile.

17.5 The opening chapter of *When Prophecy Fails* discusses unfulfilled prophecies and disappointed messiahs and has an obvious bearing on this study of prophecy.[13] But its main importance is the paradigm of conditions set out for testing Festinger's thesis about increased fervour following disconfirmation of a belief. For this will permit the biblical scholar to check his data to see if this approach can be used in their analysis. Although it is specifically designed to test a particular form of activity response to dissonance it can be used to delineate general reactions to the failure of expectations. The paradigm may be set out briefly as follows:

1. There must be conviction.
2. There must be commitment to this conviction.
3. The conviction must be amenable to unequivocal disconfirmation.
4. Such unequivocal disconfirmation must occur.
5. Social support must be available subsequent to the disconfirmation.[14]

Conditions 1 and 2 make the belief resistant to change, 3 and 4 suggest factors that would entail the discarding of the belief, and 5 allows a situation whereby the belief may be maintained or even used to persuade others of its truth. In the subsequent discussion Festinger looks at various millennial or messianic movements such as the second coming of Christ, the Sabbatai Zevi movement in the 17th century, and the Millerites in the 19th century. The main difficulty for his thesis is finding sufficient data to confirm or refute it. The ambiguity of the evidence also militates against a cogent exposition of the theory when applied to complex traditions such as the second coming of Christ.[15]

17.6 In applying dissonance theory to the prophetic traditions of the Old Testament it is necessary to restate the theory in such a way that it can be usefully applied to material outside the normal range of social psychology. The general theory of cognitive dissonance describes at least three responses to dissonance which can be readily adapted for biblical research purposes. These consist of avoidance of sources likely to increase dissonance, i.e. a tendency to associate with those who hold the same opinion, or the production of rationalisations and explanations which show how the dissonance can be reduced by new evidence, or by gaining converts to the movement whose conversion will constitute new elements of cognition consonant with the belief system.[16] Thus social support is of paramount importance in providing the individual with a secure context from which he may avoid or modify all dissonant elements. To translate these responses into suitable categories for application to prophetic movements of the biblical period I would suggest the traditional notions of exclusivity of grouping, hermeneutical systems, and various forms of missionary activity. The tendency towards exclusiveness is apparent in certain periods of ancient Israelite society. The histories of Judaism and Christianity are filled with complex hermeneutical systems explaining doctrines and dogmas in such a way as to avoid charges of inconsistent or contradictory notions. Missionary movements have been a strong feature of Christian activity over the centuries. However these elements are not in themselves responses to dissonance. But given a context of prophetic prediction their presence might indicate an area of response to the experience of dissonance among members of the group. Thus the theory may provide the researcher with another analytical probe for his material.

17.7 The paradigm set out for describing a suitable testing of the dissonance theory raises one major problem for prophecy and that is the difficulty of clearly establishing evidence for conditions 3 and 4. There are many examples of predictions in the Old Testament which have been fulfilled, e.g. Jeremiah's predictions of the destruction of Jerusalem, and predictions which have not been fulfilled, e.g. Israel's sharing power with Egypt and Assyria (Is. 19: 24) or the hopes expressed in Is. 9: 2–7; 11: 1–9. But there is little evidence of a conscious awareness on the prophet's part that his predictions have failed to materialise. Condition 4 states 'such undeniable disconfirmatory evidence must occur and must be recognised by the individual holding the belief'.[17] This lack of awareness poses the question whether the prophet seriously expected these predictions of future bliss to be actually fulfilled and if so did he expect such fulfilment in his own lifetime? It certainly seems to be the case that the prophets hardly ever anticipated the distant future (cf. Dt. 18: 20).[18] For them the immediate future was the stage on which would be played out the consequences of Israel's response to the prophetic message. The one clear example available of a prophet confronted by a positive response to his preaching and therefore a rescinding of the threat of doom is Jonah. And that presents a picture of a prophet shocked and disappointed by the success of his mission! It may be that the prophets were simply unaware or incapable of conceiving of the possibility of failure, in which case it becomes difficult to apply rigorously the conditions of Festinger's thesis. But it is the structure of the prophetic proclamation that poses the main obstacle to the discovering of dissonant elements in the prophetic traditions.

17.8 The basic structure of Israelite prophecy is the proclamation of a message designed to create a response in the people to whom it is addressed and thereby to influence their behaviour. Within the critique of society there is the call to return or repent, that is, a call to make a decision and change direction. This principle of repentance makes the people a moral agent capable of responding to the prophetic word. As such it means that prophecy cannot be simply thought of as a predicting the future irrespective of man's action in the present time. Although the literature influenced by deuteronomic ideas (e.g. Dt. 18: 22; Jer. 28) gives the impression of the prophet as a predicter of future events this is an inadequate summary of his role in Israelite society. The kernel of the prophetic summons to transformation in society may be summed up in the words of Isaiah 'cease to do evil, learn to do good' (1: 16, 17). It is, of course, necessary to add a rider to the principle of repentance by pointing out that an oversimplified notion of repentance is ruled out in certain instances, e.g. Isaiah's preaching is designed to prevent the people turning and being healed (6: 10), and Jeremiah recognises that public repentance can be a false form of repentance (3: 10). At the other end of the scale there is the example of Jonah's preaching to the Ninevites which resulted in national fasting and repentance and averted the threated doom (3: 4–10).

17.9 This principle of repentance and its effect on the prophetic proclamation is enunciated most clearly in Jer. 18: 7–10:

> If at any time I declare concerning a nation or a kingdom, that I will pluck up and break down and destroy it, and if that nation, concerning which I have spoken, turns from its evil, I will repent of the evil that I intended to do to it. And if at any time I declare concerning a nation or a kingdom that I will build and plant it, and if it does evil in my sight, not listening to my voice, then I will repent of the good which I had intended to do to it.

17.10 The element of response here controls the future so that whatever a prophet might declare about a nation's prospects was subject to that nation's response. So Festinger's simple paradigm of a prediction-fulfilment state of affairs will not cover the prophetic case. Furthermore there is built into this statement about response a fail-safe device for prophetic prediction. No prediction can ever really be falsified because whatever may be predicted of the future it will be subject to human reaction. If the future turns out to be other than expected then the principle expounded in Jer. 18: 7–10 can be utilised to show how the prediction was controlled by men's actions. There is even some evidence within the Old Testament traditions that this possibility was realised on occasion. The oracles of Jerusalem's destruction given in Mic. 1–3 are shown to have been neutralised by Hezekiah's repentance (Jer. 26: 18, 19). A similar application of the repentance principle may also have operated in the Chronicler's account of the reign of king Manasseh (2 Chron. 33: 10–20; cf. the account in 2 Kings 21: 1–18 which has no mention of Manasseh's prayer). It is also possible to see the false repentance of Jer. 3: 10 as the reverse side of this application, namely, repentance may only be a show of repentance so if disaster follows national repentance the rule remains valid.

17.11 The prophetic call to decision which can evoke man's response and bring about what Buber calls 'the extreme act: the turning to God'[19] stresses the activity of man but must not be taken to mean that God is subject to man's response in such a way that the notion of transcendence is lost. For another strand in the prophetic proclamation is the declaration of redemption, especially in Second Isaiah. Both repentance and redemption are aspects of the transformation of man, one from the human side and the other from the divine side.[20] Thus the vision of salvation in Is. 9: 2–7 is anchored in the assertion 'the zeal of Yahweh of hosts will do this' as if to suggest that the future is not entirely dependent upon man's response. The reverse of this positive aspect of transcendence is Is. 6: 10 where the proclamation subverts man's response in order to prevent his turning away from disaster. These signs of transcendence may well modify the principle laid down in Jer. 18: 7–10 and permit at some level the introduction of dissonance theory. But it must be recognised that the principles of transcendence and repentance severely qualify any application of this theory to prophetic traditions.

17.12 If the notion of repentance removes the bulk of Old Testament predictions from the possibility of falsification, particularly the salvation oracles, then the remnant motif may well protect the positive element in prophecy from total disintegration. There is, however, no agreement among scholars on the precise nature of the remnant. It is clear that in Am. 5: 3 (cf. 3: 12) it simply indicates the scale of the destruction and in Is. 1: 8, 9, it points to bare survival. But it came to mean the nucleus of the future for later writers (e.g. Is. 11: 11, 16; Hag. 2: 2; Zec. 8: 6).[21] So it became a device for retrieving the oracles of salvation from obscurity and a vehicle for new oracles of salvation. It also functioned as a hermeneutical principle in later interpretations of the prophets for a more positive evaluation of the salvation element in the canonical prophets.[22]

17.13 In practical terms the concepts of repentance and remnant expose the inadequacy of dissonance theory for dealing with the complex notions involved in prophecy. No prediction need ever fail because the repentance principle creates sufficient space for it to be modified in accordance with human behaviour. The prophetic view of human society tends to be pessimistic and critical so the proclamation of doom is dominant but because of the possibility that men will respond there is always the hope of restoration or salvation. The historical experiences of Israel and Judah reflect the disintegration of small states during the rise of the Assyrian and Babylonian empires and this fitted in with the prophetic critique of society. But after the Babylonian exile the Jerusalem community was reconstructed along different lines and the remnant motif provided a useful approach to reinterpreting the old salvation oracles of the prophets. Thus even the salvation oracles were not seen as failures but as new possibilities for the ongoing community. So these two levels of prediction expectation safely guard prophecy from a simplistic approach to failure response. Festinger's theory is fine for post-decision problems in modern society and for dealing with simple communities whose existence is grounded in predictions of a straightforward nature.

17.14 But dissonance theory can provide some positive insights into the prophetic tradition in the Old Testament. It can make the researcher aware of the problems facing any prophet in a given situation in which expectation of a particular nature comes under pressure from events outside the prophet. Where expectation can be falsified and where the prophet is embarrassed by his situation then it is reasonable to assume some experience of dissonance has disturbed the prophet. But the editing of the prophetic tradition has removed so many oracles from their social setting that it is extremely difficult to reconstruct any possible interaction between prophet and environment.

17.15 The prophetic tradition which yields the most positive material for this study is that associated with Isaiah of Jerusalem. The totality of judgment expressed in Is. 6: 9–13 is in striking contrast to the salvation oracles elsewhere attributed to Isaiah and also to the call to turn from evil in 1: 16, 17. The material in 6: 9–13 looks like mature reflection on the nature of his call in the light of his subsequent experiences of an unresponsive people. This section should probably be treated as coming from a time after his failure to persuade Ahaz the king to trust Yahweh rather than the Assyrians (7 : 1–17).[23] Thus dissonance caused by the failure of his proclamation is resolved, or modified, by the hermeneutics of his commission which demonstrate that such a failure was his mission! This general failure of preaching eventually led Isaiah to retire from active proclamation and to seal up his teaching among his disciples (8: 16–18). Here is a good example of a withdrawal from the source of dissonance and of recourse to social support among a group of sympathetic followers whose agreement with the prophet could stimulate him and detract from his failure. The response of his followers could provide him with a more positive ministry without the intrusion of harsh dissonant elements. The tendency of prophets to congregate in groups must have facilitated the avoidance of critical elements in the general public. It is clear from Jeremiah's experience that the prophet was a particularly vulnerable target to gibes such as 'where is the word of Yahweh? Let it come!' (Jer. 17: 15; cf. Is. 53: 1).

17.16 The complex traditions surrounding the Assyrian crisis in the time of Isaiah make it very difficult to sort out both Isaiah's view of the situation and the precise nature of the event described in the legendary accounts in 2 Kings 19. How the siege of Jerusalem in 701 B.C. and its stringent consequences described in Is.

1: 4–9 are to be reconciled with the triumphalist deliverance recorded in the Kings story is beyond the scope of this paper and the wit of most competent scholars. But Childs, whose study of this problem is a fine piece of form-critical work, is certainly correct in his assessment 'the oracles of Isaiah are far too complex and diversified to allow for a simple formulation of his position on Assyria which could then serve as a criterion for measuring the historical elements in the narrative material'.[24] Furthermore it is not clear at all whether Isaiah held out hope for Jerusalem irrespective of whatever its people did or whether Is. 37: 33–35 is a genuine Isaiah saying.[25] If it could be established that Isaiah did believe Jerusalem was inviolable and that Yahweh would defend it against the Assyrians then it would be possible to regard 2 Kings 19 as an outworking of that belief. In which case in the light of Is. 1: 4–9 and the terrible deprivations of the siege it is possible to regard the legend in 2 Kings 19 as a resolution of the dissonance caused by the failure of Isaiah's hopes for his city put forward by the theologian historians who believed history to be the outworking of prophecy. However the evidence is far too meagre to maintain such a view with any degree of confidence. At the most it is a possibility, but one which reflects all the uncertainty and obscurity of the prophetic tradition at its most difficult level. In the final analysis it is not the prophet's experience of dissonance but the later community's experience which involves the prophet in the situation.

17.17 Outside of the Isaiah tradition traces of dissonance reaction can be seen in the confessions of Jeremiah where the prophet considers the possibility of having been deceived by the deity (15: 15–18) and in his general adamancy against the people and the other prophets (1: 18; 15: 20; 23: 9–40). Throughout the oracles of Jeremiah there is a feeling of confusion and anxiety which suggests the prophet was struggling with inner conflicts in an attempt to resolve the problems of his role in Judean society. Further elements of dissonance can be found in the prophecies of the post-exile prophets Haggai and Zechariah concerning the community governor Zerubbabel (Hag. 2: 20–23; Zec. 4: 6–10; 6: 9–14). Here the expectations centring on Zerubbabel are in contrast with the reality of Zerubbabel's failure to realise the high hopes predicted of him. Yet the only trace of that reality would appear to be in Zec. 6: 11 where 'crowns' may originally have been made for both Zerubbabel and Joshua the high priest, or what is more likely, for Zerubbabel alone. Because the expectations for Zerubbabel were never realised the high priest has been substituted for the governor in the text.[26] Again this is only a possibility and one without further support in the text. Perhaps the case of Zerubbabel is a good example of a problem posed for later readers of the text rather than for the community which produced the tradition. But, at least, it is an indication that dissonance producing events could be dealt with by editing the text at some level so as to reflect historical outcome.

17.18 These examples drawn from Isaiah, Jeremiah and the post-exilic prophets show that there is some evidence of factors giving rise to dissonance within the prophetic experience and reflected in the written traditions. The coenobia of the earlier prophets and the disciples of the canonical prophets provided the prophetic movement with adequate social support to shield them from the onslaughts of their critics and the worst ravages of dissonant experiences. The failure of so many salvation oracles and the modifications brought about by time and reality may have helped shape Second Isaiah's vision of Israel as a servant suffering on behalf of others (Is. 53) but even that vision terminated in a hint of triumphalism (v. 12). The hermeneutic process of rationalisation and explanation is difficult to trace within the biblical tradition, though in the later prophets there are echoes of the earlier prophets (e.g. Hab. 1: 5; Zec. 7: 7; cf. Dan. 9: 2, 24–27).[27] But in post-biblical times systems of hermeneutical activity emerge which subjected the biblical text to minute examination. Thus there is the handling of the prophetic text at Qumran where the community tried to read itself in the predictions of the prophets. The New Testament is the beginning of multiple forms of exegesis on the Old Testament in which the writers expound their belief that the Christ event is the fulfilment of prophecy, and that many of the events of that period can be expressly described as 'this is what was spoken by the prophet . . . ' (e.g. Acts 2: 16). Rabbinical Judaism continued to produce exegeses of the biblical text and some of the rabbis sought in their own time the fulfilment of prophecy. Early Christian patristic interpretation followed a messianic understanding of the prophets in which all the expectations of the prophetic tradition were related to Christ and the experiences of the Christian community. Thus the failure of prophecy in its own time became the opportunity for later communities to seek in their time the unfolding of prophetic expectation.

17.19 The fundamental principle which seems to emerge from all this exegetical activity surrounding the prophetic texts is dissonance gives rise to hermeneutic. In order to avoid the failure of prophecy or because there is a strong belief that prophecy cannot fail it becomes necessary to construct a system of explanation showing how various examples of supposedly failed predictions can be rescued by reinterpretation and reapplication. Here is the main thrust of dissonance theory for biblical studies — it allows hermeneutical systems to be seen as responses to failures in prediction. It therefore theoretically poses the assertion that where there are prophetic texts there must also be, what Barr calls, a 'resultant system', i.e., 'there are two systems or levels at work: the first is the text, the second is the system into which the interpretation runs out'.[28] The resultant system may be any form of hermeneutical principle used by later interpreters, e.g. mystical approaches to the text or allegorical systems or typological exegesis in Jewish and Christian theology. Perhaps the earliest attempts at reinterpreting and therefore transforming the prophetic traditions came from the apocalyptic writers who attempted to get around the basic failure of the prophetic expectation of future salvation by grounding such hopes in a transcendental act of God imposed upon mankind (cf. Dan. 2: 44, 45; 7: 9–27).[29] The fusion of prophecy and apocalyptic eventually led to the emergence of Christianity which introduced yet another set of dissonance producing expectations.

17.20 If the structure for analysis is accepted as the text plus its interpretation within various communities embracing it as holy scripture or authoritative writ then it becomes possible for dissonance theory to be applied with fruitful results. However this means the material available for research is increased to include the fields of biblical exegesis and its history, historical theology and the multiple forms of sects deriving their existence from discrete interpretations of the Bible. It becomes a programme for historical, sociological and intellectual research and threatens to get out of hand. The difficulties of establishing the precise meaning of so much biblical material remain and therefore the legitimacy of many of the interpretations maintained in any such study is also called in question. An example of the difficulty of clearly establishing what is the nature of the case may be taken from the New Testament. On the surface it would appear that an ideal subject for dissonance analysis would be the notion of *Parousieverzögerung*, 'delay of the parousia'. The New Testament certainly seems to present a community daily expecting the return of Jesus (cf. Mt. 24: 34; Acts 1: 11; 1 Cor. 7: 26, 29–31; 1 Thess. 4: 15–17; 2 Thess. 1: 10; Rev. 22: 20). The return of Jesus is an event that appears to be easily verifiable or falsifiable. History has shown that the expected return did not materialise so there should be fairly straightforward evidence of attempts to resolve the ensuing dissonance caused by this failure. At one level this seems to be the case in that there are assertions in the New Testament which suggest that an interim period must occur before the parousia takes place, e.g. 'this gospel of the kingdom must be preached throughout the whole world . . . and then the end will come' (Mt. 24: 14) or 'that day will not come unless . . . ' (2 Thess. 2: 3). Thus explanations are arising which attempt to modify the expectation in the light of reality and show how the coming may still be expected but not before a period of time has elapsed in which must occur certain other events. On the other hand the Fourth Gospel gives the impression that there will be no second coming in the future because the parousia has already taken place.[30] The real problem for the researcher is to discover which view represents the authentic Christian belief and to what extent there was any one fixed view about the future. Some of the early churches may have had a strong belief in an imminent parousia but others probably identified that coming with the outpoured spirit at Pentecost or by regarding the church as the body of Christ had no concept of an absent Christ requiring a return to earth. Thus it becomes very difficult to establish clearly dissonance response because of the lack of strict controls on the material.

17.21 Furthermore the early Christian communities were not simply eschatologically orientated groups so expectations of future events were open to failure without catastrophic effects for the communities. Fundamental to these communities was the emergence and development of christology which became the formative element in subsequent Christianity.[31] It is the christological *kerygma* which functions as the resultant system in the New Testament.[32] Christology allied to notions of transcendence prevented Christianity becoming the slave of eschatological expectations and allowed it to develop into a complex system of transformational beliefs. Where there are dissonance producing events in the New Testament christology resolves them by hermeneutical processes. If there is cognitive dissonance in the New Testament it is created by the death of Jesus and resolved by the christology of the gospel.[33] The dissonance expressed by Lk. 24:21 acquired its resolution by way of a christological interpretation of the Old Testament (vv. 25–27). It cannot be denied that communities continued to expect some form of literal return of Jesus, e.g. the churches of Paul and the churches addressed by the Apocalypse, but slowly the christological hermeneutic won its way until by the time of Augustine christology had overcome chiliasm. Yet the subsequent history of Christianity in West Europe has been punctuated by chiliastic movements, strong in millennial expectations but rather weak in christology.[34]

17.22 Because Judaism and Christianity had strong elements of eschatological expectation within them there was always a tendency for dissonance resolving hermeneutics to emerge, but because neither structure was simply constructed around such expectations their central cores were relatively safe from the vicissitudes of failed predictions. Perhaps because Christianity has a stronger eschatological element at its roots it has been more vulnerable to millennial movements seizing it and distorting its christology. Judaism is centred around Torah and sees its existence as the way of obedience to divine commandment with the stress on the ethical mode of life. As such even prophecy was subservient to Torah and was seen as commentary on Torah. So the failure of prophecy was not a danger to Judaism, though the existence of prophetic expectation did give scope to movements within Judaism to develop messianic movements which occasionally broke away from the parent body, e.g. Qumran, Christianity, and the later stages of the Sabbatai Zevi movement.

17.23 This study has been a theoretical exploration of the possibilities of applying the theory of cognitive dissonance to the study of biblical prophecy. If it has failed to reveal startling results that is because the material to hand is strictly limited in terms of information about prophetic self-awareness and details about how the prophetic preaching was received by the people.[35] The fundamental element of repentance in the prophetic declaration also rendered clear failures of prediction rather difficult to establish.[36] Festinger's theory has great explanatory value when applied to groups constructed around simple prediction expectations characteristic of the twentieth century but it is out of its depth when applied to complex structures of belief and hermeneutic such as Judaism and Christianity. This is not to conclude that the theory has no applicatory value to the study of prophecy but to be wary of any simplistic application of a cross-disciplinary approach. It can uncover various levels of tension within the prophetic traditions and it illustrates the complexity of the interaction between prophet and society. According to some authorities 'the main virtue of dissonance theory is that its use permits so much understanding. It points to many nonobvious sources of tension'.[37] As such the theory should assist in mining the multiplex nature of the Old Testament prophetic tradition given further research into specific sets of texts.

Notes

1. Cf. G. Fohrer, *History of Israelite Religion* (London, 1973), pp. 223–291, esp. p. 272.
2. Cf. E. Würthwein, 'Der Ursprung der prophetischen Gerichtsrede', *ZTK* xlix (1952), pp. 1–16; H. G. Reventlow, *Das Amt des Propheten bei Amos* (Göttingen, 1962).
3. Cf. Wittgenstein's remark 'It is in language that an expectation and its fulfilment make contact', *Philosophical Investigations* (Oxford, 1972), I, § 445; see also §§ 437–445.
4. See O. Kaiser, *Isaiah 1–12* (London, 1972), pp. 123–130; also G. von Rad, *Old Testament Theology* (Edinburgh, 1965), pp. 169 ff.
5. *A Theory of Cognitive Dissonance* (Evanston, 1957); Festinger was then

professor of psychology at Stanford University.

6. M. L. J. Abercrombie, 'Small Groups', *New Horizons in Psychology*, ed. B. M. Foss (London, 1966), p. 386.

7. On social support see Festinger, *op. cit.*, pp. 177–259.

8. See relevant articles in *Journal of Abnormal and Social Psychology* vols. 52–60 (1956–60); also any competent introduction to psychology, e.g. M. Manis, *An Introduction to Cognitive Psychology* (California, 1971), pp. 239–53; E. E. Sampson, *Social Psychology and Contemporary Society* (New York, 1971), pp. 108–14.

9. L. Festinger, H. W. Riecken, and S. Schachter, *When Prophecy Fails* (Minneapolis, 1956; paperback edition New York, 1964).

10. *Ibid.* pp. 139–92.

11. *Ibid.* pp. 12, 28.

12. J. A. Hardyck and M. Braden, 'Prophecy Fails Again: A Report of a Failure to Replicate', *Journal of Abnormal and Social Psychology* 65 (1962), pp. 136–41.

13. *When Prophecy Fails*, pp. 3–32.

14. *Ibid.*, p. 216; a longer exposition of the paradigm is given on pp. 4–6.

15. This is acknowledged by Festinger *ibid.*, pp. 23–5.

16. See especially *A Theory of Cognitive Dissonance*, pp. 177–202.

17. *When Prophecy Fails*, p. 4.

18. Fohrer, *op. cit.*, pp. 272 f.

19. *The Prophetic Faith* (New York, 1949, 1960), p. 104.

20. Cf. Fohrer, *op. cit.*, p. 273.

21. Fohrer, *ibid.*, p. 271.

22. Cf. G. F. Hasel, *The Remnant* (Berrien Springs, 1972).

23. See H. W. Hoffmann, *Die Intention der Verkündigung Jesajas*, BZAW 136 (Berlin, 1974), pp. 77–80; cf. Kaiser, *op. cit.*, p. 82.

24. *Isaiah and the Assyrian Crisis* (London, 1967), p. 120.

25. Cf. T. C. Vriezen, 'Essentials of the Theology of Isaiah', *Israel's Prophetic Heritage*, ed. B. W. Anderson and W. Harrelson (London, 1962), pp. 139–42; O. Kaiser, *Isaiah 13–39* (London, 1974), pp. 367–412, esp. pp. 384 f., 394 f.

26. M. Noth, *The History of Israel* (London, 1960), p. 312; cf. J. L. McKenzie, *A Theology of the Old Testament* (New York, 1974), p. 288; P. R. Ackroyd, *Exile and Restoration* (London, 1968), pp. 196 f.

27. Cf. F. F. Bruce, 'The earliest Old Testament interpretation', *The Witness of Tradition*, OTS xvii (Leiden, 1972), pp. 37–52.

28. J. Barr, *Old and New in Interpretation* (London, 1965), pp. 108f.

29. See P. D. Hanson, 'Jewish Apocalyptic against its Near Eastern Environment', *Revue Biblique* 78 (1971), pp. 32–58; 'Old Testament Apocalyptic Re-examined', *Interpretation* 25 (1971), pp. 454–79; and more recently his *The Dawn of Apocalyptic* (Philadelphia, 1975).

30. Cf. N. Perrin, *The New Testament: An Introduction* (New York, 1974), p. 41; see also A. L. Moore, *The Parousia in the New Testament* (Leiden, 1966).

31. See D. Flusser, 'Salvation Present and Future', *Numen* 16 (1969), pp. 139–55.

32. Barr, *op. cit.*, p. 109.

33. See U. Wernik, 'Frustrated beliefs and early Christianity', *Numen* 22 (1975), pp. 96–130.
34. Flusser notes 'where Christology is strong, the longing for Millennium is comparatively weak', *op. cit.*, p. 155; on later movements see N. Cohn, *The Pursuit of the Millennium* (London, 1970).
35. Some useful material is contained in H. W. Wolff, 'Das Zitat im Prophetenspruch', *Gesammelte Studien zum Alten Testament* (München, 1964), pp. 30–129.
36. On repentance see T. M. Raitt, 'The Prophetic Summons to Repentance', *ZAW* 83 (1971), pp. 30–49.
37. J. W. Brehm and A. R. Cohen, *Explorations in Cognitive Dissonance* (London, 1962), p. 314.

18

Robin Scroggs
The Sociological Interpretation of the New
Testament: The Present State of Research

This Extract comprises an article which first appeared in *New Testament Studies* in 1980. Scroggs is professor of New Testament at Chicago Theological Seminary. The Extract provides a very useful and thorough introduction, firstly to the reductionist problems seemingly raised by the use of sociology in biblical research (*18.6f.*) and secondly to the Extracts from Gager, Theissen and Meeks that follow. Scroggs' discussion of social-class and socio-economic factors in relation to earliest Christianity (*18.15–22*) is relevant to a number of the Extracts (notably *Extract 4*, *Extract 5* and *Extract 20*). Since it was written, Wayne A. Meeks, *The First Urban Christians*: *The Social World of the Apostle Paul* (Yale, 1983) has brought a considerable degree of sophistication to the subject. His notion of social class is well aware of more complex stratification theories, of the multi-dimensionality of stratification, and of the way, for example, that even wealthy people may feel that they lack social status. Scroggs also provides a brief account of cognitive dissonance theory as it is understood by Gager (*18.28–33*) and an introduction to Meeks' article from which *Extract 21* is taken. Finally he has a brief account of Marxist approaches to the New Testament, which is included here simply for completeness.

18.1 It is fitting that the first major attention given by the SNTS to sociological concerns should occur in Paris, the home of Auguste Comte (often called the father of sociology) and his circle. Actually there seem to have many fathers and many more offspring, such that the present genealogy of the discipline presents an almost bewildering profusion of perspectives, goals, models, and methodologies.[1] This is a productive situation and a sign of health, but it suggests right away that I cannot analyze in this paper a single or simple sociology of the New Testament. Those of us who are experimenting — and that cautious phrase must be taken literally — with sociological approaches have come from different backgrounds

254

and perspectives, borrowing from sociology where it seems useful and tentatively trying out various methods and models. The exploration has really just begun.

18.2 Interest in the social reality of early Christianity, of course, is nothing new. Especially during the preceding one hundred years keen interest has often been expressed in such matters. This interest peaked during the first third of this century, best exemplified by scholars such as Deissmann, Lohmeyer, Cadoux, and especially representatives of the so-called Chicago School (e.g., Shirley Jackson Case and Shailer Matthews) who with great energy focused on early Christianity as a social reality and upon Jesus as a social reformer.[2]

18.3 Those were the days of liberal Christianity and the social gospel; it is hardly an accident that a socially oriented theology would cause social questions to be asked of the New Testament. By the 1930s, however, not even the Chicago School was being heard in the United States. Neo-orthodoxy, with its emphasis upon theology and the Word, displaced the social gospel. The kinds of questions the liberals had asked became unfashionable. Symbolic of this change are the fortunes of Frederick Grant's monograph, *The Economic Background of the Gospels*.[3] Published in 1926, toward the end of the era, it long remained, at least in the United States, the only major statement about the economics of first-century Palestine. In fact, the book had to be republished in unaltered form in 1973, forty-seven years later, because nothing comparable had appeared in the intervening years.[4]

18.4 Today the pendulum has swung again. Interest in social questions is again substantial in some quarters. Whether this is the result of a neo-liberalism, or social tensions such as the Vietnam war, student revolutions, and severe economic and political oppression in various parts of the world, or all of these, is not clear as yet. Nevertheless, Gerd Theissen speaks for many of us when he notes a rising *Unbehagen* [uneasiness] about a discipline which limits the acceptable methods to the historical and theological. No one doubts the supreme importance of these time-honored approaches. They do not, however, ask, let alone answer, all of the important questions, those concerning social dynamic, the relation between earthly goods and faith, and the interaction between social reality and theological assertions.

18.5 To some it has seemed that too often the discipline of the theology of the New Testament (the history of *ideas*) operates out of a methodological docetism, as if believers had minds and spirits unconnected with their individual and corporate bodies. Interest in the sociology of early Christianity is no attempt to limit reductionistically the reality of Christianity to social dynamic; rather it should be seen as an effort to guard against a reductionism from the other extreme, a limitation of the reality of Christianity to an inner-spiritual, or objective-cognitive system. In short, sociology of early Christianity wants to put body and soul together again.

Problems Confronting Sociological Analysis

18.6 This is not to say that all is easy for the new approach. Among the serious problems which the sociologist of the New Testament must deal with, let me mention three.

The Problem of Methodology

18.7 The current state of tremendous variety in sociological theories and models presents the New Testament scholar with numerous possibilities and understandable confusion at the same time. Which are valid? Which are appropriate for the data to be interpreted? If we use more than one method, are these compatible or in tension? Theissen implies by his work, probably correctly, that an eclecticism and pluralism is appropriate.[5] If the methods have true heuristic value, they should ultimately prove complementary and contribute to one's confidence in conclusions drawn from them. I suggest only two warnings here. First, we need to understand fully how the method works and to be clear that it *can* be applied to the data at hand. Secondly, we need to know both the theoretical presuppositions and implications of the use of the method. Is it compatible with other (e.g., theological) presuppositions we may hold?

The Problem of the Data

18.8 Most sociologists, particulalry those using computer methods to study contemporary societies, would probably be aghast when they learned how little in the way of data was available for the sociological analysis of the New Testament. Furthermore, what we do have is not directly sociologically access-ible. That is, most texts are speaking about theological verities, not sociological conditions. The sociologist must read the text as if it were palimpsest. This means the researcher must work with the utmost caution and strictness, with adequate guard against overenthusiasm. There can probably never be any complete sociological analysis of early Christianity. And yet there may be times when a sociological model may actually assist in our ignorance. If our data evidence some parts of the gestalt of a known model, while being silent about others, we *may* cautiously be able to conclude that the absence of the missing parts is accidental and that the entire model was actually a reality in the early church.

The Problem of Reductionism

18.9 There is no doubt that one can use sociological methods from a reductionist standpoint, that is, to explain any societal phenomenon completely in terms of hidden, unconscious social dynamic. Thus one could understand religion out of Feuerbachian, Durkheimian, or Marxist closed systems. It is at this point that the New Testament scholar should be careful about the implications of the method he or she selects, to ask whether that method implicitly or explicitly excludes all dynamic except the immanent social. For example, it is clear that the Weberian emphasis upon the charismatic prophet allows for relatively more freedom and novelty than the societal emphasis of Durkheim. Nevertheless, it is to be doubted that any sociological method, except that of the strictly orthodox Marxist, is incapable of being used by a scholar who wants to leave room for the transcendent. Let me make three brief observations on this issue.

18.10 1. Social dynamics may create the situation but may not determine the response to the situation. Jesus rejected the Zealotic option, and Paul had to decide, according to Theissen, between the rich and the poor in Corinth. He points out that a distinction must be made between the social conditions and the theological intention of a Paul.[6] (This is a solution which respects the freedom of the leader [Weber].)

18.11 2. Even a more Durkheimian approach, it seems to me, can be fitted into a theological scheme, if one takes seriously the doctrine of creation, or finitude. Subjection to social dynamic is as much a part of our finitude as any other dimension of society's impingement on individual freedoms. For example, when the exegete seeks sources for Jesus' or Paul's ideas in Judaism or Hellenism, he or she is working out of that same presupposition of finitude.

18.12 3. It also needs to be emphasized that sociological models are not to be awarded absolute objectivity as if they were natural laws. They are rather the time- and culture-bound creatures of humans. They are useful in so far as they have heuristic value, that is, in so far as they serve to illumine the *unique* phenomenon the researcher is studying.

Report on Recent Scholarship

18.13 I will now turn to an all too sketchy report on recent scholarship. For purposes of clarity I want to make a somewhat artificial distinction between historical research into social phenomena and sociological analysis. Let me illustrate this distinction. The *historian* may ask the question, 'What was the social level of early Christians?' and answer it by evaluating data which are theoretically available to the conscious perceptions of those early Christians and by putting them into causal and time-sequential structures. The *sociologist* then takes the historian's data and asks what underlying, usually *unconscious*, dynamic is at work, how that social level interacts with other levels, what conflicts usually emerge in such circumstances, and whether knowing that dynamic in turn helps us interpret certain interrelationships or even certain truth assertions in our data. Sociology thus depends upon data but works with them in ways that historiography does not. Sociology is comparative, since it will most often come to data with a model of dynamics taken from analyses of other groups and other data. It thus also tends to be synchronic rather than diachronic. I cheerfully admit that this definition of sociology is quite narrow and can easily be disputed. It will serve, I nevertheless trust, to sharpen the following analysis.

18.14 What follows is of necessity illustrative rather than comprehensive. Furthermore the emphasis will be not so much on *content* as on *methods* and *models*. I will concentrate on *how* the researcher works more than on *what* the resulting conclusions are. The full contributions to the discipline of the scholars discussed will rarely emerge — for this I ask for the sympathy of my colleagues. Hopefully what *will* come to expression are the varied possibilities of current research.

Recent Research into Social History of the Early Church[7]

18.15 The first name that comes to mind as one turns to research into social history is that of Martin Hengel. In a series of publications too well known and too numerous to name, Hengel has concerned himself with the concrete political and economic history in relation to the first centuries of the church and particularly with regard to Jesus and his followers.[8] He has, furthermore, offered us a useful model in the relevance of such social history for reflection in the church today.[9]

18.16 Recent years have seen the publication of a number of valuable studies by other scholars. A book with slowly growing influence was published in 1960 by E. A. Judge, titled *The Social Pattern of Christian Groups in the First Century*.[10] Much useful information is contained in a series of essays under the title: *The Catacombs and the Colosseum: The Roman Empire as the Setting of Primitive Christianity* (1971).[11] Most recently two books relevant to the topic have appeared in the United States: *Social Aspects of Early Christianity* (1977) by Abraham Malherbe, and *Early Christianity and Society* (1977) by Robert Grant.[12] Mention should also be made of a study group under the auspices of the Society of Biblical Literature in the United States. Under the title 'The Social Description of Early Christianity' (Wayne Meeks and Leander Keck, co-chairpersons), this group has been working for the last several years in a kind of sociological trench study of the city of Antioch, attempting to discover as much as possible about societal reality in that city, thus the better to understand the interaction of the Christian community with the larger social situations and dynamic.[13]

18.17 I can illustrate the work of these and other researchers only by one — albeit important — example, the question of the socioeconomic level of Christians. It is Deissmann who seems to get the credit for the view that early Christians were of the lower social classes — peasants, slaves, artisans.[14] In 1960 Judge mounted his, at that time somewhat lonely, protest.[15] True, he argued, the Christian community did not attract the true Roman nobility, but it did not draw to itself the other end of the spectrum either — peasants and farm slaves. Otherwise, Christians came from all strata in society.

18.18 It is interesting to note the data to which he appeals. (1) Middle- and upper-class people are mentioned in Acts and in the Pauline correspondence. (2) Barnabas, who donated the proceeds of a land sale to the Jerusalem church, is a representative of 'the foreign community in an international resort', and it can be assumed that this class would be composed of 'persons of means'.[16] (3) The church enjoyed the 'hospitality of wealthy and respectable patrons'.[17] (4) The main passage of debate, 1 Corinthians 1:26–28, shows the opposite of what is commonly concluded, namely that there *were* Corinthian Christians who were from at least relatively privileged classes. Judge can then conclude: 'Far from being a socially depressed group, then, if the Corinthians are at all typical, the Christians were dominated by a socially pretentious section of the population of big cities'.[18]

18.19 Writing seventeen years later, Malherbe shows how the pendulum, at least in his judgment, has swung.

Malherbe believes it even possible to speak of a 'new consensus' emerging which places the social level noticeably higher than did Deissmann.[19] Theissen seems to be moving in the same direction when he speaks of a leading minority of upper-class Christians at Corinth, over against a lower-class majority.[20] Hengel, basing his judgment on Paul and the Pliny-Trajan correspondence, agrees: 'Das heisst Glieder der christlichen Gemeinden fanden sich in *allen* Bevölkerungsschichten, vom Sklaven und Freigelassenen bis zur örtlichen Aristokratie, den Dekurionen, ja unter Umständen bis zum senatorischen Adel'.[21]

18.20 Robert Grant's book, while moving far beyond the New Testament period, pictures a church which is essentially conservative, both politically and economically, reflecting the main concerns of the empire at large. While Grant does not exactly say it, he gives the impression that early Christians were as snobbish about their class status as anybody else in the contemporary world.[22] Supporting the political conservatism is the article, 'Social Unrest and Primitive Christianity', by Clarence Lee in *The Catacombs and the Colosseum*. He finds no evidence to support the contention 'that Christianity swept across the Roman world on the coattails of a social revolution'.[23]

18.21 What is interesting about this 'new consensus' is that it reaches a conclusion so different from Deissmann's, while working with precisely the same data — almost exclusively that found in the New Testament (I, of course, am speaking only to the conclusion for the New Testament period). This raises the question how the same data can produce such different conclusions. Tentatively the following can be observed. (1) The 'new consensus' places relatively less emphasis upon the social implications of the Synoptic material. (2) It places relatively more emphasis upon the material in Acts *and its historical veracity*. (3) It seems, at least to this reviewer, to place almost exclusive weight upon *economic* factors to the exclusion of other sociocultural dynamics in determining social level.

18.22 The implications of the 'new consensus' for the social interpretation of early Christianity are immense and thus its conclusions must be tested with great care. Such testing is out of place in this report; I do, however, raise the following questions. (1) Should not the Synoptic material (e.g., the strong protest against wealth) be given more weight, even if it does not reflect the same Hellenistic urban context of the Pauline letters? Surely the Synoptics speak for important segments of the first-century church and in their final form do not necessarily reflect only a rural setting. (2) Is the Acts material as historically trustworthy as the proponents assume? (3) Even if it is, and granted the evidence of the epistles, should the presence of a few (is it not a universal tendency to remember and name the upper rather than the lower?) wealthier members be allowed to change, in effect, the social location of the community as a whole? Is this not an elitist definition? (4) Should economic alienation be the only alienation considered? Do not all societies have categories of outcast individuals and groups who are not economically deprived?[24] (5) Finally (and here I am perhaps out of place) is there any relation between the 'new consensus' and the change in our society from the more 'revolutionary' period of the 1960s to the more 'conventional' 1970s? Is there a need today to find a more 'respectable' (i.e., middle-class) origin for the church? I am quite aware that the followers of Deissmann can be charged with a counter question: do they want to romanticize poverty?

Sociological Analyses of the Early Church

18.23 Here again I have space only for examples of recent sociological analyses and even so will do justice to no one example. I organize the discussion around the methods used rather than the total gestalt of the researcher.

18.24 Typologies. In an article published in 1975 I looked at some Synoptic material from the perspective of the religious sect.[25] I researched post-Troeltsch analysis of the sect by British and United States sociologists who now can base their conclusions on concrete studies of sects, both past and present. It was encouraging to see that there is basic agreement among these researchers as to what constitutes the dominant characteristics of the sect (Troeltsch's insights are mostly confirmed), although the sect is now interpreted over against the established social organization as a whole, rather than a sub-category named the 'church'. I summarized these arguments under seven heads. (1) The beginning point of the sect as protest (*N.B.*, not necessarily conscious). (2) The rejection of the assumptions of reality upon which the establishment bases its world and creation of a new world with different assumptions. (3) The egalitarian nature of the sect. (4) The vitality of love and mutual acceptance within the sect. (5) The voluntary character of the group. (6) The demand of total commitment to the new reality accepted by the sect. (7) And sometimes adventist, or millenarian expectations.

18.25 I argued that most of these characteristics were evidenced in the Synoptic material, which reflected the earliest Palestinian communities in their interaction with the larger social context. If so, this analysis gives us some new insight into the social dynamic — namely *unconscious social protest* — that helped bring the church into existence and that gave it the particular shape it took in those earlier years.[26]

18.26 Graydon Snyder, in an as yet unpublished manuscript, is working from quite a different typology.[27] Borrowing an anthropological model developed by researchers at the University of Chicago, Snyder sees early Christianity always in tension between dynamics he calls respectively the 'trans-local tradition' and the 'local tradition'.[28] The trans-local tradition is the religion of the prophet, the universalist, the intellectual, the more-than-moralist (Weber). The local tradition, or social matrix, is the religion of the person rooted in land, community, family, moralism, or the one who uses religion to integrate people into the social matrix by the ceremonial marking of key-season and life-process days (Durkheim).

18.27 Any specific religious phenomenon, Snyder argues, will be a result of the tension between the two traditions in a given time and space. At times the trans-local tradition may dominate, at other times the local. Usually there will be some compromise, such that a phenomenon will rarely be a pure example of either tradition. Since writings are usually suspect as being primarily creations of the trans-local tradition, Snyder only begins in the post-New Testament period, when archaeological artifacts are available. In conversation, however, Snyder and I have concluded that it may be possible to use this typology as a grid to understand movement within trajectories in the New Testament itself. For example, it is possible that Paul himself represents a decisive victory of the trans-local tradition over the local, while the Pastorals reflect increasing assimilation by the local tradition of the Pauline thought world. At any rate, this typology should help us grasp more clearly some of the intramural conflicts within early Christianity.

18.28 **Cognitive Dissonance.** One major sociological study of early Christianity that has recently appeared in the United States is John Gager's *Kingdom and Community*.[29] In this many-faceted study the author uses varied models, unfortunately only one of which I can describe here. This is the theory of cognitive dissonance, a theory derived from sociological (or anthropological) theorists in the United States — although Gager will modify this theory in some respects.[30]

18.29 The theory asserts the following. When, in a community, religious or otherwise, a certain belief is held, specific enough for disconfirmation to be unavoidably clear, and given certain other conditions (named below), the likely result of any disconfirmation of the belief will not be the dissolution of the group but rather an intensification of its proselytizing. For example, if a community predicts the end of the world on a certain specific day, that belief can be disconfirmed, and such disconfirmation, while painful to the community, cannot be avoided by it.

18.30 In all, there are five conditions, according to the theory, which are necessary if proselytizing is to occur following disconfirmation. (1) The belief must be held with deep conviction. (2) There must be committed action on the part of the believers. (3) The belief must be specific enough that disconfirmation cannot be denied. (4) The believers must recognize the disconfirmatory evidence. (5) There must be communal support for the individual believer.

18.31 Gager claims that the community following Jesus fits all of the above conditions. The belief in question was that Jesus is the Messiah (although the author carefully hedges as to whether Jesus himself held this opinion). The death of Jesus is then the disconfirming event, for how could a messiah die? He writes:

> It would appear, then, that we are justified in maintaining that the death of Jesus created a sense of cognitive dissonance, in that it seemed to disconfirm the belief that Jesus was the Messiah . . . Thus according to the theory, we may understand the zeal with which Jesus' followers pursued their mission as part of an effort to reduce dissonance, not just in the early years but for a considerable time thereafter.[31]

18.32 To this Gager adds the disappointment of eschatological expectations. He claims that these expectations were also specific enough (the end was to come while the first generation of believers was still alive) for disconfirmation to occur. This then added to the missionary fervor of the first-century church.[32]

18.33 Gager is quick to say that he does not intend to explain the entire missionary endeavor by this one model, although he does not discuss what other dynamic might have contributed. This view of missionary dynamic may seem shocking and certainly clashes with the puristic, idealistic view so commonly held in theological circles. Ultimately both positions may have something to contribute to the complete picture of those very human early Christians making the missionary rounds. The question is whether both views can learn to live with each other.

18.34 **Role Analysis.** Surely the most prolific and provocative sociologist of the New Testament is Gerd Theissen. In an impressive series of articles and a book he has explored both the rural Palestinian setting of the *Urgemeinden* (original communities) and the urbanized church of the Hellenistic world.[33] In his writings there is a wealth of social data and luxuriant use of a number of sociological models, emering out of a basic functionalist approach to social dynamic. Although it is a disservice to the productivity of

Theissen, I can here choose only one example of his work, to illustrate the use of role analysis.[34] In role analysis one looks at the description of self-understanding of people who adopt or accept certain roles within the society, whether such roles are defined by social status, relationship of person to group, or kinds of activity expected of the role. How these roles *function* in the larger societal context is investigated.

18.35 By now most scholars are familiar with Theissen's analysis of the Palestinian Christian prophet as a 'wandering charismatic'. These were people who had given up all of their old life to proclaim the urgent gospel of the Kingdom of God. Homelessness, lack of family, lack of possessions, and lack of protection were characteristics of their new life. Jesus had commanded that they live this way and promised that they would be provided for by the people they served. To live as beggars was a sign of their trust in God.[35]

18.36 Paul, on the other hand, represents a different type — plays a different role, that of the community organizer.[36] The Hellenistic urban churches reflect a less radical, more middle-class society, in which the image of the wandering beggar would not be suitable, at least as Paul understood the situation. First Corinthians, however, reveals Paul on the defensive precisely because he would not accept payment from the Corinthians, i.e., would not put himself in the posture of a beggar. This passage has always puzzled exegetes. Why would not the Corinthians be happy not to have to pay their minister? Theissen believes he has solved the puzzle. The Corinthian situation has been created by the entrance into the church of wandering charismatics from Palestine who, living out the role of the faithful beggar, have seen Paul (and have tried to convince the Corinthians that Paul should be seen) as a faithless missionary. Paul, working independently of the community as an artisan, is not willing to follow the command of Jesus to give up all possessions. He is unwilling to put full trust in God's care.[37]

18.37 This ingenious analysis completely changes the picture we have traditionally held of Paul's opponents, and forces a radically different interpretation. The conflict is not between a good Paul and evil opponents, but between *conflicting roles*, between different understandings of the true missionary. Theissen's sociological analysis thus offers us a new perspective.

18.38 **Sociology of Knowledge.** For some of us, I suspect, the single most important approach within the field of sociology comes from the sociology of knowledge. It may also for others be the most threatening approach. This perspective teaches us that the world we live in, the world we think, or assume, has ontological foundations, is really *socially constructed* and is created, communicated, and sustained through language and symbol.[38] To denote this constructed world, whose relationship to the 'really real' is by definition unknowable, many are using the phrases 'social world' or 'symbolic world'.

18.39 What is potentially threatening is that language, *including theological language*, is never to be seen as independent of other social realities. *Thus theological language and the claims made therein can no longer be explained without taking into account socioeconomic-cultural factors as essential ingredients in the production of that language.* The difficult questions for the sociologists are, in concrete instances, *how* to move between language and social realities, and *which* social realities are to be related to *which* linguistic structures? These seem to me immensely important questions which are not yet adequately answered and thus the process does not currently have the proper methodological controls. I will, however, illustrate the immense possibilities in this approach by reporting an article which shows provocatively how one scholar believes it possible to bring language and social realities together — 'The Man from Heaven in Johannine Sectarianism', by Wayne Meeks.[39]

18.40 Here Meeks wishes to understand the Johannine christology of the descending/ascending savior. He doubts that this christology was taken over from already existent gnostic myths and suspects, rather, that it represents John's own contribution to the march toward gnosticism. To understand the reason why the motif was created, Meeks raises the question, what *social function* this myth may have had in the community itself.

18.41 Why is it, Meeks questions, that the revelatory discourses are so opaque? With regard to chapter 3, for example, he writes: 'Thus the dialogue with Nicodemus and its postscript connected with John the Baptist constitute a virtual *parody* of a revelation discourse. What is "revealed" is that Jesus is incomprehensible . . . Even for an interested inquirer (like Nicodemus) the dialogue is opaque'.[40] The motif of descent/ascent in every instance in the Gospel 'points to contrast, foreignness, division, judgment'.[41]

18.42 But these are characteristics which apply to the entire Gospel. This writing sets itself against the world and in turn appears incomprehensible to that world. The book is simply a 'closed system of metaphors'.[42] Here lies, in Meeks' judgment, the clue to the function of the Johannine christology. As the community itself feels alien and over against the world, so the book and specifically the christology express this same alienation. If the church is not of this world, then neither can be its Lord. 'One of the primary functions of the book, therefore, must have been to provide a reinforcement for the community's social identity . . . It provided a symbolic universe which gave religious legitimacy, a theodicy, to the group's actual isolation from the larger society'.[43]

18.43 Thus the christology cannot be interpreted apart from the social context of the community. Actually the movement between the two is dialectical. The christological claims of the Johannine Christians result in their becoming alienated and 'that alienation in turn is "explained" by a further development of the christological motifs'.[44] This startling dialectic should not be taken to mean that the christological language is no longer to be taken seriously. There is no reason to doubt that theological insights can emerge out of the pain of alienation. To the extent that Meeks' judgments are compelling, however, they should lead us to a greater caution about generalizing or universalizing the christological claims in John. But in this caution are there not significant measures of realism and honesty?

Marxist Interpretations

18.44 Before concluding, it is only appropriate to point to recent Marxist interpretations of early Christianity, since they at many points relate to sociological approaches. Marxist theory certainly deals with social process and dynamic, while sociological theory can accept the unconscious nature of the process. Marx himself is perhaps the first to have understood the basic premise of the sociology of knowledge.[45]

18.45 Important advances in sophistication have on occasion been made since Kautsky's book of 1920.[46] *Not* in that category is the volume by Martin Robbe, *Der Ursprung des Christentums* (1967).[47] Working from a traditional Marxist-Leninist perspective, he develops a view of Christianity's emergence purely as social process, as a protest against the class society and its injustice. The importance of the figure of Jesus completely disappears (no Weberian perspective here!); Robbe is not even concerned whether Jesus existed or not. Nothing would have been different had he not.

18.46 In sharp contrast with Robbe, however, is Milan Machoveč, the author of *Jesus für Atheisten* (1972), translated into English as *A Marxist Looks at Jesus* (1976).[48] Leaning on the humanism of the younger Marx, Machoveč goes in exactly the opposite direction to Robbe; for the Czech communist, Jesus is a supremely important, seminal figure. Kautsky is roundly criticized as reductionistic; ideas again assume an intrinsic, determinative role, particularly those of monotheism and eschatology. Jesus made his mark upon society because he taught that the future depends upon human action. 'In modern terminology we should say that Jesus turns a future which is essentially alien to us . . . into an experienced, a human future.'[49] Even more, Jesus embodied that experience in his own life; without such embodiment he could only have failed. Finally, Jesus' eschatological thinking is 'concerned with the transformation of the *whole* man . . . not just . . . oppression, need, slavery, etc'.[50] Machoveč equates Marxism with true humanism, and humanism with the total person. Here shines clearly the attempt to put all dimensions of a person together, without minimizing any element. He honors Jesus because he reads Jesus as caring for the total selfhood of persons. For Machoveč, a Marxist should not be interested in Jesus despite the fact, but precisely because he is a Marxist.[51]

18.47 The most sensational and startling production of this genre has been written by the Portuguese Christian Marxist, Fernando Belo: his *Lecture matérialiste de l'évangile de Marc* (1974).[52] Unfortunately this book and its popularization by Michel Clévenot, *Approches matérialistes de la Bible* (1976)[53] seem virtually unknown to English- and German-speaking scholars. What little discussion I have uncovered about Belo's work has been almost entirely in French.[54]

18.48 Belo needs a hearing! His book is difficult, eclectic, startling, threatening, and perhaps even offensive to some. Yet he writes with a passion and clarity of vision that has as its aim to force a '*re*-reading' of the Gospel, a challenge to us 'bourgeois scholars' to turn away from our consistently 'idealist' reading (i.e. perspective) of the Gospel to a 'materialist' reading.

18.49 When one struggles to get behind the author's erudite structuralist and Marxist symbolism and terminology, his 'materialist reading' of the Gospel can, perhaps too simplistically, be reduced to a few points. The basic tradition in Mark is susceptible to a materialist reading, although a movement toward ideological (i.e., theological) interpretation is also apparent in some of the (later?) tradition.[55] Putting the latter aside, the former, if looked at correctly, reveals a Jesus as teacher and *actor* of a messianic *practice* (act is more important than teaching, narrative than discourse).

18.50 And what is this practice? It is a rejection of the dominant code of society; thus it reflects a struggle of class. It is a rejection of the definition of the self as spirit and a reassertion of the importance of body. In the *economic* sphere the messianic practice means giving to each according to need.[56] In the *interrelational* sphere, it means the end of the lord/servant relationship and its replacement by a community where there are only 'des frères, tous enfants, tous derniers, tous serviteurs'.[57] In the *ideological* sphere, it requires a conversion from reading the Gospel according to the dominant code of establishment society to that of the 'subversive' messianic practice, which Jesus embodies and to which Jesus calls the reader.[58]

18.51 Contrary to the Zealots, however, this practice is communist (i.e., egalitarian), nonrevolutionary, and international.[59] It is a practice which remains open to the future — it is a *way*. Hence the *resurrection of the body* is perhaps the single most important symbol for Belo.[60] For this points the reader toward the future, yet a future which is life in the body (i.e., anti-idealist). This future can be realized only by following the messianic practice of Jesus. That means that any idealist reading of the resurrection which separates it from messianic practice *in* this world is to be rejected. As Clévenot comments: 'Ce n'est qu'au sein d'une pratique visant à *l'insurrection* des corps que peut se poser valablement la *question de leur résurrection*.[61]

18.52 From the perspective of critical ('bourgeois') scholarship, there is much that is perversely unscientific which can be dismissed all too easily. Yet there may also be much that is stubbornly right in its materialist reading that calls the idealistic (docetic?) reading into serious question. At the least Trocmé is correct in his conclusion about Belo: 'Il y a place pour des études expérimentales dont les auteurs s'efforcent de relire les textes bibliques à la lumière des grands débats de notre temps'.[62] Is not Belo a challenge to our scholarly world, asking whether New Testament exegesis has, in fact, anything to say about ecology, human oppression, economic slavery, mass malnutrition — or whether we can only be silent and leave *that* Gospel to others?

18.53 Even this all too brief march through recent scholarship reveals great differences and tensions among the various researchers, whether historians, sociologists, or Marxists. Do they have anything at all in common? Ultimately, it seems to me, they at least all share the aim to show how the New Testament message is related to the everyday life and societal needs and contexts of real human beings, how the texts cannot be separated from social dynamic without truncating the reality of both speaker and reader (including the reader today). In the final analysis, the issue is not whether these authors are correct, but whether they make us think about the texts in fresh ways, and in ways which are not out of tune with 'the great disputes of our age'.

Notes

1. Since in these Notes I hope to present as full a bibliography of sociological work on the New Testament as is suitable, given space limitations, it has been necessary rigorously to exclude mention, except when necessary for the discussion, of non-New Testament studies, whether those secular studies which form the groundwork for work on the New Testament, or those which deal with contiguous areas such as early Judaism or the Greco-Roman world. For the latter, the interested reader should consult the bibliography in J. Smith, 'Social Description of Early Christianity', *RelSRev* 1 (1975): 19–25.

2. E.g., Adolf Deissmann, *Licht vom Osten* (Tübingen, 1908); Eng., *Light from the Ancient East: The New Testament Illustrated by Recently Discovered Texts of the Graeco-Roman World*, trans. Lionel Strachen, rev. ed. (Grand Rapids, Mich.: Baker Books, 1965); E. Lohmeyer, *Soziale Fragen im Urchristentum* (Darmstadt, 1921); R. Schumacher, *Die soziale Lage der Christen im apostolischen Zeitalter* (Paderborn, 1924); C. J. Cadoux, *The Early Church and the World* (Edinburgh and Naperville, Ill.: Allenson, 1925); S. J. Case, *The Evolution of Early Christianity* (Chicago: University of Chicago Press, 1914); idem, *The Social Origins of Christianity* (Chicago: University of Chicago Press, 1923); idem, *The Social Triumph of the Early Church* (Chicago: University of Chicago Press, 1934; repr. facsimile ed. Freeport, N.Y.: Books for Libraries); Shailer Matthews, *The Social Teaching of Jesus* (New York, 1897); idem, *The Atonement and the Social Process* (New York, 1930).

   Some have argued that form-criticism itself opened the way for a sociological interpretation, or at least for the asking of social questions, by concerning itself with the *Sitz im Leben* of the pericopes. Cf. D. Gewalt, 'Neutestamentliche Exegese und Soziologie,' *EvTh* 31 (1971), 88f., and K. Berger, *Exegese des Neuen Testaments* (Heidelberg, 1977), p. 219.

3. Frederick Grant, *The Economic Background of the Gospels* (London, 1926, repr. New York: Russell and Russell, 1973).

4. In this statement I am referring explicitly to New Testament scholarship. With regard to the social history of early Judaism there has been and continues to be careful work. S. Baron, *A Social and Religious History of the Jews*, Vol. 1, *Ancient Times to the Beginning of the Christian Era*; Vol. 2, *The First Five Centuries* (1937; 2nd rev. and enlarg. ed., New York: Columbia University Press, 1952) has long been standard. More recent is the work of H. Kreissig, e.g., 'Zur Rolle der religiösen Gruppen in den Volksbewegungen der Hasmonäerzeit', *Klio* 43 (1965): 174–82; 'Zur sozialen Zusammensetzung der frühchristlichen Gemeinden im ersten Jahrhundert u. Z.', *Eirene* 6 (1967): 91–100; 'Die Landwirtschaftliche Situation in Palästina vor dem jüdischen Krieg', *Acta Antiqua* 17 (1969): 223–54; *Die sozialen Zusammenhänge jüdischen Krieges* (Berlin, 1970). See also E. Urbach, e.g., 'The Laws Regarding Slavery as a Source for Social History of the Period of the Second Temple, the Mishnah and Talmud',

Papers of the Institute of Jewish Studies (Jerusalem, 1964), Vol. 1, pp. 1–50. Now there is the massive *The Jewish People in the First Century: Historical Geography, Political History, Social, Cultural, and Religious Life and Institutions*, ed. S. Safrai and M. Stern (Philadelphia: Fortress Press, 1974).

5. E.g., Gerd Theissen, *Soziologie der Jesusbewegung* (Munich, 1977), pp. 9–13, Eng., *Sociology of Early Palestinian Christianity*, trans. John Bowden (Philadelphia: Fortress Press, 1978) [British title: *The First Followers of Jesus* (London: SCM, 1978)].

6. Gerd Theissen, 'Soziale Integration und sakramentales Handeln: Eine Analyse von 1 Cor. xi:17–34', *NovT* 16 (1974): 200–202.

7. The reader must understand that I must limit myself to recent work only.

8. Among Martin Hengel's many contributions one can note the following: *War Jesus Revolutionär?* (Stuttgart: Calwer, 1970), Eng., *Was Jesus a Revolutionist?* (Philadelphia: Fortress Press, 1971); *Gewalt und Gewaltlosigkeit: Zur 'politischen Theologie' in neutestamentlicher Zeit* (Stuttgart, 1971), Eng., *Victory over Violence: Jesus and the Revolutionists*, trans. David E. Green (Philadelphia: Fortress Press, 1977); *Judentum und Hellenismus*, 2 vols. 2nd ed. (Tübingen, 1973), Eng., *Judaism and Hellenism: Studies in Their Encounter in Palestine during the Early Hellenistic Period*, trans. John Bowden (Philadelphia: Fortress Press, 1975); *Eigentum und Reichtum in der frühen Kirche* (Stuttgart: Calwer, 1973), Eng., *Property and Riches in the Early Church*, trans. John Bowden (Philadelphia: Fortress Press, 1975); *Christus und die Macht* (Stuttgart: Calwer, 1974), Eng., *Jesus and Power*, trans. Everett Kalin (Philadelphia: Fortress Press, 1975). Hengel has been particularly concerned with the problems of political force and the question of war violence. This topic has been much discussed in recent years; here I can mention only Oscar Cullmann, *Jesus and the Revolutionaries* (New York: Harper & Row, 1970), and George R. Edwards, *Jesus and the Politics of Violence* (New York: Harper & Row, 1972).

9. In *Gewalt und Gewaltlosigkeit* Hengel argues that only when the social *context* bears some analogies with the contemporary setting can the teaching of Jesus about violence be relevant for today's world. See my introduction to the English translation, *Victory over Violence*, pp. ix–xxiv.

10. E. A. Judge, *The Social Pattern of Christian Groups in the First Century: Some Prolegomena to the Study of the New Testament on Social Obligation* (London: Tyndale Press, 1960).

11. S. Benko and J. O'Rourke, eds, *The Catacombs and the Colosseum: The Roman Empire as the Setting of Primitive Christianity* (Valley Forge, Pa.: Judson Press, 1971) [British title: *Early Church History* (London: Oliphants, 1972)]. Covering some of the same ground is the collection of essays by Hans von Campenhausen, *Tradition und Leben: Kräfte der Kirchengeschichte* (Tübingen, 1960).

12. Abraham Malherbe, *Social Aspects of Early Christianity* (Baton Rouge: Louisiana State University Press, 1977), and Robert Grant, *Early Christianity and Society* (New York: Harper & Row, 1977). Cf. also S. Bartchy, *Mallon chresai: First-Century Slavery and the Interpretation of 1 Corinthians 7:21* (Missoula: Scholars Press, 1973), and Richard Batey, *Jesus and the*

Poor (New York: Harper & Row, 1972); Leander Keck, 'The Poor among the Saints in the New Testament', *ZNW* 56 (1965): 100–137; idem, 'The Poor among the Saints in Jewish Christianity and Qumran', *ZNW* 57 (1966): 54–78.

13. Many papers were produced by working members of the group on various social *realia* in Antioch, processing what information is known about Jews and Christians in the early centuries. Two papers that originated the discussion of the group have been published: L. Keck, 'On the Ethos of Early Christianity', *JAAR* 42 (1974): 435–52, and J. Smith, 'Social Description' (cf. Note 1 above). The recent volume by Wayne A. Meeks and Robert W. Wilken, *Jews and Christians in Antioch in the First Four Centuries of the Common Era* (Missoula: Scholars Press, 1978), lucidly summarizes many of the findings of the group, as well as including translations of some relevant texts (Libanius and Chrysostom). Cf. also the essays of several American scholars translated in *Zur Soziologie des Urchristentums*, ed. Wayne A. Meeks (Munich, 1979).

    Two projects begun by the group are still underway. One is a bibliography, under the direction of Leander Keck, expected to be completed by 1979. Cf. L. Keck and J. Louis Martin, eds, *Studies in Luke-Acts* (Philadelphia: Fortress Press, 1980). The second is a prosopography for Antioch which is being completed by the Disciples Institut zur Erforschung des Urchristentums in Tübingen. According to F. Norris, director of the project at the Institut, completion is not expected before 1985.

14. Deissman, *Light from the Ancient East*.

15. Judge, *Social Pattern*.

16. Ibid., p. 55.

17. Ibid., p. 57.

18. Ibid., p. 60.

19. Malherbe, *Social Aspects*, p. 31. In addition to the authors cited here, Malherbe has supporters in Wilhelm Wuellner, *The Meaning of 'Fishers of Men'* (Philadelphia: Westminster, 1967); idem, 'The Sociological Implications of 1 Corinthians 1:26–28', *Studia Evangelica* 4 (1973): 666–72; and G. Buchanan, 'Jesus and the Upper Class', *NovT* 7 (1964–1965).

20. Gerd Theissen, 'Soziale Schichtung in der korinthischen Gemeinde', *ZNW* 65 (1974): 232–72.

21. Hengel, *Eigentum und Reichtum*, pp. 44–45: 'This means that the members of the Christian communities were found in *all* social classes, from slaves and freed slaves to the local aristocracy, the members of municipal and colonial senates, and possibly even to the senatorial nobility'.

22. Grant, *Early Christianity*, pp. 83–95.

23. Clarence Lee, 'Social Unrest and Primitive Christianity', in *The Catacombs and the Colosseum*, p. 134.

24. Cf. R. Scroggs, 'The Earliest Christian Communities as Sectarian Movement', in *Christianity, Judaism and Other Greco-Roman Cults*, ed. J. Neusner (Leiden: Brill, 1975), Vol. 2, p. 3. I am dependent here on Werner Stark, *The Sociology of Religion: A Study of Christendom*, 5 vols. Vol. 2: *Sectarian Religion* (London, 1967; New York: Fordham University Press, 1967 and 1972), Vol. 2, pp. 6–29.

25. Scroggs, 'Earliest Christian Communities'.

26. My analysis concerned only the rural setting of Palestinian Christianity, and it cannot without alteration be applied to the urban churches of the Hellenistic mission. Howard C. Kee, in a recent work using sociological analysis believes that the Markan church in the late sixties is still non-urban: *Community of the New Age: Studies in Mark's Gospel* (Philadelphia: Westminster, 1977), pp. 104–5.

In the Paris meeting of the SNTS in 1978, however, Wayne Meeks addressed the question whether sectarian analysis would fit a Pauline church. He concludes that the evidence is ambiguous. His address, ' "Since then you would need to go out of the world": Group Boundaries in Pauline Christianity', has now appeared in *Critical History and Biblical Faith: New Testament Perspectives*, ed. J. T. Ryan (Villanova, Pa.: Catholic Theology Society, 1979), pp. 4–29.

At least some of the suggested essential characteristics of the sect are clearly present, however, in the Hellenistic churches, *at least in the earliest period*. Recent investigations have shown, for example, the basic egalitarianism that existed within the communities — the test case being the relation between male and female. For discussion and bibliography, cf. R. Scroggs, 'Paul and the Eschatological Woman', *JAAR* 40 (1972): 283–303; and W. A. Meeks, 'The Image of the Androgyne: Some Uses of a Symbol in Earliest Christianity', *HR* 13 (1974): 165–208. Before the New Testament period is over, however, this egalitarianism has disappeared, at least in those churches representing emerging 'orthodoxy'.

27. Graydon Snyder, professor of New Testament at Bethany Theological Seminary, Oak Brook, Illinois. Cf. his 'Survey and "New Thesis" on the Bones of Peter', *BA* 32 (1969): 3–5, and an unpublished paper he presented to the SNTS Seminar on Social Background and History of the Early Church, Tübingen, 1977: 'The Great Tradition and Its Local Complement in Early Christianity'.

28. Key here are Robert Redfield, *Peasant Society and Culture: An Anthropological Approach to Civilization* (Chicago: University of Chicago Press, 1965); Melford E. Spiro, *Buddhism and Society* (London, 1971, and New York: Harper & Row, 1972); and R. Thouless, *Conventionalization and Assimilation in Religious Movements* (Oxford: Oxford University Press, 1940).

29. John G. Gager, *Kingdom and Community: The Second World of Early Christianity* (Englewood Cliffs, N.J.: Prentice-Hall, 1975) [see below, *Extract 19*]. This has stirred up quite an active response in the United States. Cf. three recent review articles, all appearing in *Zygon: Journal of Religion and Science* 13 (1978): D. Bartlett, 'John G. Gager's *Kingdom and Community*: A Summary and Response', pp. 109–22; J. Smith, 'Too Much Kingdom, Too Little Community', pp. 123–30; D. Tracy, 'A Theological Response to *Kingdom and Community*', pp. 131–35.

30. L. Festinger, H. Riecken, and S. Schachter, *When Prophecy Fails: A Sociological and Psychological Study of a Modern Group that Predicted the Destruction of the World* (New York: Harper & Row, 1964). The 'modern group' in question was an actual flying saucer cult in the U.S. The thesis,

however, does not rest primarily on study of this group alone but involves analysis of many other millennial cults. The theory of cognitive dissonance has been used by at least two other scholars in related studies. Cf. U. Wernick, 'Frustrated Beliefs and Early Christianity: A Psychological Enquiry into the Gospels of the New Testament', *Numen* 22 (1975): 96–130, and W. Zenner, 'The Case of the Apostate Messiah: A Reconsideration of the "Failure of Prophecy" ', *Archives de sciences sociales des religions* 21 (1966): 111–18, the latter dealing with the history of the Zabatean movement.

31. Gager, *Kingdom and Community*, p. 43 [below, *19.12*].
32. Ibid., pp. 43–46 [below, *19.13ff.*].
33. Gerd Theissen, 'Wanderradikalismus: Literatursoziologische Aspekte der Überlieferung von Worten Jesu im Urchristentum', *ZTK* 70 (1973): 245–71; 'Soteriologische Symbolik in den paulinischen Schriften', *KuD* 20 (1974): 282–304; 'Soziale Integration und sakramentales Handeln: Eine Analyse von 1 Cor. xi, 17–34', *NovT* 16 (1974): 179–206; 'Soziale Schichtung in der korinthischen Gemeinde: Ein Beitrag zur Soziologie des hellenistischen Christentums', *ZNW* 65 (1974): 232–72; 'Theoretische Probleme religions-soziologische Forschung und die Analyse des Urchristentums', *NZSTR* 16 (1974); 35–56; 'Legitimation und Lebensunterhalt: Ein Beitrag zur Soziologie urchristlicher Missionäre', *NTS* 21 (1975): 192–221; 'Die Starken und Schwachen in Korinth: Soziologische Analyse eines theologischen Streites', *EvTh* 35 (1975): 155–72; 'Die soziologische Auswertung religiöser Überlieferungen: Ihre methodologische Probleme am Beispiel des Urchristentums', *Kairos* 17 (1975): 284–99; 'Die Tempelweissagung Jesu: Prophetie im Spannungsfeld von Stadt und Land', *ThZ* 32 (1976): 144–58; 'Wir Haben Alles Verlassen (Mark: 10:28): Nachfolge und soziale Entwurzelung in der jüdische-palästinischen Gesellschaft des I. Jahrhunderts n. Chr.', *NovT* 10 (1977): 161–96; *Soziologie der Jesusbewegung: Ein Beitrag zur Entstehungsgeschichte des Urchristentums* (Munich, 1977) [compare *Extract 20* below].
34. Of this method Theissen says simply, 'Die Rollanalyse untersucht typische Verhaltensmuster', *Jesusbewegung*, p. 10.
35. Ibid., pp. 14–21; see also 'Wanderralikalismus', *ZTK* 70.
36. Theissen, 'Legitimation und Lebensunterhalt', *NTS* 21, pp. 202–5.
37. Ibid., pp. 205–17. Two other authors who have recently wrestled with the problem of the bases of apostolic authority in the Hellenistic churches, both of these in dialogue with the Weberian analysis of charisma and legitimation, are J. H. Schütz, *Paul and the Anatomy of Apostolic Authority*, Society for New Testament Studies Monograph Series, No. 26 (Cambridge: Cambridge University Press, 1975), and Bengt Holmberg, *Paul and Power: The Structure of Authority in the Primitive Church as Reflected in the Pauline Epistles* (Lund, 1978, Philadelphia: Fortress Press, 1980).
38. A sociological work that has had great influence, perhaps especially in the United States, is P. Berger and T. Luckmann, *The Social Construction of Reality: A Treatise on the Sociology of Knowledge* (New York: Doubleday,

1966). These authors are themselves dependent on A. Schutz. Cf. my paper read at the Tübingen SNTS meeting in 1977: 'A Theological Apology for Using Sociological Methodology'; W. A. Meeks, 'The Social World of Early Christianity', *Bulletin of the Council on the Study of Religion* 6 (1975).

39. Wayne A. Meeks, 'The Man from Heaven in Johannine Sectarianism', *JBL* 91 (1972): 44–72 [see below, *Extract 21*]. For a critique of Meeks' view, cf. K. Berger, *Exegese*, pp. 230–31.
40. Meeks, 'The Man from Heaven', p. 41.
41. Ibid., p. 67.
42. Ibid., p. 68.
43. Ibid., p. 70 [below, *21.14*].
44. Ibid., p. 71 [below, *21.16*].
45. Cf. his famous sentence, 'It is not the consciousness of men that determines their being, but on the contrary, their social being determines their consciousness'. This is from the Preface of *Zur Kritik der politischen Ökonomie*, and I take it from the translation of T. Bottomore, *Karl Marx: Selected Writings in Sociology and Social Philosophy* (New York: McGraw-Hill, 1964), p. 51.
46. Karl Kautsky, *Der Ursprung des Christentums* (Stuttgart, 1921); Eng. trans., *Foundations of Christianity: A Study of Christian Origins* (New York: International Publications, 1925). Interesting here also is B. Stasiewski, 'Ursprung und Entfaltung des Christentums in sowjetischer Sicht', *Saeculum* 11 (1960): 157–79.
47. Martin Robbe, *Der Ursprung des Christentums* (Leipzig, 1967).
48. Milan Machoveč, *Jesus für Atheisten* (Stuttgart, 1972); Eng. trans., *A Marxist Looks at Jesus* (Philadelphia: Fortress Press, 1976).
49. Ibid., p. 88; references are to the English edition.
50. Ibid., p. 97.
51. Ibid., p. 31.
52. Fernando Belo, *Lecture matérialiste de l'évangile de Marc* (Paris: Du Cerf, 1974). By 1976 there was already a third edition. English ed., *A Materialist Reading of the Gospel of Mark,* trans. Matthew J. O'Connell (Maryknoll, N.Y.: Orbis Books, 1981).
53. Michel Clévenot, *Approaches matérialistes de la Bible* (Paris: Du Cerf, 1976); Eng., *Materialist Approaches to the Bible,* trans. William J. Nottingham (Maryknoll, N.Y.: Orbis Books, forthcoming).
54. Although I am sure that this list is not complete, I have noted the following reviews: by Poulat, Herrieu-Léger, Hadot, and Ladrière in the *Archives de sciences sociales des religions* 40 (1975): 119–37; by E. Trocmé in *RHPR* 55 (1975): 293–94; by M. Bouttier in *Etudes théologiques et religieuses* 50 (1975): 89–91; by Vanhoye in *Biblica* 58 (1977): 295–98. Cf. also the interesting comments of E. Trocmé in 'Exégèse scientifique et idéologie de l'école de Tubingue aux Historiens Français des origines chrétiennes', *NTS* 24 (1977/78): 461–62. P. Pokorny discusses Belo and other Marxists in 'Die neue theologische Linke', *Communio Viatorum* 19 (1976): 225–32. From the same perspective, cf. S. Rostagno, 'Is an Interclass Reading of the Bible Legitimate?', *Communio Viatorum* 17

(1974): 1–14, see Article 4 in this volume; and the paper delivered at the Paris SNTS meeting in 1978 by K. Tagawa, 'Possibilité de l'interprétation matérialiste: un essai de l'exégèse de Marc 6:7–12'.

55. Belo, *A Materialist Reading*, pp. 233–340, references are to the English edition.

56. Ibid., pp. 244–45.

57. Ibid., p. 248: 'There will be only brothers, with everyone a child, everyone last, everyone a servant'.

58. Ibid., pp. 251–55.

59. Ibid., pp. 261–62.

60. Ibid., pp. 288–95. Cf. also Pokorny in *Communio Viatorum* 19, p. 227.

61. Clévenot, *Approaches matérialistes*, p. 152: 'It is only at the heart of a praxis aiming at the *insurrection* of bodies that it is possible to pose validly the *question of their resurrection*'.

62. Trocmé in *RHPR* 55, p. 294: 'There is a place for experimental studies in which the authors strive for a re-reading of biblical texts in the light of the great disputes of our age'. An equally provocative study is that of José Miranda, *Marx y la Biblia* (Salamanca: Sígueme, 1971), Eng., *Marx and the Bible: A Critique of the Philosophy of Oppression*, trans. John Eagleson (Maryknoll, N.Y.: Orbis Books, 1974).

19

John G. Gager
Christian Missions and the Theory of Cognitive
Dissonance

This Extract comes from the second chapter of Gager's *Kingdom and Community: the Social World of Early Christianity*, first published in 1975. The chapter is entitled 'The End of Time and the Rise of Community': Gager is professor of religion at Princeton University. *Kingdom and Community* can already be seen to be one of the most important and sophisticated in recent sociological studies of the New Testament. Throughout Gager shows that he is well aware of the strengths and obvious limits of such studies: 'any exploration of new models in a field that provides few precedents ought to proceed with caution, though not necessarily without conviction' (p. 2). It is certainly his conviction that 'the promise of this paradigm is that it will make it possible to see old facts in a new light' (p. 11). His concern throughout the study is with the way a social world is constructed and maintained in early Christianity: 'to explore . . . the relationship between religion and social status, the enthusiastic character of the earliest Christian communities, their gradual transformation into a formidable religious and social institution, and the emergence of Christianity as the dominant religion of the later Roman Empire' (p. 2). This Extract focuses upon the aspect of gradual transformation. It has been chosen partly because it can be compared usefully with *Extract 17* and partly because it is the aspect of the book which has received most attention (cf. *18.28f.*). Whereas Carroll argues, on the basis of mainly Old Testament prophetic texts, that 'dissonance gives rise to hermeneutic' (*17.19*), Gager, in contrast, argues that 'an increase in proselytizing normally follows disconfirmation' (*19.4*). To support this interpretation of the New Testament evidence, he looks at two critical moments in the transformation of earliest Christianity — the death of Jesus and the expectation of the kingdom (*19.7f.*). In both of these critical moments Gager sees evidence for the sort of rationalisation and dissonance that Festinger detailed (*19.18*). However, this still does not explain why some religious groups showing signs of dissonance react by proselytising whereas others do not. To account for this Gager makes a number of modifications to

Festinger's theory (*19.21*). Finally Gager shows that he is aware that cognitive dissonance will not 'explain' all forms of missionary activity or patterns of 'conversion' (*19.24*). Nonetheless, he clearly believes that it is a theory which can generate new insights on familiar biblical material.

19.1 Despite uncertainty about numerous aspects of primitive Christianity, the sources are unanimous in reporting certain basic traits. Among these is an enthusiastic dedication to missionary activity.[76] There was, to be sure, a protracted and often bitter debate about whether the mission should focus exclusively on Jews ('Go nowhere among the Gentiles, and enter no town of the Samaritans, but go rather to the lost sheep of the house of Israel' — Matt. 10:5f.; cf. also the story of the Syrophoenician woman in Matt. 15:21–28) or should include Gentiles as well ('Go therefore and make disciples of all nations . . .' — Matt. 28:19!). Even among those who advocated a universal calling, there was disagreement about the conditions under which Gentiles could embrace the faith. Should they assume the full burden of the Mosaic Law ('But some believers who belonged to the party of the Pharisees rose up, and said, "It is necessary to circumcise them, and to charge them to keep the law of Moses" ' — Acts 15:5) or just a partial burden (Acts 15:19f.)? Still others, like Paul, maintained that allegiance to the Christ meant freedom from the Law altogether (Galatians, *passim*). But transcending these disagreements was a consensus that a primary obligation of the community as a whole was to proclaim the gospel of Christ in the world. More than any other cult in the Roman Empire, Christianity was a missionary faith and, of course, owed its ultimate status in the empire to the success of its mission.

19.2 The fact of Christian mission is plain enough, but the underlying issue of what motivated it is far from clear. Indeed, the issue has seldom even been raised. In his classic work on *The Mission and Expansion of Christianity in the First Three Centuries*, Adolf Harnack deals systematically with every issue *except* that of motivation.[77] Almost in passing, he remarks that the churches inherited their missionary zeal from Judaism.[78] Just a few pages later he strikes a somewhat different note in suggesting that missions arose as a response to the death of Jesus and as an expression of their hope in the coming of the kingdom in the near future.[79] But why, one is tempted to ask, should the death of Jesus and the expectation of the kingdom have led to mission? More recent studies have also taken up the matter of motivation but have succeeded merely in proliferating the number of explanations: words of Jesus, a sense of responsibility for the unevangelized world, the experience of Jesus' resurrection, etc. Of these perhaps the most common explanation is that the enthusiastic anticipation of the End was the fundamental motivation for early Christian missions. F. Hahn locates the initial impetus in Jesus' own command to proclaim the message of the kingdom (Mark 6:7–13; Luke 9:1–6, etc.), and adds that the events of Jesus' death and resurrection 'awoke in the whole of the primitive Church a white-hot expectation of its [the kingdom's] imminence, and now [it] had to be made known afresh to men'.[80] Similarly, O. Cullmann has argued that early Christian eschatology, rather than paralyzing the communities, turned it outward toward the world.[81] In particular, he points to Mark 13:10 ('And the gospel must first be preached to all nations') as evidence for the connection between mission and eschatology.[82]

19.3 Undeniably the missionary zeal of the early churches was related to their eschatological consciousness. But this statement alone hardly settles the matter, for it still leaves the basic questions unanswered. Why, for instance, did the churches ignore those sayings in the Gospels that limited the mission to Israel? Why did they attach such importance precisely to missionary commands? Or, to put the matter somewhat differently, why did the communities that eventually produced the Gospels choose to represent and emphasize Jesus' role as initiator of missions? What precisely is the connection between missionary action and eschatological awareness? Why did missions persist long after most Christians had ceased regarding the kingdom as imminent? Why is it that certain Jewish communities in this period (e.g., the Essenes at Qumran), who also understood themselves to be living in the last days, did not undertake vigorous missions? Or, on a more general level, why is it that in the case of early Christianity expectation of the End did not lead, as often happens, to an isolationist or quietist stance toward the outside world? In short, explanations that appeal to eschatology as the basic motivation for missions are not really causal explanations at all. They simply note that the early communities were both eschatological and missionary and then proceed to assume that the one must have caused the other. *Post hoc ergo propter hoc.*

19.4 Rather than abandon the connection between eschatology and missions, I would contend that the precise nature of their connection can be understood by appealing to the theory of cognitive dissonance, as developed by L. Festinger and others. As presented in *When Prophecy Fails. A Social and Psychological Study of a Modern Group That Predicted the Destruction of the World*,[83] the theory states that under certain conditions a religious community whose fundamental beliefs are disconfirmed by events in the world will not necessarily collapse and disband. Instead it may undertake zealous missionary activity as a response to its sense of cognitive dissonance, i.e., a condition of distress and doubt stemming from the disconfirmation of an important belief. The critical element of the theory is that 'the presence of dissonance gives rise to pressures to reduce or eliminate the dissonance. The strength of the pressures to reduce the dissonance is a function of the magnitude of the dissonance'.[84] Among the various techniques for reducing dissonance, Festinger et al. argue that proselytism is one of the most common and effective. Rationalization, i.e., revisions of the original belief or of views about the disconfirming event, will also operate, but proselytism almost always occurs. The assumption, often unconscious, is that '*if more and more people can be persuaded that the system of belief is correct, then clearly it must, after all, be correct*'.[85] Thus, the authors argue, we find the apparent paradox that an increase in proselytizing normally follows disconfirmation.

19.5 To support and illustrate the theory of cognitive dissonance, the authors devote the bulk of *When Prophecy Fails* to a group (Lake City) in the 1950s that had predicted the destruction of the world on a given December 21 and that had made extensive preparations for the occasion. The most striking feature of the group is that when December 21 had come and gone, i.e., when the central belief of the group had been unequivocally disconfirmed, the members responded not by disbanding but by intensifying their previous low level of proselytizing. Eventually the group broke up as the result of a number of factors (legal action and ineffective proselytism), but its initial response to disconfirmation aptly substantiates the basic theory. Other examples illustrate the same sequence: the Millerite movement in the Northeastern United States of the 1840s; the messianic fervor surrounding Sabbatai Zevi in the Near East between 1640 and 1670; and finally the origins of Christianity. Although the authors regard early Christianity as the best historical illustration, they finally conclude that it cannot, because of uncertainty on one or two issues, serve by itself to validate the theory. But once the theory has been established through other, more controlled movements, should we not reexamine its relevance as a tool for investigating the source of missionary activities in earliest Christianity?

19.6 At the outset, *When Prophecy Fails* stipulates five conditions that must be present before one can expect disconfirmation to produce increased proselytism:[86]

1. A belief must be held with deep conviction and it must have some relevance to action, that is, to what the believer does or how he behaves.
2. The person holding the belief must have committed himself to it; that is, for the sake of his belief, he must have taken some important action that is difficult to undo. In general, the more important such actions are, and

the more difficult they are to undo, the greater is the individual's commitment to the belief.
3. The belief must be sufficiently specific and sufficiently concerned with the real world so that events may unequivocally refute the belief.
4. Such undeniable disconfirmatory evidence must occur and must be recognized by the individual holding the belief . . .
5. The believer must have social support. . . . If [however] the believer is a member of a group of convinced persons who can support one another, we would expect the belief to be maintained and the believers to attempt to proselytize or to persuade nonmembers that the belief is correct.

19.7 There is little need to argue that early Christianity meets the first, second, and fifth conditions. The conviction with which early Christians held to their beliefs was greeted by many pagans with a mixture of admiration (for their remarkable tenacity) and contempt (for the unworthiness of the beliefs themselves).[87] The decision to embrace the faith in the first decades often entailed the irrevocable loss of family, friends, and social status. And it is clear that missionary activities flourished primarily *after* the death of Jesus. Questions do arise, however, concerning the third and fourth conditions. Can we locate important beliefs that were specific enough to be disconfirmed by events in the world, and is there any evidence that believers regarded such events as having occurred? To answer these questions I propose to consider two critical moments in the early history of the movements, in fact the same two movements mentioned earlier by Harnack — the death of Jesus and the expectation of the kingdom.[88]

The Event of Jesus' Death

19.8 On the matter of Jesus' death, we must be able to demonstrate that it was regarded by his followers as in some sense disconfirming beliefs and hopes that they had attached to him during his lifetime. And as a subsidiary issue, our case will be strengthened if there are also indications that his death continued to disconfirm belief for a period of time thereafter.

19.9 There is no doubt that the crucifixion of Jesus constituted a major obstacle to the conversion of many Jews. Paul says as much in 1 Cor. 1:23 ('but we preach Christ crucified, a stumbling block to Jews and folly to Gentiles'), and his assertion is supported by an examination of Jewish messianic expectations prior to the time of Jesus. There are no signs that any group of Jews awaited a suffering Messiah, let alone one who would be crucified by Rome.[89] In other words, insofar as the followers of Jesus shared the messianic views of their time, they were unprepared for the death of the one whom they believed to be the fulfillment of their messianic dreams. But a problem arises precisely at this point: how far did Jesus' followers adhere to traditional messianic formulations? Jesus himself is portrayed in the Gospels as predicting his future suffering and death (Matt. 16:21 — 'From that time on Jesus began to show his disciples that he must go to Jerusalem and suffer many things from the elders and chief priests and scribes, and be killed, and on the third day be raised').[90] 'If this view is maintained', comment the authors of *When Prophecy Fails*, 'then the crucifixion, far from being a disconfirmation, was indeed a confirmation of a prediction and the subsequent proselytizing of the apostles would stand as a counter-example to our hypotheses.'[91] But the difficulties raised by this text are actually less severe than the authors recognize. There are two possible views about the origin of these predictions. Either they were created after the event in order to lend supportive meaning to the otherwise disconfirmatory event of the crucifixion[92] — in which case the text must be read as *sustaining* the theory — or they originated with Jesus himself. Even in the second case, however, there is firm evidence that the prediction was not accepted or understood by the disciples and that Jesus' death still came as a rude shock to them.

19.10 The passages in question (Mark 8:27–33; 9:30–32; 10:33–34), when read as a whole, tend to support rather than contradict the theory of dissonance. The first section (Mark 8:27–29) culminates in Peter's confession, 'You are the Christ [i.e., the Messiah]', in which Peter clearly represents the universal belief of early Christians. The confession is then followed by Jesus' command to remain silent about this (8:30) and by his teaching that he (Matt. 16:21), or the Son of man (Mark 8:31), must suffer and die. To this Peter responds with dismay, presumably at the prediction of suffering and death — Matt. 16:22 makes this explicit: 'God forbid, Lord! This shall never happen to you' — thus expressing his inability to comprehend or accept the notion of a suffering Messiah. And finally, Jesus turns on Peter angrily, calling him Satan and questioning even his loyalty to God, again presumably for his failure to understand the need for suffering and death. Here again, Peter must be seen as representing more than his own personal views. To summarize: Whether or not this scene actually occurred in Jesus' lifetime, it conveys the clear sense that the death of Jesus was a problem for his followers from the beginning and that its problematic character persisted thereafter, no doubt reinforced by Jews who maintained that a crucified Messiah was a contradiction in terms.

19.11 The relevance of this passage for the theory of dissonance is two-fold. In the first place, it obviously springs from a sense of doubt and distress about Jesus' death, and in the second place, it represents the process of rationalization that, according to Festinger et al., normally accompanies proselytism. And on this particular issue, it is still possible to trace the process of rationalization whereby the early church sought to persuade others and itself that Jesus' death was both necessary and beneficial. The Gospel of Luke records a rather striking conversation between two disciples and the resurrected Jesus, whom the disciples do not recognize: 'But we had hoped that he was the one to redeem Israel. Yes, and besides all this, it is now the third day since this [the crucifixion] happened' (Luke 24:21). To this expression of disappointment, Jesus replies, 'O foolish men, and slow of heart to believe all that the prophets have spoken! Was it not necessary that the Christ should suffer these things and enter into his glory?' (Luke 24:25). In what we may call the first stage, we find the risen Jesus himself claiming that his death was both necessary and in accordance with the Scriptures as properly, i.e., in a Christian context, interpreted. Much the same view is expressed by Paul when he affirms that 'Christ died for our sins in accordance with the scriptures . . . that he was raised on the third day in accordance with the scriptures . . .' (1 Cor. 15:3f.). Although neither Luke nor Paul cites a specific passage from Scripture, both reflect a situation in which an effort has been made to turn the disconfirmatory evidence of Scripture (traditional interpretations had not produced the idea of a suffering Messiah) into supporting evidence (correct interpretation showed that such was precisely what had been intended from the beginning).[93] A final stage appears in those Gospel passages in which Jesus predicts, *before* the event and in detail, the necessity of his suffering and death (Mark 8:31, etc.).

19.12 It would appear, then, that we are justified in maintaining that the death of Jesus created a sense of cognitive dissonance, in that it seemed to disconfirm the belief that Jesus was the Messiah. Even the event of the resurrection, which the Gospels present as having surprised the disciples every bit as much as the death, seems not to have eradicated these doubts. Thus according to the theory, we may understand the zeal with which Jesus' followers pursued their mission as part of an effort to reduce dissonance, not just in the early years but for a considerable time thereafter. Initially, it might seem reasonable to suppose that Jesus' death was most problematic for converts from Judaism, but there is good reason to believe Paul when he reports that the crucified Christ was 'a stumbling block to Jews and folly to Gentiles'.[94] Long after Paul's time, Lucian[95] and Celsus[96] continued to mock Christians for their faith in a crucified Savior, whereas Justin Martyr raises the question, surely not a rhetorical one, 'Why should we believe that a crucified man is the first-born of the unbegotten god . . . ?'[97]

The Non-Event of the Kingdom

19.13 We may now return to the issue raised at the start of our discussion, that is, the connection between mission and eschatology. Specifically, can we now envisage the continuing mission as deriving, at least in part, from disappointment and despair over the delay of the kingdom? In different terms, were the eschatological hopes of early Christians 'sufficiently specific and concerned with the real world so that unequivocal disproof or disconfirmation is possible', and are there intimations that believers sensed such disconfirmation 'in the form of the nonoccurrence of a predicted event within the time limits set for its occurrence'?[98]

19.14 Recent scholarship has given affirmative answers to both questions.[99] The earliest Christian communities stood in the mainstream of Jewish apocalyptic thinking. With but one possible exception (the Gospel of John), the earliest ascertainable traditions, i.e., the Gospel sources and the letters of Paul, present a unified picture. The kingdom would happen in the near future; and it would happen as an event in history, indeed as the final event of history in its present mode. The resurrection, the act of divine judgment, and the transformation of the physical and political orders — all were understood to be specific and unmistakable events in the real world. In this respect, Paul's description of the eschatological drama in 1 Thess. 4:16f. ('For the Lord himself will descend from heaven with a cry of command, with the archangel's call, and with the sound of the trumpet of God . . .') may be taken as typical expressions of widely shared beliefs. Whether or not Jesus himself first announced the imminent arrival of the kingdom has been a much debated matter. I am inclined to the view that Jesus shared and thus prompted the belief that the kingdom was imminent,[100] but I am even more certain that our picture of primitive Christian eschatology does not hinge on an answer to the question of Jesus' predictions about his death. As with these predictions, the texts that portray the kingdom as an event in the near future (Mark 1:15; 14:25; 11:12–14, etc.) can have only two possible sources — Jesus or the earliest Christians. Thus even if it should prove methodologically impossible to assign them with certitude to Jesus, the only alternative is the early community.[101] And from that point on, they were transmitted and received *as words of Jesus*. In either case, the structure of the problem remains unchanged: a specific and important prediction that is liable to disconfirmation.

19.15 In the final analysis, however, the surest testimony on this issue is expression of concern about the delay of the kingdom in Christian texts themselves. In 1 Clement 23:3–5 (written around 96 C.E.), the author speaks openly of such concern:[102]

> Let that Scripture be far from us which says: 'Wretched are the double-minded, those who doubt in their soul and say, "We have heard these things even in our fathers' times, and see, we have grown old and none of this has happened" '.[103]

2 Peter 3:3–9 (probably written around 125 C.E.) reflects a similar situation:

> First of all you must understand this, that scoffers will come in the last days . . . saying, 'Where is the promise of his coming? For ever since the fathers fell asleep, all things have continued as they were from the beginning of creation.' . . . But do not ignore this one fact, beloved, that with the Lord one day is as a thousand years, and a thousand years as one day. The Lord is not slow about his promise as some count slowness. . . .

19.16 Both passages reveal that the traditional chronology of the kingdom was under attack, whether by outsiders (i.e., Jewish antagonists) or by Christian revisionists (e.g. Hymenaeus and Philetus who are anathematized by the author of 2 Tim. 2:18 for 'holding that the resurrection is past already'). Paul, too, confronts the issue in 1 Thess. 4:13–5:11, where the concern appears to have arisen quite apart from any outside instigation:

> But we would not have you ignorant, brethren, concerning those who are asleep [i.e., have died], that you may not grieve as others do who have no hope. . . . For this we declare to you by the word of the Lord, that we who are alive, who are left until the coming of the Lord, shall not precede those who have fallen asleep. . . .

19.17 This passage is especially revealing because it points to the specific occasion for the concern, namely, the death of some believers. In other words, the kingdom had been expected before any believers, or at least the first generation, would die, and Paul is forced to remind his readers that the coming event of the resurrection was the positive assurance that those who had died would not miss 'the coming of the Lord'. Finally, of the many passages in the synoptic Gospels, one will serve to complete our survey.[104] The prediction in Matt. 10:23 ('Truly, I say to you, you will not have gone through all the towns of Israel, before the Son of man comes') has been variously interpreted as an authentic saying of Jesus and thus a primary *source* of later concern about the delay, or as a product of the early tradition, a word of consolation spoken in the name of Jesus, and thus a *response* to the delay.[105] Both, of course, are possible. But once again either view leads to the same consequences, for the saying entered the tradition *as a word of Jesus* at an early stage. As those who had known Jesus began to die, this saying and others like it (esp. Mark 9:1 — '. . . There are some standing here who will not taste death before they see the kingdom of God come with power') become a source for concern rather than an attempt to assuage it. In fact, it seems quite likely that the anxiety reflected in later texts (e.g., 2 Peter and 1 Clement), arose from the fact that specific prophecies like that of Mark 9:1 had been unequivocally disconfirmed. Thus we should probably conceive of the response to the delay in at least two stages: an initial disappointment among the earliest believers who had expected the end in the immediate future, a disappointment that evoked consolation in the form of sayings like Mark 9:1; and a subsequent disappointment among those who had expected the end within the first generation of the faithful, a disappointment that produced consolatory sayings (e.g., Mark 13:10 — 'And the gospel must first be preached to all nations') as well as more systematic efforts to de-eschatologize the Christian message.[106] The success of these efforts may be seen in the fact that by the year 150 C.E. not only was Christianity no longer an eschatological community, but, as the reaction to the apocalyptic fervor of Montanism clearly reveals, that it had come to regard eschatological movements as a serious threat. Toward the end of the first century Christians could still pray, 'Thy kingdom come' (Matt. 6:10). But at the end of the second century, Tertullian tells us that Christians prayed 'for the emperors, for the deputies and all in authority, for the welfare of the world, *and for the delay of the final consummation*' (*Apol.* 39.2: cf. 32.1)!

19.18 At this point it is obvious that Festinger and his colleagues' discreet glance at early Christianity is far more significant than they have recognized.[107] We may now formulate their position as follows: Rationalization in connection with important beliefs, specifically the death of Jesus and the delay of the kingdom, represents an effort to reduce doubt and despair and thus is evidence of cognitive dissonance. When, in addition, missionary activity is regularly associated with the same beliefs, it can and must be interpreted as a further attempt to reduce dissonance. In contrast to O. Cullmann, who rejects the notion that mission was 'something which has been substituted for the unrealized hope of the kingdom' and who insists that 'if this were true, then the Church has carried on its mission because it has been obliged to renounce eschatology',[108] it now becomes possible to reverse Cullmann's terms and to conclude that the church initially carried on its mission *in an effort to maintain* its eschatology. The strength of this factor in relation to other motivating forces is beyond final determination. Here we must rest content with the general principle that as other factors, such as commands of Jesus or influence from Judaism, are minimized, the factor of cognitive dissonance must be maximized.

19.19 One final question: Does our discussion suggest the need for any modification in the theory itself? Festinger et al. set out from the observation that disconfirmation of important beliefs produces a sense of disappointment, ranging from doubt to despair, as well as pressures to reduce this disappointment. One method for reducing it is to give up the belief; but in other circumstances, as they say, 'it may even be less painful to tolerate the dissonance than to discard the belief'.[109] In other words, individuals find it easier to maintain a disconfirmed belief when there is group reinforcement. Thus 'the other circumstances' must include loyalty to the group itself, so that it becomes less painful to maintain a disconfirmed belief than to abandon one's loyalty to the group. The authors point in this direction when they admit that 'there is a limit beyond which belief will not stand disconfirmation'.[110] Our examination of early Christianity suggests that this outer limit is not absolute but is rather a function of (1) the extent to which individual members have transferred former loyalties and identities (family, friends, religion, profession) to the new group; and (2) the extent to which the group itself succeeds in retaining and sustaining these new loyalties.

19.20 This last point is of particular importance because it has been questioned in a follow-up study to *When Prophecy Fails*, entitled 'Prophecy Fails Again: A Report of a Failure to Replicate'.[111] The authors, Jane Allyn Hardyck and Marcia Braden, examined a Pentecostal community (True Word) that appeared to meet the five conditions. But the group did not turn to proselytism following its prediction of nuclear destruction on a given date. This result led the authors to propose two revisions in the theory itself: first, 'that the more social support an individual receives above the minimum he needs to maintain his belief, the less he will have to proselytize';[112] and, second, 'that if a group is receiving considerable ridicule from nonmembers, one way of reducing dissonance that would be apparent to them would be to convince these "unbelievers" that the group is right'.[113] The second proposal obviously reinforces our own analysis of early Christianity and requires no further analysis. As for the first proposal it would appear that either the theory itself needs modification or that the type of social support was different in the two cases (Lake City and True Word). There is, in fact, one significant and perhaps decisive difference between early Christian communities and the Lake City group on the one hand and the True

Word group on the other. Hardyck and Braden note that 'many members of the True Word group had worked together for several years'[114] and that their prophet, Mrs Shepard, had been proclaiming her prophecy for nearly four years before the final deadline was set.[115] In other words, the fact that the identity of individuals with the group as well as their breaking of old loyalties had long been established suggests that the prophecy was less important to the members than the existence of the group itself. For the earliest Christians, however, as well as for the Lake City group, the prophet and the message were recent, the movement was new, and between them prophet and prophecy were the basic occasion for the coalescence of the groups. This situation, in which the creation of the group and the subsequently disconfirmed belief are inseparable, seems a likely explanation for the presence of proselytism in the one case and its absence in the other.

19.21 Thus we may summarize the proposed modifications in the theory of dissonance as follows:

1. Proselytism as a means of reducing cognitive dissonance will appear primarily in new groups, like early Christianity, whose existence has been occasioned by or associated with a belief that is subsequently disconfirmed.
2. Public ridicule at the time of disconfirmation may play an important role in turning such a group toward missionary activity.
3. The limit beyond which belief will not withstand disconfirmation is a function of the degree to which identification with the group supplants the original belief as the basic motivation for adherence to the group.

To these we may add one further point. Festinger mentions, though he does not emphasize the fact that rationalization always accompanies proselytism in the period following disconfirmation — the timetable was wrong; the event really did occur in some unexpected and imperceptible fashion; the disconfirming event, when properly understood, turns out to be confirmatory after all, etc. Thus the total process of adjustment includes a social (proselytism) as well as an intellectual (rationalization) component. And insofar as rationalization occurs, it will inevitably alter the shape of the original belief, whether by setting a new deadline, by recasting it in more general terms, or by relegating it to a lower rank within the total nexus of the group's beliefs and practices. In other words, what at first appeared to be a paradox in our explanation of early Christianity — that its status as a millenarian movement enables us to understand both its failure, in the sense that all such movements fail, *and* its success, in the sense that its very failure became the occasion for the intense missionary activity that ensured its ultimate survival — turns out not to be a paradox at all.

Conversion and Dissonance[116]

19.22 In the preceding discussion I have attempted to reinforce Festinger's proposal that cognitive dissonance associated with the disconfirmation of important beliefs was one among several factors behind missionary activity. Beyond this, there is a quite different area, not considered by Festinger, in which dissonance theory can be related to missions. In *A Theory of Cognitive Dissonance*, Festinger deals with dissonance in relation to the general question of decisions and their consequences.[117] Briefly, he notes that dissonance is an inevitable consequence of decisions and that the magnitude of dissonance, and thus of pressures to reduce it, depends on two elements — the importance of the decision and the initial attractiveness of the unchosen or rejected alternative. Successful reduction of dissonance, he maintains, will tend to increase confidence in the decision taken *and* to intensify the attractiveness of the chosen alternative in contrast to the rejected one.[118] These are familiar stages in the process of rationalization. What Festinger does not consider is the further possibility that attempts to diminish postdecision dissonance may also, as in the case of disconfirmed beliefs, lead to or reinforce an inclination to proselytism.

19.23 The relevance of these propositions for the question of conversion is readily apparent. Without pursuing the matter in detail, let me suggest several ways in which efforts to reduce postconversion dissonance may have influenced the experience of early Christians. In the case of Paul, for instance, one is tempted to say that his effort to play down the status and significance of the Mosaic Law (e.g., Gal. chapters 3–4) is an attempt to diminish the attractiveness of the rejected alternative. More generally, the recurrent polemic against pagan cults may express the need of pagan converts to reduce dissonance by emphasizing the discrepancy between rejected and chosen alternatives. The intensive commitment which so often characterizes new converts should also be seen in the same light. Finally, proselytism itself, again among recent converts, would serve to reduce dissonance, not only by stressing the incompatibility of the two alternatives but also by assuming, in Festinger's words, that 'if more and more people can be persuaded that the system of belief is correct, then clearly it must, after all, be correct'.[119]

19.24 Two words of caution are in order before completing this brief aside. First, I do not wish to claim that cognitive dissonance is the single explanation for either missionary activity or polemic against Judaism and paganism. Several factors were involved, and dissonance must be counted among them. Second, dissonance theory will apply only in those cases that involve conversion as defined above, i.e., a decision between incompatible and attractive alternatives. *In this sense*, not all early believers would qualify as converts. Paul would, of course, and he behaves accordingly. But for those who did not see Christianity as a choice between incommensurables, e.g., for those 'Jewish Christians' who disagreed violently with Paul as to the status of the Law, one would have to speak of conversion, if at all, in a different manner. The same would be true of 'pagan Christians' who saw in Christianity the fulfillment of Greek wisdom rather than its antithesis. This particular result points forward to the discussion of orthodoxy and heresy. The harsh attitude of emergent orthodoxy toward both 'Jewish Christianity' and syncretistic Gnosticism can thus be viewed as a process of emphasizing the discrepancy between chosen and rejected alternatives. These movements were threatening precisely because they diminished this discrepancy and thereby increased dissonance for those who had made the decision to convert.

Notes

76. In addition to the works of Harnack, Hahn, and Cullmann, noted below, see also J. Jeremias, *Jesus' Promise to the Nations* (London: SCM Press, 1958); D. Georgi, *Die Gegner des Paulus im 2. Korintherbrief: Studien zur religiösen Propaganda in der Spätantike* (Neukirchen-Vluyn; Neukirchener Verlag, 1964), esp. pp. 83–281; and M. Green, *Evangelism in the Early Church* (London: Hodder and Stoughton, 1970).
77. See below, n. 78.
78. *The Mission and Expansion of Christianity in the First Three Centuries*, 2 vols (New York: G. P. Putnam's Sons, 1908), 1:9; see also, pp. 15f. The missionary character of Judaism is also emphasized by Georgi (*Die Gegner*, pp. 83–187), although both Harnack and Georgi recognize the differences between Jewish and Christian missions. I am rather inclined to agree with the observation of A. D. Nock that 'we should be cautious in inferring widespread efforts by Jews to convert Gentiles. Individual Jews did undoubtedly try to "draw men to the Law", but in the main the proselyte was the man who came to the Law, and the duty of the Jew was to commend the Law by his example (cf. Deuter. 4:6) rather than by missionary endeavor' (from his review in *Gnomon* 33 [1961], p. 582 of H.-J. Schoeps, *Paul. The Theology of the Apostle in the Light of Jewish Religious History* [Philadelphia: Westminster Press, 1961]).
79. *Mission and Expansion*, 1:44.
80. *Mission in the New Testament* (Naperville, Ill.: A. R. Allenson, 1965), p. 51.
81. In his essay 'Eschatology and Missions in the New Testament' from *The Background of the New Testament and Its Eschatology* (Festschrift for C.

H. Dodd), ed. W. D. Davies and D. Daube (Cambridge: The University Press, 1956), pp. 409–21.

82. Cullmann, [ibid.] p. 415.

83. Jointly authored by L. Festinger, H. W. Riecken, and S. Schachter (New York: Harper & Row, 1956). See also Festinger's further elaboration of the theory in *A Theory of Cognitive Dissonance* (Stanford, Calif.: Stanford University Press, 1957).

84. *Theory*, p. 18.

85. *When Prophecy Fails*, p. 28 (their emphasis).

86. *Ibid.*, p. 4.

87. See E. R. Dodds, *Pagan and Christian in an Age of Anxiety* (Cambridge: The University Press, 1965), pp. 120f.

88. It should be noted that *When Prophecy Fails* deals only with Jesus' death and that it ignores recent critical literature on the New Testament.

89. So, for instance, O. Cullmann in *The Christology of the New Testament* (Philadelphia: Westminster Press, 1959), p. 60.

90. Mark's version (8:31) reads: 'And he began to teach them that the Son of man must suffer many things. . . .'. Mark's text can be interpreted to mean that Jesus is speaking of a person *other than himself*. In clarifying this ambiguity, by substituting 'he' for 'the Son of man', Matthew no doubt reflects the universal belief of early Christianity that Jesus was and understood himself to be the Son of man.

91. *When Prophecy Fails*, p. 24.

92. This is the view of most contemporary critics; see, for example, H. Conzelmann, *An Outline of the Theology of the New Testament* (New York: Harper & Row, 1969): 'These [sayings about the suffering Son of man] are all *vaticinia ex eventu*: not prognoses for the further development of the situation, but dogmatic assertions' (p. 133).

93. For a thorough discussion of the manner in which Christians used the Old Testament to support their views, see B. Lindars, *New Testament Apologetic* (Philadelphia: Westminster Press, 1961).

94. 1 Cor. 1:23.

95. *Death of Peregrinus* 13.

96. Origen, *Against Celsus*, 2.39f.

97. *First Apology* 53:2.

98. Festinger, *Theory*, p. 248.

99. See N. Perrin, *Rediscovering the Teaching of Jesus* (New York: Harper & Row, 1967), for a discussion of the central issues and a survey of recent literature.

100. For the contrary view that Jesus' sayings about the kingdom were intensified eschatologically by his followers after his death see E. Stauffer, 'Agnostos Christos. Joh.ii.24 und die Eschatologie des vierten Evangeliums' in *The Background of the New Testament and Its Eschatology* (above, n. 81), pp. 281–99.

101. In the second edition of his important work on responses to the delay of the kingdom (*Das Problem der Parusieverzögerung in den synoptischen Evangelien und in der Apostelgeschichte* [Berlin: Alfred Töpelmann, 1960], pp. 220–26), E. Grässer responds to his critics' charge that his false

premise (Jesus expected the kingdom immediately) leads inevitably to false conclusions (the delay created difficulties because Jesus' words were disconfirmed). By insisting on his interpretation of Jesus, however, he fails to see that the results of his study would remain valid for Christian believers even if his reconstruction of Jesus cannot be sustained.

102. Compare also 2 Clement 11:2 (usually dated between 100 and 150 C.E.), which cites the same (unidentified) passage from Scripture ('Wretched are the double-minded . . .'), but concludes on a different note: 'If we have done what is right before God's eyes, we shall enter his kingdom. . . '.

103. The translation is from *The Library of Christian Classics*, vol. 1: *Early Christian Fathers*, ed. C. C. Richardson (Philadelphia: Westminster Press, 1953), p. 55.

104. Grässer notes four types of material in the synoptics that reflect concern about the delay: first, expressions of uncertainty about precise chronology (Mark 13:32); second, commands and parables urging constant alertness in view of this uncertainty (Mark 13:33; Luke 12:35, 36–38); third, prayers and petitions that the kingdom come (Matt. 6:9–15; cf. Rev. 22:17; 1 Cor. 16:22); and fourth, direct expressions of concern (Matt. 24:45–51; 25:14–30; Luke 20:9). In addition, he details a series of texts that represent more far-reaching attempts to resolve the concern: statements of outright consolation (Luke 18:7–8; Mark 9:1; 13:30; Matt. 10:23); the so-called parables of contrast (e.g., Mark 4:30–32); and finally, actual changes in the timetable (Mark 13:10).

105. This verse is the key to Albert Schweitzer's interpretation of Jesus' ministry. In *The Quest of the Historical Jesus* (New York: Macmillan, 1959), he argues that Jesus was distressed when his words remained unfulfilled and thus turned toward Jerusalem in an effort to force God's hand (pp. 358–60). Thus Jesus himself becomes the first to express concern about the delay of the kingdom. Schweitzer's views were later taken up and expanded by M. Werner, *The Formation of Christian Dogma* (New York: Harper & Bros., 1957). Werner argues that the delay was the single most important force in shaping the development of Christian doctrine.

106. One outstanding example is the Gospel of Luke; see H. Conzelmann, *The Theology of St Luke* (New York: Harper & Row, 1960), pp. 95–136.

107. See the comment of P. Berger, *The Sacred Canopy* (Garden City, N.Y.: Doubleday, 1969), p. 195, n. 30: 'The similarity of the phenomena analysed in the case study [*When Prophecy Fails*] with what New Testament scholars have called *Parousieverzögerung* is astonishing and highly instructive'.

108. 'Eschatology and Missions' (above, n. 81), p. 409.

109. *When Prophecy Fails*, p. 27.

110. *Ibid.*, p. 23.

111. *Journal of Abnormal and Social Psychology* 65 (1962), pp. 136–41. For a more general critique of dissonance theory see R. Brown, *Social Psychology* (New York: Free Press, 1965), pp. 601–8. It should be noted that on one particular issue, our analysis has endeavored to meet Brown's

criticism. He notes that investigators have rarely made an effort, at the beginning of their studies, to determine whether a specific combination of ideas, beliefs, or actions is in fact dissonant for their subjects (p. 597). Throughout this section I have argued that the texts reveal just this awareness of dissonance.

112. *Ibid.*, p. 139.
113. *Ibid.*, p. 140.
114. *Ibid.*, p. 140.
115. *Ibid.*, p. 136.
116. I am indebted to my colleague, Alan Segal, for calling this further application to my attention.
117. *Theory*, pp. 32–83.
118. *Ibid.*, p. 83.
119. *When Prophecy Fails*, p. 28.

20

Gerd Theissen
Functional Effects of Earliest Christianity

This Extract forms the final chapter of Theissen's *Soziologie der Jesusbewegung: Ein Beitrag zur Entstehungsgeschichte des Urchristentums* (Christian Kaiser Verlag, Munich, 1977). This work is considerably bolder than John Gager's *Kingdom and Community* and has, perhaps, been far more influential in popularising the sociology of the New Testament. However, it does lack the rigour of Gager (or of Meeks, as the following Extract demonstrates) and is only thinly documented. Despite this limitation, Theissen always has the ability to raise fresh perspectives and to make telling observations. The book is divided into three parts. In the first he looks at the social role of the earliest Christians, focusing on the role of disciples as wandering charismatics and the communities that responded to them. In the second he analysed four major social variables that effected the 'Jesus movement': socio-economic, socio-ecological, socio-political and socio-cultural. And in the final part he sketches the effects of this Jesus movement on society. In this final part Theissen sometimes writes as if he is going beyond sociological analysis. So, he starts the introduction as follows: 'The analysis of factors has shown that the Jesus movement emerged out of a deep-seated crisis in Palestinian Jewish society. If it were no more than a reflection of social conditions, an analysis of its social conditioning would be conclusive; a separate analysis of function would be unnecessary. However, we proceed on the assumption that the Jesus movement not only emerged from a social crisis but also articulated an answer to this crisis which does not have a sociological derivation' (p. 97). Yet, despite Theissen's having written that, sociological factors are well in evidence in the analysis presented in this Extract (e.g. *20.8f.*). If he had explicitly adopted, at this point, a Weberian interactionist perspective (i.e. one which takes into account the *mutual* influence of society and ideas) he might not have described it in these terms, as going beyond sociology. Certainly the analysis in this Extract of earliest Christianity in relation, first to Palestinian Jewish society (*20.4–5*), and secondly to Hellenistic society (*20.6–13*), is consonant with such a sociological perspective. It is

293

only in his initial understanding of the Jesus Movement (*20.2–3*) that Theissen appears as a theologian rather than as a sociologist/social historian: indeed, it is this part which makes the sharpest contrast with Gager's approach. For Theissen it is the earliest Christians' belief in *and experience of* miraculous powers which enables them to attempt to change the world. Gager, in contrast, argues in his final chapter on 'The Success of Christianity': 'The distinctive factors that can be cited as facilitating the ultimate triumph of Christianity are two-fold: a series of *external* circumstances that were completely beyond its control (the organization of the empire under Augustus; the experience of Hellenistic Judaism; the series of armed conflicts between Rome and Judaism; and the internal crisis of the empire in the third century) and a single, overriding *internal* factor, the radical sense of Christian community — open to all, insistent on absolute and exclusive loyalty, and concerned for every aspect of the believer's life. From the beginning, the one distinctive gift of Christianity was this sense of community . . . Christian congregations provided a unique opportunity for masses of people to discover a sense of security and self-respect' (*Kingdom and Community*, p. 140). It is this social factor, rather than any of the specific beliefs or 'powers' of Christianity (which he does not regard as unique), that Gager argues are responsible for the 'success' of Christianity. The difference between Theissen and Gager here is clear: for the latter only social factors appear relevant, for the former theological factors must be used in addition.

20.1 Did the vision of love and reconciliation ever have a chance of being realized? Could it offer a constructive contribution to life in community? In giving an answer we must break the question down further and consider its chances (1) within the Jesus movement itself, (2) within Palestinian Jewish society as a whole, and (3) within the Hellenistic world.

1. The Jesus movement

20.2 Obviously the Jesus movement took its own programme seriously. The question is not so much how it was possible to obligate a group to observe such 'alien' demands as that of loving their enemies. This group was in an exceptional situation and consisted of outsiders. The early Christian wandering charismatics in particular had the freedom to put even an extreme ethical pattern into effect. The problem is, rather: how could the Jesus movement cherish the hope of permeating the whole of society with this pattern? Was that not to expect a miracle? And indeed a miracle is what they hoped for. The Jesus movement believed in miracles, in the realization of what appeared to be impossible. It had experienced miracles. For it is beyond question that Jesus had powers beyond that of a normal man. Furthermore, he had the gift of arousing these capabilities in other men. His followers had performed miracles themselves. All these miracles were regarded as signs of the great eschatological revolution: exorcisms announced the coming of the kingdom of God (Matt. 12.28).

20.3 Now if the movement had at its disposal powers which foretold a complete change in the world, might it not also have confidence in ethical extremes? Would not the faith which moves mountains (Mark 11.23) also be capable of changing the human heart? If so many miracles had taken place, would not the miracle of love be possible also? We should not underestimate the encouraging effect of miracles. Matthew 11.2–6 combines both Jesus' paranormal actions and his proclamation of the gospel. The message of reconciliation and love is given added force by the fact that the blind are made to see and the sick are healed.

2. Palestinian Jewish society

20.4 As a renewal movement within Judaism, the Jesus movement was a failure. It found so little support that the Jewish historian Josephus could largely ignore it. The primary cause of its failure in Palestine may be the growing tensions in Palestinian Jewish society. The Jesus movement had come into being in a comparatively peaceful period. All that Tacitus can write of the time is that things were quiet under Tiberius (*sub Tiberio quies, Hist.* V.9). The unrest after the death of Herod (6 B.C.) and the first development of an anti-Roman resistance movement after the deposition of Archelaus (A.D. 4) lay far back in the past. The situation was certainly not without its tensions. There is sufficient evidence of that. But there were no major conflicts, so that it is perhaps no coincidence that a new movement with a propensity towards peace-making came into being in this particular time. In any case, during the thirties, after the death of Jesus, the tensions became more acute: the controversies in Alexandria (in which Palestinians were also involved) and the turbulent events connected with Gaius Caligula's attempt to introduce his statue into the temple (A.D. 39–40) may have been symptoms of growing conflicts which were intensified further by the great famine under Claudius (*c.* A.D. 46–48). Now if a society feels threatened and uncertain, it usually resorts to traditional patterns of behaviour; the most sacred treasures of the nation are ostensibly revered, dissociation from anything alien is intensified and currency is given to fanatical slogans. We may assume that events also developed in this direction in Palestinian Jewish society in the first half of the first century A.D. However, this development diminished the chances of the Jesus movement, which encroached on the tabus of society with its criticism of the temple and the law. Its attitude to aliens ran contrary to the tendencies towards segregation that we may assume to have been prevalent. Indeed, it is even probable that the Jesus movement was often forced into the role of a scapegoat: antipathy towards aliens could easily be transferred to those who loosened or even broke through the bonds which held the Jews united against foreigners. Social tensions could be expressed in the suppression of minorities. Thus it is hardly by chance that the persecution under Herod Agrippa (A.D. 41–44) came after the unrest in Alexandria and Palestine. Nor is it coincidence that at the same time Herod Agrippa made enemies of both the Hellenistic cities and the first Christians (Acts 12.20ff.). Acts explicitly stresses that the persecution was carried out to meet the wishes of the 'Jews'. Must there not have been a need among the people to discover scapegoats? The situation of the Christians must have become even more precarious with the increasing tensions that preceded the Jewish war. The Christians belonged to the peace party. There is nothing to support the assumption that they will have taken part in the rebellion against the Romans. It is more probable that at that time many Christians left the country because the situation was becoming intolerable.

20.5 We could, of course, argue as follows: Hillelite Pharisaism, too, seems to have had little chance before the Jewish rebellion. It was too prepared for compromise. Why, then, did it establish itself after the rebellion? Why had Christianity no chance at all when it was a matter of consolidating Judaism anew? At this point we come to a second reason for the failure of the Jesus movement in Palestine: the success of primitive Christianity outside Palestine. This success must have had negative effects on the situation of Christians in the land where the movement originated. The clearer it became that Christianity transcended the boundaries of Judaism and would accept even uncircumcised Gentiles, the less chance it had as a renewal movement within Judaism. For it is impossible to reform any group and at the same time to put its identity in question. The activity of Christian missionaries among Gentiles must inevitably have given the impression that other people were being put on the same footing as the Jews. We can therefore understand why fraternization between Jews and Gentiles in the community in Antioch was noted with suspicion by the Jerusalem community (Gal. 2.11ff.), and why Paul was felt by the Palestinian churches to be encouraging compromise, so that his fellow-countrymen planned to murder him (Acts 23.12ff.). In order to understand the failure of the Jesus movement as a renewal movement within Judaism, we must therefore investigate its success in the Hellenistic world. Such an investigation would go beyond the limits of this attempt at a sociology of the Jesus movement. We must therefore content ourselves with giving a brief survey of further developments.

3. Hellenistic society

20.6 Our analysis of the Jesus movement in Palestine was based on a sociological theory of conflict: religious renewal movements develop out of social tensions and attempt to give new impulses for their resolution. In small groups of outsiders, society experimented with new forms of life, but chose only a few elements from the wealth of new possibilities which emerged, adapting them to its needs. Much remained unused. A negative selection was made even from the Jesus movement in the context of Jewish Palestinian society. In Hellenistic society, by contrast, it was given a positive welcome. A sociological theory of conflict is an inadequate explanation of this. For in comparison with other eras of world history, the Roman empire during the first two centuries of the Christian era was one of those rare exceptions, a period characterized by peace and stability, prosperity and open communications. The Hellenistic cities on the Mediterranean flourished and reached new peaks of civilization, only to be regained in modern times. Of course there were tensions, but it seems more appropriate to consider them in terms of the way in which society integrated them and balanced them out. Consequently a sociological theory of integration is a more appropriate perspective from which to approach an analysis of earliest Hellenistic Christianity and from which to assess and co-ordinate the relevant sociological data (which here too are very sparse). The basic question is: how were relatively stable and sturdy communities with considerable inner cohesion formed from a mixture of ethnic, social and religious groups? How did Jews and Gentiles, Greeks and barbarians, slaves and freemen, men and women, come to form a new unity in Christ (cf. Gal. 3.28; I Cor. 12.13; Rom. 1.14)?

20.7 The transition from the Jesus movement in Palestine to the earliest Hellenistic Christianity is bound up with a deep-seated change in role-structure. Whereas in earliest Palestinian Christianity the wandering charismatics were the decisive authorities, in a Hellenistic setting the chief emphasis was soon laid on local communities: the resident authorities to be found in them soon became the normative figures for earliest Christianity, first of all as a collegiate body, and then as early as the beginning of the second century as a monarchical episcopate (Ignatius of Antioch). On the other hand, the successors of the earliest Christian wandering charismatics were increasingly brought into disrepute, as is shown by III John. One consequence of this change in structure is that the early Christian literature which came into being in the Hellenistic communities (above all the corpus of epistles in the New Testament) is primarily oriented on interactions within the local community as far as ethical instructions are concerned. This is also true of the letters written by the wandering preacher Paul. The radical ethics of the synoptic tradition is only handed down with reservations. Paul hardly ever cites words of Jesus. And even if he had known a number of them, the ethnic radicalism of the Jesus movement, its pattern of dispensing with family, homeland, possessions and protection, would hardly have found a place in the communities which he founded. Rather, within these communities there arose a more moderate patriarchalism of love, oriented on the need for social interaction within the Christian community — on the problems of the common life of masters and slaves, men and women, parents and children (cf. Col. 3.18ff.; Eph. 5.22ff.). The restructuring of roles even extended to that of the revealer. Whereas the Son of man christology is governed by a movement in the ascendant (the one who is now despised and persecuted will become the judge of the world), the Hellenistic communities added a movement in the opposite direction: the pre-existent Son of God empties himself and humiliates himself in our world. Paul can connect this development with the social structures of the earliest Christian communities not only metaphorically, but also as a matter of fact. The humiliation of the Son of God is voluntary impoverishment: 'For you know the grace of our Lord Jesus Christ, that though he was rich, yet for your sake he became poor' (II Cor. 8.9). His manifestation in such a ridiculous fashion corresponded with the fact that most of the members of Christian communities came from the lower classes (I Cor. 1.26ff.). Here too, then, we can establish a structural homologue between the earliest Christian groups and the role of the revealer.

20.8 In the same way, an analysis of the factors in earliest Hellenistic Christianity points to far-reaching changes. Here we must content ourselves with a brief sketch of the most important factors:

20.9 (*a*) There was a fundamental change in the socio-economic situation. Although the Hellenistic communities may not have amassed great riches, they were still in a position to support the Palestinian communities (Gal. 2.10; Rom 15.15ff.; I Cor. 16.1ff.; II Cor. 8f.; Acts 11.27ff.). The place of wandering charismatics with no social roots was taken to an increasing extent by Christians with a high position in society; true, in Corinth these formed only a small minority (I Cor. 1.26ff.), but as almost all the members of the congregation whom Paul names can be reckoned as being among the upper classes (as far as we learn anything about their social status), we may conclude that the Christians who counted in a community belonged to the more privileged classes.[38] Pliny the Younger explicitly confirms that people of every class (*omnis ordinis*) were Christians (*Ep.* X. 96.9). An attempt at an effective compensation[39] between classes increasingly took the place of a rigorous criticism of property and riches. The situation in the Shepherd of Hermas seems to be that the rich supported the poor with their possessions and the poor the rich with their prayers. For the rich man is poor in his relationship to God, and the poor man is rich in faith (*Similitudes* 11.5ff.).

20.10 (b) Socio-ecological changes are no less decisive. A movement which was formerly connected with the country became a group based on the cities. When Pliny the Younger writes that Christianity spread 'not only through the cities, but also through the villages and the countryside' (*Ep.* X 96.9), it is clear where Christianity has its focal point. Developing cities with their new increase in population were more open to the new message than the country, with its traditionalist attitudes. Groups of this kind in particular, whose roots in the cities were not too deep, could find security and support in the communities. It is probably a consequence of the change from country to city that the vivid concrete pictures of the synoptic tradition increasingly give place to abstract argumentation: primitive Christian literature becomes more theological, more speculative, more reflective.

20.11 (c) The situation in Hellenistic civilization differed from that in Palestine in socio-political terms. Palestine was a powder barrel within which the Mediterranean cities kept the tensions within bounds. Earliest Hellenistic Christianity was largely in accord with the political structures of its environment, though always with the eschatological proviso that this whole world would in any case soon pass away. Paul, for example, is well integrated into Hellenistic society in this respect. He was both a citizen of the city state of Tarsus in Asia Minor (Acts 21.39) and a Roman citizen (Acts 22.25ff.). Radical theocratic ideas were quite alien to him. He seldom used the concept of the kingdom of God, and indeed it retreated well into the background in the earliest Hellenistic Christianity. It drew its strength from the socio-political tensions of Palestine and dissatisfaction with the existing structures of government. Paul is far removed from such dissatisfaction. For him all authorities are from God (Rom. 13.1ff.).

20.12 (*d*) The change from Palestine to the Hellenistic world was bound up with a far-reaching socio-cultural change. Primitive Christianity extended into an area where a new language was spoken. It had to come to grips with philosophical schools and compete with other religions. It was confronted with a wealth of new traditions, norms and values. Only now did it enter the 'wider' world. Only now were its writings addressed to a larger public, for example in the apologies written in the second century. Only now did it become an independent religion. For originally it had been a renewal movement within Judaism, an origin to which it owes a rich heritage: monotheism, a lofty ethic, the acuteness of prophetic criticism, a universalistic view of history — in short, the Old Testament and its great figures. With all this, however, it also took over the ethnocentricity of the Jewish people which it continually transformed by representing itself as the 'true Israel' and associating with this view a claim to absoluteness which was no longer restricted or toned down by ethnic boundaries. It emerged with this claim to absoluteness in a Gentile world which was characterized by a relatively great degree of religious tolerance; it put in question the foundations of a world from whose tolerance it benefited at the same time.

20.13 If we take all the factors into account, we can understand why the Hellenistic world was more favourable than that of Palestine for earliest Christianity: the vision of love and reconciliation may have been born in a society rent by crises, but it had no chances of realization here. The new vision was more in accord with the less tense world of the Hellenistic cities (here too there were considerable tensions between city and country: the cities were privileged). Here there was a considerable degree of local and social mobility, an urge for communication between very different groups of people and a need for integration. Here an eirenic movement had more chance from the start. In the relatively peaceful period down to the beginning of the third century A.D. it succeeded in building up a stable organization and establishing institutional norms like a pattern of ministry, a canon and a confession of faith. It succeeded in creating a social balance between the different classes within society and in differentiating itself from radical tendencies like Montanism and Gnosticism, so that despite massive persecutions it was able to survive the great political, social and economic crisis which shattered the Roman empire in the third century A.D., whereas the traditional political and religious institutions emerged from it weakened. When he reorganized the empire, Constantine could rely on a small, well-organized Christian minority, which had proved itself in critical situations, to give the state internal support at a time of increasing social pressure. Christianity became more and more the social cement of the totalitarian state of late antiquity. The vision of love and reconciliation faded. But it still continued to flicker. Some 'fools in Christ' pursued it, who tended to be classified as religious 'virtuosi', so that they did not have to be taken too seriously. Yet it could be that the pattern of love of one's enemy, of renunciation of power and freedom towards possessions, which are thought by many to be the 'Sunday norms' of world history, are also significant for everyday life at a time when our social relationships are becoming increasingly fluid. The necessity for inward and outward peace, coupled with the urgency of social change, perhaps requires of us more of a radical change in attitudes than we realize. What has failed to function so far may one day prove to be functional, and what has been counted as an ethical luxury may prove to be mankind's chance of survival.[40]

Notes

38. I have attempted to shed light on social conditions in the Corinthian community in a number of articles: 'Soziale Schichtung in der korinthischen Gemeinde', *ZNW* 65, 1974, 232–72; id., 'Soziale Integration und sakramentales Handeln', *NovTest* 24, 1974, 179–206; 'Die Starken und Schwachen in Korinth', *EvTh* 35, 1975, 155–72; 'Legitimät und Lebensunterhalt', *NTS* 21, 1975, 192–221.
39. M. Hengel has coined the impressive formula 'The Compromise of Effective Compensation' for the social ethos of primitive Christianity in the second century A.D. cf. *Property and Riches in the Early Church*, ET London and Philadelphia 1974, pp. 60ff.
40. A good deal more could be said, for example, on the consequences of a sociology of the Jesus movement for the quest of the historical Jesus, for christology, ethics, church practice. I hope some time to be able to present my thoughts on fundamental theological questions elsewhere. I must therefore limit myself to a few remarks which I wish were unnecessary. (1) Anyone who thinks that a sociology of the Jesus movement is a rewarding undertaking is not therefore aspiring to a theology of social structures or a sociological theology or a theological sociology or anything of that kind. (2) Anyone who learns from Marxism and finds it stimulating as a result to apply theories of conflicts in society to the interpretation of social and religious processes is not necessarily a Marxist. Remember Ralf Dahrendorf! (3) Anyone who writes about the radicalism of the early Christian wandering charismatics and finds it difficult to deny his sympathies for them is still some way from being a radical.

21

Wayne A. Meeks
The Man From Heaven in Johannine Sectarianism

The article from which this Extract is taken first appeared in the *Journal of Biblical Literature* in 1972. Meeks is professor of religious studies at Yale University and author of the very important *The First Urban Christians: the Social World of the Apostle Paul* (Yale, 1983). The article can now be seen as a landmark in the sociology of the New Testament: it represents a crucial attempt to understand biblical concepts not simply in terms of the history of ideas (the dominant pattern in theology) but also in terms of their social rootedness. Meeks' particular concern here is to understand the *social function* of the Johannine language about 'descending' and 'ascending'. He agrees with Bultmann that this language constitutes a 'puzzle'. This puzzle is caused by the fact that the Fourth Gospel 'seemed to identify Jesus as a revealer come from the heavenly world, and therefore able to communicate what he had "seen and heard" in that world — but his promise to do so was never fulfilled in the Gospel. He revealed only *that* he is the revealer' (*21.6*). Meeks is unhappy with both purely literary/theological approaches to this puzzle and with Bultmann's explanation of the Johannine group belonging to a general gnostic milieu (*21.1–7*). Meeks is intent upon attempting to establish the type of community within which such puzzling language (and the other apparent contradictions of the Gospel — *21.7*) might be located. It is at this point that he adopts a specifically anthropological approach to the social function of myth (*21.8–9*), and then, at the end of the article, an approach based upon the sociology of knowledge (*21.15–18* — see also *Extract 6* and *Extract 10*). The lengthy exegetical section of the article has been omitted because of space, and is in any case more appropriate for the New Testament specialist (for specialist criticism, see the references in *Extract 18*). For him the puzzling language suggests a social location within a counter-culture of Judaism: it provides a reinforcement for the social identity of a community that is cut off from Judaism and which sees itself as under attack, misunderstood and alien from the world (*21.13–15*). It is a counter-culture which feels itself both to be threatened and to have found a unique identity in the 'descending' and 'ascending' Christ. Whatever the merits of Meeks' detailed exegesis, his active use of an approach based upon social function offers new ways of perceiving the mixture of paradox and exclusivity in John's Gospel: such perceptions are not dependent upon any imperialist claim that social function is the *only* way to understand this mixture (*21.16*).

21.1 The uniqueness of the Fourth Gospel in early Christian literature consists above all in the special patterns of language which it uses to describe Jesus Christ. Fundamental among these patterns is the description of Jesus as the one who has descended from heaven and, at the end of his mission which constitutes a *krisis* for the whole world, reascends to the Father. Not the least of Rudolf Bultmann's enduring contributions to Johannine studies was his recognition and insistence that any attempt to solve the 'Johannine puzzle' must begin with this picture of the descending/ascending redeemer. Moreover, he saw that it is not simply a question of explaining the *concept* 'pre-existence', but rather of perceiving the origin and function of a *myth*. The solution could not be found, therefore, by comparisons with philosophical developments in the hellenistic schools, such as the long-favored *logos spermatikos* of the Stoics, or its adaptation by middle Platonists or Alexandrian Jews. Myths have a logic of their own, which is not identical with the logic of the philosophers.[1]

21.2 Nevertheless, Bultmann's own proposed solution has not commanded general assent. To be sure, his observation that the closest extant analogies to the Johannine myth are to be found in the literature of gnostic movements stands firm and has been reinforced by more recent discoveries. The problem comes in assessing the very important differences between the typical gnostic myths and that of John, and therefore the direction of the relationship between the two patterns. Perhaps the most important difference, which Bultmann did not fail to notice, is the fact that in gnostic myths most comparable with the Johannine pattern the redeemer's descent and ascent parallel the fate and hope of the human essence (soul, pneuma, seed, or the like), while in the Fourth Gospel there is no such *analogia entis* between redeemer and redeemed. Bultmann's hypothesis is that the typical gnostic myth was deliberately modified by the fourth evangelist, effectively 'demythologizing' it. The hypothesis, plausible as it is, ran into difficulties of two sorts: (1) It required the support of very complex additional hypotheses about the literary sources of John, about the relationship between the Johannine Christians and the disciples of John the Baptist, and about the latter's role in the origins of the Mandean sect. None of these hypotheses has received support from further specialized investigations.[2] (2) The *typical* gnostic myth with which Bultmann compared the Johannine pattern is an abstraction, obscuring the variety of actual gnostic myths in extant texts.[3] Furthermore, Bultmann's synthetic myth is heavily dependent on the terminology of the Fourth Gospel; there is hardly any single document other than John in which all the elements of the 'gnostic redeemer myth' listed by Bultmann in his 1925 article are integrally displayed.[4]

21.3 A number of scholars have proposed to stand Bultmann's hypothesis on its head: Johannine christology was not an adaptation of gnostic myth, they would say, but a step *towards* gnosticism. Older forms of this proposal, supported only by pointing to the lateness of the Mandean and Manichean sources used by Bultmann, are not adequate. While no extant document of definite pre-Christian date may present a descending/ascending redeemer of the gnostic type, sufficiently strong inferences may be derived from later sources to make an argument from silence highly precarious.[5] More weighty are studies which use the logic and literary form of the Johannine christological discourses to suggest a historical location somewhere between primitive Christianity and emerging gnosticism. For example, Siegfried Schulz's study of the Son of Man passages in John, despite the occasional artificiality of his 'themageschichtliche Analyse', is able to show frequently that the re-interpretation of a basic substratum of *apocalyptic* motifs serves as the center for 'Ankristallisationen von gnostisch-hellenistischen Elementen'.[6] Helmut Koester locates the Johannine farewell discourses at 'a crucial place in the development of the genre "Revelation" ' which would lead to such theophany-type revelations as the Apocryphon of John.[7] M. Jack Suggs has very plausibly argued that the identification of Christ with Sophia by Matthew, in contrast to Q, and by Paul, in contrast to his opponents in Corinth (so also Koester, against Wilckens), created a peculiar symbolic dialectic that paved the way for the developed gnostic Sophia-myths.[8] What he says could be applied *mutatis mutandis* to John.

21.4 It is now commonly agreed that the Jewish Wisdom myth in some form lies behind both the Johannine christology and the gnostic soul and savior myths.[9] The question is whether both the Johannine and the gnostic myths are independent variants of the Jewish, or whether one has influenced the other. The present essay will not attempt a direct answer to that question by re-examining the possible antecendents of John's symbolism, but will only explore the function of the mythical pattern within the Johannine literature. Such a study may have its own contribution to make to the question of inter-group influence.

21.5 The problem has been treated too one-sidedly as a problem in the history of ideas. Mythical language tends to be reduced to theological categories, and *historical* judgments are then made on the basis of the presumed *logical* priority of one or other of these categories. Where this has occurred, Bultmann's insight, that the language of myth has a special logic, has been ignored. The Bultmann–Jonas theory of myth as the objectivation of the religious person's sense of his relationship to self and world was a significant step towards a more appropriate hermeneutic for mythical language. Yet, as Jonas later observed, the categories of existential philosophy that seemed to fit the *gnostic* myths so well are by no means a universal key.[10] And even Bultmann tends to reduce the function of myth in John to theological categories; that is shown by his obsessive attempt to discover a *rational* sequence in the Johannine discourses and narratives by the incredibly complex rearrangement-hypotheses in his commentary. We have not yet learned to let the symbolic language of Johannine literature speak in its own way. It is symptomatic of the impasse in NT hermeneutics that we have as yet no adequate monograph on the Johannine symbolism as such.[11]

21.6 Bultmann's starting point was the observation that the symbolic picture of Jesus as the man who descended and ascended constituted a *puzzle* within the Fourth Gospel. It seemed to identify Jesus as a revealer come from the heavenly world, and therefore able to communicate what he had 'seen and heard' in that world — but his promise to do so was never fulfilled in the Gospel. He revealed only *that* he is the revealer.[12] Bultmann's solution involves the argument that this pattern ordinarily, in the gnostic milieu posited for the Johannine group, depicted a 'revealer'. The pattern as such therefore did not have to make sense within the literary structure of the gospel; it made sense in the extrinsic historical setting. The only thing necessary for John was to show that Jesus *was* the one and only one to whom the well-known pattern ought to be applied. If we are not satisfied with Bultmann's reconstruction of the historical situation in which the puzzle could be explained, then we are forced to ask his initial question all over again: In what situation does a literary puzzle provide an appropriate means of communication?

21.7 The problem may be best approached by complicating it: this pattern is not the only puzzling thing about the Fourth Gospel. The major literary problem of John is its combination of remarkable stylistic unity and thematic coherence with glaringly bad transitions between episodes at many points. The countless displacement, source, and redaction theories that litter the graveyards of Johannine research are voluble testimony to this difficulty. Many of the elements of the unitary style are probably not specific to a single author, but belong to the Johannine 'school', for they are frequently found distributed between portions of the gospel which, on other grounds, we would attribute to 'source', 'evangelist', and 'redactor'. On the other hand, not all the *aporiae* in the present form of the gospel can be attributed to clumsy redaction; most of them evidently were acceptable to the evangelist, despite his ability to produce large, impressively unified literary compositions (the trial and crucifixion scenario, as the most notable example). There are a number of examples not only of double entendre which are progressively clarified by repetition and modification, but also of self-contradiction that are manifestly deliberate ('I do not judge . . . yet if I do judge. . .', 8:15). Above all there are parallel, slightly varying formulations of similar thematic complexes, ranging from double Amen-sayings side by side within one didactic dialogue ('Unless one is born *anōthen* he cannot *see* the kingdom of God' // 'Unless one is born *of water and spirit* he cannot *enter* the kingdom of God', 3: 3, 5)[13] to whole compositions that seem to be alternate interpretations of the same group of themes belonging to different stages of the history of redaction of the gospel (ch. 14 // chs. 15–16).[14]

21.8 We may find a clue to the proper understanding of these peculiar relationships in the attempt of some contemporary anthropologists to get at the function of myths in the societies that create them by means of close analysis of their *structure*. For example, the distinguished English scholar Edmund Leach proposes that the way in which myths work may be understood by analogies drawn from the study of electronic communications. If a message is to be conveyed in the face of pervasive distractions — 'noise', or, in the case of myth, the overwhelming complexity of the total social matrix — then the communicator must resort to 'redundance'. He must repeat the signal as many times as possible, in *different* ways. From the repeated impact of varying signals, the basic *structure* which they have in common gets through. It is, therefore, only by paying attention to the underlying structure of the components in a system of myths that an interpreter can 'hear' what the myths are 'saying', or, to put it another way, can discover the function which the myths have within the group in which they are at home.[15]

21.9 It is astonishing that attempts to solve the Johannine puzzle have almost totally ignored the question of what *social* function the myths may have had.[16] No one, of course, is in a position to write an empirical sociology of Johannine Christianity. Nevertheless, it has become abundantly clear that the Johannine literature is the product not of a lone genius but of a community or group of communities that evidently persisted with some consistent identity over a considerable span of time. We know at least a few things about its history — all from direct allusions in the documents themselves. The group had to distinguish itself over against the sect of John the Baptist and even more passionately over against a rather strong Jewish community, with which highly ambivalent relationships had existed. It suffered defections, conflicts of leadership, and schisms. I shall argue that one function of the 'symbolic universe' communicated in this remarkable body of literature was to make sense of all these aspects of the group's history. More precisely, there must have been a continuing dialectic between the group's historical experience and the symbolic world which served both to explain that experience and to motivate and form the reaction of group members to the experience. . . .

2

21.10 So long as we approach the Johannine literature as a chapter in the history of *ideas*, it will defy our understanding. Its metaphors are irrational, disorganized, and incomplete. But if we pose our question in the form, What functions did this particular system of metaphors have for the group that developed it? then even its self-contradictions and its disjunctures may be seen to be *means of communication*.

21.11 This point can be illustrated by our attempt to understand the function of the ascent/descent motif within the Fourth Gospel. The unbiased reader feels quite sympathetic with poor Nicodemus and the 'believing' Jews with whom, it seems, Jesus is playing some kind of language-game whose rules neither they nor we could possibly know. What we are up against is the self-referring quality of the whole gospel, the closed system of metaphors, which confronts the reader in a fashion somewhat like the way a Semitist once explained to me how to learn Aramaic: 'Once you know *all* the Semitic languages', he said, 'learning any one of them is easy'. The reader cannot understand any part of the Fourth Gospel until he understands the whole. Thus the reader has an experience rather like that of the dialogue partners of Jesus: either he will find the whole business so convoluted, obscure, and maddeningly arrogant that he will reject it in anger, or he will find it so fascinating that he will stick with it until the progressive reiteration of themes brings, on some level of consciousness at least, a degree of clarity. While an appeal to the reader's subjective experience may appear highly unscientific, I have tried to show that such an experience is grounded in the stylistic structure of the whole document. This is the way its language, composed of an enormous variety of materials, from the standpoint of the history of traditions, has been organized, partly by design, i.e., by the actual composition by the evangelist, and partly by pre-redactional collocation of the different ways of talking in the life of the community. *The book functions for its readers in precisely the same way that the epiphany of its hero functions within its narratives and dialogues.*

21.12 While this function of the book is undoubtedly the hallmark of some one author's genius, it is unthinkable apart from a particular kind of religious community, in the same way (though not perhaps to the same extent) that the pesher on Habakkuk is unthinkable without the Qumran sect, and the convoluted and overlapping myths of the Mandean *Ginza* unaccountable without the perduring Nazoreans. Unfortunately we have no independent information about the organization of the Johannine group, and even the Johannine literature gives little description of the community and hardly any statements that are directly 'ecclesiological'. Nevertheless, the structural characteristics of the literature permit certain deductions.

21.13 The observation that the book functions in the same way that its Jesus functions can be elaborated. As we have seen, the depiction of Jesus as the man 'who comes down from heaven' marks him as the alien from all men of the world. Though the Jews are 'his own', when he comes to them they reject him, thus revealing themselves as not his own after all but his enemies; not from God, but from the devil, from 'below', from 'this world'. The story describes the progressive alienation of Jesus from the Jews. But something else is happening, for there are some few who do respond to Jesus' signs and words, and these, while they also frequently 'misunderstand', are progressively enlightened and drawn into intense intimacy with Jesus, until they, like him, are not 'of this world'. Now their becoming detached from the world is, in the Gospel, identical with their being detached from Judaism. Those figures who want to 'believe' in Jesus but to remain within the Jewish community and the Jewish piety are damned with the most devastatingly dualistic epithets. There can be no question, as Louis Martyn has shown, that the actual trauma of the Johannine community's separation from the synagogue and its continuing hostile relationships with the synagogue come clearly to expression here.[77] But something more is to be seen: coming to faith in Jesus is for the Johannine group a change in social location. Mere belief without joining the Johannine community, without making the decisive break with 'the world', particularly the world of Judaism, is a diabolic 'lie'.

21.14 Thus, despite the absence of 'ecclesiology' from the Fourth Gospel, this book could be called an etiology of the Johannine group. In telling the story of the Son of Man who came down from heaven and then re-ascended after choosing a few of his own out of the world, the book defines and vindicates the existence of the community that evidently sees itself as unique, alien from its world, under attack, misunderstood, but living in unity with Christ and through him with God. It could hardly be regarded as a missionary tract,[78] for we may imagine that only a very rare outsider would get past the barrier of its closed metaphorical system. It is a book for insiders, for if one already belonged to the Johannine community, then we may presume that the manifold bits of tradition that have taken distinctive form in the Johannine circle would be familiar, the 'cross-references' in the book — so frequently anachronistic within the fictional sequence of events — would be immediately recognizable, the double entendre which produces mystified and stupid questions from the fictional dialogue partners (and from many modern commentators) would be acknowledged by a knowing and superior smile. One of the primary functions of the book, therefore, must have been to provide a reinforcement for the community's social identity, which appears to have been largely negative. It provided a symbolic universe which gave religious legitimacy, a theodicy, to the group's actual isolation from the larger society.

21.15 The sociology of religion has not yet developed theoretical categories adequate for describing the formation of a 'sect' of the sort we are discovering in the Johannine group,[79] but the discipline of the 'sociology of knowledge', particularly in the form proposed by Peter Berger and Thomas Luckmann,[80] provides categories which help us to understand how a figure like the Johannine Jesus, through the medium of a book like the Johannine Gospel, could bring about a change of world. For one's 'world' in the sociology of knowledge is understood as the symbolic universe within which one functions, which has 'objectivity' because it is constantly reinforced by the structures of the society to which it is specific. Faith in Jesus, in the Fourth Gospel, means a removal from 'the world', because it means transfer to a community which has totalistic and exclusive claims. The Fourth Gospel not only describes, in etiological fashion, the birth of that community; it also provides reinforcement of the community's isolation. The language patterns we have been describing have the effect, for the insider who accepts them, of demolishing the logic of the world, particularly the world of Judaism, and progressively emphasizing the sectarian consciousness. If one 'believes' what is said in this book, he is quite literally taken out of the ordinary world of social reality. Contrariwise, this can hardly happen unless one stands already within the counter-cultural group or at least in some ambivalent relationship between it and the larger society.

21.16 I do not mean to say that the symbolic universe suggested by the Johannine literature is *only* the reflex or projection of the group's social situation. On the contrary, the Johannine dialogues suggest quite clearly that the order of development must have been dialectical: the christological claims of the Johannine Christians resulted in their becoming alienated, and finally expelled, from the synagogue; that alienation in turn is 'explained' by a further development of the christological motifs (i.e., the fate of the community projected onto the story of Jesus); these developed christological motifs in turn drive the group into further isolation. It is a case of continual, harmonic reinforcement between social experience and ideology.[81]

21.17 The dialectic we have suggested would surely continue, producing a more and more isolated and estranged group until some disruption occurred. The Johannine letters show a progression of that sort: tighter internal discipline, more hostility towards 'the world' and everything 'in the world', schism occasioned by a docetic group, whose denial that Jesus could have 'come in the flesh' would seem a fairly logical deduction from the symbols we have analyzed.

21.18 The analysis undertaken here does not answer the question of the relation between the Johannine christology and gnostic myths, but it provides clues which may be helpful in pursuing that problem. The Fourth Gospel is content to leave unanswered the question how there could exist in 'this world' some persons who, by some pre-established harmony, could respond to the Stranger from the world above and thus become, like him, men 'not of this world'. But that enigma cries out for some master myth to explain it. Both pressures from outsiders and internal questioning would assure that the cry did not long remain unheeded; the legitimation of the sect's counter-cultural stance would lead to the projection of some myth explaining that members of the group had an origin different from that of ordinary men. In gnosticism it was the Sophia myth that provided the basic images for that projection — the same Sophia myth which provided important elements of the descent and ascent of the Son of Man in John. As the archetype of the soul-to-be-redeemed, Sophia recovers her normal feminine guise, making possible the elaborate sexual imagery that in the gnostic myths describes the relations between Christ or Logos and Sophia or the soul. In the Fourth Gospel there is no trace of the usual feminine Sophia; she has become entirely the masculine Logos, the Son of Man. But the Fourth Gospel does introduce the motif of Christ's union with the believers, which comes at times quite close to sexual metaphor.[82] Thus once the Fourth Gospel had identified Christ-Wisdom with the masculine

Logos, and once the social dynamics of the anti-worldly sect were in motion, all the forces were present for the production of a myth of the Valentinian type. We cannot say that it happened that way, or that the Johannine literature was the only place where ingredients were brought into the necessary creative association.[83] But these conjectures suggest that it is at least as plausible that the Johannine christology helped to create some gnostic myths as that gnostic myths helped create the Johannine christology. A satisfactory answer may be achieved only when studies of gnosticism also begin to ask not only about ideational structure and antecedents, but also about social functions.[84]

Notes

1. See R. Bultmann, 'Die Bedeutung der neuerschlossenen mandäischen und manichäischen Quellen für das Verständnis des Johannesevangeliums', *ZNW* 24 (1925) 100–46 (reprinted in *Exegetica* [Tübingen: Mohr, 1967] 55–104), and especially his criticism of Ernst Percy in 'Johanneische Schriften und Gnosis', *OLZ* 43 (1940) 150–75 (*Exegetica*, 230–54) and C. H. Dodd in *NTS* 1 (1954–55) 77–91 (ET: *Harvard Divinity Bulletin* 27 [1963] 9–22). Dodd's focus upon 'the logos-doctrine' as the *tertium comparationis* between John and the Hermetica and Philo was particularly vulnerable to this objection.
2. For example, K. Rudolph's careful investigation of the Mandean materials convinced him that 'Johannes der Täufer und seine Jüngerschaft haben nach dem Befund der uns zugänglichen Quellen keine Beziehung zu den Mandäern gehabt' (*Die Mandäer*, Vol. I: *Prolegomena* [FRLANT, n.s. 56; Göttingen: Vandenhoeck & Ruprecht, 1960] 80). Both E. Käsemann ('Aufbau und Anliegen des johanneischen Prologs' in *Libertas Christiana: Friedrich Delekat zum 65. Geburtstag* [Munich: Kaiser, 1957] 75–99 [reprinted in *Exegetische Versuche und Besinnungen* II (Göttingen: Vandenhoeck & Ruprecht, 1965) 155–80; ET: *New Testament Questions for Today* (Philadelphia: Fortress, 1969) 138–67]) and E. Haenchen ('Probleme des johanneischen "Prologs" ', *ZTK* 60 [1963] 305–34 [reprinted in *Gott und Mensch* (Tübingen: Mohr, 1965) 114–43]) reject the hypothesis of a *Redenquelle*. See also D. M. Smith, Jr, *The Composition and Order of the Fourth Gospel* (New Haven: Yale, 1965).
3. Cf. C. Colpe, *Die religionsgeschichtliche Schule* (FRLANT, n.s. 60; Göttingen: Vandenhoeck & Ruprecht, 1961), especially 186–208. See also A. D. Nock, 'Gnosticism', *HTR* 57 (1964) 255–79.
4. This is even clearer in his article 'Johannesevangelium', *RGG*³ 3. 840–50.
5. E. Haenchen has established a high probability that the essential gnostic features of Simon Magus were developed in the Simonian sect prior to any Christian influence ('Gab es eine vorchristliche Gnosis?', *ZTK* 49

[1952] 316–49; reprinted in *Gott und Mensch* 265–98). The question of the date and interpretation of the *Hymn of the Pearl* is more difficult; see most recently C. Colpe, 'Die Thomaspsalmen als chronologischer Fixpunkt in der Geschichte der orientalischen Gnosis', *Jahrbuch für Antike und Christentum* 7 (1964) 77–93, and the survey by K. Rudolph, 'Gnosis und Gnostizismus, ein Forschungsbericht', *ThRu* 34 (1969) 214–21. The Nag Hammadi documents prove that Christian gnostics did borrow and adapt mythical elements from non-Christian gnostics — and vice versa — at a later period. While these sources cannot directly prove anything about first century gnosis, careful analysis of them is providing cumulative evidence that myths of descending/ascending revealers flourished without any Christian influence. See, e.g., G. W. MacRae, 'The Coptic Gnostic Apocalypse of Adam'. *HeyJ* 6 (1965) 27–35, and F. Wisse, 'The Redeemer Figure in the Paraphrase of Shem', *NovT* 12 (1970) 130–40. Finally, it is impossible to dismiss the question whether the NT itself may not provide the earliest documentation of pre-Christian gnosticism, depending upon one's evaluation, for example, of the opponents of Paul in Galatia, Corinth, and Colossae, and of the sources of mythical elements found in liturgical traditions that are quoted in Pauline and deutero-Pauline letters. There remain, however, many vexed questions in this area.

6. *Untersuchungen zur Menschensohn-Christologie im Johannesevangelium* (Göttingen: Vandenhoeck & Ruprecht, 1957) 179.

7. 'One Jesus and Four Primitive Gospels', *HTR* 61 (1968) 240; reprinted in *Trajectories through Early Christianity* (eds J. M. Robinson and H. Koester; Philadelphia: Fortress, 1971) 197.

8. *Wisdom, Christology, and Law in Matthew's Gospel* (Cambridge, Mass.: Harvard, 1970) 10, n. 14; 42, n. 18; 53, n. 41; and especially 58, n. 49.

9. G. W. MacRae ('The Jewish Background of the Gnostic Sophia Myth', *NovT* 12 [1970] 86–101) seems to me correct against U. Wilckens (*Weisheit and Torbeit* [Beiträge zur historischen Theologie, 26; Tübingen: Mohr, 1959]) that it was precisely the *Jewish* form of the Wisdom myth that was used by the gnostics — at least those that may be usefully compared with the Fourth Gospel. On the other hand, I doubt the propriety of speaking of a *single* Jewish Wisdom myth or one single Wisdom movement. 'Wisdom' as the ideology of a royal bureaucracy was obviously different from the 'Wisdom' cultivated in an apocalyptic conventicle, for example.

10. *The Gnostic Religion* (rev. ed.; Boston: Beacon, 1963) 320–21. The Bultmann–Jonas concept of 'objectivation' is significantly parallel to the notion of 'projection', particularly as the latter has been re-defined by C. G. Jung. The reaction of Bultmann and other kerygmatic theologians to the 'psychologism' of earlier theological Liberalism has blocked off what might have been a fruitful area of interaction, particularly in view of the Jung school's profound interest in gnosticism. However, Jung's discussion of the motif of descent and ascent as it occurs in medieval alchemy (*Mysterium Coniunctionis* [2d ed.; Princeton: Princeton Univ., 1970] 217–24) offers little that is directly useful for our present discussion.

11. The analysis by E. Schweizer in his early work *Ego Eimi* (Göttingen: Vandenhoeck & Ruprecht, 1939, Part IV) is abstruse and rather artificial. The perennial attempts to discover OT typologies in John have usually demonstrated more the ingenuity of eisegesis than the grammar of Johannine symbols. G. Stemberger's recent *La symbolique du bien et du mal selon saint Jean* (Paris: Seuil, 1970), violating the impressive canons in his own introduction, reduces the symbols to a puzzle picture where the categories of moral theology are to be discovered.

12. *ZNW* 24 (1925) 102 (= *Exegetica* 57).

13. On this form, see K. Berger, *Die Amen-Worte Jesu* (BZNW, 39; Berlin: de Gruyter, 1970) 95–117.

14. See. J. Becker, 'Die Abschiedsreden Jesu im Johannesevangelium', *ZNW* 61 (1970) 215–52.

15. 'Genesis as Myth', *Discovery* (London) n.s. 23 (1962) 30–35; reprinted in *Myth and Cosmos* (ed. John Middleton; Garden City, N.Y.: Natural History Press, 1967) 1–13. This 'structural' approach is now associated especially with the theories of the French anthropologist Claude Lévi-Strauss (see, e.g., the latter's *Structural Anthropology* [New York: Basic Books, 1963], especially chs II and XI), but Leach has brought *structuralisme* into connection with the functionalist and empirical traditions of English and American social anthropology. See his fascinating appreciation and critique in *Claude Lévi-Strauss* ('Modern Masters', ed. F. Kermode; New York: Viking, 1970). Among other recent examples of the social-structural analysis of myth-systems which I have found suggestive for developing my own method are: V. W. Turner, 'Colour Classification of Ndembu Ritual', *Anthropological Approaches to the Study of Religion* (ed. M. Banton; ASA Monographs, 3; New York: Praeger, 1966) 47–84; J. Z. Smith, 'Birth Upside Down or Right Side Up?', *History of Religions* 9 (1969–70) 281–303; W. D. O'Flaherty, 'Asceticism and Sexuality in the Mythology of Śiva', *ibid.* 8 (1968–69) 300–37; 9 (1969–70) 1–41.

16. Two partial exceptions are A. Kragerud's proposals to see certain of the symbols, particularly the 'beloved disciple', as a covert self-justification of a charismatic sect of Christianity (*Der Lieblingsjünger im Johannesevangelium* [Oslo: Osloer Universitätsverlag, 1959]) and E. Käsemann's attempts to explicate the argument between Diotrephes and the Elder ('Ketzer und Zeuge', *ZTK* 48 [1951] 292–311; reprinted in *Exegetische Versuche und Besinnungen*, 1, 168–87) and the 'naive docetism' of the Gospel (*Jesu letzter Wille* [Tübingen: Mohr, 1967]) within 'conventicle piety' in conflict with 'early catholicism'. Kragerud's thesis, however, is undercut by highly arbitrary exegesis at points; Käsemann's by the imposition of categories from post-Reformation church history on the first-century phenomena (see my review in *USQR* 24 [1969] 414–20). More important, J. L. Martyn has made a major contribution toward locating the kind of milieu in which the anti-Jewish polemic of one stratum of the Johannine materials was formed (*History and Theology in the Fourth Gospel* [New York: Harper and Row, 1968]). His position is reinforced by the investigation, from quite a different perspective, of H.

Leroy, *Rätsel und Missverständnis* (BBB 30; Bonn: Peter Hanstein, 1968). I became acquainted with Leroy's careful and provocative monograph only after I had completed the present essay; hence I shall forgo the detailed *Auseinandersetzung* with him which would be appropriate at points where our analyses run parallel. While our methods are different (but not, I believe, incompatible) and the passages and motifs he examines only partially overlap those treated here, I am delighted to find a remarkable convergence of my results with his. On the basis of a wide-ranging survey of the *riddle* in folklore and literature (pp. 13–45), Leroy describes the form of the Johannine dialogue-with-misunderstanding as a 'verborgenes Rätsel', which presupposes a tight-knit community with a 'Sondersprache' unintelligible to outsiders. In order to 'know the truth', one must join this community — probably a cluster of small congregations — hear its preaching, be instructed in its catechesis, and participate in its rituals.

77. *History and Theology* passim.
78. Against a large number of scholars, including K. Bornhäuser, D. Oehler, J. A. T. Robinson, W. C. van Unnik, and C. H. Dodd, I thus find myself in agreement with R. E. Brown that John's distinctive emphases 'are directed to crises within the believing Church rather than to the conversion of non-believers' (*Gospel according to John I–XII* [AB 29; Garden City, N.Y.: Doubleday, 1966] lxxviii).
79. I am using 'sect' here in a somewhat different sense from the classic definitions by Weber, Troeltsch, and Niebuhr. On the special problems of an adequate definition, see P. Berger, 'The Sociological Study of Sectarianism', *Social Research* 21 (1954) 467–85; also his *The Sacred Canopy* (Garden City, N.Y.: Doubleday, 1967) 196, n. 22. Eventually the work of social psychologists on the formation and functioning of counter-cultural groups may provide useful models for the historian; see the survey by T. F. Pettigrew, 'Social Evaluation Theory: Convergences and Applications', *Nebraska Symposium on Motivation 1967* (ed. D. Levine; Lincoln: University of Nebraska, 1967) 241–311.
80. *The Social Construction of Reality* (Garden City, N.Y.: Doubleday, 1966); cf. P. Berger, *The Sacred Canopy*, chs 1, 2. Also extremely helpful is the definition proposed by C. Geertz, 'Religion as a Cultural System', *Anthropological Approaches to the Study of Religion* (ed. M. Banton; New York: Praeger, 1966) 1–66.
81. This is something like the interaction between scripture text, group organization, and historical experience in the development of apocalyptic ideology proposed by N. A. Dahl in the very important essay, 'Eschatologie und Geschichte im Lichte der Qumrantexte', *Zeit und Geschichte* (ed. E. Dinkler; Tübingen: Mohr, 1964) 3–18; ET: *The Future of our Religious Past* (ed. J. M. Robinson; New York: Harper and Row, 1971) 9–28.
82. This was first pointed out to me by one of my students, the Rev. James Ameling. Note how Paul explicitly uses Gen 2:4 to express the same notion in I Cor 6:16–17.
83. Philo's peculiar dialectic between Logos and Sophia, and the successive characterization of the wise man's soul as feminine and masculine at

different stages of progress, show that such speculations were not unknown to hellenistic Judaism prior to the birth of Christianity. R. A. Baer, Jr (*Philo's Use of the Categories Male and Female* [ALGHJ 3; Leiden: Brill, 1970]) collects and analyzes the most important passages, but offers little help in discerning the pre-Philonic forms of the myths.

84. Lately there have been a few preliminary signs of a recognition of this need: E. M. Mendelson, 'Some Notes on a Sociological Approach to Gnosticism', *Le origini dello gnosticismo* [ed. U. Bianchi; Leiden: Brill, 1967] 668–75; the two essays by J. Z. Smith [above, note 15; and 'A Place on Which to Stand: Symbols and Social Change', *Worship* 44 (1970) 457–74]; H. G. Kippenberg, 'Versuch einer soziologischen Verortung des antiken Gnostizismus', *Numen* 17 (1970) 211–31 (marred by tendentious over-generalizations, coupled with a Feuerbachian 'explanation' of religion); and S. Laeuchli, 'The Sociology of Gnosticism', a paper read to the Biblical Literature Section of the American Academy of Religion, October 30, 1971.

SECTION FOUR

Implications for
Applied Theology

22

Robin Gill
Social Variables within Applied Theology

This Extract is taken from chapter 6 of my *Theology and Social Structure* which appeared in 1977. This chapter was a digression from the main theme of the book, which was an attempt to provide an account of theology in terms of the sociology of knowledge — interpreting theology as a discipline which is both socially constructed and socially significant. The chapter attempted to provide a theoretical account of applied theology which makes an integral use of the social sciences. The Extract seeks to distinguish between 'prescriptive' understandings of applied theology (both in practical theology and in Christian ethics) and 'descriptive' understandings (albeit understandings which also include a critical element). It argues that the social sciences tend to play only an ancillary role in 'prescriptive' understandings, and that if a more integral use is sought 'descriptive' understandings allow for this better. The approaches of Whyte and Rahner, from Presbyterian and Roman Catholic traditions respectively, offer the possibility of a more integral role for the social sciences in practical theology (*22.18–25*); as does that of Lehmann in Christian ethics (*22.26f.*). If applied theology is identified as the discipline which is concerned with the critical analysis of relationships between faith and activity, then the crucial role of the social sciences becomes evident (*22.31*). Naturally applied theology should not be *reduced* to sociology, anthropology etc.: but such disciplines are clearly highly pertinent to it. It is this integral relationship which is a feature of other Extracts in this Section. In the final part of the Extract, I identify three distinct ways sociology can be used in this way: to depict the social context of theology, to analyse the social structure of theology, and to assess the social consequences of theology (*22.33–35*). For a fuller acount of these approaches, see *Extract 11*.

22.1 Because of the lack of theoretical clarity in much of the 'applied theology' literature, it will be necessary to start with an account of prescriptive and descriptive approaches within it. However, no claim will be made that sociology can supply a complete account of applied theology, or that the latter can be reduced without remainder to the former. Most accounts of Christian ethics or practical theology as descriptive, rather than prescriptive, disciplines include a critical element. They are not content simply to describe: they do wish to distinguish between more and less adequate understandings of theological or ethical concepts. Thus, although their central focus is not upon it, they do contain a prescriptive element. It assumes a secondary role without being entirely absent.

Prescriptive Understandings of Applied Theology

22.2 In Christian ethics and practical theology, the common feature requiring the label 'prescriptive' is that each discipline is viewed essentially as a means of producing tangible solutions to particular problems. Each is seen as the producer of specifiable prescriptions. In Christian ethics, this has taken the form of a widespread emphasis upon decision-making as the principal object of the discipline. The theologian engaged in Christian ethics is attempting to resolve particular ethical dilemmas, albeit from a Christian perspective. In practical (or 'pastoral' — the terms are used synonymously) theology since Schleiermacher, the prescriptive emphasis has taken the form of a general assumption that the discipline is basically concerned with the 'application' of systematic theology, with the provision of prescriptions for the churches or ordinands elaborating how they should act. Frequently this has meant that practical theology is viewed merely as the 'practical' side of theology.

22.3 (a) **Prescriptive Practical Theology**: Karl Barth expressed this understanding of practical theology very clearly, when he suggested that 'practical theology is, as the name implies, theology in transition to the practical work of the community — to proclamation'.[2] For him:

> The question of practical theology is how the Word of God may be served by human words. How can this Word, which has been received in the testimony of the Bible and of Church history and has been considered in its contemporary self-preservation, be served also through the community for the benefit of the world that surrounds it? . . . The real question is the problem of the language which must be employed by those who undertake to proclaim this Word. . . . Theological speech is taught its content by exegesis and dogmatics, and it is given its form through the experiences of whatever psychology, sociology or linguistics may be most trustworthy at a given moment. . . . Practical theology is studied in order to seek and to find, to learn and to practise, this speech that is essential to the proclamation of the community in preaching and teaching, in worship and evangelisation.[3]

22.4 It is evident that Barth, like Schleiermacher, viewed practical theology exclusively as a function of the church and not as an autonomous discipline.[4] But, unlike Schleiermacher, he did not see it as the 'crown of theological studies': for him it was simply a means, albeit an indispensable means, to more effective preaching of the Word. Practical theology is regarded essentially as a prescriptive discipline, because its primary objective is to equip the preacher with the correct tools for preaching the Word.

22.5 Sociology is assigned an ancillary role within this understanding of practical theology. At the most, it is able to give theological speech its form: it cannot alter its contents in any way. From Barth's other writings, it is evident that he would have been loath to admit that an analysis of the social context of theology could in any way affect our understanding of theology. For him contemporary plausibility structures would have been irrelevant. Instead, he admitted only that sociology can exercise an ancillary role in relation to theological speech. Sociology merely provides the practical theologian with a useful tool.

22.6 It should be stressed that there is nothing methodologically improper about assigning an ancillary role to sociology *vis-à-vis* practical theology. Fernand Boulard was quite happy to see 'religious sociology' in France as an 'auxiliary science of pastoral policy', arguing that 'it is at the service of pastoral theology, which directs the work of the Church towards "the edification of the Body of Christ", by making available a better understanding of human milieus and their influence upon the behaviour of the individuals who live in them'.[5] Boulard's work is certainly open to criticism, but not, I believe, at this point.[6] It is nevertheless important to recognise that, given Barth's and Boulard's prescriptive understandings of practical theology, sociology is accorded an ancillary and not an integral role.

22.7 On the other hand, Seward Hiltner's understanding of practical theology, although still prescriptive, does appear to allow the social sciences an integral role — and this may be its weakness. Hiltner divides the theological discipline into two types of field; the 'logic-centred' field and the 'operation-centred' field. Whereas systematic theology belongs to the first, practical theology belongs to the second. He defines the latter as, 'that branch of theological knowledge and inquiry that brings the shepherding perspective to bear upon all the operations and functions of the church and the minister, and then draws conclusions of a theological order from reflection on these observations'.[7] Thus, like Schleiermacher, he locates practical theology within the context of the church's work, but, unlike Schleiermacher, he maintains that the discipline (and along with it the social sciences, from which it derives important insights) not only follows from, but also contributes directly to, systematic theology. In effect, the social sciences are given a determinative role *vis-à-vis* both practical theology and theology in general.

22.8 Whatever the particular merits of this understanding of practical theology as such, it is apparent that it risks a conflation of theology with the social sciences, which may do justice to neither discipline.[8] The social sciences areused, not simply to analyse the social context of practical theology, but actually to determine its nature. If only Hiltner had been content with a more modest appreciation of the social sciences as ancillary to practical theology, then his prescriptive understanding of the latter would not have faced this difficulty. However, given that he does have this prescriptive understanding, his allocation of an integral role to the social sciences raises serious methodological problems.

22.9 (b) **Prescriptive Christian Ethics**: Within much contemporary Christian ethics there is a parallel prescriptive understanding of the discipline. Proponents of normative, situational or even some contextual ethics, apparently agree that the primary function of Christian ethics is to be concerned with decision-making and eventually to offer 'solutions' to particular ethical dilemmas. Just as many would appear to regard practical theology as the discipline which attempts to resolve problems of praxis (and usually church praxis), similarly, many would appear to regard Christian ethics as the discipline concerned to resolve problems of morality.

22.10 Perhaps this is most evident in the instance of situation-ethics. So, for example, Joseph Fletcher offers the following brief account of this approach to ethics:

> The situationist enters into every decision-making situation fully armed with the ethical maxims of his community and its heritage, and he treats them with respect as illuminators of his problems. Just the same he is prepared in any situation to compromise them or set them aside *in the situation* if love seems better served by doing so.[9]

22.11 Fletcher contrasts this approach to ethics with 'legalism' on the one hand and 'antinomianism' on the other. In the former approach 'one enters every decision-making situation encumbered with a whole apparatus of prefabricated rules and regulations':[10] in the latter, 'one enters into the decision-making situation armed with no principles or maxims whatsoever, to say nothing of rules'.[11] In all three approaches to ethics, then, Fletcher apparently believes that the central focus is upon the individual confronted with problematic decision-making. Significantly, his characteristic method of commending situation-ethics involves the exegesis of an exceptional paradigm. The latter usually concentrates upon the individual (rather than upon society at large) faced with a seemingly intransigent moral dilemma. It is the primary objective of situation-ethics to resolve such a dilemma, albeit always taking into account the idiosyncrasies of particular situations.

22.12 The academic response to Fletcher's account of situation-ethics has been enormous — few other works in Christian ethics have created such widespread interest and criticism in the theological world. However, an examination of all the weaknesses that have been attributed to it would not be relevant here.[12] What is relevant, though, is the observation that much of the response to situation-ethics, whether positive or negative, has itself concentrated upon the individual confronted with problematic decision-making. In so far as this is the case, both situation-ethics and the response to it may be depicted as prescriptive.

22.13 A single example of this may be given. In his detailed critique of situation-ethics, Paul Ramsey suggests that, in so far as 'agapism' presents Christian ethics with an adequate model, a combination of normative and situation-ethics is necessary if the latter is to be accepted.

> It can be shown that a proper understanding of the moral life will be one in which Christians determine what we ought to do in very great measure by determining which rules of action are most love-embodying, but that there are also always situations in which we are to tell what we should do by getting clear about the facts of that situation and then asking what is the loving or the most loving thing to do in it.[13]

22.14 Ramsey's eventual position is, of course, more complicated than this, since he holds that the notion of *agape* alone is not adequate for Christian ethics. Instead, he offers a theory of 'mixed agapism', which he sees as 'a combination of *agape* with man's sense of natural justice or injustice which, however, contains an internal asymmetry that I indicate by the expression "love transforming natural justice" '.[14] Nevertheless, it is clear that he accepts Fletcher's account of the fundamental task of Christian ethics as being the study of the individual confronted with problematic decision-making. Even those, like G. R. Dunstan, who have bemoaned precisely this focus within contemporary Christian ethics, themselves tend to become involved in the self-same prescriptive debate.[15]

22.15 As with prescriptive understandings of practical theology, the various prescriptive understandings of Christian ethics again tend to relegate the social sciences in general, and sociology in particular, to an ancillary role. Although Fletcher himself makes little use of sociology, his account of situation-ethics does not preclude the sociologist from clarifying given situations in which an ethical decision is subsequently to be taken. Indeed, the assumption that we should get 'clear the facts' of particular situations before reaching decisions may well imply a prior assumption about the pertinence of disciplines like sociology. By analysing the 'is', 'was', 'will be' or 'could be' of a given situation — but emphatically not the 'ought to be' — the sociologist may be able to exercise an important function in clarification.[16] Indeed, in all but the most normative accounts of Christian ethics sociology may be able to perform this illuminatory, though essentially ancillary, role.

22.16 Whilst it may be no criticism of prescriptive understandings of Christian ethics as such, it is important, in this instance also, to recognise that the possibility of sociology becoming integrally related to the discipline, is precluded. Sociology may be afforded a status somewhat higher than the purely utilitarian one suggested by some understandings of practical theology, but it is still not an integral status. At the most, it can analyse the societal features of the situations surrounding moral dilemmas.

Descriptive Understandings of Applied Theology

22.17 Alongside these prescriptive understandings of applied theology, there have been a number of attempts to suggest a more descriptive orientation for the discipline. Within both Christian ethics and practical theology, several scholars have tried to move away from the production of tangible solutions to particular problems and towards a more analytical/critical approach to issues within applied theology. Thus, within Christian ethics, some exponents have suggested a focus upon the moral context or upon the moral actor, rather than upon moral decision-making; whereas, within practical theology, some have argued for an analysis of the relationship between belief and action in all its complexity, rather than an emphasis upon the requirements of belief for action.

22.18 (c) **Descriptive Practical Theology**: Amongst those exponents of practical theology who have advocated the abandonment of a post-Schleiermacher understanding,[17] J. A. Whyte, in particular, has argued against a 'hints and tips' for ordinands approach to the discipline. He believes that instead practical theology should become more seriously theoretical:

> Practical theology must understand itself as *the theology of practice*, and as such a properly academic enquiry. The subject matter of this enquiry is not what is *said*, but what is *done*, as an expression of faith. The data for Practical Theology are not the verbal formulations, the ideas, the language in which people express their faith (or their unbelief), for these are the concern of philosophical or systematic theology, but the activities, the practices, the institutions, the structures of life and of relationships which are, or purport to be, the outcome, embodiment or expression of their faith or unbelief.[18]

22.19 In addition, Whyte suggests, unlike Schleiermacher, that 'practice' in this context should not be restricted to ecclesiastical practice and that 'faith' should not be viewed solely as Christian faith.

22.20 In so far as it is the function of the practical theologian to analyse religious practice as it relates to religious faith, his task would appear to be identical with that of the sociologist of religion. The analysis of correlations between faith and action is, after all, one that specifically belongs to the latter. Yet the two types of analysis would appear to be distinct, in as much as Whyte believes that the practical theologian has an additional critical function. So, for example, he suggests that the theologian might wish to offer a critique, and not simply an analysis, of social change.

22.21 Whyte's account of this descriptive/critical understanding of practical theology, in terms of 'the theology of practice', is brief and open-ended. Whilst rejecting the church and Christian faith as the proper context of the discipline, he makes little attempt to relate the descriptive features of his analysis to contemporary sociology of religion, or to specify the critical criteria necessary to differentiate the latter from practical theology. Nevertheless, it is evident that this understanding of the discipline does allow the possibility of a close interaction between it and sociology. Here, sociology is no longer relegated to the role of an ancillary discipline: a closer integration becomes possible.

22.22 A similar, though somewhat more developed, understanding of practical theology as a descriptive/critical discipline is offered by Karl Rahner. Unlike Whyte, however, he does locate it within the context of the church. For Rahner, 'practical theology is that theological discipline which is concerned with the Church's self-actualisation here and now — both that which *is* and that which *ought to be*'.[19] He rejects the view of practical theology which sees it, either as 'a mere hotch-potch of practical consequences' of other theological disciplines, or 'merely as a collection of psychological, didactic, sociological rules of prudence, gained directly from the ordinary practice of the care of souls'.[20] He maintains, instead, that the discipline is both autonomous and thoroughly theoretical:

> The task of practical theology as an original science demands a theological analysis of the particular present situation in which the Church is to carry out the especial self-realisation appropriate to it at any given moment. In order to be able to perform this analysis of the present by means of scientific reflection and to recognise the Church's situation, practical theology certainly needs sociology, political science, contemporary history, etc. To this extent all these sciences are in the nature of ancillary studies for practical theology. However, although the contemporary analysis provided by these profane sciences is necessary and sufficient for its use, it cannot

simply draw on it uncritically as though it were already complete and given. Practical Theology must itself critically distil this analysis within a theological and ecclesial perspective, a task which cannot be taken over by any other theological discipline. . . . Beyond the confrontation of the Church's essence with the contemporary situation, practical theology should contain an element of creativity and prophecy and be engaged in critical reflection.[21]

22.23 It is evident, then, that, for Rahner, practical theology has two distinct, though interacting, functions. The first of these is a descriptive function. No longer content with a purely prescriptive understanding of the discipline in which the social sciences are used simply as 'tools', he argues that it is legitimately concerned with analysing the contemporary role of the church *vis-à-vis* society. The second function appears to be a critical/prophetic one, less concerned with the church as it 'is' than with the church as it 'ought to be'. Rahner maintains (although he does not elaborate the point) that the social sciences, including sociology itself, are no longer directly relevant to this second function.

22.24 Although Rahner refers to sociology as an 'ancillary' discipline in relation to the descriptive function of practical theology, it is clear that it does, in fact, exercise a more integral role than it might under a prescriptive understanding of the discipline. Certainly, in his account, sociological analysis cannot be conflated with practical theology, since the latter has a critical/prophetic function which would usually be considered inappropriate to the former. However, in so far as practical theology is a descriptive discipline and in so far as it is concerned with offering an analysis of the church's self-actualisation in contemporary society, the role of sociology is far from ancillary.

22.25 In differing ways, then, the accounts of Whyte and Rahner both present the possibility that sociological analysis may be regarded as a constituent part of practical theology. Further, both apparently differentiate the two disciplines on the basis of the additional critical function of the latter. Whether the descriptive feature of practical theology is seen, with Whyte, as the analysis of correlations between faith and action or, with Rahner, as the analysis of the church's self-actualisation within society, sociological analysis would appear to be directly relevant. Indeed, the analysis of theology as both a dependent and an independent variable within society, suggested in the previous chapters, can now be seen to be an aspect of this descriptive function of practical theology. This is not to claim, of course, either that this descriptive understanding of practical theology is the 'correct' one, or that the purely sociological analysis of theology offered until now *must* be viewed as an aspect of practical theology. It is to claim, more modestly, that, given this particular understanding of practical theology, a sociological analysis of the determinants and significance of theology can now be seen to be an important feature of the discipline.

22.26 (d) **Descriptive Christian Ethics:** Although an emphasis upon ethical decision-making and the resolution of particular moral dilemmas would still appear dominant in contemporary Christian ethics, there is also evidence of a more descriptive understanding. A similar emphasis is to be found in general moral philosophy, although, here too, R. W. Hepburn suggests that, 'there have been . . . some reminders that, whether or not rule-obedience may be the most satisfactory analysis of moral language, very different models are quite often in fact held by morally sensitive people — by those, for instance, who see moral endeavour as the realising of a pattern of life or the following out of a pilgrimage'.[22]

22.27 One of the most widely known attempts to present Christian ethics as a descriptive, rather than prescriptive, discipline is that of Paul Lehmann. He argues that the Protestant Reformation entailed for ethics, 'the displacement of the prescriptive and absolute formulation of its claim by the contextual understanding of what God is doing in the world to make and to keep human life human'.[23] As a result, 'ethics could now be a *descriptive* discipline, not in contrast to a normative discipline . . . but in the sense of providing an account of the transformation of the concrete stuff of behaviour, i.e., the circumstances, the motivations, and the structures of action, owing to the concrete, personal, and purposeful activity of God'.[24] For Lehmann, the context of Christian, as distinct from non-Christian, ethics is the *koinonia* and the task of Christian ethics is to elaborate the theological basis of this *koinonia* as it relates to its members. The following passage sets out this thesis in more detail:

> When Christian ethics is defined as *the disciplined reflection upon the question and its answer: What am I, as a believer in Jesus Christ and as a member of his church, to do?* the point of departure is neither vague nor neutral. It is not the common moral sense of mankind, the distilled wisdom of the ages. Not that we can ignore this ethical wisdom, but we do not start with it. Instead, the starting point for Christian thinking about ethics is the fact and the nature of the Christian Church. To put it somewhat too sharply: Christian ethics is not concerned with *the good*, but with what I, as a believer in Jesus Christ and as a member of his church, am to do. *Christian ethics, in other words, is oriented toward revelation and not toward morality.*[25]

22.28 This radical relocation of Christian ethics, away from ethical decision-making, ethical theories and moral dilemmas and towards its communal and doctrinal basis, has inevitably attracted critics. So, for example, Paul Ramsey maintains that

Lehmann's 'descriptive' approach to ethics suffers from two weaknesses. In the first place, it is 'contradicted by the vast difference and dialectical relation between the hidden and the empirical reality of the *koinonia*':[26] it fails to take seriously the discrepancy between the actual church, with its absence of doctrinal purity, and the *koinonia*. And in the second, it tends to yield only vague generalisations about Christian behaviour, not the detailed prescriptions of traditional Christian ethics or moral theology. Whatever its particular weaknesses as an adequate explication of Christian ethics (which are not relevant here), it does represent an important attempt to focus the discipline on the theological variables upon which it depends as a separate and distinct discipline.

22.29 A rather different attempt to relocate Christian ethics away from the individual confronted with problematic ethical decision-making is to be found in the writings of David Harned and Stanley Hauerwas. Harned, whilst agreeing with Lehmann that 'the idea of virtue cannot be explored satisfactorily without extensive reference to the Christian community',[27] seeks in his writings to focus upon 'the importance of vision and imagination in human conduct'.[28] Hauerwas' emphasis is similar although he also concentrates on the idea of 'character' as a focus for Christian ethics, rejecting the exclusive 'command-obedience metaphor' of much contemporary ethics. He believes that 'the language of character does not exclude the language of command but only places it in a larger framework of moral experience'.[29] On this understanding of the discipline, there is no longer sole concentration upon problematic decision-making. Hauerwas suggests a descriptive/critical understanding:

> Once ethics is focused on the nature and moral determination of the self, vision and virtue again become morally significant categories. We are as we come to see and as that seeing becomes enduring in our intentionality. We do not come to see, however, just by looking but by training our vision through the metaphors and symbols that constitute our central convictions. How we come to see therefore is a function of how we come to be since our seeing necessarily is determined by how our basic images are embodied by the self — i.e., in our character. Christian ethics is the conceptual discipline that analyses and imaginatively tests the images most appropriate to score the Christian life in accordance with the central conviction that the world has been redeemed by the work and person of Christ.[30]

22.30 Two functions, then, are suggested for Christian ethics — the first analytical/descriptive and the second critical/imaginative. As it happens, it is more to philosophy than sociology that Hauerwas turns for this first function, but, in principle, it is arguable that he might have chosen sociology. After all, the latter could analyse the images actually used by Christians in their moral lives and suggest ways in which these images are determined or determinative. Whereas the second function in Hauerwas' analysis belongs exclusively to the discipline of theology, clearly the first does not. Not surprisingly, then, Harned, in particular, makes frequent use of sociologists, such as Berger and sociological concepts, such as that of secularisation.[31]

22.31 There begins to emerge the possibility of an integral relationship between sociology and the descriptive function of these understandings of Christian ethics. The object of scrutiny is not so much the general correlation between faith and activity (whether exclusively within the church or not), but rather the specific correlation between faith and moral activity and even between faith and potential moral activity. Practical theology, viewed in these terms, appears as the overall discipline and Christian ethics as the specialised discipline within it. Both are concerned with the relation between faith and action, but the second has a specialised focus on moral action. Sociology, though, is integrally related to both, performing a primary task of analysis. It is the addition of a critical, evaluative element, superimposed upon a purely descriptive analysis, that distinguishes the task of the applied theologian from that of the sociologist.

Sociology Within Applied Theology

22.32 We are now in a position to isolate a number of ways in which sociology may be employed in the discipline of applied theology. These range from the most superficial and ancillary adoption of sociological techniques to an integral use of sociology as itself a function of applied theology.

22.33 First, sociological techniques may be used to denote *the social context* within which applied theology operates. At the most superficial level this need not greatly affect the discipline. If the exponent of practical theology or Christian ethics is content to communicate to the faithful alone and not to society at large, he may pay scant attention to the social context within which he operates. In this instance sociological techniques may be used *en passant* and with few clear implications for the discipline. Some of the examples of prescriptive applied theology already cited conform closely to this usage. On the other hand, if the applied theologian is concerned with communication and with the plausibility structures apparent within society, then he, like the general theologian,[32] is obliged to take sociological data more seriously.

22.34 Secondly, sociology may play an integral role in the analytical part of descriptive/critical applied theology. In assessing specific correlations between faith and activity, the applied theologian may have recourse to analyses of *the social structure of theology*. As already indicated, the specific correlations which are germane to descriptive practical theology and descriptive Christian ethics, coincide, to a large degree, with an account of theology as a dependent and independent sociological variable. Nevertheless, there is an important difference between the two, at the purely analytical level. Whereas the sociologist, in general, may tend to concentrate on the 'is' rather than the 'could be', that is, on the empirical rather than the speculative, the sociologist working within applied theology may be encouraged to give equal attention to both. Provided that he does not confuse the 'could be' with the 'ought to be', his task remains properly sociological.[33] In this way, he will be able to fulfil the condition that applied theology has seldom been content solely with an analysis of existing activity — potential activity has figured prominently as well.

22.35 Thirdly, sociology may play an integral role in assessing, but not evaluating, *the social consequences of theology*. It is at this point that the most radical effects of sociology may be felt within applied theology. Precisely because theology is an evaluative and critical discipline, it cannot ignore its social consequences. A necessary element within the 'explication of the "sequelae" of individual religious beliefs' (to return to my original definition of theology) is that this explication is 'critical'. Within descriptive/critical understandings of applied theology this entails a critical evaluation of the effect of faith upon action and of action upon faith. It is at this point that sociology can perform a crucial function in highlighting the social consequences of belief in general and theology in particular. Without itself evaluating these consequences, it can none the less supply an essential element in theology's self-evaluation.

Notes

2. Karl Barth, *Evangelical Theology: an Introduction*, London, 1963, p. 169.
3. *Ibid.*, pp. 169–70. cf. Eduard Thurneysen, *A Theology of Pastoral Care*, John Knox Press, 1962.
4. See F. D. E. Schleiermacher, *Die Praktische Theologie nach den Grundsätzen der Evangelischen Kirche*, Berlin, 1850.
5. Fernand Boulard, *An Introduction to Religious Sociology*, Darton, Longman & Todd, 1960, p. 74.
6. See R. Gill, *The Social Context of Theology*, Mowbrays, 1975, pp. 23–4 and 87–9.

7. Seward Hiltner, *Preface to Pastoral Theology*, New York, 1958, p. 20.
8. Cf. Alastair V. Campbell, 'Is Practical Theology Possible?', *Scottish Journal of Theology*, May 1972.
9. Joseph Fletcher, *Situation Ethics*, SCM, 1966, p. 26.
10. *Ibid.*, p. 18.
11. *Ibid.*, p. 22.
12. See George Wood, 'Situational Ethics', in ed. Ian T. Ramsey, *Christian Ethics and Contemporary Philosophy*, SCM, 1966, essays in ed. Gene H. Outka and Paul Ramsey, *Norm and Context in Christian Ethics*, SCM, 1969.
13. Paul Ramsey, *Deeds and Rules in Christian Ethics*, Scottish Journal of Theology Occasional Papers No. 11, 1965, p. 5.
14. *Ibid.*, p. 110. cf. Paul Ramsey, *Nine Modern Moralists*, Prentice-Hall, 1962.
15. See G. R. Dunstan, *The Artifice of Ethics*, SCM, 1974.
16. Cf. David Martin, 'Ethical Commentary and Political Decision', *Theology*, Oct. 1973 [below, **Extract 23**].
17. e.g. Campbell, *op. cit.*
18. J. A. Whyte, 'New Directions in Practical Theology', *Theology*, May 1973, p. 229.
19. Karl Rahner, *Theological Investigations*, Vol. 9, Darton, Longman & Todd, 1972, p. 102.
20. *Ibid.*
21. *Ibid.*, pp. 104–5.
22. R. W. Hepburn, 'Vision and Choice in Morality' in ed. Ian T. Ramsey, *op. cit.*, p. 181.
23. Paul Lehmann, *Ethics in a Christian Context*, SCM, 1963, p. 14.
24. *Ibid.*
25. *Ibid.*, p. 45.
26. Paul Ramsey, *op. cit.*, p. 46.
27. David Baily Harned, *Faith and Virtue*, Pilgrim, 1973, p. 14.
28. *Ibid.*, p. 9. cf. David Baily Harned, *Grace and Common Life*, University of Virginia, 1971.
29. Stanley Hauerwas, *Character and the Christian Life*, Trinity University, 1975, p. 3.
30. Stanley Hauerwas, *Vision and Virtue*, Fides, 1974, p. 2. cf. Keith Ward, *The Divine Image*, SPCK, 1976.
31. See ed. James F. Childress and David Baily Harned, *Secularisation and the Protestant Prospect*, Westminster, 1970.
32. See Gill, *op. cit.*
33. Cf. Martin, *op. cit.*

23

David Martin
Ethical Commentary and Political Decision

David Martin, professor of sociology at the London School of Economics (see *Extract 13*), wrote this Extract as an article for the journal *Theology* in 1973. It expresses very succinctly the role that sociology can play in ethics (I pursue this at length in my *Textbook of Christian Ethics*). Martin identifies two distinct ways it can be used in this context. The first depends upon the interactionist account of the relation between ideas and behaviour apparent elsewhere in this reader (*23.1–6*). This approach attempts first to analyse the likely empirical consequences of particular ethical policies (cf. *22.35* and *11.23f.*) and then their social antecedents (*23.5*). By now this will be familiar ground: it is a sociological approach clearly dependent upon Weber (*Extract 1*). The second approach seeks to use sociology as a means of differentiating roles in a socio-political situation. Here Martin distinguishes between the ethical commentator and the political decision-maker (*23.7f.*). Whereas the latter is involved in a 'quagmire of compromises' (*23.10*), the ethical commentator can be concerned to restate first principles, ignoring partisan interests, and can even afford to be speculative in ways not open to the politician (*23.10–15*). Role analysis is an important contribution that social scientists (it is obviously not limited to sociologists) can make in a number of areas within applied theology — especially those of liturgy and ministry (see *Extract 26* and *Extract 28*).

23.1 The purpose of this short paper is two-fold. It aims to comment on the morality of corporate bodies, in particular Church or State, in so far as they deliver themselves on the ethical aspects of political decisions.[1] It also aims to compare and contrast the role of ethical commentary performed on behalf of a corporate body like the Church with the role of the actual decision-maker. In other words, I am discussing the general difference between corporate morality (whether in Church or in State) and individual morality in so far as it relates to the further difference between commentator and performer, political moralist and politician. The argument is going to be that all corporate morality, whether it consists in political moralizing by a Church or in political decisions claiming some ethical justification on the part of the State tends to lay its stress on consequences. That being so it introduces a strong empirical element in the form of scientific predictions about the likely consequences of alternative policies. This empirical element will be economically labelled sociology. And it is sociology which may perhaps enable us to locate the difference between ethical commentary and political decision, since it can contrast the type of consequence which concerns the commentator with the type which concerns the politician — and also indicate perhaps the extent to which they must overlap. The arguments just set out must now be presented in more extended fashion, beginning with the point made about the estimation of consequences.

23.2 One of the major traditions of ethical reflection lays its prime stress on the consequences of acts rather than on their intrinsic nature or on the motives lying behind them. No doubt it is true that a stress on the intrinsic qualities of actions hardly avoids some calculation of consequences just as a stress on the consequences of actions must include some estimation of the intrinsic worth of particular sets of consequences when weighed against other sets. Nevertheless, I hope the broad distinction still holds. At any rate I presume there is agreement on the supposition that whatever the emphasis of different ethical traditions they all must concern themselves with consequences to some extent.

23.3 It seems to me that a shift of emphasis occurs when the focus of concern moves from individual to corporate ethics. Presumably there is less interest in the *motives* of an action: whether or not, for example, the intentions of an ecclesiastical or political agency were good. And so far as the contrast between intrinsic and consequential is concerned I suppose that not only is a stress on the consequences of a decision so much the greater but that the main attention is on the ability of whole *sets* of decisions when integrated together to produce an approved state of affairs. Thus the primary questions turn on an organized relation between whole ranges of decisions and recommendations and an envisaged condition of communal well-being.

23.4 If this is the case — and I make all these suggestions with extreme diffidence having regard for the immense complexities involved — then the science of social consequences, sociology, comes to play an even greater role in the decisions of corporate bodies and in the ethical commentary made by one corporate body on the decisions of another.

23.5 There is no difficulty in stating how sociology enters into the decisions of corporate bodies. It can provide social information, and set the context of a problem. It can, at least in principle, estimate the likely results if course (*a*) is followed rather than course (*b*). It can bring within the scope of intentionality what previously might have been the unintended consequences of action. And, finally, it is capable of tracing the antecedents of a situation, a peculiarly important function so far as ethical commentary is concerned and one which raises some profound problems. These services which 'sociology' may provide represent the combined resources of economics, political science, etc., and are only new in that nowadays such services are explicitly sought and are systematically performed. Presumably in the past every politician and ethical commentator was an amateur political scientist and economist, more explicitly perhaps after Machiavelli in the European experience but implicitly everywhere and at all times. What is now understood in the multidimensional perspectives of sociology as systematized, verified propositional knowledge has always been practical knowledge, even if working with a 'Ptolemaic' rather than a 'Copernican' perspective.

23.6 I take it there is no dispute about the relevance of this type of information in shaping ethical commentary and political decision.[2] I am not saying, of course, that such information and such predictions enter into the ethical substance so as to leap over the chasm between is (was or will be) and ought. However, there is an important aspect worth noting just at this point and it relates not to 'is' and 'ought' but to 'ought' and 'can'. To some extent ethical commentary can only say that a politician should do thus and thus if it can be shown that it was possible for him to do so. Sociology provides an analysis of practical limits in given situations and to that extent restricts the range of justifiable free-ranging finger-wagging. And of course to the extent that it shows an action as part of a whole *system* with a particular 'drift' then ethical commentary shifts away from particular actions to discuss a whole system of relationships, a whole history of tendencies, a whole semi-determinate course of likelihoods.[3] This is a complex point which must be taken up below since it relates to the degree to which ethical commentary may take up alternative perspectives outside the 'system', how far such alternative perspectives need to represent a genuine empirical likelihood (or at least possibility) and how far *back* the tracing of a history of tendencies should go — inasmuch as the last Conservative government is too near and Adam too far.

23.7 I hope I have begun to indicate how sociology can enter into ethical commentary and the kind of problems it raises. If so I can now move on to my contrast and comparison between ethical commentary and political decision. The appropriate point at which to begin is one which at least illustrates the difference and which also most brings out the element of the intrinsic as distinct from the consequential. Commentators and politicians alike agree in being against sin and on the side of the angels. Actually, to say that everybody is against sin is somewhat of a rhetorical exaggeration since in situations which are sufficiently crucial most moralists and actors agree that ends justify means. They apologize, maybe, for violence, falsehood and promise-breaking but argue that such things are necessary in the circumstances. But at any rate they very seldom apply this argument to those of their opponents who utilize the same escape clause. Moreover, those who regard any means as justified usually adopt the attitude of moral scold towards their enemies.

23.8 Clearly sociology is not relevant to a basic evaluation of truth-telling, promise keeping, etc., though it might provide an estimation as to the point where things had so deteriorated that one had to utilize the moral escape-hatch: as regards truth-telling this point of deterioration can be reached very quickly.[4] But sociology is relevant at the next level of commentary and decision, which might most usefully be illustrated by the proposition that colour, race and religion are irrelevant. As regards the point about the irrelevance of colour and race, sociology can usually erode racist arguments in their empirical form though clearly not in the form of a basic attitude towards blackness or colour. On the other hand it can replace the false arguments about inferior moral and intellectual qualities by much more plausible arguments regarding tolerable degrees of cultural heterogeneity. As regards the point about religion the same argument based on cultural heterogeneity holds, and sociology could obviously bolster a position which stated communal peace as an overall aim and predicted that a given degree of religious heterogeneity would lead to an intolerable degree of disruption.

23.9 In this area of discussion one has left behind the level of immutable principles and entered the murky level of compromises, varied estimates of likely tendencies, calculations of ultimate and immediate political benefit or popularity, and so on. Presumably it is here that the difference between ethical commentary and political design can emerge. As I attempt to delineate these differences I shall use language favouring the politician. This is not because I wish to support State rather than Church, but because there is at large in our society, particularly on its leftward margins, a form of ethical comment which abuses its advantages and manages to create a false image of moral superiority which a proper disdain for the attractions of office enables it to maintain untarnished. So it seems worth while to set out these advantages in such a way as to be at least fair even to politicians, on the supposition that as individuals they are not inferior to the rest of us, either morally or intellectually. As I do this some of the advantages listed may seem to be incidental, others more inherent in the whole mode of ethical comment, but I shall not attempt to differentiate between them.

23.10 In the first place ethical commentary can afford to restate first principles when politicians are already lost in the quagmire of compromises and would rather not hear about such things. It can point out the colour *is* irrelevant, the promise breaking *is* improper and so on. An allied advantage, which is in a sense the reverse side of the coin, consists in the ability to admit that first principles are *continually* broken, whereas politicians pretend this only occurs under pressure of the direct necessity. Ethical comment can show empirically, for example, that a government has over-extended itself in terms of promises, so that if it keeps one it *must* break another. Or it can show that solemn pledges are made with unstated reservations about 'vital interests' (variously defined) on the part of participants, and that the solemnities are to some extent a kind of mutually deceptive confidence trick which is also for the benefit of dangerous third parties. In other words comment can be both more naïvely moral than politicians and more sophisticatedly honest about the actual processes involved. Both possibilities are immensely satisfying to their practitioners.

23.11 Comment can ignore survival as a primary value, a point related to the issue of 'vital interests' just raised. It need not think in terms of party survival or national survival, whereas a politican must think in terms of both. And if one can ignore survival one can also ignore immediate and ultimate electoral considerations, the appropriate garnishing of images, the buying-off of crucial pressure groups and so on. Indeed, comment can ignore the sometimes mendacious demands of the great democracy to which politicians must at least pretend to give ear. One further refinement open to ethical commentators is the offering of morally prestigious advice in the sure and certain hope that it will not be taken.

23.12 However, although the commentating role can ignore the more restricting types of empirical consideration forcing themselves on politicians, yet presumably it must in turn recommend policies or alternative social systems which are empirically viable. The alternatives must be possible and should preferably constitute an option currently open. No doubt social science is relevant to a decision about what is a possible alternative and a genuine immediate option, although this may require precisely that very extensive analysis of the total range of financial and political pressures and historical obligations operating on a government which ethical commentary prefers to avoid. To speak too cautiously within the actual limits of choice gives the politician a chance to avoid a consideration even of possible alternatives. So ethical commentary must not publicly overprize empirical analysis, otherwise it tends to assimilate its position too closely to that of the decision-maker, thereby losing its impact and relinquishing the essential complementarity of role and division of labour between commentary and political decision. After all, even a clearly unrealistic assessment can *sometimes* help a politician to acquire a little more leeway. However, to perform in this way requires a great deal of empirical political understanding from the commentator, which he often either lacks or does not choose to have.

23.13 Another gain of commentary *vis à vis* politics is derived from the above and consists in the capacity to ignore opportunity costs. These costs may be immediate or they may be the ultimate opportunity costs of choices between degrees of emphasis on either hierarchy or equality, power or justice, wisdom or democracy.[5]

23.14 An empirical situation is the one which confronts a politician *now*, but ethical commentary can say that policy (*y*) would not need to be followed *now* if policy (*x*) had not been implemented in the past. However, although the past can be undone verbally there is a limit on the extent to which it can be undone practically. Moreover, the politician often cannot even undo the past verbally since this would detract from the viability of his current efforts. As noted earlier the commentator must make a choice as to how far he traces back 'bad' decisions and how far he condemns this or that decision as distinct from condemning the system within which they occur.

23.15 Finally, the commentator has the ability to snipe without revealing his own position in full. A politician is more easily forced to state the criteria with which he is operating with regard to a whole area of politico-ethical discussion whereas the moralist can engage in a moral guerilla warfare from which he cannot quickly be flushed out.

23.16 In sum, I have attempted to show the importance of empirical consequences for both ethical comment and political decision and the difference in mode between the two types of activity. I have further suggested that these differences, where the commentator has the advantage of irresponsibility and the politician the responsibility (not to say consolation) of power, are complementary roles in any politically and morally conscious society. It may be thought immoral or unfair of a commentator to utilize the advantages just outlined, but the alternative is a total assimilation to the considerations most pressing on the actual power holders. It may be that an analysis of empirical pressures and possibilities does lead one logically to such an assimilation but sociologically it is clear that this course would blacken one's own image, reduce one's impact, and therefore eliminate precisely that element of pressure which oneself can contribute to a situation — and which is both an additional restriction and an additional freedom for the politician, according to circumstances.[6]

Notes

1. These are not the only corporate bodies which might be discussed: trades unions also come in the same category.
2. Perhaps I may anticipate one criticism in so far as I am discussing two out of a possible four boxes, as shown by the following diagram:

	State	*Other Organizations*
Action	X	
Ethical Talk		X

I have omitted the two unmarked boxes.

   If this were a more extended piece I should no doubt have to consider the restrictions which operate not only on the 'politicians' in the State but those operating on 'politicians' in other organizations (e.g. unions) and the ethical commentary to which they in turn are subject, both within and outside their organizations. Pressure groups like unions are usually restricted by their material interest and by an external ethical commentary based on notions like the rules of the game and the 'national interest'. Pressure groups whose primary *raison d'être* is a critique of a given political system achieve much higher degrees of freedom, and need consider only their own internal cohesion. They have no responsibilities outside their critique, except of course that once they try *effective* political action they must consider tactics in relation to activities which could prove counter-productive, and this consideration of tactics often eventually reacts back to modify their philosophical strategy. The Church lies between these two positions, having both material interests (usually) and philosophical strategy. Its critical perspective is restricted by opinion within its constituency (impact depends on representing *somebody*) and the degree of integration it hopes to maintain with other sub-sections of society (e.g. the education system).
3. No doubt one can still say that, given the 'system' and its tendencies, nevertheless politician *x* could have done better than he did.
4. As Aron has pointed out, all democratic societies are bound to be hypocritical. [See next note.]
5. Cf. Chap. 4 of R. Aron's *Eighteen Lectures on Industrial Society*, Weidenfeld & Nicolson, 1967, for a discussion of these basic political dilemmas.
6. To give just one example, one could cite Lloyd George secretly asking to be attacked by newspaper commentators when at Versailles so as to give him more elbow-room at the conference table.

24

Mady A. Thung
An Alternative Model for A Missionary
Church: An Approach of the Sociology of
Organisations

The article which forms this Extract appeared originally in Dutch in
Wereld en Zending (Amsterdam) and then in English in the *Ecumenical
Review* in 1978. Mady Thung, a sociologist with considerable theological interests, wrote it to explain the socio-theological model of a
missionary church that she argued at length in *The Precarious Organisation: Sociological Explorations of the Church's Mission and Structure*
(Mouton, 1976). This model involves one of the most sustained uses
of the sociology of religion and the sociology of organisations in
applied theology. In effect she produces a blueprint, or 'ideal' construction (see *8.10*), for a church that is oriented towards mission in
the world. She is clear that her assumptions about what such a church
ought to be, are grounded in theology. However, having established
that, she then uses sociology to assess what patterns of church
structure would be most effective in furthering this church. She thus
uses sociology as a predictive, but not a prescriptive, discipline (cf.
23.6). More specifically, the sociology of organisations is seen by her
as 'the planned, conscious structuring and restructuring of social
groups, with the intention to achieve, in the most efficient way
possible, a number of special objectives' (*24.7*) — that is, in this
context, objectives that have been specified by theologians (*24.13–
14*). She is well aware of the research in the sociology of religion
suggesting that the political convictions of church members are
largely shaped by society at large (*24.16f.* — see *Extract 5*), and sets
out to devise a model of the church which could actually overcome this
determination whilst still 'turning towards the world' (*24.19f.*). She
argues that there are three essential areas of concern in her vision of
the church — faith, ethical reflection and practical action — each of
which must be given a distinct and separate sub-organisational structure within a missionary church (*24.30f.*). Her overall aim she sees as

'quite simply to discover what kind of division into subgroups would be conducive to the practical realization of "the turning of the Church towards the world" ' (*24.39*). This is an admittedly speculative, but nonetheless properly sociological, task.

1. Various forms of resistance to sociology

24.1 Anyone who attempts to make a contribution to the discussion of the problems of the Church from a sociological angle will meet with quite a few forms of resistance. One of these also exists in other parts of society — outside the Church. Sociology is concerned (as is, for instance, psychology) with people's daily experience of reality. Its approach is different, however (more systematic and detached), and has a different aim (explanation) from that of those who are more directly involved. It uses a special set of concepts and perceives inter-relationships in which the people involved do not recognize themselves, and which may threaten the image which they themselves have formed of the world as they experience it. This discrepancy does not differ basically from the one between, for example, the medico-scientific picture of the human body, and our own experience of it, but we have been used to this discrepancy much longer. This is why we grant the medical profession the privilege of having its own (somewhat disillusioning) image of our bodies. Perhaps our image has gradually been so influenced by popularizations of medical thought that the medical profession cannot really upset it very much. There was a time, however, when this was very much the case, and it is not by accident that, just at that time, Church and theology were up in arms against medical science.

24.2 This leads to a second type of resistance, which is met particularly in the Church. It has to do with the difference between the way of thought of sociology and of theology. As a separate article would be needed to deal with this, I will merely indicate the difference by pointing to a few key words: explanation as against interpretation, analysis against synthesis, empirical against normative, sceptical against utopian. Or, in a brief definition: the sociologist attempts to *explain* our experience of reality; he therefore analyzes it into its component elements, formulating hypotheses concerning possible connections, which are then, in turn, tested against the facts of reality, whereby he limits himself to one aspect (i.e. that of inter-personal relations and processes). The theologian, however, seems to be engaged in *interpreting* this same experience of reality, understanding its meaning in the context of a vision of what God wants from us in this reality and how He deals with it. In doing this, the theologian is concerned with the *whole*, and not with the aspects which have been 'anatomically' analyzed. His interpretation carries a normative and utopian slant, against which the reasoning of the sociologist can only show up as disillusioning, desecrating and threatening.

2. Assumptions

24.3 These remarks are necessary because conversations have shown again and again that sociological images of the Church and of church life are taken as equivalents of, or alternatives to the theological ones. On the basis of this assumption, they are then weighed and found wanting. What the sociologist has to offer is, however, intended as entirely different. His analysis of our (common) experience of reality does not in any way exclude a theological interpretation. No more than an anatomical analysis of the human body excludes the interpretation of human beings as creatures bearing the image of God. In this respect, the sociologist makes no special claims and, in his own view of life, he will himself adopt numerous theological interpretations if he is of the Christian persuasion.

24.4 The threat which the sociologist poses comes in a different guise: it concerns the implicit models of society, the intuitive but untested notions of social phenomena, which are concealed in many theological explanations. The sociologist is concerned that, before there is any interpretation of the empirical reality of daily life, the perception of this reality should be clarified as much as possible. Otherwise one risks interpreting phenomena which cannot be found in empirical reality at all, or assuming inter-relationships in social life where none exist. The consequence could well be that anyone employing these interpretations might in practice repeatedly founder on this empirical reality. The confrontation of sociological and theological views may thus, indeed, lead to a request to change the latter, or at least to reinterpret them.

24.5 It is, however, not so that the sociological approach will always furnish irrefutable explanations of the empirical reality. On the contrary, there is much that is not clear; moreover, in the social sciences, it is impossible to achieve the same degree of certainty and precision as is, for instance, possible in the natural sciences. On top of this, in so far as we are concerned with the *churches*, very little research indeed has been done in the Netherlands, and there is very little factual knowledge available.[2] The theologian or church worker who does take sociological insights into account has, therefore, no guarantee that he will *not* founder on the empirical reality. But he is given a tool which improves the way of understanding it, and helps to approach it closer. He can also build on the work which has been accomplished by generations of researchers who have specialized in understanding social reality. He does not need to be caught in the traps which they have negotiated. This is why it seems useful to me that theologians should attempt, in collaboration with sociologists, to arrive at new interpretations which seem satisfying to *both* parties. In the nature of the case, this would mean that they would go beyond the domain of sociology.

24.6 What has just been said does not nearly cover everything.[3] For the sake of brevity, I must confine myself to this, however, before introducing some of the concepts of the sociology of organizations. I hope that it suffices to clarify the nature of these concepts: they illuminate one aspect (just as anatomy illuminates one aspect of human body), leaving to other disciplines, such as psychology, social psychology, political science, economics, etc., the task of studying other aspects.[4]

3. Some remarks about the sociology of organizations

24.7 The sociology of organizations is a relatively new field of specialization: it is concerned with a phenomenon which may be called peculiar to modern western society: the planned, conscious structuring and restructuring of social groups, with the intention to achieve, in the most efficient way possible, a number of specified objectives. This activity, this conscious and planned structuring, can be found throughout history (as for instance in the history of churches, states, armies), but in our time it has become the object of increasingly careful, explicit and exact research. This has also led to the development of separate disciplines, such as management theory and organization consultancy. Moreover, since the nineteenth century, the number of organizations has grown continually, so that now in nearly every sector (economy, recreation, health care, education, etc.) social life is almost entirely lived within specialized groups which have been created for that purpose, that is to say, within an *organized* context.

24.8 Where the sociology of organizations is concerned with such groupings, it considers, among other things, the *formal* systems of:

— division of labour between people, between subsections or subgroups;

— direction, management, decision making, coordination;
— leadership, control, available sanctions;
— recruitment, incorporation, withdrawal of members, selection of leaders;
— recruitment and internal division of assets (money, goods, goodwill); and other, similar conditions for the common achievement of objectives.

24.9 It seems that these conditions can be provided for in a number of highly diverse ways, and that the method adopted can influence the other events which may take place in an organization: for instance, the way people associate with each other; the extent to which there is harmony or conflict; the extent to which effective work is carried out; the growth or decrease of membership, etc. It also appears that the inter-relationships which are found differ for different sorts of organizations: the social processes to be observed in hospitals are partly the same and partly different from those in business; both differ to a certain extent from organizations in the field of leisure-time activities, and so on.

24.10 It is clear that insights gained from this area of study can be of use when considering questions related to churches and congregations. It should, however, first be made clear in which *direction* answers are sought, that is to say, what *kind* of organization one has in mind when posing these questions.

4. What is meant by a missionary church?

24.11 This issue of *Wereld en Zending* is concerned with the missionary character of churches and congregations. In this context, it could be of importance to ask whether they are forms of organization which either promote or impede missionary action. For a sociological approach, it would be necessary first to define what is meant by missionary; that is to say, when is a church to be described as a missionary church? Now this is exactly the kind of problem we discussed in section 2: a theological interpretation which may conceal implicit images of social phenomena. Obviously, some churches are missionary while others are not. That is to say, we have here concrete (actual or possible) differences between churches. Are they supposed to be empirically observable? If so, then it must be possible to describe them in sociological terms. But in what terms?

24.12 The sociologist can only make guesses here — and offer some propositions. In doing this, he will rely, on the one hand, on such clues as he can catch from theological discussions in order to determine the direction in which the search is being carried on. On the other hand, it is necessary to establish what seems to be realistic in practice. Only after this inquiry will it be possible to make concrete suggestions about interpretations of the word 'missionary' which are acceptable both to the sociologist and to the theologian. The latter will, of course, have to decide for himself whether or not he can accept the suggestions made.

24.13 The clues which the present author has caught about the concept of the 'missionary congregation' came mostly from the well-known study-project of the same name of the World Council of Churches.[5] For the readers of this magazine [i.e. *Wereld en Zending*, tr.] this will hardly need any further explanation; it will suffice for me to make a few key points: the relation perceived between God's action and changes in history, the emphasis on *shalom* as the aim of his action, the invitation to men and women to participate in that action. For the *Church*, this means that, 'since God is constantly active in the world, and since it is his purpose to establish *shalom*, it is the Church's task to recognize and point to the signs of this taking place'.[6]

24.14 In my opinion, we may conclude from this that we are faced here with the same concern as that which can be traced from the end of the last century in the Christian movements for social work, in Christian socialism, the American Social Gospel Movement, the Movement for Practical Christianity, the WCC programme on Church and Society, etc., that is to say, all the things which Berkhof called: 'The Church's turning towards the world'.[7] In this respect, the ecclesiology of the 'missionary congregation' had nothing new to offer. What was new, in my opinion, was the connection which was made between this concern and the question about the structure and the working methods of the Church. This offered a good point of entry for an approach to the Church from the angle of the sociology of organizations. As will become clear later, this approach led to a proposal for a theological interpretation of the 'mission' of the Church which does *not* completely cover the ideas of those who advocate the concept of the 'missionary congregation'.

24.15 Unfortunately, there is no room to go into the details of this approach by the sociology of organizations. I shall confine myself to indicating some of the sociological problems, and to sketching some systems one may think of for the division of labour between the subsections. For all the other aspects of organization, as mentioned in section 3, I refer to another publication.[8]

5. An issue in the sociology of religion

24.16 If one considers the actual practice of church involvement in politics and social affairs, one perceives great problems. The convictions of church members in this field vary from the extreme left to the extreme right, and the expectations concerning the action which their church ought to take vary accordingly. The sociological explanation of this is that the political convictions of church members are, at the moment, not determined by what the Church is saying, but by their place in society, the influence exercised by their background, the interests that their position entails and all sorts of forces in their close environment which help to form their opinions. Research has confirmed this up till now, and the investigations show even more: there is a suggestion that the social positions and environments of church members do not only influence their *political* but also their *religious* convictions.[9]

24.17 For the sociologist, this is related to the question of how religion functions in society. It is a question in which Marx's well-known dictum may be recognized, that 'religion is the opium of the people'. If formulated in this extreme way, the proposition is not usually accepted, but it did lead to intensive discussion of the problem of whether a religion can furnish any impetus for change. Is it not true, rather, that all religions, including Christianity, are themselves so profoundly influenced by society that they change as and when society changes?

24.18 An author who has probed somewhat further into this matter, is Lewy.[10] He comes to the conclusion that religion is a phenomenon with a Janus face: in certain circumstances, it may have a revolutionary influence; but in other circumstances it legitimates, it confirms the *status quo*. Lewy considers that the organizational form is one of these latter circumstances.

24.19 Can this give us any help with respect to the problem indicated earlier, that of the way in which the political and religious convictions of individual church members are determined by social factors? In my view it can: this social determination is never absolute; there is always a (small) margin within which it is possible to take up a divergent attitude, which allows for personal choices. It is therefore important that, over against all the influences and pressures which the environment brings to bear on church members, the Church should exert its own counter-influence. If the Church fails in this, its members will soon succumb to the temptation to forget about the free margin and to conform to their everyday environment and the convictions which most nearly coincide with their daily interests. In that case, the faith can be enlisted to soothe the conscience, because it provides a complex of familiar phrases, rituals and customs which create a feeling of safety and comfort.

6. Operational and non-operational goals[11]

24.20 The question is, however: do the churches, in fact, exert any such counter-influences at the moment? In other words: do they provide leadership; have they got the authority to deal with the complicated social problems of our era? Here we are confronted with a new problem. The sociology of organizations distinguishes two kinds of organizations: those with operational goals, and those with non-operational goals. Examples of the first are sports clubs, a society for the preservation of the Wadden Zee [off the Frisian coast, tr.] or a dairy cooperative. These are organizations with more or less concrete aims, which do not need much discussion as to ways and means that must be employed to achieve them. In the case of non-operational goals, on the other hand, it is not directly obvious how they might be achieved. Organizations which nail such goals to their mast (community organization or adult education, for example, or the promotion of development cooperation), will need special tools and procedures in order to transform their vague goals into practical action programmes. This should be done annually or for the span of one planning period. A political party, for instance, formulates a new party programme at certain set periods; at election time this programme is given concrete form in the shape of an election manifesto; and if the party is incorporated in the government, it will attempt to give it an even more concrete form in the shape of government policy. To achieve all this, however, investigations are needed, as well as internal discussion and decision making, and all this is done in ways to which the churches are entirely unaccustomed. Nor do the churches have the necessary organizational equipment.

24.21 Anyone who has become aware of the distinction between operational and non-operational goals becomes increasingly uncomfortable when listening to all the things preached, written and discussed in the churches about social problems. They are almost exclusively formulated in non-operational terms.[12] The result is that the church member receives from the side of the *Church* only extremely *vague* counter-influences, over against all the other appeals, social pressures, suggestions and other influences which he receives daily from his environment. He is left with some vague feeling that things ought to be different, but he has no concrete indications as to how this is to be achieved. It is therefore not surprising that he ignores them when his family expects him to vote for a certain party, to make disparaging remarks about political figures which are talked about at the family dinner party, to join in with the complaints about high taxes and coloured immigrants or to conform thoughtlessly to generally-accepted attitudes in other ways.

7. Is it possible to engage in operationalizing social goals?

24.22 The reaction to all this will be: what then? Should the Church pronounce itself for or against membership of NATO; for or against specific taxation policies; for or against trade-union participation in industrial management? This is a subject about which the last word has by no means been said. My position (for the time being) is that this is a matter of a choice between two evils:

— either the churches continue to move on the level of non-operational pronouncements, appeals and sermons where social problems are concerned. There is then the serious risk, however, that they will have no influence whatsoever on the conduct of the church members, as their political convictions have been fixed long ago;
— or the churches venture out on the slippery path of the (relatively) concrete choices and clear guidelines of what they regard as responsible political behaviour at a given moment.[13]

24.23 It seems to me that the second alternative affords a great deal more chance of exercising influence, both on the members of the Church, and on society in general. It is even possible that the path might be less slippery than it now seems, because a number of important conditions have not been fulfilled at the moment. The average church members do not consider it a matter of course that their church should act in this way; religious education in the past has *not* made them familiar with the idea that the formation of a responsible political opinion should be part of Christian morality. The Church also *lacks* systematic and regular adult education in the course of which social and ethical subjects would be considered. Above all, however, there is *no* apparatus for research, reflection, seeking advice or making preparatory studies, as would be needed in order to assume a leading role in educating the church members' conscience with respect to political issues.

24.24 Nor are we in the churches used to the idea that ethical concepts must be constantly re-operationalized. We tend to think that prophetic language is needed, irrefutable pronouncements, along the lines of: 'thus says the Lord . . .'. Our changing and complicated society demands an entirely different way of proceeding. There are not so many certainties. We can only guess from one moment to the next what will look like the best way. Often, that is a way of compromises and recognition of the 'not yet' — recognition also of the fact that nearly every political programme has its drawbacks.[14] Political and ethical choices which are recommended with these limitations in mind, are often much more palatable than anything that is offered with great ethical or prophetic pretension.

8. A precarious undertaking

24.25 A church which ventures into the political arena in this way will not escape internal conflicts. These conflicts may be made more manageable, however, if the basic social and political problems are made the subject of joint study, discussion and education. Democratic decision-making procedures can also help to make them more fruitful than they are at the moment. There is, after all, even now, a vague awareness that we cannot opt out of politics in the Church. Because of the way our church work is organized at present, this concern is not met in any systematic way, so that it only leads to disastrous polarization at the moment. Every minister and every church member interprets it in his own way, according to his own judgment.

24.26 But even if it were done more systematically than is the case at the moment, the political involvement of the Church would continue to be a precarious affair. It makes high demands on the leaders of the Church;[15] it requires the use of expert research and the careful collection of information; at times, it requires the making of hazardous decisions; it may often cause the Church to defend unpopular standpoints, or to join a losing party.

9. 'Deeds' and 'words'

24.27 It might seem that all this will not get us very far. However, we must be aware that there should be much more going on in the Church than political study, education and action. If the proclamation of the Gospel, the announcement of the *shalom* which God has promised, only were to take place in these ways, then it would not amount to much. Our political activities are too defective for this, our knowledge about their effectiveness too incomplete, and our choice between this or that course of action is based on too many uncertainties. In my opinion, it is an indication of the shortsightedness of the so-called 'horizontalists' that they do not take the defectiveness of all our practical efforts into account. Without the complementary dimension of 'words', it is impossible to convey what is meant by *shalom*. Much more is needed for that — everything which traditionally was conveyed by preaching and celebration, as well as Bible study, reflection on the faith, training in prayer and meditation. To be sure, we may well raise the question — not in the present article, however — of whether we do not need new forms for all this.

24.28 In order to prevent misunderstanding, we must remind the reader at once of sections 5 and 6: the phenomenon that the *same* religious conviction may serve to legitimate the most divergent social aims. The nature of religious language causes this, in my opinion. It makes pronouncements about the meaning, the ground, the aim of our entire existence. It must be applicable to all the situations in which we may find ourselves, and it is by definition non-operational. It is therefore *just as much* a misunderstanding to believe that a sermon or a celebration which makes use of this language will motivate people to behave responsibly in society. Put differently: 'words' are equally insufficient to convey what the Gospel is all about. The complementary dimension of 'deeds' is also indispensable. The social consequences of what we express in religious terms, we argued above, are not immediately evident.

24.29 At this point, we may perhaps be permitted a short digression. Much of the misery connected with the 'horizontalist' and 'verticalist' interpretations of what a church should do, can, in my opinion, be traced to a lack of awareness, among both horizontalists and verticalists, of the great distance between morally-responsible action and religious language. Anyone who starts from this premise, however, will not assume too easily that faith will lead to the right kind of action, or that our faith will be deduced from our actions. This awareness will also mean that not too much is expected — as far as the clarification of ethical problems is concerned — from renewed study of the Bible. Bible study is necessary, because we must also face the important question of what to do with the words which have been handed down to us. And Bible study will certainly serve to remind us that we must take the ethical questions of the moment seriously. For the execution of this latter task and the choice between one way of action or another, it is necessary to study society, to reflect, to make painful guesses as to the effect of our choices and to attain agreement in a common decision-making process. The individual church member cannot be left to do this unaided; he will need the support of the whole fellowship of believers.

10. Three areas of concern

24.30 All this has led me to the conviction that the 'turning towards the world' by the Church cannot be brought about unless there are forms of organization and fixed procedures for the purpose. But that is not the only thing which needs organization; as far as I can see there are three areas which need attention:

— the faith itself, the reflection upon it, the understanding of the Bible;
— ethical reflection, the search for directives for socially-responsible action in different situations and for successive periods;
— practical action in connection with (at least some) social problems to which, after common consultation, priority has been given for a certain period of time.

24.31 These three areas of concern are all essential: reflection on the faith, without ethical reflection or action, could easily lead to a retention of non-operational language. Ethical reflection alone, without action, could easily remain uncommitted. Ethical reflection combined with action, but without reflection on our faith, would easily cloud the vision of a more perfect peace and a more perfect justice that man can ever achieve with his action.[16]

24.32 Because they do not follow on automatically from each other, and because work in one area does not guarantee that all is well in the other fields, it is necessary that each of the three areas has its own procedures and apparatus. One could, therefore, visualize the life of the Church as grouped round three centres:

— two educational centres — synagogues, if that seems preferable — where reflection on the faith and on ethical matters can take place; and
— a centre for church action, which can serve as the base for the organization of political activities (such as lobbying by pressure groups, collections, demonstrations and other actions like that).

24.33 Perhaps these should not be separated from each other in a physical sense, but it is important that there should be three *separate* sub-organizations, each with its own staff (ministers, if that seems preferable), and its own procedures for planning, investigation and evaluation. Otherwise, there is the possibility that one area of concern is sacrificed for the sake of another, depending on the individual preferences of the minister. Under certain circumstances, there may be a fourth centre necessary, for:

— charitable work;

Different models of sub-division and coordination

I. Unitary organization

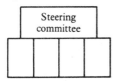

—one goal
— mutual dependency
  between departments
— constant membership in each

II. Federal organization

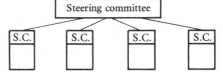

— several goals
— separate management;
  independent departments
— constant membership
  in each department

III. 'Composite' organization

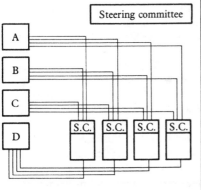

Steering committee

— several goals
— specialized divisions (for
  personnel, accounts, etc.)
  providing services for all
  departments
— constant membership in each
  department

IV. Project organization

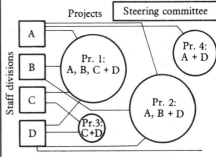

— successive goals realized
  in successive projects
— specialized divisions make
  contributions as needed
— members grouped in changing
  units responsible for specific
  projects (e.g. members from
  C and D divisions work
  together on Project 3)

Model of a missionary church in a region

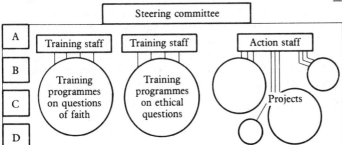

— three major goals
— project organization
  in action department
— members
  temporarily
  grouped in
  ad hoc units
  participate in
  all kinds of
  activities

but in our western welfare states, it is doubtful whether there is still a task for the Church here.

11. Forms of organization

24.34 Such an elaborate structure cannot be financed and manned by one single congregation. One should, however, raise the question of whether the churches are not somewhat obsessed with this one organizational model and, in consequence, lay unnecessary and, in fact, fatal emphasis on the significance of the local congregation. The result of this is that it is heavily over-taxed, so that it is submerged by a range of tasks and expectations which is much too wide. I have already argued that the individual church member should not be left to cope alone with all the study and guesswork necessary for morally-responsible action. Neither should the isolated *congregation* be left to cope with these matters.

24.35 From the drawing on p. 351, it is clear that there are many possible variations of organizational forms. The models which have been designed here could occur successively in a small village school with a few classes (I); an association with local divisions (II); a business firm or a hospital, with separate 'staff divisions' for domestic affairs, purchases, sales, bookkeeping, etc., (III); a large building concern which regularly takes on new projects for which *ad hoc* forms of organizations are set up (IV). Church organization is usually thought of as being like II. But there are elements of a 'composite' organization to be found (such as, building committees, advisory councils, bookkeeping services), and there are quite a number of offices and bodies (a publicity section, a printing firm, a seminary) which have the form of a unitary organization. Often *ad hoc* projects (Christian Aid, Nairobi Follow-up, cf. IV) are also undertaken, to which all sorts of church bodies give assistance according to the needs. There is no reason why the *local* congregations, in particular, are considered as such important instruments for the realization of the missionary task of the Church. What can the congregation achieve without all these other church bodies? Would the later not have a great deal more influence in society in many cases?

24.36 There is another factor, however. Many people believe that the local congregation affords a chance of creating some kind of community bond of solidarity, a spiritual home. Now there is, first, the question of whether this will succeed; quite a few clergymen have been disappointed in this matter. But, if it does come off, it is not even certain that this is the most desirable form of solidarity. Here, one should compare the first three models of organization with the fourth. In the first three, the same members will continually meet each other in each department. This may lead to the development of good personal relations (or, of course, to violent conflicts!). But it also means that they do not become fully aware of the other parts of the organization. Contacts with these other parts go through:

— the head of department, appointed from above, in the case of a hierarchical organization;
— the representative of the department on the steering committee, in the case of a democratic organization. Protestant congregations, with representatives in the Assembly or Synod are well aware how little is passed on to the congregation through such a contact. The 'Church' for the average congregational member is the local or parish church; anything beyond that is too far away to be grasped.

24.37 Model IV, however, would permit a person to get to know the rest of the organization through personal experience. One day, he would meet the members from department A, at another time those from department B, etc. Personal ties may develop from this, but, over and above that, there would develop solidarity with the organization *as a whole*. In sociological research, this has been observed in the great social movements; it leads to identification with the founders, the history and the symbols of such a movement. This is a more abstract solidarity than that of the face-to-face relationships in the local congregation. For that reason, it also implies greater stability: less vulnerability to the fluctuations caused by accidental quarrels, personal idiosyncrasies or the capricious behaviour of some minister or other. In the nature of the case, it is not for the sociologist to lay down whether this is the kind of solidarity which is the most desirable for the Church. It is offered here as one possibility in order to show that there are many more variations of organizational forms than is usually realized.

24.38 Assuming that the kind of solidarity which develops in a project-type organization is valuable for the Church, it is possible to combine organization models III and IV into a kind of 'church model' on the understanding that, at this point, we are only concerned with the division of tasks between the subgroups (that is, we are *not* thinking here of the type of staff, the kind of leadership needed, or how this should be appointed or chosen, how it will carry out its tasks, etc.). The main point in all this is the idea that there must be adequate organizational space for all three of the areas of concern discussed in section 10.[17] The implication of this is that the necessary equipment can only be made available on the level of a region or a city. It also means that church members will have the opportunity to gain experience in a larger sphere, will get to know more of the Church and will have a more varied experience than is possible within one small congregation. It does not at all exclude the formation of small groups at the local level: this can be set up from the three centres. Moreover, the programmes for education and action will often work through small groups. It does, however, reduce the chance that people cut themselves off from the rest of the Church in one group.

12. Reinterpretation of the idea of the 'missionary church'?

24.39 Before I finish, I must once again underline that this has been a purely analytical approach. The aim was quite simply to discover what kind of division into subgroups would be conducive to the practical realization of 'the turning of the Church towards the world'. For this, it was necessary in the first place to discuss the obstacles to this turning, as observed by the sociologist, namely, the problem of the 'Janus-face' of every form of religion, and the non-operational character of our religious language. Thus, a fundamental problem was indeed raised, but apart from that, this article was confined to one single aspect of 'organization'. Nor were questions concerned with liturgy, pastoral care, religious education raised at all. The only point I made here was that the last mentioned would be more effective in some form of adult education than in the form of school teaching. Apart from that, I am well aware that the organizational side only accounts for one aspect of the life of the Church. The faith itself, the inspiration, have been completely left aside. Is there any point, then, in going into such a mass of detail about organizational forms, *when the inspiration is the essential thing?* In my opinion, there is; these forms of organization can either support or frustrate the inspiration, depending on the way in which they have been structured. Besides, forms of organization can be planned and manipulated, while we cannot control the inspiration. What is there to prevent us from giving the best form possible to that which we can shape ourselves?

24.40 It has already been shown that the 'turning towards the world' remains a precarious undertaking, even when we tackle it in the best way possible. Is it possible, then, that this is the specifically 'missionary' dimension which, theologically speaking, seems to be the order of the day? This brings us to our last point: the promised suggestion of a new interpretation of 'missionary', which follows here; it consists of two parts.

24.41 My first suggestion is that we no longer speak of the 'missionary congregation' but of the 'missionary church'. We demand far too much from the local congregation when we expect it to bring about the laborious 'turning towards the world' by itself alone.[18] Besides, it would be far too easy for the higher levels in our churches if they were *not* expected to make this turn!

24.42 But what is to be said about the concept, 'missionary'? Gradually, a hopeless confusion of tongues has developed around this concept. Due to theological manipulations, at least three connotations have gradually come to be understood by this term, each indicating an entirely different activity, so that there is no hold whatsoever for the concrete job:

1) work overseas;
2) recruitment of new members;
3) service in society.

24.43 It is high time that we cease to give all these activities the same name. Why can we not speak of 1) 'service overseas'; 2) 'publicity'; and 3) 'Christian action' — or some such similar terms? If the 'missionary' character of the Church must have anything to do with our faith in God's action in history, then we should reserve the term for that. To represent *that* belief in society, *in combination* with the aspiration to give it form through practical action programmes might well be a trait which would make a church unique. Perhaps this is what its 'mission' consists of. A church with a concern of that nature would be quite distinct from quietist churches concentrating on devotion, on the one hand, and from political parties and action groups, on the other. It is a trait which should permeate every activity of the Church, and not just the three mentioned above.

Notes

2. There are a great many questions which have not been researched. For instance: *which* people attend church regularly and *why*; *which* people stay away from church consciously and *why*; how the service is experienced; how the sermons are interpreted; what the so-called pluriformity of religious experience consists of, *i.e.* who *does* and who does *not* appreciate ecumenical services; *what* political options are favoured by which people; and whether there is any connection there with the various religious attitudes; how much of the discussions in Synods or Assemblies gets through to the congregations, etc.
3. The sociological analysis of inter-relationships may also take in the theological interpretations themselves. Moreover, the question as to when theological interpretations are based on images of society which are not verified or insufficiently thought out may receive different answers in specific cases.

4. The integration of different disciplines, which is insisted upon nowadays, requires that the various specialized disciplines examine the extent to which their presuppositions and conclusions tally with those of other disciplines, or need to be corrected. However, in my opinion, it is impossible to escape their 'aspect' character.

5. Successively called 'The Missionary Structure of the Congregation', and 'Structures for Missionary Congregations'. A report of the West-European and American working groups on this topic can be found in *The Church For Others and the Church For the World*. Geneva: WCC, 1967.

6. *The Church For Others and the Church For the World, op. cit.*, p. 15.

7. H. Berkhof, *Christelijk geloof: Een inleiding tot de geloofsleer (The Christian faith: An Introduction to Dogmatics)*. Nijkerk, 1973, pp. 429ff.

8. Mady A. Thung, *The Precarious Organisation, Sociological Explorations of the Church's Mission and Structure*. 's-Gravenhage: Mouton & Co., 1976.

9. This phenomenon is well-known; the Dutch Reformed Church is said to be 'middle-class', the Remonstrant and Mennonite Churches in the Netherlands count relatively more of the higher professional groups among their members. In the so-called Neo-Calvinist churches in the Netherlands, the working classes are poorly represented while the agricultural groups are over-represented. In the United States of America, this is even clearer; advance on the social ladder often leads to transition to a better situated church, such as the Presbyterian or Episcopal Church. (See further, Thung, *op. cit.*, section 5.1.)

10. G. Lewy, *Religion and Revolution*. New York: Oxford University Press, 1974.

11. This subject needs to be studied in further detail. There are degrees of operationality to be distinguished (Thung, *op. cit.*, p. 139).

12. Dr H. M. de Lange drew my attention to the fact that my description of this phenomenon does not do sufficient justice to a number of recent pronouncements of the sub-unit on Church and Society of the World Council of Churches: these are much more concrete and detailed than I suggested on, for example, pp. 136, 139, in Thung, *op. cit.*

13. This does not necessarily lead to the position of some political party; sometimes important political options are to be found with more than one party.

14. The tendency, found among many politically involved pastors, to deny this, is probably one of the most important reasons why political action by the churches arouses so much opposition. Such action is often presented with an air of moral excellence and infallibility.

15. This is elaborated further elsewhere. Thung, *op. cit.*, pp. 265ff., pp. 312ff.

16. For a more detailed argumentation, see Thung, *op. cit.*, pp. 222ff.

17. The reproach has been made that this leaves no room for pastoral care. But there is ample room for pastoral counsellors, people who have been trained for personal counselling, and who might have consulting hours to which anyone could come (as I have advocated elsewhere; see in P. E. Kraemer and others, *Gemeente in Meervoud*: Amsterdam, 1969, pp. 113 ff.). In my opinion, pastoral care in the sense of care, attention, sensitivity to the personal distress of the people one is in contact with ought to be

a dimension of all the intercourse we have with each other in the Church. People in positions of leadership have an extra responsibility here, even though they may not always have the opportunity to respond to the signals of distress and do something about them personally.

18. For the same reason, the report of the study project on the 'missionary congregation' was finally called *The Church For Others and the Church For the World*.

25

E. Mansell Pattison
Systems Pastoral Care

This Extract was originally an article in *The Journal of Pastoral Care* in 1972. Pattison was then associate professor in the Department of Psychiatry and Human Behaviour, University of California, and deputy director of training, Orange County Department of Mental Health. He subsequently set out his social model of pastoral care more fully in *Pastor and Parish — A Systems Approach* (Fortress, Philadelphia, 1977). In advancing a specifically social understanding of pastoral care Pattison notes that the general movement in the discipline has been towards an individualistic and clinical model (*25.3–8*). In contrast, the perspective in social psychiatry has been that 'social and cultural forces' can 'serve to maintain personal integration or serve to promote personal disintegration' (*25.10*): a general systems theory has been used to see all human behaviour as a 'total unitary system' and any clinical intervention 'must always take into account the total system characteristics' (*25.16*). Such a view of psychiatry clearly goes well beyond the one-to-one patient–doctor model and may even involve political and epidemiological considerations (*25.23f.*). Applying this perspective to pastoral care, Pattison argues that it is the church and the congregation, rather than the individual pastor, which can be seen as the location of pastoral care (*25.30f.*). The church as a sub-system can be seen as a moral agency and as a learning-growth centre (*25.31–32*): it can serve to sustain and maintain social groups, and even to reintegrate and help them (*25.34f.*). Like Thung, Pattison is aware of some of the deficiencies of existing churches, but like her he projects a model of a church actively engaged in the community, which can sustain, support, accept and assist that community (*25.44*). His terms are naturally drawn from social psychiatry rather than sociology, but amongst the skills required for those engaging in systems pastoral care he includes 'knowledge of community organization, structure and function' (*25.50*). However, in contrast to Thung, his approach tends to assume the functional understanding of religion characteristic of Durkheim (*Extract 3*), whereby religion appears as a major source of social integration. Thung's understanding derives more from the prophetic role that Weber sometimes accorded religion (*Extract 2*).

A Perspective on Pastoral Care

25.1 It is apparent from recent articles that the nature of pastoral care is being examined afresh, as those active in the field take pause to look back on the major developments since the pioneering days of Boisen forty years ago.[2]

25.2 From my vantage point as a somewhat peripheral observer the term *pastoral* care has been somewhat of a misnomer, for it seems to me more a development of the field of *clinical* care. To be sure, there is the long tradition of the 'cure of souls', the pastoral concern for sick, needy, wounded, alienated, deprived. But many of these pastoral functions have been taken over by other new professions and supported by the state which has acquired the mandate for such services. Two major polar reactions ensued. One was a retreat, holding that the church could and should provide for the care of its membership, holding fast to an insular separation from the secular developments of society. The other extreme was to embrace the secularization of the pastoral functions.[3]

25.3 The field of pastoral care seems to be characterized by the predominant motif of secularization. Thus the major developments have not been pastoral but clinical. This is exemplified in each of the three major movements within pastoral care. First, the chaplaincy movement began as a ministry to the medically and emotionally ill. But the chaplain, qua pastor, has had a difficult time establishing himself within the social structure of organizations: either remaining a functionally social isolate as in general medical hospitals; or being coopted in the mental health organization as another helping hand when he has demonstrated usable clinical skills. Second, the pastoral counseling movement began as an adumbration of pastoral skills, but quickly moved to a specialized 'ministry' of counseling which was but a short step into full-time counseling, the organization of separate pastoral counseling programs, and finally the exodus from the religious context altogether into private practice. Third, the most recent movement of social action, with the action network and social change training and service programs, has seen the same progression. The emphasis on pastoral skills in community action led to specialized ministers of social action, to separate programs of 'community ministry', to autonomous programs of community organization and social action indistinguishable from social work and other poverty programs under governmental aegis.

25.4 From the point of view of professional mental health I would not decry any of these developments. They represent additional manpower and programs that are sorely needed for the total national mental health endeavor. Indeed, there well may be demonstrable advantages in certain instances for such mental health programs with the religious label attached in one way or another. Elsewhere I have described a number of roles and functions of the clergy in relation to mental health programs, and in particular the new developments in community mental health.[4]

25.5 There are two major deficiencies in the developments described. First, if we seek to recruit and utilize religiously oriented mental health personnel, the present circuitous routes through seminary, pastorates, *ad hoc* courses, and heterogeneous curricula seem an expensive, haphazard, and unpredictable method for the development of needed manpower.

25.6 But the most important issue is that we have lost the *pastor* in all this. Here is the man in the parish, with his people, his vocation, his commitment. The pastoral care movement does not address him. Rather it tells him that the model of success is the psychotherapist, or the physician, or the social worker. It tells him that the most important tasks are to deal with the sick, deviant, and deprived. It tells him that further training and skill acquisition will provide him with status and function when he functions outside the pastoral role. And it tells him that personal satisfaction, monetary reward, recognition and status are not found within the church context, but in the specialized context outside the church as a chaplain, counselor, or community organizer.

25.7 In my observations, the pastoral care movement has been eminently successful in recruiting pastors out of the church, and out of pastoral care, into clinical care. It has been less successful but still influential in diverting pastors from the acquisition and practice of pastoral skills to clinical skills while remaining within the pastoral context. The movement has failed to facilitate and enlarge the roles and functions of pastoral care.

25.8 Therefore, the concern of this paper is not with the typical concerns of the clinical enterprise, even expanded in the context of community mental health. Rather, it is a focus upon the nature of pastoral tasks and skills within the traditional notion of pastor. The reason for this concern is not solely out of interest in the welfare of the pastor — although he surely merits our concern! Rather, we have tended to look upon the church and the clergy as handmaidens of the mental health movement *per se*, and thereby fail to look at the particular and special contributions of the church and clergy in the overall context of the society. I shall endeavor to illustrate that the most important contributions of pastoral care may lie in quite another area not directly related to sickness, dysfunction, rehabilitation, and treatment.

A Perspective on Social Psychiatry

25.9 The academic discipline of social psychiatry represents not so much a professional role but an area of intellectual inquiry. Sharing the same arena are the applied anthropologists, applied sociologists, the action-oriented social psychologists, and the community organization-social segment of social work.

25.10 The common shared interest is upon the social and cultural forces that either serve to maintain personal integration or serve to promote personal disintegration. Simply put, what sociocultural variables promote mental health and what produce mental illness?

25.11 This viewpoint can then be extended into the applied clinical context — namely, what types of sociocultural interventions can be made to influence and change sociocultural factors? We may seek to strengthen positive sociocultural influences, modify or eradicate negative influences, or change the influence from negative to positive.

25.12 Much of the work in social psychiatry is grounded in *general systems theory.*[5] Briefly stated, systems theory is an attempt to organize all data about human behavior into a total unitary system. Any one element of the system must be placed in juxtaposition to all other elements. Each element influences, interacts, and is mutually reciprocal with all other elements.

25.13 For example, any one piece of behavior — say how I behave on a Saturday afternoon — will reflect the total system of my existence, with discrete influences from each part of the system: My physiological system will have an immediate determinant effect — whether I feel well or have a cold. My internal psychological system — whether I reap rewards internally from reading professional journals or enjoy escaping to gardening. My immediate family social system — whether my family plans for outings or each person does his own thing. My local community system — whether Saturdays are neighborhood project days, or everyone goes to the beach, or people traditionally plan family get-togethers at that time. From the geographic system — whether winter is different from summer as in the north, or much the same as in Florida. From the economic system — whether I must work regularly on Saturdays, or have only a four-day work week. From the social system of marketing — whether I can shop any evening and every Sunday as in California, or must shop on Saturday afternoon or not all all. From the religious system — whether I am Jewish, Adventist, Mormon, agnostic, or religious-none. And so on.

25.14 In terms of general systems theory, then, human behavior is the sum outcome of the total system at any given point in time. No one subsystem is predictive nor determinative by itself. All subsystems are necessary, but none sufficient. With different persons, the determinative influence of each subsystem will vary in overall relative importance. And the relative importance of subsystems will vary over time with the same person.

25.15 In like manner, system intervention may be made at one or with several subsystems. The method and effectiveness of intervention will vary with the subsystem involved. For example, curing my cold may require medication, may be effective in changing the physiological subsystem, but may not influence my behavior on Saturday afternoon. Or if I move from one geographic part of the country to another, the change in the climatic subsystem, the neighborhood subsystem, and the marketing subsystem may profoundly influence my Saturday afternoon behavior. But subsystem interrelationships may be more complex. For example, if my intrapsychic rewards from reading hold extremely high valence, that subsystem influence may counterbalance the influence of the geographic, neighborhood, and marketing subsystems. In this instance, the whole system of the person does not remain static. The move to a new area produces change in several subsystems and throws my system into dysequilibrium. In order to satisfy the intrapsychic subsystem, accommodations and readjustments will have to be made in order to bring the system as a whole back into ongoing functional equilibrium.

25.16 To summarize, intervention must always take into account the total system characteristics. Intervention with only one subsystem must take into account the effect on the other subsystems, and the requirements for re-equilibration. The most accessible subsystem may not be the most critical subsystem influencing specific behavior. Or the most critical subsystem may not be available for entry or change. Thus, interventions may be framed in terms of availability, potency, and change-potential of all subsystems.

25.17 At this point it may be instructive to compare the more conventional orientation of clinical psychiatry and the orientation of social psychiatry. From a general systems point of view, conventional clinical psychiatry has been preoccupied with one subsystem dysfunction — intrapsychic organization, and intervention with only that subsystem — to effect change in intrapsychic subsystem function.

25.18 In contrast social psychiatry is concerned not only with one subsystem but all subsystems, and the possible interventions with various subsystems. For example, family therapy is an intervention with an intimate social system. An extended family including grandparents, children, in-laws, and cousins would be a more extensive social system intervention. The organization of a group of neighbors or friends to work with a dysfunctional person or family is still further social system elaboration. Self-help groups, such as Alcoholics Anonymous, Recovery, Parents without Partners, represent the development of a nurturant social system that enables members to maintain function. Thus we may look at clinical intervention in terms, not of working with an individual *per se*, but working to organize a social system, or intervene in existing social systems, or provide entry for a person into effective social systems.

25.19 The basic theoretical assumption here is based in Kurt Lewin's famous field theory, namely, personal behavior is a *product* of *both* the internal organization of the person and the social field of forces in which he is existent. To produce behavioral change, we may intervene in the personality *and/or* intervene in the social field of forces. It should be emphasized that we are discussing basic changes in the field of forces — not merely petty environmental manipulation or environmental management.

25.20 It should now be evident that the skills and methods of system intervention go beyond the typical clinical skills of one-to-one psychotherapy. The first step would be skills involved in group therapy and family therapy. But that is only a beginning. We must move to additional skills in system intervention that include the ability to organize new social systems to gain entry and effect change in existing social systems, and rehabilitate social systems.

25.21 What we are describing can be seen in part in the Maxwell Jones model of the manager of the therapeutic community, in community organization work, in the model of community mental health consultation, in group work with natural community groups, in organizational consultation and organization change. All of the above contain characteristics of social system intervention, although addressed to one or another subsystem. But the unitary theme is that intervention is aimed at change in the structural-functional characteristics of the social system.

25.22 Within the clinical context, if we seek to treat or rehabilitate an individual patient or client, we may not necessarily focus our intervention on the individual person, rather we may elect to work with a variety of social systems that comprise the general system field of the person. Various innovators in this field have labeled this social network therapy, ecological therapy or field therapy. The essential characteristic, again, is therapeutic intervention with social systems on behalf of a patient, changing the sociocultural field of forces that significantly determine the target behavior. In my own theoretical and clinical elaboration of this perspective I label this *social system psychotherapy*.[6]

25.23 Another major concern of social psychiatry does not deal with individual persons, but rather with *populations*. Here we are concerned with epidemiology — the incidence and prevalence of mental health and mental disorder in specified groups of people. We are concerned with the sociocultural forces that will affect the general distribution of mental health/illness for that population. In particular, we are interested in high risk populations: populations that are especially vulnerable to noxious sociocultural forces, or populations that are exposed to high sociocultural stress.

25.24 Here our model is not clinical medicine and the clinically ill. Rather our model is public health and preventative medicine. We are concerned with the sociocultural forces that will produce and maintain mental health in a population, and the sociocultural interventions that will prevent or deter adverse effects to a population exposed to sociocultural risk situations.

25.25 Several brief examples must suffice. A vulnerable population might be the families of military serving in Vietnam. These wives and children are deprived of the father in their family social system, experience increased anxiety in the family system; hence they are more vulnerable to any additional stress on the functional system of family integration. In contrast, a population exposed to high risk might be a successful executive's family with good system coping skills who move because of the father's promotion. This relatively non-vulnerable family system will be exposed to unusually high system and subsystem disturbances as they move and relocate.

25.26 Our concern for populations then will lead us to consider interventions on the basis of the population. We will not be content to wait for dysfunctional symptomatic persons to appear, but rather we will develop system interventions that will prevent the development of personal dysfunction.

25.27 A broader example of population intervention is the issue of alcoholism and drug abuse. If we are to reduce the number of persons in the general population who abuse chemicals we cannot just treat the obvious abuser. We must change sociocultural attitudes that influence patterns of chemical use. Alcohol is a good example. The rate of alcoholism in specific populations has been shown to be directly related to how, when, where, and why alcohol is consumed. Social system intervention will be aimed at changing attitudes and behavior in the use of alcohol.

25.28 To recapitulate, a second major concern of social psychiatry relates to sociocultural intervention aimed at specific populations, for the development and maintenance of mental health, and the prevention and reduction of personal dysfunction in specific target populations.

25.29 In conclusion of this perspective, social psychiatry does not leave traditional clinical skills behind, but places such skills and clinical problems in perspective as one part of the general system of human behavior, human dysfunction, and intervention. The direct clinical aspects of social psychiatry concern interventions with proximate social systems of the patient, while problems of populations and prevention may lead to non-clinical work *per se*. In this latter instance the social psychiatrist may be concerned with social systems that directly deal with human services, or he may work with larger sociocultural forces such as informational media, governmental agencies, and public policy bodies.[7]

Pastoral Care from the Social Psychiatry Perspective

25.30 The two lengthy prologues set the stage for some applications of principles. First, we will address the nature of the church as a social system in the general sociocultural milieu. What are the possible functions of the church as a subsystem, and how might this subsystem be seen as a sociocultural force influencing human behavior?

25.31 **The church as a moral agency.** Every culture requires a system of checks and balances — a cultural ego system if you will. Every culture maintains an ongoing process of moralizing. As sociologist Philip Rieff notes: 'The process by which a culture changes at its profoundest levels may be traced in the shifting balance of controls and releases which constitute a system of moral demands'. Talcott Parsons has called the church a cultural 'boundary structure'.[8] Hence he focuses on the function of the church in maintaining established moral values. That is important. We all must be able to maintain limits and boundaries on our behavior. But we must be able to express ourselves, question, assess, and reevaluate. This is the 'liberation' function of the moral process. Unfortunately the church as a social institution has been a moral constrainer but not a moral liberator. Both are needed. The church as a social system can be an agency of *moral dialogue*.[9]

25.32 The church as a learning-growth center. In our culture learning and growth have too often been seen as attributes of the young alone. Indeed learning and growth have often been seen as painful and onerous. When we became adults we did not have to learn or grow anymore. We were free! But is not the reverse the truth? If we stop learning and stop growing do we not ossify, stagnate, and become the bound captives of our past? The schools of our culture do not yet really take continued adult learning as vital, nor do schools at any level explicitly address the vital matter of human growth as a person. That only happens through the backdoor as a by-product of intellectual cognition and specific skill acquisition. The church has traditionally addressed itself to education, but more often it has been *reinforcement* of that already known, instead of *educo* — the 'leading forth' into newness.

25.33 In his 1969 H. Paul Douglass memorial lectures, social psychologist Milton Rokeach gives a back-handed recognition to the learning growth potential of the church as social system: 'If religious institutions taken as a whole are indeed, at best, irrelevant, and, at worst, training centers for hypocrisy, indifference, and callousness . . . (it) would probably require a profound reorganization of the total social structure of organized Christian religions'.[10] Thus Rokeach recognizes that the church social system has a profound learning-growth influence. They are training centers. But are the results in the desired direction? Here is a potent subsystem of the culture. What will be its learning-growth input?

25.34 The church as a sustaining-maintaining center. No man is sufficient unto himself. One major demonstration of social psychiatry has been the vital necessity of ongoing human relations. People who have no natural groups, no meaningful and intimate personal groups, no stable matrix of meaningful social systems are quite likely to become and remain dysfunctional. All of us are maintained, sustained, restrained, corrected, and nourished by a variety of human groupings. In the past the church was often the major or central source of many human group relations. The huge urban church and the occasion-oriented suburban church have often lost the intimate human grouping experiences that once enriched the lives of many. Only a minority in our culture will perhaps locate much of their group nourishment in the church. Or maybe this vital aspect of the church social system may prove a major avenue of revitalization. Certainly the excitement of the new radical and underground churches may in part relate to the fact that such churches provide this ongoing human group nurturance function. We need nurturing groups in our society. The church may provide such as a social system.[11]

25.35 **The church as a reparation center**. The term reparation is deliberately chosen to avoid a too clinical overtone. We all experience being torn apart. How we cope with dysfunction, dysequilibrium, and failure to cope effectively relates not only to our own personal capacities, but again to our sociocultural matrix. The effective marital partner can nurse, nourish, and help repair the other. The family can absorb and help reintegrate the distraught, torn member. The neighborhood can help a family weather a crisis. The Mormon church as a social system has said 'we can take care of our own'. The church as a social system has the potential for providing aid in the reparation process for its constituency and also for others not closely affiliated in the community. How do we maximize the church as a reparative social system in the community? We need such subsystems. The mental health systems, welfare systems, and other human services agencies are artifices compared to the potential of natural social systems of the community. Indeed, the clients of governmental reparative programs may be seen as the fall-out population — those who have no natural reparative systems, or for whom such systems have not been effective. An analogy can be made here. The healthy marriage is not one that is problem- and conflict-free. Rather the healthy marriage can in part be measured by its reparative capacity. In like manner, the social system of the church may be in part measured by its reparative potential.

25.36 The second element of pastoral care will be discussed in terms of the notions of prevention: primary, secondary, and tertiary. Primary prevention is concerned with elimination of conditions that produce emotional illness and with the promotion of conditions that promote mental health. Secondary prevention is concerned with the early and effective detection of emotional problems when they do exist, so that such problems can be resolved before producing serious disruptions in a person's life. Tertiary prevention is concerned with rehabilitation that will prevent the development of chronic disability as the consequence of serious dysfunction.

25.37 First let us examine the role of the church in primary prevention. The teachings of the church regarding human nature and human relationships may foster either mentally healthy attitudes or destructive neurotic attitudes in its members. Inevitably a church presents models of human behavior, how to deal with aggression, anger, pride, sexuality, competition, social relations, child-rearing, and marital relations. The church must reexamine its implicit and explicit models. It can be a major constructive force in the community if its preaching, church school curricula, and formal and informal social gatherings provide a cohesive and coherent sense of healthy human relationships that will guide, sustain, and encourage healthy emotional behavior in its members.

25.38 Another positive aspect of primary prevention is in the provision of group activities that offer intimacy, support, and relationship. The church in its programming can provide opportunities for participation in a number of formal and informal groups that provide this normal and necessary human nurture.

25.39 The church can also provide group social relations to persons who are exposed to particular life stresses that make them emotionally vulnerable. Through participation in church-sponsored groups a vital contribution can be made to sustaining such persons. Such groups would include adolescents, old people, single middle-aged adults, divorcees, and servicemen. Such groups are intended not to be therapy experiences, but rather to provide opportunity for human contact and relationship to people who are relatively isolated and need structured means of participating in human relationships.

25.40 Another area of primary prevention is the provision of material and human assistance to people in the midst of life crises. It is to be expected that people will experience unsettling emotional crises in their lives. We need not be considered neurotic if we need help in living through and effectively coping with crisis. Here the church and pastor can assist in natural human ways. For example, the family that moves to a strange city can find advice and assistance in the church during their relocation. The family that has suffered a death can find support and comfort in their bereavement. The family that is unemployed or has had their house burn down can obtain shelter, food, clothes, and human concern. These are common predicaments. Yet it is in these common life crises that emotional stress can either be generated or averted, depending upon the human resources available during the crisis.

25.41 And finally there is the arena of social concerns. The church may lend official public support, supply monies, provide clerical and lay leadership, volunteers and facilities to programs aimed at redressing social problems in the community which are contributory factors in producing emotional distress and mental illness. Churches may collaborate in interracial dialogue programs, preschool education, nursery schools for working mothers, alcohol and drug education, sex education, open housing programs, health and education programs for migrant workers.

25.42 In each area of primary prevention we do not deal with the mentally ill, but rather with the provision of relationships and assistance in dealing with the development and maintenance of healthy styles of relationships, the management of life crises, and response to undue malignant societal stresses.

25.43 In the area of secondary prevention we come to the issue of identification. It's like the childhood rhyme — a stitch in time saves nine. The human contacts in the church arena often provide early contact in the course of progressive disability. One problem of identification is the stigma of labels. If a person is identified as 'ill' he is shunned and ostracized. At issue, can we identify disabling or dysfunctional behavior and keep the person within the system? With emotional distress it may be more important to activate the reparative forces in the church social system than immediately to refer the person to an external mental health system. In fact this already happens. Mental health facilities would be immediately swamped if every emotional disturbance were referred to them. Secondary prevention entails an effective response once the dysfunction is defined. Here is an analogy. If a child shows disturbed behavior we do not want to extrude him from the family, but rather help the family to change its pattern of interaction with the child. With family or church, we seek to enhance its reparative potential.

25.44 The problem of tertiary prevention is one of rehabilitation. Those who are mentally ill, or criminal, or on welfare for a time, or unemployed for extended periods, may be seen as sociological 'dropouts'. They lose their acceptance and involvement in the community. Reentry becomes a major problem. There may be difficulty finding a job, being received back into social gatherings, renewing friendships, feeling comfortable participating in community activities. The church can afford an atmosphere of acceptance, receptivity, and interest. Members of the church can reach out to draw the person back into human relationships, assist in vocational and social relocation. The church can provide a liaison with treatment and rehabilitation programs and services. A crucial need exists for a community to which the expatriate can return and receive acceptance, support, and assistance. The church is a major institution that can provide just such a community of human relationships.

Implications for the Field of Pastoral Care

25.45 What I have described in the preceding section is my definition of pastoral care. First, I described the potential subsystem characteristics of the church as part of the general sociocultural system. Second, I described specific activities of the social system of the church as they relate to ongoing human needs.

25.46 I have emphasized these aspects of human life that are *nonclinical, normal, developmental, life-process oriented*. I have described the various ways in which the church as a social system can relate to these aspects of human behavior.

25.47 From these emphases flow implications for pastoral care. The clinical tradition in pastoral care does not provide the necessary skills, nor define the appropriate roles and functions of the pastor in this perspective. (Similarly, the traditional clinical psychiatric tradition does not provide the necessary armamentarium for social psychiatry).

25.48 Just as clinical psychiatry provides a necessary but not sufficient background for social psychiatry, neither does clinical pastoral training in any of its dimensions provide the sufficient background for pastoral care.

25.49 If we may frame pastoral care in the context of the church as a social system at the local level, and as a subsystem in terms of the larger society, we can project certain requirements for preparation in pastoral care.

25.50 I would include the following: A basic grounding in normal human development throughout the life cycle. An orientation to normal and unusual life crises and crisis intervention. Basic knowledge of normal family and group dynamics. Working knowledge of community organization, structure and function. Functional knowledge of social and cultural determinants of human behavior. And a reasonable working armamentarium in social system intervention.

25.51 The intent of this preparation is to equip the pastor to deal with social systems at several levels — to equip him to become an enabler and catalyst. Unfortunately, clinical pastoral education has prepared the pastor to do more things himself, as counselor, group leader, community organizer. But that is a dead-end in systems theory. One man by himself does not go very far. The pastor who does it all himself soon runs out of gas. 'If only I had the time.'

25.52 The whole perspective of systems theory is based on existent and continuing social systems. Those systems become the object of major concern. We are much more deliberate in this than mere administration. We are describing a mode of operation that produces self-sustaining, effective systems of human relations. The aim of pastoral care then is to produce a pastor who is capable of dealing effectively with social systems for which he is 'shepherd'.[12]

25.53 From this perspective we may then seek to train pastors who can enable the church to become a center of moral enquiry, a center for personal learning and growth, a center for human sustenance and nourishment, and a center for human reparation. The pastor will not do this himself. He will work to craft a social system that performs the above system functions.

25.54 It also follows that a pastor who is a shepherd of systems will seek to place his given social system (church) in context as a subsystem vis-à-vis other major subsystems, neighborhood, community, city-state, nation, and world.

25.55 All of this may seem a big order — as indeed it is. The case may be overstated. But it may be that the historical tradition of clinical pastoral care with its focus on the individual and his vicissitudes may also be an overstatement. Clinical pastoral care has looked at the trees. I shall coin a new phrase — 'systems pastoral care'. It is to call attention to the configuration of the forest.

Notes

2. T. W. Klink, C. W. Stewart, and E. E. Thornton, 'Ministry: 1970 — and a Journal in Search of a Name', *Journal of Pastoral Care*, 1970, **24**, 1–3. Also background and perspective are found in the following: C. E. Hall, Jr, 'New Thrusts for the Association for Clinical Pastoral Education', *Ibid.*, 1968, **22**, 203–205; P. E. Johnson, 'Fifty Years of Clinical Pastoral Education', *Ibid.*, 1968, **22**, 223–231; and E. E. Thornton, 'Some Hard Questions for Clinical Pastoral Education', *Ibid.*, 1968, **22**, 194–202.

3. E. M. Pattison, 'Social and Psychological Aspects of Religion in Psychotherapy', *Journal of Nervous and Mental Diseases*, 1966, **141**, 586–597.

4. E. M. Pattison (Ed.). *Clinical Psychiatry and Religion* (Boston: Little, Brown, 1969); 'The Chaplain in Community Mental Health: Agent of Program and Community', *Association of Mental Hospital Chaplains Newsletter*, 1970, **23**, 14–25; 'An Overview of the Church's Roles in Community Mental Health' in *Community Mental Health: The Role of Church and Temple*, ed. by H. J. Clinebell, Jr (Nashville: Abingdon Press, 1970), Chap. 1, pp. 20–27.

5. A general introduction can be found in the following recent books: F. K. Berrien, *General and Social Systems* (New Brunswick, N.J.: Rutgers University Press, 1968); C. W. Churchman, *The Systems Approach* (New York: Delacourt Press, 1968); K. de Greene, *Systems Psychology* (New York: McGraw-Hill, 1970); M. D. Mesarovic, *Views on General Systems Theory* (New York: Wiley, 1964); T. Parsons and E. A. Shils (Eds), *Toward a General Theory of Action* (Cambridge, Mass.: Harvard University Press, 1951); H. M. Proshansky, W. M. Ittelson, and L. G. Rivlin, *Environmental Psychology* (San Francisco: Holt, Rinehart, and Winston, 1970); L. von Bertalanffy, *General Systems Theory* (New York: Braziller, 1968); J. M. Yinger, *Toward a Field Theory of Behavior* (New York: McGraw-Hill, 1965).

6. E. M. Pattison, 'Social System Psychotherapy', *American Journal of Psychotherapy* (in press). Other examples of clinical implications are found in these books: W. Gray, F. Duhl, and N. Rizzo (Eds), *General*

Systems Theory and Psychiatry (Boston: Little, Brown, 1969); R. R. Grinker (Ed.), *Toward a Unified Theory of Human Behavior* (New York: Basic Books, 1957).

7. E. M. Pattison, 'Residency Training Issues in Community Psychiatry', *American Journal of Psychiatry* (in press).

8. P. Rieff, *The Triumph of the Therapeutic: Uses of Faith after Freud* (New York: Harper and Row, 1966).

9. This point is the main focus of a new book: J. M. Gustafson, *The Church as Moral Decision-Maker* (New York: Pilgrim Press, 1970). See also E. M. Pattison, 'The Development of Values in Children', *Pastoral Psychology*, 1969, **20**, 14–23.

10. M. Rokeach, The H. Paul Douglass Lectures for 1969: Part I. 'Value Systems in Religion'. Part II. 'Religious Values and Social Compassion', *Review of Religious Research*, 1969, **11**, 3–40.

11. E. M. Pattison, 'Group Psychotherapy and Group Methods in Community Mental Health', *International Journal of Group Psychotherapy*, 1970, **20**, 516–539; L. A. Gottschalk and E. M. Pattison, 'Psychiatric Perspectives on T-Groups and the Laboratory Movement: An Overview', *American Journal of Psychiatry*, 1969, **126**, 823–839: E. M. Pattison, 'The Role of Adjunctive Therapies in Community Mental Health Center Programs', *Therapeutic Recreation Journal*, 1969, **3**, 16–25.

12. A few of many possible citations in the pastoral care literature will indicate how these concepts are being implemented in pastoral care: T. W. Klink, 'Epidemiology and Prevention in Pastoral Work', *Journal of Pastoral Care*, 1967, **21**, 220–228: T. W. Klink, 'An Experiential Introduction to Social Systems', *Journal of Religion and Health*, 1971, **10**, 346–358: W. E. Hulme, 'Concern for Corporate Structures or Care for the Individual?' *Journal of Pastoral Care*, 1969, **23**, 153–163: W. R. Voelkel, 'Creating Human Environment: Mission for the Seventies', *Journal of Pastoral Care*, 1970, **24**, 14–29: H. Seifert and H. J. Clinebell, Jr, *Personal Growth and Social Change* (Philadelphia: Westminster Press, 1969).

26

Robert Bocock
Religious Ritual in the Church of England

This Extract comes from chapter 4 of Robert Bocock's *Ritual in Industrial Society: A Sociological Analysis of Ritualism in Modern England* (George Allen and Unwin, 1974). He was at the time lecturer in sociology at Brunel University. This book seeks to distinguish between four 'types' of ritual: religious (the subject of this Extract), civic, life-cycle, and aesthetic. Whilst admitting that there are obvious links between these four types, he argues that the 'usefulness of the analytical distinction lies in making it possible to identify the elements of actual ritual action, and to make the richness of some ritual action more comprehensible' (p. 48). It is this which he considers to be one of the main services of sociologists looking at liturgy and worship. For Bocock, 'all ritual action is distinguished from other types of action on the basis of the action being oriented to sacred or charismatic objects (material things, persons, or animals), that is objects which are set apart from the profane world, the everyday world of routine and utilitarian action' (p. 60). By adding the term 'charismatic' Bocock adds to Durkheim's understanding of ritual: he broadly accepts Durkheim's distinction between the 'sacred' and the 'profane' as distinguishing specifically religious ritual (*26.5*), but includes 'charismatic' to cover civic forms of ritual which do not involve a specifically sacred object (e.g. army parades). This allows him to avoid the tautology of Durkheim, whereby religion and society become almost interchangeable (cf. *8.5f.*), but still to see connections between religious and other forms of ritual. A clear connection in this Extract can be seen in the way Bocock applies Weber's concept of the routinisation of charisma (see *Extract 2*) to Durkheim's concept of the sacred (*26.9*). In addition, in a changing society which has little contact with formal religious ritual, the Church of England still supplies a life-cycle ritual for the population of England (*26.12*). Bocock then provides an account of the Eucharist, the Stations of the Cross, and the feast of Corpus Christi, from this perspective of the sociology of ritual (*26.14–21*). His account of the last two can be compared usefully with Turner's understanding of the social role of pilgrimage (*Extract 27*).

26.1 'Liturgy' will be used here to refer to the whole complex of ritual actions in the narrower sense of specific acts, such as making the sign of the cross, together with readings from the sacred scriptures, singing hymns and psalms, prayers and sermons which make up acts of worship. During the 1960s the Church of England, along with other Churches, has been revising its liturgy. There are a number of experiments going on at present with these revised liturgies in various churches, where the vicar and church council have agreed to try them for a period of time. This period of change has been problematic for some members of the laity, for it makes it very clear that liturgies are man-made, they are not absolute for all time, nor God-given. It is particularly problematic for some of the Anglo-Catholic congregations who have previously looked to the Roman Catholic Church as the authority and standard in these matters and have found the Roman Church changing its liturgical forms; and rules. For example, catholics in the Church of England had always paid a great deal of attention to fasting before taking communion, but the Church of Rome relaxed its rules on this matter when it introduced evening mass, and requires those taking communion to fast for one hour only before communion. The traditional rule had been not to eat anything before taking communion on the *day* of communion, hence the early morning communion, or mass, in the Church of England.[1]

26.2 In the process of liturgical reform there is a stress on the importance of both 'religious ritual' and 'civic ritual' where the church congregation is the reference. For example, the stress on the value of a general communion of all at the Eucharist has the intended consequences of increasing awareness of the collectivity assembled together (civic ritual).

26.3 One of the unintended consequences of the reform is to focus attention on the impact the liturgy makes on the congregation. Its efforts on them becomes a major criterion for judging changes. This will in turn entail more concentration on what has been termed here 'civic ritual' where the group becomes the major object of concern and symbolism is interpreted in relation to the group. 'Religious ritual' would be judged by the criterion of its relevance to the worship of the Holy; this may mean in practice examining whether a particular liturgy has been used by the Church in the past, and whether it has a capacity to evoke spiritual feeling of the Holy in those regarded as most competent to judge this in the Church at a particular period. There is an appeal to both traditional authority — the undivided Catholic Church of early Christianity — and to the charismatic authority of contemporary liturgical specialists.

26.4 The liturgical changes which have been made in the Roman Church and in the Anglican Churches have been concerned to reduce the element of 'natural religion'[2] and of 'mystery cult' in the services of the Church, and to introduce changes that symbolise and evoke the view of the Church as a 'sacred community', with a participating laity, instead of the reliance on the words and actions of the priest alone. Thus the westward-facing position for Mass emphasises and symbolises the priest as representative of the community of believers, in place of the mystery cultus figure far away at the altar, with his back to the congregation. The Kiss of Peace, which involves the priest taking the hands of fellow priests and servers around the altar, and the congregation doing the same action, stresses the brotherly love of the Christian community, and the value of 'Peace which passes all understanding'.

26.5 Having established that religious ritual is distinct from ritual in which the group is the focus of worship, it is necessary to look in more detail at how religious ritual is itself differentiated, how it is produced and sustained, and what its effects are on the participants. Here the work of Durkheim and his group, especially H. Hubert and M. Mauss, is a useful starting point, even though the fundamental assumption of Durkheim, that religious ritual has the group as its focus always, has been rejected. Durkheim's fundamental distinction between the sacred and the profane is an important starting point. His claim that such a distinction can be found in all religions may not be entirely true of every human group studied by Western anthropologists, but it is certainly very widespread empirically, and has not disappeared in modern industrial society. Religion is built fundamentally on this division between sacred and profane things, places, times, people; they radically exclude each other. Sacred things are set apart by interdictions, and negative rites, from profane things.[3] Durkheim goes on to distinguish religion from magic in terms of the nature of the relation between those who use a magician, as relatively isolated individuals seeking help on specific issues, and those in the same religious group united into a Church, a single moral community.[4]

26.6 There are difficulties in using Durkheim's distinction in the way he formulated it in examining a Church such as the modern Anglican Church, and even the Roman Catholic Church, in that their new liturgies are not built on the basis of ideas which make the same radical distinction which Durkheim suggests between sacred and profane. Rather, the new liturgies rest on the idea of bringing the common and the holy together. 'The marks of the liturgy in future are likely to be informality, flexibility and continuity with ordinary life-style, so that there is no forced sense of stepping out of one world into another, no compulsory cultural circumcision as one "enters church".[5] Here there are complex theological issues involved about the nature of Christianity and its ultimate aims; suffice it to say that there has always been a push towards making the common holy, sanctifying the secular, and breaking out of the rather rigid sacred–profane dichotomy as formulated by Durkheim.

26.7 Organised religious groups in Christianity have nevertheless had a tendency towards this separation of sacred and profane, and the Church of England still had this in modern England. Anglicans, like other denominations, still dress in their 'best' clothing when they attend church, and the atmosphere in most Anglican churches is one of separation from the ordinary world, especially in those with stained glass windows and organs playing. The new ideas of liturgy are still ideas of the religious virtuosi, although some younger members of congregations often welcome change from the old style of 'sacred' services.

26.8 In order to understand more adequately what is happening today in religious ritual it is necessary to develop the Durkheimian distinction more fully, and in some respects rather differently. Thomas O'Dea distinguishes eight characteristics of Durkheim's notion of the sacred: it has superior seriousness and dignity when compared with the profane; it involves the recognition of a power or force behind nature and cosmos, attractive and repugnant, helpful and dangerous to me; it is non-utilitarian, non-empirical and does not involve knowledge, but rests on feelings and experiences of a non-sensory kind; it gives support and strength to the worshippers; and finally, it impinges on human consciousness with moral obligation. O'Dea goes on to suggest that this set of characteristics is remarkably similar to Rudolf Otto's analysis of the holy, the numinous experiences. It is remarkable because Durkheim is normally seen as a positivist, and yet here, his analysis of the sacred experience in life is described in more phenomenological terms, and with results very like those of more 'religious' phenomenologists such as Otto and G. van der Leeuw. For Otto the holy is not just the very good, but independent of our moral notions initially; and it is also non-rational. It is 'wholly other', quite beyond the usual, the intelligible and the familiar. What is involved is the 'element of majesty or absolute overpoweringness' and it evokes a 'peculiar dread' but is at the same time attactive and inviting to the beholder.

> The coincidence of many strategic elements of the analysis of Durkheim's and Otto's treatment of the sacred, or holy, is worthy of our attention. These elements are the extraordinary character of the phenomenon, its implication of power, its ambiguity in relation to man, its awesome character and the feeling of dependence it arouses.[6]

26.9 This experience of the sacred is fundamental to organised religion, but the latter has ritualised the relationship with the sacred powers, the Holy, in ways which, as O'Dea has argued, can never be final. Yet religious experience tends to lead to the formation of specifically religious groups, partly through the process Max Weber termed the routinisation of charisma. The notion of 'charisma' is very closely linked with the idea of the 'sacred' and the 'holy' as outlined.[7] A person who has had a very fundamental religious experience or encounter with the holy may become the founder of a new religious group which may be contained within existing organisational frameworks, like Saint Francis, or lead to new organisations, such as happened with Luther, Calvin and John Wesley. The process of new religious groups emerging involves the idea of 'religious virtuosity' as Weber called the quality possessed by people with a peculiar 'ear' for the holy, and sacred experience.[8] Such people will tend to develop a following in their own lifetime, which may or may not lead to a new and long-lasting religious organisation with its own rituals to evoke the peculiar religious experience with which the original founder was primarily concerned.

26.10 There are more studies of breakaway religious movements which later become organisations than of the ways such new experiences are contained within a Church. Catholics are more prone to remain within the church structures if possible than are Protestants, because they believe that the Church is not just a man-made organisation, but a sacred one, with the power to dispense grace through its sacraments. The Anglican Church sought to contain some religious virtuosi, and has been relatively more successful with those with a Catholic type of theology than with a Protestant one. When Newman left the Anglican Church, there was not a mass exodus of Anglo-Catholics, but rather a consolidation of the new ideas centring to some extent around Pusey. Joachim Wach's work contains a useful typology for examining the ways in which new charismatic movements can be contained within the Church — Ecclesiola in ecclesia is the main category for Protest movements within a Church, with three sub-categories: the Collegium pietatis; the Fraternitas; and the Monastic Order.[9]

26.11 The ritualists within the Church of England, and especially those with Socialist political views, were the most important recent example of such a movement in the last hundred years.[10] More recently there has been the liturgical movement, and the new theology of the Bishop of Woolwich, John Robinson, now in the University of Cambridge. This movement has been contained within the Church of England.

26.12 Many people in any society undergoing a large degree of social change, such as modern England, will find that the organised religious groups do not provide for their experience of the sacred, the holy dimension, assuming that they are in contact with it all. In England there is still considerable use made of life-cycle rituals provided by the Church of England, and almost no one dies without some kind of religious ritual being performed after their death. Even the old who die without any known family are buried, or cremated, with a religious functionary performing a religious rite of burial. In other, more regular, forms of worship the social class differences between the people living in England are basic to the formation of congregations at specific churches, and in affecting who stays away from church altogether. Young people who have had drug experiences often turn to various forms of oriental religion, as more in keeping with their 'religious' experiences. Apart from this exception and obviously that of ethnic minorities, class differences seem to be the most important in England in creating such different values and ways of life, that worshipping together is not easy, or even possible. The Church of England is a Church of the upper classes and the middle classes, and very rarely do working-class people attend its regular services of worship. Where they do, it is in parishes with a sense of community among the working class themselves. Ordinary working people are the church wardens, and fill the other lay offices in such parishes. Where there are middle-class people in a parish, they will tend to dominate and fill the lay offices in the parish system, and the working-class people come to feel left out, and do not go regularly to the services.[11]

26.13 There are some ritual acts which are still central to Christianity, and which have not changed basically for at least two thousand years. The use of water at baptism is one such, which is discussed in the chapter on life-cycle rituals. The other basic act is that of taking bread and wine, blessing them in some way, and breaking and eating the bread and drinking the wine, among the members of the congregation.

> Was ever another command so obeyed? For century after century, spreading slowly to every continent and country and among every race on earth, this action has been done, in every conceivable human circumstance, for every conceivable human need from infancy and before it to extreme old age and after it, from the pinnacles of earthly greatness to the refuge of fugitives in the caves and dens of the earth. Men have found no better thing than this to do for kings at their crowning and for criminals going to the scaffold; for armies in triumph or for a bride and bridegroom in a little country church; for the proclamation of a dogma or a good crop of wheat; for the wisdom of the Parliament of a mighty nation or for a sick old woman afraid to die; for a schoolboy sitting an examination or for Columbus setting out to discover America; for the famine of whole provinces or for the soul of a dead lover; in thankfulness because my father did not die of pneumonia;

for a village headman much tempted to return to fetich because the yams had failed; because the Turk was at the gates of Vienna; for the repentance of Margaret; for the settlement of a strike; for a son for a barren woman; for Captain so-and-so, wounded and prisoner of war; while the lions roared in the nearby amphitheatre; on the beach at Dunkirk; while the hiss of scythes in the thick June grass came faintly through the windows of the church; tremulously, by an old monk on the fiftieth anniversary of his vows; furtively, by an exiled bishop who had hewn timber all day in a prison camp near Murmansk; gorgeously for the canonisation of St Joan of Arc — one could fill many pages with the reasons why men have done this, and not tell a hundredth part of them. And best of all, week by week and month by month, on a hundred thousand successive Sundays, faithfully, unfailingly, across all the parishes of christendom, the pastors have done this just to make the *plebs Sancta Dei* — the holy common people of God.[12]

26.14 Theological interpretations of this act have varied, and still do, but the ritual seems to continue as basic to Christian groups. The actions surrounding it vary from time and place, but the basic act is usually recognisable. The central theological problem has been about the nature of the act, whether it is a new sacrifice each time it is done, or a remembrance of one sacrifice, that of Jesus. As Durkheim points out in his study of Australian aborigines' religion, '. . . a *sacrifice* is composed of two essential elements; an act of communion and an act of oblation. The worshipper communes with his god by taking in a sacred food, and at the same time he makes an offering to his god. We find these two acts in the Intichiuma . . .'[13] Given this as the definition of 'sacrifice', then the Anglican ritual of the Eucharist, or Holy Communion, is a sacrifice, for sociological purposes. It contains the two essential actions, the eating of sacred food in the actual communion itself, which is believed by some to be the body and blood of Christ present in some way in the bread and wine, and is thus an eating of a human sacrifice as well as a communion with God. The congregation also make an act of oblation, symbolised in the giving of money during the collection, and the offering of the bread and wine at the altar, which is often done by two members of the congregation to make the point clearer that the laity are giving these. The priest says, over these objects on the altar — 'Pray, brethren, that this our sacrifice may be acceptable to God the Father Almighty'. The people: 'May the Lord accept the sacrifice to the praise and glory of His name for our good also, and for that of all His holy church' (Series 2), And during the Prayer of Consecration — 'And here we offer and present unto thee, O Lord, ourselves, our souls and bodies, to be a reasonable, holy and lively sacrifice unto thee: . . .'.

26.15 This sacrificial act is the centre of the worship of the Christian Church, and has been for nearly two thousand years, and will continue to be, no doubt, whatever the future of the organisations at present called the Church. Such ritual acts of sacrifice are extremely ancient, existing long before written, sacred texts, as can be seen from the Australian aborigine societies. There seems every reason for thinking that the same basic type of ritual act will continue in the future in most human societies. It may not be specifically Christian always, but the symbolism of sacrifice is basic to man's psychic life, and to his social life, as Durkheim maintained. There are civic rituals which attempt to motivate men to make sacrifices for a social group, such as the rallies of political movements, various expressions of nationalism, and army rituals. Civic rituals of this type are not, analytically, part of the sacred. Often, historically, they have been, of course, in that the Christian Church has been involved in persuading men to die for their country, or for a prince, or a group of rulers, as part of their duty to God, and their sacrifice to Him. Communist societies are able to motivate people without an appeal to the old gods, and it may be that neither Church nor Party can do this without people feeling motivated in some ways independently of such ideological appeals. The latter may serve rather as legitimating ideologies. Nevertheless, they are important, for without such legitimation it is difficult to keep up the momentum in a war, for example. Within Christianity there has always been a minority who have claimed that their allegiance to the faith does not allow them to kill anyone at all, and most societies have been forced to recognise this claim sooner or later. 'Sacrifice' in this context is interpreted by the believer to mean risking persecution for his pacifism.

26.16 Even communist societies have not been able to fully eradicate some section of their populations from wanting to meet as a religious group to perform some act of sacrifice and worship. These meetings are potentially a threat to any totalitarian regime of the Western or Eastern blocs in Europe, for they can lead to values and action stemming from the religious group and its experience which are contrary to those of the ruling élites in those societies.

26.17 Within Anglican Catholicism, there is a rite derived from both modern Roman Catholic sources and from the pre-Reformation English Church, which is more clearly a *commemorative ritual* than the Eucharist, or Mass, which as has been said is a sacrifice.[14] *The Stations of the Cross* is a mythic drama, portrayed in pictures, of the events of the Founder's torture and death. It involves people moving from one station to another, praying at each of fourteen images of a scene from the Passion of Jesus. Such commemorative rites in Christianity are primarily religious rituals. There are civic rituals of a similar type, both of national heroes, such as Henry VIII, portrayed in a recent television series in England, and of a political party type, the most important case being Lenin in his tomb in Moscow and the ritual events which take place, such as pilgrimage, past his tomb.

26.18 Another set of rituals which have been revived by Anglican Catholics in the Church of England during this century, derive from their conception of the Real Presence of Christ in the consecrated bread, from the Eucharist. One central and controversial issue has centred around the *Reservation of the Blessed Sacrament*. When Anglican Catholic clergy first introduced it, the practice was condemned by bishops, unless it was for the purpose of communion of the sick.[15] However, many of the Anglican Catholics also introduced ritual acts of Adoration of the Blessed Sacrament, in a service called '*Benediction*' in which the congregation is blessed by the priest holding the bread, after a series of ritual devotions have been made in front of the tabernacle in which the bread is kept, with a light always in front of it. The practice of Reservation has spread quite widely within the Church of England in the last few decades; for example, in a cathedral in one of the areas used for participant observation for this study, the Reservation of the Sacrament has been introduced in the 1960s, and people pray in front of it, although there is no service of Benediction, which is considered theologically suspect. This is because it can lead people to attend Benedictions, rather than take communion at a Eucharist. (Sometimes Benediction is at a more convenient time, namely early evening, after Evensong. Roman Catholics can now go to Evening Mass, a practice not very widespread in Anglican churches at present, i.e. 1973.)

26.19 *The Feast of Corpus Christi*, with its procession of the Blessed Sacrament through the streets of the parish, was also introduced by clergy who were committed to the dogma of the Real Presence. This is a feast for Thanksgiving for the institution of the sacrament of Holy Communion which is not done on the Eve of Good Friday itself, for the ritual for Maundy Thursday is, if anything, the Washing of Feet.

26.20 Holy Communion or the Eucharist, as the central ritual act of Christianity, is worth examining further in terms of the effects it may have on the participants through its symbolism and emotional structure. It is partly a ritual in which people hear the Word of God, through the reading of the Bible, and through the sermon. The first part of the revised liturgy in the Church of England is termed the Ministry of the Word, followed by the other sections of the rite. The sermon is usually seen as a teaching situation, in which the congregation is taught something of the faith, based on the gospel of the day. This may be ethical in its orientation, or more 'spiritual'. Usually, though, there are implications from the gospel and the sermon, and sometimes in the epistle, and the lesson from the Old Testament when this is used, which are meant to affect people's behaviour in the world morally. There are here, therefore, the moral implications of the 'sacred' which Durkheim mentions as being one of the important consequences of worshippers' participation in the sacred area, through ritual. This does not necessarily mean that people live up to their ideals and moral values but that they are guided by them, and by the preacher's interpretations to some extent. The value implications of the gospels are often seen in terms of middle-class radical-liberalism, in the churches where the most articulate preachers are heard. Full conservatism, like full-bodied socialism, is much rarer, but the latter is if anything growing as a political position among clergy.

26.21 The rest of the rite is concerned with the preparation of people, and the bread and wine, for the act of communion. At a Mass during which incense is used there is a point in the rite where the priests and congregations are censed, after the offertory and before the consecration section begins. This is a clear ritual act in which all the things, and people, involved in the ritual action to follow, are shown symbolically to be able to approach the 'sacred'. The ritual of censing is not essential; the prayers, and being present for the first section, seem enough to allow the people and clergy to contact the sacred. In some churches holy water is used at the beginning of the rite in a ritual called the Asperges, in which the priest walks through the congregation sprinkling them with holy water. Again this is not essential. The *confession* of sin by the congregation is. There is a public confession before the consecration and communion, and individuals in the Church of England may go for individual confession before the service if they wish. The rubric on confession is 'None must, all may, some should'. After either private or general confession, the people are blessed and forgiven their sins. They are thus able to be brought into contact with the sacred itself, the consecrated bread and wine, believed by the Catholic groups to be the Body and Blood of Christ; in some sense an instance of God incarnate in the world now. For some this is almost a literal truth, for others it is a more symbolic truth. In any case it is the most sacred ritual of the Church; the consecration, the breaking of the bread, and communion.

Notes

1 See I. Clutterbuck *What's happening to Our Discipline* (Church Union, Church Literature Association, London — no date, but late 1960s).
2 For this term see M. Weber *The Sociology of Religion* (Methuen, London 1965) chapters II and X.
3 E. Durkheim *The Elementary Forms of the Religious Life* (Collier Books, by arrangement with Free Press, New York 1961) book 1, chapter 1, section 3.
4 ibid., section 4.
5 J. A. Robinson *Christian Freedom in a Permissive Society* (S.C.M. Press, London 1970) p. 162 of paperback edition.
6 T. O'Dea *Sociology of Religion* (Prentice-Hall, Englewood Cliffs, New Jersey 1966) quotation p. 21.
7 See. T. Parsons *The Structure of Social Action* (Free Press of Glencoe, New York 1937) chapter XVII, section IV on Max Weber, 'Ritual', pp. 637–7 of the 1964 printing.
   See also R. Nisbet *The Sociological Tradition* (Heinemann, London 1967) chapter 6.
8 Max Weber *The Sociology of Religion* (1922, German edition; 1963, Beacon Press; 1965 Methuen, London).
9 J. Wach *Sociology of Religion* (University of Chicago Press, 1944).
10 See R. J. Bocock, 'Anglo-Catholic Socialism: A Study of a Protest Movement within a Church' in *Social Compass*, vol. XX, 1973.
11 See, for example, D. B. Clark *Survey of Anglicans and Methodists in Four Towns* (Epworth Press, London 1965) and R. Frankenberg *Village on the Border* (Routledge & Kegan Paul, London 1957).
12 Dom Gregory Dix *The Shape of the Liturgy* (A. & C. Black, London 1945) p. 744.
13 Durkheim op. cit. (note 3) book 3, chapter 2, section 4.
14 ibid., book 3, chapter 4.
15 See, for example, M. Reynolds *Martyr of Ritualism* (Faber, London 1965). About the trials of Fr MacKonochie of St Albans, Holborn, London, in the 1860s.

27

Victor Turner
Pilgrimage as a Liminoid Phenomenon

In this Extract, from the introduction of *Image and Pilgrimage in Christian Culture* (Columbia, 1978), the distinguished American anthropologist Victor Turner (together with his wife Edith who carried out much of the library and field research) views Roman Catholic pilgrimages from a specifically anthropological perspective. He outlines the key concept of 'liminality' (*27.1–5*), which a number of social scientists have used to denote a time or stage of crisis, transition and potentiality that is so crucial to individual and cultural change (religious conversion, for example, can be analysed in terms of liminality). He points to the ways tribal societies have sought to control this liminality and contrasts this with situations in European societies (*27.6f.*). He then looks at ways pilgrimages can be seen as occasions related to liminality. In the discussion not included in this Extract he sets this discussion into a wider anthropological setting as a prelude to the detailed studies of Mexican, Irish and mediaeval pilgrimages that form the main part of the book. However, in the second part of the Extract he concludes his introduction with an examination of some of the social differences between Catholics and Protestants (*27.9f.*) Some of the key theological and political differences that constitute the varying social and cultural contexts of pilgrimages are isolated. Of particular interest for this Reader are the way differing theological stances shape attitudes towards rituals, the links and tensions between popular piety and official orthodoxy, and the transposition of elements of the pilgrimage into supposedly secular society. Victor Turner held the William R. Kenan Jr chair of anthropology at the University of Virginia at the time of his death in 1983.

27.1 Pilgrimages are probably of ancient origin and can, indeed, be found among peoples classed by some anthropologists as 'tribal', peoples such as the Huichol, the Lunda, and the Shona. But pilgrimage as an institutional form does not attain real prominence until the emergence of the major historical religions —

Hinduism, Buddhism, Judaism, Christianity, and Islam. In view of its importance in the actual functioning of these religious, both quantitatively and qualitatively, pilgrimage has been surprisingly neglected by historians and social scientists. But perhaps it has merely shared in the general disregard of the liminal and marginal phenomena of social process and cultural dynamics by those intent either upon the description and classification of orderly institutionalized 'facts' or upon the establishment of the 'historicity' of prestigious, unrepeated events.

27.2 It was Arnold van Gennep (1908; 1960), the French folklorist and ethnographer neglected by the pundits, savants, and mandarins of the French school of sociology in his own time, who gave us the first clues about how ancient and tribal societies conceptualized and symbolized the transitions men have to make between well-defined states and statuses, if they are to grow up to accommodate themselves to unprecedented, even antithetical conditions. He showed us that all *rites de passage* (rites of transition) are marked by three phases: separation, limen or margin, and aggregation. The first phase comprises symbolic behavior signifying the detachment of the individual or group, either from an earlier fixed point in the social structure or from a relatively stable set of cultural conditions (a cultural 'state'); during the intervening liminal phase, the state of the ritual subject (the 'passenger' or 'liminar') becomes ambiguous, he passes through a realm or dimension that has few or none of the attributes of the past or coming state, he is betwixt and between all familiar lines of classification; in the third phase the passage is consummated, and the subject returns to classified secular or mundane social life. The ritual subject, individual or corporate (groups, age-sets, and social categories can also undergo transition), is again in a stable state, has rights and obligations of a clearly defined structural type, and is expected to behave in accordance with the customary norms and ethical standards appropriate to his new settled state.

27.3 By identifying liminality Van Gennep discovered a major innovative, transformative dimension of the social. He paved the way for future studies of all processes of spatiotemporal social or individual change. For liminality cannot be confined to the processual form of the traditional rites of passage in which he first identified it. Nor can it be dismissed as an undesirable (and certainly uncomfortable) movement of variable duration between successive conservatively secure states of being, cognition, or status-role incumbency. Liminality is now seen to apply to all phases of decisive cultural change, in which previous orderings of thought and behavior are subject to revision and criticism, when hitherto unprecedented modes of ordering relations between ideas and people become possible and desirable. Van Gennep made his discovery in relatively conservative societies, but its implications are truly revolutionary. In the liminality of tribal societies, traditional authority nips radical deviation in the bud. We find there symbolic inversion of social roles, the mirror-imaging of normative secular paradigms; we do not find open-endedness, the possibility that the freedom of thought inherent in the very principle of liminality could lead to major reformulation of the social structure and the paradigms which program it. But in the limina throughout actual history, when sharp divisions begin to appear between the root paradigms which have guided social action over long tracts of time and the antiparadigmatic behavior of multitudes responding to totally new pressures and incentives, we tend to find the prolific generation of new experimental models — utopias, new philosophical systems, scientific hypotheses, political programs, art forms, and the like — among which reality-testing will result in the cultural 'natural selection' of those best fitted to make intelligible, and give form to, the new contents of social relations.

27.4 It has become clear to us that liminality is not only *transition* but also *potentiality*, not only 'going to be' but also 'what may be', a formulable domain in which all that is not manifest in the normal day-to-day operation of social structures (whether on account of social repression or because it is rendered cognitively 'invisible' by prestigious paradigmatic denial) can be studied objectively, despite the often bizarre and metaphorical character of its contents. In *The Ritual Process* (V. Turner 1969), certain modes of liminality in preindustrial society were examined, and further studies in more developed cultures were suggested. The present book is an attempt to examine in some detail what we consider to be one characteristic type of liminality in cultures ideologically dominated by the 'historical', or 'salvation', religions.

27.5 When we first began to look for ritual analogues between 'archaic', or 'tribal', and 'historical' religious liminality, beginning with the Catholic Christian tradition which we know best, we turned, naturally enough, to the ceremonies of the Roman rite. But in the liturgical ceremonies of the Mass, baptism, female purification, confirmation, nuptials, ordination, extreme unction, and funerary rituals, though it was possible to discern somewhat truncated liminal phases, we found nothing that replicated the scale and complexity of liminality in the major initiation rituals of the tribal societies with which we were familiar. One obvious difference was seen in the spatial location of liminality. In many tribal societies, initiands are secluded in a sacralized enclosure, or *temenos*, clearly set apart from the villages, markets, pastures, and gardens of everyday usage and trafficking (see Junod 1962: vol. 1, pp. 74–94; Wilson 1957:86–129;

Richards 1957; Turner 1968:210–39; Barth 1975:47–102). But in the 'historical' religions, comparable seclusion has been exemplified only in the total life-style of the specialized religious orders. In other words, the progressive division of labor made of the liminal phase a specialized state, complex and intense enough to involve the entire lives of the deeply devoted. Of course, as the history of monasticism has shown, the orders become decreasingly liminal as they enter into manifold relations with the environing economic and political milieus. That, however, is matter for a different book. But the religious, though relatively numerous in the heyday of the historical religions, were easily outnumbered by the ordinary worshipers, the peasants and the citizens. Where was their liminality? Or was there indeed any liminality for them at all?

27.6 In European societies with a rurally based economy and feudal political structures, life for the masses tended to be intimately localized. Indeed, for Christian serfs and villeins the law itself ordained their attachment to particular manors or demesnes. Their religious life was also locally fixated; the parish was their spiritual manor. Yet during its development, Christianity generated its own mode of liminality for the laity. This mode was best represented by the pilgrimage to a sacred site or holy shrine located at some distance away from the pilgrim's place of residence and daily labor. Beginning with the pilgrimage to remote Jerusalem (*Palestine Pilgrims' Text Society*, 1887; 1889; 1891a,b,c; 1893) — made by a few choice, pious, and relatively well-to-do persons — to which was swiftly joined the pilgrimage to the shrines of Peter and Paul in Rome (Jusserand 1891:374–78; Sigal 1974:99–110), the map of Europe, particularly after the Saracenic occupation of the Holy Land and domination of the Mediterranean sea routes thither, came to be crisscrossed with pilgrim ways and trails to the shrines of European saints and advocations of the Holy Virgin (varieties of mode of address, such as Our Lady of Walsingham) and to churches containing important relics of Christ's ministry and passion (Turner 1974a: 224–26). Such pilgrim centers and ways, frequented increasingly by the poor, can be regarded as a complex surrogate for the journey to the source and heartland of the faith.

27.7 The pilgrim trails cut across the boundaries of provinces, realms, and even empires (Jusserand 1891:362–71, 393–95). In each nascent nation certain shrines became preeminent centers of legitimate devotion. But since the church laid claim to universality, pilgrims were encouraged to take up staff and scrip to travel to the great shrines in other Christian lands. In time this international religious tourist traffic became organized. (Venice became the model for later secular tourism, as well as for modern agencies of pilgrim travel.)[2] Many Englishmen made the pilgrimage to St James the Apostle's shrine in Spain, while French and Dutch pilgrims swarmed across the Channel to visit St Thomas's tomb at Canterbury. Within each country one can detect a loose hierarchy, or at least a rough scale of priorities, among its shrines. In plural societies, each linguistic or ethnic group has its favored pilgrimage places. Provinces, districts, even the shrines themselves, have their focal devotions. All sites of pilgrimage have this in common: they are believed to be places where miracles once happened, still happen, and may happen again. Even where the time of miraculous healings is reluctantly conceded to be past, believers firmly hold that faith is strengthened and salvation better secured by personal exposure to the beneficent unseen presence of the Blessed Virgin or the local saint, mediated through a cherished image or painting. Miracles or the revivification of faith are everywhere regarded as rewards for undertaking long, not infrequently perilous, journeys and for having temporarily given up not only the cares but also the rewards of ordinary life. Behind such journeys in Christendom lies the paradigm of the *via crucis*, with the added purgatorial element appropriate to fallen men. While monastic contemplatives and mystics could daily make interior salvific journeys, those in the world had to exteriorize theirs in the infrequent adventure of pilgrimage. For the majority, pilgrimage was the great liminal experience of the religious life. If mysticism is an interior pilgrimage, pilgrimage is exteriorized mysticism.

27.8 The point of it all is to get out, go forth, to a far holy place approved by all. In societies with few economic opportunities for movement away from limited circles of friends, neighbors, and local authorities, all rooted alike in the soil, the only journey possible for those not merchants, peddlers, minstrels, jugglers, tumblers, wandering friars, or outlaws, or their modern equivalents, is a holy journey, a pilgrimage or a crusade. On such a journey one gets away from the reiterated 'occasions of sin' which make up so much of the human experience of social structure. If one is tied by blood or edict to a given set of people in daily intercourse over the whole gamut of human activities — domestic, economic, jural, ritual, recreational, affinal, neighborly — small grievances over trivial issues tend to accumulate through the years, until they become major disputes over property, office, or prestige which factionalize the group. One piles up a store of nagging guilts, not all of which can be relieved in the parish confessional, especially when the priest himself may be party to some of the conflicts. When such a load can no longer be borne, it is time to take the road as a pilgrim. . . .

2

27.9 The development of a pilgrimage may be accelerated or retarded by the intellectual and political climate. Just on the point of flourishing, for example, a pilgrimage may be denounced and destroyed by representatives of church or state, or even by revolutionary groups who see it as an organ of church or state. Pilgrimage systems are peculiarly vulnerable in that they do not have their own means to defend themselves by force. But they have one immense advantage: unless a pilgrimage center is systematically discredited and destroyed, the believing masses will continue to make their way to the shrine. Mexico provides many examples of the perseverance of pilgrims in the teeth of antireligious governmental pressures. Some call this inertia, others faith, but the fact remains that on the great feast days pilgrimage centers have never been so crowded as today. Thus, a popular pilgrimage, supported by a range of homeostatic institutions, both formal and customary, may long resist the countervailing tendencies of an unpropitious environment. Something in the human condition, particularly as it is exemplified in the poor, responds to the root paradigms which nest within one another in any great pilgrimage. Regardless of the progress of the division of labor, the nature and degree of social stratification, the division between urban and rural milieus, and the distribution of wealth and property, human beings are subject to disease and death, and experience guilt as a result of their dealings with one another. From all these ills and sins, pilgrimage systems furnish relief — as well as the increased prospect of ultimate salvation, since the performance of pilgrimage is considered by Catholics to be a supereminently good work. Pilgrimage provides a carefully structured, highly valued route to a liminal world where the ideal is felt to be real, where the tainted social persona may be cleansed and renewed.

27.10 It is significant that Calvin, who declared that pilgrimages 'aided no man's salvation', believed in predestination and shared the general Protestant emphasis on faith rather than good works as the key to salvation. The orthodox Catholic view, of course, has always been that no one can be sure of salvation until the very last gasp: on the one hand, the believer is plied with graces by God; on the other, he continually exerts his free will by accepting or rejecting them. Faith without good works is regarded as useless. Good works are performed in response to graces — the initiatives of God, who desires the salvation of all. Good works are defined as the 'observance of the precepts and counsels'. 'Precepts' are rules of life and conduct necessary for all who wish to obtain salvation. The Ten Commandments are examples of such rules. 'Counsels' are rules of life and conduct for those who, not satisfied with the bare minimum, aim at greater moral perfection by means of good works not commanded but commended — for example, abstinence from lawful pleasures. Observance of the counsels is held to be meritorious only if done out of a desire for salvation, rather than out of a wish to be highly regarded by one's fellow men. Protestantism, which professes justification by faith alone, naturally ignores the distinction between precepts and counsels. For Catholics, going on pilgrimage is a good work in response to a counsel. We mention this peculiarly Christian instance of theological infighting merely to emphasize that pilgrimage, though having initiatory features, is not, strictly speaking, an initiation rite (that is, 'an irreversible, singular ritual instrument for effecting a permanent, visible cultural transformation of the subject'). Pilgrimages resemble private devotions — like those to the Sacred Heart of Jesus or the Immaculate Heart of Mary — in their voluntary character, but differ from them in their public effect. The decision to go on pilgrimage takes place within the individual but brings him into fellowship with like-minded souls, both on the way and at the shrine. The social dimension is generated by the individual's choice, multiplied many times. On pilgrimage, social interaction is not governed by the old rules of social structure. When a pilgrimage system becomes established, however, it operates like other social institutions. The social takes precedence over the individual at all levels. Organized parties make the journey; devotions at the shrine are collective and according to the schedule. But pilgrimage is an individual good work, not a social enterprise. Pilgrimage, ideally, is charismatic, in the sense that pilgrim's decision to make it is a response to a charism, a grace, while at the same time he receives grace as he makes his devotions.

27.11 For this reason, orthodoxy in many religions tends to be ambivalent toward pilgrimage. The apparent capriciousness with which people make up their minds to visit a shrine, the rich symbolism and communitas quality of pilgrimage systems, the peripheral character of pilgrimage vis-à-vis the ritual or liturgical system as a whole, all make it suspect. Pilgrimage is too democratic, not sufficiently hierarchical. In Catholic Christianity the sacramental system does have something of the irreversible character of tribal rites of passage, giving direction to social and personal life, and coordinating sacred and secular processes. Baptism, confirmation, ordination to the priesthood, all are irreversible, once-only rites of passage, which are declared dogmatically to 'imprint an indelible character on the soul'. It is significant that the sacraments most closely associated with pilgrimage are the Eucharist and penance. Neither of these is a rite of passage, and both are indefinitely repeatable. These sacraments in one aspect form an admirable system of instruments of social control. This is not true of pilgrimages, at least in their early stages. As we shall see when considering historical cases, there is something inveterately populist, anarchical, even anticlerical, about pilgrimages in their very essence. They have at times been linked with popular nationalism, with peasant and anticolonial revolt, and with popular millenarianism. They tend to arise spontaneously, on the report that some miracle or apparition has occurred at a particular place, not always a place previously consecrated. Pilgrimages are an expression of the communitas dimension of any society, the spontaneity of interrelatedness, the spirit which bloweth where it listeth. From the point of view of those who control and maintain the social structure, all manifestations of communitas, sacred or profane, are potentially subversive. We shall see, in this connection, how religious specialists have attempted to domesticate the primitive, spontaneous modes of peregrination, with their freedom of communitas, into orderly pilgrimage, more susceptible to ecclesiastical control. Their model is the structured ritual system. Individual Catholic pilgrimages have in the course of time been transformed into extended and protracted forms of such sacraments as penance and the Eucharist. Their voluntaristic, even miraculous, essence has been subjugated to doctrinal and organisational edict. Their charism has been routinized; their communitas, structured. Nevertheless, like Etna, old pilgrimages are apt to revive unexpectedly; and new ones erupt like so many Paricutíns — indeed, miracles attributed to the crucifix rescued from Paricutín village in Mexico have made of its present refuge, the church in San Juan near Uruápan in Michoacán state, a new pilgrimage center!

27.12 There is no simple answer to the question of how pilgrimages begin. Some pilgrimages indeed have no traceable ultimate origin, but are known to antedate the historical religions with which they are currently associated. Other pilgrimage centers exist today which have been superimposed on known older centers, like scions on a stock. This is true not only for the Mexican Catholic shrines of Guadalupe, Ocotlán, Chalma, and Ízamal, pilgrimage sites, but also for such world-renowned centers as Mecca, Islam's 'navel of the world' (which was a pilgrim shrine long before Muhammad), and Jerusalem, frequented by Jewish pilgrims long before the birth of Christ. Wherever communitas has manifested itself often and on a large scale the possibility of its revival exists, even when linked to a different religious system. Recognition of this fact perhaps underlies Gregory the Great's injunction, via the monk Mellitus, to St Augustine of Canterbury, missionary to the Anglo-Saxons — to tolerate those pagan practices which were not directly repugnant to Christian notions of morality, and to attach them to some feature of Christian belief or practice. To this letter may be owed the preservation of many wells held sacred to pre-Christian deities, wells which were later incorporated into the shrine-complex of local Christian saints. Such a practice of incorporation is referred to colloquially as 'baptizing the customs'.

27.13 However, the oldest pilgrim centers of the historical religions are generally places mentioned in sacred narratives as connected with the birth, mission, and death of the founder and his closest kin and disciples. In Hinduism, pilgrim shrines are associated with the cults of deities. The sacred narratives are paradigms of the salvific process. They concern the relationship between the timeless message of the founder, whose words and works show how to obtain release from time's suffering or how to use it to one's eternal advantage, and the concrete circumstances of time and place. Believers in the message seek to imitate or to unite with the founder by replicating his actions, either literally or in spirit. Pilgrimage is one way, perhaps the most literal, of imitating the religious founder. By visiting the sites believed to be the scenes of his life and teaching mission, the pilgrim in imagination relives those events. As we have noted above, pilgrimage may be thought of as extroverted mysticism, just as mysticism is introverted pilgrimage. The pilgrim physically traverses a mystical way; the mystic sets forth on an interior spiritual pilgrimage. For the former, concreteness and historicity dominate; for the latter, a phased interior process leads to a goal beyond conceptualization. Both pilgrimage and mysticism escape the nets of social structure, and both have at various times been under attack by religious authorities. Pilgrimage has its inwardness, as anyone who has observed pilgrims before a shrine can attest; while mysticism has its outwardness, as evidenced by the energetic, practical lives of famous mystics such as St Theresa of Ávila, St Bernard of Clairvaux, St Catherine of Siena, William Law, al-Ghazali, and Mahatma Gandhi.

27.14 In the early stages of a religion's development, the prototypical shrines tend to predominate. Later, the places where saints and martyrs lived and died may become pilgrim shrines. Later still, places where visions, or apparitions, of the founder and those close to him — or of some manifestation of God or divine power — presented themselves to a believer, may become pilgrim shrines. All these types of shrines provide evidence for the faithful that their religion is still instinct with supernatural power and grace; that it has objective efficacy derived from the founder's god or gods and transmitted by means of miracles, wonders, and signs through saints, martyrs, and holy men, often through the medium of their relics.

Summary

27.15 Pilgrimage, then, has some of the attributes of liminality in passage rites: release from mundane structure; homogenization of status; simplicity of dress and behavior; communitas; ordeal; reflection on the meaning of basic religious and cultural values; ritualized enactment of correspondences between religious paradigms and shared human experiences; emergence of the integral person from multiple personae; movement from a mundane center to a sacred periphery which suddenly, transiently, becomes central for the individual, an *axis mundi* of his faith; movement itself, a symbol of communitas, which changes with time, as against stasis, which represents structure; individuality posed against the institutionalized milieu; and so forth. But since it is voluntary, not an obligatory social mechanism to mark the transition of an individual or group from one state or status to another within the mundane sphere, pilgrimage is perhaps best thought of as 'liminoid' or 'quasi-liminal', rather than 'liminal' in Van Gennep's full sense.

27.16 Tribal rites know nothing of modern distinctions between 'work' and 'play' or 'work' and 'leisure'; episodes of joking, trickery, fantasy, and festivity mark the rituals of tribal societies. Yet within tribal societies ritual activities are themselves clearly considered to be a form of 'work' and are thus described by any modern preliterate societies, as in the Tikopia's 'work of the gods', quite as necessary to the group's welfare as subsistence activities and the judicial process. The ludic (as in Huizinga's term, 1950), or play, aspects, as well as the most solemn aspects of ritual, are most vividly represented in liminality — for example, in the masked dancing, with clowns of various kinds, in the riddles, joking speech, rites of reversal, and practical joking, found in puberty initiations, side by side with the telling of myths about the sometimes obscene and often tricky behavior of deities and founding ancestors. Now, in postindustrial societies, the spheres of work and leisure are sharply divided by the clock but, at least in the cities, have little to do directly with the seasonal cycle — being determined instead by the rational organization of industrial production, mainly mass production in factories (V. Turner 1974b:67–70). Religion generally has been moved into the leisure sphere, more and more subject to individual option ('a person's free time is his to do as he likes with'). Even weekly attendance at religious services is becoming increasingly voluntary; failure to attend is no longer a sin. Games, sports, pastimes, hobbies, tourism, entertainment, the mass media, compete to fill the leisure sphere. On the other hand, work, perhaps originally under the influence of the Protestant ethic, has itself become rationalized, highly serious, almost ascetic in its regulation of productive time, like canonical hours in a monastery, and has been totally segregated from religion. But leisure activities have been so influenced by the prestige of work that many of them are pursued with the same solemnity as work and demand at least an equal outlay of attention. Even leisure has become professionalized, and some pastimes require more technical skill and know-how than many jobs. Thus, under the influence of the division between work-time and leisure-time, religion has become less serious but more solemn: less serious because it belongs to the leisure sphere in a culture dominated by the high value set on material productivity, and more solemn because within that sphere it has become specialized to establish ethical standards and behavior in a social milieu characterized by multiple options, continuous change, and large-scale secularization.

27.17 The history of pilgrimage illustrates this progress from the 'ludergic' liminal to the 'ergic' liminoid (V. Turner 1974b:83). The great medieval pilgrimages, in Islam as in Christianity, were usually associated with great fairs and fiestas as indeed they are in Shinto Japan. For example, in his article 'Ḥadjdj' (hajj) in the *Encyclopaedia of Islam*, A. J. Wensinck (1966:32) writes: 'Great fairs were from early times associated with the ḥadjdj, which was celebrated on the conclusion of the date-harvest. These fairs were probably the main thing to Muḥammad's contemporaries, as they still are to many Muslims'.

27.18 The Christian medieval fairs at such pilgrim centers as Chartres, Zaragoza, and Cologne on important feast days of Jesus, Mary, or major saints have their present-day successor in Latin America. We have seen almost at the portal of the church of Naucalpan (on the outskirts of Mexico City), where the venerable image of Our Lady of the Remedies is kept, troupes of brightly feathered Conchero dancers mime fights between Aztec warriors and French troops, while a skull-headed Death clowns wildly for the amusement of pilgrims. Fifty yards farther on, a full-blown fair was taking place, with ferris wheels, shooting galleries, and bumper cars, beside peddlers selling a wide range of goods. In describing the northern Brazilian pilgrimage to the shrine of Bom Jesus da Lapa in Bahia, Daniel E. Gross (1971:132–34) has given us a vivid picture of the juxtaposition of worship and commerce:

> [Lapa is a] raw river town whose chief *raison d'être* is the annual flow of thousands of pilgrims to its religious shrine. . . . As the major festival of August 6 (which is, incidentally, the Feast of the Transfiguration of Our Lord Jesus Christ) draws near, more and more vendors from outside Lapa arrive and set up stands selling a great variety of wares. Some of these depend on the local trinket distributors, but others bring a large part of

their merchandise, including a few items of artisanry such as saddles, leather hats and vests, hammocks, horse-blankets, spurs, and innumerable items fashioned from tin cans. . . . I used to count the numbers of stands on my way down a single street about one-half km in length. On June 20, 1966, there were only five temporary stands set up on this particular street. By July 11, there were 43; a week later 78 had appeared, and by the end of July, 187. On August 5, the day before the procession, 346 vending stands could be counted along the same street, which became choked with pilgrims admiring the wares.

Gross also mentions that cabarets and bars thrive in the pilgrimage season.

27.19 Pilgrimage devotion, the market, and the fair are all connected with voluntary, contractual activities (the religious promise, the striking of a bargain, the penny ride on the merry-go-round), and with a measure of joyful, 'ludic' communitas (see V. Turner 1974a:221–23). This extends even to the religious activities proper, for comradeship is a feature of pilgrimage travel. Chaucer noticed this aspect six centuries ago, and we have experienced it personally as members of pilgrim groups in Yucatán, Ireland, Rome, and Lourdes. Those who journey to pray together also play together in the secular interludes between religious activities; sightseeing to places of secular interest is one common form of 'play' associated with pilgrimage. Anthropologists have learned that it is necessary to study the total field of a great ceremony, the nonritualized factors surrounding it, as well as the liturgical or symbolic action. If one applies this method to the study of pilgrimage, one finds that play and solemnity are equally present. Indeed, it is the ludic component which excited the wrath of many Christian critics of pilgrimage and perhaps prepared the way for the virtual abolition of pilgrimage in Protestant lands. One has only to name William Langland, John Wycliffe, Erasmus, Hugh Latimer (bishop of Worcester in Henry VIII's time), and John Calvin, among the host of detractors.

27.20 Today, pilgrimages, like so many other leisure-time activities, have been organized, bureaucratized, and subjected to the influence of the modern forms of mass transportation and communication, mediated by full-time travel agencies. On the whole, they have become more solemn in tone, especially in the Western European lands, where once they combined devotion with pastime and mirth. However, recent changes in the Christian outlook have aimed to transform pilgrimage by encouraging more informal dress, sermons with contemporary themes, and a relaxed atmosphere outside the precincts of the shrine.

27.21 One fact is certain and striking. The numbers of pilgrims at the world's major shrines are still increasing. That this phenomenon is not due merely to tourism can easily be seen in the voluminous literature published in connection with pilgrimage centers (Lourdes, Guadalupe, and Knock come immediately to mind as Christian examples).[3] The papers, journals, and annuals of these centers abound with devout articles, fervent religious poetry, and news about visits to the shrine by organized pilgrimages and celebrities of church and state. Sermons delivered on feast days at the shrine by famous preachers and bishops are printed verbatim. There are lively correspondence columns on questions of doctrine and on the social role of the Church. Despite obvious resemblances and historical connections between archaic, medieval, and modern pilgrimages, we would argue that there is a significant difference between pilgrimages taken after the industrial Revolution and all previous types. In the scientific and technological age, pilgrimage is becoming what Geertz (1972:26) has described as a 'metasocial commentary' on the troubles of this epoch of wars and revolutions with its increasing signs of industrial damage to the natural environment. Like certain other liminoid genres of symbolic action elaborated in the leisure time of modern society, pilgrimage has become an implicit critique of the life-style characteristic of the encompassing social structure. Its emphasis on transcendental, rather than mundane, ends and means; its generation of communitas; its search for the roots of ancient, almost vanishing virtues as the underpinning of social life, even in its structured expressions — all have contributed to the dramatic resurgence of pilgrimage. It is true that bureaucracy has been pressed into the service of pilgrimage, and that comfortable travel has replaced penitential travel. Here, too, the stress has been on the communitas of the pilgrimage center, rather than on the individual's penance on the journey thither. In the earlier periods, pilgrimage still had liminal, even initiatory, aspects. Though it was one of the first forms of symbolic religious action to assign an important role to voluntary action, it was still, especially in its penitential aspect, deeply tinctured with obligatoriness. This was because the earlier pilgrimage systems, in all the major religions, were highly consonant with both the social and the religious systems, which in some measure they served to maintain. But in the present age of plural values, increasing specialization of function and role, and potent mass communication (the publication explosion, in particular, has brought the whole of man's past within the range of all literate people, in cheap paperbacks), pilgrimage — with its deep nonrational fellowship before symbols of transmundane beings and powers, with its posing of unity and homogeneity (even among the most diverse cultural groups) against the disunity and heterogeneity of ethnicities, cultures, classes, and professions in the mundane sphere — serves not so much to maintain society's status quo as to recollect, and even to presage, an alternative mode of social being, a world where communitas, rather than a bureaucratic social structure, is preeminent. Thus, out of the mixing and mingling of ideas from many traditions, a respect may grow for the pilgrimages of others. These may be seen as providing live metaphors for human and transhuman truths and salvific ways which all men share and always have shared, had they but known it. Pilgrimages may become ecumenical; and more devotees than the Swami from Madras, whom once we met in Chicago, will become palmers to the pilgrim shrines of all great religions.

Notes

2. For a first-rate account of the late fifteenth-century Venetian pilgrimage 'trade', readers should consult M. Margaret Newett's Introduction to her book *Canon Pietro Casola's Pilgrimage to Jerusalem; in the Year 1494* (1907:1–113).
3. According to René Laurentin (1973a:145), there are 'about a thousand [Christian] sanctuaries which [each] receive a hundred thousand pilgrims a year'.

28

Edward Schillebeeckx
Sociology, Theology and Ministry

This Extract comes from chapter 4, entitled 'Tension Between Actual Church Order and Alternative Practices in the Ministry', of Edward Schillebeeckx's *Ministry: a Case for Change* (SCM, 1981 — from the Dutch original *Kerkelijk ambt*, Bloemendaal, 1980). Schillebeeckx is a distinguished Dominican and was at the time professor of theology and the history of theology in the University of Nijmegen. In the earlier part of his book, Schillebeeckx argues that in contrast to the loose differentiation of function apparent in the New Testament (with a clear link between the local community and ministry), formal 'orders' began to emerge with the closer relations of the church with the Roman empire. Thus, 'in the Roman empire, *ordo* had the connotation of particular social classes differing in status . . . : after the time of Constantine the church *ordinatio* or appointment to the "order of office-bearers" clearly became more attractive because the clergy were seen as a more exalted class in the church in comparison with the more lowly "believers". The clericalization of the ministry had begun' (p. 39). This process became more rigid in the mediaeval period, especially after the Third Lateran Council of 1179 and the Fourth of 1215. In this Extract Schillebeeckx considers the implications for contemporary ministry within the Roman Catholic Church (and, by association, other churches) of this socio-historical analysis of the process of clericalisation. He is aware that the most obvious implication is that 'the church's ministry is always to be found only in specific, historically changing forms' (*28.1* — this compares interestingly with Baum's similar understanding of the impact of sociology upon doctrine in *Extract 10*). He believes that this perspective on ministry makes it 'clear that the actual order of the church has now become fixed as an ideology and itself hinders the original purpose of the church' (*28.7*): alternative forms of ministry can no longer simply be discounted. He points out that the church has in fact always found ways of allowing for changes in ministry (*28.9f.*): indeed, changes take place whether or not they are officially sanctioned by the church.

He stresses that these changes must themselves always be regarded as provisional (*28.18*) and is fully aware that some will regard his understanding of ministry as being too concerned with social factors (*28.20*). Nonetheless he is convinced that a 'sacral' view of priesthood is a historically limited understanding of ministry which satisfies neither his sociological nor his theological critique.

1. Church order as a historically conditioned means of salvation

28.1 It emerges from the historical theological sketch which I have given that the constant in the church's ministry is always to be found only in specific, historically changing forms. In this evaluation I am beginning from the insight that is really shared by all Christians: that church order, though changing, is a very great benefit for Christian communities. In one form or another church order is part of the specific and essential manifestation of the 'communities of God', the church. However, this church order is not an end in itself. Like the ministry, it too is at the service of the apostolic communities and may not be made an end in itself, or be absolutized. That is all the more the case because it is evident that at all periods of the church it is utterly bound up with a specific conditioned history. At a particular point in history, moreover, certain forms of church order (and thus also criteria for the admission of ministers), called into being by earlier situations in the church and in society, come up against their limitations; this can also be demonstrated in sociological terms. These limitations can clearly be shown in terms of specific experiences of their shortcomings and faults, in other words, from negative experiences with a particular church order in changed circumstances. With a shift in the dominant picture of man and the world, with social and economic changes and a new social and cultural sensibility and set of emotions, a church order which has grown up through history can in fact hinder and obstruct precisely what in earlier times it was intended to ensure: the building up of a Christian community. Experiences of contrast then give rise to spontaneous experiments in possibilities of new forms of life for Christianity and the church (which also happened in New Testament Christianity). Experiences of defects in a given system in fact have a regulative force. Of course even a largely unanimous experience of what has gone wrong within a valid system which has grown up through history by no means amounts to agreement over the positive steps that must be taken. The specific direction in which things can change can only emerge from tests made through a large number of models, some of which will succeed and some fail. These can and may also fail; they are precise experiments with that possibility in view. Failure is nothing to be ashamed of, but a phase within the quest for a new discovery of Christianity. In these manifold attempts the binding character of the new possibilities for Christian life and the life of the church, which have been brought to life but still not given a completely specific form, will gradually become evident. This will happen in the case of the ministry also.

28.2 On the other hand it is also a sociological fact that in changed times there is a danger that the existing church order will become a fixed ideology, above all by reason of the inertia of an established system which is therefore often concerned for self-preservation. This is true of any system in society, but perhaps in a special way of the institutional church, which, rightly understanding itself as a 'community of God', often wrongly shows a tendency to identify even old and venerable traditions with unchangeable divine ordinances. Here Vatican II was more careful than people perhaps thought at the time. Whereas at the Council of Trent (see above) there was at least a suggestion that the tripartite division of the ministry into episcopate, presbyterate and diaconate went back to divine law, the Second Vatican Council replaced the *ordinatione divina* ('through divine dispensation') which had already been weakened at Trent, by the still more relativistic 'it was like this from antiquity'.[1]

2. Illegality

28.3 Thus against the background of the existing church order, new and perhaps urgently necessary alternative possibilities can usually be seen only through the medium of what must provisionally be called 'illegality'. This is not a new phenomenon in the church; things have always been that way. Furthermore, the old, mediaeval scholasticism, which was still very free (in contrast to later scholasticism, which ignored this fact), sometimes elevated this provisional illegality to the status of a theological principle, especially in its theory of the *non-acceptatio legis*, the rejection of the law-from-above by opposition from the grass roots. Whatever the value of the law may be, in particular instances it is rejected by a great majority and therefore in fact is irrelevant. Thus from the history of the church it seems that there is a way in which Christians can develop a practice in the church from below, from the grass-roots, which for a times can compete with the official practice recognized by the church, but which in its Christian opposition and illegality can eventually nevertheless become the dominant practice of the church, and finally be sanctioned by the official church (whereupon the whole process can begin all over again, since time never stands still). That is how things have always been!

28.4 What each of us hears about practices in the ministry which diverge from the official church order therefore: 1. has a diagnostic and dynamic effect, and serves to criticize ideology: and 2. itself has a normative power. This latter is not, of course, on the basis of the fact that these alternative practices actually exist. It is to be justified by the nature of Christianity, in that on the one hand they anticipate the future in a utopian way and on the other hand they express a Christian apostolic conviction which is to be tested by the whole history of Christian experience.

28.5 The normative force of facts as such — 'hard facts', as the sociologists say — reigns supreme in our secular, bourgeois society. But none of us would claim that facts or statistics in themselves have any normative authority. Such a position would in fact be a blunder, because it would also and even *a fortiori* have to attribute even more massive authority to the even greater factual dimension of the church order which exists at present. But just as the official church order must be justified in the face of the ups and downs of the historical experiences of Christians, and in our time in the face of the negative way in which Christians experience this church order, so too must the critical, new alternative forms of practice in the church and in the ministry also be justified over against our historical experiences. An alternative, or the new for its own sake, is nothing. A particular practice of the Christian community, whether old or new, always has authority only in so far as it is indwelt by the Christian 'logos', that is, by what I have called the apostolicity of the Christian community. Furthermore, 'All things are lawful, but not all things are helpful' (Paul).

28.6 Historically, accounts of new, alternative practices in Christianity and the church are always connected with reminiscences and experiences of what is faulty and sometimes even absurd in the existing system: with the obstructions which are in fact there. In assessing the authority of an alternative practice it is certainly possible to begin from present-day experiences of the situation: from demands made in the name of humanity, human rights and so on. This is a legitimate and even obvious way. However, because of the experiences I have been through, and in view of the toughness of any system, I have preferred to adopt another way which also seems to me to be a more strategic one, namely to choose as my starting point what has been accepted and defended by both sides of the church with a view to building up the Christian community: both by representatives of the official church order, which is still in force, and by the protagonists of the critical, alternative practice. To put it briefly, this is the right of the Christian community by itself to do everything necessary to be a true community of Jesus and to be able to develop itself intensively, albeit in connection with and in the light of mutual criticism from all other Christian communities. This situation can lead to genuine restrictions both from above and from below (Vatican II). To make the same point in a more limited way: this is the right of the community to the eucharist as the heart of the community (Vatican II). Alternatively, it is the apostolic right of the community to have leaders: i.e., a leader (male or female) or a 'significant other figure' who, on the basis of the fundamental values of the group, clarifies, dynamizes and also is able to criticize the community, and in so doing can also be subject to the criticism of the community. Fundamentally, the official church also accepts these apostolic affirmations, but at the same time in respect it begins from decisions which have already been made at a prior stage of history (e.g. on criteria for admission to the ministry). However, when circumstances change in the church and the world, these can in fact obstruct this original right which belongs to the community. Thus, for example, the present shortage of priests (which itself can partly already be explained in terms of pre-existing historical conditions) leads to all kinds of substitute forms of church ministries. Alongside an authentic multiplicity of ministries which have become necessary because of the present-day situation of the community, i.e. the more differentiated ministry in the church, there is also an inauthentic multiplicity — simply because consecration or sacramental accreditation has in fact been withheld.

28.7 This approach, in terms of what is commonly accepted, serves to show more clearly the dilemma in which the so-called modern view of the priest now finds itself. On these grounds it must have become clear to everyone that in modern conditions, for example, the actual celebration of the eucharist has come up against fundamental difficulties; it is sometimes trivialized and often completely blocked. A whole series of accounts of negative experiences which have been brought about by the actual functioning of the 'service' priest within a sacral vision of the ministry shows that at the moment this view of the priesthood often makes the community and the eucharist look utterly ridiculous in the context of Christianity and the church. And this happens when there is an abundance of pastoral workers, men and women, who sometimes have already spent many years in full-time work for the community. These negative experiences make it quite clear that the actual order of the church has now become fixed as an ideology and itself hinders the original purpose of the church. And the only reason for this problem over the sacraments is the absence of a male, celibate, priest — both non-theological concepts. Many Christians can simply no longer take this. Consequently such negative experiences are an occasion for particular Christians and their ministers for the moment to take it into their own hands to begin an alternative practice. This is the reason why the phenomenon of an alternative form of ministry, which is in fact making itself felt everywhere, serves to provide a diagnosis of symptoms of sickness in the existing system, and in addition functions as a criticism of the ideology which is bound up with traditional practices. For many Christians it has become clear meanwhile that the alternative practice is a clear expression of the New Testament datum of the priority of the community over the ministry (and *a fortiori* over criteria for admission to the ministry which are not necessary in themselves). Furthermore, it is a sociological fact that existing ordinances in a particular society, even when that society is the church, remain intact as long as they carry intrinsic conviction, i.e. as long as no one doubts their (Christian) 'logos' or 'reason'. In itself, the fact that at a particular moment a wave of alternative practices sweeps over the church throughout the world indicates that the existing church order has lost a structure of credibility and is in urgent need of being revised. For many believers it no longer carries any conviction, so that spontaneously, and on all sides, we find the social and psychological mechanism of the *non-acceptatio legis*. This is what we now in fact see happening on a large scale. If despite this the church wants to maintain its existing church order, then from this point it can do so only in an authoritarian fashion (because it carries no conviction with a great many 'subjects'). This course would simply make the situation more precarious, because in turn the authoritarian way of exercising authority conflicts with the basic themes of the way in which life is experienced today, and is also experienced by Christians.

28.8 Finally, this alternative practice also has a dynamizing effect. At any rate, particular Christians are gradually recognizing the new structure of credibility; furthermore, as time goes on, they come to identify with it more and more. It is not the bare fact of an alternative way of exercising ministry which has dynamic force, but the way in which, by virtue of the 'Christian reason' which can be found in it, Christians almost infallibly recognize a modern form of 'apostolicity' here. It is precisely because a new practice of this kind carries conviction that in the long run it acquires authority and the power to attract. Nevertheless, we cannot claim that this experienced conviction, which now already inspires and determines the lives of many communities and ministers even before it has been recognized openly by the official church, does not possess an inherent Christian apostolicity, and can only acquire this when it is sanctioned by the church at a later stage. On the contrary, it is recognized later when, and in so far as, it already has in fact an innate Christian 'logos' or apostolicity: when it in fact provides the possibility for a meaningful Christian life today.

3. The traditional reception of practices which diverge from church order

28.9 Through the long history of its experience, the Western church has also had to refer to all kinds of principles on the basis of which practices that diverge from existing church order might nevertheless be regarded as being 'in order'.

28.10 First of all there is the principle of the 'extraordinary minister',which sanctioned what was often originally an 'illegal practice'. According to the anti-Donatist Council of Arles (314), in the absence of priests, deacons may preside at the eucharist;[2] at the time of the persecution of Diocletian (303–311) they replaced not only priests but bishops. Furthermore, it is known that for more than a century, abbots consecrated priests, with papal permission.[3] We can say that in additional to the 'ordinary minister' (in terms of church order) there have always in the end also been 'extraordinary ministers' for the administration of virtually all the sacraments.

28.11 Another principle of the Western church is above all the *supplet Ecclesia*.[4] This applies particularly in the case of mistakes in form, in which the sacrament has not been administered in accordance with the rules of church order. Here the church as it were compensates for these lacunae. From the history of this practice since the Middle Ages it seems that the Latin church appeals to this question less in cases of the absence of the power of consecration (*potestas ordinis*), and above all when it is a matter of the absence of the power of jurisdiction (which has clearly been distinguished from the power of consecration in the Latin church from the Middle Ages to the Second Vatican Council — in contrast to the Eastern churches).

28.12 There is also the principle of *intentio faciendi quod facit Ecclesia*.[5] Here someone can have the intention of wanting to do what the church does (e.g. baptize) though without in fact taking account of the form prescribed by church order. In this case, too, the action is valid in terms of both Christianity and the church. This means that there are traces of the sacramental church outside the area dominated by its church order, e.g. in marginal 'grass-roots communities' which have sometimes grown up outside the sphere of authority of the bishop. Although these stand apart from existing church order, they nevertheless seek to be in the great tradition of the church.

28.13 The appeal to a *sanatio in radice* (healing at the roots), and above all a reference to the power of dispensation held by the church authorities, is specifically connected with the theory of the *plena potestas* which has emerged since the Middle Ages. This relates to the powers which the Pope in particular is said to possess, so that in the last resort he can diverge from all church order currently obtaining (albeit within certain limits).[6] Despite any illegality in respect of existing church order the Pope can subsequently declare what has been done as nevertheless valid. However, for the time being alternative grass-roots communities will not be able to make much of this principle.

28.14 Finally there is the ancient doctrine of the *non-receptio legis*, on the basis of which a church law, while being valid, can in the long run become irrelevant because it is in fact no longer accepted by the great majority of believers.[7] Laws only in fact have force if they are also supported by the community and have a plausible structure.

28.15 Most of these principles can in fact be invoked even in the case of a modern 'illegal' practice, which nevertheless respects the intention of the great church (in other words, which means to remain in line with the main church tradition). This is the case on one condition, which has been properly formulated by the Council of Trent: *salva eorum substantia*, in other words, provided that the 'substance of the sacrament' is preserved.[8] However, when it comes to the 'sacrament of consecration', the question has arisen as to precisely what belongs to the substance of the church's ministry and what does not (though the so-called 'substance' will always be found in a specific liturgical form, through which it is 'given substance'). Now it has emerged from the theology of the ministry in the first millenium that the sacramental substance or nucleus of *ordinatio*, appointment to an office, lies in the fact that as a minister a believer is recognized and accepted by the church (the local community and its leaders) and is called to the service of the ministry in and for a particular community, along with the gift of the Spirit which is bestowed in such an instance. The rights of a local church can of course be 'moderated' (above all by Pope and Council) with an eye to what the Latin church calls the *utilitas Ecclesiae* or the welfare of the church; however, this last is in that case part of historically changing church order, and not the substance of the sacrament concerned, so that here in particular instances an appeal can be made to the principles outlined above. Thus in 1088 Pope Urban II sanctioned deviations from existing church order with an eye to very specific situations in the church and the world.[9] However, quite apart from historical ecclesiastical rules for *communio* among all local churches, concern for this bond of love in the church is of the *substance* of each separate community. With these principles in mind we can now come to an evaluation of present-day alternative practices in respect of the ministry.

4. An evaluation of present-day alternative practices in the ministry

28.16 The alternative practice of critical communities which are inspired by Jesus as the Christ is 1. possible from an apostolic and dogmatic point of view (I cannot pass judgment on all the details here). It is a legitimate way of living a Christian life, commensurate with the apostolicity of the church, which has been called into being by the needs of the time. To talk of 'heretics' or those who 'already stand outside the church' (on grounds of this alternative practice) seems to me to be nonsensical from the church's point of view. Furthermore, 2. given the present canonical church order, the alternative practice is not in any way *contra* (against) *ordinem*; it is *praeter ordinem*. In other words, it does not follow the letter of existing church order (it is *contra* this letter), but it is in accordance with what church order really set out to safeguard (in earlier situations). It is understandable that such a situation is never pleasant for the representatives of existing church order. However, they too should take note of the negative experiences of Christians with church order and above all be sensitive to the damage which these do to the formation of communities, to the eucharist and to the ministry. Otherwise they are no longer defending the Christian community and its eucharistic heart and centre, but an established system, the purely factual dimension. At a time when people have become extra-sensitive to the power-structure of a system, a hardening of attitude in the existing system to the luxuriant upsurge of all kinds of experiments (even if some of them are perhaps frivolous) would be a very painful matter for all those who are well disposed towards the church.

28.17 Given that the alternative practice is not directly *contra ordinem*, but generally speaking merely *praeter ordinem*, in difficult circumstances in the church it can also be defended in an ethical respect (of course no one can pass judgment on subjective intentions). In this connection, too, to talk to 'members who have placed themselves outside the church' is not only a distressing phenomenon which has no place in the church, but also smacks of what the church itself has always called heresy. Even the Second Vatican

Council had difficulty in defining where the limits of church membership really lie. Of course they can be found somewhere; but how can they be defined precisely? Furthermore, talk like this makes posthumous heretics of authentic Christians of earlier centuries and above all condemns the New Testament search for the best possibilities of pastoral work.

28.18 I also want to say here that no one may pursue this alternative practice in a triumphalist spirit: this also seems to me to be un-apostolic. It remains a provisionally abnormal situation in the life of the churches. Personally (but this is simply a very personal conviction) I think that there is also need for something like a stategy or 'economy of conflicts'. Where there is clearly no urgent necessity for an alternative practice because of a pastoral need felt by the Christian communities, ministers must not put into practice everything that is possible in apostolic or dogmatic terms. In that case, of course, there is a danger that, for example, in critical communities, the communities are again put in second place after the problems of the ministry and begin to be manipulated on the basis of problems arising from the crisis of identity among ministers themselves. In addition, we must not turn alternative forms of ministerial practice into a mystique. We need a degree of realism and matter-of-factness. Of course renewals in the church usually begin with illegal deviations; renewals from above are rare, and are sometimes dangerous. Vatican II is an illustration of both these points. In its Constitution on the Liturgy, this Council largely sanctioned the illegal liturgical practice which had grown up above all in France, Belgium and Germany. On the other hand, when after the Council the Vatican programme of renewal was put into effect in other matters, largely on promptings from above, many people proved to be unprepared, so that there was resistance in many communities.

28.19 One often hears the objection that changes or an alternative practice are not justified by the fact that they are different or new. That is quite correct; but the implicit presupposition here is wrong. In changed circumstances this is equally true of the existing church order. It too cannot be legitimated on the basis of the inertia of its own factual existence. When views of man or the world change, it too can come under the suspicion of deterioration, i.e. of actually falling short of authentic Christian and church life. Even the old and venerable does not enjoy any priority because it is old and venerable.

28.20 Some people will criticize my views for being too one-sided and seeing the church in 'horizontal' terms, exclusively in accordance with the model of a social reality which can be treated in sociological terms, and not as a charismatic datum 'from above'. I must reject this ecclesial dualism, on the basis of the New Testament. Of course we may not speak about the church only in descriptive empirical language; we must also speak about the church in the language of faith, of the church as the 'community of Jesus', as 'the body of the Lord', the 'temple of the Spirit', and so on. And this language of faith expresses a real dimension of the church. However, in both cases we are talking about one and the same reality: otherwise we should split up the church in a gnostic way into a 'heavenly part' (which would fall outside the sphere of sociological approaches) and an earthly part (to which all the bad features could evidently be transferred). Vatican II already reacted against this with the words: 'We may not see the earthly church and the church enriched with heavenly things as two realities' (*Lumen Gentium* I, 8). In my view, the obstacles to the renewal of the official ministry in the church are grounded above all in this dualistic conception of the church (which is often described in pseudo-Christian terms as 'hierarchical'). The consequence of this is that because of the shortage of priests Christian laity are allowed to engaged in pastoral work as much as possible but are refused the sacramental institution to the ministry which goes with this. The question is more whether this development in the direction of pastoral workers (whose existence can only be understood in the light of the historical obstructions which have been placed in the way of the ministry) who are not ministers and have not been appointed sacramentally is a sound theological development. It maintains the exaggerated sacral view of the priesthood, as will emerge even more closely from what follows.

Notes

1. *Lumen Gentium*, no. 28.
2. Mansi II, 469.
3. J. Beyer, 'Nature et position du sacerdoce', *NRT* 76, 1954, 356–73, 469–80; Y. Congar, *Sainte Eglise*, Unam Sanctam 41, Paris 1963, 275–302; W. Kasper, 'Zur Frage der Anerkennung der Ämter in der katholischen Kirche', *TQ* 151, 1971, 97–102. Cf. F.J. Beeck, 'Extraordinary Ministries of All or Most of the Sacraments', *JES* 3, 1966, 57–112.
4. See Y. Congar, '*Supplet Ecclesia*: propos en vue d'une théologie de l'économie dans la tradition latine', *Irénikon*, 45, 1972, 155–207; H. Herrmann, *Ecclesia supplet. Das Rechtinstitut der kirchlichen Suppletion nach can. 209. C.I.C.*, Amsterdam 1968.
5. See F. Gillmann, *Die Notwendigkeit der Intention auf Seiten des Spenders und des Empfangers der Sakramente nach Anschauung der Frühscholastik*, Mainz 1916; A. Landgraf, *Dogmengeschichte der Frühscholastik*, Regensburg 1955, III-I, 109–68; IV-2, 223–43.

6. F. Planzinski, *Mit Krummstab und Mitra*, Buisdorf 1970; M.A. Stiegler, *Dispensation*. *Dispensationswesen und Dispensationsrecht in Kirchenrecht geschichtlich dargestellt*, Mainz 1908; A. Schebler, *Die Reordinationen in der altkatholischen Kirche unter besonderer Berücksichtigung der Anschauungen Rudolphs Sohms*, Bonn 1936; L. Saltet, *Les réordinations*, Paris 1907; L. Buisson, *Potestas et Caritas. Die päpstliche Gewalt im Spätmittelalter*, Cologne-Graz 1958. The Western principle of dispensation differs on a number of points from the common Eastern *oikonomia* principle. See M. Widmann, *Der Begriff Oikonomia im Werk des Irenaeus und seine Vorgeschichte*, Tübingen 1956; F.J. Thompson, 'Economy', *JTS* NS 16, 1965, 368–420; Mgr J. Kotsonis, *Problèmes de l'économie ecclésiastique*, Gembloux 1971; Mgr P. l'Huillier, 'Economie et Théologie Sacramentaire', *Istina* 17, 1972, 17–20; K. McDonnell, 'Ways of Validating Ministry', *JES* 7, 1970, 209–65; K. Duchatelez, 'De geldigheid van de wijdingen in het licht der "economie" ', *TvT* 8, 1968, 377–401; P. Dumont, 'Economie ecclésiastique et réitération des sacrements', *Irénikon* 14, 1937, 228–47 and 339–62; Y. Congar, 'Quelques Problèmes touchant les ministères', *NRT* 93, 1971, 785–800.

7. Y. Congar, 'Reception as an Ecclesiological Reality', *Concilium* 8, 1972, no. 7, 43f.; there is a more extended version in 'La "reception" comme réalité ecclésiologique', *RSPT* 56, 1972, 369–403; see also Congar, '*Quod omnes tangit ab omnibus tractari et approbari debet*', *Revue historique de Droit français et étranger* 36, 1958, 210–59; A. Grillmeier, 'Konzil und Reception' in *Mit ihm und in ihm. Christologische Forschungen und Perspektiven*, Freiburg 1975, 303–34.

8. Denzinger-Schönmetzer no. 1728, see E. Schillebeeckx, *De sacramentele heilseconomie*, Antwerp-Bilthoven 1952, 416–51.

9. Mansi, 20, 970. See A, Schebler, *Die Reordinationen* (n. 6), 277f.

29

Clare Watkins
Ecclesiology and Sociology

The final extract in this section is taken from Clare Watkins' longer article 'Organizing the People of God: Social-Science Theories of Organization in Ecclesiology' (*Theological Studies*, 52, 1991, pp. 693–700, 701–3, 706–11). In that article, she reviews some of the more substantial attempts to use the social sciences in the service of ecclesiology.

At the start of the longer article she rehearses a number of methodological issues which will already be familiar from earlier parts of this Reader. Above all, she is concerned that 'both ecclesiology and sociological theory should alert us to the danger of oversimplifying the complex reality of the Church ... [I]f we are to remain primarily theologians (and that is our primary perspective here), we must fully appreciate the Church as a peculiar sort of organization, first of all by virtue of its involvement in a living tradition and faith based on divine revelation, but also on sociological grounds' (p. 693). She writes as a Catholic, but she also draws widely from a broad ecumenical range of offerings in this area.

In **Extract 29** Watkins looks first at Dietrich Bonhoeffer's very early work of 1927, *Sanctorum Communio: A Dogmatic Enquiry in the Sociology of the Church* (English translation, Collins, London, 1963). Unlike a number of other approaches, Watkins argues that Bonhoeffer's approach 'remains properly theology, and not some kind of religious sociology' (*29.8*). None the less, she is not sure that it actually enters into dialogue with the social sciences. Turning instead to a Catholic writer, Patrick Granfield, she identifies the opposite tendency. Unlike Bonhoeffer, Granfield 'fails to give a detailed theological account of [his] ecclesiological perspective' (*29.14*). Nor does she believe that he offers a sufficiently distinctive view of church activity: 'nowhere does Granfield take up the issue of ways in which the Church might be critical of secular changes; nor does he highlight the significance of the fact that the Church's identity is grounded in revelation' (*29.16*).

She is apparently more sympathetic to the work of Rudge, and especially of Thung. However, she does conclude (correctly I believe) that Rudge has a tendency to over-simplify differing types of organizational theory — at both sociological and theological levels. Thung, too, is seen as having similar tendencies to over-simplify — although in her case her theological and sociological model of the church is set out at considerable length and in considerable detail. Although Watkins finally does not offer an elaborated alternative to the attempts she criticizes, she does at least present some of the bones of this alternative. For her, this is based on an equal 'dialogue', with theology neither conceding too much to sociology nor seeking to vanquish sociology. This is precisely the issue which dominates the final part of this Reader.

29.1 In exploring the ecclesiological literature which tries to relate social-science theories of organization to the Church, we must be aware of the variety of theological traditions at work. But 'organization theory' also exhibits variety, for 'organization theory' is really a set of theories, which adopt different perspectives and approaches in dealing with their common subject. This variety reflects not so much the existence of discrete schools, but rather the complexity of actual organizations,[1] which may be discussed on the levels of their individual members, their small groups, their inevitable bureaucracy, or their institutional power structures; furthermore, theories can choose to concentrate on one particular process common to all organizations, such as authority, communication, or goal structure. It is well for the ecclesiologist attempting to work in this field to start by studying a few of the general introductions.[2]

29.2 Some of the works we will discuss are significant enough to be considered individually, whereas others have been grouped under general headings. Together they represent the present state of this interdisciplinary field and provide us, despite their variety and lack of formal interrelation, with a number of common questions, consideration of which will allow a more systematic enquiry into the area.

Dietrich Bonhoeffer: The Theology of Sociality

29.3 The importance of Bonhoeffer's *Sanctorum Communio*[3] for this discussion lies particularly in the method implicit in his bringing together a highly sacramental ecclesiology and what can only be called a social philosophy. It needs to be pointed out also that this work stands apart from the rest, both chronologically and in the kind of sociological ideas employed. Writing in the late 1920s, the sociological material available to Bonhoeffer was limited, and he drew most of his 'sociological' insight from 'formalist' sociologists such as Simmel and Tönnies, with their abstraction from empirical reality. By contrast more recent works in this field emphasize, in theory at least, the concrete structures of the Church.

29.4 Bonhoeffer's lack of empiricism and his dominant use of Hegelian concepts have led Berger to accuse him of 'theological imperialism' and 'social mythology,'[4] and it is true that *Sanctorum Communio* is more concerned with social philosophy than with sociology proper.[5] But the work is of theological interest to us, as it explicitly deals with the problem of how to talk of the reality of human social existence within the Church. If we come to Bonhoeffer's work expecting, as Berger seems to have done, an attempt to understand the Church sociologically, we will be disappointed; rather, *Sanctorum Communio* uses reflection on sociology so as to open up an ecclesiology based on a theology of human sociality. For this reason it is a useful introduction to the field of organizational ecclesiology.

29.5 One of the primary questions for the enquirer into this field concerns the methodology employed in bringing together the two disciplines, and this is the major question to be asked of our texts. In fact *Sanctorum Communio* does not attempt to develop an explicit methodological rationale for the use of sociology, and we must rely on a number of significant 'hints' if we are to understand the theological reasons for Bonhoeffer's sociological interest. His method appears to be based on a strongly incarnational understanding. Thus in his Preface to the 1930 edition, Bonhoeffer argues that it is the historical nature of Christianity that justifies the theologian's taking a sociological view of the Church. This is developed in a Christological way in the body of the book, where Bonhoeffer clearly asserts that the Church must be treated empirically 'because Christ entered into history.'[6] It is important for us to note that this Christologico-ecclesiology works two ways: it is used to encourage a realistic, 'incarnational' perspective in ecclesiology; but it also makes clear the peculiarity of the ecclesial community, a peculiarity which disallows a straightforwardly sociological approach to the Church. This is clear when Bonhoeffer writes that 'the empirical church is the Body of Christ, the presence of Christ on earth. It is possible to understand the empirical church only by looking down from above, or by looking out from the inside, and not otherwise.'[7]

29.6 This rigorously theological approach to the sociology of the Church deeply affects Bonhoeffer's use of sociological concepts. For example, the 'sociological' ideas concerning sociality based on human relationships are transformed by a consideration of a specifically Christian anthropology; for there are within the Church 'new basic social relationships,'[8] transfigured by the participation of the church members in Christ's Body. Indeed, the unique structures of the Church are transformed, above all, by the action of the Holy Spirit, 'which means that this uniqueness can only be theological and not morphological and sociological.'[9]

29.7 It is important for the student of organizational ecclesiology to notice the way in which Bonhoeffer's particular ecclesiology acts as a formative, shaping influence on his interdisciplinary work. For Bonhoeffer is no less insistent than Barth on the peculiarity and mystery of the Church, based on revelation and the Spirit but, unlike Barth, he binds this mystery close to the actual reality of the Church, adopting a more sacramental ecclesiology. This gives the human nature of the Church, or its 'objective spirit,' a relative value and authority as *the* instrument of the Holy Spirit.[10] Once this is asserted, then the social reality of the Church has a properly theological importance.

29.8 For all this, it remains unclear what actual difference Bonhoeffer's ecclesiology might make within the Church; his quasi-interdisciplinary study does not present us with a 'concrete ecclesiology,' one which really talks theologically of the experienced reality of church life. But it does describe for us an ecclesiological type which, as distinct from Barth's, not only allows, but demands the theological consideration of church structures. It is an ecclesiology rooted in incarnational and sacramental concepts, one which holds together the human and divine without falling into thoroughgoing immanentism. Such an ecclesiology encourages social-science insights into the Church, but it remains properly theology, and not some kind of religious sociology. Social-science insights are critically examined within a theological context, and they are brought into tension with the ecclesiological realities of the Spirit, revelation, and sacrament.

29.9 How we evaluate Bonhoeffer's contribution to this field depends on the acceptability of his sacramental ecclesiology. For many, this involves too ready an identification of the ecclesial institution with the mysterious Body of Christ,[11] and a 'usurpation of sociology by theology.'[12] It may be due to such criticisms that Bonhoeffer's ecclesiological position has not been adopted by recent writers working with the social sciences. On the whole, recent writers have a somewhat different model of Church, which leads to a distinctly different use of social sciences. We turn now to these writers, to see whether their ecclesiological models work any better than Bonhoeffer's in the search for a concrete ecclesiology through the use of theories of organization.

Patrick Granfield and the Democratization of the Church

29.10 It is not surprising, sociologically speaking, that there have been increasing numbers of 'democratizing' reforms in Western churches in modern times; the Church, as a more or less 'open system,'[13] an organization with an active relationship with wider society, can be expected to take up general societal trends. Indeed, there is a long tradition of popular participation in the Christian community, from the Acts of the Apostles to the commendable attempts of congregational churches to get all Christians actively involved in the Church.[14] In the last twenty-five years both the Church of Rome, and the churches of the international Anglican Communion have seen reforms which, to a greater or (generally) lesser extent, have increased the participation of laity in governmental matters and decision making. This long and pervasive tradition is the context for the works we consider in this section, all of which, interestingly, are rooted in the Roman Catholic tradition.

29.11 The years immediately following the Second Vatican Council saw a number of changes in the way ecclesiological issues were addressed in Catholic theology. Among these can be identified a growing concern for structural reform in the Church, along the lines of increased participation and democratization. Hans Küng is the most prominent write in this respect, with his study of councils and the involvement of laity,[15] and his argument that, if the Vatican II vision of an empowered laity is to be actively expressed in the Church, it requires radical reforming of decision-making structures so as to include lay people and their representatives.[16] Most of the theologians who attempted, like Küng, to develop some theological basis for structural reform did not directly employ theories from the social sciences (perhaps that is part of the reason for the failure of these models for reform). However, it was within the context of emphasis on structure and democratic models of power sharing that a number of more socio-logically involved ecclesiologies emerged in the Roman Catholic tradition.

29.12 One of these is Patrick Granfield's *Ecclesial Cybernetics.*[17] Granfield begins with an outline of cybernetic theory — that is, the science of communication and control within organizations. The first thing to note is that Granfield stresses the nature of organizations as open systems: because all organizations are 'open' to their societal environment, they constantly respond to the wider society, changing in relation to changes within that environment. Such essential change depends on a complex system of communication, in which information from outside the group can be brought into critical contact with the norms and authorities of the organization; the 'output' of organizational decisions and policies depend in some way on the 'input' from the environment which is 'the raw material of authoritative decision.'[18] The central component in this communication system is the 'feedback loop,' by which the organizational members can properly respond to the organizational decision, so as to reform or renew it in some way or other.

29.13 After this account of cybernetic theory, Granfield discusses its general applicability to the Church. We must notice the way he relates the theory to theological considerations. He asserts that the Church is not merely a human organization like any other; it is sacramental and peculiarly bound to revelation as the 'given' communication input. Further, he highlights the importance of a properly expressed theology of the laity for his cybernetic system; lay people above all are involved in communicating environmental information to the organization as a whole, and that is essential for the Church's continuing relevance and ultimate survival.

29.14 Granfield exhibits a genuine concern for the doctrines of ecclesiology, whose integrity and roots in revelation must be sustained in the interdisciplinary exercise. He chooses to focus on a particular aspect of ecclesiology, the importance and mission of lay people in the Church; but because he fails to give a detailed theological account of this ecclesiological perspective, he is unable to move beyond a generalized understanding of Church. So the rather sweeping idea of participation or democracy is deduced somewhat simplistically from a general, almost impressionistic, picture of the Vatican II ecclesiology which emphasizes its theology of laity; it is this broad theme of participation which Granfield uses to lead us into a cybernetic analysis of a number of ecclesial controversies and decisions. Important theological questions remain. And we look in vain for a really critical synthesis of a detailed and complex ecclesiology with a comparably complete social-science theory.

29.15 One of the strengths of Granfield's work is his attempt to conclude his study with practical suggestions as to how greater participation, or democratization, might be achieved in the Church. Among these suggestions elections of clergy by laity, lay councils and congresses, and the expression of public opinion in the Church through the various media channels find a place. No doubt some of these practical reforms would help resolve communication problems in the Church, but there remains a certain naivety, both theological and sociological, in this study.

29.16 First of all, Granfield does not appear to emphasize sufficiently the distinctiveness of the Church's activity. For example, in introducing his interdisciplinary work, he sees as the context of his method 'the modern world,' with its increased information flow and widespread democratizing forces. The Church, like any other open organizational system, does well to take note of this. But nowhere does Granfield take up the issue of ways in which the Church might be critical of secular changes; nor does he highlight the significance of the fact that the Church's identity is grounded in revelation. Failure to bring the doctrinal base of the Church's existence into the discussion leads to other curiously uncritical assumptions, such as seeing in the use of computers a 'new possibility' for the *consensus fidelium*, as if this ecclesiological theme can be straightforwardly translated into a matter of majority opinion.

29.17 Parallel to this, there is in Granfield's work a sociological naivety typical of many ecclesiologists who work with ideas of participation and democracy. For, in fact, studies in the social sciences highlight the power of democratic forms as a management tool. Given that there is an 'iron law of oligarchy,'[19] an inevitable tendency of the majority to apathy, which allows the energetic few a real power under the semblance of democracy, an organization's management might well adopt structures of participation so as to reduce out-and-out conflict and satisfy the members' need to feel involved, while remaining in control themselves.[20] Indeed, the study of Vaillancourt[21] into the manipulation of lay opinion at the Roman Catholic Third Congress of the Laity should alert us to the real possibilities in the Church, as elsewhere, of 'the management' winning the day precisely through the use of democratic structures; it is no coincidence that Vaill-ancourt is noticeably well read in sociological studies of organizational power from Weber to Etzioni. Certainly the tendency to mass apathy in all human organizations is an insight from social-science research which our more idealistic ecclesiological ideas must grapple with in some way or other ...

Peter Rudge: Ecclesiastical Administration

29.18 The work of Peter Rudge[22] is central to this field for several reasons. First, Rudge is unusual in his dual qualification as both social scientist and theologian. In addition to this, and perhaps because of it, he makes the clearest attempt of all the writers to discuss the practicalities of organization theory under the headings of systematic theology.

29.19 Rudge's starting point is the experience of attitudes toward administration in the Church. He points out that pastoral work is often valued as the 'real' work of Christian ministers, in contrast to administration, and he reacts against this by asserting the dignity and importance of administration in the Church as elsewhere. For Rudge, educated in business studies, administration is an important aspect of any large organization, and one which is to be treated seriously and thoroughly by those who wish life in the organization to fulfil its potential.

29.20 This high estimation of the administrative sciences on Rudge's part goes hand in hand with a deep awareness of the way in which an organization's structures are integral to the whole. His writings convey a stronger sense than other works discussed so far that the formal institution is not just a matter of structures, but is the real context of the human lives and ideals which form the dynamic of organizational life. Awareness of the way in which structures are rooted in the complexities of the human group distinguishes Rudge's method in applying social-science theory to the Church.

29.21 Rudge's ability to combine organizational approaches and Christian doctrine depends on his identification of five distinct organizational theories: the traditional, the charismatic, the classical, human relations, and the systemic.[23] After describing these theories, he discusses each of them in the light of certain Christian doctrines, namely the doctrines of the Church, of Church and society, of ministry, of God, and of man (sic).[24] The nature of each doctrine is outlined, and theological sources given, and then the organizational theories are examined in terms of their affinity or incompatibility with the tenets of the doctrine. Rudge concludes that there are distinct similarities between the organizational and theological perspectives (each, after all, describes the same human realities, albeit in rather different ways), and he singles out the systemic theory as that most appropriate to ecclesiastical administration on theological grounds. The final (and longest) part of Rudge's book examines the practicalities of administration in the Church, comparing the approaches of the various theories, and concluding, once again, that the systemic approach is the most appropriate to church life.

29.22 All this is particularly refreshing for its clarity of approach, its practicality, and, above all, for the way it combines organization theory and theology. However, some criticism needs to be made if the value of Rudge's method is to be properly assessed.

29.23 It is, perhaps, inevitable that the attempt to bring together two quite differently constructed realms of thought will tend to lead to caricature. Certainly, the way in which Rudge presents five distinct organizational theories does little justice to the complexity of this sociological field and the interdependence of the different approaches. Theorists increasingly recognize that no single approach can adequately describe the real organization, and that each approach reflects some different aspect of organizational reality.[25] In the light of this, Rudge's championing of what he has termed 'the systemic' theory seems unnecessary; it obscures the fact that all the theoretical approaches are needed, as we come to terms with the complex realities of human social life.

29.24 Similarly the depth at which Rudge examines the Christian doctrines is limited. No one can do justice to 'the doctrine of the Church' in a few pages, and it would be unreasonable for the reader to expect too much from this interdisciplinary endeavour. But one may fairly criticize the separation of the theological discussions of the theories from the practical considerations of the major part of the book. Ultimately the interrelating of theological and sociological perspectives remains on a general level, while the particularities of ecclesiastical administration are dominated by the organizational theories. The question remains: How can theology find its own way of talking about these concrete facts of organizational life? But Rudge's work has emphasized the real importance of these matters for the life of the Church and has opened the way for theological discussion of them ...

Mady Thung: Church Renewed or New Church?

29.25 Like Peter Rudge's work, that of Mady Thung[26] is outstanding for its thoroughness, rigorous method, and knowledge of social sciences. Indeed, the sociological emphasis tends to dominate the theological considerations, which are less prominent in the structuring of the argument. Yet Thung's work undoubtedly represents the most detailed attempt to date to employ organization theory in ecclesiology.

29.26 Thung's approach has a number of features in common with those already considered. Like Granfield and others, she is motivated by the reality of the Church in the modern world, with its task of proclaiming its gospel message to the society in which it finds itself. Like Rudge, she recognizes the need to be honest about the theological nature of her work, and so makes clear that the problems she examines and the concepts she employs are drawn from a properly ecclesiological concern. However, moving along these not unfamiliar lines, Thung constructs a highly detailed picture of Church organization, drawing on a considerable knowledge of both organization theory and the sociology of religion, as well as some broad theological concepts.

29.27 The ecclesiologist, however, is likely to find Thung's work dissatisfying because of the breadth and generality of her theological concepts. Thung does recognize the importance of theological ideas in her argument. She concentrates on working out the idea of a missionary church,[27] defined by commitment to Christian action and witness in society, that is the basis of the ecclesiology she employs as a critical guide to the organizational themes. We witnessed a similar synthesis of theological themes and organizational concepts in Rudge's work, and we noted its advantages over less theologically structured interdisciplinary ecclesiologies; but, in Thung's case, the description of the theological side of the dialogue suffers by being both too general and undetailed.

29.28 There is also a certain utopianism evident in Thung's description of the ideal missionary church, and in her appeal to this ideal while treating ecclesiological theories of organization. She makes little attempt to relate her image of the missionary church to actual ecclesial structures in the here and now, and so the organizational ideas are employed, once again, in an ecclesiological context where the only language for the concrete, the experienced, the structural belongs to the social sciences. Theology may be allowed to point the way along general ethical and idealistic lines, but it does not contribute otherwise to the language of the empirical and institutional.

29.29 A particularly helpful feature in Thung's work, however, is her clear identification and discussion of particular organizational detail for an ecclesial organization. For example, her treatment of the question of what a church's goal is, and how the goal might be expressed in terms of workable aims,[28] makes clear the problems faced by an ecclesiologist who reads the social-science theories on goal structure and its manipulation. Other organizations might be able to set a number of more-or-less straightforward tasks for their members in the pursuit of a particular goal, but the goal of the ecclesial organization, whether described eschatologically, evangelistically, or otherwise, is, by nature, a permanent focus of debate and renewal, and might be served by a wide variety of apparently conflicting activities. Theologians are aware of all this; but those who study theories of organization also become aware of the necessity and inevitability of institutional goals being set one way or another.

29.30 Something of this paradoxical position for an interdisciplinary ecclesiology is recognized in Thung's writing, in her discussion of goals,[29] of control,[30] of leadership,[31] etc., and this makes her work particularly valuable. For here we come close to the heart of the problem involved in employing social-science theories in the ecclesiological sphere — as theological ideas and ideals, often developed with little relation to concrete actualities of church life (though none the less sure for all that, the theologian would argue), come up against the science of the concrete and empirical. If Thung's analysis is correct, and if our appraisal of her work and that of others is valid, then it would seem that the ecclesiologist who wishes to employ organization theory faces two alternatives: either she must work with simplified and generalized theological concepts, implying a weak ecclesiology which allows the particularities of the social-science theories to dominate; or she must abandon the search for any rigorous interdisciplinary method and merely pick up certain useful sociological concepts, which can be used theologically in a superficial, although still potentially helpful, way.

29.31 Yet there is, perhaps, a third alternative which presents itself from the discussion so far; it is possible that an ecclesiological language and understanding of structure could be developed, so that eventually each detail of organization theory could be matched with concrete ecclesiological (i.e., properly theological) detail based on doctrine, revelation, and the faith of the Church. This would seem to me to be the necessary

beginning to a well-balanced and theologically satisfying interdisciplinary dialogue.

Concluding Reflections

29.32 Our main purpose has been to introduce the complex and not clearly defined field of 'organizational
ecclesiology.' Our consideration of the texts has been critical and
not without its own biases and beliefs, but ultimately any student of
this field must come to her or his own conclusions about these
writings. I have tried to engage critically with the literature in such a
way as to illustrate certain problems and weaknesses, and to achieve
an overall sense of what is being done in diverse, but related,
organizational ecclesiologies. Some brief general considerations are
in order as a conclusion to this study, but also, and more importantly, as a preliminary to further creative work in the area.

The Problem of Detail

29.33 A recurrent weakness in the studies considered
here has been the simplicity and generality of the
theological side of the conversation, compared with the concrete
detail of the organizational side; this lack of theological detail
ultimately undermines the properly interdisciplinary nature of the
endeavor and results in a dominance of the social sciences in the
discussion. Is this universal weakness inevitable?

29.34 Each theologian's answer to that question will
depend on their particular ecclesiology, on how
elaborately they have developed their theology of power, of laity, of
ministry, of the Holy Spirit in the Church, and on their understanding of the human person, of revelation, and so forth. Before we
can combine theories of organization and ecclesiology in a balanced
and satisfying way, a good deal of straightforward ecclesiological
work must be done. Only after developing our theological understanding of how the people of God is organized and explaining how
our ecclesiology works in terms of power, the interaction of human
and divine, the place of the individual and small groups — only then
can we engage in detailed dialogue with social-science theories of
organization.[32] The possible effectiveness of such dialogue is illustrated by the work of Bonhoeffer and Rudge. Both of them, but
particularly the former, concentrate on holding together the quite

different, but not incompatible, languages and traditions of theology and sociology, giving some witness to theology's proper depth and thoroughness. Each of them is handicapped, though in different ways, by the size of the task.

29.35 One manner of dealing with the problem of detail is to restrict the subject of the interdisciplinary dialogue. The language of the social-science theories would seem more intelligible in relation to a clearly defined ecclesiological problem in a concrete context and tradition. Such is the complexity of organizational life, in the Church as elsewhere, that to talk clearly and effectively means to talk about a limited and defined area, and not to deal in general and grand theory.

Ecclesiological Models

29.36 The majority of the writings considered here have been shown, in practice at least, to employ an understanding of Church in which the concrete structures are detached from the theological 'ideal' Church, while still reflecting it in some way. Within such a Brunnerian-type ecclesiology structures may be changed along theological lines once the 'true' nature of the Church has been theologically described. Such an approach is distinct from that of Bonhoeffer, which implies a more theological or sacramental approach to the structures themselves. Working with this ecclesiological model means that suggestions for actual change in the Church must be constrained, or partly conditioned, by the Church's own theological understanding of those structures and what they embody.

29.37 Either ecclesiological model is coherent within an organizational ecclesiology; but it is as well to point out the difference in methodology that will result, so as to be clear as to what is being aimed at. If the Church institution is seen as a thoroughly human expression of a certain faith, then the organizational ecclesiologist may take a fairly adventurous approach to structural reform, in which, almost inevitably, the social-science view will dominate in the actual conclusions drawn. A more sacramental ecclesiology, in which the relation of the divine or transcendent to the here-and-now Church is not so clear, will feel itself more restrained in its consideration of concrete change, and will tend to emphasize the theological in its conclusions. If the organizational ecclesiologist is clear about his or her own position on this at the outset, the nature of the interdisciplinary task and its hoped-for results will be clarified and more highly defined.

Is Organizational Ecclesiology Theology?

29.38 This question arises because of the general lack of clarity concerning what the writers considered here are doing. At the outset I made it clear that we would be concerned with works of *ecclesiology* which employ theories of organization, and not consider the large body of sociological literature on the Church. In fact this division of material is not so clear, as the attentive reader will appreciate. A good deal of the writing of Rudge, Granfield, Thung, and the others is more properly sociological than theological; it is perhaps only Bonhoeffer's *Sanctorum Communio* which is theological to the core — arguably to the point of being hardly interdisciplinary at all.

29.39 Every theologian who 'borrows' from, or enters into conversation with another discipline — and it seems to me that theology must continually do so — runs the risk of either being seen as a 'theological imperialist,' or as an 'amateur' in the other field, and not properly a theologian. The interdisciplinary theologian needs, then, to invest some energy in sorting out what exactly she is doing in using another discipline. Is it a matter of simple borrowing of terms and ideas? Or is it a matter of whole-hearted adoption of another logic and language, in which theology proper, with its revelational and transcendent reference, becomes thoroughly immanent? One model of this interdisciplinary relationship that I have found helpful is that of *conversation*: the theologian cannot stop being properly theological (talking of faith- and God-matters) but always needs to learn more about human realities, in which there are other experts, with whom he or she engages in conversation. Being an amateur in other disciplines, as long as we know ourselves to be such, does not prevent us from being proper theologians, conversationalists who rely on our friends, but who retain our own logic, traditions, and language.

29.40 This is just one possible model of what is going on in the ecclesiological use of nontheological sciences; there are many others. Which model is adopted is important, as it will deeply affect the way the organizational ecclesiology is pursued; but it is still more important for the field in general that the nature of what is being done is made clear, giving the work a necessary coherence and consistency; out of such clarity a properly critical attitude and creativity can come.

29.41 These remarks amount to a call for deeper consideration of the use of theories of organization in ecclesiology. Each point mentioned indicates some fundamental premise on which organizational ecclesiology is based; these premises, however, remain undiscussed in many of the works to date. If this interdisciplinary field is to develop and offer insight into the nature of the Church (and even now it seems clear that it has crucial insights to offer), attention must be given to basics such as these, so that a proper foundation can be laid for future work.

Notes

1. Not everyone would agree with this and, as we shall see, a number of the writers considered here do treat different organizational approaches as discrete schools. The idea that these approaches are actually complementary and depend upon one another is particularly argued in more recent social-science studies; see, e.g., the comments on recent organizational theory in the general work of Herbert G. Hicks and C. Ray Gullett, *Organizations: Theory and Behavior* (New York: McGraw-Hill, 1975) 220.
2. These would include the work of Hicks & Gullett and the following: Amitai Etzioni, ed., *A Sociological Reader in Complex Organizations* (New York: Holt, Rhinehart & Winston, 1961); Gouldner, 'Organizational Analysis' in *Sociology Today*, ed. Robert K. Merton et al. (New York: Harper Torchbooks, 1965); Sherman Roy Krupp's critical and enlightening *Pattern in Organization Analysis* (Philadelphia: Chilton, 1961); William R. Scott's *Organizations: Rational, Natural and Open Systems* (London: Prentice-Hall, 1981).
3. There have been many useful studies of this work; particularly helpful is Peter Berger's essay 'The Social Character of the Question concerning Jesus Christ: Sociology and Ecclesiology,' in *The Place of Bonhoeffer*, ed. Martin E. Marty (London: SCM, 1963).
4. Berger, 'Social Character' 63, 76.
5. Bonhoeffer himself goes some way toward recognizing this when he argues for the necessity of a 'social philosophy' as the grounds of any sociology; see *Sanctorum Communio*, chap. 1.
6. Ibid. 146.
7. Ibid. 145.
8. Ibid. 88.
9. Ibid. 183.
10. Ibid. 173–4.
11. Compare the similar view described by Emil Brunner in *The Misunderstanding of the Church* (London: Lutterworth, 1952) that the 'true' church is not, and cannot be, identified, even in a partial way, with a human institution.
12. Berger, 'Social Character'.
13. The term 'open system' has been extensively used by social scientists in describing one of the facets of the relationship between an organization and its environment.

14. This is clearly set out in Robert William Dale, *A Manual of Congregational Principles* (1884; 11th ed., London: Hodder and Stoughton, 1920), which displays a commendable realism concerning the limitations of democratic practice once its context has become a larger, more anonymous group than the local congregation.
15. See Hans Küng, *Structures of the Church* (New York: Thomas Nelson & Sons, 1965); and his article 'Participation of the Laity in Church Leadership and in Church Elections,' *Journal of Ecumenical Studies* 6 (1969) 511–33. Others who should be mentioned besides Küng include Leon Suenens, *Corresponsibility in the Church* (London: Burns and Oates).
16. This is particularly clear in his article 'Participation' 571 f.
17. Patrick Granfield, *Ecclesial Cybernetics: A Study of Democracy in the Church* (New York: Macmillan, 1973). The main pattern of Granfield's ideas is also to be found in his article, 'Ecclesial Cybernetics: Communication in the Church,' *TS* 29 (1968) 662–78.
18. See Granfield, 'Ecclesial Cybernetics' 665.
19. The term 'iron law of oligarchy' comes from Robert W. E. Michels, *Political Parties: A Sociological Study of the Oligarchic Tendencies of Modern Democracy* (London: Jarrold & Sons, 1915). It should also be mentioned that there is equally evidence for an 'iron law of democracy,' according to Alvin W. Gouldner, 'Organizational Analysis,' in *Sociology Today*, ed. Robert K. Merton (New York: Harper Torchbooks, 1959). Both 'laws' actually witness to the same reality, that the majority of organizational members are content not to be involved in decision making, except in situations of extreme oppression or crisis.
20. The study of James G. March and Herbert A. Simon, *Organizations* (New York: Wiley, 1958), is a good example of the way a theory can be worked out around an understanding of the members' indifference and apathy, and how this can be exploited by managers.
21. Jean-Guy Vaillancourt, *Papal Power* (London: Berkley, 1980).
22. Peter F. Rudge, *Ministry and Management: The Study of Ecclesiastical Administration* (London: Tavistock, 1968).
23. Ibid. 21–23.
24. Ibid. 37–39.
25. I share this view with a number of theorists, notably Sherman Krupp, whose work *Pattern in Organizational Analysis* (above n. 2) gives a critical and probing account of the social-science field.
26. Mady Thung, *The Precarious Organization: Sociological Explorations of the Church's Mission and Structure* (The Hague: Mouton, 1976).
27. Ibid. 44–74.
28. For a good introduction to the sociological importance of goals in an organization, see Charles Perrow, 'The Analysis of Goals in Complex Organizations,' *American Sociological Review* 26 (1961) 854–66.
29. Thung, *The Precarious Organization* 121–3.
30. Ibid. 161–72.
31. Ibid. 237–9.

32. This is the approach of my own unpublished study in which a very particular ecclesiological problem is addressed and a good deal of space devoted to working out the appropriate ecclesiological approach to power and communication, e.g., before the interdisciplinary conversation can take place: Clare Watkins, *Laity and Communication: Some Implications of Organization Theory for the Vatican II Church* (PhD diss., Cambridge, England, 1990).

SECTION FIVE

Implications for Postmodern Culture

30

Fergus Kerr
Milbank's Thesis

This extract comes from Fergus Kerr's article 'Simplicity Itself: Milbank's Thesis', *New Blackfriars*, Vol. 73 No. 861, June 1992, pp. 306–10. The Dominican Kerr uses his theological and philosophical skills to give a summary of John Milbank's *Theology and Social Theory* — a summary which Milbank himself recognizes as accurate (*34.1*). Since it is written more concisely than the original, it acts as a useful introduction to Milbank's formidable work. Kerr is the author, among other works, of *Theology After Wittgenstein* (Oxford: Blackwell, 1986).

30.1 A book entitled *Theology and Social Theory* in a series containing titles such as *Theology and Philosophy, Theology and Politics* and the like, would naturally be expected to bring together in a mutually illuminating way what everyone is likely to think of as two radically different disciplines, each with its own autonomous method and distinctive discourse — 'naturally', that is to say, in the cultural environment of carefully protected academic specialisms which we inhabit and which the author means to disrupt. Theologians, peering through the machicolations of faith-engaging scholarship, would learn from sociologists about the ways in which ideas are shaped by social processes. Sociologists, at least those few who specialize in religion, might glean a serendipitous insight in conversation with a friendly theologian as they set up research programmes or interpret their results, but, as scientists, their approach would of course be completely open-minded, impartial, neutral and above all 'secular'.

30.2 'Beyond Secular Reason', the subtitle runs. John Milbank's simple but ingenious thesis is that, far from being two separate and self-sustaining disciplines, theology already contains a great deal of social theory while the social sciences are steeped in theology. Theologians have become increasingly (if reluctantly) aware, since they discovered the idea of the development of doctrine, that their constructions and even their paradigms are inescapably contingent and historical; but that does not go very deep. On the whole, according to Milbank, they suppose that most of what is to be known about social processes must still be learned from social scientists. He is thinking in particular of theologians who seize on some social theory of (usually) Marxist inspiration and work out what place remains for religion within the situation authoritatively described, as they suppose, by the social theory. Theology would thus deal only with what 'secular reason' leaves free — another version of 'God of the gaps' theology.

30.3 Milbank is struck, however, by recent developments within social theory itself which suggest that, contrary to the Marxist thesis about the priority of the economic base over the ideological and hence theological superstructure, there is *no* socio-economic reality which is more 'basic' than the reality of religion. Social theorists, influenced by Nietzsche, trace the formation of social structures to the will-to-power. While they mostly want to get rid of religion they acknowledge the subterranean presence of the mythic-ritual elements that social structures characteristically contain. (These are, of course, mostly French theorists: British sociologists would mostly be wary, and even uncomprehending, of this type of literature.)

30.4 The Nietzschean legacy is ambivalent. On the one hand it seems the last word in post-Enlightenment rationalism, a 'truly non-metaphysical mode of secular reason'. On the other hand, for all the declaimed scientific positivism and evolutionary naturalism, Nietzsche's work also embodies an ontology of non-human power and primordial conflict which is simply a return to a pagan perception of life. It looks as if something metaphysical, and thus in some sense something theological, rears its head in even the most obsessively pagan 'genealogy of morals' so far invented.

30.5 Paradoxically, then, post-Nietzschean social theorists have recognized that the mythic-religious dimension of social structures cannot be treated as superstructural, while most theologians go on naively submitting to the authority of the supposedly secular discipline of the social sciences. While post-Nietzschean social theorists become suspicious of allegedly secular rationality, post-Enlightenment theologians go on innocently working under the constraints of their respect for precisely that. Theologians accept the autonomy of secular reason, and thus place themselves under the rule of methodological atheism, whereas social theorists now recognize the practical inescapability of theistic or anti-theistic elements, however disguised and displaced, in any social order they study.

30.6 In one sense, then, Milbank's thesis is simplicity itself. There is no need to bring theology and social theory together, theology is *already* social theory, and social theory is *already* theology. The task is to lay bare the theology, and anti-theology, at work in supposedly non-theological disciplines like sociology, and, analogously, to uncover the social theory inscribed in theology — not just the methodological humanism mistakenly respected by modern theologians but the theory of society which Christian theology, properly practised, always already is. Whether one agrees in the end, or even succeeds in following much of Milbank's extremely learned and densely argued exposition of this thesis, is another matter. One cannot doubt the brilliant simplicity of the thesis itself.

30.7 The epigraph offers a second clue to the simplicity of Milbank's thesis: 'For both "civil" and "fabulous" theologies are alike fabulous and civil'. The quotation comes from St Augustine's great book, *The City of God* (the reference needs to be corrected: it is to chapter 8, not chapter 9, of Book VI). One way into Milbank's book is to read the last chapter first, where it becomes clear that *Theology and Social Theory* is essentially a creative retrieval of Augustine's *De Civitate Dei*. Briefly, Augustine argued that the peace of the earthly City (the Roman empire) was a peace created by arbitrary limitation of a preceding state of conflict, whereas the true peace of the heavenly City (the Catholic Church) was a state of harmonious agreement indistinguishable from a community of love and a realization of justice for all. However various the customs and institutions which bring human beings together and divide them, there are, Augustine thought, in the final resort, only two kinds of human association: the alliance of those who live according to the flesh and the community of those who live according to the spirit, each in the 'peace' appropriate to their kind. For Milbank, as for Augustine, peace and non-violence are onto-logically prior to, and more basic than, the anarchy and strife which, on most views of the world, including gnostic forms of Christianity, are primordial and foundational, so that religious strategies (if any), like political ones, can do no more than hold it in check. On a proper ('Catholic') understanding of the Christian doctrine of creation, on the other hand, sin of any kind has to be secondary: reality is fundamentally good ('And God saw ... '), evil is *privatio boni* and 'violence is an unnecessary intrusion'. Again, whatever one makes of it, the thesis is simplicity itself: Christianity is committed to the ontological priority of non-violence, harmony and peace over anarchy, aggression and war.

30.8 The third preliminary clue to entering Milbank's book is the table of contents. Theology is played off against 'liberalism' (Part I), 'positivism' (II), 'dialectics' (III) and finally 'difference' (IV). In effect, we are being offered a post-Nietzschean history of modern western views of reality as a prelude to retrieving Christian theology.

30.9 'Liberalism', in this connection, is a Bad Thing. It is a commonplace, across the spectrum from socialists and feminists to conservatives and neo-ultramontanist Catholics, that liberalism is to be rejected for its 'individualism' — for occluding the manifest ways in which human beings are 'situated' in a network of social roles and communal relationships. In a misguided attempt to protect the autonomy and the natural rights of the individual, liberalism as a moral and political philosophy only undermines the communities which alone enable human beings to flourish. So the story goes. Theologically, at least since Newman's denunciations of it, liberalism in religion operates on the assumption that believers are free to use, or change, or discard, religious symbols and doctrines, according to their current experiential value for the individual. Politically, as Nicholas Boyle showed in his 'Understanding Thatcherism',[1] the belief in the primacy of individual desires has driven the ideology of British central government since 1979.

30.10 Historically, according to Milbank, in seventeenth-century thinkers such as Grotius and Hobbes, the concepts of sovereignty, autonomy, property, power, and so on, which were to generate the new 'secular' disciplines of political theory, economics and sociology, emerged from the late-medieval theological matrix of an effectively non-Trinitarian theism which celebrated a notion of the absolute will of the divine monarch. The 'anthropology' which celebrates human beings as atomistic individuals, with their individuality defined essentially as will, would thus be the spin-off of a (distinctly non-Thomist!) voluntarist monotheism. The modern liberal-individualist conception of the human person would thus be a product of a heretical (because barely if at all Trinitarian) conception of God.

30.11 In Part II of his book Milbank introduces us to the notion of 'positivism': that supposedly non-metaphysical concentration on the facts, on the given, which, in Comte and his progeny, has encouraged the idea of sociology as almost (if not quite) one of the natural sciences. At about the same time, indeed rather earlier, such conservative Catholic thinkers as de Bonald, de Lamennais, de Maistre and Ballanche, were reasserting the social nature of human beings, reacting so strongly against the liberal doctrine of the autonomy of the individual will that they created an ecclesiocentric positivism, usually labelled 'traditionalism', which was officially ruled out at the Vatican Council (1870). Just as Marx famously stood Hegel on his head, so Milbank nicely says, Comte did the same to de Bonald. The ferociously royalist Catholic's mystical corporatism turned quite easily into the methodological humanist's cult of the *fait sociale*. (For that matter, Comte borrowed a great deal from Catholic liturgy when he invented the new religion he regarded as essential to the spread of altruism, including even a 'Positivist Calendar' in which the names of scientists replaced those of the saints.) For the positivists as for the Catholic reactionaries, the social order is a totality which is prior to the creative activities of human beings. Once again, then, social theory and theology mirror one another, and the latter even generates the former. In effect, as Milbank says, theology encounters in sociology only a theology in disguise.

30.12 In Part III, in which theology is confronted with 'dialectics', Milbank deals with Hegel, Marx and some liberation theologians. The trouble with these last, briefly, is that they remain imprisoned in Karl Rahner's non-historical metaphysics of human subjectivity ('Not without distress do I realize that some of my conclusions here coincide with those of reactionaries in the Vatican'). In effect, they remain trapped in liberalism. They should have followed Blondel, Milbank argues, 'perhaps the boldest exercise in Christian thought of modern times' (*L'Action* appeared in 1893, when he was thirty two). By embracing his absolute historicism and perspectivism they would have escaped from the illusions of the quasi-divine solitary human subject.

30.13 The welcome and brilliant excursus on Blondel prepares the way for devastating criticism of Hegel, who turns out to remain trapped in the Cartesian myth of the autonomous self. He is 'still a liberal'. Like Hobbes, he traces the origins of human society to individual self-seeking. The new element is a gnostic myth, taken over from the Lutheran mystic Jakob Boehme, about the self-estranged and self-returning deity, but of course only one more deviation from a properly Christian understanding of creation.

30.14 In Part IV we turn to 'the thinking of difference', in effect French and German philosophy in the post-Nietzschean mode. All these thinkers, including Heidegger, Foucault, Derrida, Deleuze and Lyotard, corporately labelled 'nihilism' here, assume that reality is ultimately anarchy, which, in the absence of God, cannot be controlled except by subjecting it to the will

to power in some form or another. Plurality of meaning is necessarily equivocation, contingency is fate, difference is rupture, and so
on. In effect, the unity sought by previous generations of thinkers
gives way to irrepressible plurality. What Nietzsche called *Mono-
tonotheismus* yields to crypto-polytheistic views of reality. Alasdair
MacIntyre, in *Whose Justice? Which Rationality?*,[2] has sought to
retrieve a Christian moral philosophy which breaks with modern
nihilism (otherwise known as emotivism, relativism, subjectivism,
pluralism and so on). Milbank, offering us another clue, describes
his book as 'a temeritous attempt to radicalize the though of
MacIntyre' — which, in the end, he finds too close to Aristotle and
thus insufficiently Christian.

30.15   His own proposal, finally, is that, in contrast to all
(*sic*) other views of the world, Christianity alone,
properly understood, denies the ultimacy of chaos and conflict.
Only Christianity — 'and perhaps Judaism' — affirms that peace
(*shalom?*) is coterminous with Being. Christian theology, properly
understood, is alone capable of exposing and overcoming the liberalism, positivism, dialectics and nihilism inscribed in the ideology of
western society, and so in our social and political theory essentially
because all four of these configurations are themselves versions, or
subversions, of theology.

30.16   A brilliantly simple thesis, then. But to see if it is
sustainable, of course, one has to read the book.

Notes

1. Nicholas Boyle, 'Understanding Thatcherism', *New Blackfriars*, vol. 69,
   no. 818, July/August 1988, pp. 307–24.
2. Alasdair MacIntyre, *Whose Justice? Which Rationality?* London: Duckworth, 1988.

31

Rowan Williams
A Theological Critique of Milbank

This extract comes from Rowan Williams' article 'Saving Time: Thoughts on Practice, Patience and Vision', *New Blackfriars*, Vol. 73 No. 861, June 1992, pp. 319–26. Williams is now Anglican Bishop of Monmouth. Previously he was a professor of theology at Oxford, where he was also John Milbank's tutor. In this extract he offers a characteristically gentle theological critique of *Theology and Social Theory*. Among his other works are *The Wound of Knowledge* (Darton, Longman and Todd, London, 1979), *Resurrection* (Darton, Longman and Todd, London, 1982) and *Arius* (Darton, Longman and Todd, London, 1987).

The central criticism that Williams makes concerns ecclesiology and praxis. He repeatedly notes a gap between Milbank's understanding of the church and the church as it is realized in history. Williams is 'concerned to keep in view ... the danger of setting the common life of the Church too dramatically apart from the temporal ways in which the good is realized in a genuinely contingent world' (*31.8*). He argues that Milbank tends to fuse historical narrative about the church with an essentialist, ideological model of the church. This fusion does not finally do justice to 'the specific points of strain' that have characterized the history of the church (*31.2*). In the process, Milbank's account of Christian distinctiveness tends to become ahistorical (*31.4*); his understanding of Christian 'peace', for example, is in danger of becoming 'vacuous' and 'fictive', precisely because he underestimates historical processes (*31.5*). In contrast, for Williams, 'the peace of the Church as an historical community is always in construction' (*31.6*). He also argues that Milbank's criticism of liberation theology tends to be over-simplified, ignoring important differences among liberation theologians themselves (*31.10*).

31.1 *Theology and Social Theory* is a book that prompts conversation on almost every page — conversation of both the 'yes, and ... ' and the 'yes, but ... ' kind, as well as something like a 'no, but ... ' on occasion. An adequate review would have to be a kind of gloss, a talmudic margin. It is no small tribute to Milbank that this work is so hard to discuss briefly. What follows is not a review, but a few fragments of this reader's side of the conversation, assembled round a focal area of unease within an overall admiration for the learning and boldness of the enterprise. My title will hint at something of my discomfort: is Milbank's commitment to history and narrative, to time as the medium of benign creativity and non-competitive difference, fully realized in his exposition? Does he 'save time' in a theological sense or only in the colloquial one of getting more expeditiously to his goal than the circumstances might seem to warrant?

31.2 The project of reconstructing a Christian ontology by retelling the story of the Christian Church's origins, so as to display it as the history that makes sense of all histories, is heralded as one of the indispensable moments in the rehabilitation of a properly theological critique of secular order (e.g. p. 381). 'The metanarrative ... is the genesis of the Church' (p. 387). This is an intriguing and exhilarating prospect; I am not sure if it has been carried through. Christian universalism is opposed to the 'orders' of non-Christian antiquity — the Roman sacralization of dominion, with its programmatic refusal of a properly common good, and the Jewish commitment to law as the defining structure of a common good, at least for one specific community. The Church witnesses to a community without dominion, bonded by charity and forgiveness rather than law, ethnically unrestricted: in this definition of its ideal self, it uncovers what other orders characteristically lack, and the story of its emergence over against empire and synagogue begins to shape the kind of metanarrative now required for a critique of modern order (and presumably of the sacral order of other religious traditions, an entailment of Milbank's scheme worked out more fully in a later essay[1]). But the problem here is, I think, the trap of fusing historical narrative with 'essentialist', diagrammatic accounts of ideological options. The history of 'ecclesial origination' here offered is a narrative constructed from a position determined as outside the Jewish and Roman worlds of reference; and while Milbank would (rightly) reply that we cannot but tell the story from where we now are, from the standpoint of the *achieved*, the realized difference of the Church, we are not given any purchase on the specific points of strain or collision that gradually constituted the Church as historically and tangibly other than the orders it contests. It is as if this origination is the birth of a full-grown Minerva; and if narrative is *plotted*, a structured sequence of transformations, the metanarrative that is being sought is in danger of flattening out into a bald statement of timeless ideal differences.

31.3 To carry through the project more adequately might involve, for example, attention to the variety of ways in which Jewish identity in particular was constructed in the Second Temple period and after; to how and why the practice and teaching of Jesus came to conflict with the *politically* dominant definitions of Jewish probity and loyalty — which would in turn need some analysis of the economic role of the Temple and its administrators in occupied Judaea; to the specific character of the resurrection narratives as stories about the reconsolidation of Jesus' practice, especially in terms of the offer of forgiveness and unrestricted hospitality; to the characteristic crises of the early communities over issues of inclusion and purity and the relation of ethics to eschatology. It might also need to reckon with the fact that Mishnaic Judaism, which is definitive for practically all later developments, is itself shaped by response to a variety of first century problems and ruptures in the Jewish world — a sister rather than a mother to the Church, and not necessarily representing in its sophisticated views of law precisely what the Jewish world before 70 AD would have taken as axiomatic.[2] And we should have to trace the way in which Christian communities worked out an understanding of their unity and coherence, and how exactly this proved uncontainable within the Roman state (what were Christians tried for and why?).[3]

31.4 Now I am not, of course, complaining that Milbank should have written a social history of the first two Christian centuries; but I am concerned that the specific process by which Christian distinctiveness became aware of itself is occluded by the rather ahistorical framework of this narrative of origins. The telling of the story as a narrative of learning or discovery and of particular (economic or social or ritual) crises and conflicts would not weaken the 'metanarrative' project: on the contrary, it might well give it more substance. For the risk Milbank's exposition runs is, rather paradoxically, of slipping into a picture of history as the battlefield of ideal types. He notes (p. 163) the oddity of the fact that in Hegel's system there is no real ground for the necessity of the Idea's appearance in an historical individual (I am by no means sure that he has fully got hold of what Hegel has to say about the historical Good Friday, incidentally);[4] but a malign interpreter might say that the specificity of the first century Mediterranean world had been no less sacrificed here. The very faint suggestion that ecclesial life is determined by its negation of prior forms imperils just that historical gratuity and contingency that is essential to the whole project. There are some excellent observations (p. 234) on how historical 'plot' can outrun 'character', yet be retrievable, narratively, as destiny. But if that destiny blurs the edges of the contingency of the plotting itself, we are landed back in a caricature version of Hegel, a vulgar dialecticism. Milbank emphatically does not want this outcome, nor does he give it explicit houseroom; but there is an unmistakable grid imposed on the vagaries of late antique social and intellectual history that does not help the case. There is more thought to be given to how the story of the Church's beginnings is to be adequately told.

31.5 The insistence on thinking Christ in inseparable relation with the Church is, however, one of the most important constructive elements of the book. Milbank's reservation (p. 398) about Girard, that he is inclined to deal with Jesus rather than the Church and so fails to say enough about the 'idiom' of the peace adumbrated by the preaching and death of Jesus, is a searching point for the Girardian to answer. But this issue of idiom is one that again raises some questions about Milbank's procedure. The Christian imagination is of 'a state of total peace', enabling us 'to unthink the necessity of violence' and reaffirm the ontological priority of non-violence (p. 411). It is a culture of corporate virtue, instead of competing heroisms, of difference without menace, and of forgiveness (earlier on — pp. 168, 172 — this has been contrasted with the merely formal reconciliations of Hegelianism). The recovery of a genuinely Augustinian political ethic, the virtues of God's *polis*, is another real achievement in the work; but some of the questions already hinted at return here, questions that would need to be put to aspects of Augustine as well. It seems that we are again confronted with something 'achieved', and left with little account of how it is learned, negotiated, betrayed, inched forward, discerned and risked. To speak of 'total peace' (and Derrida's anxiety about Levinas' comparable apocalypticism may be recalled here)[5] is not in fact to speak of a culture or an idiom — or really an *ethic*. Milbank boldly and obstinately contests the haunting of ethics by the tragic, to the extent that this might suggest an inevitability, a non-contingency, about evil. Yet I wonder whether the very ideas of culture, idiom and ethic insist on the tragic in some form. If our salvation is cultural (historical, linguistic, etc.), it is not a return to primordial harmonics, purely innocent difference. We are always already, in history, shaped by privation, living at the expense of each other: important moral choices entail the loss of certain specific goods for certain specific persons, because moral determination, like any 'cultural' determination, recognizes that not all goods for all persons are *contingently* compatible. The peace of the Church is going to be vacuous or fictive if it is not historically aware of how it is *constructed* in events of determination which involve conflict and exclusion of some kind.

31.6 This is really to say no more than that the minimalist theodicy of Augustinianism needs a hearing too: an authentically contingent world is one in which you cannot guarantee the compatibility of goods. That's what it *is* to be created. And when that contingency becomes meshed with rational beings' self-subverting choices of unreality over truth, the connectedness of human community becomes life-threatening as well as life-nurturing. That is what it is to be fallen. Grace does not give innocence, as Milbank is generally well and eloquently aware, it gives absolution, and the Church's peace is a healed history, not a 'total' harmony whose constructed (and thus scarred) character doesn't show. And in our history, healing is repeatedly imperilled and broken by new decisions. The Church actually articulated its gospel of peace by speaking the language of repentance: failure can be 'negotiated' into what is creative. But this means that the peace of the Church *as an historical community* is always in construction. It does not promise a new and finished innocence in the order of time, but focuses the freedom of God constantly to draw that order back to difference that is nourishing, not ruinous.

31.7 Is this to succumb to a myth of necessary violence? Two points: first, the word 'violence' is both loaded and vague, and sometimes it is being made to do duty for any voluntary limiting of another's unrestricted will, while still retaining extreme pejorative connotations not necessarily appropriate to such a more general account. It ought to be possible to say that a contingent world is one in which contestation is inevitable, given that not all goods are 'compossible', without saying that there can be no healing or mending eschatologically, or that conflict and exclusion have either a sacred or a necessarily liberative character. Second, part of the problem lies in how to read the doctrine of creation itself. In God, according to orthodox Christian theology, there is difference without collision or competition, in the generating of the Word and the procession of the Spirit: this has often been agreed to be the ground for understanding the positing of difference 'outside' the divine life. But this positing is not a *repetition* of divine generation; it is the making of a world whose good will take time to realize, whose good is to emerge from uncontrolled circumstance — not by divine enactment in a direct sense, but by a kind of interaction of divine and contingent causality, entailing a divine responsiveness such as the doctrine of the Trinity again authorizes, in letting us think both a divine giving and a divine receiving. Creation itself is not to be thought of as a moment of tragic rupture, a debauching of divine Wisdom, but it is surely pregnant with the risk of tragedy, conflicting goods, if the good of what is made is necessarily bound up with taking time. The Fall is not necessary, logically or ontologically, but (in Milbank's own language) its story can be 'retrieved' as one outworking of what creation (logically) cannot but make possible if it really is *other* to God.

31.8 What I am concerned to keep in view is the danger of setting the common life of the Church too dramatically apart from the temporal ways in which the good is realized in a genuinely contingent world. We might remember Simone Weil's insistence[6] that the attaining of goals in a material environment by timebound beings entails a 'mediation of desire': to get what we want, we have to perform actions that are not what we want, not themselves desirable — boring physical labour, for example. But this suggests that a theology of Church history involves theologizing the risks taken by the Church in constructing its peace; and so too theologizing about its misconstruals, its repeated slithering into premature totalizations, and, ultimately, theologizing about the victims of the historical Church — even where this risks sharpening some of the particular conflicts of the Church's present life. The imagining of 'total peace' must somehow be accessible to those whose history is not yet heard or even heard in and by the Church (how might a woman tell this story as a story of peace or promise?).

31.9 Which leads me to some final reflections on Milbank's discussion of political theologies, European and Third World. Here the great strength of the treatment is its full and lucid exposition of something Gutiérrez touched on in his earliest work, the close correlation between political options and theologies of grace and nature. A certain sort of chastened Thomism, vaguely inspired by Maritain, helps to legitimize 'Christian Democrat' parties of a liberal-centrist kind; a more 'integralist' view of grace and nature impels to a more revolutionary politics. Milbank brilliantly demonstrates the ambiguities at work here. The problem with integralism is that it can suggest a definition of corporate and individual good in which the role of explicit reference to the saving action of God is obscure; statements about revelation, conversion, grace or holiness are always in danger of melting into supposedly univeralizable beliefs about human goodness. There is no clear place from which the Church can call secularity to account. There is, in fact, an ersatz peace invoked here between the city of God and the earthly city. Add to this the effect of a poorly digested Marxist-Leninism, and you have a virtual abandonment of political ethics: necessary conflict necessarily delivers an advance in the realizing of justice. Economics and politics are kidnapped by a new doctrine of providence (pp. 244–5). And the familiar justification for contemporary use of (Marxist and other) social science to ground a political theology, the claim that this is simply a modern version of what Aquinas did with Aristotle, is sharply rebutted: modern social science is precisely what *replaces* authentic political ethics such as Aristotelianism provided, and so cannot serve a political theology (p. 248).

3.10 Milbank's dismantling of much of the rhetoric of liberation theology is an impressive critique, chiefly because it is done out of a conviction that liberation theology is *insufficiently political*, still caught in the Weberian trap of seeing cataclysmic social change as the condition for improved individual liberties — i.e. it fails to imagine what creative sociality is. There is some weight in this, and Milbank's impatience with some of the woolly nonsense that passes for theology in this context is readily intelligible. I think too that he has identified some serious difficulties in the project of the early Gutiérrez and Juan Luis Segundo. But I also read these pages wondering how seriously they had grappled with more recent developments in Latin America debates about folk piety, about the suspicion and retrieval of popular images, about Christology. Increasingly, it has become impossible to generalize usefully about liberation theology as a project that makes Christian language and practice instrumental to a programme whose norms come from elsewhere. Taking a couple of examples almost at random from a collection published as long ago as the late 1970's,[7] we can find Galilea and Assmann both insisting on the emptiness of what Milbank calls the 'instrumental enclosure' (p. 242) of liberation theologies, and calling for a deepening of the charismatic and prophetic life of Christian communities as places where equality and forgiveness are realized locally and specifically, grounded in eucharistic worship and reflection on scripture.

31.11 Milbank's own conclusion, indeed, seems to envisage the Church's political calling very much in terms of the sustaining of paradigm creative political societies, like the Latin American base communities. But this might have led to some nuancing in the treatment of theologies of liberation, which, as it stands, will bring comfort to some whom Milbank would find unwelcome bedfellows (as he is clearly well aware). And even the unbalanced instrumentalism of some early liberationist writing should make us recall the sheer scale of corruption, repression and political infantilism which it confronted. Was it really so easy in 1970, say, to believe in the avoidance, the contingency of struggle, even armed struggle? Somewhere behind the romanticizing and rationalizing of futile, disorganized violence so typical of that era lies a harsher recognition that *here* the gospel cannot but be adversarial in respect of existing power; the question is how to handle that adversarial role without colluding with state violence by mirroring it (think of Peru in the last decade) or becoming totally marginal to any imaginable political process at more than local level. What *force* is entailed in realizing peace?

31.12 Milbank's Augustinianism allows this question to be raised, certainly; and perhaps the important thing is to avoid, as he does, an answer in anything other than negative, regulative or minatory terms. But this issue is a significant part, surely, of his campaign for real ethics; and my point throughout this brief essay has been to press the question of whether the kind of ethic he so evidently wants doesn't require rather more attention to the tragic implications of contingency itself, if the peace it constructs is not to be totalizing and ahistorical. This is, in fact, something to which Milbank gives exemplary attention in an essay on Donald MacKinnon,[8] which ought to be read in tandem with any pages in *Theology and Social Theory* that might suggest an undifferentiated or timeless model of ecclesial virtue. There too, I think, he says, very obliquely, more of what I would like him to say about the distinctions between divine generation, creation and fall. We can expect further clarification from the work he is evidently now engaged in to do directly with trinitarian and Christological themes. In any case, it will, I hope be clear that these (Lutheran? MacKinnonesque?) queries are designed not to challenge the project, but to ask how fully its own leading themes are enacted in its exposition; how much place is systematically given for the patience that contingency enjoins.

Notes

1. 'The End of Dialogue', in G. d'Costa, ed., *Christian Uniqueness Reconsidered: The Myth of a Pluralistic Theology of Religions*, New York 1990, pp. 174–91.
2. Practically all of these issues are addressed expertly in J. D. Crossan, *The Historical Jesus: The Life of a Mediterranean Jewish Peasant*, Edinburgh 1991; see especially pp. 422 ff. on the parallelism of Christianity and Mishnaic Judaism.
3. For some reflections on this, see R. Williams, 'Does it make sense to speak of pre-Nicene orthodoxy?' in R. Williams, ed., *The Making of Orthodoxy: Essays in Honour of Henry Chadwick*, Cambridge 1989, pp. 1–23.
4. It seems fairly clear from the relevant section in the *Lectures on the Philosophy of Religion* (ed. P. Hodgson, Berkeley, Los Angeles and

London, 1985, vol. III, pp. 124ff.) that the overthrowing of the constructions of meaning typical of Roman society and religion requires precisely the trauma of God's manifestation in the body of an individual maximally devoid of sacrality and significance within the Roman system — thus in the corpse of a man suffering a slave's death at the hands of imperial authority as well as at the instigation of his own traditional religious authorities.

5. J. Derrida, *D'un ton apocalyptique adopté naguère en philosophie*, Paris 1983; ET in *Semeia: An Experimental Journal for Biblical Criticism* 23 (1982), pp. 62–97, from the text as given at a conference in 1980.

6. See especially some articles published in *Libres Propos*, May and August 1929; some very good discussion of the issue in Peter Winch's book, *Simone Weil: 'The Just Balance'*, Cambridge 1989, chs. 5–9, 11, and cf. the present writer's review article on Winch's book, *Philosophical Investigations* 14.2 (1991), pp. 155–71, especially 158ff.

7. *Faces of Jesus: Latin American Christologies*, ed. J. M. Bonino, Maryknoll, NY, 1984 (the Spanish original appeared in 1977).

8. ' "Between purgation and illumination": a critique of the theology of right', in K. Surin, ed. *Christ, Ethics and Tragedy: Essays in Honour of Donald MacKinnon*, Cambridge 1989, pp. 161–96, especially 183–92.

32

Aidan Nichols
An Ecclesial Critique of Milbank

This extract comes from the Dominican theologian Aidan Nichols'
article 'Non Tali Auxilio: John Milbank's Suasion to Orthodoxy',
New Blackfriars, Vol. 73 No. 861, June 1992, pp.326–32.

Despite his obvious admiration for the intellectual stimulation of
John Milbank's *Theology and Social Theory*, Nichols makes two
forceful criticisms. First, he believes that Milbank's overall position
is 'hermetic': 'there can be no argument to the truth of Christianity
from shared premises with non-Christians, for no such premises
exist' (*32.3*). In effect Milbank replaces 'dialectic' simply with
'rhetoric'. For the radically postmodern Milbank, unlike Nichols,
there are no 'universal structures of reason' (*32.4*). In the process
the church becomes for Milbank 'the only possible bearer of human
community' (*32.5*). Like Gregory Baum (see my 'Introduction'),
Nichols argues for a Catholic position founded upon natural law —
that is, for a system of rationality which does see continuities
between the ecclesial and the secular.

This point leads to Nichols' second criticism: Milbank's position
appears finally to be theocratic. It is theocratic in the sense that it
seeks to restore Christendom and in the sense that 'it systematically
writes out of the social script all clauses — based on natural law,
human rights, or whatever — which should safeguard in a Christendom society the protected place which, in conscience, unbelievers,
and those of other faiths, should be accorded' (*32.6*). Although
Nichols does not use Baum's term 'exclusivism' to depict Milbank's
position, it is clear that his opposition is very similar and just as
forceful. For both men 'Milbank goes too far' (*32.7*).

32.1 I finished this breath-taking book lost in admiration
for the breadth of intellectual culture that lies behind
it; for its situating of different enquiries — theological, philosophical, sociological — in illuminating inter-relation; for the masterly
way in which it weaves together negative analysis and positive
proposal so as to commend Christian faith as the only world-view,

and recipe for social living, truly worth having. That a British author, writing at the end of the twentieth century, could take on, in profoundly informed fashion, every major proponent of autonomous thought and religiously emancipated social action ('secular reason'), from the Athenian enlightenment to the Parisian *nouveaux philosophes*, all with a view to showing the inadequacy — not simply *de facto* but *de jure* — of their projects, and, correlatively the sole adequacy of a religious, and more specifically a Christian, alternative in both theory and practice; this is, evidently, a publishing event of considerable magnitude. Moreover, the subtlety and sophistication of Milbank's criticisms of a range of secular constructs for both thought and social action so broad as to include virtually the entire contemporary intelligentsia of Western Europe and North America, will require a response of equal incisiveness from the inhabitants of these systems, and, as such, makes his book an event in intellectual history as well. That his critique of secular rationality in its various guises is mounted in the name of Christian *orthodoxy* and Catholic *tradition* can, it seems, only gladden the heart of a Catholic believer, a priest, a Dominican . . . In the hour of Catholic Christianity's desperate intellectual need (a glance at the pages of the *Times Literary Supplement* is enough to show the disappearance of Christian orthodoxy, as a source of meaning and truth, from high culture in Britain), God has, apparently, visited his people.

32.2 'It seems', 'apparently' . . . My second, and equally strong, reaction was a shudder of aversion. *Non tali auxilio:* 'not by such help' is Christian, and especially Catholic, faith to be recommended. Despite the numerous true judgments, good maxims and beautiful insights to be found scattered through this book, its overall message is deplorable. My objections can be summed up in two words: 'hermeticism' and 'theocracy'.

32.3 By 'hermeticism' I mean the enclosure of Christian discourse and practice within a wholly separate universe of thought and action, a universe constituted by the prior 'mythos' of Christianity — that is (I take it, the word is never explained) an overarching, supra-rational, vision of the world, within which alone particular truths can be set forth, particular exemplars of action set up for imitation. For Milbank there can be no such thing as an intellectual indebtedness of the Church to natural wisdom. Every putative form of such wisdom as can be named is not extraneous to the Christian *mythos*, and without a role in the dramatic narrative, from Genesis to Apocalypse, in which that *mythos* is expressed. Also, all natural wisdom is legitimately liable to deconstruction. Its own story of interpretation is poised unhappily between the pre-Socratic Heraclitus, with his view of Being as flux, and the contemporary French post-modernists, with their anarchic nihilism, and at no point can the history of its degeneration be halted, so as to provide the play of signifying that is human language and culture with a stable foundation. Only supernatural revelation, itself equally 'unfounded', yet, as *super*-natural, invulnerable to such attack, can reliably disclose what Christian Scholasticism has called the transcendentals — the beautiful, the good, the true — in their interconnected unity. Otherwise there is (literally) nothing. No common ground exists, therefore, between natural wisdom either in its philosophical form or (presumably, this goes undiscussed by Milbank) such non-philosophical forms as the other world-religions, their rites, beliefs, norms for action, literature and art. At best, from *within* the Christian *mythos* and narrative we can reclaim fragments of another tradition, such as that of the Greek *polis*, in the way that Christian exegetes have allegorically exploited the Hebrew Bible as the Church's 'Old Testament'. There can be no *argument* to the truth of Christianity from shared premises with non-Christians, for no such premises exist. There can only be *persuasion* to accept the Gospel, whether negatively, by showing up the vacuousness of the (Western) alternatives, or positively, by evoking its beauty. 'Dialectics', discourse based on reason, is to be replaced by 'rhetoric', that is, in the last analysis, an appeal to taste.

32.4 It is no use my protesting that such an ordinance is inhuman, or at least anti-humane, for Milbank recognizes no shared 'human nature' to which appeal might be made, but only the endlessly different outcomes, whether good or evil, of the action of a creature whose single *proprium* it is to be a (finite, though open-ended) creator. What counts as the authentically human — for Milbank, the *charitable* — can only be identified within the Church, indeed only exists there. But I can at least protest in the name of ecclesial tradition, which he does accept. The Catholic theologians on whom he relies above all, Henri de Lubac and Hans Urs von Balthasar, with, behind them, the seminal philosophical figure of Maurice Blondel — though concerned, as he rightly says, to 'supernaturalize the natural' — did not suppose that they were thereby *eliding* the natural, rubbing it out on the Church's map of the world. It is an incorrect interpretation of De Lubac's thought to say that, by insisting on the essentially supernatural orientation of human nature, and denying the existence of two parallel sets of ends for that nature in the concrete order, he rejected any formal distinction of nature from the supernatural. Though Balthasar may move at times perilously close to such an erasure of the natural (and so of natural wisdom, and natural law), owing to the centring of his theology in the incarnate, not the pre-existent Logos 'by whom all things were made', the literary practice of both men as historical theologians shows that they were far from denying a relative autonomy to the expression of the transcendentals found outside the Judaeo-Christian order. One need only think of De Lubac's account of the Renaissance scholar Pico della Mirandola, with his love of the *pia quaedam theologia* of the antique sages, and the fourth volume of Balthasar's *Herrlichkeit*, on 'the realm of metaphysics in antiquity'. Or, taking a longer view, we can think of Justin Martyr's encomium of certain Greek philosophers as men who lived with the Logos, an early testimony to an appropriation of ancient philosophy by Christian thinkers more intimate and constitutive than Milbank cares to admit. Its justification lies precisely in the doctrine of creation, as the making of one world for all human beings, a commonwealth founded on God's primordial self-disclosure in the creative act. Nor was this simply a matter of the initiatives of individuals, for the utilization of the patrimony of ancient thought by the great conciliar definitions of faith (first, in the patristic period, in Trinitarian theology and Christology, and then, in the middle ages, for sacramental theology and theological anthropology) amounts to the ecclesial ratification of this *démarche*, a ratification that privileges, as it happens, just those features of the ancient conceptual vocabulary — substance, person, presence, soul — which Milbank finds most problematic. Analogously, individual exegetes, in drawing on the Hebrew Bible not only allegorically but also typologically — thanks to the conviction, found in the 'rule of faith', of the unity of the two Covenants, and the consequent non-desuetude, though surpassedness of the First — witnessed to the distinct value of the pre-Christian Jewish tradition as an expression of God's saving purpose, and did not simply treat it as a source of illustration for the Second. Here again, the Church sanctioned the claim (already anticipated in the canonical New Testament itself) that the Christian tradition internally incorporated — and did not merely externally exploit — that of Judaism by transposing such typological exegesis into her liturgical prayer where *lex orandi* equals *lex credendi*. Although it is important to draw attention to the way in which the Gospel innovated on the conceptual world of antiquity in the conciliar definitions, where the key terms to which Milbank objects undergo a seachange thanks to their pressing into the service of a truine, christocentric, eucharistic, resurrection-oriented faith, as also to the transcendence of the Gospel in its active fulfilling of the Torah, nonetheless it is imperative as well to keep open the commerce of the Church's doctrine with more universal structures of reason as with the faith of Israel. And notably, in posing the question of God, Milbank cannot do justice to the affirmation found in the 'Catholic reading' of Scripture (especially the Wisdom literature and the Letter to the Romans) at the First Vatican Council that the divine existence is naturally knowable by human reason; like Hans Küng in *Does God Exist?* he could only maintain that, at any rate, trusting oneself to an ultimate mothering reality is the sole alternative to Nietzsche's nihilism.

32.5 Before moving on to my second objection to *Theology and Social Theory* — namely, its espousal of theocracy, let me raise the query suggested by the above criticism: What Church *is* this to which Milbank makes appeal? For Milbank the Church is not only, as already seen, the teller of the Christian narrative, and thus the transparency of humanity to the uniquely valid *mythos* of Christianity. She is also (and for this reason) the key to all proper social co-existence, the only possible bearer of human community, the *altera civitas* or 'alternative City' in whose peace alone the otherwise ineliminable conflicts of the human *polis* are assuaged. In his programme, all sociology is to be replaced by ecclesiology, just as all philosophy is to be replaced by the doctrine of the Trinity. But granted that, as he tells us, the Church he is describing is not some ideal Church (that would be to fall victim to those sins of illicit reification and misplaced abstraction which count high on his list of intellectual evils), then which of the historic churches must bear the weight of saving truth and redeeming action which he would offload? 'Protestantism', usually diminished with a minuscule initial letter, is treated derisively throughout, not least for spawning the individualism, liberalism and secularism celebrated in the 'Whig' interpretation of history. Milbank protests the 'Catholic' (exalted in majuscule) character of his faith, ethics, exegesis. There are, accordingly, three main contenders: (Eastern) Orthodoxy; (Roman) Catholicism; Anglo-Catholicism. Despite occasional passing references to such Greek fathers as Gregory of Nyssa and Maximus the Confessor, Milbank betrays little understanding of, or sympathy for, the Orthodox East. Speaking of the pastoral role of the emperor in the unified Christendom society of Charlemagne, he dismisses the corresponding Byzantine practice as beneath attention since at Constantinople the Church was but a department of the State. Such a description might serve for the Church of Russia in the period between Peter the Great and the Revolution of 1917, but it hardly fits Byzantium where, though no single model of relationship pertained, the notion of *symphonia* of emperor and patriarch predominated. So far as the (Roman) Catholic Church is concerned, there are insuperable obstacles to any reconciling of Milbank's theology with the doctrine of the Church of Rome. Not only is it hard to see how his 'counter-ontology' can be squared with the conciliar pronouncements of the first six ecumenical Councils (Nicaea I to Constantinople III), with the Council of Vienne on the soul–body relationship, with Lateran IV and Trent on the holy Eucharist. His outright rejection of a non-ecclesial rationality and morals (natural wisdom, natural law) also go against (Roman) Catholicism's grain, as visible not only in conciliar monuments of Tradition but also in a wider practice. His remarks on the papal claim to a 'plenitude of power', founded on the dominical promise (and command) to Peter, with their echo of the pervasive anti-Romanism of non-Anglo-Papalist Anglo-Catholicism, suggests what local enquiry confirms. Milbank's Church is Anglicanism — which is to say, in effect, the Church of England, together with its diaspora, and assorted appurtenances, abroad. The difficulties which must surely be involved in getting members of the *Church of England* at large to accept Milbank's thesis, and to act, in respect of English society, as though it were true, must to some degree call into question his credibility as a commentator on the politically possible.

32.6 What Milbank desires indeed — and here I come to my second (and closing) theme, that of 'theocracy', is the restoration of the Tudor polity in England, shorn of those monarchical, aristocratic and proto-bourgeois features which militated against its (as it were) 'socialist' character. His ideal (the term must *malgré lui*, with the discovery of his Anglicanism, be reinstated), as his section on Church–State relations indicates, is Richard Hooker's *respublica christiana*, at once, and, in the concrete, inseparably, Church and civil society, the English people in their twin offices as temporality and spirituality — the second, evidently, prior to and summoned to transfigure the first. Garnering a harvest cut from a great swathe of intellectual history, from the Greek tragedians on the conflicting allegiances of city and household, law and loyalty, to the post-Nietzschean, post-Freudian French analysts of desire and the will-to-power, Milbank concludes that the city of the State, the secular city, *the civic itself* is irredeemably given over to violence, whether overt or covert, and incapable of either formulating or, more vital still, granting effectively to itself the conditions of a social peace. Nothing remains but for the secular to yield, not as theoretical reason only but also as practical reason — the justice of the State, and to allow the Church to fill the vacuum which, in reality as distinct from the façades and stratagems of power, civil society already is. Only the Christian *mythos*, the Christian narrative, the Christian (ecclesial) community, can secure the human good — the beautiful pattern of living — which always eludes the secular ruler's grasp. Milbank's social programme is not 'theocratic' in the sense of necessarily requiring the apostolic ministry to be the guardians of the State (there is in his book, for a 'Catholic' writer, remarkably little treatment of the role of the ordained). But it is theocratic in that, on the one hand, it seeks to restore Christendom (*Theology and Social Theory* is dedicated to 'the Remnant of Christendom') and on the other it systematically writes out of the social script all clauses – based on natural law, human rights, or whatever — which would safeguard in a Christendom society the protected place which, in conscience, unbelievers, and those of other faiths, should be accorded. In adopting his hermeticism, Milbank has left himself no language — other than that of charity, with its indefinitely flexible creative constitution of its own ethos — in which the distinct place of these 'others' could be articulated, and his theocracy, accordingly, mitigated. Were all members of the Church saints, such a régime of charity might suffice. But as the history of the Church, that mingled story of grace and sin, indicates, charity is not enough. Nor can the Church, as the non-plenary extension of the Incarnation (she is the body, not the Head!) and the only partial manifestation of Pentecost (the Spirit is her soul, not her hypostasis!), legitimately claim to *absorb* the world by her Christic and Pneumatic energies. A remainder is left, a realm for the play of the *free will* of God's creatures, though this be not yet the eschatological *freedom* of the children of God. The Church 'pro-exists' for all humanity; but in the meanwhile, before her mission is divinely completed, she must 'co-exist' with other aggregates of the human members of the creation.

32.7 I want, however, to conclude this article by saying — the reader may think paradoxically — that *Theology and Social Theory* represents in its broad lines, and despite my criticisms, the *general direction* in which (Roman) Catholic Christianity should move. Both in its high doctrine of the supernatural and of 'special' revelation, and in its willingness to entertain the recreation of a Christendom society, where the secular is transformed into a culture penetrated by that revelation, in the service of that (sole, concrete) supernatural end of man, Milbank's book points the right way. It restores the guts to a Christianity often eviscerated by unhappy marriages with predatory ideologies — whether they take the strong form of such positive philosophies as Marxism, or the weak one of a negative counterpart like liberalism. Unfortunately, Milbank goes too far: in attempting to persuade to the faith of the Great Church he damages it, and not with some light scar but a grave wound. Hence I respond to his suasion to orthodoxy: *non tali auxilio*.

33

Kieran Flanagan
A Sociological Critique of Milbank

This extract comes from Kieran Flanagan's article 'Sociology and Milbank's City of God', *New Blackfriars*, Vol. 73 No. 861, June 1992, pp. 333–41. Flanagan is an academic sociologist at Bristol University. In his two books *Sociology and Liturgy* (Macmillan, London 1991) and *The Enchantment of Sociology* (Macmillan, London 1996) he writes, as here, explicitly as a Catholic.

Flanagan begins this extract helpfully by putting this debate into the context of the wider debate about the Enlightenment (of which classical sociology is a part). Like the other critics, he is clearly impressed with John Milbank's book. He develops the insight that some sociology, at least, 'contains an implicit theology which is a fraudulent legacy of the Enlightenment' (*33.4*) himself in *The Enchantment of Sociology*. However, his central sociological difficulty with Milbank is that he does not believe that all sociology can be characterized in this positivist manner. He considers that Milbank 'tends to confuse the reception of sociology as perceived by theologians in modern culture with what sociologists themselves have tried to argue' (*33.12*). For example, Flanagan believes that 'Weber's attitude to religion was far more hesitant and complex than appears in Milbank's account' (*33.13*). Present-day sociology of religion is certainly not dominated by a positivist functionalism: 'demolishing sociology on the basis of its concern with functionalism is to rejoice over a corpse sociologists, themselves, have long abandoned' (*33.15*).

Flanagan's theological difficulty is finally knowing 'which Church does Milbank have in mind. The theology he uses is almost totally Catholic and this leads him to occupy some odd positions for an Anglican' (*33.9*). Finally, both Milbank's sociology and his ecclesiology are considered by Flanagan to be 'wrong headed and naive' (*33.21*).

33.1 Sociology is a necessary evil on the academic landscape. It is the discipline we all like to hate. Somehow,

sociology fits everywhere and yet belongs nowhere in particular. It does not have the finesse of philosophy, the vision of theology or the grace of classics, but as a mongrel child of the Enlightenment it plays about with their deepest insights. Sociology reflects modernity, but in a way that confirms an instinctive dislike of its basis. In the academic game of musical chairs, sociology is left standing, when the waltz ceases, and other disciplines sit awaiting the next score. Yet behind this facade of dislike, an odder and deeper crisis confronts sociology.

33.2 In the past two decades, philosophy, literary studies, history and classics have all become entwined in sociology which stands at the analytical crossroads directing a busy traffic in concepts up the high road of modernity. But as its rhetoric becomes woven into the humanities, the distinctive voice of sociology has become muted. Critical theory, embracing linguistics, post-structuralism, phenomenology and post-modernism, to name a few, now has squatter's rights within sociological theory. Textual exegesis forms the basis of much critical philosophy which sociology has to recognize, but is uncertain how to use. Whereas Dilthey laid the philosophical basis for the autonomy of the cultural sciences against the clutches of the natural sciences, an equivalent exercise has yet to be undertaken for sociology in relation to the competing demands of other disciplines also to speak of culture. Despite their sophistication, modern philosophers such as Rorty, MacIntyre, Derrida and Levinas yield slight sociological insights. There are two sides to the analytical coins to be spent in the cultural marketplace. Sociology makes its own purchases, and these are not the debased offerings of the 'thick', incapable of reading the classical texts of philosophy in all their nuances. Too often one gets thick philosophical works with a very thin amount of sociology sandwiched in the centre. Anyhow, sociology has its own problems in dealing with culture.

33.3 Recently, the issue of culture has moved into the centre of contemporary sociology. Prior to the past decade, culture was the reserve of the anthropological, the primitive and the exotic, classified and kept safe on the margin. Althusser and Poulantzas left the issue of culture wrapped in a structuralist paradigm. When fashions changed, Gramsci and Benjamin were resurrected to speak of its autonomy. But as culture was moved into the centre of sociological discourse, issues of judgement, aesthetics and ethics emerged especially in the writings of the French sociologist, Pierre Bourdieu.[1] His approach to the symbolic basis of cultural reproduction relies heavily on theological metaphors to inform his approach to judgement and distinction. It is a debatable point as to how far he secures an autonomy for sociology against the rival claims of theology and philosophy. Nevertheless, issues of theology are emerging on the fringe of sociology in an unexpected manner. Understanding, reflexion and self are back on the sociological agenda in its approaches to culture.[2] A further sign of change is that the statue of that sociological sphinx Max Weber is now turned away from Marx to face Nietzsche. His approach to power, modernity and the heroic was based on a deep hatred of Christianity, and to that degree, his resurrection places theology unexpectedly into the centre of sociological theory. There is also a lot of theological baggage attached to an equally important theorist of culture, Walter Benjamin. These point sociology to beyond its narrow analytical concerns with modernity, in a theological direction that is as profound as it is unexpected.

33.4 Milbank's book is timely, significant and is likely to generate a vast and deserved debate. It is a brave, tough complex, dense and difficult work that should keep theologians, philosophers and sociologists wrestling with it, and with each other, for some time to come. In theory, sociologists should dislike this book intensely. It seeks to dethrone the discipline, arguing that it contains an implicit theology which is a fraudulent legacy of the Enlightenment. Through a dense exposition of philosophers such as Plato, Aristotle, Kant, Hegel, Nietzsche, Blondel and Heidegger, to name a few, sociology is marked out as the villain which has secularized the sublime in a manner that has bedazzled theologians. In his ruthlessly pursued narrative, where analysis is used like a scythe, the sociological field gets flattened. A modified version is admitted under sufferance into Milbank's vision of a Church which encompasses all matters social.

33.5 Writing from within systematic theology, Milbank is concerned with the issue of public and private virtue. Modifying MacIntyre's Aristotelian concern with ethics, Milbank seeks to place a vision of Augustine's City of God in modern culture, so that violence is overcome and peace reigns. This is a holy end for a ruthless philosophical tour de force. His work is more than an exercise in urban sociology with celestial overtones. It is an unabashed tract of Christian apologetics whose unfashionable conclusions will disturb those who would detach belief from analysis.

33.6 Any cross disciplinary exercise will attract criticism for caricaturing the tenets of rivals. Milbank's origins are in theology, his expertise is in philosophy, and sociology is his target. A serious critical evaluation of this study would presuppose a rare working knowledge of all three disciplines. For this reason, criticisms of the work are likely to be specific and partial. Although sociology is only treated as an episode along the route, in Part II, where it is hitched to positivism, this strand does seem the weakest part of the book. To echo a striking phrase of John Orme Mills, there is an 'epistemological imperialism' abroad in this study.[3] Through sheer philosophical cleverness, he strikes home points by default, that are not always convincing.

33.7 The theological and philosophical denseness of the study makes sociological redress difficult. Sociology is lumped in with issues of politics, ethics, post-structuralists and post-modernists, so that its autonomy is denied. To some extent, this book is a collection of discrete essays, written in highly detailed sections, where the narrative flow gets clogged in some very fine philosophical tuning. Perhaps this is a price to pay for such subtle expositions of Hegel, Kant, Heidegger and Nietzsche, and for driving with such force through a number of philosophical thickets few sociologists stay to inspect.

33.8 The study is a peculiar mixture of piety and pungent philosophical analysis that yields some unexpected insights. It is a modern *Apologia pro Vita Sua*, a ruthless passage through a vast range of philosophy. Beneath the cleverness there is a subtext lurking, heavily coded, that makes one wonder where Milbank will go next. The answer is perhaps rather obvious. There is an unexpected grace of witness in this work, whose sophistication precludes its defence of peace and harmony from the callowness this stance might embody on a more simple evangelical terrain. One can agree with many of its targets: that the Enlightenment failed to produce an authentic moral consensus; that nihilism is a phoney option, a myth, that has emerged from post-modernism; that the vision of a holy city is a worthy pursuit, where a self-forgetting communality will operate with virtue and peace in harmonious public and private relationships; and that theology should be re-enthroned in a Church that embodies and transcends all matters social. All these are wondrous things to wrest from the present inchoate state of philosophy. What is awesome about Milbank is that he is not afraid to attack. Thus, against Lyotard, he posits the need for a metanarrative for theology, one based on the foundations of a counter-ontology, that suggests an active strike against modernity, and not its passive incorporation in the manner of liberal theologians.

33.9 There is a redemptive cast that runs as a theological thread through this work. This is discernible in the stress on areas, such as sin and sacrifice, unfashionable to the liberal Protestant, who Milbank clearly despises. This dark side of the human condition leads Milbanks to nail his own faith to the text at repeated intervals. Social life has theological implications. Thus, he asserts that 'mutual forgiveness and bearing of each other's burdens becomes the *modus vivendi* of the Church: an "atoning" way of life'.[4] But there are also some passages which suggest Milbank is less occupying a Church than a bathing hut on Dover Beach. The issue of ecclesial authority is seldom raised. A question is continually begged as to which Church does Milbank have in mind. The theology he uses is almost totally Catholic and this leads him to occupy some odd positions for an Anglican. The use of Pascal's wager which he imposes on contemporary philosophy could also be applied to his own dithering with matters ecclesial. At one point, he does seem to realize he has fallen more deeply into a Catholic camp than might seem desirable when he ruefully reflects, in a crucial chapter on politics and modern Catholic thought, that 'not without distress do I realize that some of my conclusions here coincide with those of reactionaries in the Vatican'.[5] The severe and effective criticisms Milbanks makes of Boff, on liberation theology, cause one to wonder how Ratzinger will regard this unexpected theological friend in the Anglican court. This failure to find an ecclesial home lends an artificial cast to some of the problems he encounters. It is peculiar that a continual plea for forgiveness and healing, that runs as a theme through the book, seldom confronts the solutions offered in sacramental theology. This also is an area where sociology can be of considerable use in supporting his concerns.

33.10 There are many illuminating sections on theology and philosophy that clarify some very shadowy areas for the wandering sociological mind. The choice of Blondel is apt as the progenitor of a social theology best suited to deal with the nihilism that emerges like a fog from post-modernism. If the treatment of von Balthasar is disappointingly thin, his assessment of Rahner is penetrating. The human anthropology he advocated in his theology has seemed impenetrable to sociological intervention for reasons Milbank touches on, which one would have liked developed.

33.11 Heidegger has loomed as a great unread figure for many sociologists, but, who, nevertheless, has had a paralysing effect on its theory. Existentialism and phenomenology had a profound effect on the humanization of sociology in the 1960s and 1970s. Heidegger hovers around this change of direction and has to be taken into account in approaches to hermeneutics. Milbank supplies a splendidly accessible account of Heidegger in a notable chapter on ontological violence and the post-modern problematic. This forms the basis of his effort to establish a counter-ontology for Christianity, and represents a notable achievement that will generate much debate. The secular is portrayed as another form of 'religion', one with its own mythology, shaped against Christianity, but in a way that disguises its debts. This chapter 10 and the sections dealing with Marxism and Christianity display an admirable power of analysis.

33.12 Providing a critical response to this work from a sociological perspective is difficult, mainly because its relationships to philosophy and theology are so inchoate. Milbank presupposes this connection is more advanced than it seems. He tends to confuse the reception of sociology as perceived by theologians in modern culture with what sociologists themselves have tried to argue. This is despite a close and intelligent reading of quite a number of sociological and anthropological texts that relate to the study of religion. Common thinking has not even commenced on the terms of reference that should govern the relationships between the two disciplines, which will generate issues of considerable hermeneutic complexity. Because of the lack of such links, many of the philosophical and theological aspects of Milbank's analysis will seem like clouds high above the sociological fields, casting shadows of varying density over its capacity to analyse. Unfortunately, in his account, sociology is rendered a prisoner of a highly textual analysis. The capacity of sociology to intervene and to generate understandings of contemporary culture is needlessly diminished. Indeed, Milbank makes sociological enemies he does not need. He pushes with great philosophical violence at a number of open sociological doors.

33.13 Milbank demonstrates a significant competence in handling Weber, Luhmann and Durkheim in the three chapters devoted to what he conceives to be the pernicious influence of sociology in policing, and thus misrepresenting, the sublime. There are many valuable aspects to his response to sociology. The chapter dealing with the efforts of Comte and Durkheim to escape a theological influence provides a valuable exploration of the French philosophical background to their writings. More mileage could have been made out of Comte's inversion of Catholicism in a Positivist religion which Lepenies has explored with such effect.[6] Milbank is quite clever at exposing theological cracks in sociological approaches to the social, whose treatment involves an element of deification and reification that inadvertently implicates sociology in a wager with the Divine. He is not the first to discover the ambiguity of Durkheim's legacy to sociology in its dealings with religion. He is a bit harsh on Weber in claiming that his sociology involved nothing but a spurious promotion of the secular culture of modernity.[7] Weber's attitude to religion was far more hesitant and complex than appears in Milbank's account.

33.14 A continual argument he makes is that a fixation of sociology on modernity places issues of Christianity on the margin. It suggests religion can only be understood in a technical sense, but, one whose foundational basis within the social sciences is open to suspicion. Presumably his point to theologians is that they do not need to enter this sociological gate, but should establish their own for passage into the social. Yet, at this point flaws arise in his argument. Milbank reads a functionalism into contemporary sociology of religion that does not exist in the dominant form that gives him so much metaphysical angst. It is perverse to argue that Talcott Parsons, mediating between Weber and Durkheim, is exemplary for sociology of religion.[8] There is a fatal confusion in this chapter between sociology of religion as conceived in its classical format, following Durkheim and Weber, and its specific concerns as a branch of the discipline dealing currently with religious sects, Fundamentalism and renewal. This failure to distinguish traditional and contemporary interests of sociology of religion is exemplified in Milbank's odd treatment of Peter Berger, described as a 'modern American sociologist'.

33.15 Berger has made his career policing the sublime, less against marauding sociologists, than against liberal Protestant theologians. In his pursuit of a rumour of angels, and his notion of 'signals of transcendence', Berger has directed his energies against reductionist definitions of the social that would close off a sense of the transcendent. He has re-centred religious belief into sociology in a way that marks a crucial break with Weber. More importantly, he has mapped out a sense of the sublime in terms of religious experience in a way that is connected to social transactions that do require a sociological intervention. There are ambiguities buried within modern culture that have theological roots which can be turned to sociological advantage. These are endemic in a manner that justifies the necessity of a type of sociology that could be squared with Blumenberg's critique of secularization.[9] Rather than finding some idea of a City of God, where antinomies are overcome, and the need for a critical sociology is abolished, Milbank should have explored how these signs of contradiction could be harnessed to holy advantage. Because sociology speaks from within the modern world, the emptiness it encounters points to the price of religious disbelief. This is too important a witness to be abolished by a utopian vision of the City of God. Demolishing sociology on the basis of its concern with functionalism is to rejoice over a corpse sociologists, themselves, have long abandoned. Milbank's approach to sociology is too simple and too negative. Its present consensus can be converted to theological use. In his seminal work, *Theo-Drama*, von Balthasar has shown the way the question 'who am I' can be turned from sociological assumptions into theological speculations.[10]

33.16 Milbank's failure to confront the substance of contemporary sociology of religion is exemplified in his choice of biblical studies and liberation theology as examples of the distorting effect of sociological thought on theology in general. But these examples are misplaced. Some of the strongest critics of liberation theology have come from within sociology.[11] Sociology has cast its own marker on liberation theology, a point Gutiérrez recognized, when he affirmed the need to place Marxist analysis within the context of the social sciences, if enlightened analysis is to proceed. Because liberation theology cannot provide concrete analyses, sociology has a negative function of remedying this deficiency. This gives it a distinctive and autonomous relationship with theology which Gutiérrez, for instance, noted, when he observed that 'use of the social disciplines for a better understanding of the social situation implies great respect for the so-called human sciences and their proper spheres. . .'[12] Later, he makes a point that deserves further exploration, that 'theology must take into account the contribution of the social sciences, but in its work it must always appeal to its own sources'.[13]

33.17 Again, sociology cannot be held responsible for its reception and misuse in biblical studies. Milbank's strictures against sociology would have been more persuasive, if he had examined the general methodological problems governing historical sociology. If Milbank had explored the range of research in anthropology and sociology of religion, rather than concentrate on some dominant figures, his conclusions on policing the sublime might have been more catholic.

33.18 Through philosophy, Milbank has made a deductive case against sociology's relationship to religion, but in a way that masks its own distinctive approach to theology. There is a reductionist strand in sociology towards belief, but that can point to an analytical pit in modernity whose only exit is ascent. Speaking of the distinctive task of sociology, Bourdieu commented on the 'wretchedness of man without God or any hope of grace — a wretchedness the sociologist merely reveals and brings to light, and for which he is made responsible, like all prophets of evil tidings. But you can kill the messenger: what he says is still true, and has still been heard'.[14] Acceptance of analytical limits in approaches to understanding of religion is far more apparent in Simmel's writings than Milbank seems to realize. This points to another sociological tradition in handling religion, one more open to its claims for authenticity than the form of closure exemplified in functionalist approaches.

33.19 Milbank is wrong to argue that Simmel illustrates the way the social sciences tend to 'promote "ontology of conflict" in radical antithesis to Christianity'.[15] Writing as a Jewish agnostic, Simmel had the most sympathetic attitude to religion in general, and to Christianity in particular, of all the great sociologists. Writing during the First World War on the crisis of culture, and of its soul, by which he meant man's intellectual accomplishments, Simmel bleakly noted a turning away from Christianity as part of a failure to regulate priorities, where the relative and the provisional were elevated into ultimate values. If Christianity was affected by this crisis, Simmel felt this applied even more so to philosophy. In a point with which Milbank would agree, Simmel noted that 'if the signs do not deceive us, our entire system of philosophy is beginning to become an empty shell'.[16]

33.20 In Luigi Sturzo, Milbank finds a Catholic sociologist who permeates the social with a notion of the supernatural. Religion is located in social forms and practices that bind.[17] At this point, Milbank makes an odd and arbitrary point that vitiates the possibility of arriving at a modus vivendi between sociology and theology. Instead of accepting the analytical limits of sociology, the methodological atheism that makes negative theology its particular brand, Milbank dismisses Sturzo's 'sociology of the supernatural'. Rather than accepting with Blondel, in relation to philosophy, that sociology can only approach theology through negative means, Milbank seeks to establish the issue of social understanding within the Church which is regarded as a truly universal society. Sturzo's endeavour becomes a 'social theology', one which Milbank fails to spell out coherently at the end of the book.

33.21 In the final chapter, where theology is treated as a social science, too many targets are pursued. Frankly his notion of 'ecclesiology' as 'sociology' is wrong headed and naive. The philosophical route through which he arrives at a social theology is persuasive, but not at the price of rejecting some form of sociology that has the method, the conceptual apparatus and capacity to discern the contours of change and the corruptions of the cultural that make disbelief possible. Like many philosophers,

Milbank ends on a question that marks the beginning of a fascinating sociological problematic; how is Christian praxis to be restored to its freshness and originality, to give them a quality of strangeness that makes them of the world, but not in it?

Notes

1. For an accessible account of his significance, see Derek Robbins, *The Work of Pierre Bourdieu*, Milton Keynes: Open University Press, 1991.
2. See Anthony Giddens, *Modernity and Self-Identity: Self and Society in the Late Modern Age*, Cambridge: Polity Press, 1991.
3. John Orme Mills, 'God, Man and Media: on a problem arising when theologians speak of the modern world', in David Martin, John Orme Mills and W. S. F. Pickering, eds, *Sociology and Theology: Alliance and Conflict*, Brighton: The Harvester Press, 1980, p. 136.
4. John Milbank, *Theology and Social Theory: Beyond Secular Reason*, Oxford: Basil Blackwell, 1990, p. 397.
5. *ibid.*, p. 208.
6. Wolf Lepenies, *Between Literature and Science: the Rise of Sociology*, trans. R. J. Hollingdale, Cambridge: Cambridge University Press, 1988.
7. John Milbank, *Theology and Social Theory, op. cit.*, p. 97.
8. *ibid.*, p. 109.
9. Hans Blumenberg, *The Legitimacy of the Modern Age*, trans. Robert M. Wallace, Cambridge, Mass.: The MIT Press, 1985.
10. Hans Urs von Balthasar, *Theo-Drama: Theological Dramatic Theory*, vol. I, trans. Graham Harrison, San Francisco: Ignatius Press, 1988, see especially Part III B.
11. See, for example, David Martin, *Tongues of Fire: The Explosion of Protestantism in South America*, Oxford: Basil Blackwell, 1991.
12. Gustavo Gutiérrez, 'Theology and the Social Sciences' in Paul E. Sigmund, *Liberation Theology at the Crossroads: Democracy or Revolution?* New York: Oxford University Press, 1990, p. 219.
13. *ibid.*, p. 221.
14. Pierre Bourdieu, *In Other Words: Essays towards a Reflexive Sociology*, Cambridge: Polity Press, 1990, p. 15.
15. John Milbank, *Theology and Social Theory, op. cit.*, p. 81.
16. Georg Simmel, 'The Crisis of Culture' in P. A. Lawrence, *Georg Simmel: Sociologist and European*, London: Nelson, 1976, p. 259.
17. John Milbank, *Theology and Social Theory, op. cit.*, p. 225.

34

John Milbank
A Response

This extract comes from John Milbank's article 'Enclaves, or Where is the Church?', *New Blackfriars*, Vol. 73 No. 861, June 1992, pp. 341–8 and 351–2.

Milbank responds to his critics somewhat obliquely. Apart from acknowledging a lack of attention to ritual, he ignores Kieran Flanagan's criticisms of his use of sociology. Instead, he is more concerned to address the ecclesiological questions raised mainly by Rowan Williams and Aidan Nichols. He does admit that 'between my "formal" or ideal descriptions of the Church and rather minimal attempts at "judicious narrative"', there may exist a certain tension' (*34.5*). Yet he sees such tension as characteristic of the earliest church and seeks to show this in a detailed exposition of Paul's letters to the Corinthians. For Milbank, and as he believes for Paul, 'the Church is, uniquely, not a community constituted by judgement, but by the acknowledgement that judgement is not yet possible' (*34.6*). Indeed, 'the only Christian approach here must be a persuasive attempt to recite particular cases, particular biographies as authentic embodiments of the *logos staurou*, the logic of the cross' (*34.9*). He concludes that 'Paul's letters to the Corinthians ... exhibit the way in which extreme attention to formal categories which detail a "heterotopia" of non-exclusion and non-domination, actually demands supplementation by precise and particular appeals to contingent histories' (*34.10*).

By setting his response at this level it is quite difficult to see whether or not he is addressing the central concerns of his critics. Although he concludes by noting Paul's 'non-exclusion', it is not clear how his own position avoids the charge of exclusivism. And although he concedes ground to Williams' historical criticisms, his use of Paul's letters to the Corinthians may not cope with the weight that the church must finally bear in his account of the role of the Christian meta-narrative.

34.1 It was not the purpose of *Theology and Social Theory* (whose argument has been so accurately précised by Fergus Kerr) to imagine the Church as Utopia. Nor to discover in its ramified and fissiparous history some single ideal exemplar. For this would have been to envisage the Church in spatial terms — as another place, which we might arrive at, or *as this* identifiable site, which we can still inhabit. How could either characterize the Church which exists, finitely, not in time, but as time, taken in the mode of gift and promise? Not as a peace we must slowly construct, piecemeal, imbibing our hard-learned lessons, but as a peace already given, superabundantly, in the breaking of bread by the risen Lord, which assembles the harmony of peoples then and at every subsequent eucharist. But neither as a peace already realized, which might excuse our labour. For the body and blood of Christ only exist in the mode of gift, and they can *be* gift (like any gift) only as traces of the giver and promise of future provision from the same source. This is not an ideal *presence* real or imagined, but something more like an 'ideal transmission' through time, and despite its ravages. Fortunately the Church is first and foremost neither a programme, nor a 'real' society, but instead an enacted, serious fiction. Only in its eucharistic centring is it enabled to sustain a ritual distance from itself, to preserve itself, *as* the body of Christ under judgement *by* the body of Christ, which after all, it can only receive. In a sense, this ritual distance of the Church from itself defines the Church, or rather deflects it from any definition of what it is. In its truth it *is* not, but has been and will be. (Here I am much indebted to Kieran Flanagan for pointing out that my book omitted the ritual dimension.)

34.2 And yet it is, or believes itself to be, a true rite of passage from redemption to judgement. The eucharistic elements are given to the Church, but not only may one eat to damnation, the very eating and drinking of Christ can be nullified by human greed (1 Cor. 11:20–22). For even ritual forms are entrusted to our transmission, presentation and elaboration: to receive Christ, to receive the flow of time as embodied God, is in some minimal way to receive the Church as itself an adequate mode of reception. Since the wine must unavoidably be carried in a chalice if it is not to be spilt, we can only be *persuaded* that this is indeed the blood of Christ if we are also persuaded by the performance (despite the performance) and persuaded by the preacher (despite the preacher).

34.3 Therefore the short answer to where is the Church? (or where is Milbank's Church?) might be, on the site of the eucharist, which is not a site, since it suspends presence in favour of memory and expectation, 'positions' each and every one of us only as fed — gift from God of ourselves and therefore not to ourselves — and bizarrely assimilates us to the food which we eat, so that we, in turn, must exhaust ourselves as nourishment for others. But the long answer could never be completed, since it would be nothing other than the Church's own act (which *also* defines it) of self-judgement and self-discrimination: all the stories of true and failed transmission, of more or less adequate persuasions and receptions. An ecclesiology of the kind which Rowan Williams demands, which involves critical narratives of the (endless) genesis of the Church. Not a judgemental history which measures the Church against the pre-established standard of Christ, but a history which in detailed judging raises us to a better perception of the pre-given standard — which can only be pre-given in the mode of promise. I willingly concede that my steps in this direction have been too hesitant (to the extent, as Williams implies, of distorting my intentions) and would only add that such 'theological Church history' is not a task for academics only, nor one which finally privileges the first beginnings of the Church, but one which is also dedicated to many obscure, 'private' and scarcely traceable happenings. If one neglects the 'micro-temporality' of the Church, its proper precariousness, then a new kind of narrative essentialism might intrude, ignoring the fact that the Church is present as much in an obscure but precise act of charity as in the deliberations of epochal councils. Paradoxically, I would wish to argue that the 'formalism' of my metanarrative, of my ethics and ontology, operates precisely as a safeguard *against* such an essentialism. For two reasons: first, the metanarrative which declares that all other histories are judged by the story of the arrival of a community of reconciliation is in a sense an 'anti-metanarrative' as it tells of an *end* to (the rule of) imagined fateful logics, destined sacred identities and so forth. From henceforward there will, indeed, be only multiple and complexly interweaving stories to tell: what makes these stones nonetheless one, is no principle of hypotactic subordination but a peace, which (faith experiences and hopes) will shine amidst their parataxis.

34.4 Second, the 'formal' descriptions (which I do not claim could ever be exhaustive — even within the confines of formalism) — in terms of peace, forgiveness, harmony etc — describe structural relations, and *do not* isolate essences (i.e. what substantive ingredients are necessary to an identity) nor prescribe 'what is to be done'. In a sense, indeed, I am *not* concerned to provide an 'ethics' (and doubt even the desirability of doing so) but rather to describe a supra-ethical religious affirmation which recasts the ethical field in terms of a religious hope: we may think of the good as infinitely realizable harmony if we believe that reality can finally receive such an imprint. This faith sustains ethical hope, but it also *overthrows* every 'morality': every prescription in terms of such and such an inviolable law, uniquely valuable virtue or exemplary politics. To say 'universal peace' is to say, everything has its place and its moment: every person's position can be judged equally by all others and must finally be judged by herself from her own unique and irreplaceable perspective (of course one needs general examples and conventions and norms, but none are *inviolable*). Therefore the ecclesiastical task of judgement (the Church is to judge itself and the world, as St. Paul makes clear) cannot be academically pre-empted. Which is not to deny that the last chapter of *Theology and Social Theory* requires (infinite) supplementation by judicious narratives of ecclesial happenings which would alone indicate the shape of the Church that we desire.

34.5 Nor do I want to deny that between my 'formal' or ideal descriptions of the Church (of an 'ideal' happening, and 'ideal' yet real, if vestigial transmission) and rather minimal attempts at 'judicious narrative', there may exist a certain tension: close to the tension between ritualized and improvised (supposedly more 'real' and 'historical') action. However, it seems to me that the Church has always lived with this tension and that it already surfaces to view in the New Testament itself. Consider, for example, Paul's letters to the Corinthians. They are characterized by what one might describe as 'ritual priority'. The Church is only the Church because it imbibes and becomes Christ's body, and re-articulates his earthly performance (1 Cor. 10:16–17). What a cumbersome and taxing re-conception of social life! This new community has no 'head' but a man once crucified, who only speaks again in the mute form of food. Unlike previous pagan (Indo-European?) rule he is not, as head, over-against the body as the superiority of reason (which from time immemorial has governed 'desire' and 'passion' with aid of auxiliary 'force'), but also as his (already) own body, at a 'distance' from his (not yet) own body, which he rules. His reasons are not commands to his body, but undergoings of his body, by which his body is given to us. This wisdom is not 'of this age', and not in this age does it exercise its power (2:6). It is as radically absent as a dead, exhausted body can be, and its power only that of a promise. Such wisdom can therefore only operate as 'hidden, foreordained' (2:7). It is the creative wisdom of God which as, J.-L. Marion has pointed out,[1] can for Paul make 'to be' the things that are not and 'as nothing' the things that are, which seem to be solidly before us (1:28). This wisdom (*pace* Aidan Nichols' plea for 'natural law', 'common wisdom' and other yogic delights)[2] *ruins* the 'wisdom of this age'; the Greek philosophic wisdom which rests on a secure grasp of what is 'present' (and so what 'is', simply) to intellectual sight (1:18–29).

34.6 The crucified Lord only rules by giving himself over to us for our future nourishment. He refused the temptation of *present* power, and his post-ascended availability by no means reverses that refusal. To be governed by this Lord, to internalize his rule, can only mean to come under his sign of the reversal of all worldly norms of knowledge and authority. Self-knowledge (the basis of self-command) is impossible, every image we make of ourselves illusory. But when we love, then we gradually come to know 'as we are known', not as we *are*, but under the transformative gaze of uncontingent love itself (8:2–3). Without self-understanding we should not judge even ourselves, and certainly not others on the basis of our own norms. Judgement has occurred with Christ, and is radically suspended till the *parousia* (4:3–5). The Church is, uniquely, not a community constituted by judgement, but by the acknowledgement that judgement is not yet possible. Only out of such acknowledgement, which is its possessing of the mind of Christ, its waiting on love, is it alone fit to judge the world. And its members, for now, should only submit to judgement within the Church (for violations of the suspension of judgement? For lack of love?). To enter into judicial litigation with other Christians, is supremely to betray the character of the Church as community (6:1–8).

34.7 Without knowledge, without judgement, there can be no economy for the restriction of loss (endemic to our finite temporality). This, presumably, is why Christians are *moroi* not *phronimoi* (not prudent, *not* ethical) and only *phronimoi* in Christ according to an economy in which loss turns out to be gain (4:10). Fools, because they give themselves away, and not for a cause, not to a city, not to a place, only as links in a continuous, non-teleological chain of givings-away. Fools, because indifferent to worldly circumstance whose *reality* under the *sign* of the cross is transposed: slavery is freedom, self-giving freedom is slavery, our bondage to the truly desirable (7:20–23). Likewise, we must be joyful as if sorrowing, for this joy is not ours, does not belong to us. And be sorrowful as if rejoicing (7:30); for every sorrowing misses something, and is our possession after all of love, and can be received as love by whomsoever is thereby loved (2 Cor. 7:7). In this way (as Marion indicates) love goes 'further' than loss of being, of presence (at least of the other). Faith in creation, in resurrection, is faith in the deeper power of love over the apparent power of destruction.

34.8 If the 'head' is a self-giving body, then no-one is submitted to anyone else, but all are submitted to all. Paul may be an apostle, but the Corinthians can be kings without him and he will be happy to rule with them (1 Cor. 4:8). The only rule of the Christian economy must be sharing for the sake of equality (2 Cor. 8:2), and in the case of sexual exchange, each spouse must give unstintingly since each 'rules' over the other (1 Cor. 7:3–4). Most communities are 'identified' by legal codes which distinguish the pure from the impure, the ethically allowed from the disallowed (the two categories, ritual and ethical may not finally be distinct). However, Paul begins to see, tentatively and inconsistently, that this is not properly true of the Church. Those who eat the body of Christ do not eat this food *rather than* other foods, since Christ's food is uniquely not used up and uniquely 'claims us', rather than vice-versa (6:13). Other foods are but temporarily useful, even if they have been offered to idols, who have no real power, and therefore are reduced to mere ontological indifference, and the innocence of actuality (8:1–13). (In the sexual sphere, Paul's intimations of apurism are less marked: Christ *can be* the rival of whores, having already paid for our bodies, just as he can be the rival of our spouses (6:15–20; 7:33–34).) To say *this* (positive being) rather than *that* (positive being) is to say rift, exclusion, and violence: in this fashion only *law* can 'empower' sin, which otherwise would remain an inert possibility of destruction (15:56). 'Morality' is complicit with death, as it is only the fragility of the world which requires a coded shoring-up against loss. Death itself, however, or temporal disappearance, or the way we must indeed necessarily feed off each other (as Williams says) is not 'sin', for it may be the distance of love. Yet as intended or resigned-to death, as absolute loss and diminution, it is to be decoded as venomously invaded by sin, as a self-justificatory will to the annihilation of the other.

34.9 All this complex 'formal' characterization of the Church is for Paul pre-given in ritual enactment. And *yet* even the latter can only be guaranteed as an authentic repetition if it is genuinely reflected in the improvised 'real-life' of those who transmit and perform it. Paul is obsessively concerned with his own credentials as an apostle, in part because only authentic apostleship will guarantee authentic founding, authentic eucharistic performance. He therefore seeks to supplement the formal categories with rehearsals of his own missions to and dealings with the Corinthians. Sublime imagery of death and resurrection, atoning substitution and undying corporeality is harnessed without mediation to the diurnal matters of fund-raising, moral discipline and claims to authority. The character of the gospel as gift — the gift that is only of gift — is in part authenticated by Paul's own Socratic boast to have preached it *gratis*, or rather with the support of the Macedonians (9:15–18). Does this impress, as evidence of disinterest? Whether it does or not, the persuasive *content* of the gospel is here not separable from a persuasive mode of *communication*. Inversely, severely practical matters depend upon decisions regarding ineffable theological categories. Are the apostles entitled to their bread for working only at apostleship (9:3, 11)? This depends upon their direct knowledge of Christ and their bearing in their lives the Christ-like marks of substitutionary suffering: hence they also — like the body and blood of Christ — stand judgementally over-against the Church (4:16). Appeal to one's endurances (4:10–13) then constitutes also a claim to power, for all the redefinitions of power as self-denying ordinance, for all the assertions of ultimate equality, and for all the paradoxical vauntings of 'the least member', compared specifically to our genitalia, the weakest, most lacking and desiring (and therefore most responsive to Christ?) (12:22–26). Will Paul efface himself (and his 'rational' headship) this far? And is such effacement shown in his claim to the right to judge harshly mere drunkards and sexual offenders (5:1–5; 6:9–10)? Does he not fall into the trap of wanting the Church to excel in a purity understood all too conventionally and exclusively? Whatever the answers, it is clear that formal specifications of *ecclesia* do not readily serve to resolve complex issues of everyday routine, discipline and authority. Nonetheless, the only Christian approach here must be a persuasive attempt to recite particular cases, particular biographies as authentic embodiments of the *logos staurou*, the logic of the cross. Whereas, indicates Paul (in an astonishing reversal), all philosophy is reduced to the level of mere persuasion (*peithois*), this *logos* alone is truly *demonstrative* (*apodeixei*) since it is realized in power in resurrection and the emergence of the Church (2:4). Yet such power is itself first effective through persuasive preaching and this priority constitutes the ineradicable hierarchic claim of the apostle.[3] However, for his persuasion to become apodeictic, for his gift to be discerned in the Holy Spirit as gift, this authority must collapse in pace with its exercise. Unlike space, which may be democratic and merely consensual, time demands asymmetrical power and aristocratic rule; but unlike space also, which may persist in oligarchy, time demands the handing over of power as the only mark of its achievement. Apostolic power is self-cancelling. And if Christ, by virtue of his proleptic character does, nonetheless, (through his apostles) continue to exercise headship over his body, which is his bride, then all the same the distinction of the Spirit, which is *from* Christ, yet also received as that 'other' gift in which he may be discerned as gift, concurs with the impossibility of ever including a later, interpretative, temporal moment merely 'under' a past authority which it is to interpret. Christ is himself more disclosed through the Spirit at work in the Church. And as mother and bride, the Church asymptotically approaches (without ever reaching) the perfection of the response of the Holy Spirit to the Logos in the Trinity, in which the Logos *is* through this response, which not only bears the Logos through desire, but as desire yet in excess of the Logos, becomes its now *equal* bride. St. Paul even seeks to locate gender relations within this suspense. As the Church is for Christ, so woman is for man and should go veiled in church — nevertheless, he can add, in parentheses, *in the Lord* neither are independent, and both are 'from' each other (11:11–12). For now, the priorities of time and its subordinations, but eschatologically, mutual generation. How, practically, can one instantiate such a strictly temporal logic? When, precisely, should equality supervene? But no rules here, for Church governance: rather we are handed over to all the many particular pleas of claimed authority, all the kenotic measures of its truth.

34.10   Paul's letters to the Corinthians, therefore, exhibit the way in which extreme attention to formal categories which detail a 'heterotopia' of non-exclusion and non-domination, actually demands supplementation by precise and particular appeals to contingent histories, if these categories are not to remain empty. The categories are not, however, purely paradigmatic: in a sense they detail an ideal yet also real diachrony, a 'uchrony', or process of peaceful transmission which is *how* time falls out, despite the universal contamination of sin (since this in Christ has been fully suffered, such that even violent abuse and rupture, now traversed by love, can itself be transmitted as gift). In Christ peace has not, indeed, been totally achieved (a building remains to be built), yet it is proleptically given, because only the perfect saving of one man from the absolute destruction of death, this refusal of the loss of any difference, can initially spell out to us perfect peace. The latter validates the individual as being in excess of any achieved totality, so that the community of infinite peace ('total', I concede, is a misleading qualifier) must be first inscribed in this space of the single element, the discarded stone, which yet now frames the whole future construction ...

34.11   Against Williams' 'tragic' emphasis, which seems too allied to political projects, the writhings of committees and the identification of the many roads not taken by a single individual with moral 'goals', I would want to stress the 'absurdity' of faith, its non-resignation to loss and scarcity, and its augmentation of the Platonic vision of good as precisely the harmonious 'fitting in' of all roles and options, where these have come to constitute peoples' very identity. All the same, he is wholly right to say that we only act in a history which is (exhaustively if contingently) 'shaped by privation': and if *Theology and Social Theory* appears to play this down, then it is much at fault. Original innocence is indeed wholly lost, and only leaves its trace as suffering. Yet it *is* still innocence that suffers, and *only* innocence (the children we are to become), because what must be suffered is the senselessness of evil, and those who know evil, having 'learned from experience', have learned precisely nothing. Furthermore, to surpass the tragic, to make the Christian gesture of faith beyond (but not without) renunciation, is not to embark on a premature celebration. On the contrary, it is to *refuse* to cease to suffer, to become resigned to a loss. Only at the price of an augmentation of suffering does a complete joy and peace begin to shine through.

34.12 And this is why Christ came to visit the lost. He sought out those who dwell in tragic enclaves, those who, through privation, enjoy goods which paradoxically cannot be goods because cut off from communication, from universal resonance. I mean something like honour amongst thieves, love in brothels, wisdom in the councils of state, Utopia constructed on the ravaged hunting-grounds of Indians. But we *all* dwell in enclaves, within founding dishonesties and deprivations which no later virtue can truly undo. Christ suffers this enclosure and so loves it and discloses it for us and to us. The enclave is henceforwards our hospital and asylum. Here — nowhere yet — is the Church. Everywhere.

Notes

1. Jean-Luc Marion, *God Without Being*, trans. Thomas A. Carlson, Chicago: University of Chicago Press, 1991, pp. 53–108. Marion's book has further warned me that in any talk of 'theological ontology' one should not mean that one has access to the nature of being as something present, graspable through intellectual sight. While I am not sure that I can follow him in his account of a priority of charity as the 'pre-ontological' (though love creates from nothing, *is* it not also always already a relation?) something like an 'equal priority' of the pre-ontological with the ontological is hinted at in my critique of *actus purus* in *Theology and Social Theory* (p. 423).

2. One wonders how Nichols would respond to the Pascalian theology of a Marion, with whom he might find himself more ecclesiastically in harmony. I suspect that his Englishness renders him more insular than my (never concealed!) Anglicanism.
3. Here and roundabouts I'm trying to make some sort of response to Nichols' complaint about my neglect of the ordained ministry.

35

Richard Roberts
Globalized Religion?

This extract comes from Richard Roberts' article 'Globalized Religion?: The "Parliament of the World's Religions" (Chicago 1993) in Theoretical Perspective', *Journal of Contemporary Religion*, Vol. 10 No. 2, 1995, pp. 121–2 and 127–37.

Theologians have recently taken considerable interest in the social process (or perhaps processes) of postmodernity. However, they seldom pay much attention to the social process of globalization. In this respect Richard Roberts, formerly a professor of theology at St Andrews University and now at Lancaster University, is an important exception. For the last decade social scientists, and particularly those specializing in international relations, have been exploring the cultural implications of increasing global contacts in the media, electronic communication, travel and trade. Roland Robertson's *Globalisation* (Sage, London, 1992) and Peter Beyer's *Religion and Globalisation* (Sage, London, 1993) provide useful accounts of this process. If postmodernity tends to foster fragmentation — and here David Harvey's *The Condition of Postmodernity* (Blackwell, Oxford, 1989) traces this fragmentation very helpfully across a number of academic disciplines — globalization, paradoxically, may increase uniformity and homogenization. Richard Roberts seeks to take account of both processes in his analysis of the potential social significance of inter-faith dialogue.

Roberts' article was prompted by his attendance at the 'Parliament of the World's Religions' in Chicago. In the longer article he provides a much fuller account of this occasion, but here only the theoretical discussion has been included. He starts this discussion by looking first at globalization theory. In these terms, global religion 'becomes a means, possibly one of the few remaining means, of outflanking globalized and totalizing power' (*35.5*). It has an important function 'when confronting the absence of an adequate immanent critique of the modern world system' (*35.6*). Global religion can also offer a means of confronting some of the more extreme fragmentations of postmodernity. It 'celebrates diversity whilst honouring and seeking to articulate universal exigencies' (*35.11*). Global religion represents a crucial tension between universal and particular. Roberts argues that this observation gives the specialist in religious studies an important role within other academic disciplines. If Milbank tends as a theologian to confront the social sciences, Roberts seeks rather their recognition and respect (*35.19*, and see, especially, his note 17). He believes that global religion could become 'an effective cultural capital, a dynamic resource for a modern/post-modern world system' (*35.22*).

35.1 In the late summer of 1993 I was able to attend the 'Parliament of the World's Religions' held in the Palmer House Hilton, Chicago. This event, planned over some five years by a Council (chaired by Cardinal Joseph Bernardine of Chicago), celebrated and re-enacted the first Parliament held in 1893. The first Parliament is generally credited with having introduced Eastern world religions to the United States in ways which were to have a growing impact on the level of mass culture and society, rather than upon a small eccentric or academic élite. The traditions then planted underwent an enormous boost in the 1960s when esoteric religious and mystical religious experience began to feature in global popular culture, not least following the Beatles' association with the Maharishi. The second Parliament of 1993 was a global event in which indigenized religions from within the United States and Canada, including not only official representatives of Buddhism, Christianity (mostly Roman Catholic) and Judaism (predominantly Liberal), Hinduism, Islam, Sikhism, and so on, encountered their root communities and traditions of origin. There was also an impressive array of more esoteric groups of many kinds. The much remarked and controversial participation of Neo-Pagans was indicative of the opening up of the religious 'market' at the Parliament. Co-religionists from all over the world converged upon Chicago in a highly diversified, complex, and sometimes conflictual encounter . . .

Theoretical Contextualization: Emancipatory Global Religion?

35.2 What, however, can be made of the Parliament in a wider context? An evaluation on the level of political consequences, or of an advanced synthesis between spiritual values and scientific discourse might well prove disappointing. If, however, the Parliament is taken on its own terms as a global religious event, then there are sociological grounds for considering that its socio-cultural importance could be more considerable. It is this latter dimension that is now opened up to analysis in the three following sub-sections concerned with globalization, an economy of space and signs, and post-modernization, respectively.

Religion and Globalization Theory

35.3 In an era after the 'End of History',[1] that is in a post-Marxist world order where 'capitalism has triumphed', the interpretation of religion as part of the socio-cultural capital of humankind involves the juxtaposition of the global (and globalization) with the local (and with processes of localization) of resurgent indigenous cultures.[2] It is at this juncture, in a fraught and complex tension between conflicting tendencies, that globalization theory advanced over the last decade by the sociologist Roland Robertson[3] of Pittsburg, and developed by the Canadian Peter Beyer,[4] proposes a more substantive role for religious beliefs, values and practices in the world system than had hitherto been sanctioned by both world system theory and post-war secularization theory.[5] World system and globalization theory (from the economic materialism of Sergei Eisenstadt, Immanuel Wallerstein and Leslie Sklair to the more 'humanistic' interpretations of Robertson and Beyer) has important relevance to the task of interpreting the relations between religious belief systems and religious cultural practices and the global economy and transnational business.[6] Peter Beyer has gone farthest in this direction and applied globalization theory in a series of test cases.[7] Correspondingly, it is Beyer's ideas which touch most closely upon our concern with the Chicago Parliament.

35.4 Beyer's presentation of his conception of the role of religion in globalization is constructed around an extended definition of the nature of religion that draws upon the insights of Niklas Luhmann:

... religion is therefore, sociologically speaking, a certain form of communication. Many sociological definitions of religion operate with a basic dichotomy such as profane/sacred (Durkheim), natural/supernatural (Parsons), nomos/cosmos (Berger), and empirical/super-empirical (Robertson). Others speak about religion as dealing with ultimate 'problems' (Yinger) or a 'general ... uniquely realistic' order of existence (Geertz), implicitly defining it by contrast to a more proximate and equivocal domain. The common thread through most of them is that religion is primarily about something beyond the normal, the everyday, the perceptible; and that somehow this radically other conditions human existence.[8]

Beyer maintains that religion comprises the juxtaposition of 'otherness' of transcendence with the 'indeterminacy of the immanent'. The latter term is perhaps not wholly satisfactory. This is because it is precisely the ever-extending power of the modern world-system and its tendency to normalize individuals and social structures in terms of 'managerialism',[9] or, more contentiously, global 'Macdonaldization[10] that threatens to create a totalized — even a totalitarian — reality from which the deviant and unpredictable should be excluded. Examined from this standpoint, the Parliament understood as a global religious event takes on significance as an exercise in benign deviance, a 'dangerous circumstance' (Roland Robertson), assimilable only with difficulty into a hegemonic managed modernity.[11] Beyer continues:

> I prefer to use immanence/transcendence to label the central religious dichotomy. What is definitive about this polarity is the holistic nature of the first term. The immanent is the whole world, the whole of perceptible reality, all meaning communicable among human beings. The whole, however, cannot as such be the object of communication because we cannot distinguish it from anything that it does not encompass. The transcendent, as the polar opposite, serves to give the immanent whole its meaningful context. In this sense, it acts as the condition for the possibility of the immanent. The central religious paradox lies in the fact that the transcendent can only be communicated in immanent terms, and this by definition: communication on the basis of meaning is always immanent, even when the subject of communication is the transcendent. Religion, therefore, operates with sacred symbols, ones which always point radically beyond themselves. It deals simultaneously with the immanent and the transcendent.[12]

35.5   Global religion thus understood becomes a means, possibly one of the few remaining means, of outflanking globalized and totalizing power. Placed in this context the 'Parliament of the World's Religions' was correspondingly a corporate, yet also individual and differentiated act which reclaimed human values and interests through symbolic and mythopoeic functionalization of immanence/transcendence distinctions (which are of course conceived in many ways).[13] Beyer contends that,

> religion posits the transcendent to give the immanent world meaning; and makes the requisite distinction between the two by further postulating that the transcendent is not subject to the root indeterminacy of the immanent.[14]

and,

In sum then, religion is a type of communication based on the immanent/transcendent polarity, which functions to lend meaning to the root indeterminability of all meaningful human communication, and which offers ways of overcoming or at least managing this indeterminability and its consequences.[15]

35.6 According to the perspective outlined in this section, the 'Parliament of the World's Religions' may be understood as a challenge to globalizing hegemony inasmuch as it succeeded in enacting the emancipatory distinctions between immanence and trancendence central to much world religion in conjunction with the articulation of total global threats. Global religion confronts alienation,[16] it even negotiates with it in special ways; but this engagement implies no capitulation either to hegemonic ideologies or to the seamless consumerism of late capitalism. It may function as a powerful, and globally well-dispersed resource to be drawn upon when confronting the absence of an adequate immanent critique of the modern world system.[17]

Religion and Differentiation in an 'Economy of Signs and Space'

35.7 A second theoretical resource upon which this paper draws is Scott Lash and John Urry's (1994) *Economies of Space and Time*[18] in which important connections are made between economic systems and their cultural analogues. Whereas some influential globalization theorists ascribe more than an epiphenomenal role and status to religious beliefs and practices in the global system, Lash and Urry evince little overt interest in the sociocultural role of religion in their magisterial study of the state of the world system after 'organized capitalism'.[19] This marked divergence is despite an implicit convergence of concerns between the study of religion and explorations in social science: religion may exemplify emancipatory differentiation; Lash and Urry seek out differentiation as the opportunity for emancipation.

35.8 The following passage provides a sense of the postmodern context in which Lash and Urry are to propose an emancipation driven by an ever more efficacious 'reflexive modernization':

Analyses of (such) post-modern economies and societies have dominated debate on the left and the right for the last decade. If modernism came to cut away the foundations of the Western tradition with the death of God, then post-modernism proclaiming 'the end of Man' removed even those few foundations that remained. The abstraction, meaninglessness, challenges to tradition and history issued by modernism have been driven to the extreme in post-modernism. On these counts neo-conservative analysts and many Marxists are in accord. In any event not just are the analyses surprisingly convergent, but so too are the pessimistic prognoses.

In response to this scenario Lash and Urry stress subjectivity and a conception of 'reflexive modernization' as agents of emancipation in a de-traditionalized post-modern world. Whilst it is possible to concur with the maximization of critical reflexive consciousness this is nevertheless an intellectualistic response and they are arguably unduly optimistic when they consider that the social process can be challenged or changed simply at the level of consciousness. Lash and Urry supplement their argument and thus expose the basis of a congruence and a potential elective affinity between globalized religion as exemplified in the 'Parliament of the World's Religions' and their emancipatory intent. Lash and Urry continue:

> Now much of this pessimism is appropriate. But it is part of the aim of this book to argue that there is a way out. It is to claim that the sort of 'economies of sign and space' that became pervasive in the wake of organised capitalism do not just lead to increasing meaninglessness, homogenization, abstraction, anomie and the destruction of the subject. Another set of radically divergent processes is simultaneously taking place. These processes may open up possibilities for the recasting of meaning in work and in leisure, for the reconstruction of community and the particular, for the reconstruction of a transmogrified subjectivity, and for heterogenisation and complexity of space and everyday life.[20]

35.9   There is insufficient space to take this argument much further here[21] save to suggest that it is precisely global and globalized religion of the kind functionalized in the 1993 Parliament which not only, following Lash and Urry, provides 'heterogenization and complexity of space and everyday life' but also, as Beyer proposes, affords a dynamic way of articulating comprehensive issues concerning the human condition in ways accessible to groups lying outside the subjectivity of the virtuoso reflexive modernizer.

Religion, 'Meta-Theory' and the 'Condition of Post-modernity'

35.10   Whilst Beyer's approach requires modification, enlargement and a measure of recontextualization, it nevertheless points to a way of satisfying the demand for post-Marxist 'meta-theory' articulated at the core of the debate concerned with the 'condition of post-modernity'. Likewise, it is necessary to take even greater liberties with Lash and Urry's procedure which is narrow in its admission of real possibilities for emancipation in a differentiated world order. Nevertheless, in the two preceding subsections of this paper the 'Parliament of the World's Religions' has been presented as a symbolic collective act that embodied a set of distinctions correlatable with those made in recent globalization theory and in the idea of an 'economy of space and signs'. The Parliament may thus be construed as having a role in the world system which should not be underestimated, and which could well be developed further. In a third theoretical contextualization the Parliament is further related to arguments concerning aspects of the so-called 'condition of post-modernity'.[22] Here the threads can be drawn together in David Harvey's (1989) fuller argument for a political conditioning of post-modernity:

> Postmodernism, with its emphasis upon the ephemerality of *jouissance*, its insistence upon the impenetrability of the other, its concentration on the text rather than the work, its penchant for deconstruction bordering on nihilism, its preference for aesthetics over ethics, takes matters too far. It takes them beyond the point where any coherent politics are left, while that wing of it that seeks a shameless accommodation with the market puts it firmly in the tracks of an entrepreneurial culture that is the hallmark of reactionary neoconservatism. Postmodernist philosophers tell us not only to accept but even to revel in the fragmentations and the cacophony of voices through which the dilemmas of the modern world are understood. Obsessed with deconstructing and delegitimating every form of argument they encounter, they can end only in condemning their own validity claims to the point where nothing remains of any basis for reasoned action. Postmodernism has us accepting the reifications and partitionings, actually celebrating the activity of masking and cover-up, all the fetishisms of locality, place, or social grouping, while denying that kind of meta-theory which can grasp the political-economic processes (money flows, international divisions of labour, financial markets, and the like) that are becoming ever more universalizing in their depth, intensity, reach and power over daily life.[23]

35.11 This is an humane and influential characterization of the process of post-modernization. There are many ways in which the global religion of the Parliament might be understood to intersect with, yet challenge Harvey's vision. Of these, perhaps the most important is that global and globalized religion confronts deconstructive fragmentation because it does not itself seek to avoid juxtaposition of the extremes of universality and particularity: its management of this tension is both problematic and paradigmatic; yet it does not offer easy answers (there are none, despite what a consumerist capitalism might lead us to believe). It celebrates diversity whilst honouring and seeking to articulate universal exigences. Harvey's demand for a 'meta-theory' that may grasp and resist totalizing power is enabled by the admission of the global religion dimension when this is appropriated along the lines suggested by Beyer and implied (contrary to their explicit agenda) by Lash and Urry. This is not a question (as in, for example, the former East Germany where religious societal space was temporally exploited) of using religiosity as a vehicle for political goals, but of understanding more fully the role of religion as a resource, as 'cultural capital' that creatively, yet ambiguously and unpredictably refracts the human condition through myth, ritual, symbol, narrative and complex cultural practices. The peculiar and distinctive ways in which religion represents the global condition acknowledges the relativity of all validity claims, yet it does not abandon them; it cannot, because tensions between universal and particular are endemic and acknowledged in religion.

Religion as Resource: A 'Cultural Capital' Approach

35.12 In this paper the argument has been advanced that in the 1993 Chicago Parliament forms of consciousness designatable as 'reflexive mythopoesis' and 'reflexive spirituality' were apparently analogous to the 'reflexive modernity' required by contemporary theorists as both the price of, and the opportunity for emancipation in late modernity and postmodernity. In other words, seen from a socio-linguistic standpoint informed in a provisional way by the three theoretical positions outlined above, the Parliament was not characterized by regressive pre-modern traditionalism, but a dynamic, emancipatory postmodern-tending discourse in which a variety of 'genres' (in the Bakhtinian sense) were dialectically combined, not least through a repeated, yet transformed ritual diachronic structure.

35.13 It is possible to maintain, moreover, that the Parliament was more politically conscious in its own distinctive way than Lash and Urry in *Economies of Space and Signs*, despite their explicit emancipatory agenda. This was because the Parliament was able both to admit a truly extreme heterogeneity and complexity of space and signs way beyond anything conceded by these sociological writers and then to assimilate them, albeit proleptically, under a single global agenda. In other words, in the crudest terms, can 'reflexive modernization' on its own (albeit understood as an improvement on naked instrumental reason) be an adequate agent of emancipation in the context of the global crisis such as that addressed by the Parliament?

The Chicago Parliament and the Study of Religion

35.14 The interpretation of such a global religious event raises important questions for the academic study of religion. The theorization and interpretation of religion in such sub-disciplines as the sociology of religion is, however, in a state of partially-acknowledged crisis. The isolation of such a sub-discipline from the core activities of the parent disciplines is problematic. In this paper we have tried to show that contemporary religion need not necessarily be understood as pre-modern residuum, of interest only to specialists in something close to intellectual necrology.

35.15 Furthermore, the socio-scientific study and normative evaluation of contemporary religious phenomena can now only be adequately undertaken in ways which imply a critique of internal, endogenous approaches to the study of religion. As the sociologist James Beckford remarked at the Easter 1993 meeting of the Sociology of Religion Group of the British Sociological Association, recent analyses of modernity neglect religion as a social factor, but this need not necessarily be the case. Our contention has been that despite the distance between the study and analysis of religion and the socio-scientific representation of the contemporary human condition, there is evidence of the existence of important elective affinities between both fields of activity. We have tried to illustrate and expound this with regard to an extremely important recent example of global religion.

35.16 The move we have made from description to explanation in the foregoing account of the 'Parliament of the World's Religions' confronts a problem elucidated by John S. Cumpsty in one of the most substantial recent contributions to methodology, *Religion as Belonging: A General Theory of Religion* (1991). Cumpsty's impassioned plea for a return from the disciplinary dispersal of religious studies into its *Hilfswissenschaften* needs to be treated with some caution. Cumpsty asserts that:

> Wherever Religious Studies has sought to move beyond description to explanation, it has been heavily dependent upon sociology, anthropology and psychology, for both definition and theory.[24]

In order to counter this tendency which appears to endanger and lose the distinctiveness of 'religion' itself, Cumpsty proposes a systemic, self-referential method for the study of religion, based upon the assumption that,

(a) it become truly a discipline in its own right, by

(b) defining its own object of study (however tentatively) in terms of the object itself, that is as non-reductively as possible, or it will not be in a position to fulfil the other criterion of a normative discipline, which is to:

(c) develop and evaluate its own theory in terms of what enriches understanding of its own object of study.[25]

For, he concludes:

> In short, one needs to have a feeling for what is the really real and some way of assuring one's relation to it. That, in human terms, is the religious drive.[26]

35.17 Such a *sui generis* definition of religion is problematic for obvious reasons. A definition of religion as appropriating the 'really real' directs us into at least three major areas of difficulty: (i) an evasion of an array of hidden and begged questions concerning realism and constructivism in the human and social sciences that confront anyone seriously engaged in social representation and the construction of social facts in and through disciplines; (ii) confinement *ab initio* within the commonplaces of a discourse which may well then suffer from an immediate methodological foreclosure; (iii) an uncontrolled slide towards the abyss represented by the search for a watertight definition of religion (Was it 95 or 96 such definitions at the last count?). This is an unsatisfactory procedure, and one challenged long ago by Max Weber when he argued that the definition of 'religion' should be attempted, if at all, only at the conclusion of an investigation.

35.18 In more positive terms, Ursula King's observations made some years ago in an important study of the historical and phenomenological approaches to the study of religion are worthy of reiteration:

> The study of religion, as currently conceived, is undergoing a great deal of change involving much critical self-examination and a search for clearer definition.[27]

35.19 The approach adopted in this paper has been conducted in the spirit of such critical self-examination. Indeed, it is basic to the foregoing argument that narrative and systemic, purely self-referential accounts of religion do not tell us much more about religious phenomena in the contemporary world than any informed student could construe on the basis of prolonged participant observation. When Religious Studies is

involved in empathetic yet critical participant observation, responsibly and flexibly practising the disciplines of the human and social
sciences in ways recognizable and respected by main-line exponents
of those disciplines, drawing upon the history of religions and the
apposite linguistic tools, and when it is concerned with what are
rightly called 'first-order normative issues in religion', then it may, I
believe, play its part in engagement with problems of universal
human import. To achieve this is not easy, for it requires not least
credibility within disciplines and across disciplinary boundaries,
besides an awareness of the processes involved in the history and
formation of those disciplines in the context of the modernization
process itself.[28]

35.20   In conclusion, in this paper we have sought to
show that the Chicago 1993 'Parliament of the
World's Religions' was a remarkable expression of global spirituality which embodied and enacted forms of reflexive consciousness
with important emancipatory potential. As such it lends substance
to an eventuality sketched out by Peter Beyer:

> All in all, then, we might provisionally conclude that 'global civil' religion
> is both possible and likely; but there will be more than one of them and
> these will simply be more religious offerings beside others, both systemic
> and cultural . . . We live in a conflictual and contested social world where
> the appeal to holism is itself partisan. That paradox alone is itself enough
> to maintain the religious enterprise, even if with more risk and less self-
> evidence.[29]

35.21   Ninian Smart remarks in his concluding reflections on global religion[30] in *The World's Religions*
(1989):

> Though we may not achieve a global religion, we may achieve a global
> civilization in which values from the great traditions are woven together
> in a glittering net. Perhaps it will turn out like the jewel net of Indra, of
> which Hua-yen so eloquently speaks: each stone reflecting every
> other.[31]

35.22   This is an idealistic vision portrayed with imagery
which recalls much of the experience of the 1993
Chicago 'Parliament of the World's Religions'. Since Smart wrote
these words, it has become even less plausible to hope for a 'global
civilization'. Nevertheless, although the 'Parliament of the World's
Religions' was not immune from the experience of the conflicts
pervasive at both global and local level in the world system, there
was evidence of serious, negotiated convergence of concerns. When
global religion becomes a global religiosity, that is when as a form of
critical reflexivity it has access to, and refunctions the resources of

ancient traditions and engages in diverse, but commensurable cultural practices in the context of shared universal concerns, it becomes an effective cultural capital, a dynamic resource for a modern/post-modern world system.

35.23 The 1993 Chicago 'Parliament of the World's Religions' may be counted as an important step on the path towards the recovery of the use-values of religion in a threatened world. In the glittering lobby of the Palmer Hilton many jewels in the net of Indra reflected and refracted each other's light. World religion drew itself together for a moment; much of what it saw was good, not least in the experience of the multitude of 'Others' who experienced each other both as difference and likeness — but also as complementarities within the greater community of religions and of humankind itself.

Notes

1. Fukuyama, Francis. 'The End of History', *The National Interest*, 16, 1989, 3–18; Francis Fukuyama, *The End of History and the Last Man*, London: Hamish Hamilton, 1992. Fukuyama (1992) is less than helpful on the religious issue: 'Religion has thus been relegated to the sphere of private life — exiled, it would seem, more or less permanently from European political life except on certain narrow issues like abortion', yet in the revival of nationalism, 'identity would be expressed primarily in the realm of culture rather than politics', p. 271. In other words, Fukuyama's prescriptive approach to contemporary history signally fails to grasp the integral character of the ethno-religious revival of nationalism.

2. For discussion of communitarian as opposed to individual and liberal, universal ethics, see Taylor, C. *The Ethics of Authenticity*, Cambridge, Mass: Harvard University Press, 1991, ch. V, 'The Need for Recognition'; and Roberts, R. H. (forthcoming), 'Identity and Belonging', in *Nation, State, and the Coexistence of Different Communities*, Societas Ethica volume to be published by KOK PHAROS.

3. Robertson, R. 'The Globalisation Paradigm: Thinking Globally', *Religion and Social Order*, vol. I, 1991, 207–24 and many other articles. Robertson's recent book, *Globalisation: Social Theory and Global Culture*, London: Sage, 1992, draws together his thought. See also Featherstone, M., ed., *Global Culture: Nationalism, Globalisation and Modernity*, London: Sage Publications, 1990, and a growing further literature.

4. Beyer, P. *Religion and Globalisation*, London: Sage, 1993.

5. See Acquaviva, S. *The Decline of the Sacred in Industrial Society*, Oxford: Blackwell, 1979; Blumenberg, H. *The Legitimacy of the Modern Age* (orig. 1966) Cambridge, Mass.: MIT, 1983; Cladwick, O. *The Secularisation of the European Mind in the Nineteenth Century*, Cambridge:

CUP; Dobbelaere, K. 'Secularisation: A Multi-Dimensional Concept', *Current Sociology*, 29(2), 1981; Dobbelaere, K. 'Some Trends in European Sociology of Religion: The Secularisation Debate', *Sociological Analysis*, 48(2), 1987, 107–37; Fenn, Richard *The Dream of the Perfect Act: An Inquiry into the Fate of Religion in a Secular World*, London: Tavistock, 1987; Glasner, P. E. *The Sociology of Secularisation: A Critique of a Concept*, London: Routledge & Kegan Paul, 1977; Luckmann, T., 1967, 'The Decline of Church-Oriented Religion', in Robertson, *Readings*, 1969, 141–51; Martin, D. *A General Theory of Secularisation*, Oxford: Blackwell 1978; Martin, D. 'Towards Eliminating the Concept of Secularization', in *The Religious and the Secular: Studies in Secularization*, London: RKP, 1969, ch. 1, 9–22; Stark, R. & Bainbridge, W. S. *The Future of Religion — Secularization, Revival and Cult Formation*, Berkeley: University of California Press, 1983, ch. 2, 19–37.
6. Given the real power of these factors the critical study of managerial and business ethics in the context of global managerialism becomes, contra Alasdair MacIntyre, a central rather than a peripheral issue.
7. This is a very difficult area. Robertson and Beyer's arguments for taking seriously the claim that culturally entrenched religious discourse is now taking on substantive significance in a post-Marxist world order merit very careful scrutiny. For present purposes it is assumed that the attribution of epiphenomenal status to religious (and many other) phenomena in an ideological 'superstructure' or *Überbau* is now under challenge. For comparative studies of global fundamentalism relevant to these considerations see: Kepel, G. *The Revenge of God: The Resurgence of Islam, Christianity and Judaism in the Modern World*, Cambridge: Polity, 1994; and Riesebrodt, M. *Pious Passion: The Emergence of Modern Fundamentalism in the United States and Iran*, Berkeley: University of California Press, 1993.
8. Beyer, P., 1994, 5.
9. Enteman, W. F. *Managerialism: The Emergence of a New Ideology*, Madison: University of Wisconsin Press, 1993.
10. Ritzer, G. *The MacDonaldization of Society*, Thousand Oaks/London: Pine Forge Press, 1993.
11. On the discussion of 'modernity' see: Anderson, P. 'Marshall Berman: Modernity and Revolution' in *A Zone of Engagement*, London: Verso, 1992, ch. 2; Bauman, Z. *Modernity and Ambivalence*, Cambridge: Polity, 1991; Bauman, Z. *Modernity and the Holocaust*, Cambridge: Polity, 1989; Beck, U. *Risk Society: Towards a New Modernity*, London: Sage Publications, 1992; Berger, P. L. *Facing Up to Modernity: Excursions in Society, Politics and Religion*, New York: Basic Books, 1977; Berman, M. *All that is Solid Melts into Air: The Experience of Modernity*, London: Verso, 1983; Bernstein, R. J. *The New Constellation: The Ethical-Political Horizons of Modernity/Post Modernity*, Cambridge: Polity, 1991; Giddens, A. *The Consequences of Modernity*, Cambridge: Polity, 1990; Giddens, A. *Modernity and Self-Identify: Self and Society in the Late Modern Age*, Cambridge, Polity, 1991; Habermas, J. *The*

Philosophical Discourse of Modernity: Twelve Lectures, 1987, Introduction, Preface, Lectures I and II; Luhmann, Niklas 'The Paradox of System Differentiation and the Evolution of Society', in Alexander, J. & Colomy, P., eds., *Differentiation Theory and Social Change: Comparative and Historical Perspectives*, New York: Columbia University Press, 1990, 409–40; MacIntyre, A. 'Why the Enlightenment Project of Justifying Morality Had to Fail' and 'Some Consequences of the Failure of the Enlightenment Project', in *After Virtue: A Study in Moral Theory*, London: Duckworth, 1981, 49–75; Touraine, A. *Critique of Modernity*, London: Routledge, 1994; Vattimo, G. *The End of Modernity: Nihilism and Hermeneutics in Post-Modern Culture*, Cambridge: Polity, 1988.

12. Beyer, P. 1994, 5.
13. There is much that is unclear concerning the sociological interpretation of such distinctions, especially when the gender perspective is brought into consideration.
14. Beyer, P., 1994, 6.
15. Beyer, P., 1994, 6.
16. It will be necessary to re-engage with the nature(s) of alienation in a post-Marxist world order. The anti-totalizing critique of globalized religion and its comprehension of the global/local matrix is an important starting-point.
17. Milbank, J., has attempted such a critique in *Theology and Social Theory*, Oxford: Blackwell, 1990, but his solution is a Pyrrhic victory involving a retreat from serious worldliness. See Roberts, R. H. 'Transcendental Sociology? — Article Review of A. J. Milbank's *Theology and Social Theory*', *Scottish Journal of Theology*, 46(4), 1993, 527–35.
18. Lash, S. & Urry, J. *Economies of Space and Sign*, London: Sage, 1994.
19. See Lash, S. & Urry, J. *The End of Organized Capitalism*, Cambridge: Polity, 1987.
20. Lash & Urry (1994), p. 3.
21. See Roberts, R. H., ed. *Religion and the Transformations of Capitalism*. London: Routledge, 1995, and Roberts, R. H. *Religion and the Resurgence of Capitalism*, London: Routledge (forthcoming 1997).
22. See, for example, Harvey, D. *The Condition of Postmodernity: An Enquiry into the Origins of Cultural Change*, Oxford: Blackwell, 1989, chs. 1 and 2; Küng, H. *Theology for the Third Millenium: An Ecumenical View*, London: HarperCollins Academic, 1991, 1–12; Milbank, J. *Theology and Social Theory: Beyond Secular Reason*, Oxford: Blackwell, 1990; Roberts, R. H. *A Theology on Its Way? Essays on Karl Barth*, Edinburgh: T. & T. Clark, 1992, chs. 1 and 6.
23. *The Condition of Postmodernity*, Oxford: Blackwell, 1989, 116–17.
24. Cumpsty, J. S. *Religion as Belonging: A General Theory of Religion*, Lanham: University Press of America, 1991, p. xxxvi.
25. Cumpsty, J. S. 1991, pp. xxxvi–xxxvii.
26. Cumpsty, J. S. 1991, p. xxxvii.

27. King, U. 'Historical and Phenomenological Approaches', in Whaling, F., ed., *Contemporary Approaches to the Study of Religion* in 2 Volumes, Vol. I: *The Humanities*, The Hague: Mouton, 1984, 71.
28. See Co-Editor with Good, J. M. M. *The Recovery of Rhetoric: Persuasive Discourse and Disciplinarity in the Human Sciences*, Bristol: Bristol Classical Press/London: Duckworth/Charlottesville, VA: The University of Virginia Press, 1993.
29. Beyer, P., 1994, 227.
30. Note the six dimensions of religion: ritual; mythological; doctrinal; ethical; social; experiential in Smart, N. *The Religious Experience of Mankind*, London: Collins, 1969, 15–25.
31. Smart, N. *The World's Religions: Old Traditions and Modern Transformations*, Cambridge: Cambridge University Press, 1989, 561.

36

Stephen Pattison
Mystical Management

This extract comes from Stephen Pattison's article 'Mystical Management: A Religious Critique of General Management in the Public Sector', *MC* (now entitled *Modern Believing*), XXXIII, 3, 1991, pp. 17–27. Pattison is the author of *A Critique of Pastoral Care* (SCM Press, London, 1988), *Alive and Kicking* (SCM Press, London, 1989) and *Pastoral Care and Liberation Theology* (CUP, 1994).

Within the last decade, management studies have assumed an increasingly dominant role in the social sciences. So it is fitting to conclude this Reader with a theological interpretation of management. Less ambitious than the differing postmodern roles for theology offered by Milbank and by Roberts, Pattison's analysis nevertheless offers some sharp observations about recent management theory and practice. For some years he lectured in pastoral theology at Birmingham University. However, in the 1980s he retrained in management studies and is now a lecturer in the School of Health and Social Welfare of the Open University. In this extract he shows that, despite this career move, he has lost none of his interest in theology.

He sets out to show that 'the new managers are deeply involved in religious activity ... indeed in religious activity which has close analogies with charismatic evangelical Christianity' (*36.3*) of which they are largely unaware. Pointing to the immense changes in the British National Health Service resulting from the recommendations of Roy Griffiths in 1984 (*36.10*), Pattison argues that quasi-religious language often accompanied these changes (*36.14*). He traces the roots of this language to the connection in the United States between the business and evangelical worlds (*36.16*). This language contains significant eschatological features (*36.17*) as well as clear elements of 'faith' (*36.18*). In particular, the process of management by objectives is an area in which 'the vivid apocalyptic language of early Christianity has its greatest contemporary currency' (*36.22*). Having made this analysis, Pattison argues that managers need to learn to refine and scrutinize the metaphors that they use, just as critical theologians have learned over the years to do this with their language (*36.24*). Thus 'if people are involved in what is in many ways religious activity with important faith assumptions and a language of faith ... they should be self aware and self-critical' (*36.32*). In effect, 'managers should become much more openly and honestly theologians' (*36.35*).

36.1 In the summer of 1988 I gave up agonizing about the relevance and practicality of religious belief and Christian theology as a university teacher of practical theology to enter the 'real' world of the National Health Service. Here, where billions of pounds are spent by powerful managers in the public interest, I thought more certainty, direction and security of identity was sure to be found.

36.2 Two years later I find, to my surprise, that while I may have left one area of life concerned with metaphysics I am now in another. Behind the imposing (if decrepit) walls of the hospitals, beneath the impressive mounds of statistics, reports and other papers and within the well-pressed pin-striped suits of the public servants an experiment in values and metaphysics is taking place. The somewhat unlikely protagonists of this experiment are a new breed of public sector manager — the general managers, introduced in 1984.

36.3 I want to argue that the new managers are deeply involved in religious activity (using this term in the widest sense), indeed in religious activity which has close analogies with charismatic evangelical Christianity. Unfortunately, they are largely unaware of this and the implications which follow from this kind of enterprise.

36.4 To do this, I will draw on books, personal experience in the NHS, conversations and lectures culled from undertaking a course in Public Sector Management at Birmingham University, and from my native disciplines of theology and ethics to construct a critique of the values, nature and context of public sector management. The sources upon which I draw are necessarily selective, as are the areas of practice considered. For the sake of exhibiting partial knowledge rather than total ignorance I shall concentrate on the NHS in my exemplifications.

36.5 Inevitably, I must allow an element of caricature to creep into my discussion. Only by a caricaturing, 'ideal-typing', or stereotyping certain traits in management theory and practice can I attain the heuristic clarity needed to make my point. I am fully aware of the dangers of partiality and distortion which this entails. The justification for it will lie in whether others can recognize something of value within it which illuminates their own perceptions. This is a suggestive and exploratory exercise, not a definitive analysis.

36.6 My conclusion is that if managers are involved in a kind of religious activity they should become conscious of this fact and work with it rather than denying or ignoring it. By becoming more self-consciously critical practical 'theologians', i.e. students and practitioners of deep values, metaphors, hopes and assumptions, they will be more self- and institutionally-aware.[1] They might or might not become 'better' managers (though the adjective 'better' begs the question in this context). They will certainly have more potential for examining their own values and choices, essential prerequisites for effective judgement and practical action.

The Faith of the Public Sector Managers[2]

36.7 For the majority of the sophisticated, well-educated ruling classes in Britain, religion in its conventional, Christian, dogmatic, church-going forms is largely a thing of the past.[3] Although it may well be the case that the welfare state owes something to traditional religious values such as compassion and fellowship and there are undoubtedly those amongst the managers who have a personal faith (which may even have motivated them to join the public sector in the first place), it is probably true to say that in a pluralistic society conventional religion has become marginalized and privatized.[4] Any attempt to start a District Health Authority with prayer, for example, would be greeted with unease and be perceived as intrusive, inappropriate and irrelevant.

36.8 The assertion that public sector managers are conducting a religious experiment is, therefore, not an assertion that they practise overt, conventional religion. A wider understanding of religion is required. The anthropologist, Geertz, suggests that religion is

(1) a system of symbols which acts to (2) establish powerful, pervasive, and long-lasting moods and motivations in men by (3) formulating conceptions of a general order of existence and (4) clothing these conceptions with such an aura of factuality that (5) the moods and motivations seem uniquely realistic.[5]

36.9 While definitions of religion are extensively disputed, this definition serves my heuristic purpose well.[6] Clearly, there are many aspects of social life which could be described as religious in these terms. So, for example, the capitalist market economy with its belief in the real value of symbolic pound notes backed up by extensive ideologies formulated by economists would be a religion. In more specific terms, I suggest that religion in this sense acts as 'a panacea, a blessing, a comfort, a source of all meaning, a path to identity, morality, wholeness, progress, worth'.[7] I hope that even if these words cannot be easily applied to all public sector managers or management in toto (so, for example, it might be maintained that management understandings and beliefs do not permeate the whole lives and experience of managers), their validity in this context can be provisionally accepted. I want now to pursue the concept of management as a religious activity. More particularly, I want to suggest that the kind of religious activity it has become in present-day Britain is a charismatic, evangelical religious activity.

36.10 Perhaps the best way of highlighting this is to quote from an account of the introduction of general management into the NHS. Before 1984, management in the NHS was consensual. Broadly, the service was run in a syndicalist way by a tripartite arrangement between doctors, nurses and administrators. Individual clinicians had most influence. There were a number of parallel hierarchies and no-one had overall control. This was radically changed by the introduction of general management from the retailing part of the private sector on the recommendation of Sir Roy Griffiths, at the time Managing Director of Sainsbury's. The general management revolution of 1984 created a single operational hierarchy with one person in overall charge at each level of the NHS. It was greeted with dismay by some — by others with almost religious enthusiasm:

> Chairmen of health authorities, directors of finance and personnel, community physicians, nurse managers, general managers and aspirants to management would sit, several hundred strong, and listen to the *prophets* of the *new order* ... In the heady atmosphere that a day off work can induce, a *dream* was outlined; a *vision* that was both organisational and *moral* ... but this was not just another way of restructuring the health service, it was also a *crusade* ... Down the tatty corridors of the NHS, new and dedicated heroes would stride — the general managers. Inspired by their leadership a new sort of staff would arise.[8]

36.11 I assume that the use of words which have extensive religious, moral, even millenarian connotations in this description is not satirical or exaggeration.

36.12 At a later point in their examination of general management into the NHS, Strong and Robinson go on to describe general management as 'a *doctrine*, not just of firm leadership and corporate structure, but of cost and quality too'.[9]

> General management is both a theory and a practical discipline. As a theory, it is not something that has been conclusively and scientifically demonstrated to be superior; nor, perhaps, could it ever be for it operates in that most complex of worlds, the social arena, the home of the soft, not the hard sciences. Thus the only way practical managers can proceed is by using a subtle brew of hard evidence and gut feeling, of official statistics and qualitative data, of both careful analysis and the charismatic enthusiasm of management gurus, variously stirred. *General management, in short, is a philosophy, a paradigm, a doctrine.*[10]

36.13 Strong and Robinson approach general management in the NHS as dispassionate ethnographic researchers. The fact that they use language with religious overtones to describe some facets of the management revolution would seem, *prima facie*, to confirm my own view that it is worth exploring this phenomenon in religious and theological terms rather than just accepting it at face value. I shall, therefore, now go on to explore the religious style, content and language of the faith of the managers.

The Religious Style of General Management

36.14 General management has many of the features of a charismatic, fundamentalist, aggressive, conversionist, evangelical North American sectarianism;-[11]
— *Commitment* is required from all members of the organization, however low down or badly paid;
— A strong sense of *corporate identity* is required — members of the organization must stick together and adhere to a set of common values over against the world (the customers?) outside;
— The *individual* is important to the organization — he or she must believe in what he or she is doing and be *converted* to the aims of the organization. Thus she will find a sense of purpose, community and belonging;
— *Perfection* (quality assurance, excellence) is to be sought by all members of the organization;
— *Leadership* is directive, and comes from above (cf the place of God in Christianity);
— There is no long or elaborate *hierarchy* of leadership but the short hierarchy is very clear and definite;
— Leadership is based on *charismatic authority* not on professional training or knowledge. Anyone, from any part of society, can be a

manager so long as they are qualified by personal gifts and competences;

— No-one can say what the *essential features* required for management and leadership are with any certainty. Instead, the manager, like the true prophet, is known by his fruits, or what is more popularly known as meeting individual performance targets;[12]

— Managers, especially senior managers, are required to exercise extreme *inner asceticism*. They must be devoted to the organization and give to their jobs unlimited time as a sign of the seriousness with which they accept their vocation. Only thus will they receive the manna of performance-related pay and experience the fruits of organizational salvation;

— Before the judgement seat of individual performance review the manager is *personally and uniquely responsible* for the success or failure of his organizational stewardship. Sin and salvation are ultimately personal;

— *Evangelizing* the organization and clientele is important — hence the emphasis on what are enigmatically called communication skills and organs such as corporate newspapers and leaflets;

— *Theories and statements* about the organization must be clear, simple and indisputable. They should be accepted and retailed by all organization members;

— Because of their charismatic authority managers are in a unique position to *identify the vision* towards which the organization should be working and to empower their followers to bring this vision to reality;

— To reinforce their own authority and confirm their own *identity, vision and inspiration,* managers may from time to time go to a rally at which they will be inspired by a wandering charismatic leader who will give them a simple, practical and uplifting session on the need for excellence or time management. This will be easily assimilable within 6–8 hours and will not require further elaboration. The wandering charismatic will have his own vocation confirmed by the size of the cash collection from participants (NB Convention centres are preferred to tents for these occasions, but the media and messages used will be similar to those of Christian evangelists);

— *Pour encourager les autres,* from time to time successful charismatics like Tom Peters will write easy-to-understand popular tracts explaining in narrative form, with concrete personal examples and testimonies, how they have succeeded and how others can appropriate the grace of success and become heroes of faith if only they can become like the author.[13]

36.15 I have drawn on a number of personal impressions and different sources to create this caricature or ideal type of management style. Of course, it is a gross distortion and over-generalization, but I believe it contains some elements of truth.

36.16 At this point, it might be objected that the style traits I have outlined are drawn immediately from the ideology of business in the private sector, not from American charismatic religion. This is true. It must, however, be remembered that management theory in the private sector is heavily influenced by American thinking. In the US, protestant religion is much more central in society and there is often a symbiotic relationship between religion and business. Evangelists run their organizations like big businesses while big business retains something of the value-driven charismatic fervour of the protestant optimism which arguably helped to fuel capitalism in the first place and to bring about the American dream.[14] It should also be recalled that the present British government has itself set out on a quest to restore values, some of them overtly religious, in British society which has itself responded to this quest in successive elections.[15] The direct, uncomplicated style and thinking of business evangelists such as Peters and Waterman who talk the language of values richly blessed by worldly success, thus finds fertile soil in this country.[16]

The Faith Content of General Management

36.17 The faith content of the management revolution is characterized principally by a forward looking optimism (what theologians would call eschatology). The forces of humanity and nature can, given the right motivation, reasonable resources and clarity of purpose, be harnessed towards a desired future. Combining elements of ratio-technological instrumentality such as breaking down problems into soluble goals and targets which can then be dealt with by individuals or groups, the management revolution is also suspicious of reason and rational planning.[17] Too often in the past, it is believed, rationality has led to paralysis by analysis, abstraction and heartlessness, negativity, an unwillingness to take risks and a denigration of the role of values.[18]

36.18 The rediscovery of values lies at the heart of the management revolution. Peters and Waterman wax lyrical as they claim that 'so much excellence in performance has to do with people's being motivated by compelling, simple — even beautiful — values'.[19] They suggest that 'good managers make meanings for people, as well as money'[20] and they argue that 'Instead of brain games in the sterile ivory tower, it's shaping values (management's job becomes more fun) through coaching and evangelism in the field — with the worker and in support of the cherished product'.[21] The company or organization should become a community of the faithful finding meaning and productivity together as they colonize an ever-expanding future and wrest from it blessing for themselves and their customers. Having developed their key values the point is then to act, for actions speak louder than words and, of course, they reinforce faith.[22] The faith of the managers can be summarised as 'I believe, therefore I can do'.

36.19 A number of critical points can be made here. First, the teleology of the managers is unclear. It is one thing to have and to seek visions and values but these are not a virtue in themselves. Presumably Hitler and armaments companies have or had clear visions and values, but they are not necessarily socially acceptable or useful. This is a vital point in relation to public service management, as is the issue of how these values are arrived at and by whom. In the private sector the values and faith of managers is tested against the concrete reality of consumer demand and response. 'False' visions in terms of the market are extinguished by bankruptcy. This is not a corrective which is available in the public sector.

36.20 Secondly, the grounds for managers' optimism and faith in the value of their own enterprise and its future beneficial effects is open to question. The concepts of economy, efficiency and effectiveness have now become almost reified within the faith of the managers but, in practice, it is difficult to assess these. While it is relatively easy to measure inputs, financial and other, into the public services it is still almost impossible to measure outputs. Despite all the information technology now available to managers it is still not possible to assess whether outcomes are becoming better or worse. This is, of course, enormously complicated by the fact that much public service must have a qualitative component rather than simply assuming that quantity is the key indicator. Ultimately, general managers (and their critics) do not know whether their assumptions, goals, objectives and values are improving things or not.[23] Like all true believers, they have to believe that they are. They, too, wait for some kind of final revealing of a future which they believe themselves to be participating in constructing but whose real nature cannot really be predicted or known.[24]

36.21 Thirdly, and emerging from the previous two points, managers, like many other groups in society, e.g., counsellors, priests, politicians, accountants, businessmen and women, are involved in the metaphysical realm of deep hopes, values and assumptions. Even as they talk of elements of 'realism', practicality and pragmatism entering the public sector and they scan spread sheets and accounts, the managers are acting on a faith in the transcendent world of values, hopes and assumptions. Part of what managers manage, perhaps ultimately the most important part, is this reality shaping transcendent dimension through which they and their subordinates perceive needs, tasks, their own place in the world and the nature of their organisation. This could be designated the spiritual aspect of management if 'spiritual' is understood to mean something like:

> the way in which a person (or organisation SP) understands and lives within his or her historical context that aspect of his or her religion, philosophy or ethics which is viewed as the loftiest, the noblest, the most calculated to lead to the fulness of the ideal or perfection being sought.[25]

Religious Language in General Management

36.22 The religious nature of general management reaches its apotheosis in the language used in association with this activity. Here evangelical revivalism appears to have unbridled sway. The process of Management by Objectives, i.e. the process whereby a vision is turned into goals and objectives which are then implemented, is governed by visions (what people most want to bring into being), mission statements (very short statements of what the organization believes itself to be trying to do) and doom scenarios (what will happen if desired action to achieve objectives is not taken). It is possible that the vivid apocalyptic language of early Christianity has its greatest contemporary currency with the British public service at the moment, quite leaving churches and overtly evangelical groups in the shade!

36.23 It could be argued that this language is used ironically, that it has nothing to do with religion and that it just forms a convenient short-hand for discussing the future. For my own part, I am not so sure.

36.24 But this brings me to a general point about the use of language in management which is very significant in considering it as a religious phenomenon. The point is this. Religious and theological language used by theologians and religious believers has been refined over many centuries. Because the subject matter of theology, God, is certainly not available for direct objective scrutiny, theological language perceives itself to be ironical and metaphorical.[26] Metaphors in theological discourse are intensively scrutinized, accepted refined, and compared with other metaphors. They are not uncritically accepted or employed in an undisciplined way (except by fundamentalists or poor theologians). There is a recognition that metaphors and models carry with them unintended and possibly harmful or distorting secondary meanings. A similar awareness and sensitivity is not usually to be found in the language of management.

36.25 In general terms, managers seem cheerfully undisciplined and unaware of the language they use to describe what they are doing. Metaphors streak across conference tables and board rooms like bright comets, making points vividly and excitingly. Unfortunately, like their physical counterparts, these comets have tails of slush and mud in that they have important secondary and perhaps unintended meanings. So, for example, perhaps it is good to have a mission in an organization. But are those who use this metaphor aware of, for instance, the implicit radical, militant, invasive, sectarian, dualistic overtones of this concept which may energize 'outreach' at the expense of seeing people outside the organization as being objects to be saved? Is this an appropriate metaphor to use in the context of an organization which is supposed to serve the public and in which the public may feel they have a right to participate?

36.26 Similarly, 'crusading' may be a very good thing to do if you are really bringing salvation to other people. The problem is that the dualistic, aggressive, 'us and them' world view which spawned the crusades led to a denigration of the 'heathen' and ended up in many of them losing their lives.

36.27 Many of the metaphors used by public sector managers are implicitly dualistic, aggressive, male and 'red-blooded'.[27] They are used to rally the troops to the vision. Perhaps this is as it should be. It is certainly consistent with the competitive world of the capitalist market place and big business, whence it emanated. The point I am trying to make, however, is that language and the way it is used is important. It shapes the fundamental way in which people perceive their worlds and the organizations in which they work. It forms their reality. If managers are to engage in the religious activity of helping shape fundamental world views, values and assumptions, they would do well to consider and discipline their metaphors lest their secondary meanings shape a reality which may even be counter-productive to their primary intentions.[28]

Conclusion

36.28 I have tried to argue that contemporary general management appears to be in some significant respects a broadly religious activity with instructive similarities and resonances with North American sectarianism. This may or may not be deemed to have been an interesting and convincing exercise, but in any case I must now tackle the question, 'So what?' What are the advantages and disadvantages of seeing management in this way? If being broadly religious in character helps management do a better job on behalf of the public, what does it matter?

36.29 I certainly do not wish to suggest that public sector management should not have religious characteristics or use religious language. In my opinion, it may be necessary in the present climate that it should be so. Before 1984 in the NHS, for example, there were a number of crucial problems which could not be solved by parallel hierarchies trying to implement consensus management.

36.30 Although the NHS had demonstrated its value in being reasonably fair, reasonably effective and very cheap, it had failed to address certain key problems. First, being organized as a rationing system, there were inevitable delays and long waiting lists. Money did not follow patients and so a) there was a lack of client control and b) the costs of treatment were unquantified. Finally, the medical profession had an undue dominance within the service which distorted all attempts to manage it.[29]

36.31 In this situation, it was perhaps necessary that a new, post-welfare state consensus, sect of general managers with a clear sense of their own vision, purpose, power, high morale and control should be born.[30] There is some evidence that these problems are being addressed by the new religion, even if they are not proving particularly tractable.

36.32 However, it does seem important that if people are involved in what is in many ways religious activity with important faith assumptions and a language of faith that they should be self-aware and self-critical. I will conclude with some practical theses about the importance of metaphysical or mystical management.

36.33 1. If managers are engaged in activity with important religious overtones and resonances this cannot be avoided. It may or may not be beneficial to their organizations or to the public, but in any case there is no point in denying this aspect unless one wishes to be self-deceived or to deceive others.

2. Religions have often been used to deceive self and others, particularly in the interests of the socially powerful who wish to control the world, by presenting a seamless robe of meaning which is internally consistent and which cannot be challenged. Such religions can be narrow and oppressive. They over-simplify the nature of reality and can be morally vicious. It seems undesirable that public service should unwittingly adopt this approach.

3. The way to avoid narrow religious fundamentalism is to mature into a self-aware, self-critical, more ironical position whereby commitment and action are not abandoned but more factors are taken into account and assumptions are vigorously interrogated (this is fundamentally the task of the critical theologian).[31]

4. Once it is acknowledged that one is indulging in quasi-religious activity it is then possible to criticize and learn from other religious activities. So, for example, critical examination of other religious movements' attitudes to, say, evil, may illuminate and correct one's own assumptions. It may be, for example, that it could be useful to think more directly about the 'spirituality' of an organization, thus embracing its material and immaterial, its internal and external reality rather than hiding behind more partial and vaguely militaristic terms such as staff morale.[32]

5. As self-conscious 'theologians', managers would open themselves up more directly to external scrutiny and internal debate about their 'mystical management'. They could dialogue much more directly about their attitudes, hopes and assumptions. They might also be able to recognize the essentially artistic and creative aspects of their work, enriching and deepening it with legitimized and self-conscious metaphor manufacture. Their authority might then become more the authority of the artist who creates through imaginative performance in human relationship rather than that of the commander who coerces.[33]

6. Ultimately, if managers fail to recognize the religious nature of their activity and to work self-consciously with it, they will be in danger of being unrealistic and other-worldly in the worst sense.

36.34 One of the most criticized aspects of evangelical Christianity is that it cuts people off from the world and fixes their lives within a sectarian community where all attention is fixed on the world to come, not the world as it is with its present needs. The mystical manager who is unselfconsciously absorbed in shaping the vision of her sectarian organization according to the tenets of the latest wandering charismatic pamphleteer stands in danger of failing to see the real needs of the world outside. While the implicit spirituality of the organization may be growing strong, she may fail to hear what the Bible would call 'the cry of the poor' — what might be called the needs and voice of the public. These people, particularly the most needy and vulnerable, cry now, as they have for thousands of years, 'How long, O Lord, how long?' It is this cry which must ultimately determine the validity, fruitfulness and effectiveness of the faith of public sector managers.

36.35 Managers should become much more openly and honestly theologians, with some degree of irony and detachment from their own presuppositions and activities. The desire to control the public sector and deliver a valued service should not be allowed to supplant the need for understanding the nature of the transcendent world of values in which the public sector is situated.

36.36 Managers need to understand and be aware of their own values and assumptions, what I have called their 'faith', if they are not to become blinkered ideologues of the worst sort, inflicting a service on the public rather than offering a service to it. To ignore this dimension is to be unrealistic and 'theological' in the ideological sense of that term!

Notes

1. For more on critical practical theology, which I take to be the study of and formulation of action guiding metaphors and principles, see D. Browning, *Religious Ethics and Pasoral Care*, Fortress Press, 1983; ed., *Practical Theology*, Harper and Row, 1983.
2. I have adapted this title, and taken my direction to some extent here, from P. Halmos, *The Faith of the Counsellors*, Constable, 1965.
3. See further, D. Martin, *A Sociology of English Religion*, Heinemann, 1967.
4. For the influence of Christian values on the welfare state see, e.g., D. B. Forrester, *Christianity and the Future of the Welfare State*, Epworth, 1985.
5. C. Geertz, 'Religion as a Cultural System', quoted in R. Cooter, *The Cultural Meaning of Popular Science*, Cambridge University Press, 1984, p. 368, n. 86.
6. L. Kolakowski, *Religion*, Fontana, 1982, for example, argues that worship must play a part in any religion worthy of the name.
7. Cooter, *op. cit.*, p. 190.
8. P. Strong and J. Robinson, *The NHS Under New Management*, Open University Press, 1990, p. 3. Emphasis mine.
9. *Ibid*, p. 165. Emphasis mine.
10. *Ibid*, p. 187. Emphasis mine.

11. For a characterization of sectarian views and attitudes see, e.g., M. Hill, *The Sociology of Religion*, Heinemann, 1973, chs. 3 and 4, especially pp. 77f. See also, B. Wilson, *Religion in Secular Society*, Penguin, 1969, ch.11.
12. R. Stewart, 'Studies of management jobs and behaviour: the ways forward', *Journal of Management Studies* 26, 1989, 1–9; D. Rea, 'A jolt for the apple cart', *Health Service Journal*, 7th Sept. 1989, 1104.
13. For such tracts see, e.g. M. Edwardes, *Back from the Brink*, Pan, 1984; J. Harvey-Jones, *Making it Happen*, Collins, 1987.
14. Cf. J. Rifkin, *The Emerging Order*, Ballantine Books, 1983. It is interesting to note that a whole section in T. J. Peters and R. H. Waterman, *In Search of Excellence: Lessons from America's Best Companies*, Harper and Row, 1982, is entitled 'The Saving Remnant', evoking the theology of the Old Testament. Cf Hill's observation of sects: 'the self-concept is of an elect, gathered remnant with special enlightenment' (Hill, *op. cit.*, p. 78).
15. Cf H. Young, *One of Us*, Pan, 1990.
16. Peters and Waterman, *op. cit.*
17. Cf Peters and Waterman, *op. cit.*, Cf also S. Leach and J. Stewart, *Approaches to Public Policy Making*, Allen and Unwin, 1982, for a discussion of rational planning.
18. Peters and Waterman, *op. cit.*, ch. 2. I am aware of leaning very heavily on this one text in the present context. There are, of course, many different and some more complex texts in this area. However, it seems to be that the popularity of this book indicates the general acceptance and assimilation of ideas like those of Peters and Waterman in the public sector. It is perhaps the most overtly evangelical tract with the most religious overtones within the serious management literature.
19. *Ibid*, p. 37.
20. *Ibid*, p. 29.
21. *Ibid*, p. xxv.
22. *Ibid*, p. 74.
23. See further, Strong and Robinson, *op. cit.*, ch. 11. A. MacIntyre, *After Virtue*, Duckworth, 1982, challenges management effectiveness as a metaphysical value which functions rather like God: 'I am suggesting that "managerial effectiveness" functions much as Carnap and Ayer supposed "God" to function. It is the name of a fictitious, but believed-in reality, appeal to which disguises certain other realities; its effective use is expressive' (*op. cit.*, p. 73).
24. Like the hoped-for coming Kingdom of God in the New Testament the vision of the managers is strong and compelling, but also helpfully vague!
25. Walter Principle, quoted in U. King, *Women and Spirituality*, Macmillan, 1989, p. 6.
26. Cf, e.g., S. McFague, *Metaphorical Theology*, SCM Press, 1983.
27. For more on metaphors and their crucial importance in shaping world views, secondary meanings, etc, see G. Lakoff and M. Johnson, *Metaphors We Live By*, University of Chicago Press, 1979.

28. For more on how language shapes and determines the reality of the world in which we live and affects, therefore, their fundamental orientation to life see, e.g., R. Rorty, *Contingency, Irony and Solidarity*, Cambridge University Press, 1989; D. Cupitt, *The Long-Legged Fly*, SCM Press, 1987. One of the very few management texts which draws and points up the limits of metaphors is G. Morgan, *Images of Organisation*, Sage, 1986.

29. See Strong and Robinson, *op. cit.*, ch.2.

30. For descriptions and analysis of the decline of the post-war welfare state consensus see, e.g., Forrester, *op. cit.*, R. Klein, *The Politics of the National Health Service*, Longman, 1983.

31. For more on the critical, ironical stance see Rorty, *op. cit.*

32. For more on the 'spirit' of organizations see W. Wink, *Unmasking the Powers*, Fortress Press, 1986.

33. For more on religious and ethical activity as artistic performance see Cupitt, *op. cit.* There are some resonances with this in relation to creative managerial authority in C. Handy, *The Age of Unreason*, Hutchinson, 1989.

Select Bibliography

The Blackfriars Symposium produced one of the first select bibliographies focusing specifically on methodological discussions of the relationship between theology and sociology. This was the product of the meeting of the Symposium in 1979 and was published in David Martin, John Orme Mills, and W. S. F. Pickering (eds), *Sociology and Theology: Alliance and Conflict* (Harvester, Sussex, 1980) (the Symposium also produced a rather less useful, because less defined, bibliography entitled 'Method and Understanding in Sociology and Theology'). Because of the representative nature of this select bibliography, it is reproduced here, albeit in a revised form which includes more recent material. Those requiring bibliographies in the detailed study areas can refer directly to the notes of the various extracts in this Reader.

Banning, W. *Theologie en Sociologie. Een Tereinverkenning en Inleiding* (van Gorcum, Assen, 1936).

Banning, W. *Over de Ontmoeting van Theologie en Sociologie* (Amsterdam, 1946).

Baker, E. 'Sciences and Theology: Diverse Resolutions of an Interdisciplinary Gap by the New Priesthood of Science', *Interdisciplinary Science Reviews*, 4, 1, 1979.

Barker, E. 'The Limits of Displacement' in *Sociology and Theology: Alliance and Conflict, op. cit.*, 1980.

Baum, G. 'Sociology and Theology', *Concilium*, 1, 10 (91; *The Church as Institution*), 1974, pp. 22–31.

Baum, G. *Religion and Alienation: A Theological Reading of Sociology* (Paulist Press, New York, 1975).

Baum, G. 'The Impact of Sociology on Catholic Theology', *Catholic Theological Society of America: Proceedings*, 30, 1975.

Baum, G. *The Social Imperative: Essays on the Critical Issues that Confront the Christian Churches* (Paulist Press, New York, 1979).

Baum, G. 'The Sociology of Roman Catholic Theology' in *Sociology and Theology: Alliance and Conflict, op. cit.*, 1980.

Baum, G. *Theology and Society* (Paulist Press, New York, 1987).

Baum, G. *Essays in Critical Theology* (Sheed & Ward, Kansas City, 1994).

Bellah, R. *Beyond Belief* (Harper & Row, New York, 1970).

501

Bellah, R. (ed.) *Postmodern Theology: Christian Faith in a Pluralist World* (Harper, San Francisco, 1989).

Berger, P. L. *The Precarious Vision* (Doubleday, New York, 1961).

Berger, P. L. 'The Social Character of the Question Concerning Jesus Christ: Sociology and Ecclesiology' in M. Marty (ed.) *The Place of Bonhoeffer* (SCM, London, 1963).

Berger, P. L. 'Sociology and Theology', *Theology Today*, 24, 3, 1967, pp. 329–36.

Berger, P. L. 'A Sociological View of the Secularization of Theology', *Journal for the Scientific Study of Religion*, 6, 1967, pp. 3–16.

Berger, P. L. *The Sacred Canopy* (Doubleday, New York, 1967): British title, *The Social Reality of Religion* (Faber & Faber, London, 1969), Appendix.

Berger, P. L. *A Rumour of Angels* (Doubleday, New York, 1967, Pelican, Harmondsworth, Middx, 1969).

Berger, P. L. 'Secular Theology and the Rejection of the Supernatural: Reflections on Recent Trends', *Theological Studies*, 38, 1, 1977, pp. 39–56.

Berger, P. L. *The Heretical Imperative* (Anchor/Doubleday, New York, 1979, Collins, London, 1980).

Berger, P. L. *A Far Glory: The Quest for Faith in an Age of Credulity* (Free Press, New York, 1992).

Birou, A. *Sociologie et Religion* (Les Editions Ouvrières, Paris, 1959).

Bonhoeffer, D. *Sanctorum Communio* (SCM, London, 1963; orig. 1927).

Burns, G. *The Frontiers of Catholicism* (University of California Press, 1994).

Cairns, D. 'The Thought of Peter Berger', *Scottish Journal of Theology*, 27, 2, 1974, pp. 181–97.

Chenu, M. D. 'Sociologie de la Connaissance et Théologie de la Foi', *Recherches et Debats*, 25, 1958, pp. 71–4.

Cox, H. *Religion in the Secular City: Toward a Postmodern Theology* (Simon & Schuster, New York, 1984).

Davis, C. *Theology and Political Society* (CUP, Cambridge, 1980).

Defois, G. 'Sociologie de la connaissance et théologie de la croyance', *Le Supplément*, 112, 1975, pp. 101–25.

Dekker, G. 'The Relation Between Sociology and Theology' (privately circulated, 1978).

Desroche, H. 'Sociologie et théologie dans la typologie religieuse de Joachim Wach', *Archives de sociologie des religions*, 1, 1956, pp. 41–63.

Desroche, H. *Sociologies religieuses* (Presses Universitaires de France, Paris, 1968), ch. 8.

Dhooghe, J. 'Quelques Problèmes posés par le dialogue entre sociologie et théologie pastorale', *Social Compass*, 17, 2, 1970, pp. 215–29.

Dumont, F. 'La sociología y la renovacíon de la teología' in *Teología de la renovacion, 2: Renovacíon de las estructuras religiosas* (Sígueme, Salamanca, 1972).

Edwards, A. 'Life as Fashion Parade: The Anthropology of Mary Douglas', *New Blackfriars*, 58, 682, 1977, pp. 131–9.

Fenn, R. K. *Liturgies and Trials* (Blackwell, Oxford, 1982).

Fenn, R. K. *The Secularization of Sin* (Westminster/John Knox, Louisville, Kentucky, 1991).

Fiorenza, F. 'Critical Social Theory and Christology', *Proceedings of the Convention of the Catholic Theological Society of America*, 30, 1975, pp. 63–110.

Flanagan, K. *Sociology and Liturgy: Re-presentations of the Holy* (Macmillan, London, 1991).

Flanagan, K. *The Enchantment of Sociology: A Study of Theology and Culture* (Macmillan, London, 1996).

Fortmann, H. M. M. *Als Ziende de Onzienlijke*, II (Gooi en Sticht, Hilversum, 1974).

Franco, R. 'Teología y sociología', *Proyección*, 61, 1968, pp. 203–9.

Friedrichs, R. W. 'Social Research and Theology: End of the Detente?', *Review of Religious Research*, 15, 1974, pp. 113–27.

Gablentz, H. O. 'Soziologie und Theologie', *Zeitschrift für Evangelische Ethik*, 4, 1960, pp. 56–8.

Garrett, W. R. 'Troublesome Transcendence: The Supernatural in the Scientific Study of Religion', *Sociological Analysis*, 3, 1974, pp. 169–80.

Gestrich, C. 'Theologie und Soziologie — Zwei Grenzwissenschaften' in J. M. Lohse (ed.), *Menschlich sein mit oder ohne Gott?* (Kohlhammer, Stuttgart, 1969).

Geyer, H. G., Jasnowski, H. N. and Schmidt, A. *Theologie und Soziologie* (Kohlhammer, Stuttgart, 1970).

Gill, R. 'British Theology as a Sociological Variable' in M. Hill (ed.), *A Sociological Yearbook of Religion in Britain*, 7 (SCM, London, 1974), pp. 1–12.

Gill, R. 'Berger's Plausibility Structures: A Response to Professor Cairns', *Scottish Journal of Theology*, 27, 2, 1974, pp. 198–207.

Gill, R. *The Social Context of Theology* (Mowbrays, Oxford, 1975).

Gill, R. *Theology and Social Structure* (Mowbrays, Oxford, 1977).

Gill, R. 'From Sociology to Theology' in *Sociology and Theology: Alliance and Conflict, op. cit.*, 1980.

Gill, R. *Prophecy and Praxis* (Marshall, Morgan and Scott, London, 1981).

Gill, R. *Competing Convictions* (SCM Press, London, 1989).

Gill, R. *Christian Ethics in Secular Worlds* (T. & T. Clark, Edinburgh, 1991), especially ch. 2.

Gill, R. *Moral Communities* (Exeter University Press, Exeter, 1992).

Goddijn, H. and Goddijn, W. *Sociologie van Kerk en Godsdienst* (Het Spectrum, Utrecht and Antwerp, 1966).

Greeley, A. 'Research and Debate: Theology and the Social Sciences', *Social Compass*, 17, 1970.

Green, G. 'The Sociology of Dogmatics: Niklas Luhmann's Challenge to Theology', *Journal of the American Academy of Religion*, L, 1, 1982, pp. 19–33.

Guinness, O. 'Towards a Reappraisal of Christian Apologetics: Peter L. Berger's Sociology of Knowledge as the Sociological Prolegomenon to Christian Apologetics', D.Phil. thesis, Oxford University, 1981.

de Haas, P. *The Church as an Institution: Critical Studies in the Relation Between Theology and Sociology* (Boek- en Offsetdrukkerij, N. V., Apeldoorn, 1972).

Habgood, J. *Church and Nation in a Secular Age* (Darton, Longman and Todd, London, 1983).

Harris, C. 'Displacements and Reinstatements' in *Sociology and Theology: Alliance and Conflict, op. cit.*, 1980.

Holl, A. 'Max Scheler's Sociology of Knowledge and his Position in Relation to Theology', *Social Compass*, 17, 2, 1970, pp. 231–41.

Hollweg, A. *Theologie und Empire. Ein Beitrag zum Gespräch zwischen Theologie und Sozialwissenschaften in den USA und Deutschland* (Evangelisches Verlagswerk, Stuttgart, 1971).

Homan, R. 'Theology and Sociology; a Plea for Sociological Freedom', *Theology*, 84, 1981.

Houtart, F. *et al. Recherches Interdisciplinaires et Théologie* (Editions du Cerf, Paris, 1970).

Hudson, W. D. 'The Rational System of Beliefs' in *Sociology and Theology: Alliance and Conflict, op. cit.* 1980.

Hummel, G. 'Religionssoziologie und Theologie: Traditionelle Ansätze und zukünftige Perspektiven' in U. Mann (ed.), *Theologie und Religionswissenschaft. Der gegenwärtige Stand ihrer Forschungsergebnisse und Aufgaben im Hinblick auf ihr gegenseitiges Verhältnis* (Wissenschaftliche Buchgesellschaft, Darmstadt, 1973) pp. 207–21.

Hunter, D. 'Theology and the Behavioural Sciences', *Religious Education*, 55, 1960, pp. 248–64.

Jackson, M. J. *The Sociology of Religion. Theory and Practice* (Batsford, London, 1974), Chapter 4.

Kaufmann, F.-X. *Theologie in Soziologischer Sicht* (Herder, Freiburg, Basel and Vienna, 1973).

Laeyendecker, L. 'Sociologie en Theologie' in K. Dobbelaere and L. Laeyendecker, *Godsdienst, Kerk en Samenleving* (Universitaire Pers, Rotterdam, 1974), pp. 341–61.

de Lavalette, H. 'Repères conflictuels. Du champ de la théologie à celui de la sociologie', *Recherches de sciences religieuses*, 4, 1977, pp. 589–612.

Lindner, R. 'Über die Zusammenarbeit von Soziologie und Theologie — eine Auseinandersetzung mit Helmut Schelsky', *Zeitschrift für Evangelische Ethik*, 10, 1966, pp. 65–80.

Lion, A. 'Theology and Sociology: What point is there in keeping the distinction?' in *Sociology and Theology: Alliance and Conflict, op. cit.*, 1980.

de Loor, H. D. 'Sociologie und Theologie', *Zeitschrift für Evangelische Ethik*, 11, 1967, pp. 159–68.

Luhmann, N. *Funktion der Religion* (Suhrkamp Verlag, Frankfurt am Main, 1977).

Luhmann, N. and Pannenberg, W. 'Die Allgemeingültigkeit der Religion: Diskussion über Luhmanns Religionssoziologie', *Evangelische Kommentare*, 11, 350, 1978, pp. 355–7.

Lyon, D. *Sociology and the Human Image* (Inter-Varsity Press, Leicester and Downers Grove, Illinois, 1983).

Mannheim, K. *Diagnosis of Our Time* (Routledge, London and Boston, 1943), Chapter 7.

Martin, D. A. *The Religious and the Secular* (Routledge and Kegan Paul, London, 1969).

Martin, D. A. 'The Secularization Question', *Theology*, 76, 1973.

Martin, D. A. 'Ethical Commentary and Political Decision', *Theology*, 76, 1973, pp. 525–31.

Martin, D. A. 'The Sociological Mode and the Theological Vocabulary' in *Sociology and Theology: Alliance and Conflict, op. cit.*, 1980.

Martin, D. A. *The Breaking of the Image* (Blackwell, Oxford, 1980).

Martin, D. A. 'Comparing Different Maps of the Same Ground' in A. R. Peacocke (ed.), *The Sciences and Theology in the Twentieth Century* (Oriel, Stocksfield, 1981), pp. 229–40.

Martin, D. A. 'Sociology, Religion and Secularization: An Orientation', *Religion*, 25, 4, October 1995.

Martin, R. 'Sociology and Theology: Alienation and Original Sin' in D. E. H. Whiteley and R. Martin (eds), *Sociology, Theology and Conflict* (Blackwell, Oxford, and Barnes and Noble, New York, 1969), pp. 4–37.

Mathews, S. 'The Social Origin of Theology', *American Journal of Sociology*, 18, 1912, pp. 289–317.

Mayer, H. -C. 'Plädoyer fur die Freiheit der Theologie von der Soziologie', *Scheidewege*, 4, 2, pp. 179–200.

Mehl, R. 'Bedeutung, Möglichkeiten und Grenzen der Soziologie des Protestantismus in Theologischer Sicht' in *Probleme der Religionssoziologie*, Sonderheft 6 of the *Kölner Zeitschrift fur Soziologie und Sozialpsychologie*, 1962, pp. 112–22.

Mehl, R. 'Sociologie du christianisme et théologie', *Social Compass*, 10, 3, 1963, pp. 285–92.

Milbank, J. *Theology and Social Theory: Beyond Secular Reason* (Blackwell, Oxford, 1990).

Mills, J. O. 'Of Two Minds' in *Sociology and Theology: Alliance and Conflict, op. cit.*, 1980.

Mol, H. *Identity and the Sacred* (Blackwell, Oxford, 1976).

Monzel, N. 'Die Soziologie und die Theologen', *Hochland*, 41, 1948–9, pp. 259–72.

Neal, M. A. *A Socio-Theology of Letting Go* (Paulist Press, New York, 1977).

Niebuhr, H. R. *The Social Sources of Denominationalism* (Henry Holt, New York, 1929, and Shoe String, Hamden, Connecticut, 1954).

Niebuhr, H. R. *Christ and Culture* (Harper, New York, 1951, and Faber, London, 1952).

Nineham, D. 'A Partner for Cinderella?' in M. Hooker and C. Hickling (eds), *What About the New Testament?* (SCM Press, London, 1975), pp. 143–54.

Northcott, M. S. *The Church and Secularisation* (Lang, Frankfurt, 1989).

Pannenberg, W. 'Signale der Transzendenz — Religionssoziologie zwischen Atheismus und religiöser Wirklichkeit', *Evangelische Kommentare*, 7, 1974, pp. 151–4.

Pannenberg, W. *Theology and the Philosophy of Science*, trans. from German by F. McDonagh (Darton, Longman and Todd, London, 1976).

Pellegrino, U. 'Teologia e Sociologia', *Atti del XIX Convegno del Centro Studi Filosofici* (Morcelliana, Brescia, 1965), pp. 301–7.

Pickering, W. S. F. 'Theodicy and Social Theory' in *Sociology and Theology: Alliance and Conflict*, op. cit., 1980.

Radcliffe, T. 'Relativizing the Relativizers' in *Sociology and Theology: Alliance and Conflict,*, op. cit., 1980.

Richard, G. *Sociologie et théodicée; leur conflit et leur accord* (Les Presses Continentales, Paris, 1943).

Rousseau, A. 'Emploi du terme "sociologie" dans les textes du magistère central de l'Eglise', *Social Compass*, 17, 2, 1970, pp. 309–20.

Rousseau, A. and Leconte, J. -P. 'Les Conditions sociales du travail théologique', *Concilium*, 135, 1978, pp. 19–27; trans. as 'The Social Conditions of Theological Activity', *Concilium*, 115 (*Doing Theology in New Places*), 1979, pp. 12–21.

Savramis, D. *Theologie und Gesellschaft* (List Verlag, Munich, 1971).

Schelsky, H. 'Religionssoziologie und Theologie', *Zeitschrift für Evangelische Ethik*, 3, 1959, pp. 129–45.

Schillebeeckx, E. 'Theological Reflections on Religio-Sociological Interpretations of Modern "Irreligion" ', *Social Compass*, 10, 3, 1963, pp. 257–84.

Schreuder, O. 'Works on Sociology and Theology', *Social Compass*, 17, 2, 1970, pp. 329–34.

Schrey, H. H. 'Neuere Tendenzen der Religionssoziologie', *Theologische Rundschau*, 38, 1, 1973, pp. 54–63; and 38, 2, 1973, pp. 99–118.

Seguy, J. 'Histoire, Sociologie, Théologie', *Archives de sociologie des religions*, 34, 1972, pp. 132–51.

Sellers, J., 'Theological Belief and Sociological Enquiry', *Journal of Religions*, 45, 53, 1973.

Shippey, F. W. 'The Relations of Theology and Social Sciences according to Gabriel Le Bras', *Archives de sociologie des religions*, 20, 1965, pp. 79–93.

Siebert, R. 'Religion in the Perspective of Critical Sociology', *Concilium* 1, 10 (91; *The Church as Institution*), 1974, pp. 56–69.

Siebert, R. *The Critical Theory of Religion: The Frankfurt School* (Mouton, Berlin and New York, 1985).

Spiegel-Schmidt, F. 'Theologie und Soziologie' in K. G. Specht *et al.*, *Studium Soziale. Ergebnisse sozialwissenschaftlicher Forschung der Gegenwart* (Westdeutscher Verlag, Cologne, 1963), pp. 385–96.

Stroup, H. 'Theological Implications in Anthropology', *Encounter*, 21, 1960, pp. 464–8.

Towler, R. 'Many Voices' in *Sociology and Theology: Alliance and Conflict, op. cit.*, 1980.

Tracy, D., Gilkey, L. and Ogden, S. M. 'Responses to Peter Berger', *Theological Studies*, 39, 3, 1978, pp. 486–507.

Utz, A.-F. 'Theologie und Sozialwissenschaften' in J. Feiner, J. Trütsch and F. Bückle (eds), *Fragen der Theologie heute* (Benziger Verlag, Einsiedeln, Zürich and Cologne, 1958), pp. 447–62.

Various. 'Research and Debate. Theology and Social Sciences', *Social Compass*, 17, 2, 1970, pp. 261–308.

Whitley, O. R. 'Sociological Models and Theological Reflection', *Journal of the American Academy of Religion*, 45, 1977, Supplement J, pp. 333–65.

Williams, J. A. 'Church, Religion and Secularization in the Theology of Christian Radicalism, 1960–69: Critical Perspectives from the Sociology of Religion', PhD thesis, Durham University, 1986.

Acknowledgements

Extract 1
Max Weber, 'Luther's Conception of the Calling': from pp. 79–92 of *The Protestant Ethic and the Spirit of Capitalism* (1930), published by George Allen & Unwin, 40 Museum Street, London WC1A 1LU.

Extract 2
Max Weber, 'Prophets and the Routinisation of Charisma': from pp. 60–69 of *The Sociology of Religion* (1963), reprinted by permission of Beacon Press, 25 Beacon Street, Boston, Massachusetts 02108.

Extract 3
Emile Durkheim, 'Theology and Egoistic Suicide': from pp. 156–64 and 168–70 of *Suicide: A Study in Sociology* (1952), reprinted by permission of Routledge & Kegan Paul Ltd, 11 New Fetter Lane, London EC4P 4EE.

Extract 4
Ernst Troeltsch, 'Churches and Sects': from pp. 331–43 of *The Social Teaching of the Christian Churches*, Volume I, reprinted by permission of both Allen & Unwin (Publishers) Ltd, 40 Museum Street, London WC1A 1LU, and the University of Chicago Press, 5801 Ellis Avenue, Chicago, Illinois 60637.

Extract 5
H. Richard Niebuhr, 'The Churches of the Disinherited': from pp. 26–39 of *The Social Sources of Denominationalism* (1929), published by Henry Holt, New York.

Extract 6
Karl Mannheim, 'Theology and the Sociology of Knowledge': from pp. 35–42 and 74–80 of *Ideology and Utopia* (1936), reprinted by permission of Routledge & Kegan Paul Ltd, 11 New Fetter Lane, London EC4P 4EE.

Extract 7
Peter L. Berger, 'Sociological and Theological Perspectives': from pp. 181–90 of *The Social Reality of Religion* (1969) (US edition: *The Sacred*

Canopy) reprinted by permission of both Faber and Faber Ltd, 3 Queen Square, London, WC1N 3AU, and Doubleday & Company, Inc., 245 Park Avenue, New York 10167.

Extract 8
Roderick Martin, 'Sociology and Theology: Alienation and Original Sin': from pp. 19–36 of *Sociology, Theology and Conflict* (1969), edited by D. E. Whiteley and R. Martin, reprinted by permission of Basil Blackwell, 108 Cowley Road, Oxford OX4 1JF.

Extract 9
Robert N. Bellah, 'Theology and Symbolic Realism': from the *Journal for the Scientific Study of Religion* 9, no. 2 (1970), reprinted by permission of the Society for the Scientific Study of Religion, Inc., Catholic University of America, Washington, DC 20064.

Extract 10
Gregory Baum, 'The Impact of Sociology on Catholic Theology': reprinted by permission of Catholic Theological Society of America, c/o Loyola University, Chicago, Illinois 60626, from their *Proceedings* 30 (1975); reprinted in Gregory Baum, *The Social Imperative* (1979), published by Paulist Press, Mahwah, NJ.

Extract 11
Robin Gill, 'Sociology Assessing Theology': from pp. 94–113 of *Prophecy and Praxis* (1981), reprinted by permission of Marshall, Morgan & Scott Publications Ltd, 3 Beggarwood Lane, Basingstoke, Hants RG23 7LP.

Extract 12
Timothy Radcliffe, 'A Theological Assessment of Sociological Explanation': from pp. 151–62 of *Sociology and Theology: Alliance and Conflict* (1980), published by Harvester Press, reprinted by permission of the editors David Martin, John Orme Mills and W. S. F. Pickering.

Extract 13
David Martin, 'Transcendence and Unity': from pp. 1–16 of *The Breaking of the Image* (1980), reprinted by permission of the author and Basil Blackwell Limited, 108 Cowley Road, Oxford OX4 1JF.

Extract 14
Garrett Green, 'The Sociology of Dogmatics: Niklas Luhmann's Challenge to Theology': from pp. 19–33 of the *Journal of the American Academy of Religion* L, 1 (1982), reprinted by permission of Scholars Press, PO Box 1608, Decatur, GA 30031–1608.

Extract 15
Norman K. Gottwald, 'Sociological Method in the Study of Ancient Israel': from pp. 69–81 of *Encounter with the Text: Form and History in the Hebrew Bible* (1979), ed. M. J. Buss, reprinted by permission of the Society of Biblical Literature, c/o Perkins School of Theology, Southern Methodist University, Dallas, TX 75275.

Extract 16
Cyril S. Rodd, 'Max Weber and Ancient Judaism': from pp. 457–69 of the *Scottish Journal of Theology* 32, 5 (1979), reprinted by permission of the author, the Journal and Scottish Academic Press Ltd, 33 Montgomery Street, Edinburgh EH7 5JX.

Extract 17
Robert P. Carroll, 'Ancient Israelite Prophecy and Dissonance Theory': from pp. 135–51 of *Numen* 24 (1977), reprinted by permission of E. J. Brill, Postbus 900, 2300 PA Leiden, Netherlands.

Extract 18
Robin Scroggs, 'The Sociological Interpretation of the New Testament: The Present State of Research': from pp. 164–79 of *New Testament Studies* 26 (1980), reprinted by permission of Cambridge University Press, The Edinburgh Building, Shaftesbury Road, Cambridge CB2 2RU.

Extract 19
John G. Gager, 'Christian Missions and the Theory of Cognitive Dissonance': from pp. 37–49 of *Kingdom and Community: The Social World of Early Christianity* (1975), reprinted by permission of Prentice-Hall, Inc., Englewood Cliffs, NJ 07632.

Extract 20
Gerd Theissen, 'Functional Effects of Earliest Christianity': from pp. 111–19 of *The First Followers of Jesus* (1981), reprinted by permission of SCM Press Ltd, 26–30 Tottenham Road, London N1 4BZ.

Extract 21
Wayne A. Meeks, 'The Man from Heaven in Johannine Sectariarism': reprinted, by permission, from the *Journal of Biblical Literature* 91 (1972), c/o Perkins School of Theology, Southern Methodist University, Dallas, TX 75275.

Extract 22
Robin Gill, 'Social Variables within Applied Theology': from pp. 106–19 of *Theology and Social Structure* (1977), reprinted by permission of A. R. Mowbray & Co. Ltd, Saint Thomas House, Becket Street, Oxford OX1 1SJ.

Extract 23
David Martin, 'Ethical Commentary and Political Decision': from pp. 525–31 of *Theology* LXXVI, 640 (October 1973), published by SPCK, London, reprinted by permission of the author.

Extract 24
Mady A. Thung, 'An Alternative Model for a Missionary Church: An Approach of the Sociology of Organizations': from pp. 18–31 of *The Ecumenical Review* 30 (1978), reprinted by permission of The World Council of Churches, 150 route de Ferney, PO Box 66, 1211 Geneva 20, Switzerland.

Extract 25
E. Mansell Pattison, 'Systems Pastoral Care': from pp. 3–14 of *The Journal of Pastoral Care* XXVI, 1 (March 1972), reprinted by permission of The Journal of Pastoral Care, Inc., PO Box 2967, 901 N Kings Highway, Myrtle Beach, SC 29578–2967.

Extract 26
Robert Bocock, 'Religious Ritual in the Church of England': from pp. 73–84 of *Ritual in Industrial Society: A Sociological Analysis of Ritualism in Modern England* (1974), reprinted by permission of A. D. Peters & Co. Ltd, 10 Buckingham Street, London WC2N 6BJ.

Extract 27
Victor Turner, 'Pilgrimage as a Liminoid Phenomenon': from pp. 1–7 and 29–30 of *Image and Pilgrimage in Christian Culture* (1978), reprinted by permission of both Basil Blackwell Ltd, 108 Cowley Road, Oxford OX4 1JF, and Columbia University Press, 562 West 113th Street, New York 10025.

Extract 28
Edward Schillebeeckx, 'Sociology, Theology, and Ministry': from pp. 75–85 of *Ministry: A Case for Change* (1981), reprinted by permission of both SCM Press Ltd, 26–30 Tottenham Road, London N1 4BZ, and Crossroad, 370 Lexington Avenue, New York 10017.

Extract 29
Clare Watkins, 'Organizing the People of God: Social-Science Theories of Organization in Ecclesiology': from pp. 693–700, 701–3, 706–11 of *Theological Studies* 52 (1991), reprinted by permission of Theological Studies, Georgetown University, Box 571136, 37th and 0 Streets, NW, Washington DC 20057–1136.

Extracts 30–34
Fergus Kerr, 'Simplicity Itself: Milbank's Thesis'; Rowan Williams, 'Saving Time: Thoughts on Practice, Patience and Vision'; Aidan Nichols,

'Non Tali Auxilio: John Milbank's Suasion to Orthodoxy'; Kieran Flanagan, 'Sociology and Milbank's City of God'; John Milbank, 'Enclaves, or Where is the Church?': from pp. 306–10, 319–48 and 351–2 of *New Blackfriars*, Vol. 73 No. 861 (June 1992), reprinted by permission of Blackfriars, Oxford.

Extract 35
Richard H. Roberts, 'Globalized Religion?: The "Parliament of the World's Religions" (Chicago 1993) in Theoretical Perspective': from pp. 121–2 and 127–37 of *Journal of Contemporary Religion*, Vol. 10 No. 2 (1995), reprinted by permission of Carfax Publishing Company, PO Box 25, Abingdon, Oxfordshire, OX14 2UE.

Extract 36
Stephen Pattison, 'Mystical Management: A Religious Critique of General Management in the Public Sector': from pp. 17–27, *MC*, XXXIII, 3 (1991), reprinted by permission of *Modern Believing*, King's College, Cambridge, CB2 1ST.

Index